THE SECRET HEART

THE SECRET HEART

John le Carré: An Intimate Memoir

SULEIKA DAWSON

MUDLARK

Mudlark
HarperCollins*Publishers*
1 London Bridge Street
London SE1 9GF

www.harpercollins.co.uk

HarperCollins*Publishers*
1st Floor, Watermarque Building, Ringsend Road
Dublin 4, Ireland

First published by Mudlark 2022

1 3 5 7 9 10 8 6 4 2

A catalogue record of this book is available from the British Library

HB ISBN 978-0-00-853302-1
TPB ISBN 978-0-00-855737-9

Printed and bound in the UK using 100% renewable electricity at CPI Group (UK) Ltd

This book is produced from independently certified FSC™ paper
to ensure responsible forest management.

For more information visit: www.harpercollins.co.uk/green

CONTENTS

*For Graham Goodwin again, and this time
for Jeremy Lloyd as well.
Remembering George Greenfield, too.
And for David, of course.*

And the human heart is a very mysterious thing.

Ford Madox Ford, *The Good Soldier*

BY WAY OF AN INTRODUCTION . . .

I've never let anyone this far in, David told me once, quite early in our relationship. His voice was earnest, his expression suddenly concerned. We might have been in bed, or perhaps just sitting together, I forget. We were certainly post-coital, I remember that. We almost always were. *You are safe to love, aren't you, Sue?* he urged. *I need you to be safe.*

'Safe'. A loaded word. This, after all, was the man who educated the world about safe houses. We were in one of his at the time. So – safe that I loved him as much as he loved me? That I would continue to be a safe haven for him, whenever he wanted respite from his world? Or safe, meaning I'd never call his wife? There could have been another dozen interpretations. There almost always were.

Before I could answer, he laid the underside of his forearm along my thigh.

Look, he said. *We have the same skin. The same grain. Cut from the same bale. We'll go away again soon. I think we need some more time together under our belts.*

David always pressed the 'we' of things, sparing no word or gesture to conjure up an enveloping us-ness around our times together. He was good at it, too; *really* good. I have yet to discover a word for the mistress-attending equivalent of 'uxorious', but there ought to be one, just for him. It was wholly beguiling to be an audience of one for the powerful up-close magic he could

1

summon. Nor was it entirely illusory. Real rabbits do emerge from top hats, however they get there to begin with, and large parts of our relationship, whole stretches, were as real as anything has ever been in my life. In his too, I am certain. But I have since come to wonder whether, for David, it was the illusion itself – and his own power to invoke it – that was most real of all.

There is one further interpretation of what he meant by 'safe' that may have accounted for his worry at the time. David did take me very deep into his world, into his thoughts and hopes, his memories, his besetting concerns and fears, into his carefully guarded private reality. So he might have meant safe that I wouldn't write about him. As indeed I didn't, not for the longest time, until it *was* safe – even if this book may yet constitute a breach of the Unofficial Secrets Act I never actually signed.

So – what follows is how it went. With us. This is the story of my time with le Carré the writer and with David the man; with Ronnie the father, too, whom David sent me on a secret mission to find, and in finding the father I discovered still more about the son.

My story, then, just the way I remember it happening, my memory fortified by the many dozens of letters David sent me and by my diaries and notebooks from those years. I've withheld a few details to spare some blushes – most of them my own – but otherwise this is a pretty full account of what has unquestionably been one of the most significant relationships of my life. Of his too, I like to think. And right at the beginning of it, as perhaps ought always to be the case in any last moment before things change forever, I remember I yawned …

FIRST APPROACH
September 1982

SOHO

It was an early start at the sound studios and I wasn't good with mornings in those days. But Graham had said, *Make sure to get your lovely arse round to Woodsie's for eight o'clock sharp, honey, all right?,* so there I was. Prior to that day we'd never begun a session before ten. Actors usually aren't so good with mornings, either, but that day we weren't going to be recording with an actor.

I yawned again as we sat amicably together, mostly in silence, on one of the well-worn blue banquettes in the seventh-floor reception of John Wood Studios at Broadwick Street, Soho. It was just the two of us there, with the senior engineer Derek French – Frenchie – setting up in his studio.

'Why the dawn run anyway?' I asked, since I hadn't been told.

'The Great Man requested it,' Graham replied.

Good to know. We'd been waiting for twenty minutes and the Great Man had yet to appear.

'Yes, but why?'

'Dunno. Maybe he gets going in the morning – unlike some. Maybe he wants to finish early so he can go home and give his wife one. Dunno.'

Graham Goodwin – a tall, silver-haired and habitually laid-back Gent-about-Town; the man who single-handedly started the whole audiobook business; my friend, mentor and employer for the last two years – was sounding less bothered than he looked. He'd been getting up periodically, smoothing his jacket collar, shooting his cuffs, checking his tie. That he was wearing a jacket in the studio at all was indicative of his state of mind. The only other session he ever smartened up for was when the reader was Prince Philip.

'Anyway,' he added, standing up again, 'he asked me nicely so I said yes.'

'*Starfucker*' Frenchie called out genially through the open door of the studio.

We heard the lift draw up just then, always heralding its own arrival with such a resounding thud that the rates for the studio nearest to the lift-shaft were significantly lower than for the other two studios on the same floor.

'Here we go,' Graham said, nudging me to get up too.

But when the lift door slid back it was the receptionist who stepped out, looking less than pleased with the early start. I sat down again and Graham went back to shooting his cuffs.

Audiobooks were known as talking books or books-on-cassette in those days, the pre-digital age, and Graham had started the whole trade. He devised the two-cassette, three-hour abridged reading as a product that was marketable at the price of a paperback and would suit factory requirements in production – C90 cassettes being the longest that were reliable for copying from the master tapes – then pitched the first six titles to EMI in the late seventies. The new product took off at speed, especially once Walkmans and car cassette players arrived, and has continued its acceleration from analogue to digital to today's download. What is currently the vast catalogue at Audible was originally just Graham Goodwin and a great idea.

With more and more clients wanting in on the business, Graham had taken me on as his abridger and assistant producer, and I had never been happier than working with him. Actors liked the work too, with the great and the good from stage and screen all keen to be signed up to read. But it wasn't every professional actor who could sight-read effectively – we'd already had a few surprising big-name duds – and a completely non-professional reader, even reading his own work, was a real wild-card. This was why Graham was so twitchy that morning.

'Has he really not read anything?' I asked, trying to get a picture of what the day might hold.

'Not a dickie bird that I know of. Apparently he's done a couple of bits of radio for the Beeb.'

Though this meant that our new reader had at least read in front of a microphone before today, Graham didn't take it as a great recommendation. He relayed the information with the same degree of disdain he normally reserved for men who wore pocket squares that matched their neckties. The BBC had their own studios, edit suites and staff engineers, with the licence-fee revenue on tap to pay for everything. Our productions had the pressure of real-world commercial budgets and deadlines, yet we were still expected to match the BBC radio standard. Ours was the tougher gig by a long way.

'But Uncle George assures me he can deliver the goods,' he added, 'so we'll have to take a punt on his judgement.'

George Greenfield was the doyen of London literary agents, handling a long list of major authors at the John Farquharson Agency. I didn't know him then – we would meet later – but he was already a staunch ally of our work, hence the fond moniker. George had fully embraced the potential of the new medium, releasing the recording rights to a lot of top titles. One of them – *The Moon's a Balloon*, David Niven's memoir, read by Niven himself – had been Graham's greatest success to date. But Niven was an actor; the Great Man was not. I could sense Graham's mood was slipping.

'Maybe he'll be all right,' I offered.

'Maybe. But he'll have to give it a helluva lot of wellie to match the pros. And he can't *possibly* do Guinness better than Jayston.'

The first and only other le Carré title we'd put on tape was *Tinker Tailor Soldier Spy*, the meticulously plotted tale of the unmasking of a long-term Soviet double agent – a mole – by the ageing spymaster George Smiley. This was le Carré's reworking of the Kim Philby story, the real-life double agent whose treachery, in the writer's own phrase, had turned the nation's secret services inside-out. There had been a massively successful BBC dramatisation, with Alec Guinness giving an iconic portrayal of the hitherto faceless Smiley. Michael Jayston played Smiley's younger right-hand man, Peter Guillam, and did a sterling job reading the book for us, particularly nailing the sepulchral voice of Guinness. It had been another big success for Graham and today's booking had the potential to be bigger still – John le Carré himself reading *Smiley's People*, the conclusion to his trilogy, in which the elusive figure behind the original double-agent operation, Soviet spymaster Karla, is finally brought down. A new BBC dramatisation was on the TV schedules, with Guinness revisiting his role as the lugubrious Smiley. So everything was set for another Goodwin spoken-word bestseller – as long as the Great Man could actually *read*. Graham was anticipating the fix he'd be in if it turned out he couldn't. Diplomatic forbearance was never his strong suit. He once told a renowned knight of the theatre who was unexpectedly fluffing an easy read that he could supply him with a copy of the script in Braille if it would help …

'He's bloody late too,' Graham announced, making it official by checking the reception clock against his watch. A perky whistling of the theme from *The Great Escape* drifted towards us from the studio.

'Have you met him?' I asked.

'Nope. Talked to him on the jelly-bone a couple of times, that's all.'

'Nice voice?'

'Yeah, s'pose. A bit Oxford. Touch of the Bridesheads, maybe – bit prissy on the esses. But nothing that Frenchie here can't EQ.'

'*And the rest,*' our disembodied engineer chimed in softly again.

'So's you know,' Graham said finally, forgetting he'd told me when he assigned me the abridgement a few weeks earlier, 'his real name's David Cornwell.'

'Right.'

'Like the place, but with an "e".'

'Right.'

'Right. So don't call him John.'

With that, he let the silence settle in again.

There's a sort of protective, padded-cell hush peculiar to recording studios that comes from being cocooned in an unnatural amount of sound insulation. Over the years I've made audiobooks in London, Paris, New York, Miami and LA, and the ambience is universal. I find it the most welcoming atmosphere in the world and feel instantly at home whenever I walk into a sound studio. But that morning, with the business day not yet underway, there was a distinct edge to the empty quiet. We might have been keeping watch on the deck of the *Mary Celeste*, staying frosty for whatever it was that was going to happen …

And yet somehow – although the reception area wasn't much more than six yards by five and despite our entire focus having been at all times on his arrival – the former spy managed to take us by surprise. With no sound at all, a figure appeared in the doorway; a sandy-haired individual about six feet tall, wearing a neat dull suit and offering a slight all-purpose smile. He was carrying an old-fashioned tan leather briefcase that he seemed to be holding a little ahead of himself, as if what had really arrived was not his unassuming person but what he brought with him – my abridgement of his book, our script for the day. It was only then that I realised neither of us had really known what he looked like. The world-famous name belonged to a largely incognito face. If we hadn't known better he might have been a Fuller Brush salesman with a case of samples, calling on spec.

We did know better, of course. John le Carré, our reader of the day, had joined us at last. We couldn't possibly have missed hearing the lift, so for some reason he must have taken the stairs up to the studios. All seven flights of them, soundlessly, and he wasn't even out of breath. Graham shot me a lightning-quick look, to mark that this was an altogether sneaky way to make an entrance. Thankfully, I saw that the Great Man's pocket square didn't match his tie.

'Hello, sir!' Graham said, offering his hand and his best *mea casa, sua casa* grin. 'Welcome—'

'Ah—' came the quiet-spoken reply. There was a momentary pause. Then the one-size-fits-all smile broadened out. 'Hullo!'

They moved to clasp hands as they met for the first time and before my eyes were instantaneously transformed into old chums, David and Graham, who've known each other for years, haven't we, old man? Graham could always do that. It was astounding how quickly he could determine the pitch of the hall with a reader, especially one who seemed anxious on arrival, as le Carré had just then. He had a keen sense of the exact tuning required each time, a knack which, in his cups and waxing lyrical, he was happy to call his 'whore's finesse'. More than once, after seeming to be great pals with a reader all day, he had waited until the lift doors closed on the unsuspecting actor then turned to me and muttered, 'Prick'. What he'd immediately sensed with this particular reader was that he needed to establish his credentials to handle the material – the 'deathless prose', as we less than reverently referred to it between ourselves – and had done just that in a matter of moments. He'd simply slapped all his considerable bona fides into that burly handshake – the 'sir' didn't hurt – and was now officially licensed to record le Carré on tape.

Sadly, my own credentials were established just as fast. Graham introduced me as his abridger and co-producer, but there was no handshake for me. What I received instead was what another writer – James Kennaway, whom I'd yet to read – had previously received from him and dubbed 'the wrist-watch brush-off'. It was clearly a practised manoeuvre, the hand that had readily grasped Graham's being smoothly withdrawn to adjust the watch-strap, making it conveniently unavailable to take mine. A deflected glance completed the gesture and told me more plainly than any words that I was to have no status in the day's proceedings. As a signal of the Great Man's acknowledgement of my existence, it was so distant that radio location would have been required to pick it up.

I can't say this especially troubled me. I wasn't a spurned fan; the only le Carré books I'd read at that time were the two Smiley titles Graham had paid me to abridge. Some guys could be like that about working with women, though Graham wasn't one of them and our own working relationship had been happy and equitable from the start. But now, as I watched the pair of them file into the studio ahead of me, the ho-ho-ho of new-forged male camaraderie ringing in their voices, it suddenly felt as if I'd become the *girl* of the outfit. The transformation had happened within seconds of the arrival of the Great Man, Mr David Cornwell (with an e), the so far rather uncharming international bestselling author I had a suspicion I might yet decide to call John.

Derek French was a tall chap about Graham's age, with dark brown twinkling eyes and a high forehead racing to meet his fast-receding hairline. No matter what was presented to him in the studio, his face had a permanently pleasant expression and his eyes had a look of *I'm ahead of you* in them, which, like all first-rate audio engineers, he invariably was. He and Bob Baker – until Bob moved to Magmasters – were the two engineers at John Wood whom

Graham and I most often worked with, and every session with either of them was a masterclass in How Things Should Be Done.

While Frenchie was busy in the sound booth, adjusting the microphone and making sure the new reader was comfortable at his table and chair, Graham and I lined up our scripts in the control room next door. If I wasn't directing in another studio myself, Graham always liked me in with him as an extra pair of ears (his own stereo not being so good since his wife bought him a brace of Purdeys for Christmas) and to straighten out any hitches that might crop up in the script. Not that we knew it right then, but this session was going to give all three of us a run for our money.

Once he was happy with the set-up in the sound booth, Frenchie closed the connecting door and took his seat with us in the control room. He checked all the settings on the desk in front of him, flicked a couple of dials with his fingernail for good measure and gave the thumbs-up. Graham engaged the talkback mic that fed into the reader's headphones, cleared his throat authoritatively and undertook the exposition of our recording procedures – *la méthode Goodwin* – for the benefit of his new pal.

'George tells me you're not entirely *virgo intacta* when it comes to reading your own stuff, David,' he began. 'Apparently you've done a spot of radio for the Beeb, so you'll be used to their way of recording – take one, take two, and so forth – then they edit out all the fluffs after you've gone. Well, just to let you know, we don't work that way. We use continuous editing, which means we make finished product as we go along. We call it rock and roll, it's really very simple—'

The author sat motionless at the table in the booth, staring with an expression of gravest concentration at the copy of my abridgement propped up in front of him, as Graham launched into his standard spiel for new readers. This was Gooders where he was most at home, captain of the ship of his own making, sitting comfortably at the helm in the control room, about to steer another audiobook steadily out of port. The spiel amounted to about a minute and a half of expansive and only mildly condescending instruction, ending with, '—and there you have it, my dear. Continuous editing – rock and roll. Got it?'

He sat back and waited for any of the usual first-time queries.

But there was no response from the other side of the soundproof glass. The writer still sat motionless at his table. It seemed quite as if Graham hadn't spoken. Something must have gone wrong.

'He hasn't heard a word I just said,' Graham said crossly to Frenchie. 'The bleeding talkback must've cut out.'

But Frenchie wasn't having it. He pointed to the channel light, glowing red for ON. The talkback, like everything else in his studio, was working perfectly, thank you very much. If anything had cut out, it was the bleeding reader.

This was what Graham had been worried about; the perils of using a non-professional. It was looking as if the Great Man had lost his bottle before we'd started.

'Er, do you copy that, David?' he asked hesitantly.

Still no response. The silence stretched out for further ragged moments.

Then David said simply, 'Yes.'

Graham exhaled.

'You sure? It's a lot to take in first time—'

'Quite sure, thanks. Stop recording at a mistake, rock the tape back, then roll forward and drop in at the agreed point. I think that's clear. Shall I read some for level?'

The silence was now on our side of the glass. We had just witnessed what could rightfully be called 'the microphone brushoff' – as masterful a way of saying *So fuck you, Sunshine* to Graham's hegemony in the studio as any yet devised. The captain of the ship couldn't have spoken with the barrel of one of his own Purdeys to his head.

Frenchie stepped discreetly into the breach. 'Any time, David,' he said into talkback and didn't need to hear more than a half paragraph before stopping him and offering another thumbs-up through the glass. The microphone level was bang on. He started up the Studer, and as the big reels turned, threading the quarter-inch magnetic tape silently over the recording heads, said quietly, 'Recording now.' After a few more moments of silence, a voice began to descend from the control-room speakers.

We listened spellbound – to the oh-so-persuasive tone and the just-so-effortless delivery, each phrase so beautifully modulated – as John le Carré began to tell us of the seemingly unconnected events that had brought the elderly British Cold Warrior out of retirement to finally bring down his Soviet nemesis. Graham grabbed my arm, clutched his heart and pulled a face of strangulated, ejaculatory bliss.

'Fuck me,' he groaned. 'Fuck *me* – the bloke can't half read!'

To which Frenchie, adding his own technical imprimatur, remarked quietly, 'And the rest.'

It was an anxious start, but now we were off and running and the going was just fine. As the narrative took flight from the page, like the descant from a hymn sheet, it was clear that our hitherto untested reader was as good as any card-carrying actor Graham had ever put a client's money on, bar none. As well as having such a beautiful voice, he was technically faultless, never moving off mic and barely misreading a word. We never once heard him turn a page or swallow or even breathe. His pace was perhaps a little studied, but seemed exactly right for the material. He read his own words with such absolute authority that the listener was bound to want him to take his time. The quality of the voice and the skill in the delivery was what our business of storytelling was all about. This particular voice had a sort of do-me-gently quality to it and the delivery was like a fabulous seduction in the back of a luxuriously upholstered high-end motor, taking us just exactly where we needed to go (or perhaps that was just me).

Soon all the familiar characters from the book were with us in the studio, the whole Circus and more,[1] each player emerging from the speakers in true form. As for Smiley himself, Graham needn't have worried. The extraordinary truth was that the Great Man didn't just do Guinness better than Jayston – he did Guinness better than *Guinness*.

Two hours into the session, after the second reel change, Graham began to do his usual calculation. X pages read, divided into Y minutes of finished tape, equalled how long it was taking the reader to deliver an average page of script. Multiplied by the total number of pages, it gave a reliable estimate of how long the finished reading would be. On a standard two-cassette pack anything between two and a half and three hours was acceptable to the client, anything under or over was not. Graham's brow contracted when he had the final figure.

'It's running long,' he said to me. 'What did you cut it to?'

'Thirty thousand words, same as always.'

'Then he's reading it long. I thought he might be.'

'Can't you get him to crank it up a bit now the plot's going?'

'Don't want to try. He's brilliant but he's still not a pro. The bloke's got no training. I don't want to lean on him in case it puts him off his stride.' He scratched his head. 'No. I think what we have to do is you take the rest of the script out into reception and make some more cuts.'

What *we* have to do? I gave Graham an *are-you-kidding-me?* stare. It was trial enough to render the convolutions of the near-four-hundred-page original down to thirty thousand words in the

---

[1] For a glossary of le Carré terminology used throughout, see page 337.

first place. This wasn't a Dick Francis or a Jeffrey Archer we were working with; it was clever stuff for grown-ups. The script was tight as a drum already; there was nothing left to cut.

'What else am I supposed to take out?' I asked. 'Main verbs?'

'You're the abridger – you figure it out.'

'Gooders—' I started to protest, immediately seeing what it would entail.

But Graham held up his hand.

'Sorry, honey, that's how it is. At the rate he's going, I reckon we need to lose forty minutes. That's twenty-four pages, twenty-five for comfort. Better get started. *Byee*—'

I suppose it was a compliment that Graham simply assumed I could do what he asked, but I wasn't sure it was possible. With about eight thousand words already recorded and allowing two thousand or so as a buffer so they could keep rolling in the studio, the task before me was to remove about thirty per cent of the twenty thousand words that remained. I got stuck in with a red pen out in reception, doing what I could to shave a phrase here, cut a description there, while trying not to nick the many connective arteries that supported any le Carré narrative but particularly this one, which carried the blood-flow of the whole Karla trilogy through its veins. And I had to do it at a gallop, to keep ahead of the recording, all the time staying mindful that my new cuts would have to pass the scrutiny of the writer himself. I had to stop every few pages to make three copies of each re-edited section and pass them back in, only to have them get through the pared-down pages a lot faster, so that I had to make the next new cuts faster still.

I kept grimly at it until the two of them emerged laughing from the studio just before noon. Graham kissed the top of my head as I sat surrounded by pages of script, and blithely announced that they'd decided to break for an early lunch at La Capannina, to give me time to work on the rest of the cuts in peace. *So order a sandwich or something, honey, and see you when we get back. Byee*—

Something rankled as I watched them go. It wasn't being denied the company of the Great Man over lunch, though I felt I'd more than earned a break at the Italian tratt on the corner of Frith and Romilly that Graham used as the staff canteen. It was that I'd been working my allegedly lovely arse off against the clock all morning in the clear understanding that it was entirely down to the Great Man that the script was over-running and entirely down to me that it would come out on time, yet I hadn't received a single appreciative word from him in return. My first instinct was right. There *was* something going on with this guy about working with women, or at the very least about working with *me*—

A considerate touch on my shoulder interrupted these discontented rumblings. It was the receptionist asking whether I wanted egg and cress or prawn salad when she went out to Marks & Spencer for sandwiches.

Though there seemed no scope for further deterioration, things grew actively worse when the session resumed in the afternoon. By three o'clock, I'd only managed to cut the script down to about twenty-eight thousand words and some seventeen thousand of them were already in the can. It felt as if I were careening downhill without brakes as I tried to wrest every last spare word from what was left. The final straw came when Graham poked his head out of the studio door, decided at a cursory glance that the *receptionist* was too busy to be disturbed and asked *me* if I wouldn't mind bringing them in some coffee – two white-no-sugar for him and Frenchie and one black for the reader, sugar requirement unknown.

'How many teaspoons of powdered glass do you take in your coffee, David?' I asked brightly as I brought in the tray.

If he realised I was playing one of his own lines back to him he showed no sign, but Graham caught my tone and cut in.

'D'you know what, David? I think we may have overworked our girl here today.'

He stroked my arm fondly, but I was unapologetic for being snippy.

'Listen,' he went on. 'I think her Oxbridge brain is probably getting a little overwrought with the task in hand. We've got about three-quarters of the show in the can already, but she still has a major chunk left to cut from the rest. Do you think we could call it a day and come back for another short session tomorrow morning, to finish up? That would give her overnight to remove the last of the deathless prose before her MA runs out. What do you say?'

The Great Man considered this for a moment.

'I don't see why not,' he said at last. 'Yes, I think we could manage that.'

Graham checked the studio log in reception and booked a ten-thirty start. That's all settled then, he announced, I could go.

It was all I needed to hear. I scooped up my script, called out to an actor I recognised to hold the lift – a *real* reader who had just finished a session in one of the other studios – and I was out of there. *Byee—*

Some other guy turned up at the studio the next day, without the bad suit and briefcase. The Fuller Brush man must have sent his younger brother.

I left my flat as late as possible, part of me hoping to find the session cancelled, and reached John Wood at the stroke of ten-thirty, not a second before, with my defences raised. Graham and the Great Man were already there, talking like they'd been pals forever and both dressed more casually; the writer wearing a russet-coloured soft suede windcheater over an open-necked shirt and slacks, Graham minus his jacket and back in his standard soft checked shirt, knit tie and cords. They looked up as I came in and straight away I picked up on an odd buzz of excitement. It felt as if someone were about to open a bottle of champagne, though nothing special appeared to be going on.

'Hello, *Sue*! How *are* you?'

This, against all conceivable likelihood, was le Carré, eagerly greeting me like a long-lost and much-missed friend. He was actually smiling, not a thing he'd done once in my direction the day before. In fact, his whole demeanour had changed. His eyes were brighter and seemed to have new colours in them, sparks of amber and green that I would swear weren't there yesterday. His voice, previously restrained in conversation, if not downright clipped, was warm and filled with enthusiasm. And all of it was directed at me.

This was another man.

After yesterday I might have suspected a set-up of some kind, a practical joke pre-arranged between the two of them, but that wasn't Graham's style. He only greeted me in his usual bluff and cheery way.

'Hi, honey – how'd it go?'

'It went,' I said neutrally, not yet on board with the prevailing mood, and produced three freshly minted copies of the end tranche of the script – the all-time *final* edit of *Smiley's People*. 'Finished word count as requested.'

'Oh, goodie, you managed to cut it down,' Graham said, taking the copies and already chuckling at a gag he couldn't resist. 'Does Karla still defect?'

And to make a start on another happy day on the farm, he set down his copy on the desk, handed a second one to the author and flipped the third unceremoniously over to Frenchie, who, as ever, raised a thumb and got on with setting up.

But the writer wasn't quite so ready to start. He was scanning the new pages closely, fingers held pensively to his lower lip as his eyes darted over the lines. I waited for the verdict, ready to counter anything he said. If he wasn't happy with what I'd spent my whole evening working on – even going back to the book to search for more nimble passages that better suited the shorter cut – then he could damn well fix it himself. I might even have suggested where he could put the rolled-up pages if he found them unsatisfactory. It took him a while to say anything as he studied the text, but when he did there was a very gratifying trace of awe in his voice.

'How *wonderful*,' he said. 'You've done it. I didn't think it possible but you've actually *done* it. How clever of you. Thank you so much.'

And with another smile of what seemed genuine appreciation cast towards me, he took the final cut into the sound booth and we were once more ready to rock and roll.

The rest of the recording went off without a glitch, and in barely an hour and a half we were all done and dusted. The very first commercial production of le Carré reading le Carré was in the can.

'*Alors – fin d'histoire*,' Graham said heartily, in his favourite phrase of Franglais, as the writer let himself out of the booth for the last time. 'Thanks, David, and well done for sticking with it. I'll let George know when we've got a release date from the client and I'll make sure they send you some complimentary copies. I expect you'll want to be off now.'

'Well, I'm happy it's done,' David said, and for the first time he did actually seem happy. 'But what I really want to do is ask your lovely co-producer if she'll have lunch with me. Will you, Sue? I'd be so pleased if you would.'

And he turned to me with an expression of such keen yet wistful anticipation that I could no more refuse him than disappoint a puppy.

We started giggling on the stairs – again, for some reason, he didn't attempt the lift – seven flights spiralling dizzily downwards. It wasn't anything specific that made us laugh or decide to race each other down, except that it suddenly felt like Finals were over and we had both passed with flying colours and anyway why not and who cared?

By the time we spilled out onto the street David had wrapped my arm in his so that we had to walk closely side by side, weaving in step through the Soho backstreets while we talked breezily about a million things at once, kicking at dropped fruit from the nearby vegetable market as we went along, two kids out on a spree. We were exactly the same height, with me in my not very high heels and him in his enormous desert boots. We moved along together fluidly, hip to haunch, matching our strides in a mutual gear. We felt – unaccountably – like a *pair*.

A surge of something deliciously exciting had taken me over. Had taken *us* over, apparently, since David's excitement seemed to mirror mine. An irresistible fizz had bubbled up between us, that champagne-cork-about-to-pop atmosphere I sensed when I first arrived. I could no longer remember what I so particularly didn't like about the man less than twenty-four hours earlier and had absolutely no idea how the transformation had happened.

La Capannina was a proudly unreconstructed 1960s Soho trattoria, with white rough-plastered walls hung with lumpy amateur oil paintings and fake-rustic ceiling beams festooned with straw-cased Chianti bottles and lengths of plastic vine. Graham used it as the regular lunch place for productions, and John – Giovanni – and Linda, the couple who ran the restaurant, began to glad-hand us the moment we stepped over the threshold. They knew me from being there so often with Graham, but I don't think they had any idea who the reader *du jour* was. John showed us straight to Graham's usual table in the corner by the bar.

'Will Mr Goodwin be joining you?' he enquired, asking me.

When I said that he wouldn't, the third place-setting was regretfully removed. But being considered part of Graham's gang evidently didn't sit well with David. For a man who made such a point of keeping his identity largely unknown, it seemed also that he didn't like travelling on anyone else's coat-tails. To set his own seal on the proceedings he immediately declared that we must have champagne.

John dispatched a waiter to bring a bottle, asking courteously, 'You are celebrating?'

'Yes!' David confirmed, giggling like a wayward fourth-former. 'End of term! We want everything on the menu twice over and still have room for *gelati* after!'

'Certainly,' John nodded with his knowing maître d' smile, and ducked discreetly away as the champagne bucket promptly arrived.

'That got rid of *him*!' David said in a conspiratorial stage-whisper across the table, while the waiter deftly poured.

Then the mood shifted again, becoming calmer and more intimate as we sipped our drinks and affected to study our menus. I already knew the Capannina offerings by heart and at that point didn't care what I was going to eat. For David, too, the menu seemed mostly a prop. Something was clearly happening here and food, if not the champagne, was the least of it.

'Tell me, Sue, were you actually at Oxenford?'

He'd picked up on Graham's remark yesterday. But – *Oxenford?*

'I was.'

'Which college?'

'Somerville.'

'Ahh, *Somerville*—' he repeated, tilting his head back judiciously, an intellectual Bisto Kid savouring the aroma of whatever it was this told him about me. (W. Somerset Maugham, the original spy-turned-novelist, had given his secret agent Ashenden the cover name Somerville, which may have contributed to David's reaction. And in one of his own novels he'd had the daughter of a hotel night waiter go there ...)

'And did you wear a long gown?'

He was asking, albeit rather affectedly, if I'd been given an award. The university offers two kinds: exhibitions and scholarships. They seldom carry much money with them – mine was a princely £50 a year, barely enough to buy my books – but bestow academic status. Scholars rank higher than exhibitioners, but both are entitled to wear long gowns. The remaining bulk of undergraduates wear short gowns and are known as commoners. David had himself been a commoner at Lincoln College.

'A scholar!' he exclaimed when I told him. 'How marvellous! What subject?'

'English Language and Literature,' I said. 'Course Two, starting with *Beowulf*. Course One pretty much ends with it.'

'And did you take a brilliant first or a debauched fourth?'

We seemed to have slipped back a few decades in our terms of reference. Perhaps John should have left the extra place-setting for Sebastian Flyte's teddy bear Aloysius, or John Betjeman's original, Archibald Ormsby-Gore. The university had dispensed with fourth-class degrees long before I got there.

'Neither,' I told him. 'I got a sleepwalking second.'

He took a moment to absorb this detail, though I couldn't quite see the problem. I imagined that would be the end of the topic, but he regrouped.

'And what did you make of your dons? Were there any great heroes, any good friends?'

He looked taken aback by my mirthless snort.

'Didn't you care for any of them?' he asked.

'Not much.'

'But didn't they inspire you to love your subject?'

I tried not to gag. 'On the contrary.'

Generally speaking, I'd had to protect my love of the subject *from* my dons.

David was looking mildly horrified now so I expanded my position, gently pointing out that the tradition of dons becoming friends and mentors was as lost to the overall picture of Oxford by the time I got there as the traditional skyline of dreaming spires was lost to the developers. At least for me. I went up anticipating that sort of dynamic, everyone does, but didn't find it with any of my tutors. Nor they with me, I'm sure.

'I see,' David said, but I didn't think he did. From his reaction he appeared never to have encountered the idea before. He took another moment, then asked, 'So did you only have tutes in college?'

Ah. I could see where this was heading. The man who elbowed me – the *girl* – out of his working environment yesterday was ready to believe it was my all-women's college that must have let the side down.

'We did,' I confirmed, and caught the *thought as much* glint in the back of his eyes. 'But we also had seminars with a don at one of the men's colleges. I didn't like him any better. He wore corduroy suits.'

'The fiend,' David said supportively, though wanker had been the settled opinion at the time.

'But how disappointing for you,' he concluded.

'Not really. I dare say I was far more disappointing for them.'

'But why? They must have considered you an alpha-plus mind, surely, to have awarded you the scholarship?'

'Of course. Alpha-*plus*-plus, actually.' This was the top *women's* college we were talking about, I reminded him. Because of the historically disadvantageous ratio of female-to-male admissions at the time, Somerville was multiple times harder to get into than any of the top men's colleges. *Let alone Lincoln*, I forbore to add. 'It's just that I soon developed a gamma-minus attitude to go with it.'

'But surely you wanted a first?'

'Not really,' I said again. My achievement, as I saw it, had been getting *into* Oxford – with a *scholarship* – in the first place. After that, it was axiomatic that I was going to come away with a degree *from* Oxford. I appreciate this wasn't the attitude 'my dons' expected of me, but they really were an unappealing lot, so frankly, too bad. Or, as my Classics mistress at school was given to remark, *dolendum est*. The books would always be there – and have been, in all aspects of my life since – but everything else Oxford had to offer would be gone in three short years. So I put my energies into enjoying all the rest of life at the university instead, which was as much an Oxford tradition as any other. As Christopher Hitchens once put it, 'I wasn't going to piss away my time at Oxford studying.'

Much as people seem ready to be impressed by an Oxford degree – and I claim no false modesty to suggest they shouldn't be – it's mostly the fact that you went there at all that carries the weight. I've only once been asked to prove I actually graduated and it wasn't for work, but for documentation when I almost emigrated to Canada some years ago. David is still the only person who ever cared what class of degree I obtained. To employ le Carré terminology, I could just as well have invented the 'legend' for myself all along. So, no, I didn't want a first; not for the kudos then and not for bragging rights afterwards. If a second was good enough for Graham Greene – as just one example – it was more than good enough for me. Hitchens got a third.

But David had taken a first, in German (though, as I later discovered, after a year out before his final year and with his first wife as a full-time study-buddy). He couldn't seem to take any of my attitude in. He seemed to have a built-in regard for the institution itself, something I only ever partially acquired. I was quite a recent graduate, but Oxford already seemed distant to me, while for David, who had graduated decades before me, it seemed still to occupy a very vibrant place in his mind.

'What was your special subject?' he asked. 'Old English?'

'God, no.'

It was Classical Greek Literature, in fact, which I had loved at school and which even another unedifying college tutor couldn't spoil for me. I would tell David this another time, but right then he so badly wanted me to join him on the academic-purity-test high-ground that wild horses wouldn't have made me say so.

'No,' I told him. 'My special subject was balls.'

His chin shot up. 'Balls?'

'Big Commemoration ones, mostly. And all the Winter Balls at Merton. Even one May Ball at Cambridge. About a dozen altogether.'

'I think you're amazing—'

'Thank you.'

'Have some more champagne—'

'Thank you.'

'And you're so beautiful—'

'Thank you.'

'Not at all. It would be rude not to mention it. And so clever with the script in the studio. I think I shall appoint you my Recording Angel, do you mind?'

Beating the watchful waiter to the ice-bucket, David refilled my surprisingly empty glass, which I was sure was full only a few minutes ago, then replenished his own. I realised I was keeping pace with the writer, who appeared to have gills to be able to drink and talk so efficiently at the same time. As he talked, his vocal range remained as flexible as it had been in the studio. Just now his voice was delicate and light. Deceptively light, I was beginning to think, since I was vaguely aware of being debriefed – if not vetted.

There was a break while the waiter took our orders and then the close questioning resumed.

'Tell me – did you have lots of handsome young squires when you were at the university?'

Still with Oxford – and *squires* now?

'Not lots. Just one lovely Canadian doctoral student the whole time.'

'Canadian! Beast! It was all that deep snow they have out there.'

'What was?'

'His treating you to such spectacular balls.'

I laughed. It was cute of him to play back my own joke.

'And what was his college?' David persisted in mock fury. 'Not that I care. I hate him.'

'He was in the MCR at Christ Church. My second home.'

'A House man! Ha! I hate him! And what was he doing his DPhil on? Apart from female anatomy, the beast.'

'I doubt I ever really knew,' I confessed. 'I remember it was all Old Norse sagas and runes. *Irregular Verbs in Heimskringla*, or something.'

'Well, you would think there'd be enough. So how did you come to know Graham?'

How funny. Just when he'd got me laughing over all this Oxford nonsense, he dropped that question out of the blue. I'd only read those two of his books, so was hardly a maven in le Carré trade-craft at the time, but it crossed my mind even then that this was all interrogation technique. In which case, it was just further nonsense, because he only needed to ask me straight out whatever he wanted to know.

So I told him how I met Graham through his best friend, the comedy writer Jeremy Lloyd, whom I'd dated when I first arrived in London (after Jeremy picked me up in the Picasso café on the King's Road …). Jeremy and I went out briefly, were even more briefly engaged, and the three of us had been great friends ever since.

'So you and Graham are chums?'

'Enormous.'

'And he's married?'

'To Audrey.'

'No kids?'

I shook my head. The notion of Graham with offspring didn't compute.

'Just Millie, a big red Irish water spaniel. And a manor house and sheep farm in Wiltshire bought with Audrey's money.'

'I thought you were his bird at first.'

'Did you?'

That seemed an odd reading. Graham and I were always happy and schmoozy with each other in the studio – exactly as we always were outside of it – but not in any way that would particularly suggest we were involved. Was it the kiss on the top of my head yesterday that did it? Perhaps people were usually more formal around the Great Man. Perhaps those wrist-watch and microphone brush-offs were supposed to sober us up. *Dolendum est.*

'Is that why you were so mean to me yesterday?' I asked.

'Oh. Was I mean to you? I'm sure I didn't mean to be – mean to you, that is.'

This was as close to an apology as I was going to get, I felt, so I let it pass. In any case, the man sitting opposite me bore virtually no resemblance to the previous fellow. The two personae appeared to be on non-intersecting orbits, the contrast between them like the light and dark sides of the moon. David was even physically different. He was just six months younger than Graham, something they established yesterday, and it was easy to imagine them in the same class at school; Graham a little taller and bolder, David a little more reserved. But now David seemed far more youthful, with a sharpened vigour about him that dispelled the years. Yesterday he'd seemed bland and nondescript, a figure cast in bare plaster. Today his features were coloured in and glazed. His sandy fairness had a gingery sparkle, his skin and eyes had a heightened tone; his whole bearing was buffed up. Today he was positively *glossy*.

He reached out across the table and gently began to stroke the back of my hand. Moments before the waiter brought our food, he lifted my hand up, leaned in and kissed the tips of my fingers.

*   *   *

After lunch we stood outside on the pavement in the breezy September sunshine and looked at each other. We were talked out for the moment and needed a different venue for the next episode, if there was going to be one.

'Let's go to a movie or something,' David offered, moving a strand of hair from my face. 'What shall we see?' he mused, then answered himself. 'I know – *Bambi*!'

'No, not *Bambi*,' I countered, matching his mock-solemn tone. 'I know – *Rambo*!'

'No, not *Rambo*. I know – *Bambo*! Let's see where it's showing!'

We laughed and walked on, David's arm once more snaking through mine. We wandered down to Piccadilly Circus, managing to linger over the exotic *affiches* covering the windows of the Raymond Revuebar on the way, before finally stopping on the pavement opposite Eros, where we stood looking at one another again.

'Well—' David said.

'Well—' I echoed.

I couldn't see his expression properly because his hand was over his brow against the sun. I smiled back, but something in me told me suddenly that I was going to decline whatever might be coming next. David dropped his hand and smiled too, but he had read my inner prompting and it was a different, rueful little smile.

'You'll get those books I mentioned, won't you?' he pressed. 'They're important to me. I'm sure you'll enjoy them.'

I confessed to forgetting the titles he told me about over lunch, we'd talked about so many different things. He took a note card and pen from inside his windcheater and wrote them down, then gave me the card. His address in Hampstead was printed along the top and underneath he had written: *The Good Soldier* – Ford Madox Ford, *The Horse's Mouth* – Joyce Cary. Titles which had somehow escaped my reading up till then.

'Do read them,' he pressed again. 'Particularly *The Good Soldier* – it's the book of my life.'

'Thanks,' I said. 'Yes, I will.'

He hailed an oncoming taxi, which promptly drew up. Then, without prelude, he kissed me urgently on the mouth, turned to the taxi, heaved open the door and got in. As the black cab pulled away, he looked back at me from the rear window for as long as he could, until the curve of Shaftesbury Avenue carried him out of sight.

So that was how my life was when David first walked in. I was a tall, blonde city girl not long out of college and generally up for anything. (I was happy to consider myself *a* girl, just not to be designated *the* girl.) I lived in Chelsea, worked in the West End and shopped in Knightsbridge, albeit in the sales. I saw friends, dated great guys and took frequent trips to the continent and the States. I had a happy, exciting career in audio with Graham and in television as a freelance programme researcher. In short, I was the confident, striding media-girl-about-town that I had always envisioned myself being. Everything in my world was wonderful.

David simply offered to make it more wonderful, by an order of magnitude, with that fizz of extra-super-special excitement and intensity he supplied and the way he insisted it was all just for me.

To this day, I don't know what barely registering impulse made me deflect the start of it; what transient misgiving David saw at the back of my eyes, or felt reciprocated at the back of his, that ensured we parted in front of Eros that blowy sunny afternoon. Perhaps on some inner level I knew, perhaps he did too, that I needed another year of life BC – Before Cornwell – another year under my own control, on my own terms and territory, before I surrendered to David, the perfect spy, and let him run me.

SECOND ENCOUNTER
August 1983

SOHO ZURÜCK

For ... there is no man who loves a woman that does not desire to
come to her for the renewal of his courage, for the cutting asunder
of his difficulties.

Ford Madox Ford, *The Good Soldier*

It was almost a year after our first encounter with the writer and
Graham and I were once again waiting for him to arrive at John
Wood Studios. It was the start of a leisurely three-day session that
was sure to go well, so this time Graham had no nerves. This time,
the apprehension was all mine.

During the eleven months since I watched David get into that
taxi at Piccadilly Circus, I had wondered more than once what I
might have missed by not picking up on his suggestion that we 'go
to a movie or something'. He didn't push the notion and I didn't
really decline; we just let the possibility of what might happen
linger a little, then drift away. But the notion kept drifting back.
I'd already known some lovely, special men, all stars in their own
right, but I had the feeling that David was in a constellation of his
own. As this next recording approached – of *The Little Drummer
Girl*, the latest le Carré international bestseller – I caught myself
hoping that unspecified 'something' would still be on offer. I knew
I wasn't going to pass on it a second time.

But as before, the abridgement was not without its difficulties.

In January I'd cut a proof copy of *Drummer Girl*, which wasn't yet published, down to a very workable twenty-six thousand words, four thousand short of the standard length to allow for our reader's rather stately pace, and sent off a copy of the finished typescript to George Greenfield for author approval. This was a contractual obligation, customarily only a rubber stamp, and since we weren't going to be in the studio with it until the end of the summer I thought no more about it. The novel was published to great acclaim at the end of March and was seen as a timely treatment of the Israeli–Palestinian conflict, with the atrocious days-long massacre at the Sabra and Shatila refugee camps in Lebanon having occurred less than six months earlier. When the American Embassy compound in Beirut was subsequently devastated by a terrorist truck bomb on 18 April, just weeks after publication, the book was seen not just as timely but as extraordinarily prescient. Barely two weeks after that, at the beginning of May, I received an unexpected phone call from Jane Cornwell, the Great Man's wife.

She began by complimenting me on the abridgement, then added, 'But you have left rather a lot out.' She made it sound as if this were something David had just noticed, though he'd had the script for four months by then.

'It's a twenty-six thousand word abridgement,' I replied, as tactfully as I could while stating the obvious. 'That's really all I could leave in.'

'Yes,' she said quickly. 'We appreciate that. But we feel there's rather *too much* missing. For instance, right at the beginning – the girl who delivers the bomb in Bad Godesberg. We feel she should have more of a presence …'

Jane continued with a long list of the many scenes that would improve the script by their inclusion and, when she gave me the chance, I said I agreed with every one of them, but pointed out that every addition would necessitate the subtraction of something else. I asked for suggestions, but she had no views about what could be cut to make way for the extra scenes. Evidently that wasn't in her brief.

'Well, you see, it's a big, complicated book,' she told me finally, as though that were something I might not have appreciated.

Actually, even judged by previous le Carrés, it was an extraordinarily complex narrative. Charlie, a disaffected young British actress looking for a cause to believe in, is recruited by Mossad and elaborately trained – virtually re-programmed – to infiltrate the cell of a Palestinian terrorist so that the Israelis can locate and kill him. And that was just the core story. There were layers and layers built around it to reinforce the whole.

'We want to be sure we do it justice in the recording,' Jane continued. 'What we really feel is that it needs longer to tell the story. Would that be possible, do you think – for you to make the abridgement longer?'

'Certainly,' I replied. 'I can *cut* it to any length you like, but we *record* to three hours. Graham will need to square it with the client if you want to change that. You'll really have to talk to him.'

As is usually the case with someone who tries to tell you your job, Jane retreated once I held my ground. She attempted chit-chat next, but it was still about the Great Man's work. She began to tell me about the Hollywood film that was going to be made from the new book. She said that David had started working on the script with the director, George Roy Hill of *Butch Cassidy* fame. I forbore to ask whether the girl who delivered the Bad Godesberg bomb had much of a presence in the screenplay.

'They're casting now,' Jane said. 'We understand Meryl Streep is keen to play Charlie.'

'Great,' I said. 'She's terrific.'

'Oh, yes, of course. But we feel she might be a little *icebergy* for the character. What do you think about her?'

What did *I* think? Who cared? Although, since she asked, what I thought about actors in general – after working with so many in audio and television and having a number as friends – was that they seldom pursued parts they weren't up to playing. No actor wants a pratfall unless it's in the script. What I thought about Meryl Streep in particular was that they would be lucky to have her. Le Carré movies hadn't yet proved to be Oscar-winning material, but Streep was already an Oscar-winning actress. As for *icebergy*, I couldn't see how her portrayal of the frail and damaged heroine in *Sophie's Choice* warranted that judgement, or her double role in *The French Lieutenant's Woman*. Both films were based on bestselling quality novels and Streep seemed able to suggest that in her acting, bringing a subtle sort of literary undertow with her. In short, what I thought was – how can you *not* want Meryl Streep?

But I didn't see the point in saying any of that to the writer's wife, who was only making a poor fist of being nice to me after putting her foot in it before. I simply remarked that I thought Streep would be great for the part. The conversation drew to a close with Jane saying that David would speak to Graham about getting a longer reading and with me not saying that was what should have happened in the first place. David must have known that was how to sort the issue if he felt so strongly about it, so I couldn't see why he'd directed his wife to speak to me when it wasn't my shot to call. She'd had to phone Graham in the first place to get my number. Finally, I was left wondering what it must be like to live your life in complete surrender of the personal pronoun. In the fifteen minutes we'd been talking, Jane Cornwell had said 'we' about thirty times but hadn't once used 'I'.

So David did speak to Graham and Graham did square it with the client. Now there was going to be a special six-hour, four-cassette pack of *Drummer Girl* and my next task was to make the new cut. Graham, in best bishop-to-actress mode, said he was sure I'd agree that longer was always more satisfying than shorter, especially since he was going to pay me a full second fee, given that I had to include all the specific extra scenes that David wanted, listed in a closely typed eight-page memo I promptly received from Jane. It appeared she was the Great Man's secretary – his amanuensis – as well as his wife. The passing image I had of her was as one of the uncharacterised 'Mothers' who looked after the 'boys' on the fifth floor of the Circus. I took another week to finish the second version and it received the rubber stamp without further comment. I'd never had that kind of run-around over an abridgement before – and never did again, not even when I worked on the latest Frederick Forsyth and cut a hundred and forty-eight pages out of the first hundred and forty-nine – so it puzzled me why David had suddenly become so picky about this one. There was a reason, as things turned out; I just didn't have enough clues at my disposal yet to work out what it was.

David arrived at John Wood wearing a different zip-up jacket, this one in cream leather, over the same sort of soft checked shirt and dark corduroys that Graham favoured. He looked as if he felt at home in the studio this time, even seeming somehow relieved to be with us, as though he'd reached a safe mooring after a choppy sail. He slapped Graham solemnly on the back and then, before saying a word, without even a smile, wrapped his big arms around me and hugged me right off my feet. After only a very few mild pleasantries he took his script into the sound booth and sat down at the mic. Once again, we were ready to rock and roll.

As before, his microphone level was bang on, the only difference being that David requested slightly more volume in his headphones. His hearing was going, he said, adding woefully that he might soon have to start wearing a hearing aid.

'Oh, magic,' Graham muttered to me, as the engineer – not Frenchie this time – made the adjustment. 'Talking books – read by the deaf, bought by the blind ...'

*   *   *

The new reading was quite as faultless as its predecessor. With no need to push ourselves we soon took a break, but when David came through to the control room to join us for coffee he already seemed rather washed out. The downbeat vibe he'd brought with him when he arrived didn't seem to have lifted. Even Graham noticed.

'Are we working you too hard, old love?' he asked, not very seriously, since he'd booked three full studio days for what was barely two days' work.

David took a deep breath and expelled it slowly.

'It was a rough summer.'

'Counting the money?'

Graham was incorrigible.

David smiled wanly at the joke and knocked back a gulp of black coffee as though it were neat Scotch. 'The thing is,' he said quietly after a moment, with an odd sort of throw-away solemnity, 'the thing is, I don't think I'm going to write again.'

Well, here was news. One of the world's most successful, most renowned, most admired authors, at the very summit of his career, had just told us he was thinking of jacking it all in. And the way he said it was strange. This wasn't Hillary planting the flag at the top of Everest; nor was it Alexander lamenting the want of fresh worlds to conquer. There was nothing either triumphant or regretful about David's manner. It was just flat, without affect. It was as if, since I'd last seen him, something had knocked the wind clean out of him.

As usual, Graham saw it from a different angle.

'Well, it's not like you *have* to write any more, my dear, is it?' he said. 'I mean, you can't need the money. You must have a few mill stashed away by now.'

Although it was entirely unwitting, there was nevertheless something therapeutic in the high sweep of Graham's misapprehension. David managed a slightly stronger smile and played along.

'Yeah,' he agreed mildly. 'I suppose. A couple.'

'Right.' Graham was confident he'd hit the nail of the situation right on its head. 'So why not chuck it in? Go out at the top.'

'Um, well—'

'Why not? Just fuck 'em, I say. Leave while they're still wet for more.'

'Mmm – that's certainly one approach,' David agreed mildly again. 'Shall we make a start on the next reel?'

The whole three-day recording was such a walkover it was really just one marathon boozy lunch with a few reel changes between courses. On day one, Wednesday, David treated Graham and me to a champagne lunch at La Capannina. In our tender care he seemed to have perked up over the course of the morning and was cheery enough to regale us with an account of being invited to lunch at Buckingham Palace, putting us into uncontrollable hysterics with his impression of HMQ, which he executed in a respectful but scrupulously accurate falsetto.

He also told us about the film, which had just started shooting.

'Who's playing Charlie?' I asked, wondering who they'd eventually decided to cast.

'Diane Keaton,' he replied.

Ah. From my studies in Classical Greek literature, I recalled that this was what happened when the gods offered their best thing first and you demurred.

'I think she'll be really good,' he went on. 'She's got a quality about her that I like.'

Well, yes, indeed. There were her wonderful performances as the doomed free-loving Theresa in *Looking For Mr. Goodbar* and as the neurasthenic wife of the next Don Corleone in *The Godfather*. Woody Allen's two most memorable (and most misogynistic) films are unimaginable without her. But for the feisty, maladjusted Charlie, who has to hold her own with a bunch of Mossad heavies while they train her to go after some Palestinian terrorists, perhaps you'd want an actress who could pack rather more of a punch. Maybe Meryl Streep?

But again I said none of this and Graham only said what he always said about actresses, which was to name the performance he fancied them in most.

'I thought she was magic in *Annie Hall*. But why didn't your sister get the part? You based it on her, didn't you? I fancied her madly in *Rock Follies*.'

David's sister was the actress Charlotte Cornwell; *Rock Follies* was a seventies drama series about an all-female rock band, made by Thames Television, where I'd worked myself as a researcher some months earlier.

'Well, you know how it is in Hollywood,' David answered with a diplomatic shrug. 'They don't know the English talent. But I think it's a really strong cast with Keaton heading it. And Klaus Kinski playing Kurtz—'

I continued to hold my counsel. Who cared what *I* thought? *Icebergy* – hah.

Day two, Thursday, and lunch was again, at his insistence, David's shout. He certainly loved a bash. This time the three of us went to L'Escargot in Charlotte Street and drank even more champagne than we did on day one – shampoo, as David invariably called it – and soon, in Graham's favourite phrase, were feeling no pain.

'So you've finally come out with it, then,' Graham noted. He had genned up on the massive coverage David had been receiving for the new book. 'You finally confessed that you were a spy.'

'I thought it was time to stop pretending otherwise,' the writer replied lightly.

'And great publicity.' Graham wasn't going to let that pass.

'I suppose. The conspiracy theorists had me down for a cross between Mata Hari and Himmler's aunt, so I thought now would be as good a time as any to come clean with the rather more mundane truth about my career. Frankly, I only ever had a worm's eye view of the trade.'

Immediately after playing down his espionage career, David then dropped the biggest name in the annals of 'the trade'.

'I was in Bonn, of course, when the news broke about Philby.'

'You mean over the Burgess–Maclean affair?' Graham asked keenly.

It was funny. David's astonishing announcement that he was planning to give up writing for good held far less interest for Graham than this insider tid-bit about a decades-old story of Soviet-run British double agents. It made me think that if David really did intend to forsake writing he ought to take up the lecture circuit. He had Graham on the edge of his seat as he continued with his foray into the history of Cold War treachery.

'If you recall, after their joint defection to Moscow in 1951, the hunt was on for whoever it was who had tipped them off – the person the papers were predictably calling the Third Man.'

David was sounding rather donnish now, that elevated and somewhat godly tone which was working on Graham because he hadn't met with it before. I was paying close attention too, but because David piqued my interest as a man, not because of all that spy stuff, which rather left me cold.

'So there was an enquiry,' he went on, 'a trial of sorts, and by 1955 we have so august a person as the foreign secretary, one Harold Macmillan, telling the House of Commons that he had – and I quote – "no reason to conclude that Mr Philby has at any time betrayed the interests of this country".'

David nailed Supermac's patrician drawl perfectly. Then his voice changed again, slip-streaming from lofty lecture to music-hall banter on the turn of a phrase.

'Now, I ask you, ladies and gentlemen – who briefed Macmillan?'

'The Foreign Office?' Graham guessed.

'Correct. And who briefed the FO?'

'Your lot?'

'Correct again. Give the man a bun.'

Reverting to his standard narrative voice, David continued to breeze through his topic, every detail as readily at his fingertips as a copy of Bradshaw's to a Victorian traveller. 'It *had* to be Kim, of course,' he concluded. 'No one else had the connections to all parties, no one else could have tipped off Maclean. The simple truth was that none of us wanted to *believe* it was him. Here was someone at the very heart of *our* counter-espionage operations, who controlled everything *we* knew about the Russians. If he was the Third Man then there was no Tooth Fairy, no Santa Claus and Dumbo never could fly. If it really was Kim, then it was the end of the world as we knew it.'

'So how did you find out, in the end?' Graham asked.

'I was duty officer the night the coded wires started coming in, about the sudden disappearance of one of ours in Beirut. No name, of course. Then two messages came in together. First: *Identity of person now confirmed, see my next.* Second: *Find a word of six letters, first letter P.*' David spread his hands and raised his eyebrows to convey his astonishment at the time. '"Christ—!" I said. "It's Kim!"'

Graham's mouth may actually have been open. The quality of the voice and the skill in the delivery was what storytelling was all about.

In the hiatus between courses Graham spotted someone he knew at a nearby table and got up to exchange a few words. While we were briefly alone David asked me softly, 'Will you have supper with me tomorrow, Sue?'

'Yes,' I answered in a sudden mild daze, 'of course.'

'Good. I'll pick you up at your flat at seven.'

There was no time to say anything more before Graham rejoined us and David moved smoothly on to another topic of conversation. I'd never had a secret from Graham before. Now I did.

We wound up the session on Friday by late morning, with the whole six-hour recording securely in the can. To mark the occasion, David presented us all – including the engineer, which was a nice touch – with boxed presentation copies of *The Little Drummer Girl*, very grand, ornately tooled volumes that he called the 'human skin' edition. He quickly wrote little dedications in the copies for Graham and the engineer, then paused elaborately to chew on his pen before writing in mine.

'Now, what shall I write in this one—?' he mused stagily, getting a laugh all round. 'Ah – I know!'

He scribbled furiously on the title page, slapped the book shut and handed it to me with a little bow. I took a look inside at the fresh inscription while David watched my reaction, apprehensive that he'd overstepped the mark. I gave no sign but passed the open book to Graham, who read it out loud.

'*For lovely Sue, who shortened it …*'

The Great Man must have worked all night on that one. Graham guffawed and cranked up the double entendre another notch.

'Well, she's certainly performed the service on enough grateful authors, so she should be pretty good at it by now,' he said. 'And I'm sure she particularly appreciated your extra length, David – or was it the thickness?'

In the general mirth that ensued, David seized me in another whole-body hug and whispered fervently in my ear – 'I adore you!' – before we both joined in the next wave of laughter.

In return for the previous two days of sybaritic feasting courtesy of David, Graham was going to take us to Harry's Bar for our third and final lunch and we were all gussied up for the occasion. I was wearing a dress featuring buttons from the hem to the upper thigh – quite all of which, for reasons of public order, Graham insisted I didn't keep undone – and he and David had ditched their casuals for suits. If David's wasn't the same suit as last year, then it was another one that looked just slightly less off the peg. This wasn't my observation alone. Graham's sartorial verdict, while David was in the loo during a break, had been that although the writer doubtlessly spent the earth on bespoke tailoring, he nevertheless managed to look as if he had just stepped out of a Marks & Spencer menswear department. It was a brutal observation, though not brutally meant (and intending no offence to M&S), but it wasn't wrong. Beside Graham's easy man-about-town suavity, David – trying his best – passed for a suburban accountant. It seemed a personal blind spot, at odds with his ability to draw the appearance of his fictional characters with such detailed precision – though, ironically, it quite closely matched his most characteristic description of Smiley.

The clubby sophistication of Harry's Bar soon ran to riot once the three of us were installed. I lost count of the bottles we up-ended as we ploughed our way through the menu, laughing and raising lunatic toasts to ourselves and generally becoming the sort of table that our fellow diners didn't want to sit next to, but would rather have liked to sit at. Our camaraderie was at its convivial post-wrap peak, particularly between the two men. When they discovered they had skiing as a common passion, David promptly offered him the use of his chalet in Wengen in the coming season and Graham promptly accepted.

As for me, David was just so hugely attractive it was as if he had an industrial magnet inside him, drawing me close. It wasn't too different for Graham. We were both smitten. We both wanted as much of him as he would give, and he appeared ready and willing to give us his all. There was such beguiling candour in his manner towards us, as though we had been specially selected for his confidences, were specially qualified to be the secret sharers of his domain. Yet even so, even with his opening up to us and drawing us to him, it was clear that this was just the headland. The greater part of him, like a land-mass shrouded in mist, was still held in enigmatic reserve. This man, I now knew, was going to become my lover.

HAMPSTEAD

We met at seven as planned, but not at my flat. David called me a little before six, the phone ringing just as I'd stepped out of my bath.

'You do still want me to turn up, don't you?'

'Yes, of course.'

'Suddenly I wasn't sure.' He sounded as nervous as a youth. There was a faint tremor in his voice, coupled with a sense of urgency under restraint, which I felt too. 'So we're still on?'

'Yes – of course.'

Standing naked by the phone I realised we couldn't possibly meet here, because I would simply wait like this to greet him at the door and we would never leave the flat. There was no shortage of nearby places for a more conventional, not to say more conventual, meeting. I mentioned one, a New York-style cocktail bar and restaurant which had recently opened in the Pheasantry, a storied old building with a triumphal arch to its forecourt and caryatids holding up the main portico, just a little way down the King's Road from my flat.

'It sounds perfect,' David said. 'I'll be there. Till seven, then. Gosh.'

We sat in a corner booth while our waitress brought us our drinks. More champagne, but this time as cocktails. As she set the tall sparkling glasses down on our table David tipped her a large note as an inducement to look after us with special care.

'We may need some more of these,' he told her confidentially. 'I think a pretty steady flow would work best.'

She cast a professional eye over us and sussed the situation at a glance. Smiling sweetly, she nodded at David, palmed the note, tucked her tray under her arm and left us with a suitably American 'Enjoy!'

So – here we were at last. But for the immediate moment we seemed to have no conversation. We were like tongue-tied teenagers at a school dance. I couldn't bear the suspense.

'We are going to spend the night together, David, aren't we?'

'Oh, yes – yes, please.'

'Good. Excellent. Now I can relax. Phew.'

'Phew. You're amazing, did I tell you?'

'You did. And the rest, as Frenchie would say.'

'Yes. *And* the rest.'

We raised our glasses and half-emptied them at a single draught. The tension was broken, or at least the nervy first-date worst of it, and now we could just schmooze. Talking and laughing once again – David lightly dropping in and out of topics, receiving anything I said as if it offered a fresh vista on his own thoughts – we soon got through a couple more glasses each. Or it might have been more. Excitement and anticipation gave us the edge over the alcohol and no one except our waitress was keeping count. After a little over an hour, David checked his watch.

'Do you think it might be time we moved on to solids?'

'Why not?' I said. 'There's a restaurant upstairs here.'

'Let's move somewhere else, shall we? I always like to venture on from first places. In fact, I booked us a table at Daphne's for ten minutes ago.'

'Wonderful. I love Daphne's. Let's go.'

'Yes, let's – only – not right this minute.'

'Why not?'

'Because I have an erection.'

Perfectly aware that it wouldn't speed our departure, I nevertheless leant over to kiss his cheek.

'That's all right,' I told him. 'So do I.'

At Daphne's we ordered everything on the menu and, with the debauch of Caesars, tasted it all and finished nothing. Given our blow-out at Harry's Bar barely six hours earlier, this was hardly surprising and, anyway, just as at our first lunch a year ago, food was the least of what was going on.

'Tell me,' David said, apropos of nothing we had spoken about so far, 'where does a girl go for a holiday in the late summer sun these days?'

It was funny he should ask the question, uncanny in fact, because friends of mine had just offered me the use of their holiday home in Greece that autumn.

'Mainland or one of the islands?' he asked when I told him.

'One of the islands.'

'Which one?'

'Lesbos.'

We both failed to resist the Pavlovian snigger. My friends Priscilla and John always pronounced it with a 'v'. A Lesvian holiday home probably didn't invite the same run of gags.

'When were you thinking of going?'

I hadn't thought about it at all yet. Priss had only mentioned it recently, saying they were going out for one final late-summer trip and that I was welcome to use it any time after that.

'They claim the weather is always fine till the end of October,' I said, 'even for swimming.'

'Ah. That's good,' David said sagely. 'I'd consider it a great shame otherwise.'

'Why's that?' I asked. Jeremy had taught me never to do feed-lines, but I needed to know.

'Because I want to imagine you walking naked out of the sea. Venus rising from the foam.'

'Aphrodite,' I corrected him, laughing, though David had seemed to speak quite seriously. 'Since it's Greece.'

'Yeah. But walking naked out of the sea.'

'Aphrodite Anadyomene, then.'

'Yeah. That too. As long as it's with lots of foam.'

*   *   *

It was miles up to Hampstead from Chelsea and the taxi seemed to take forever to get us there. We could have been at my place in five minutes, but something told me all along that David wanted to be on his own territory that night. While we were dining, a pale balmy evening had turned into a silky black night. All the long journey north I stared out of my window and David stared out of his while on the seat between us our hands were locked together. We didn't face each other or speak. The physical anticipation was too intense, too achingly fierce for words or looks.

Finally, a private roadway sign slipped by and our cab drew us round the circumference of a communal garden. I thought I caught a glimpse of a tennis court among the shrubs. David told the driver where to pull up and swiftly paid him as we got out. He made a show of putting away his wallet and fishing for his latchkey until the ticking cab circled away, then immediately dropped the pretence and took me by the hand and walked us a little further along. He hadn't let the driver pull up in front of his exact address or see us walk towards it.

'Come into my *Schloss*,' he said, as the house rose up out of the darkness, solid and massive in the night. A fleeting vision from Bram Stoker came to me as he stood on the unlighted threshold and beckoned me inside.

Few places are deader to the senses than an unfamiliar unlighted house at night, but this house felt particularly dead right then. David didn't turn on the hall light until he had shut the front door securely behind us, so I couldn't immediately tell why it was so. When he finally flicked the switch, the answer became apparent. The light fixture was covered with a cloth and cast a dim eerie glow over a hallway full of what looked like lurking stage ghosts. Heavy dust-sheets were draped over everything.

'I've got some workmen in,' he said apologetically.

'But not right this minute?' I asked – stupidly, since it was close to eleven o'clock on Friday night. Over his shoulder, in the uncovered hall mirror, I saw a dimly reflected face filled with an edgy mix of anticipation and apprehension. It took me a moment to realise it was my own.

'No, not right this minute,' he reassured me. 'And they won't be here in the morning either. It's quite safe, everyone's away, we're quite alone.'

He took my hand again and led the way upstairs.

'I thought we'd use Tim's room,' he said. This was the youngest of his three grown-up sons from his first marriage, who he'd said during one of the lunches was an undergraduate at his old Oxford college. 'I made sure he'd be staying at his girlfriend's pad over the weekend.'

It must have been my apprehensiveness that made me mark the quaint expression. His girlfriend's *pad* – like a line from a fifties film, where someone was about to fix a pink gin.

'Just in case, of course,' he added quickly. 'Don't worry, I changed the sheets when I came back from lunch. Strictly on the off-chance, you understand.'

David was apprehensive too, these little explanations catching in his throat as he attacked the stairs in twos and even threes while I followed in different shoes, trying to take each step quickly in order as he hurried me up behind him, still holding my hand.

'Here—'

He threw open the door to an unremarkable studenty room, dark-painted, with wardrobe doors hanging ajar, books scattered across a desk, and posters held up with Blu Tack. A newly made double bed, rather too big for the room, took up most of the floor space. An Anglepoise lamp was already on, shining over the desk, but David turned its head to face the wall, as if even the lightbulb shouldn't know we were there.

'We're here at last,' he said, turning back to me. 'I can't believe it. Oh, my *darling*—!'

*   *   *

Our clothes lay in an incontinent heap on the floor, fastenings gaping wantonly, arms and legs tangled together, a tumbled conundrum of hotly vacated shapes to which our bodies on the bed were the answer. It was as if we had always been lovers. There was no shyness between us, only an infinite familiarity. Everything about us formed an inextricable physical union. This was sex as I had never encountered it before, the sex I had determinedly pursued all my adult life, the sex I truly believed I had always been enjoying, until then. But this was different from anything before, by an order of magnitude. This was sex that only the hero and heroine can have; sex for the cameras, sex for the Olympics, sex for the gods.

'There's not a spare inch of you, Sue, not one anywhere,' David claimed, marvelling, and it was the same for me, looking at him. He was strong and muscled and quite beautiful. 'And your legs,' he added. 'They simply don't stop. They go all the way up to heaven—'

Some time later I was lying on my stomach – between rounds – and David was lying behind me, tracing his fingers over my skin. He had huge workman's hands but his touch was feather-soft.

'I'll do anything for you, my darling,' he said softly in my ear. 'Anything to please you, anything you want. Just tell me.'

So I whispered two words over my shoulder; something he hadn't attempted thus far. He made no immediate reply but there was a thoughtful pause as – so I imagined – he planned his best route forward. I anticipated being gently turned over on to my back, my knees being moved up and parted. Instead, I received a hard smack as the full flat of his big hand landed sharply on my rear.

'What was *that* for?!' I yelped, sitting up in bed and rubbing the offended part, completely confused.

'You asked me to do it,' David answered, now totally perplexed himself.

'I absolutely did not,' I objected.

'Yes, you did – you said *beat me*.'

'No, I did *not*!' I told him again, but I was already laughing and David's hand shot to his mouth as he realised his mistake.

'Oh!! Oh, I know what you said now! Oh, my darling—! Oh, my Gawd—! I *knew* I needed a hearing aid!'

At first I thought I was dreaming the noise. It was early morning and we'd been sleeping at most for a couple of hours. The rest of the night had continued as it began, until the extraordinary blitz of erotic sensation left us both finally incapable of more.

Then I heard the noise again and knew it was real; a faint rustling clatter coming from downstairs, as though someone were trying to move around quietly. David was asleep, but when I gripped his shoulder his body instantly translated my touch and he came awake in the same second, fully alert. He rose on one elbow, listening intently. The gentle clatter started again.

'Christ,' he said under his breath, 'it's Tim—'

He was out of bed and at the bedroom door in one movement. Leaving me with the superfluous gesture of a raised finger – as if I were likely to make any noise myself – he took the stairs naked, calling out ahead as he descended.

'Timo – that you? Tim? Hullo—?'

There was about a minute's silence, long enough for me to wonder how my new lover's legendary talent for compelling narrative would get us out of this one. Then I heard another brief burst of the same erratic noise, a little louder, followed by a deep laugh from David.

'Hey, Sue – it's all right,' he called up. 'Come downstairs. We've got a visitor, but it's not what you think.'

Since the master of the house had just taken the stairs buck naked, I felt authorised to do the same. By then I was sure it couldn't be the son, or indeed anyone else higher up the food chain. If it was the builder, who'd turned up to do some overtime first thing on Saturday morning, then it was his lucky day.

I tracked David's voice to the kitchen. He was standing by the window at the sink.

'Come on,' he beckoned. 'Quick.'

The tiles were cold under my feet as I crossed the floor. Everything was new and shiny, but designed to look old and Italian-farmhousey. A high-end Hampstead kitchen. David indicated a row of herb pots on the windowsill.

'Here's our intruder, look—'

I looked, but could only see parsley and basil and chives. Then something fluttered madly among the leaves and shot up to the corner of the ceiling. A tiny black eye shone down at us like a spot of liquid terror.

'Oh, David—' I looked up at the minuscule creature clinging for its life to some invisible flaw in the decor, a bundle of dun feathers the size of a large moth. 'It's a wren—'

'Is that what it is? Well, he's a clever sod – he got in past my security. MI5 probably trained him to shit micro-listening-devices into concealed areas. I think it's time we encouraged him to go back to base and file his report.'

David opened the window and we both stood back. The bird took a moment to gather itself and dropped back to the cover of the herbs. But when it tried to escape, it flew against the closed side of the window, too disoriented to make the simple sideways move to freedom. We watched it repeatedly hit the glass, with more desperate force at every attempt, each time falling back again into the herbs. I never could bear the sight of an animal in distress and couldn't stand to watch.

'It'll kill itself if we don't get it out,' I said.

'I should think he'll definitely go home with a headache. Here—'

David made to shoo the bird with his hand, but I stopped him.

'No – you'll frighten it to death. Let me—'

I grabbed a glass towel from the side of the sink and threw it gently over the wren as it skimmed frantically up the window pane yet another time. The bird dropped to the windowsill and lay unmoving beneath the cloth. I scooped up the cloth in a soft bundle, held it still for a second, then shook it lightly out of the window. A moment later I was relieved to see the wren fly away.

'That was a good trick,' David said, wrapping his arms around me. 'Where'd you learn that?'

'MI5,' I replied. 'Advanced wren-wrangling. Course Two.'

'You're amazing.'

'*You* are. *We* were – last night.'

'I know. Phew. Hey, Sue, we're standing naked together in my kitchen. How about that?'

'Yes, hey, how about that. But you are sure the builder's not coming now, aren't you?'

If I had to wrangle a workman, I was going to need a bigger cloth.

'Well, if he wasn't coming already, he soon would be, looking at you. Wow. Talk about Venus rising—'

David held me closer.

'Something's rising—' I noted.

'I know, like Lazarus from the dead. But let's not attend to him right now. I've got a better idea. Why don't we get dressed and go for a walk on the Heath, then come back and take our breakfast upstairs and see if he still wants to play?'

'Sounds good to me,' I agreed. 'We'll probably spot our wren.'

And like the comic double-act it behoves all new lovers to become, we instantly chorused together, 'If he doesn't spot us first!'

Hampstead Heath appeared to open up almost immediately through a gate at the end of David's back garden. It was still early and joggers and dog-walkers were our only companions, but already the sun was beaming down on the grass and trees. The Heath should have been looking a little tired and worn at the height of summer, but the pathetic fallacy had beaten us to it and everything was fresh and spring-clear, bright with new possibilities.

I wasn't dressed for a ramble, but last night's cocktail shift didn't look too morning-aftery and I found I could manage the grass pretty well in my shoes. David had thrown on his Graham-ish cords and a casual shirt. He took slow, heavy strides at my side, his hands thrust deep into the pockets of his trousers. Just as he had many voices, he seemed also to have many walks, perhaps many moods to go with them. He was more pensive now, as though some temporarily dismissed trouble had crept back upon him. I felt it must be what he'd told Graham and me earlier in the week.

We continued walking for a while, stopping when we got to the crest of the Heath. A hazy-bright view of London appeared in the distance. Hampstead has always been known for its writers, and many have walked the Heath and written about it. But in those years, with Smiley in such ascendancy on page and screen, David had managed to make it his own. It was impossible to stand there and not half-see the elderly spymaster walking along the winding lamp-posted paths in his expensive ill-fitting clothes, stopping to polish his glasses on the fat end of his tie. Yet his creator had said only three days before that he might never write again.

'Were you serious on Wednesday?' I asked.

'About not writing anymore?'

'Yes. I've been wanting to ask you ever since.'

'Mmm,' he said after a pause. 'I think I might be.'

'You looked all-in at the start of the session. What made it such a bad summer?'

David scanned the horizon from under a furrowed brow.

'We should've gone to that movie, you and I,' he answered obliquely. 'We really should.'

I realised he meant the extra step we didn't take after our first
lunch a year ago. But it looked as though we'd taken that extra
step now. I couldn't see how the delay might have caused a
problem.

'Last year, you mean. Why?'

'Because I met someone after you, out in Lebanon, when I was
researching *Drummer Girl.*'

'Oh.'

I hadn't stopped to think about it, but of course David must
have had other girlfriends, despite being permanently married. He
was too good at it with me to be a tyro.

'Did you have a bad break-up with her?' I asked him. 'Is that
what upset you?'

No other explanation crossed my mind. For all that David was
self-evidently unfaithful to his wife, I intuitively knew he would
be entirely faithful as a lover. He had given so much more of
himself to me last night than just the extraordinary physical
element. Whatever relationship he'd had in Lebanon, I was
certain it was over. But with a thousand guesses I could never have
imagined why.

'No,' David answered, still looking out at the view, his voice
expressionless. 'She died. In the embassy bombing in April. Blown
up. Gone.'

He made a strangely dispassionate '*Boom*' gesture with his
hands, then picked up his dogged stride and began to tell me the
story.

It had been late in the day for research, but following the
massacre at Sabra and Shatila in September, he'd gone back to
Lebanon. He'd felt he had to, after an atrocity of such terrible
dimensions. Wanting someone to show him around the camps
in the aftermath, through his CIA connections at the US
embassy in Beirut he met an American journalist named Janet

Lee Stevens, a Middle Eastern Studies graduate working with Amnesty International.

'She took me around,' he told me. 'Showed me where the authorities sent in the bulldozers after the massacre. It was appalling, what had happened. Bodies mutilated, women raped, pregnant ones disembowelled. The clean-up made it worse.'

They soon began a relationship. 'She was just a little plain bit of a thing,' he remarked, 'not tall and blonde and beautiful like some. But she was a wonderful lover.'

'Did you love her?' I asked.

'Yes,' he replied. The word seemed to come out of him from a distance. 'She had a fierce heart and was passionate about so many things – I loved her for that. She was devoted to the Palestinians, especially the refugees and their children. And they loved her.'

We walked on for another while before he stopped again to tell me more.

'We'd planned a holiday in the middle of April, to celebrate the end of the book. She was taking leave and coming from Lebanon, so we agreed on Cyprus. So I'm waiting for her at Larnaca airport when a couple of uniforms come up and ask me if I'm who I am. I thought, hullo, Jane's on to me. They escort me to a back room and some official sits me down and tells me that the person I'm waiting for has been killed in the embassy bombing.' He paused again before adding a final detail. 'She wasn't supposed to have gone in that day. She went back for something for me …'

David was telling me the story exactly as it had unfolded for him, in real time, and I couldn't ignore the irony that this was exactly how he would have written the scene himself, for maximum impact on both the character and the reader. The very novel he had just set in that region, which took him there for research, began with a bombing and then the new relationship, which had arisen out of that research, ended with one. It seemed unbearable that his own life had so cruelly played back a facsimile of his own art.

He'd gone over to America afterwards, to attend Janet's funeral and meet her family. She had a twin sister, he said. Her 'double', I thought automatically.

What he didn't say was how the authorities had known to find him; how they'd known who he was waiting for and that she'd been killed. How they knew any of it so quickly, in what must have been utter chaos in Beirut. The bombing was breaking news worldwide, yet they located David before he'd heard. *They who?* I should have asked, of course, but didn't. It was hardly the moment to request clarification, but I'd already begun to notice how he always left so much to inference, how there were always so many possible interpretations to anything he said. I was trying so hard, even at that early stage, to catch them all, and somehow already knew that asking him anything directly wouldn't work. There was, in fact, one huge detail he was leaving out, something I wouldn't discover until years later. But on that blameless sunny summer morning, standing on Hampstead Heath next to my new-found lover, it was as much as I could do to register the impact of his sad story, made all the more moving by his unadorned and expression-less telling of it. Who else had he been able to unburden himself to in the months since it happened? Clearly not his wife, possibly no one in his family. Did he have a trusted friend to confide in? It seemed likely that I was one of just a very few to whom he'd been able to open up. But imagine how many people he *couldn't* have told, how many he'd had to keep it *from*. How many times in all the publicity for his new book must he have been asked about the embassy bombing and had to respond as though he saw it only as a consequence of inexorable geopolitics, not also as a source of terrible personal loss. Consider how many times he must have had to force a modest smile after being congratulated for writing so presciently about the very conflict which brought it about. I was beginning to see why it had been such a rough summer for him. It was my first glimpse into how entirely constructed from secrets David's private life was and the emotional price he paid for it.

And there was one specific secret aspect he could only share with me; the notion in his mind – and now in mine – that it might never have happened if we'd begun our own relationship a year earlier. If we'd only gone to see that movie.

David stood like a sentinel, still looking out at the hazy city-scape on the low horizon, his hands deep in the pockets of his cords. Was he remembering her? Reliving the moment he heard? Recalling her funeral and meeting her twin? I slipped my hand into one of his pockets and threaded my fingers through his. We went back to the house, breakfast forgotten, and spent another long session in bed. This time it was gentler and quieter, though no less intense. It felt like a requiem for a young woman who had died before her time.

David called me at my flat at nine fifteen on Sunday morning. Scaling the north face of the Eiger couldn't have left me more exhausted than the events of the previous four days, and after coming home from Hampstead on Saturday I could have used an early night. But I had a supper date that I didn't want to cancel – with the friends who were letting me use their holiday home on Lesbos – and went out again that evening. It was good to see John and Priscilla and I was glad I made the effort, but I was running on fumes. I fell into bed once I was home and was still sleeping at a depth of some fathoms when he called.

But David's voice didn't have a trace of weariness. He was bounding with energy.

'You're a miracle worker, my darling,' he exclaimed. 'You've got me writing again! You've swept away the cobwebs. It's all wonder-ful and it's all you. Go back to sleep. I've written you some lovely letters, you should get them on Tuesday. I'll call you very soon and we'll make some dates.'

He rang again on Sunday afternoon. I was just about awake by then.

'Is the Lesbos holiday promised to anyone? Because if it isn't I wondered whether we might go there—'

'Together?'

'Well, yes. Honeymoons are usually more fun that way. I figured we needed one. And George Roy and the crew are going to be on location on Mykonos, so after our trip I might go and see how they're doing.'

He didn't call again until Wednesday.

'Did you like my letters?'

'They haven't arrived yet.'

'Really? They should have.'

'Well, they haven't – sorry.'

'No – I'm sorry. They were lovely letters and I wanted you to read them. Hmm. I wonder—? Tell me your address again.'

I told him and heard pages being hurriedly turned.

'Oh, Gawd! Hang up your boots, Cornwell. You know what I've done, don't you? I gave you a coded entry in my master address book and I've only gone and misread my own bleeding code! I've sent two very long and graphic love letters off to you at the same number King's College Avenue, SW3.'

'Oh, dear,' I said. 'I don't think there's any address like that near here.'

'I *know* there isn't. I put you down as King's College Road, NW3, up here – only I was too stupid to decode it the right way!'

Later on there was a courier at my door handing me an envelope. Inside was a single sheet of notepaper; David's chalet address in

Wengen was embossed at the top and it was closely written on both sides. He wrote that he was ashamed of himself for having misread his own code and felt he must hurry to write to me again to make everything real, in case the things he whispered to me that night were only dreamed. He said he turned my body over and over in his memory, marvelling in the recollection, yet not quite believing it. He told me that I had roused him from a time of terrible self-doubt, given him back his manhood and his confidence, and that he felt as if he were writing with my hand on him, telling him, *You can, you can.* Admiration, tenderness, sweet gratitude; the words were like a rarefied ether as I breathed them in. My astonishing new lover, this massive talent, this writer of international estimation and renown, was thanking *me* for restoring him to a belief in his life and work. And he was telling me that he loved me.

He ended by saying there was much more in the originals and it was a shame that I would never see them, but at least the lads in the lost-letter department at the Post Office would have a good time going through them, looking for a return address.

This episode with the letters was so perfectly emblematic of David's whole life, it seems to me now. That he encoded my address to keep it secret in his own home, hiding it out of a lifetime's habit of secrecy whereby he instinctively treated his domestic environment as enemy territory. That he mangled the deciphering of his own code because he had been too long out of the field, away from the real world of secrets, even though the compulsion to create secrecy was as strong as it ever had been. That there was never any real need to encode my address in the first place, since his wife already had it to send me the *Drummer Girl* memo and would most likely have thought nothing of it even if she had seen it in his own 'master' address book (presumably he didn't keep a separate 'mistress' one). That the very first letter I received from him, of the

61

many dozens that would follow, was actually a 'double', a hasty copy rushed out by courier to testify to the existence of the lost originals that he'd sent to what he called 'a non-existent address' – a 'dead letterbox', one might say. And yet at the same time, because he never did relay the 'much more' he had originally written – despite his facility for recalling every word – the 'double' managed also to become the 'official version'. I see all this now as a reflection of how entirely fractal David's life was, how each separate part was just a smaller replica of the whole. The perfect multifaceted reflection of the perfect spy.

ZURICH

'I very badly want to fuck you,' David told me earnestly, as we sat together in a low-lit corner of the airport bar, his hand below the table, earnestly between my thighs.

He had raised our departure to 'operational status' and there was a high-alert buzz about him. His eyes were constantly scanning the sight-lines of the room, the entrances and exits, watching who came, who stayed, who went. He was in the field, where he operated best. The married man eloping with his new mistress. The lifelong spy for whom everything was a matter of cover. I hadn't seen this version of him before. I was beginning to understand there were many versions of David.

It was late September and we were on our way to Greece. We were in Zurich because David seemed to fly everywhere by Swiss-air. The city was where his European agent, Rainer Heumann, had his offices, making it a useful cut-out for covert onward journeys like this. The AmEx credit card he used for our trips and treats was in the name of his Swiss-based company, Authors Workshop, which Rainer oversaw, so his extracurricular running costs were rerouted there too. This was already our second trip away together. The first was also in Switzerland, at a grand hotel in Vitznau on Lake Lucerne. Our delightfully *fin-de-siècle* room opened on to a stone terrace with wide-stretching views across the water to the mountains beyond. A vast canopied bed held us in a luxurious embrace while we drank champagne and made love in almost continuous rotation throughout our three-day stay, David passing the first mouthful from his glass to me in a kiss and giving me the first of many pieces of jewellery. 'Have some flowers,' he said sweetly as he laid the small red box in my lap. It was an antique piece from a Bond Street jeweller, a gold necklace set with garnets arranged as petals. We took walks by the lake, found wonderful local cafés and restaurants, and on Sunday morning let the Rigi cogwheel train take us up the steep rise to the top of the world – or so it seemed – as we sat on its articulated wooden seats among local passengers who sang folk songs to the impromptu accompaniment of an old man with a ukulele. We found a grassy slope to eat a picnic of *Bündnerfleisch* and chèvre and Swiss white wine, before taking the Rigi-Bahn back down.

Once we returned I received deliveries of huge bouquets and more letters and two more books: Malcolm Lowry's *Under the Volcano* and Budd Schulberg's *What Makes Sammy Run?* As with the titles he'd recommended last year, David seemed to be suggesting that these also held parts of the puzzle of his own character for him. I didn't know whether he wanted to have me work him out for myself, or just to share his own puzzlement at the way he was, as he put it, inside his own head.

It was only about forty minutes till our Athens flight, but David had ordered a bottle of Krug and directed me to open the fresh-cream Sprüngli truffles he'd bought while he was waiting to meet my flight from London. He explained that one would go down better with the other and wasn't wrong. By the time the flight was called both the shampoo and the chocs were gone. I pointed to the empty packaging as we left the table.

'The truffe,' I said. 'The whole truffe and nothing but the truffe.'

David laughed as we headed for the gate, but it was a tight, nervous laugh. He had a lot of nerves near the surface. The Krug he'd downed hadn't touched the sides. If anything, his watchfulness was even keener. We hadn't made our destination yet and in David's lore, as he'd explained it to me, *they could still get us before we do*. (And indeed, before we got home, they very nearly did.)

At the time, I dismissed this as a little paranoid. I didn't understand why he couldn't shed the perpetual secrecy, couldn't see what he had to lose by openly owning all the parts of his life. He was a big famous guy with a secure place in the world and all the money he could possibly need to meet any contingency in this and another dozen lifetimes. Yet so often he acted like a man on the run.

I had a lot to learn and it would be a long lesson learning it. It would take me years to arrive at even a partial answer to the one elementary question that was so central to his existence. What was he so afraid of? What was he so worried would catch up with him? *What made David run?*

This second trip could already have been our third, all in about a month and a half of being together. He'd wanted me to join him on a trip to Munich, but at the last minute decided to go alone. I went with him to Heathrow, so we could spend the night together at an airport hotel.

'Where you off to then, guv?' the cabbie asked in the time-honoured formula, as he drove us out along the Cromwell Road.

'Oslo,' David replied without missing a beat, then whispered the explanation of his tradecraft into my ear. *If you're going south, tell them north.* A simple but effective technique of inversion.

Ah. So if your girlfriend lives in *SW*3, put her down in your address book as living in *NW*3, in case your wife goes looking to find you out. (Chances were, if you couldn't decipher your own code, then she wouldn't be able to either ...)

All our other meetings since that first night in Hampstead had been ad hoc at my place, whenever his schedule allowed. My own schedule frequently allowed, since I had given up two other lovers for David. But then, I wasn't a famous writer, married with encumbrances.

For this trip, the big one, David had left for Zurich a day or two ahead of me. More business with Rainer, ostensibly. He called me from the city to check everything was in order at my end.

'It's going to be wonderful, my darling,' he said, with a sort of joyous reverence in his voice, like a young groom-to-be in a

Victorian novel. 'It'll be our honeymoon, I can't wait.' Then his tone switched to business-as-usual. 'Now, did my spook travel team send you all your documents?'

'Spook' was a word David used liberally, long before it was popularised, to indicate someone with an Intelligence background (or foreground, I was never sure). He had previously told me that the private travel agent he used was an ex-operative of some sort. He'd also said that George Greenfield had been with Military Intelligence in the war. *Uncle George was a spy? Well, I never.* My first thought was, *I must tell Graham.* But then I realised I couldn't tell Graham, because I hadn't yet told him about my relationship with David. (George always denied it, by the way.)

I confirmed that the tickets had arrived. 'Don't worry, David,' I said, 'the lamplighters made the drop.'

'Good,' he answered. 'So they should have. They know I like my covert operations to run by the rules.'

'Moscow Rules?' I asked, thinking he was just playing along with my use of le Carré-speak. But he was deadly serious.

'Naturally. No one can know about us. I've made that plain to them. They have my instructions.'

I heard him exhale forcefully at the other end of the line, sounding for all the world like a wanted man who'd been holding his breath against a threat of detection that had just passed. I realised then that there was no irony or playfulness in David's use of his own argot. He even insisted next that we have a fallback.

But first he asked suddenly, 'You will be there, won't you?'

A strange question out of the blue. What on earth made him think I might *not* be there? Was it because of the woman in Beirut? Did this remind him of the last time he had waited for her?

'Of course I'll be there,' I assured him. 'Of course.'

'Good,' he said, and breathed another great sigh into the phone. 'Good. A chap doesn't want to go on his honeymoon alone.'

'David, don't worry. You know I'll be there.'

'Yes, I'm beginning to – know things about you. We can get to know each other properly, can't we, when we're there. Stretch out by ourselves, just the two of us.'

'Yes. On the beach in the sun.'

'Anywhere, as long as it's away. Away from everyone.'

'It will be. My friends tell me all the tourists should have gone by now – even the German lesbians who are always the last to leave.'

'I'm glad of that,' David said, still immune to any kind of humour. 'I shouldn't want the competition. So now, listen, my darling, about our fallback. Take Rainer's number—'

Rainer, as I've said, was David's main man. If he wasn't technically another former spook, then he had lived a life that was definitely spook-friendly. (He was German-born, half-Jewish, and as a young man during the war had escaped from a Nazi labour camp.) Which meant that all three of David's agents about whom I had any information so far – his British agent, his European agent and his UK travel agent – had probably been, well, agents. This went a long way to explaining why we had to have a fallback, why the lamplighters had to deliver my tickets and why our affair had at all times to be conducted under Moscow Rules. David's own spy rubric appeared to be as indispensable to him in his life as in his writing; perhaps more so in his life. Was I in a relationship with David Cornwell or John le Carré? Right then, I had no idea if there was any clear difference between the two.

So our fallback, should my lover not be there to meet me in Zurich, was for me to call Rainer, who was presumably briefed on all contingencies. David had already couriered me a thick wad of Swiss francs – probably from the reptile fund – which was more than enough to put me up in the bridal suite of the most expensive hotel in the city while I awaited his arrival or further instructions.

The simple notion that I might go on to Lesbos by myself and start the holiday as originally planned, with David joining me when his life let him, didn't enter the discussion.

I didn't need to call Rainer. David was waiting for me at the connecting flights area, the box of Sprüngli clamped under his arm. He was wearing his favourite zip-up leather jacket and casual slacks with desert boots underneath. I had already noticed how he seemed to get a much better look about him whenever he was in Switzerland. He even brushed his hair a different way, straight back from his forehead, instead of the less flattering parted-the-way-nanny-did he favoured in London. He could have passed now for a savvy, good-looking Swiss professional leaving his apartment in the city for a long weekend in the mountains; a photo-journalist perhaps, or the kind of cool university lecturer that lithe young female undergrads work especially hard to earn good grades from. Regrettably, the kind I never had myself.

But despite the cool-guy gear, David's body language exposed him at fifty yards as an anxious suitor. It hadn't occurred to me that he might actually have *meant* the whole 'honeymoon' thing. I'd thought it was just his way of joking about our first long trip away. But I was gradually coming to understand something. For all the genuine good humour he could generate, David didn't ever really *joke* about anything; not about his life and work, not about the spy stuff and not about whatever it was that this relationship we'd started meant to him. I had to get it into my head. This was a man who took everything in his life – even our love and our laughter – in deadly earnest.

Seeing the look of extraordinary relief on his face, the sudden release of strain in his expression when he saw me, I realised he truly *had* worried that I wouldn't come. Christ – didn't he know? How could he *not* know? As if anything could have *stopped* me.

*   *   *

The flight to Athens was long enough for yet another bottle of Krug and quantities of smoked salmon pressed on us by the smiling Swissair cabin crew, who intuitively treated us like newly-weds. The ongoing flow of champagne eventually overtook any reserve I had left – never a great deal to begin with – and I quietly suggested we might attempt post-prandial membership of the Mile High Club. Our section of the plane was nearly empty and the Swissair onboard loos were immaculately clean. Short of a private jet – *and where was his, I'd like to know?* – this had to be the ideal scenario.

David took a moment to digest what I'd said, then regretfully declined, giving me an odd sidelong look.

'You've done that before, have you?' he asked.

The way he posed the question told me he wouldn't be happy with the answer either way. If I said no, he wouldn't like failing the challenge to be first. If I said yes, he wouldn't like knowing someone had beaten him to it.

'I have,' I confirmed.

At this, his eyebrows knitted together in hilarious mock fury. It seemed the truffe wasn't always easy to swallow.

'Lots of times?' he pressed, demanding the whole truffe now.

'A couple.'

He said nothing for a while, but looked thunderously at me out of the side of his eye. I trusted it *was* mock-fury. It wasn't terribly easy to tell.

'Have you any idea how much I hate him?' he fumed in a stage whisper.

'Hate who?' I asked back. Again, I knew from Jeremy never to do feed-lines, but I was laughing too much not to oblige.

'The swine you did it with. It was that Canadian, wasn't it?'

And nothing but the truffe! My mind flashed back to a Wardair flight to Ottawa and the inevitable effect of copious amounts of free Seagram's upon two students.

'Yes,' I confirmed. 'It was.'

'Well, *fuck* him, the swine,' David growled out of the corner of his mouth. 'Him and his runes.'

The more he fumed, the more I laughed. It was as well I didn't mention a more recent incidence, on a Christmas trip to New York with the television exec I'd been dating immediately before him, or he might have blown a fuse. But what a memory the man had, to remember not just my Oxford boyfriend, but also my passing remark about his doctoral thesis. Our conversation at La Capannina had happened over a year ago. But I would learn that about him too. David remembered everything.

For the last hop to Lesbos we left the safe charge of the Swissers, as David always called them, and boarded an aircraft that looked as if its original purpose had been crop spraying. We landed at Mytilene airport without event and the moment we stepped out of the spindly little plane the sweet, soft local air washed over us in welcome. We'd arrived on Sappho's fabled isle and were going to be there for twelve whole days, just the two of us. It already felt like a trip to heaven.

Was I in love with David? Oh, yes, to be sure. But was it true love or simply the most wondrous fling? Could it even be both? I was too enveloped in the thrilling up-close magic of it all to know the answer. But then, as I think David had already planned, that was what the honeymoon was for – so that I would find out.

PLOMARI

As Exhibit A in defence of David's insistence on the perpetual need for cover, we found that our taxi driver knew exactly who we were and where we were heading. He was just the next in line at the airport cab rank, but recognised the address in Plomari straight away. He lived there, he told us over his beefy shoulder as we slid onto the hot black leather of his back seat, and knew very well the lady Priscilla and her husband, the nice man John. Sure. They had even left his number for us at the house. They were good in England, yes?

Yes, they were very good in England, I said, mildly amazed at the coincidence, while David gave me a *You see?* look.

We must call him Tony, our driver said, and while David leaned forward over the back of the front passenger seat and made an instant chum of him, expertly feeling out all the pressure points of trans-European male bonding, I poked my elbow out of the window and watched the dusty countryside wind by, as the passing air flushed up smells of hot stone and straw.

The road twisted and turned for some miles, climbing and dipping over the hills, until after a good hour Plomari rose up to greet us, its streets running higgledy-piggledy between the last hill and the sea. As we entered the town on the long harbour road, passing locals stirring out for their evening promenade, David laid a hand on Tony's shoulder. Could he let us out here so we might have a drink and something to eat? Maybe he could take our bags to the house and come back for us in a couple of hours?

'Sure. Is good idea. Is no problem.'

Excessively large Greek banknotes exchanged hands as we got out. David seemed to be a compulsively heavy tipper. As I handed over Priscilla's house-keys, he asked Tony to recommend a restaurant.

'Sure. Costas'.' He pointed up the street to where the local stores were pulling up their shutters ahead of the coming evening's trade. 'Is best place in town.'

'Let's find a place for a snoot first,' David suggested as Tony drove off with our luggage.

Not to over-patronise first establishments, we found two, both facing the harbour about fifty yards apart. We downed large cloudy ouzos in each place and sweet black coffees thick enough to chew. Before heading to the restaurant we took a few moments to lean out over the harbour wall and watch the low red sun dip finally out of sight, Apollo riding his chariot into the sea, turning the sky into an impossibly lovely purple streaked with gold.

David stared into the darkling view as if somewhere in its far reaches a searchlight had finally gone out. He put his arm around my shoulder and pulled me tightly to his side.

'We made it,' he said, in barely a whisper.

Leaning into him as he held me close, I could feel coils of tension leave his body, the disengagement of inner cogs that had been running in high gear for far too long. I wanted to believe that this release was down to our being there together, was down to *us*, and that was a big part of it, no doubt. But there was another factor in play as well. It wasn't only our arrival that had brought him this relief. It was what he'd left behind. David gave off the unmistakable scent of *escape*, of having *made it*, as he'd said. But escape from what?

Costas himself showed us to a little marble-topped table for two in the corner of the terrace of his busy taverna. Our fame had gone before us, not David's at all, but ours, as Priscilla's chosen guests. Tony must have tipped him off. We were brought further ouzos on the house, to be followed, at David's request, by a bottle of the best red Costas could find in his cellar. My own request was for a bottle of spring water. I had schooled myself not to keep up with David's monumental capacity for alcohol during this trip, but I'd been doing just that, pretty much glass for glass, since arriving in Zurich.

'Don't you ever drink plain water?' I asked, as he filled my tumbler but not his own.

'Not usually as a first choice of beverage, no. You know what W. C. Fields said about water, don't you?'

I shook my head and gulped down the clear contents of my glass, while David executed a perfect impression of the old deadpan actor.

'Never touch the stuff. Fish fuck in it.'

As David was finishing the last of a generous snifter of brandy, Tony drew up on schedule to take us up the hill to the house. It must have been all of three hundred yards. When we got out he refused any further payment from David and handed the keys back to me.

'*Kalispera*,' he said to us respectfully and drove off.

'Oh, my darling, *look*—' David said wistfully, his arm circling my waist as he scanned the front of the little brick house with its green shutters. 'It's our first house.'

We made a swift recce of our new quarters. The stone-flagged front hall led to a shower room and loo and a storeroom behind. Next floor up were the living room and kitchen, with all kinds of provisions got in for us by a neighbour as Priss had promised. And finally, above that, was the bedroom, where a big double bed lay under the rafters.

'Come here,' David said softly, pulling me on to the bed. 'I must have you now – now and forever after. Happy honeymoon.'

Our first day should be spent exploring, David declared next morning. But before that we had to shop, *so let's get a move on.*

Right-o. *Poop-poop!*

'What are we shopping for?' I asked as we headed down the sunny street, thinking there couldn't be much more than fresh squid to buy on the whole island.

'Beach gear, for me. I didn't bring any.'

'Why not?'

He looked at me as though I'd asked a very stupid question – which of course I had.

'I thought it inadvisable to be seen packing any.'

'Oh – yes, of course.'

It was strange, given the circumstances of our relationship, but for long tracts of time when we were together I managed completely to forget that David was married. Since his infidelity didn't appear to trouble him, it didn't trouble me, though frankly even had it troubled him, it still wouldn't have troubled me, since I wasn't the one who was married. But sometimes, as just then, the reality would intrude.

'Doesn't she know you were coming here?'

'No. Certainly not the beach bit of it. And naturally not the tall blonde bit of it either.'

I was almost entirely incurious about David's relationship with his wife. I understand this isn't how many women in an equivalent situation would feel, but it was nevertheless true for me. I never had the nesting instinct, I suppose, or much of the coupling-up one either. A voluntary union of two individuals for as long as it works has been about the scope of my ambition with any man. As one subsequent lover felicitously put it, I have no tentacles. Regarding David's marriage, it was axiomatic that it had its limitations or he wouldn't have been there with me, or indeed, wherever he'd been with those who had preceded me. By then I was sure that the woman who died in Beirut wasn't the first by a long way. (About a year and a half later, David would actually introduce me to another of my predecessors.) But I couldn't help wondering what tale he'd spun for his wife. A research trip, most probably, so naturally he couldn't be seen packing a pair of trunks. Swimming in the sea off a Greek island wasn't anything a fellow needed to do for research, not even the famously meticulous John le Carré. It explained why he was still dressed like a Swiss weekender; it was how he left Hampstead. If you're going somewhere warm – as I now knew the inverted operational reasoning went – let your wife see you packing for somewhere cool. I assumed Jane believed what he told her, because God help her if she didn't, the suspicion would surely eat her alive. David called her every day while we were away, for ten minutes or so. Checking in with base, he termed it, but it was one-way signals only. In exchange for his uxorious diligence, she wasn't allowed to call him. I expect he lied very effectively.

This set me thinking about the phone call I'd had from Jane myself back in May, about making the *Drummer Girl* abridgement longer. It must have been on David's instructions, though he knew I had no say in the matter. I began to see now that it was for cover, to put her off the scent of what he was really planning, which was his second approach to me. I could even imagine the sort of thing he would have said to her, to seal the false narrative. If you're going south, tell them north. If you plan to seduce another woman, make sure your wife thinks you have no regard for her. *Give that tedious abridger a call, will you?* I could hear him telling her. *See if she can sort the script out **before** they get me into the studio this time. I can't go through the nonsense we had with Smiley's People again.* Something like that; something off-hand and plausible and just deadly enough to kill any suspicion. For cover, to get what he really wanted, which was more days in the studio to be able to cast his spell over me. All of which, I also began to realise, carried one further implication – that he'd already been lining me up then, with that other poor woman not even a month dead.

I've thought about this a lot since then and I believe I'm right. I don't think David ever had a problem with the first *Drummer Girl* abridgement. Most probably it was lying dormant on his desk while he pursued his new love interest in Beirut. Perhaps the Cyprus holiday was already planned. The truth for me, meanwhile, was that almost immediately after we parted at Piccadilly Circus – in front of Eros, for goodness' sake – I'd seriously regretted not taking David up on his offer. I looked him up in *Who's Who*, wanting to find out more about him, and when I discovered his birthday was coming up I decided I would try to re-engage him by sending a card. I spent ages selecting just the right one from the endless array at Paperchase, then carefully honed what I'd put inside – something crafted to be witty and appreciative about the books he'd recommended, particularly *The Good Soldier*, and just sufficiently appealing and open to inference without tipping off anyone else who might open it first. I wanted him to know that my hesitation had been only momentary and that I still wanted to go to that movie. I posted the card to Hampstead, hoping to hear back, and was hugely saddened when I didn't. I couldn't know he'd returned to Lebanon by then and had probably already met Janet …

Then on 18 April, *Boom*—

When I received the phone call from Jane, David must have just arrived back in Hampstead from the funeral in the States, full of secret grief and guilt – *She'd gone back for something for me* – and feeling as though he might never write again.

What we really feel is that it needs longer to tell the story, Jane had said to me.

It was only after I'd confirmed that I could cut the book to any length required – as if it needed saying, though possibly David needed his wife to *hear* me say it – that he called Graham to arrange things. And when it came to fixing the studio dates, he made sure Graham booked three days in the studio for what was only an easy two-day read. Wednesday to Friday, furthermore, so that we would finish in time for the weekend. The instructions Jane sent me were dated 16 May, not even a month after the bombing. She wrote a covering paragraph, stressing that if I didn't think I could manage to fit in all the extra scenes into the new abridgement *exactly* as he requested, then David felt we should probably call it a day ...

Given the state he must have been in after the bombing and the funeral, I think he hadn't wanted to risk turning up at the studio for a single day's reading, only to find that I was no longer interested in picking up where we'd left off the year before. So he turned the whole thing into a subtle sort of test. Very subtle, in fact, because I quite failed to realise I was taking it. I only knew that if he did 'call it a day' then I might not see him again and the possibility of that hit me hard. That single stark phrase galvanised me to make sure I delivered the second script exactly as his notes directed – no small feat, I might add – so that he *wouldn't* call it a day. Because I really *did* want to see him again. He must have told himself – *If she makes the effort, I'm in with a chance.*

So yes, what I began to realise on our holiday is what I sincerely believe now; he *was* lining me up then. Not selfishly or cynically and by no means heartlessly, but simply in desperation to mend what had been so broken in him – beaten up, as he wrote in that first letter – and to restore his faith in his creative life. I don't think I flatter myself. There was an extraordinary bond between us, which we both felt from that first lunch – which David, whose life had been a constant search for love, perhaps felt even more forcefully than I did. After Beirut, I think he knew he needed something that strong to pull him through. A few days into our holiday he would call me his last love. I didn't fully understand this claim when he made it, but subsequent events would prove him more right than even he knew.

There were only two local shops that sold swimming gear, the first one we tried catering predominantly for scuba-diving, with goggles and snorkels and flippers hanging around the walls.

'They can do me a wetsuit or a pair of Speedos,' David announced after a close conversation with the proprietor. 'You'll be pleased to hear I'm only going to try on the latter.'

As he edged himself into the cubbyhole changing room, drawing a shabby curtain behind him, I could hear Graham's voice in my head irreverently asking why he hadn't popped into the men's department at M&S on his way out to Heathrow for a pair of their swimming trunks to complete his wardrobe.

After a couple of minutes he drew back the curtain and stood with his hands cupped over his crotch, looking acutely embarrassed and appearing to be naked below his shirt. He huddled next to me and removed his hands. He was wearing the Speedos, in fact, but there was so little of them – and such a pleasing amount more of him – that one might hardly have known. David's build leaned more towards yeoman farmer than athlete and the streamlined trunks had some stretching to do, leaving absolutely nothing to the imagination. Anyone curious to know whether John le Carré was circumcised wouldn't even have had to guess.

'I can't wear *these*—' he told me in an appalled whisper, as the cottage-loaf-shaped Greek wife who ran the shop with her barrel-shaped Greek husband craned over the counter to cop an eyeful. 'They show my bush!'

I said I rather liked them, but agreed there was definitely nowhere for him to keep his sandwiches. David made his apologies to the proprietor and hurriedly changed back into his sensible German slacks. We went along to the second store, a dingy little lock-up with children's day-glo tiddler nets on long canes hanging up outside, which had precisely two pairs of trunks on offer, one in school-uniform black nylon that were a size too small and another in mustard-coloured cotton that were a size too big. David promptly told the shopkeeper he would take both.

'What about some tops?' I suggested.

We looked along the rails. From a sorry end-of-season selection, David picked a standard cotton T-shirt that was either dark green or sun-faded black and a completely weird top with short sleeves and a soft collar, made of nasty shiny synthetic fabric with hideous broad horizontal stripes.

'This one was too ugly even for the German girls to buy,' he lamented. 'They kept it specially for me.'

As the shopkeeper cheerily made a neat paper parcel of four items he'd thought he would never off-load, David asked him where the main beach was.

'Ah, Katerina's beach,' the man offered helpfully. 'Down there, please, and turn right.'

'Thanks very much,' David answered genially, taking up his parcel. Once we were out of sight of the shop he turned us around and we headed off in the opposite direction.

We walked a small distance, leaving the main part of the town behind and following a cliff path, until a little secluded bay revealed itself like a bite out of the shoreline. It was completely deserted.

'That's our place,' David declared. 'Come on!'

We clambered down, scratching up yellow dust as we descended to the pebbled beach. David swiftly changed into his new cotton trunks and I took off the shirt and cut-offs I was wearing over my bikini. We swam lazily for a while, the water warm and buoyant under us with the heat of the whole summer stored in it, and then got back to the beach to dry off.

'We're tarts,' he said, as the ticklish autumn breeze found our wet skin. 'That's what we are, stupid tarts. We didn't bring anything to dry ourselves with.'

'Or anything to lie on,' I added, sitting on my shirt. 'Or anything to eat or drink. Yes, I know.'

'Then why didn't you say something?'

'I assumed it was all part of the master plan.'

'Knowing cow.'

This was my first visit to any part of Greece and fragments from my classical studies were coming back to me. Sitting on the shingle and looking at David sprawled on his back beside me – sand and tiny pieces of shell clinging to the lines of his body, the mustard-coloured trunks clinging too, beautifully translucent from the water – I chased a scene from Homer through my mind.

'What're you thinking, Sue?' he asked me with his eyes closed. 'It's salacious, I'm sure.'

When it came to detecting a private thought process, David was more than a little uncanny.

'I was thinking of Odysseus when he washes up on the shore somewhere around here and wants to approach Nausicaa. But he's naked, so he has to break off a large leafy bough with his great hands to cover his manhood.'

'I can see why a girl might remember that from her studies.'

'I definitely remember his "salt-grimed nakedness",' I said, looking at how well the description fitted my own lover now. 'And that he had huge hands and needed a large bough.'

'Well, naturally,' David agreed matter-of-factly. 'They're renowned for their donkey-knockers, these Greeks. But can you tell me one thing, my darling – I'm sure you'll know. Was this Homer's island as well as Sappho's? I mean, did she come here to write poetry because it was already famous for him?'

I gave him a squinty look – which he didn't see because his eyes were still closed – at his implication that a woman writer would need to have been inspired by a man.

'No,' I told him. 'Homer was from Chios, by tradition. This was Sappho's own patch.'

'She lived here?' he asked.

Again, I had to chase the details for a moment.

'I know she was born here ' I said, groping for the rest from some long-forgotten essay. 'But if I remember, she became an exile. Plenty did in those days. I think she died in Sicily.'

'I see,' was all he said, thereby drawing our discussion of the island's world-famous female poet to a close. 'So I was making you think of Odysseus, was I?' he went on. 'An older version, I suppose.'

'Not so much, I don't think. Let's see – he was ten years away fighting in Troy, then another ten on his travels and he was already king of Ithaca with a wife and son before he went. He must have been quite close to your age now by the time he got back.'

'Such scholarship!'

'Not really. It's all in the text.'

'And why did he go on his odyssey after the Trojan war in the first place? I don't think I've ever known. What was he doing all that travelling for?'

That too was in the text, and though David's classical studies were considerably farther behind him than mine were behind me, it struck me as another peculiar blind spot.

'He didn't mean to go anywhere,' I explained. 'The gods were against him. He was only trying to get home.'

'I see,' he said again. I imagined he'd be pleased to have the answer at last, but his tone suggested I'd rather spoiled the plot. He turned over on to his stomach and put his chin on his folded forearms. He was looking at me now. 'You'll let me write while we're here, won't you, my darling? It won't get in the way, I promise.'

I asked him a question in return.

'Why do you imagine I would want to stop you?'

'Well, this is your place, your holiday.'

'You can write and make love in the same day, can't you?'

'With you, yes. Several times every day. All night, too, if pushed.'

'Well, then – what's the problem?'

'Don't have one. You're amazing. Beautiful. Funny. Knowing. I think I'll make you my Muse as well as my Recording Angel. I'm sure you can be both.'

'I'm sure I can, too, but you don't get to choose us, I'm afraid. We're appointed.'

'Then I'll apply for appointment.'

'Ha! Take a number and get in line.'

'I adore you, my darling. I really do. And I want to fuck you right now something rotten.'

As David began to stroke my thigh and the salt waves lapped against the shore, another well-learned line came back to me from my studies:

ἔστιν θάλασσα – τίς δέ νιν κατασβέσει;
(Here is the sea – who will drink it up?)

It felt like we lived there. It was the little house, nudging us into the sort of unassuming domestic routine that no grand hotel or big villa ever could, but it was David too. He seemed to have an innate capacity to turn native wherever he was. I saw this first in the studio, the way he just slotted in like one of the regulars, then at my flat where he moved around as much like a room-mate as a lover. He had a way of automatically adapting to his environment, becoming instantly familiar with it. He could fit into a new situation with the ease of slipping on a pair of old shoes. It was from years of living his cover, I imagined, first in his spook years and later in his personal life. In fact, first of all in his personal life, as he would soon begin to tell me, for sheer survival as he grew up in the ever-shifting crooked sham world of his father.

All the same, there was an undeniable process going on between David and me, something he was constantly urging on: the establishment of 'us'. The word was one I hardly used in the normal way and was cautious of its application then, but David's conversation was peppered with the joint pronoun in all its forms. And the more he said things like '*they love us*' when the waiters at Costas' extended special favours, or '*we live here*', or indeed '*our house*', which he said all the time, so the more it began to feel as if there might be something to it.

David's days began – as they probably had for more than twenty years before I met him – with writing. I would feel him stir around five. He would get out of bed and steal downstairs, leaving me to turn over and finish sleeping, which was just as well since, after strolling home from Costas' around ten the night before, we usually didn't finish what we did best any time before midnight, often later. By around eight I would lean over the edge of the bed and look down through the inch-wide cracks in the old floorboards, to see him sitting at the dining table, fixed in concentration, his pen flying over the sheets of white A4.

'It's about my dad,' he told me. 'I'm writing about me and my dad.'

While he was still writing, I rose and showered and went out for milk, or yoghurt, or honey, or whatever other item we'd run short of at the house. There was a local daily English-language newspaper that I always bought at David's request. It was no more than a couple of sheets folded to tabloid size but I noticed that it usually carried a piece about either attempted or successful Turkish espionage. I supposed – erroneously, as it turned out – that it was his way of keeping his hand on the local spook tiller, in the same way that he always seemed to have a little short-wave radio with him in his suitcase wherever we went, perhaps, though I never caught him listening in, so that he could tune in to the BBC World Service at a pre-arranged time for a message in code. He had brought a serious-looking Zeiss camera with him as well and took endless pictures of me, usually half-dressed or completely naked, and frequently from the rear. Much as David never tired of telling me how beautiful he thought I was – a compliment I never tired of hearing – I was coming to think he considered that to be my best side. In his defence, I had forbidden him ever to take a picture of me when I was wearing my glasses, so perhaps it was just his way of getting a candid shot.

'Why don't you get contacts?' he asked me as I shied away from his camera yet again in my specs.

'Funny you should ask. I was just going to make an optician's appointment when this big famous writer chap came along and whisked me away to a Greek island.'

'Really? Are you really going to? I mean, I love your glasses because it's such pure but-Miss-Jones-you're-beautiful when you take them off. But I do worry sometimes,' he said wryly, 'that you can't properly see the full extent of my manhood when we're in bed.'

'I'm short-sighted,' I assured him. 'I can see things close up perfectly well.' This provoked a purring sound from the writer at the recent memory of just how close up close up could get. 'But if you're worried,' I said, deciding he needed teasing on the subject, 'you can always get me a magnifying glass.'

'Cow. Shan't. But just you be sure to get those contacts when we get back. And tell them to give you extra-strong bifocals so as to enlarge your lover's microscopic member.'

We shared a mutually appreciative smile. I loved him when he was being ironic.

'And you'll let me pay for them, of course.'

When he finished his morning's writing, David always went out by himself for a while 'to radio base', meaning use the payphone at the local post office to call his wife, choosing not to use the phone in the house. UK landlines didn't have incoming number display or last-number redial then, but I shouldn't have been surprised if he already had that kind of advanced tech and more at home.

Either that, or he just didn't need me around when he lied to his wife, though it wasn't as if I had any desire to listen in. There was always an unnatural brightness about him when he came back from calling home, a deflecting veneer over something brittle underneath. 'Decompression', he would call it, after a few more trips. But his dealings with his wife were none of my concern and I asked no questions.

Then one morning he went off for a longer spell.

'You don't mind if I go off for a while, do you, my love? Just for a walk and to read the paper? I won't be long – an hour at most.'

He tipped me an odd artificial little salute with the folded newspaper, then tucked it neatly under his arm like a pace-stick, for all the world like a retired half-colonel getting his pass from the little woman before heading out for a pint at the village pub.

'That's yesterday's paper,' I said, noticing an article I'd read on the front page.

'Doesn't matter,' he said breezily. 'I'll catch up. See you.'

He came back after an hour, without the day-old newspaper and looking happy, elevated even, but still in an odd unnatural way. I even thought I heard him humming – for the first and last time ever – as he came in downstairs. I was quite oblivious to what he was doing. I hadn't yet cottoned on to his act-it-first/write-about-it-later creative process, but the whole performance would end up in his new novel. He would use snatches of our conversations, too, filleting elements from them like a sushi chef extracting the edible part from a blowfish, taking a single turn of phrase, a random observation, anything that drew his ear. At this early stage of his book he seemed to be a sort of Autolycus, snapping up all manner of otherwise unconsidered trifles.

Then we headed out for the day, with David offering his usual mild admonishment for what we should have been doing by now – getting air, going for a walk or a swim or an explore – even though our timetable was entirely of his making. He had this habit of rebuking one scenario with another and was always keen to move on to the next thing whenever he deemed any particular activity to be over. Consequently, we did a lot of moving on to the next thing, even when the current thing should have been about relaxing and doing nothing much at all. We never really relaxed, even after sex. We either did something else afterwards or had more sex to the point of exhaustion. Satiation had a strange way of making David restive, as if he were resentful of having his desires met, of letting consummation take away his want of whatever he'd just had his fill. And so we moved on.

Poop-poop!

We bought fresh-baked bread and fabulous local cheeses and fat olives and ate lunch on the beach, or sometimes up in the hills if we decided to hike inland. And vino. And vodka. David sank both like there was no tomorrow, but neither ever seemed to touch him. He never got that soft focus of the happy drinker. For every coil that unwound in him when the alcohol hit there seemed always to be another, just as tightly compressed, that it didn't reach. Then we'd head back to the house for more of what we liked to do at least three or four times a day, frequently more. David's powers of recovery were prodigious. I'd known some fine lovers before – and would again – but never one quite like him.

After we showered and changed we made for Costas', who welcomed us like family and kept the same table for us every night. We'd take ourselves for a walk along the harbour on the way, to 'have a snoot' at one of the promenade cafés first, David scribbling in his notebook as the locals strolled by.

I respected his writing time in the morning as sacrosanct – I slept through most of it anyway – but at this end of the day I felt we needed to keep it light. One evening I took photos of him as he huddled over his pen and pad, just to let him know he wasn't to get too immersed. The beginnings of a smile crept in at the corners of his mouth, but he kept jotting. Then I saw something I couldn't resist and pointed to the long arm of the harbour wall that stretched out into the water.

'What do they call that then, David?' I asked.

He still didn't want to be distracted, but he looked up to see where I was pointing. Despite himself he laughed.

'It's a *mole*,' he said appreciatively, as if I'd scored an unexpected point in a game with rules of his own devising, and closed his notebook.

Once or twice in the evening we stayed in and made something simple for ourselves, salad and omelettes or the like, puttering around semi-naked in the kitchen. We only ever seemed to dress our top halves in the house – each of us wearing one of the two sweaters David had packed, ostensibly for the cooler clime of Zurich – preferring to keep the lower parts ready for action, which indeed could happen at any time.

And one time, when we were half-dressed in that way and I was getting ice for our drinks from the top of the fridge and David was squatting down below me looking for something in the larder section to add to the salad dressing he was making, I ducked down behind him and put an ice cube on his scrotum. Everything was just hanging there in free suspension and I simply couldn't resist. I'd only planned to give a glancing touch and pull the ice cube away the moment he flinched – only he *didn't* flinch. Not believing his reaction – or rather, his astonishing lack of one – I kept the ice cube *in place*, even pressing it *more firmly* in place. But he only continued looking for whatever it was he wanted in the fridge. I was mystified.

'Can't you *feel* that?' I asked.

'Well,' he replied steadily, 'it's not the most agreeable sensation in the world, I'd have to say that.'

But he still didn't flinch, though his testicles had definitely decided to come in from the cold. He just coolly (well, yes) located a jar of mustard, while in glassy disbelief I continued to hold the ice-cube against his ever more tightly shrivelling sack.

'Do you think,' he said after another few seconds, 'we could say that this particular experiment is over?'

I finally took the ice cube away. I even sucked it, to make sure it was as cold as it should have been. The laws of physics failing to pertain to Priscilla's freezer seemed altogether more plausible than David's unflinching control over what should have been his autonomic nervous system.

'*Training*?' I asked after another moment or two. It was the only thing that made any sense.

'Mmm,' he confirmed lightly and went on with fixing the dressing.

Gradually, David told me things about himself and his life, and he began by taking me through his rather large family. I was an only child and my parents chose not to have a great deal to do with either of their own large families, so I hadn't much personal experience on that front. My various aunts and uncles and grandparents and cousins were perfectly kind to me whenever they appeared, but essentially mine was a family of just three. What I had noticed about people with large families, however, was that they only ever seemed to want to tell me about them when things weren't to their liking. But David said he wanted to tell me about his family and so I listened. We were having a mid-day 'snoot' at one of the harbour-side bars and he began by telling me about his four sons, the oldest three of whom were now grown young men. Simon, the eldest, was already married and lived in the Far East with his Thai wife. 'He's a mystery to me,' David proclaimed, as though that were explanatory. Stephen was 'the middle one', a birth detail he presented as an intrinsic difficulty, though he added, 'He seems to have found photography, thank God.' George Roy Hill had given him the job of official stills photographer on the *Drummer Girl* shoot and I'd already noticed his credit underneath David's author photograph on some of the books. Timothy was the youngest of the first three and an undergraduate at David's old college. Tim, he said, was 'the sensitive one'. These were by his first wife, Ann, whom he'd divorced a dozen years ago and who, I learned next, was definitely *not* the model for Smiley's Ann.

'No – Smiley's Ann isn't *my* Ann,' he corrected me quickly when I suggested it. 'Not at all.' He pointed out a standard-looking Greek woman who was walking away from us a little further down the road. 'There—' he said. 'That's like my Ann. Short. Long back and low saddle.'

David watched the unwitting woman walk out of sight before letting his gaze drift out across the bright noontide sea.

'I think *his* Ann,' he said dispassionately, but quite affirmatively, 'may be *you*.'

He didn't turn to me when he said this, but kept looking out – and it was as well, because I was momentarily without the capacity to sensibly respond.

'Oh, yes,' he said in the same factual tone, intuitively reading my silent astonishment and dismissing it as an invalid response. He might have been expanding a point in a lecture on his work. 'Yes – beautiful, intelligent, self-motivated, sexy. Even admiring. My dream woman. The girl on the beach I can't have.'

'But you can,' I said after a moment. 'You can have me.'

'No,' he corrected me again, still staring out. 'Like this, yes. But no, not now. You're my last love, you see. I know that now. You should have come to me earlier. Years ago, before I married again. Before I got myself banged up for life.'

'I was still at school,' I said meaninglessly.

'Yes, I'm quite aware of that. It's all your fault for being so young and so perfect.'

The fourth son, he continued, seamlessly resuming his original discourse after this diversion, was Nicholas, by second wife Jane.

He was presently a pupil at University College School, an independent day school in Hampstead. All his sons were *marvellous*, he insisted, in case he might have given me a different impression. He said it a second time with greater emphasis, managing to sound a little like Connie Sachs. *All wonderful, marvellous boys.* He mentioned his younger half-brother Rupert, the journalist, Charlotte's full brother by their father's second wife, Jean. He had an older full brother himself, Tony, who lived in the States, was an advertising executive and had been a promising cricketer in his youth. David didn't speak about either of his wives, though not, I felt, out of any delicacy towards me. It was as if he were primarily concerned with giving me the Cornwell bloodline, to which the women who had borne its members were auxiliary at best, ancillary in general.

(This may seem rather a harsh observation on my part then, but it was backed up – indeed reinforced – by what I subsequently saw in the books. All women, but particularly wives, get a very rough ride in le Carré. One way or another, they invariably bring about their husband's or partner's downfall. Elsa Fennan's treachery gets her husband killed in *Call for the Dead*. Stella Rode, the murder victim in *A Murder of Quality*, is the bar to her husband's ambition, while another schoolmaster's wife, Shane Hecht, is described in far more vicious terms than the unrepenting paedophile who is the murderer of the piece. Liz brings about Leamas's death at the very end of *The Spy Who Came in from the Cold*, just as Riemeck's girl brings about his right at the start. In *The Looking Glass War*, Turner's wife constantly derides the value of his work, and in *Tinker Tailor Soldier Spy*, Ann Smiley's affair with Bill Haydon is what blinds Smiley to the fact that his colleague is the double agent. His eventual success in getting Karla to defect in *Smiley's People* derives from his exploitation of the Soviet spymaster's only weak spot – the deranged daughter his wife bore him. Even in the book David was writing then, the wife of his hero would reveal his secret hiding place to the authorities, thereby bringing about his suicide. Meanwhile, blood relatives in le Carré, even of the women, are almost invariably male. Ann Smiley has a male cousin or two and Connie Sachs has a genius father and a string of brainiac brothers, but there is no mention of either woman's mother. Both of his directly autobiographical heroes, like David himself, only have sons. I could go on ...)

David sighed heavily after going through this roll call, assuming a sort of noble weariness at the responsibility of such a large encumbrance, as though he'd been achieving greatness under superhuman strain. A literary Atlas weighed down by the burden of the related world. Poor David, I half wanted to say, half guessed I was supposed to say, but resisted. He had the means to make his life how he wanted it, if it wasn't currently to his liking. If he didn't want to be 'banged up' then he shouldn't have married for a second time. There was rather more to his use of prison terminology than I realised at the time, however, so it was good that I held my counsel. In any event, commiseration would have been superfluous, because he next began to talk about Ronnie, his late father and present subject, and at a stroke his whole manner revived. The weariness lifted, the weight of the world was shrugged off. He was suddenly bursting with Ronnie.

'He was a conman, you see,' David explained, his enthusiasm renewed. 'He'd set up companies, dozens and dozens of them, with nothing more than string and sealing-wax, and promise investors the earth, then cheat them out of their money. He did time for it, on and off, at their various Majesties' pleasure. Olive, my mum, ran off when I was about five – she couldn't stand it anymore. Tony and I were sent off to school, but we'd never know if the school fees were going to be paid or where we'd be spending the holidays or who we'd be calling our new mum. So the book's about Ronnie. I've called him Rick, Rick Pym. My hero's Magnus, his son. I've been trying to write about him for years and failing to for even longer. Now I *am* writing about him and it's got a lot to do with a tall and lovely girl. You've made it possible, Sue. You've helped the process come alive. You see, my darling, you *are* my Muse – appointed or not.'

'I'm just a writer, you know?'

This was another tone I hadn't heard before. Laid back. Cool with things. 'I'm happy if people like my stuff,' he went on. 'It's just good when they get it.'

We were sitting on the beach after a swim, alone on another deserted little bay with just the ever-present Greek look-out patrolling the bluff above us for company.

'Ten books,' he went on. 'It's not nothing.'

He made the claim prettily and quietly, but with a touch of *Weltschmerz* in his voice, as though his underlying wish was to be understood at rather lower cost to the self.

'They should give you the Queen's Award for Industry,' I said, attempting to jolly him gently away from what sounded like a little patch of the blues on the horizon. But I should have learned not to do that by then, because he took my suggestion quite seriously.

'Mmm. They offered me a K this year. I turned them down.'

'Really?' No Sir David Cornwell, then. But it was a little incongruous, I thought, after he'd just said he liked it when people 'got his stuff'. Wouldn't a knighthood have been an acknowledgement of that?

When I asked him why he turned down the honour – and he didn't specify whether the offer had come from the Palace or from No.10 – he only shrugged gnomically. *Of course you did, David*, I think I was supposed to say, *quite right*.

'It's just not my scene,' was all he said.

The uncharacteristic sixties expression didn't ring true. The older pink-gin vernacular from the fifties that I'd heard him use before suited him better. Something didn't square. Before I could think what and why, he added, 'It wasn't the first time.'

I heard a touch of something else in his voice now. Surely not *pride*?

'You mean you've turned them down before?'

'Mmm.'

'And they asked you again?'

'Mmm.'

I nearly said, *Well, next time you'd better make sure you mean it*, but I could see he still wasn't up for the funny side. His expression as he sat on the pebbly strand, holding his knees and staring fixedly out to the horizon, told me that we'd reached a new level of high seriousness. For a man who could giggle like a schoolboy, make love like a god and write like a demon – and who had clocked up twenty years at the very top of his chosen tree – David seemed nevertheless to have the sensitivity of a virgin (to borrow his own phrase for Smiley) when it came to his status in the literary world.

He looked my way, waiting to see if I would ask anything else, but I didn't. I was treading cautiously that afternoon, having already fallen foul of David's touchy sensibilities first thing in the morning. The events of the previous evening seemed to have set it all in motion.

After another long schmoozy supper at Costas' we'd somehow got into a joke-swapping contest, which started when David asked me if I knew any good ones. I've never been especially keen on the set-piece joke, preferring humour that arises spontaneously, but I did have one special favourite, which I told him. It was the gorilla joke, with its great punchline: *He never calls, he never writes ...*

'I was going to tell you that one,' David said, with a slightly peevish pout.

'Well, then,' I replied, as one does with little boys who want to be thought cleverer than anyone else, 'you tell me another one.'

So he did, and it went on from there. David's best effort was pretty good, but I think I won in the end, because the punchline of my last one – originally told to me by Jeremy – had David rolling on the floor.

But then, next morning – and there was no way to see it coming – he suddenly claimed that I was without proper seriousness in how I lived my life.

'You have great intellect, great capacity, many strengths, but you lack *gravitas*,' he declared, from a donnish height he must have scaled in his own mind overnight. Losing a joke-telling contest was obviously no laughing matter for the Great Man. I concluded that I really should have let him tell the one about the gorilla.

So, in the context of our present conversation on the beach, if he wanted me to take what he said at face value – even though it all seemed some little way up his own lower orifice – then that's what I'd do. It was a lucky decision, coming not a moment too soon, because after a pause he added an extra detail.

'And I've told Rainer I don't wish to be considered for the Nobel.'

I decided David's special subject at Oxford must have been Advanced Cognitive Dissonance, because basic logic didn't seem to enter anywhere into that last statement (although *gravitas* looked as if it already had, all the way up to the third joint).

Would that be the Nobel Prize for Literature, David, I so badly wanted to ask, *or for World Peace?*

But I gave no voice to this dissent. By then, I was certain I wouldn't see my lover for dust if I did. Once David pronounced on a matter it seemed to go straight onto the statute books, at least in his own mind, after which it would be treason to demur. The cast was *really strong*; his sons were *all wonderful*; and now, I *lacked gravitas*.

I had to bite down hard to stay silent, all the same. Why on earth did this extraordinary man, with his talent, his fortune, his fame, need to give himself such ridiculous conceits? Not that the idea of his being awarded the Nobel was ridiculous; far less likely candidates had been chosen over the years. But to make specific provision to head them off at the pass, just in case they did? That definitely *was* ridiculous. How did it work, anyway? Had Rainer sent a pre-emptive letter to the committee? *Dear Sirs, My client wishes me to let you know that under no circumstances are you to consider him as a recipient for your prize ...* Or was it more of a standing instruction, that Rainer was automatically to turn them down if – sorry, *when* – they did? In which case, how the hell did *that* work? Did he enclose a note with the Authors Workshop annual report – *FYI, David, just to let you know they didn't nominate you again this year ...*? It was all too farcical to contemplate, either the whole or any part. I don't know how I held my tongue.

But David was untroubled by my silence. Far from suspecting me of harbouring thoughts of such outlawed *levitas*, he had clearly taken my lack of response for what he expected to receive, what he must actually *have* received from other quarters, in order to feel free to come out with this stuff with me – namely, full assent. *Of course you did, David, quite right.* But it was just so ludicrous. And if I applied his go-to technique of south–north inversion here (which he shouldn't have explained to me if he didn't want me to do just that), then stressing he really didn't want these awards must have meant, in fact, that he really rather did ...

As he sat beside me on the bay he absently clawed up a handful of pebbles and began strafing them into the waves. In that unconsidered action, I started to see the beginnings of an answer to the conundrum. Somewhere deep inside the vast and, so one would think, impregnable edifice that was John le Carré, there was a little boy named David sitting in splendid isolation, king of his own self-built castle, and he was letting the big boys of the world know that he wasn't coming out to play – just in case they weren't going to ask. He got up and waded out hip-deep into the water, which was beginning to grow dark – wine dark, as the poet said – under the slanting sun. He skimmed some more stones for a while, not very expertly, they didn't bounce much, but perhaps he needed to try and show me he could. (Alternatively, perhaps it was only for cover, so that he could go back into the water to pee.) Then he left the water and did a clumsy cartwheel back up the beach.

'Come on,' he said, regaining his tone of cheery admonition. 'We're dallying. The look-out will think we're waiting for a Russian sub disguised as a Greek trawler. Let's grab an early supper at Costas' and go back to our place and fuck all night.'

Next day was our last full day on the island and the moody atmosphere David had started to generate remained inexorably on the slide. At first I suspected my continued though now certainly chastened *levitas* was to blame – the unpardonable crime of enjoying myself on holiday – but gradually I came to see it wasn't that. Whatever was going on with him now was nothing of my making. It was a downbeat purely of David's internal drumming.

That morning we hiked inland until we reached a local peak, the highest place it was possible for us to get to without Tony taking us halfway there by taxi first. It was David's idea, a joyless yomp; I had no say in the matter. We'd brought our lunch with us and ate it without communion, hunched on separate tussocks like marines chowing down K-rations. Without any words being spoken it was suddenly wretched between us and it was David who had generated the change. His mood was powerful enough to drag both of us down to whatever depths he had decided to plumb. We were in it together but only one of us had any idea of what was going on. It was like a dark dream version of being in the studio, with David hermetically sealed in his own communication-proof zone. I could see him right in front of me, but my talk-back had cut out and he wouldn't look at me through the glass. Staring resolutely out to the horizon, he was wilfully oblivious to any reality except his own. He had retreated to some point of internal geography to which I had no map, focused on who-knew-what bleak vistas; Xerxes looking at his troops laid waste; Prospero contemplating the disaster of his island universe. There was a storm coming. The atmospheric pressure was building up and a dark cloudbank was following the wind-line, heading onshore. David's mood was so palpable, the weather felt like his creature, a thing of his summoning.

Something told me not to say anything. His mood was too intense. My voice would be discordant to his thoughts however gently I spoke, my words rejected and derided as inferior to his own however carefully I chose them. I sensed I mustn't touch him, either. My lover's willingness seemed to have shrivelled up into itself, like a slug in salt.

Writing. It was the only way in.

His ever-present notepad and pen jutted out of his shirt pocket and I reached over with cautious fingers, feeling like a cutpurse at work. But he let me take them.

Tell me, I wrote, and handed pen and pad back.

It took a long minute – it may have been three or four – but then he began to respond. He turned to a clean page.

The problem, he wrote, *is with David as the writer and with Pym as the man.*

Then he stopped cold. I took the pen from him and drew a ring around *Tell me* as he held the pad, then offered the pen back. He took it, but with an odd look, a suspicious lift of the lip as though I had laid a trap, then he started to write again.

How to continue caring about the destiny of others after entering a contract to renounce one's own.

The neat little epigram was sewn up tightly, but meant for me to unpick. I'd made sense of oblique lines of prose before, I'd spent three years doing it at bloody Oxford; I had to be up to understanding *this*. The key word seemed to be *contract*. His marriage had to be what he meant; how he was 'banged up' in Hampstead.

He began to write something else.

Only course of action is to break the fucking contract. But then the problem—

Nothing followed for a long while. When I couldn't stand to wait any longer I took the pen again.

Don't want to enough? I scribbled despairingly, hoping against hope to be contradicted.

Grabbing the pen from me this time, he wrote *Must*. My heart lifted madly until I watched two more words appear in large capitals:

MUST RUN

I felt hot tears on my cheeks before I knew I was crying. Run from me, did he mean? Run from us?

But suddenly he smiled – for the first time all day – and was once more busy with his pen. I was no longer watching. I couldn't stand to see the blue-ink words emerge and couldn't have focused anyway. Everything was just a blur. Now it was my turn to look out to the portent-laden horizon, where the clouds were still advancing in a slow smothering swarm.

I felt a sly nudge in my ribs, the sort of surreptitious poke that always came before you were slipped a note along the back row in class and, sure enough, David was passing the pad back to me. He had drawn a little cartoon rabbit, bug-eyed, running for his life across the page. Underneath he had written a new line,

Rabbits get scared when they have to run in new fields.

And beneath that, as my heart lifted again,

They need Sues.

*   *   *

To test David's new resolve, the storm followed us home. Trying to beat the rain back, we thumbed a lift in the back of a clapped-out Toyota pick-up truck and were rattled to our bones as the driver took the rocky downhill run at full throttle. We could finally laugh, now that we were on this breakneck descent, and our laughter was as fierce as the battering we were taking. Our driver was a madman, damning himself as only a Greek could by challenging the gods who commanded the weather to race him back to town. And we were every bit as crazy as he was, trusting life and limb to his maniacal driving, and knowing it made us laugh all the harder. It was all just a desperate divine joke and if death or injury were to pounce out at us from behind a sudden rock or tree, then it would only be the punchline hitting us where it hurt.

By the time we were dropped off at the harbour we'd been shaken clean out of our senses and could only continue to laugh like fools as we struggled to get our legs back under us for the last climb up the road to the house. But by then it didn't matter how hard we laughed, because the dark clouds – and the ancient beings who directed them – knew where we lived. Hubris, and all that.

First Rule of taking a secret honeymoon with your married ex-spook lover in Greece: Don't talk about making it safely home.

Inside the house the electricity supply had blown, but the static continued to build, charging us both. Somehow we made it through a thrown-together candlelit supper without ravaging each other, but when the storm finally broke David threw us both onto the living-room couch and drove himself into me like a ploughshare.

Afterwards, we climbed the stairs without speaking, hand tightly in hand, as the storm hurled itself around us. Priscilla's thin floorboards creaked wildly and the hastily fastened shutters heaved on their hinges as we lay in bed, huddled like refugees in each other's arms, staring blindly up at the rafters while we waited for the first heaven to pass away.

Within the hour things seemed to quieten down, but the storm hadn't passed, only retreated somewhere to regroup. The present lull was just a fake-out.

'Shall we say it's over?' David asked, in the trick of the calm, and at first I thought he meant the storm. 'Shall we call it the best holiday in the world but say it's over? And just stay friends?'

'No!' I cried out, rejecting the awful meaning of his words, 'God, no!'

I sat bolt upright in bed with the shock. I didn't believe he could be saying that. He'd just spent the last fortnight talking about us, us, us, making it all so lovely and so, so real. I was certain of my feelings for him now. I loved him more than I had ever thought possible. David had buried himself deep inside me with his love and his love-making. He had imprinted himself indelibly on to me in his pale blue ink. Yet *now* he wanted to give it all up?

'No,' I insisted again shakily, trying to gain some modicum of control over my voice. 'No, David – why on earth should we do that? Why on earth would you want to?'

'Because it won't ever get any better than this, my darling. And it won't get any easier. This way we'd just have the fun of it. We wouldn't have any of the pain.'

Not have the pain? I already felt as if I had a steel bolt through my ribs. How much more painful could it get?

'I thought you loved me?' I said.

It was either the stupidest thing to say or the truest. Perhaps both.

'I do, my darling, I do,' David protested. 'I've never loved anybody more and I never will. You're my perfect woman. The most beautiful, the most desirable, the wittiest, wisest, the most loving – ever.'

'Then why end it now? It's madness. I won't let you.'

'You want to go on then?'

'Of *course*. Of *course* I do. We've only started – *of course* I want to go on. Don't you?'

'I want to badly, but I don't know if I can. If we stay together I should have to get out.'

'Out?'

'From Hampstead. From the slammer I've made for myself there. I'm a born architect of slammers.'

Break the fucking contract. It *was* what he meant. He had returned to the language of escape. Our trip had begun with it and now was ending with it too.

'So do it,' I said simply. 'Find a way. I'm sure you can.'

'Will you be there if I do?'

'Of course – *yes*. I'm not going anywhere, David.'

'It may take a while.'

'It doesn't matter.'

'Really?'

'Really. I love you, David.'

'And I love you, my darling, but—'

'I'll be there. Before and after. And during. Just do it. Just do whatever you have to.'

'It's a rocky path you've chosen, you can't know.'

'Then I'll find out. But let's not cross any bridges before we have to.'

'Or burn any boats.'

'Particularly not tonight.'

'No. Not tonight. You're so wise. Much more than me. I get such blacks. Such dreadful thoughts. I'm just a scared rabbit, you see, and I need my girl.'

He was scared and needed *me*? Dear God. Where was the reassurance for *my* fears, from the sudden whiplash of 'let's just be friends'? Or was this it – the new commitment to escape? Was David set on his course now, regarding his marriage? Did he really mean to 'get out'?

ATHENS

We woke up next morning to find that a pair of Priscilla's shutters had blown away in the night.

'They're probably in Ephesus by now,' David remarked. 'We'll leave some of the folding stuff with the neighbours before we go and ask them to get new ones put up.'

I was a little groggy from last night, I couldn't remember when or if we ever stopped talking or drinking or fucking. As I packed I couldn't quite get the exact run of our storm-tossed conversation in my head. Did David say he was actually planning to leave his wife? Did I get that right? The possibility of our being able to meet up whenever we wanted to, go away whenever we wanted to, without his having to lie to anybody about it and without his fear of discovery dictating how we conducted our relationship – well, it put a spring into relinquishing the house and the island, that was for sure. Two weeks earlier this had been the big trip to look forward to. Now it felt like just the start of the journey.

Actions, however, still had to follow words. As I checked round the house to see if we'd overlooked anything, I noticed both pairs of David's swimming trunks lying on top of the bag of kitchen rubbish waiting to be thrown out. He had jettisoned the incriminating evidence and kept the rest, including the hideous stripy top. Clearly he still preferred to be suspected of bad taste than adultery.

As a farewell gesture to the house, David picked out the one le Carré paperback that had been lurking between all the Jeffrey Archers and Frederick Forsyths and Jackie Collinses on Priscilla's holiday reading shelf – a sun-bleached copy of *The Honourable Schoolboy* – and wrote a little dedication in it to her and John. He had already said he would send them a case of something nice and a big tin of caviar when we got back.

We locked up the little house and left the keys and a wad of money for new shutters with the people next door and piled into the back of Tony's taxi to take us to the airport.

'It was good, your holiday?' he asked with a big proprietary smile.

Yes, I answered. Yes. It was very good.

As we re-crossed the spice-coloured countryside, Tony tried to engage David in the same sort of man-to-man chit-chat they'd enjoyed on the way in. But David politely deflected each attempt. We were leaving now and he didn't need an instant chum on the way out.

David had given up the idea of going on by himself to join the film crew in Mykonos. The plan now was for us to spend the last night in Athens before leaving for Zurich together in the morning. When our flight got in we moved straight to the carousels for our luggage and stood chatting amiably while we waited. There was a nice easy calm between us. It had been a really good trip and, after our big conversation during the storm, we knew there was a lot more good stuff to come once we got back.

Second Rule of taking a secret honeymoon with your married ex-spook lover in Greece: Do *not* talk about making it safely home.

I'd been about to put my hand through his arm as we waited, with David making his habitual scan of the area, when he suddenly turned on me.

Don't touch me! he whispered sharply.

The out-of-the-blue severity of his tone made me pull back automatically, as if I'd brushed against a live wire. I felt him stiffen inexplicably at my side and when I looked at him for explanation all identifiable expression had vanished from his face. I had no notion what was wrong.

Then he told me, in another harsh and now also appalled whisper.

It's Steve and the whole fucking crew. They've just arrived.

Of all the airports in all the world … I glanced over to the far side of arrivals, where a group of folk had gathered by another carousel. Now that my attention was drawn to them, I could see they were surrounded by stacks of heavy black equipment cases that some burly biker-looking guys were off-loading from the conveyor. I could vaguely discern the wispy outline of Diane Keaton and a gnome-like figure who might have been Klaus Kinski. I didn't know what George Roy Hill looked like, but he was probably there too. The only one looking our way was a pale expressionless young man who had to be David's son, Stephen; 'the middle one'.

After our long secret holiday by ourselves, I could see why David was so shocked. It was a shock for me too, but mostly because of David's response to spotting them. That *Don't touch me* had a vicious edge.

'I have to go over and see them,' he declared, adding another nasty warning shot. 'Wait here.'

'Hi, Dad. Did I see you with someone over there?'

'Mmm? Oh, yes. Some tedious girl who started talking to me on the plane. Her boyfriend deserted her, so I said I'd help her with her luggage. Probably thought she was in with a chance with me. Ha-ha! So, Steve – how's the movie—?'

Something like that. It wasn't hard for me to imagine some further exposition of the fiction I was fairly certain he'd initiated with Jane over the recording of *Drummer Girl*. More south–north inversion technique. If you've been caught in the company of your secret dream woman who you've been balling night and day for nearly two weeks on a Greek island hideaway, make them think she's just an inconvenient stranger.

After a few minutes he came back to join me at the carousel. He said nothing, but the mood he brought with him was off the barometric scale. He fetched a trolley and started loading our bags onto it, acting as if it was all a royal pain in the arse – acting as if I were one too, taking any piece away from me as I attempted to lift it, the way you remove your valuables from a meddlesome child.

'What did you tell them?' I asked shakily. David's impenetrable and frighteningly cold volte-face towards me was beyond unnerving. I'm sure I'd gone pale, despite what only that morning my then enthusiastic lover had so admiringly called my 'end-of-honeymoon light-honey tan'. He offered no reply, just continued to treat me like an inconvenient stranger, maintaining his steely method acting for the benefit of the distance shots, since the others were easily thirty-five yards away.

'I'll check you in to the hotel and leave you some money,' he said curtly. 'Get room service or something. I've said I'll have supper with George and the crew. I'll stay over with Steve and come back for you in the morning—'

For one split second – the kind that has 'irreversible' stamped on it – I very nearly said, *Don't fucking bother.*

But I didn't and I wish I could claim this was because my better senses prevailed. But it wasn't the case. In that moment I had no better senses. I was completely off balance, out of kilter with any true sense of my own core self. David had seen to it that I was. He had suddenly breached all the terms we'd been operating under up till then and I'd simply lost my bearings as to how to act at all. It was brilliantly effective. He must have passed-out from Sarratt with another first: How to Keep Your Joes in Line, Course Two.

So instead of telling him where he could shove his money and exposing his rotten little charade to all present, I submitted to 'the carousel brush-off'. Once again, David had reduced me to 'the girl' – though, unlike my namesake who delivered the Bad Godesberg bomb, I suddenly had almost no presence at all in his new screenplay. Maybe I was just 'some girl' this time. But even as an extra, without a line of dialogue to my name, I still had to take direction.

'And let's have less of the marooned body language, shall we?' he told me out of the side of his mouth.

To be clear, I wasn't expecting an introduction. But I was blindingly furious with him all the same. This was a man who had lied fluently to his wife on the phone every morning of the 'honeymoon' he'd been enjoying with me for twelve days straight. A man who only a few weeks earlier had managed to manipulate another of his adult sons clean out of the family home for the weekend so that he could fuck me for the first time in that same son's own bed. A man who less than six months earlier had grieved undetectably for his *last* lover while he continued to share the marital home – and presumably the marital bed – and drafted his all-unwitting wife to help execute his plan to line me up as his *next* lover. A man whose own *nom de plume* – lest we *ever* forget – was an international byword for intrigue and plot construction on the most labyrinthine scale. Yet *this* man couldn't find a way to handle the unexpected situation decently all round? Had all the fabled subtlety of tradecraft by which he'd conducted his life and work for decades suddenly deserted him? Or had it only deserted *us* and moved on to the next scene; the one where the hero dumps the incriminating baggage (that would be me) and so manages to maintain his cover.

I had no issue with the fact that David had needed to come up with an instant cover story. I understood only too well that I was in a secret relationship with a famous married man. I hadn't even told Graham about it, for Christ's sake. But he so easily could have been sweet to me about it. It would only have taken a few words. *I can't get out of this one, my darling. We're blown if I don't go with them. Just make out we're strangers for now. Don't worry, I'll make it up to you, I promise—* Anything like that would have been fine, just to acknowledge the obvious need for subterfuge and to include me in it. But David didn't seem willing to play *that* double game. Perversely, he'd decided to start living the cover he was going to use for being caught with me *with me*, dishing out this shitty treatment to limber up for the part he was going to play with his son and the rest of them. If this was the first test of his resolve to 'get out' of the 'slammer' he'd built for himself in his second marriage, then he'd flunked it abysmally.

'I must go and look after my baby,' he announced, jamming the last of our bags onto the trolley and heading for the taxi rank, sounding less like a concerned parent than a Norland nanny under the delusion she was in charge of national security.

Even when we were out of sight of the crew, there was still nothing in his tone of voice for me, or in his face. Nothing at all in his self-serving 'theatre of the real' acknowledged the truth of my existence. I hated his putting me through this performance, but cravenly raised no objection. David's psychological hold over the scenario was so complete that the words wouldn't come and I knew I couldn't have withstood the response from him if they had. *Of course you must, David*, I might as well have been saying, like the rest of the Greek chorus he was so used to having around him in his life. *Of course.*

The farce continued to the hotel, David insisting I take a cab by myself, even separating our luggage though no one from the film could still see us, while he followed in another behind. I was trapped in David's movie now – the Saturday twelve noon first show – and there was no longer any 'us' in the scene that was playing. All the magical powers of 'us-ness' that he could summon had been moved on to the next scene, with the cast and crew. Our 'us' was a literary fragment abandoned on a Greek island.

I only wish it had occurred to me to order a large tub of caviar and any bottle of extortionate vintage from room service that night, just to make a point. David picked me up from the hotel next morning and we had a surprisingly un-moody and upbeat journey home. Without any reference to how he had left things between us, he gleefully told me everything about his evening; how wonderful Steve was, how marvellous his stills were, how splendid the cast was, how brilliantly the film was going. I listened, answering intermittently with variations of the only authorised response – *Yes, David, of course* – as he rattled on, oblivious to how the evening had been for me. At one point, as though the thought had just struck him, he paused to say, 'Do you know, my darling – I think you'd probably make *quite* a good continuity girl if you wanted to work in the movies.'

It was no use even contemplating anything to say in reply. At Heathrow he saw me into a black cab with a breezy wave. No *It was wonderful*, or *I can't wait to see you again*. Just – *Byee.*

SECOND ENCOUNTER

CHELSEA

It is very difficult to give an all-round impression of any man.
Ford Madox Ford, *The Good Soldier*

David sent me a bleak letter a couple of days after we got back from Greece, to let me know that he was 'progressing' in his efforts to extricate himself from his domestic situation. It surprised me, after Athens, that he still intended to 'get out', but the whole episode at the airport appeared to have passed from his mind. Perhaps the two things were only connected in mine. I wasn't usually given to overthinking relationships – it's usually never a good idea – but there were so many elements to David's behaviour, so many moving parts to him, that overthinking barely kept me abreast.

He said in the letter that the plan was for them all – meaning him and Jane and their son; 'poor all', he actually wrote – to go down to the house in Cornwall over half-term, after his birthday, 'and hammer something out down there'. It sounded pretty grim. But he said the writing was going really well and still claimed this was down to me. He asked me to give him time and space. He said he knew I would. He called his marriage 'indescribable' and said he couldn't see me any time soon.

Well. Less than two months earlier I'd been perfectly happy – deliriously happy would be no overstatement – at the prospect of becoming David's mistress. Without giving it too much thought, if any at all, I'd assumed he would be keeping his life and I'd keep mine and, whenever circumstances allowed, we'd meet up at home or abroad to blow the walls out in bed and generally have great times together. That, to me, would have been the perfect arrangement. But since our last day on the island those no longer appeared to be the terms of engagement. Perhaps for David they never were, right from the start.

Recording Angel, Muse, Best Girl Ever – I was fine with all that. A new lover's hyperbole can hardly ever go too far and who wouldn't want to be claimed as all those things by one of the foremost writers of our time? As for getting out of his marriage, however he envisioned achieving it, it was likely to have been something he'd been considering long before I entered the scene. For myself, I've never quite understood the notion of marriage. I'd already had two proposals before I met David, from really great guys whom I sincerely loved, so I wasn't looking for a third from him. To borrow the phrase he'd used regarding a knighthood, it just wasn't my scene. I might have taken a different view had I wanted children, but procreation wasn't my scene either. Despite my glimpse of how ruthlessly his fear of discovery could make him act, I loved David with a hitherto un-guessed-at and all-but-inexpressible intensity. I knew he loved me back, just as truly and just as passionately. But none of that meant our lives had to be integrated on any other level.

Except now – to believe the import of this latest letter – in six weeks flat I'd also become the sole repository of his hopes for the immediate future, for the resurgence of his writing and of his fantasy of the perfect woman, the 'girl on the beach' he'd claimed he couldn't have but now identified as the key to unlocking his way forward. And since he'd declared I wasn't going to see him 'any time soon', he seemed to expect me to be and to do all of it while waiting for him like a faithful war bride. I was only in my mid-twenties and hadn't long cast off from the moorings to embark on the journey of my own life. I wasn't at all sure if I had the sea legs to navigate my way – or even stay afloat – on the choppy waters of his.

But then, as he'd made such a dispassionate point of telling me on the island, it was all my fault for being so young and so perfect …

*　　*　　*

I was in John Wood Studios later that week, recording nursery tales by myself – that is, with Frenchie and the actor who was reading the script, but minus Graham. Now I was back he felt free to stay down in Wiltshire on the farm, as he told me in his own inimitable style when he rang to give me the session.

'Tail it round to Woodsie's for ten on Friday morning, will you, honey? I've got better things to do than listen to some poxy actor read me *The Three Bleeding Billy-Goats Gruff*. I'd rather de-louse the sheep. How was the holiday?'

'Fabulous,' I told him truthfully, though I was still maintaining the fiction that I went with a girlfriend. Moscow Rules, David had said. 'Just fabulous.'

'I expect you're golden brown all over,' Graham remarked, his voice going treacly down the phone. 'Gorblimey, a tall blonde brainy bird with demon specs and a tan – it's just as well I'm staying on the farm till it wears off.'

When I told him that the demon specs were about to be swapped for contacts I heard a throaty groan.

'Oh, do me a favour, honey, don't get contacts. I know we've kept it clean so far, but if you get contacts I won't be answerable. I'll be all over you like a rash. And keep your legs crossed in front of the reader. The client wants a recording that's suitable for the under-fives, so no heavy breathing, OK?'

I loved Graham.

David called me at the studio late morning, which was clever of him given we hadn't spoken since Graham gave me the booking. He managed to time the call on a reel change too. He sounded chirpy, but for all the reasons above – and the fact that I was working – I was feeling the need to sound a little cool towards the Great Man.

'I guessed you were there,' he said. 'What are you recording?'

'We're just about to start on *Red Riding Hood*.'

'Crikey. Weighty stuff. Well, just you be sure not to let the wolf eat you, my love. That's my job.'

'I'll tell the reader. He's an obliging chap.'

'I hate him already, the lucky swine, having you there to make encouraging noises and laugh with him all day. I miss you, my darling. I miss your smile – and, of course, the rest.'

Had I been at my flat I most likely would have said *I miss you* back, my coolness evaporating under the appeal of David's voice and the persuasive spell he could so effortlessly cast when he was happy, when things were fine with him. (And how come things *were* fine with him anyway? What happened to 'indescribable' and 'poor all'?) But with Frenchie within earshot it was easier to maintain the hint of frost. If he'd heard me saying anything remotely lovey-dovey down the phone it would have licensed him to do Pepé Le Pew impressions for the rest of the session. I told David that we'd just got the next reel up.

'Yes, of course. I don't want to keep you. I really only rang to say I feel very mature about our relationship and it's all wonderful and is a girl having lunch with me next Tuesday and maybe a movie after?'

I noted the date. His birthday was next Wednesday. I hadn't expected to see him anywhere close to it and he'd already told me not to get him a present. Seeing him the day before would be an unexpected treat, though I managed to say, 'Sure, great,' nonchalantly enough for Frenchie to pay no attention.

'Good,' David said, sounding very pleased. 'Tuesday then. I'll pick you up at twelve thirty.'

Graham called from the farm that evening for an update on the session.

'By the way, David rang me down here and asked for your number at the studio. At least, he asked for the studio number and I assume he wanted you, 'cos Frenchie's not that kind of girl. Did he offer to play the Big Bad Wolf?'

'I told him the part was taken,' I said, going along with the joke, 'but if he was interested we were still auditioning for Humpty Dumpty.'

'As long as he brings his own wall – hardy-har.' Graham left it there. He probably wasn't overcurious, but even if he had been he still wouldn't have pressed. He was just the perfect friend in so many ways; Gooders by name and Gooders by nature.

'We've just signed Jacobi for *1984*,' he announced. 'He's going away skiing in the middle of December, which means we've got to book him in well before then. So cut the Orwell straight away, will you? The full thirty-thou, as per. Makes a difference having a pro lined up to read your stuff, doesn't it? Hardy-har. Catch you later, honey.'

David took me to Odin's, the famous Marylebone bistro, where the lunchtime crowd was made up entirely of expense-account suits. I wasn't quite the only woman there, but I was very likely the only side-order girlfriend and, except for staff, definitely the only person under thirty.

'I thought this might be fun,' he said confidently as we were given menus the size of pillowcases. While I looked down the list of fashionable offerings, thinking none of them had half the appeal of Costas' simple nosh, David made one of his oblique sidelong remarks.

'Don't think I don't notice when a girl swallows on her disappointment and says nothing.'

Were there three negatives in that construction or only two? And did he mean in regard to this self-conscious watering hole he'd decided to take me to for lunch – I didn't think my nose had actually turned up – or did he mean Athens? Was that a sly acknowledgement of his ditching me for his son and the crew?

I know it might seem the simplest thing to have asked *what do you mean?* But it wasn't at all. Querying what David, John le Carré, *meant* – asking him to clarify his characteristic ellipsis – would have been offering a challenge to the very essence of the man. Besides irritating him profoundly, the question would probably have received only another riddle of the sphinx for answer anyway, so I let the remark pass. Viewed from a certain angle it might have been an apology, or at least an acknowledgement of my not having demanded one myself.

After we gave our orders he made his habitual scan of the terrain.

'Hah!' he said with a slight lift of his lip. 'Do you see Pinter at his usual table?'

I followed the direction of his nod and recognised the black-browed playwright lunching with another suit. He didn't look over our way, but had probably seen us when we came in. (It was *years* before I realised that David had taken me to that restaurant precisely *because* Pinter would be there; a new twist on literary rivalry!)

'The Great Poet,' he said coolly, in reference to Pinter's most recent publication. From his impeccably balanced tone, it could equally have been thinly veiled irony or thickly veiled praise. 'He's a great fan of Charlotte's.'

I could not have said the same myself. I found David's sister quite unwatchable, which may well have been why Pinter thought so highly of her.

'Graham fancied her madly in *Rock Follies*,' was all I could think to say, knowing David had heard it before. (Though in fact, as I subsequently discovered, it was actually Julie Covington Graham fancied; he'd confused Charlotte's character with hers in the credits …)

'Yes, so he said. Though I doubt she'd go for him. My sister says she loves you very much, by the way.'

'Me? Why?'

'Because she loves me very much and you make me happy. She said so. And she wants us to go round to her place for supper sometime soon. She really wants to meet you. Shall we do that, my darling?'

'Any time,' I answered. 'Tell her I'll look forward to it.'

So. David had written that he couldn't see me any time soon, yet here we were having lunch a week later. He'd insisted we conduct our affair by Moscow Rules, yet was openly displaying me 'on the Town'. He'd disowned me in front of one member of his family, yet told another all about us. A theatre of the absurd play came to mind, where all the chairs are shifted around for no discernible reason, when there's not even a discernible reason for all the chairs in the first place. Perhaps Pinter could have explained.

'Now, on to far more important matters. First, I thought you should know I'm buying a flat. I've told my chief scout in these matters that I want a pad where I can write and get away from my family to entertain my bird. I said I needed a small but elegant bolthole far enough away from the *Schloss* in Hampstead to create some space between me and it, but close enough so that I can get back in a hurry if so required. He thinks he's found me a place.'

Not giving me a moment to process what he'd just said, which was simply *huge*, he continued.

'And second, I thought a girl might like something for her birthday.' He reached into his jacket and withdrew a red jeweller's case. 'Here,' he said, passing it across the table. 'Happy Birthday for tomorrow.'

'But it's your birthday tomorrow,' I said, 'not mine.'

'I know. Happy Birthday. Open it.'

'You told me not to get you anything.'

'I know. Happy Birthday. Open it.'

I lifted the lid and saw a delicate cage-link gold necklace lying on a satin cushion.

'It's late eighteenth century,' he explained. 'They made things to last in those days. I got it for the clasp, look—'

I looked. There was a little gauntleted hand, set with a tiny turquoise, valiantly clutching the last link of the chain.

'It's to say hold on, my darling. It's not going to be easy and it's not going to be quick. I'm like poor old Odysseus, the gods are against me. But I'm heading for shore. Just hold on until I can get out,' he urged me. 'Can you stand it? Can you wait?'

'I said I would,' I managed to say. My eyes were brimming with all that I felt for this extraordinary, paradoxical, unlike-any-other man. I loved him desperately and desperately wanted to understand every aspect of him, as much the parts that hurt him as the parts that I already knew would hurt me. 'I suppose I can spin thread like Penelope,' I said, trying to hold my reactions back. 'I love you, David. Happy Birthday. I love you so much.'

'And I love you too. Massively. But don't make me blub in front of Pinter or he'll think I've read his latest volume.'

After lunch, David said he couldn't make a movie. Jane had to attend to an unexpected situation with her mother, so he'd have to collect their son from school. He must have known this before lunch, since he'd been nowhere near a phone while he was with me. He asked would I instead please help him shop for something for Timo's twenty-first?

'I'd an idea to get him a gold ingot with his signature engraved on it,' he told me in the taxi. 'But I was advised that if you put any markings on them it devalues the bullion. So I thought I'd take a look around Phillips in Bond *Strasse* instead. You won't mind coming with me, will you?'

The gold necklace I'd just received was in an S. J. Phillips box, as was the flower-petal one he'd given me on our trip to Vitznau and which I'd made a point of wearing to lunch. My first ever job in London was as a temporary sales assistant at Asprey in Bond Street. (I was dating Jeremy at the time, who had used his own early experience as a sales assistant in Simpsons of Piccadilly for

116

his long-running BBC comedy series *Are You Being Served?* He took great delight in strolling up to the pens-and-diaries counter where I was stationed to ask me 'Are you free, Miss Dawson?') Asprey is super-chic now, since its 2004 revamp, but then had an old-style elegance, with acres of pale green carpet, brightly lighted display cases and a cohort of courteous well-spoken staff, to which I had happily, if briefly, belonged. I was rather shocked, therefore, to see the inside of S. J. Phillips, with its dark wood floors and panelling, and with every available inch crammed with what seemed, to my Asprey-trained but otherwise untutored eye, to be a load of old stuff. There appeared to be no staff on the premises; the only person inside when we entered was the proprietor, Nicholas Norton, who was busy attending to something in a cabinet. He looked over briefly as we came in, offered an informal 'Hullo!' and resumed what he'd been doing. Compared with the ultra-polite greeting all customers received at Asprey, this was the Bond Street equivalent of 'You again!' to David. Were they pals? Was Nolan another ex-spook? Or was David such a frequent shopper there that they treated him like family?

We poked around for a bit, but nothing looked particularly promising. There was something a little strange about the process, too – the father's secret mistress helping to pick out a gift for the son – though David didn't appear to see a problem. Then I spotted a two-inch length of slim well-turned arm protruding from the clutter of *objets* lodged on top of a high cabinet. Taken down, it proved to be an art deco statuette of a golden near-naked sylph posing athletically on a plinth.

'Oh, my love, how clever of you,' David declared. 'You get a lot of Brownie points for that. Look at her, she's perfect. Timo will love her.'

The piece was set aside and we left. I assumed it would be boxed and delivered, though David left no instructions. He didn't even leave his signature, another huge contrast to Asprey. Even James Goldsmith had to sign his account there.

Once again, it was *years* before I realised David had no intention of buying his son a birthday present from Phillips, the least likely shop for the purpose in the entire West End. The statuette was merely a fortuitous find and who knows whether he cancelled the purchase later. Or he may have just added it to what he was already getting him. Whatever mark-up Nolan had put on it would have been peanuts next to what David had been prepared to shell out for a gold bar. He must have bought the necklace for me there just before lunch – it's the only way to account for the '*You again*' welcome – then took me back on the birthday present ruse expressly to show Nolan who it was he'd bought it *for*. I was even *wearing* the other one he'd bought there! I had no idea. Was that his plan all along, once he knew he didn't have time for a film? Or had it occurred to him only when he saw that I was wearing the first necklace at lunch? (I can't believe he would have been so crass as to have me wear the one he'd just bought.) Did he get a secret kick out of my being so oblivious to his manoeuvring? How would he have reacted if I'd been able to tell him I knew what he was doing? The possible permutations of his thinking can make my head spin even now – though I have to concede he was paying me quite a substantial compliment, albeit in a characteristically covert way.

We went straight back to my place next, for what David had taken to calling *a full and frank exchange of views*, apparently one of his father's expressions. We ought to go away again soon, he said before he went an hour or so later, leaving me to try and digest the main take-away from our lunch date. Was he really getting a bolthole where we could meet? Was this his first step towards getting out of the slammer?

David rang at ten to nine next morning.

'I'm fifty-two, my darling. I just rang to say Happy Birthday.'

He sounded thin somehow, stretched out on what he'd given me to believe was the rack of his life at the other end of the line in

Hampstead. It was the school run just then, so he was alone in the house. It was a detail from his domestic life I could have done without realising, but I loved him for using what were probably the only free minutes he'd have to himself that whole day to call me.

'Happy Birthday,' I said back.

'Thanks,' he said with a small sigh.

'I'm picking up the contacts today,' I told him, trying to cheer him up.

'Oh, how wonderful. That's the best birthday present ever.' It probably was, all things considered, but he didn't sound even a little bit cheered. 'I'm just so much older than you and it's terrifying,' he went on. 'Do you realise that in thirteen years I'll be sixty-five?'

'Then you can come and see me on your OAP bus pass.'

'Cow. Shan't. I love you.'

I told him I loved him back. David said he really rang to ask if I would spend the weekend at the end of half-term with him at the house in Cornwall. He said his wife and son would have gone back to London by then. They would have 'had their talk', would have 'hammered something out'. He said he'd really need me after that. He wanted me to meet some of his friends down there too. So Saturday to Tuesday inclusive, then, in ten days' time, if that worked with my schedule.

I checked my diary.

'That would work,' I confirmed. 'Graham doesn't want me again until Thursday.'

'And I want you now,' David replied. 'So that's perfect.'

That weekend I received my first-class rail tickets by courier from the spook travel agent. Next Saturday morning I was to take the 'Cornish Riviera' train from Paddington to Penzance, arriving mid-afternoon. David's wife and son mustn't have been due to

119

leave until after lunch, or else I could have taken the Friday over-night sleeper and got there first thing; another domestic detail I didn't need in my head, yet found myself calculating. David said he would be waiting for me at the station. The fallback this time, should anything go wrong and he not be there, was for me to take a taxi to Sancreed House, a few miles away from his own place at Land's End, where the painter John Miller lived. Miller was his best friend, he said, and one of the people he wanted me to meet.

Not long after the tickets arrived, there was another courier at my door, this one bearing a diva-sized bouquet from an exclusive West End florist. The card read *Hurry up, love David*. The flowers filled all the vases I had in my flat and I had to run across the road to Habitat to buy more.

LAND'S END

David picked me up from Penzance station and we drove to his house at Land's End. While driving he held my hand on his knee, pressing it, kneading it, as if he couldn't quite believe in its reality. He was so glad to see me here, he said. This was where he really lived, he said, not Hampstead. This was his real home.

As an urban type living in the heart of London, I could never see the benefit in travelling for hours just to end up somewhere else in 'the country' for the weekend, especially when Heathrow was so handy for a real getaway to so many other wonderful cities. I'd never visited this last tip of England and the end of October was not the best time for a favourable first impression. The sky was low and grey, the sea was flat and grey, and the light was already falling as we drove. Everything seemed wind-blasted and bare. Shortly before we reached the house we passed through a bleak little village built of colourless local stone. I paid it no attention until I saw the sign saying St Buryan, which rang a distant bell for me, though I couldn't have said why. As if he'd read my mind, David filled in the connection.

'Peckinpah filmed *Straw Dogs* here,' he told me.

In regard to how the visit was going to go, that should probably have been my first clue.

David's house, Tregiffian, stood virtually on the cliff's edge facing the vast waste of the Atlantic. Originally a row of derelict workmen's cottages he'd bought in the waning years of his first marriage, it had been knocked into one dwelling and completely refurbished, with the suitable gentleman's additions of sunroom, terrace, an extra wing and landscaped gardens. His two dogs appeared in the hallway as we arrived – Whisper and Mach, a father and son pair of whippets – and introduced themselves by rolling over for belly rubs. I bent down to oblige, but their master told them to stand down, saying they'd have to wait their turn if they were after that kind of attention from me. He took my coat, set it with my bag on the stairs, then put my arm through his to guide me round the house.

'Do you like it?' he asked, gleefully showing me around, and once again I could see the little boy in him, this time the one who wanted to parade his stuff.

I said it was lovely. And it was. But the moment I crossed the threshold, I was assailed by the same sensation that confronted me in the *Schloss* at Hampstead. There I had ascribed it to the dust-sheets and building work, but I couldn't see evidence of builders here. I thought perhaps it was the last of the daylight reflecting eerily off the ocean, but when David switched on the lights it didn't make much difference. There was a heavy colour scheme, a lot of deep red and dark wood, grey flagstones and more lifeless local stone. But I knew what I felt wasn't really down to the decor or fading coastal light, or even the pervasive Cornish damp. It touched me the minute I was inside.

David particularly wanted to show me his workroom. (This was the word he always used, not office or study.) It was down a corridor from the main body of the house, in a part which seemed more recently built. His attitude changed as he eased open the door. Gleeful became reverential. It was a privilege, his body language seemed to be saying, to be admitted. I followed him into a large lofty room with more than a little of a chapel about it. A wooden lectern stood pulpit-like against the back wall and at the other end of the room, by a tall narrow window with a long view of the sea, lay a writing desk the size of Robinson Crusoe's raft. Like surf left by a receding wave, pages of David's blue-ink hand-writing drifted across it, along with other desk jetsam – some pens and a notepad and a small cushion for his non-writing arm to rest on as he worked. Apart from his work chair, the only other item of furniture was a long pale sofa against one of the walls. The room seemed austere and comfortless, but must have been how he liked it. Perhaps comfort hindered David's writing. Perhaps not only his writing.

'I've made it lovely, don't you think?' he asked me again when the tour of the ground floor concluded. Again I answered that he had and it was. But I couldn't shake the feeling that for all the money he must have spent, all the evident time and careful effort to get everything just the way he wanted (he never once mentioned input from either wife, by the way), the whole place felt desolate.

We would be sleeping in the master bedroom, he announced, but right now we had to go back into the main sitting room, which he'd only let me glance at on the tour. I'd caught a glimpse of large comfy sofas, upholstered in a red chinoiserie pattern, all arranged in front of a stone fireplace with a log fire blazing in the hearth. Now I saw what he'd done. Before coming to pick me up he'd laid out a picnic on the rug in front of the fire; feta and stuffed vine leaves, olives and hummus and crusty bread, yogurt and honey, with a bottle of extremely serious red wine warming on the stone hearth.

'I thought I'd do us a Greek,' he said. 'And by the way, aren't you ever going to have sex with me? You've been here five whole minutes—'

We were happily post-coital and post-prandial, sitting on the rug with our backs to the sofa and our feet to the replenished fire, drinking the last of the wine, when David asked me lightly, 'Have you been calling the house, my darling?'

As was so often the case when he said things out of the blue, choosing the most incongruous moment, I didn't immediately take his meaning. I thought he meant *this* house, Tregiffian.

'You didn't give me the number here.'

'Not here. Hampstead.'

I did have that number. Jane had supplied it with her notes for the longer *Drummer Girl* abridgement, cautioning *not on general release*. I began to see what David was suggesting.

'No – I haven't been calling the house in Hampstead. Why should I?'

'Jane's been getting calls,' he continued, sidestepping my question. 'Somebody ringing and not speaking when she picks up. She lives in terror of kidnappers.'

'Then maybe it *was* kidnappers,' I returned smartly, 'because it wasn't *me*.'

He gave me a steely look. If I couldn't be condemned for nuisance phone calls, he might consider pressing charges for flippancy. Over the lunch at Odin's, he'd told me of a recent bomb scare at the Hampstead house. *Jane saw wires hanging underneath the car and a smashed tail light*, he said, *and she called Scotland Yard*. The police had cordoned off the area, apparently, but it was a false alarm, so he made light of it in the telling. *While the Bomb Squad checked it out, we had the regular bobbies hiding in the bushes, as if, by not being seen, they wouldn't be blown up!*

With factors like that in play, I didn't care for the idea that he considered me a possible suspect for the silent calls.

But for David the moment had passed. He went straight to what I would come to learn was always his next move after he'd knocked me off balance.

'I think I need to fuck you some more,' he said, nuzzling in.

Next day we drove over to Sancreed for Sunday lunch with John Miller and his partner Michael Truscott. Miller was David's best friend and a well-known artist; prints of his stylised local beachscapes were immensely popular at the time. David said that Michael was also well known as a local potter.

The two men seemed to share a joshing closeness with David and were both very sweet to me. Miller was David's age, a spare, silver-haired, almost ascetic figure with a wry humour to his conversation. Michael was younger, slim, dark-haired and quietly spoken, also with a clever wit. It was good to meet them and it was all happy enough.

But still—

It didn't *feel* right. Something about the lunch rang hollow. I don't mean to suggest that either of them was insincere or inhospitable or ungracious. I had a really nice time in their company. But somehow they were both in performance mode. David was too. I'd already spent too many hours working with actors and performers not to recognise the element of *show*, however subtle and polished, and the lunch was a well-paced three-hander. They seemed to have gone into girlfriend-drill, a sort of coded understanding between the three of them. I wondered, and instantly doubted, whether it was different when he brought Jane over. Perhaps it was wife-drill then, the performances just as polished, but with a less lively script. Or perhaps he didn't bring Jane over.

Despite the continuously maintained 'anyone for tennis?' patter, Miller did let one thing slip right at the end. After we finished the leisurely meal at their long refectory table, Michael suggested we take coffee in the sitting-room. No thanks, David replied; he had to get back to make some calls. Seeing us to the door, Miller said to me, 'David always has to have a reason for leaving.'

Back at the house, after I'd been equipped with a spare waxed jacket – David seemed surprised I hadn't brought one with me, as if I owned such a garment myself – we walked Mach and Whisper on the footpath along the edge of David's own mile of cliff. The dogs rocketed through the bracken, tearing off at mad tangents on their master's attack command – 'Critics!' – in search of kill.

'So how did it go at half-term?' I asked pleasantly after we'd been walking for a while. He'd previously made such a big issue of telling me how he and his wife would 'talk' then, but so far hadn't made any reference to it.

That probably was clue number two.

Suddenly a tangible chill descended over him. I might just have asked him how much money he had in the bank, or the consistency of his last bowel movement.

'What do you want to know?' he asked me back.

I suppose I ought to have said *never mind* and brushed it off, though most likely the damage was already done by my having had the temerity to ask. But I felt entitled to. He was getting out, he'd told me – he was getting a bolt-hole, he'd told me – 'Wait, my darling' and 'Hold on' while he 'hammered something out' over half-term. If he was going to be so touchy about it, he shouldn't have told me anything at all. I didn't want a blow-by-blow re-enactment, he didn't have to betray any confidences. I was simply asking whether he felt he'd made progress with what he set out to do. So I repeated what I'd said.

'Just – how did it go?'

He let the silence set in again for a long minute as we continued walking, then finally answered.

'We talked.'

He said nothing more for the rest of the walk. He still issued commands to the dogs, who were unperturbed by their master's sudden drop in body temperature. They probably thought he was in search of kill, too. This barren heath wasn't my kind of place to begin with, but now it felt like an alien planet. Other than the dogs and any unlucky rabbits they might find, there was no sign of warm-blooded life for miles around, though my lover was only paces away from me. I might have been walking along his damn-awful cliff top, wearing his damn-awful hacking jacket, going back to his damn-awful house entirely by myself.

David didn't speak to me again until we got back inside. As we sloughed off our coats he told me oh-so softly, 'I don't need you here, you know, if you're going to be moody.'

Maybe I didn't need to be there at all.

*　　*　　*

The tension continued through most of the next two days. The tripwires I'd witnessed David laying around himself towards the end of our stay in Greece, which I'd managed mostly to avoid, were much more sophisticated devices on his own turf. He seemed to have a cat's cradle of invisible sensor beams strung all around him, regulated to his body readings, to his moods and sensibilities, whatever they happened to be. But the alarm they triggered was silent, so not only could I never see which wire I'd tripped, I never knew when I had. I only knew that I'd done or said something to set off the alarm when David would freeze me out at random intervals. But with no way to tell what I'd done or said, there was no way for me to know what to do or say next, what not to do or say again. Even so, I kept trying and must have succeeded some of the time, because just as randomly he would wrap me in his arms and draw me close with a smile, as if I'd passed some undisclosed module of his ever-escalating test. Sex was the only constant, the only point of true contact. Everything else was in ever-shifting flux.

The bed in the master bedroom was rock hard and about ten feet wide, the sort you acquire either because your nights are given over to copious amounts of acrobatic sex or, more likely, you want to sleep five feet away from your wife. I'd have preferred we were in the guest room, but perhaps the laundry considerations were too tell-tale. Or perhaps David wanted to be reminded of our acrobatics next time he was sleeping five feet away from his wife.

He took little sleeping pills every night but they didn't seem to be much help to him. I'd noticed he was an uneasy sleeper in Lesbos, but he was far worse in this house, where he moaned and talked in frantic mumbles in the night. Was it the foghorn that racked his dreams, droning like a beached whale, or the beam from the nearby lighthouse strobing relentlessly through the blinds? Both disturbed *my* sleep. I didn't see how he could think of this place as a haven. It felt to me like a site of banishment and exile.

David's writing regime played out much as it had in Greece, only without the sunshine and shingle. In the morning he rose at about five and went downstairs to his workroom. Around eight, he came back to the bedroom, woke me up and made love to me without a word. Afterwards he gently told me I was keeping him from his work and went back to his room.

I rose soon after and took a hot bath in the pine-panelled chalet-style bathroom, to draw out my lover's fluids and shake off the emanation – perhaps it was just pervasive Cornish damp – which I still felt in the house. As I was getting dressed something impelled me to look in Jane's side of the long bedroom wardrobe. I can only say in my defence that I had never before and have never since so much as opened a bathroom cabinet in anyone's home, but on that sole occasion I felt something close to a compulsion to look through Jane's clothes. It seemed a necessary deviation for survival at the time. Like the bear who went over the mountain, I had to see what I could see. But there was nothing *to* see; just the other side of the wardrobe. Nothing that told me anything worth knowing or gratified my deviant impulse.

Then one garment caught my eye. It was the dreadful striped top David bought with his trunks in Plomari. Did Jane see it among his clothes when he came home and take a liking to it? Did he say he'd brought it back for her? Or was claiming it for herself a way of establishing a connection to the latest of his long foreign trips that she hadn't been allowed to accompany him on? And when she wore it, seeking that connection, did it remind David of our secret 'honeymoon'? Was that why he'd brought it back? I closed the wardrobe on my questions, wishing sincerely I hadn't looked. I finished dressing and went downstairs.

*   *   *

My only strategy for coping with David's kaleidoscopic moods was to stay in some sort of quiet balance myself. But it wasn't easy to do. He could spring a trap from any direction.

He'd asked me to compile a list of quotations from *The Good Soldier* that might be useful for his new book. I'd brought the list and gave it to him, receiving what seemed genuine thanks. I'd also brought *1984* with me, to finish cutting, and sat with it by a window overlooking the terrace while he remained cloistered in his workroom. At about eleven he made one of his silent entrances when I was in the middle of a word count. After a morning's writing he always looked strangely insubstantial, almost transparent, as if he'd beamed down from some other planetary surface and stepped too quickly off the teleporter pad, before his atoms had properly gathered themselves.

'Hullo,' he said dully, interrupting my count. 'What're you reading?'

I raised the book amicably so he could see the cover.

'Hah. Haven't you read that before?'

You see? Not *Are you reading that again, my love?* or *Has Graham got you taking work away with you?* which he might easily have guessed from the pen in my other hand. Only the familiar tone of mild rebuke.

I kept my reply pleasantly neutral, saying it was a rush job for the studio. The reader had asked to record as soon as possible, because he was going skiing in December.

'Who's the reader?'

'Derek Jacobi.'

'Hah!' he said again, this time with greater animation. 'Well, you know why that is, don't you? He came to a party at my house and I lent him my chalet in Wengen for two weeks then, that's why. Fancy a snoot?'

While we sat with our drinks, he announced we'd be going over to see some more of his friends, Derek Tangye and his wife Jeannie, for lunch. They lived about a mile away at Minack, we'd walk over. Again, I recognised the name. Tangye was author of such lending library stalwarts as *A Donkey in the Meadow* and *A Gull on the Roof,* a series known collectively as the 'Minack Chronicles', the sort of pastoral reminiscences my mother liked to read.

It was another blowy cloudy day, the pale grey sky and dark grey sea stretching for unbroken miles all round. David suggested I wear the windproof jacket again, and though I could never stand that type of garment – 'country lifestyle' and all that – I was grateful for its protection as we stomped along the clifftop path in the headstrong wind. After twenty minutes we neared a tumbledown cottage, which I first took to be a donkey shelter until David turned in at what might once have been a functioning gate.

'*This* is their place?'

The Tregiffian cottages had been transformed into a gentleman's abode. Sancreed was a restored Georgian rectory. I'd expected Minack to be something similar, but instead, I was looking at what must have been the inspiration for Connie Sachs' tin-roofed shack in *Smiley's People.*

'This is their place,' David confirmed. 'Don't eat any more than you have to and drink absolutely as much as you can.'

He'd brought along a brace of heavyweight premier cru reds, one in each pocket of his waxed jacket. I'd assumed this was simply his bringing our welcome with us, but now I saw it as an ominous sign.

Ahoy!

A rumpled figure, a good stretch older than David and far more worn, hailed us like a dry-docked sea captain from the ramshackle front porch. Tangye – for it was he – was wearing a faded blue fisherman's smock over somewhat less disreputable rust-brown cords that were rather baggy on him (and which I instantly suspected were David's cast-offs), with a gaily spotted neckerchief knotted at his throat. He clamped David's hand then turned to me.

And this is the lovely Sue!

He would have embraced me freely, I could see. There was a rheumy glimmer in his eyes and his mouth was moistly open, ready for an introductory, not to say exploratory, kiss. His battered Boxing Blue nose had a burst of purple grog-veins on its end. I quickly offered my hand before he could close in.

Here's Jeannie!

Everything Tangye had said so far was an exclamation, at the pitch of Captain Bligh ordering ratings in a Force Nine gale. Somehow I was already certain it was going to be the tenor of the whole visit. Jeannie, who became visible when he stepped aside, was a tiny bird of a woman with a permanently smiling trilby mouth and pink dumpling cheeks. In contrast to Tangye's raddled fly-blown appearance, she possessed a girlish glow, her unlined fresh complexion and her eager bright eyes quite belying the fact that she was well into her sixties and married to Tangye for north-wards of forty years. Within moments of looking at her, it came to me that this was the agelessness of the certifiably insane.

'Come in, won't you?' she said.

As we crossed the threshold, David gave me a quick *told you* dig in the ribs, which he had no right to do since he'd done no such thing.

'Jeannie's been cooking!' Tangye cried, at a slightly lower volume inside, and took my coat. 'Marvellous! What'll you drink?'

Milk of magnesia, I wanted to say as the smell from the oven hit me, *a large one*. The kitchen was a narrow galley to one side of the cramped main room and mad little Jeannie began to show me proudly around. It was simply disgusting. There wasn't a surface without a stack of dishes on it and not one dish in any of the stacks that wasn't caked with leftover food, from how far back I dared not consider. The place couldn't have been cleared for weeks, not cleaned for far longer, and as I edged along behind our hostess the soles of my shoes were sticking to the floor. David caught my eye and passed something to me over the counter; a shot glass with greasy smudges down the side, filled with clear liquid.

'Vodka,' he told me softly as Tangye bellowed **Down the hatch!** from across the room. David had brought that bottle with him too, 75cl of Stoly in an inside pocket. He and Tangye downed theirs in one gulp, like Cossacks, and for the first time in my life I did the same. David produced a corkscrew he'd also brought along – *what, no glasses?* – and started to open the wine. With my instincts flying, I realised why. If he hadn't opened both bottles immediately, Tangye would have squirrelled the good stuff away and served up some evil plonk of his own, most likely a home-brew. God, they were appalling, these two. It was all simply appalling. And on one level in particular – there was another – it was also infuriating. People who lived like this didn't do so out of genuine hardship. People who are genuinely hard-strapped will most often take every care to look after their surroundings so that their true circumstances don't show. Cornwall being the neglected backwater it was in those days, they could have lived like princes on as little as five thousand a year, so it was glaringly clear to me that the Tangyes lived this way because they were both as mean as mouse-shit with money and too bat-crap crazy to think anyone noticed.

My other level of infuriation, for the record, was with how David was treating it all as though it were a minor lapse in house-keeping, rather than a gruesome pathology. Did he think he was helping these people by ignoring how they lived? He could have donated an annual five grand to their upkeep out of his back pocket. Did he believe, by bringing me over and knowing I would follow his lead and act as if everything were normal, that he was protecting their finer sensibilities? They didn't *have* any finer sensi-bilities – and he certainly wasn't protecting *mine*! I knew from my mother's reading that Tangye had written upwards of a dozen books and when we were walking over David told me that Jeannie had written several herself. But as I looked around at the squalor this pair lived in I could only wonder how many copies they would have to sell between them before either one prioritised the purchase of a bottle of bleach. Why hadn't David invited them over to his place, for God's sake? What on earth made him decide to bring me *here*? Was it another test, to see how I'd react? Wasn't it enough for him to see me 'swallow on my disappointment' – did he have to see me swallow lunch with this God-awful pair as well?

Jeannie reached down into a kitchen cupboard and held up the latest thing they'd discovered in culinary convenience; a vacuum pack of salmon.

'Look at this,' she said, still smiling inanely. 'We get all our meat and fish this way now.'

'Marvellous firm!!' Tangye exclaimed, with the glee of a Crusader spearing a Saracen. He refilled our shot glasses till the vodka spilled over the sides. 'Send you anything you like in the post – meat, fish, poultry, game – all in vacuum packs. Marvellous!'

Their enthusiasm was due to the fact that the kitchen had no refrigerator. *Of course it didn't.* Their rancid shack wasn't connected to the power grid, because you have to *pay* for electricity. But what neither of them seemed to have noticed – since, as I may have mentioned, *they were both completely insane* – was that the seal on the vacuum pack wasn't sound and the plastic wrapping had inflated to the dimensions of a rugby ball. Ptomaine poisoning by post – *marvellous!*

'Would you like their address?' Jeannie asked me.

Like the condemned at their last meal, David and I took our places at the table with deliberate cheer. David shared local chit-chat with Tangye while from the disgusting kitchen Jeannie brought out the disgusting food she was preparing to kill us with. She covered the entire surface of the rickety dining table with her offerings: potatoes with a greyish gleam, spinach (or something green and steaming) and two great pies, one for each course, with crusts on them like village kerbstones. The savoury one, when she cut into it, had a filling that smelled like hot dog food and which I would have eaten rather more easily if I'd known for sure it *was* dog food. Each mouthful wanted to rise again as I swallowed it, but to prove to David that I could be what he wanted me to be – whatever *the fuck* that was in this loathsome scenario – I managed to eat every last fetid lump our demented little hostess piled on my plate. The second pie, our dessert, with the luxury of tinned cream on the side, contained berries. Locally gathered, Jeannie announced blithely. They could have been brambles, they could have been deadly nightshade, she didn't say. But she did add that they were cutting down on sugar – *of course they were,* these raving misers – meaning I could feel the skin on the roof of my mouth begin to blister at first bite. But by that stage of the ordeal nothing mattered any more. David was bound to have antacid tablets at his place and if he didn't then I would go straight to the bathroom once we were back and – also for the first time in my life – stick my fingers down my throat.

Tangye was another old spook, it transpired, with MI5 during the war. *Of course he was.* Could there possibly have been another reason for David wanting to keep the company of this ghastly old fart and his no-sharp-objects asylum escapee of a wife? Was Miller too? As ever, I didn't ask and by then couldn't have cared. I just assumed that anyone David knew with any degree of familiarity could be placed somewhere on the spook spectrum, even if they were mad as hatters and ten times as dreadful – *zum Beispiel, unser Host.*

When David and Jeannie took the dishes to the kitchen, disgusting old Derek felt me up under the table.

'Come over any time David's too busy to entertain you properly, won't you?' he told me in a phlegmy growl with his hand firmly on my knee.

'My mother loves your books,' was all I could think to say.

(By the way, I didn't ever ask David how he came to know Miller, demonstrating conclusively that I would have made the world's worst investigative reporter. But on the other hand, David didn't ever tell me and I suspect he would have deflected my question if I'd asked. I first learned the truth of their original connection from Adam Sisman's exceptional book, *John le Carré: The Biography* (Bloomsbury, 2015), where he writes, 'One of David's agents, John Miller, would become a lifelong friend.')

That foul experience actually brought us closer together and for a while dispelled David's weekend-long moodiness and distance. We headed back at marching pace, laughing away the worst of it as we walked off mad Jeannie's appalling garbage of a meal. (I found a convenient clearing in the bracken to pee, since I would have preferred risking the need for a catheter to using the facilities *chez* Tangye. David evidently took the same view, availing himself of a nearby gorse bush.) The minute we were in we promptly downed more neat vodka as a digestive aid and managed to have a happy, funny, sexy evening together. This was the way it could always have been between us, if David would only have let it happen that way, if he could have found it in himself to save the misery for the part of his life that engendered it and just enjoy the good stuff, the bonus, with me. That was what he claimed he wanted, what he always seemed to start off aiming to achieve. But there was something lurking deep within him that would emerge to take a stab at our good times, something that wasn't ever content until it had spread the old contagion to the fresh wound.

At the end of the day we fell asleep in the middle of the huge unyielding bed, lying together like spoons. But even so, David's ghosts still stalked him through the night.

When George Greenfield and his girlfriend Gigi arrived on Tuesday afternoon, I quite unexpectedly found myself close to tears with relief. It was like the moment in those 1950s science-fiction films when the hero's girlfriend discovers that not all of the townsfolk have been turned into pod-people. For the first time since arriving I felt I was among friends, though, as with all the others, I hadn't met either of them before. George brought a welcome camaraderie with him and an elegant city ease. He greeted me cordially, as though we were already established colleagues. He was older and shorter than David, but lean and trim, with dark twinkly eyes and a tight but broad smile under a thin moustache. I'd been feeling caught up in something decidedly *Rebecca*-ish the whole weekend – the young *ingénue* deeply in love with the brooding older man, on a first visit to his daunting Cornish pile where everyone was in on the big secret except me.

But with George's arrival all that vanished and my sense of the real world returned. I hardly realised how far it had receded until then. Now I *knew* there was something odd and encoded about the lunch with Miller and his boyfriend – I hadn't imagined it. Even the barking Tangyes had been part of the pre-arranged show. George proved it to me with his easy genuine affability. So did Gigi, who was just wonderful. She was vibrant and glamorous and witty, and I instantly felt we could become great pals – as indeed we later did. (She asked not to be identified here, so I've named her after George's initials.) But as David had arranged things, one good evening was all I got. I could have taken the sleeper back on Wednesday night and still made it to the studio on Thursday. But David made no offer to change the arrangements. I was to leave first thing on Wednesday morning, as planned.

The renewed confidence I was starting to feel needed more shoring up than it could get in a few congenial *normal* hours. *Had I been moody*, as David charged? I didn't know, there was no way to tell. David certainly had been – and far worse for most of the time. His reality was always the dominant one, though he only seemed to see the depth of his own dark eddies when the backwash spilled on to me. No previous lover – no one in my life until then – had ever accused me of being like that before. If I was guilty as charged, then it was only the natural response to my current lover knocking the living *levitas* out of me for three days straight.

All the long way back to London I stared out of the train window, feeling lost and confused and somehow worn away.

David's next letter was dated 5 November and was a suitable powder-keg for the occasion. He began ominously by saying he wished he could write a happier letter, then dived headlong into a description of all the tensions and problems and bad things the weekend had left him with. He felt a failure, he said, and concluded that I must too. (Perhaps so, but at least I knew I'd tried for success. And anyway – *failure*? It was just a weekend in the damned country, not UN peace talks.) Then he declared that we must not fall victim to our own rhetoric. (*Our* rhetoric?) Said he couldn't shake off the bad memories despite a happy last night. (I was only surprised he didn't write happy last *supper*, his letter was such a self-awareness- and irony-free zone.) He claimed to be going ahead with the flat nonetheless, but finished by saying that he didn't like being pushed around. (*He* didn't like it?) I was to write back *poste restante* Hampstead, he insisted, citing our first official dead letter-box, though still without any trace of irony. He said he wouldn't call me again until I did.

Christ Almighty. All that *Sturm-und-Drang* just because I asked him 'what happened?' over half-term.

Thank God I didn't ask him 'what happens next?'

I had entered into this relationship thinking of David as an enigma; a man whose hidden heart and complex mind would be an enormous challenge to interpret but an even greater reward to ultimately understand. Now, after the visit to Cornwall, I had modified my view. I still didn't doubt the reward, but the complexity and the challenge were both far greater than I'd imagined.

I had first assumed that secrecy – with its corollary, encryption – was simply David's *modus operandi*, his standard method of approaching the world, left over from his training and career as a spy. I hadn't taken the issue too seriously, seeing it as a professional habit of mind, nothing more.

But that was a hopeless misinterpretation. What I'd taken for David's *m.o.* was his essential self. Secrecy was a survival instinct deep within him and encryption was the mechanism by which it was maintained. I'd seen it in relentless operation that weekend. Just when I thought I understood some part of him, the mechanism would re-encrypt with a fresh turn of his inner cogs and I'd be confounded once more. As I began to grasp the next new element, the cogs would turn again. So now I began to see David not so much as an enigma, but rather as an Enigma machine, with uncountable combinations lying within him, just waiting for the gears of limitless permutation to engage. Only *I love you* seemed to escape the obscuration of code – and the sex which invariably followed, in limitless permutations of its own. If I wanted the relationship to continue – and I had never wanted anything more – there was one vital thing for me to do. I had to try and crack the code.

I took a couple of days to decompress, from the trip and from the letter, then wrote back. I have no idea now what I wrote; I had precious little idea even then. I just let my pen cover the page and posted it as soon as it was done. All I could do after that was wait.

David called me a couple of days later.

'Wow. You can't half write a letter, my girl, I'll say. That one doesn't go in the shredder, I can tell you. I love you, my Sue, I love you enormously. What are you doing tomorrow night?'

I was enormously relieved, of course, that it was all fine again. But was that all it took to get him right-side-up – a good letter? I didn't believe what I'd written could be entirely responsible for the turnaround any more than I felt entirely responsible for his despondency in the first place. If David could haunt himself without supernatural help – as I'd seen he could, perfectly well – then he could probably capsize and right his own emotional boat all on his own too.

We met 'for a quick Chinese' somewhere in Paddington, before he caught the train back down to Penzance. He was sweet and kind and loving during the meal and plainly desperate to be with me again. He said he could hardly stand to see me for a meal and not make love to me afterwards, but something had cropped up so this was the only time he had and he couldn't stand not to see me at all.

Something so often did crop up. His accountants, his lawyers, the movie, the script, the builders – even his babies, as he persisted in calling his grown-up sons, though never the one who was actually still a child. Any of these had a claim on his time and attention prior to mine and, since he'd already complained to me about their depredations into his life, I didn't feel I could say anything. I loved him for spending what free time he did have with me and trusted that the process he was going through would eventually free him substantially, partly for us but most importantly for him. His most abiding lament was that he was constantly being taken away from the new book. I always sympathised, but his schedule at times resembled the plate-spinning act that used to appear on old TV variety shows, where the guy kept spinning more and more plates on top of more and more poles and then had to race around madly trying to keep them all from crashing to the ground. I couldn't understand why David arranged his life in such a way, though Miller had already told me the key to it. I just hadn't caught on.

After some more calls, all of them loving and reassuring – *It's all good, Sue, all good* – and promises that he'd write me *lovely long letters*, which actually were lovely when they arrived, he returned briefly to London. (The frequency of his travelling was dizzying. In the three and a half months of our relationship, I'd been abroad with David twice, knew of three other European trips he made by himself and he'd been to Cornwall more times than I could count.) A further cancelled lunch became dinner, with a movie first, something David said he was keen to see – *Zelig*, Woody Allen's latest. He watched with great attention throughout, but afterwards said he didn't think much of it. The irony of his choosing that particular film – about a man who is a perpetual chameleon, slotting into moments in history without really being part of them – wasn't a line he pursued. He saw the thesis in the film, but not the irony of his choosing it. Some prod of intuition made me decide not to point this out.

After the cinema we went to Fakhreldine, the big Lebanese restaurant overlooking Green Park. As we dug into a gargantuan meze starter, David advised me that I really shouldn't raise anything to my mouth with my left hand.

'Why not?' I asked.

'Because it's the one you wipe your bum with.'

'But it isn't,' I replied, before realising he was speaking culturally.

I might have added, *Aa-ow, me bloomin' beads!* David had a pretty wide streak of Henry Higgins running through him, at least with me. But it was odd that he should care what a bunch of waiters in a Lebanese restaurant might think of my otherwise standard table manners. It wasn't as if we were in Beirut, and even if we had been, so what? I was sure none of them cared about anything we did as long as it didn't involve a food fight and he left a good tip.

After the restaurant we headed to Paddington station. David was going back to Cornwall *again*, in advance of a family weekend for his youngest son's birthday, but not until the first train next morning. He'd booked us in for the night at the Great Western Royal.

What was once an ornate stuccoed Victorian hotel was now a tired old Miss Havisham's wedding cake of a place. Our room looked as though it had last been decorated for the Coronation. But David seemed to like the dilapidated grandeur.

'Lady Docker has a suite here, I believe,' he announced, as if that were a recommendation. (Her name had been a byword for extravagance a couple of decades earlier, when she was a notorious spendthrift, most notably on a string of luxuriously personalised Daimlers. Her husband, Sir Bernard, was the Daimler chairman until he was ousted for charging his wife's excessive running costs to the firm.)

David surprised me by saying he wanted me to go down to Cornwall again at the end of the month. Well, well. Tangye and Miller must have filed favourable reports. George probably put in a good word for me too. Or maybe the time he'd spent back in the bosom of his family since then had made my lover re-evaluate whatever problems he thought he had with me.

I agreed to go – on one non-negotiable condition.

'No Tangyes this time,' I said flatly.

'No Tangyes this time,' he confirmed. 'So you needn't bring a stomach pump.'

Meanwhile, Graham and I were in the studio with Derek Jacobi and *1984*. Jacobi was an instant sweetheart and a first-rate reader. He apologised for making us rush the recording because of his skiing trip, but said he was going to Wengen just before Christmas. Graham said what a coincidence, he was going skiing in Wengen just after the New Year. It took them about four seconds to realise what I already knew, that they'd both be borrowing David's chalet.

'He's a lovely bloke, isn't he?' Graham said, adding rather artfully, 'My co-producer and I have both rather taken to him.'

Jacobi readily agreed. 'Delightful,' he said. 'Simply delightful.'

I went along with the Cornwell love-fest, chiefly because they weren't wrong. David *was* lovely, he *was* delightful. He was just, well … *and the rest.* They had seen only one aspect of the man; I'd already seen so many more. Neither of them was sleeping with him, of course, which accounted for most of the difference, though I dare say Jacobi wouldn't have minded having his name in the hat.

David called that night from Cornwall to ask how the recording had gone. He was once more *tout seul* and rang after having supper at Miller's, saying he'd left the first pages of the new book with him. He sounded fine but broke off after a few minutes to take a call on another line. When he rang back, his voice had changed.

'Book's no good, Our Sue. Miller says so. He just rang. Told me all about Job.'

(I can't quite remember when David started that variant for my name. It was one example of a sort of mock-Cockney lingo he would sometimes lapse into and would brand it 'Belgravia-Cockney' in his books. There was a lot of this going around the smarter areas of London at the time, with Chas & Dave riding high in the charts and the BBC about to start a new soap opera called *EastEnders*. But I think David may have been using it since his army days, although his usage was never quite as convincing to my ear as Graham's, whose expressions were drawn from real Londoners like Frenchie and the other engineers in the studios. But anyway, 'Our Sue' stuck as an endearment for me.)

He didn't seem to want to say anything further about his book – or about Job, for that matter – but asked if I'd watched Alan Bennett's film, *An Englishman Abroad*, based on actress Coral Browne's unlikely association with defector Guy Burgess, which had aired that night. He'd missed it, being out at Sancreed, and this was before the general advent of video recorders. He asked if it was good and I said it was terrific. The waspish actress played her even more caustic younger self and the once-beautiful Alan Bates had gone full-throttle as the degenerate and impossibly fruity Burgess. The two had met in 1958, when Browne was touring Russia with the Shakespeare Memorial Theatre Company and Burgess stumbled drunkenly into her dressing room in Moscow after the first night of *Hamlet* and vomited prodigiously into her sink. I relayed the scene to David, expecting him to laugh, but he still sounded wan and distant at the other end of the line. His mind was on Miller's critique and, though he'd asked, what I was saying didn't help. The subject of Burgess was too close to Philby and, as I didn't yet know, Philby was too close to the central matter of the new novel. And Miller had just trashed his first attempt.

It seemed to me – perhaps in my prejudice, but I don't think entirely – that Burgess's life in the USSR was something like David's life in Cornwall, the bleak and inhospitable location where he took himself to evade capture and confinement in the Hampstead slammer, with only a couple of fellow ex-spooks who'd also defected from civilisation for company. But even in his self-imposed exile, David couldn't escape a domestic situation which – I hesitate to say Kremlin-like – seemed to monitor his every move.

Cornwall was more than a little lovelier the second time around. Not that I was ever going to warm to the locale, but David was lovely again himself, all right inside his head as he would so often put it. This time I took the overnight sleeper, the train that Smiley takes to see Ann before setting off on his final quest for Karla. David was waiting for me at the station, but on the wrong platform, and it took him a while to pound his way over to the right side of the track. (Sometimes the metaphors write themselves …)

He made me a little breakfast when we got in and then we hastened to bed. The book was going well now, he told me, which was probably as much the root of the easy atmosphere as anything. He was over a false start, he said, meaning the book but quite possibly meaning our relationship as well.

'There's only deeper with us, my darling – it's the only way.'

As before, David wrote in the mornings while I read, but this time when he came to find me for lunch it was with an easy, contented expression on his face, asking *Fancy a snoot?* with a sweet smile, or *Would a girl like a quick fuck? Or even a slow one?* We talked and talked the whole time I was there, then had a lot more sex and then talked some more. We walked and walked too. David was a huge walker and told me that when he was down there with Jane he would get her to drive him ten or fifteen miles out from the house and then leave him to walk back. He offered this detail as something constructive, as I suppose it was, for him. But it struck me as being just one more thing his wife couldn't join him in. There were already his foreign research trips – from which, of course, I was currently benefitting – but there was also what he'd described as his daily routine at Hampstead. He wrote all through the morning, then passed his hand-written pages to Jane to type while he went off for whatever lunch and afternoon refreshments he'd arranged for himself, which were also currently to my benefit much of the time. I'd already concluded they had no sex life and, although David gave parties at the house and seemed to know a lot of people, he'd told me Jane didn't really like socialising. All in all, at this point I couldn't quite see what the marriage was *for*.

We went over to Sancreed again for lunch with Miller and Truscott and this time were joined by Miller's elderly but very sprightly mother, Reni. It was a nice, cheery, easy occasion. Real, instead of show.

There was evidence of building work at Tregiffian now. David showed me floor plans and talked about new wings. His aim was to have the house divide easily between all his sons and their families in the years to come. This wasn't really his place, he said, although only last month he'd expressly insisted it was. This place, he said, was for his sons. His place was really the chalet in Wengen.

Poop-poop!

'Do you ski?' he asked.

I confessed I did not.

'Really? Ah, well – you're no use to me if you don't ski. We could go there all the time if you did.'

He gave me another red box from S. J. Phillips. My Christmas present; a gold pendant, set with a delicate coral and lapis carving of Venus rising from the sea.

'It was something to do with a girl on a beach,' he said sweetly.

Next morning a tiny piece of history repeated itself when a wren needed rescuing in the kitchen. I did my wrangling act again and it co-operated like an old hand. Perhaps it was even the same bird and had flown down specially to deposit some more micro listening devices. Or perhaps it was simply that the living metaphor of imprisonment and escape accompanied David wherever he went.

At the end of my visit we took the train back to London together. As we sat across the little table from each other in first class, David announced that he had an idea for me. I heard this with a certain trepidation, with no clue to what he had in mind.

So, he asked after a careful pause, why didn't I help him with some research for the book?

Oh. In a million years I wouldn't have guessed that.

'I need you to find out about my dad,' he told me. 'There's a mass of stuff about his life that I don't know. Official stuff. The phoney businesses he started, the court cases when he was up on fraud charges, the slammers he was in when he got sent down. He agented for parliamentary candidates during the war. You got leave from the services to do it, you see. It was a good wheeze – I don't think he ever finished basic training. He had race horses, too, and knew radio and showbiz sorts. He entertained the Australian cricket team when they were on tour. Think about it and let me know. It might be fun and the pay will be excellent, though one of the terms of your contract will be that you are required to engage in frequent bouts of intensely inventive sex with your employer. And, of course, more seriously, it means I would give you a credit in my book. That could be quite a good qualification, if a girl decided she wanted to do more literary research afterwards.'

I said yes, it did sound fun (though privately I wasn't so sure) and I would think about it and let him know. David seemed pleased with my answer and looked contentedly out of the window as the West Country slipped away.

David's sister Charlotte lived somewhere south of the river and David picked me up from my flat in a cab. It was a long, slow journey in the evening traffic and on the way he informed me that Lady Docker had been found dead in her suite at the Great Western. Recalling how neglected the hotel had seemed, I wondered whether she might already have been dead when we stayed there. Then he told me that he'd visited his mother a couple of days earlier and asked her about her sex life with his father.

'She told you?' I asked, though whether I was more incredulous that David had asked her or she had answered him, I couldn't have said.

'Oh, yes.' David shifted to the county matron voice he always used for his mother. '"It was pure Krafft-Ebing, dear. Pure Krafft-Ebing."'

For once, my failure to ask a follow-up question was quite intentional.

For myself, I was in high good spirits; Cornwall had been wonderful, Cornwell had been wonderful. I anticipated an enjoyable evening ahead with David's sister, who had already expressed her approval of our relationship. But it didn't go like that. After an initial hello, Charlotte completely blanked me out. She had eyes only for David, wanted to talk only to David, make him listen to her problems and her family stuff. Seating me awkwardly at the head of the table, she sat down directly across from him, leaned forward on her elbows and talked intently to him for the rest of the night. It seemed like a deliberate snub at first, but I began to think she didn't know she was doing it. Had we been in a restaurant – and this was possibly why we weren't – unwitting diners would have picked Charlotte, not me, for the new girlfriend at our table. And yet, for all that, she didn't crack a smile once through the whole evening.

At one point Charlotte's infant daughter took herself out of bed and came downstairs. The girl's father, Charlotte's partner, actor Kenneth Cranham, hadn't joined us that night, most likely by deliberate design. The presence of her actual lover might have cramped Charlotte's unwholesome focus on her brother, who in any case had been less than complimentary about Cranham in the cab coming over. When she spotted the small figure at the foot of the stairs she quickly scolded her, saying sharply that it was long past her bedtime and she had no business getting up. David greeted the little girl with an odd fixed smile, a little like the Queen Mother accepting a posy.

'Hello, Nancy Grace,' he said. 'How are you?'

Nancy Grace didn't appear to recognise her uncle. Charlotte scooped her up and carried her back upstairs.

After the evening was over – whatever that evening *was* – we headed to Heathrow to spend the night at an airport hotel. David was leaving for Zurich again in the morning. More business with Rainer. In the cab he said scornfully, 'Charlotte has no idea how to present a face to children.'

I gave his remark no thought. I was just glad to be out of yet another Cornwell house full of deeply weird vibes.

He called from Switzerland the next evening to say he'd spoken to Charlotte and she'd told him how very much she liked me.

'She says you're lovely and that you have a gentle heart.'

That couldn't be right. I suspected he was making it up. But I was wrong.

With David's insistence on Moscow Rules, I'd told only a very few people about our relationship and those few I'd sworn to secrecy. One of them was a girlfriend I'd met when I was working as a researcher at Thames Television. She shared a flat with an actress whom I'd met briefly once or twice and unbeknownst to me, but arguably Exhibit B in the case for David's insistence on the perpetual need for cover, was a great chum of Charlotte's. Shortly after that supper, my friend rang me with a story. The flatmate had just taken a long call from Charlotte about her famous brother's new girlfriend and was astonished when she heard her give my name. She eagerly repeated everything to my friend – all of it really good – only to be put out to discover that she already knew all about it and hadn't said a word.

'I was sworn to secrecy,' my friend told her flatmate in her defence.

So David hadn't made it up. His sister actually did think well of me. Yet I'd spent a whole evening in her company feeling like I wasn't even in the room.

Next time he called from Zurich there had been an IRA bombing in London and he was concerned in case I'd been anywhere in the vicinity. I told him I hadn't and didn't know anyone who had.

'Well, I want you to keep safe, Our Sue, so just you stay away from all that.'

I wasn't sure how to implement his advice, but was touched that he'd instantly worried for my safety when he heard the item on the news.

A new spy series called *Chessgame*, based on novels by English author Anthony Price, had just started its run on ITV. (Along with the Bennett film, this was part of the ongoing vogue for espionage drama in the wake of the huge popular success of the BBC's two big Smiley series.) I hadn't watched it, but one review in particular had made me chuckle and I passed it along.

'They're saying it's like Smiley with sex,' I told David.

'Well,' he replied simply, 'that's what you've got.'

I also relayed the story about Charlotte, thinking he'd appreciate it as a funny little tale and be glad to hear that a friend of mine could be trusted with our secret. (As they all could. If I'd put them all in a room together and plied them with drink they still wouldn't have breathed a word even to each other.) But David's reaction was suddenly very clipped. He told me to wait by the phone and rang off. Ten minutes later he rang back, saying he'd called Charlotte 'to have words'.

'So *that's* all settled,' he said with a snort. I pictured him dusting himself off after the fray. 'Don't let anyone think I'm *cross* ...'

He hadn't liked Charlotte spreading the good news. He must have sworn her to secrecy too.

Then it was nearly Christmas and school holidays. That meant radio silence till the New Year, David told me, using that exact phrase.

'But don't worry, my darling. Our love is singing.'

Just before the start of the holidays he called one last time.

'I've got a flat! I'll show it to you when I'm back – Happy Christmas! It's going to be a wonderful New Year – I promise!'

1984

ST JOHN'S WOOD

Mistress and wife can well supply his need,
A miss for pleasure, and a wife for breed.

John Gay

A man who has two women loses his soul.
But a man who has two houses loses his head.

Proverb (epigraph in *A Perfect Spy*)

The new flat wasn't quite finished by the start of the New Year, but David couldn't wait to show it to me anyway. He told me to meet him at the exit to the tube station at St John's Wood. I was to be there at four o'clock.

It was a cold gloomy day, not meant for hanging around outside, but as I came up the escalator to the street, digging my gloves out of my pockets and turning up my coat collar against the icy north London wind, David was waiting for me. There I was *at last*, he said, though it was only a couple of minutes past the hour. He'd been waiting for me *for ages*, why wasn't I here *hours ago*? He wasn't scolding me, I realised. He'd been waiting ahead of time because it was so important to him. There was exhilaration in his expression. He seemed oblivious to the whipping cold.

'So hurry up and come with me – I want you to see my new pad.'

This was why he'd directed me to come by tube, not a cab. He wanted to *take* me to his new place himself, not have me arrive at the door. We raced along hand in hand, David in high gear, and turned into a side road off the High Street, turning again into a small courtyard. Like so much of London at the time, it was 'under development'. It might once have been an old mews or a merchant's yard, but now it was new and spiffy and residential, almost college quad-looking. David unlocked an outer door to a stairwell, releasing the smell of fresh paint and plaster, and geed me up three flights to the apartment on the top floor.

'Here—!' he said, excitedly turning his latchkey and flinging the door wide. 'This is it—!'

Inside was even colder than outside. Our breath was fogging ahead of us as we went in. The flat was small and neat but an unfinished shell, sans heat, sans light, sans everything except painted walls and new carpet throughout. There was a narrow hall, with a bathroom to the right, a bedroom to the left, and five paces ahead lay the main area, an all-in-one living room and kitchen. The ceiling was high and sloping; dormer windows set into the front overlooked the street and skylights at the back gave a rooftop view over the courtyard. The whole place had plainly been an attic not so long before. Now, post-developers, it was David's new bolthole.

'You're the only one I'm ever going to let in here,' he declared and kissed me to set the seal on it. Within minutes we were lying on the factory-fresh wool twist, doing what we did best – better than anybody ever, even fully clothed in the tomb-like cold, overcoats and all – sending up steam that was visible in the hazy yellow light from the street-lamp outside.

'It's hard to imagine without you,' he told me as he locked up when we left.

A lunch date we made for a couple of days later became tea at my place instead. I said I was taking myself off to the States for ten days to see some friends and David made an only half-joking joke that he was sure it was to see my other lover, that *much older* fellow with *nothing like* his staying power. You're so good at guessing, I said, though he wasn't even close. He said he awarded me *a lot of Brownie points* for taking myself away like that, by which I understood he was tired of people waiting for him to tell them when to jump. (Not that he didn't like it when they deferred to him and asked how high …) I gave him my best friend Barbara's phone number in New York as a contact. He stayed until very late, probably later than he'd intended now he knew I was going away.

Graham rang me the next day with some new titles for me to abridge. By the time I was back from the States he would have just left for two weeks in Wengen and he wanted me to have them done for his return. So I should probably make a start on the plane. He wished me a happy trip, then added as a cheery afterthought that he'd been driving along the King's Road the previous night and *saw a bloke coming out of your place at midnight*.

We were going to have to tell him, I realised; it wasn't right that he still didn't know.

I flew TWA to Boston Logan to meet up with Roger, a pal from Oxford who had moved Stateside. We hit the nearest supermarket and liquor store, piled the brown paper grocery sacks along with our stuff into the trunk of a rental and headed up to New Hampshire, where one of Roger's friends had lent him his ski lodge in the White Mountains. Mindful of David's only partially lighthearted remark that I was 'no use' to him if I couldn't ski, I'd decided it was time to learn.

Next morning I surrendered all dignity and joined a total beginners' class made up entirely of seven- and eight-year-olds. By lunch I was able to descend the barely discernible gradient on the green baby slope in a wide plough at about two miles an hour. By the end of the week Roger took me down the easiest of the grown-up slopes, so that I could say I'd done my very first blue run.

We celebrated as we'd always celebrated the end of exams, with – what else? – quantities of champagne. We were only half of our old Oxford foursome – Roger and his then girlfriend, me and my lovely Canadian – and instead of getting rowdy in Christ Church Meadows we were sitting modestly in swimsuits in the hot tub at the lodge, but it was a sweet moment nonetheless. As we chinked glasses Rog declared, 'The *gurrrl* dun *guuuhhd*,' in an excruciating John Wayne impersonation he had saved for the occasion. Then, reverting to best English, he added, 'This has to beat getting an alpha-plus in Anglo-Saxon, wouldn't you say?'

Not that I ever had, but he was so right.

I took the shuttle down to New York to spend the last two days of my stay with Barbara. We'd met on my first trip to North America in the summer before I went up to Oxford. Barbara was the Harvard room-mate of an American girl I'd become friends with at school and she'd insisted I come to stay with her in her NYC summer sublet – at the exalted address of 45 Fifth Avenue – so that she could show me the city. It was the beginning both of our beautiful lifelong friendship and, with Barbara as my guide, of my unshakeable love affair with New York. Barbara was a staff writer at *Time* magazine and lived with her (first) husband, a reporter on the *New York Post*, in an apartment on Horatio Street in Greenwich Village. As we hugged on my arrival, the first thing I saw over her shoulder was a vase of purple orchids on her dining table.

'They're from David,' she told me. 'They came yesterday. He called as well, a couple of days ago.'

'Did he ask where I was?'

'He did.'

'What did you say?'

Barbara shrugged. 'I told him you were out.'

'What did he say to that?'

'He wanted to know where.'

'Did you manage to put him off the scent?'

'Yeah. Kind of.'

'What did you tell him?'

Barbara shrugged again. 'I said you were at Bloomingdale's.'

Barbara's husband joined us for supper. He was a big le Carré fan, so we let him in on the secret.

'Wow,' he said, taking it in. 'Well, I know one thing. You must be a very special lady. And you're very lucky – 'cos he's the best.'

When I said that David had asked me to help him with the research for his new book – I was circumspect about the details – he gave me a further 'Wow' and continued to listen avidly as I passed on what I knew about the *Drummer Girl* movie. Basking in the vicarious admiration, I went on to say that David had also told me he thought I would make a good continuity girl in films. But that instantly triggered the city-desk reporter's bullshit sensor.

'I thought you had a *master's* degree from *Oxford*,' he said scornfully.

I was suitably chastened by his remark. It was only what I should have said to David at the time.

Back home after the overnight flight I heard the phone ringing as soon as I opened my front door. David was calling from Hampstead, starting with an urgent apology.

'I didn't mean to call you from here, but I couldn't wait. I never want to call you from here again.'

Did I have a good trip? Did I get the orchids? Had I finally done the decent thing and given up my other far inferior lover? Had I decided to do the Ronnie work? Would I let him fuck me soon and then again immediately afterwards?

Yes to all the above, I said, and heard him sigh with contentment.

I was to keep my passport handy then, he said, because we were going to Zurich the day after next. He'd have the spook travel agents send the plane tickets round by courier, with some of the folding stuff just because, and by the time we returned the flat would be ready.

'Then,' he declared, 'our new year can really begin.'

Soon after the tickets and money arrived there was another courier at my door. David had sent a couple of his sleeping pills to help me over my trans-Atlantic jetlag.

We stayed at the Dolder Grand, another one of David's magnificent *Schloss* hotels, set high on the Adlisberg and commanding a sweeping view down to the city and the lake beyond. As soon as we were in our room, I made him a present of my ski pass from the White Mountains, gift-wrapped in coloured tissue paper and ribbon.

'Oh, my *darling* – that's so wonderful, so absolutely wonderful,' he said, holding the little laminated card in his hands as though it had been a fragment of the rood. 'I adore you for doing that – my darling girl – I really do.'

Of all the people I have ever known – of all the people *you* have ever known, I guarantee – only David could make you feel so good about paying him his tribute. Only David could spoon-feed you with such tender and glowing appreciation that it made you want to please him all the more, just to have him spoon-feed you all over again.

And yet, even though he was being so lovely and was evidently so truly and deeply touched by what I'd done, some weasel suspicion at the back of my mind was already laying odds that he would never utter the word 'ski' in my presence again.

David was his best Swiss self for the whole trip, Zurich suiting him like the more stylish clothes he was wearing, the more attractive way he brushed his hair, the way his whole appearance seemed to flesh out in that country. For me, though the city was cold and stark and wintry, it spoke to my profoundly urban soul. There was a crisp elegance to the light, a pewtery sheen to the surface of the river, a reassuring historical solidity to the buildings that was a bulwark to the cold. If David had decided on the spot to leave Hampstead for this place, I would have moved there with him in a heartbeat.

He took me to meet Rainer at Mohrbooks on Klosbachstrasse. As we passed through the bustling corridors of the old building, Rainer appeared from his office, looking like a wise court adviser from a previous epoch; tall and spare, beautifully *soigné*, he was elegance and urbanity personified. He took my hand as David introduced me and bowed over it with the first and so far only '*gnädige Frau*' I have ever received. He had a particular smile for David – Miller had it too – that said they went way back and he knew it all. Several of the more senior female staff joined us – Swiss 'mothers', I couldn't help thinking, but on the second floor there, not the fifth – to say a cooing hello to David and to cast a smiling but 'we have to remember this for later' eye over me. One of them had a little dog with her which, at a rather wordy command in German from Rainer, promptly rolled over onto her back with her legs in the air, drawing oddly girlish giggles from the assembled staff. David translated for me.

'Rainer said, *Show them what the little ladies in the red-light district do—*'

The magic wand of money had been waved over the flat by the next time I was there, on a day that was positively beaming with unseasonal sunshine. (That darned pathetic fallacy.) In the intervening few weeks since our chilly but heated session on the carpet, the place had been plumbed in, wired up and fully furnished. The bathroom and kitchen were appointed in rather sail-boat scale, as the dimensions were tight, and the bedroom proved big enough to hold a double bed if it was wedged against one wall. In the main room a slouchy sofa and two armchairs were arranged around a coffee table under the skylight, while the space at the dormer window was entirely taken up by a large table for David to work at. (So large it had to be sawn in half to get it up the stairs and reconstituted *in situ.*) A whole team of fitters must have been tasked with perfecting this miniature Camp David and the last member of it was leaving as I arrived for lunch. He appeared to have been working on the front door.

The man promptly packed up his power drill and left, but David kept the door open once he'd gone, smiling proudly. I was supposed to notice something, I realised; the tilt of his chin tipped me off, but it didn't help me guess what he was so pleased with. A thousand guesses wouldn't have got me close.

'Bulletproof!' David declared happily and rapped his knuckles on the door, generating a hard metallic ring. 'Solid steel facing, a quarter-inch thick.'

There was a spyhole too – naturally – and when he shut us inside, the door closed with a heavy jailhouse clunk, which seemed to please him tremendously.

'By the way,' he said, undoing my blouse in the process of taking my coat, 'I didn't mention it, but you are going to spend the whole of the day and night here with me, aren't you? I bought a spare toothbrush.'

There was champagne along with caviar and other goodies chilling in the little fridge in the little kitchen, but it all had to wait while we christened the new area rug. After that we made a picnic on the rug and after that we needed to launch the bed. Then I lay with my head on the crook of David's arm while for the very first time he read me the pages that he'd written there that morning. He read to me in a softer tone than in the studio – Frenchie would have wanted to adjust his level – but with no less power to transport. I closed my eyes and let him take me on a magic carpet ride to Vienna, to spy on the shambles of the Pyms' diplomatic residence, whence his new hero Magnus had vanished overnight.

Afterwards, David began to tell me more of the story he was creating.

'So it starts with my guy disappearing. They fear the worst, of course. He's a diplomat – read spook – so they think he's defected. But he's really gone back to his roots to write his life down in a letter to his son. Rick, his old man, has died and he's just buried him. Now, suddenly, he feels free. The rules don't apply any more. He wants to tell it all, set down his life, now that he can. The life he had to lead because of Rick – what Rick made him into. It's a sort of atonement, but it's also his ticket out. So there's the story of his past as a baby spook and I want to wrap it round the story of his adult spook life and what they're doing to try and find him – what they turn up in the search.'

As with all our conversations, although I learned so much there was still so much more to know. But I didn't probe further. I knew David would read me the pages as they emerged, most likely as we were now, lying together in bed. It was thrilling – astounding, in fact – to be so close to the man and to his process as he created what he was determined should be his finest book yet. I asked whether he had a title. In Greece he'd said his initial idea had been *Agent Running in the Field* until Rainer pointed out that the word-play wouldn't work in the foreign editions.

'Yes,' David answered contentedly. 'Now I do. It's called *A Perfect Spy*. It's going to be wonderful, I think. Yes, I really think so. I'm finally writing the book I want to be buried with.'

This seemed to me to be a strange expression of satisfaction. But of course I knew nothing of how it must feel to have created a literary legacy – beginning when he wasn't much older than I was then – such that your pen name became a byword for the real-world version of what was in your fiction. Graham Greene was the senior example of the ex-spook turned world-renowned novelist and 'Greeneland' was often used to describe the instantly identifiable doubt-ridden internal landscape of that writer's narrative. But no one ever said of a scenario in real life that it was 'just like a Graham Greene novel', as they so frequently did with le Carré. After *Tinker*

Tailor, David's own spook argot had entered the general vocabulary and you couldn't count the variants of his *The Spy Who Came in from the Cold* title that turned up in everything from Hollywood scripts to newspaper headlines. (For the first article ever written about this book, in fact – The Spy Who Came into the Bedroom; *Sunday Times*, 5 June 2022 – and there was a genius tabloid take on another of David's titles in 2016, when Taylor Swift was photographed in a surreptitious clinch with *The Night Manager* leading man Tom Hiddleston: TINKER TAYLOR SNOGS A SPY!) It all spoke to David's power to conjure such tangible authenticity in his writing. (Sisman, by the way, gives an entirely different origin story for the novel's title in his biography – which is not to say, given the nature of our subject, that either of us is wrong.)

I asked which of his books he considered the best to date, meaning the one which would have accompanied him into his casket up till then, and he seemed pleased that I'd joined him on this patch of his own psychological terrain. But, as was so often the case, he didn't quite answer the question.

'Well, we know which one is generally held to be the *worst,* don't we? That would be *The Navy and Sentimental*, wouldn't it?'

I chuckled at his own little twist in the title, something he often did with names. Waterstone's, the bookseller, was invariably Wasserstein; his publishers were Odders and Sodders.

'Have you read it?' he asked.

'No,' I confessed. I'd only reached *A Small Town in Germany* in my 'required reading'. 'Do you want me to?'

'You might like it if you did. It's a pretty little book. You know what it's about, don't you?'

A *ménage à trois*, I seemed to think, but I wanted David to tell me his own way.

'It was about my time with James Kennaway and his wife, Susan. He was this big Scottish brawler, a drinker, but a fine writer. *Tunes of Glory* was his big book. He wrote the screenplay, too; Guinness

162

was in the film. After a while of knowing him, I realised he was trying to feed me his wife, just to watch the drama unfold ...'

I watched his face as he revisited this landmark episode from his past. I could see he was giving me just the top notes while the full score played privately in his mind. As he lay on his back staring up at the bedroom ceiling, his amber-flecked eyes were seeing scenes projected there, his pupils wide black pools of memory despite the bright winter sun that was streaming into the bedroom. (This was the second time I observed his unlikely control over his autonomic nervous system, the first being the episode with the ice cube.)

'Susan wrote a memoir a few years ago,' he told me. '*The Kennaway Papers*. You might be interested in reading that too.'

No, I thought immediately; I didn't want to read an account of one of David's past affairs at this stage of ours. I did read it, of course, and Kennaway's own novel about their sparky threesome, which was his last publication before he died in a car crash and prophetically titled *Some Gorgeous Accident*. It was also the first of their three accounts to be published, though David didn't mention it.

My guess then – that David was revisiting moments from his love affair – was both right and wrong at the same time. He *was* recalling the love affair, but it was only once I'd read *The Naïve and Sentimental Lover* that I realised which of the Kennaways had left the deeper impression on his heart. David's self-hero Cassidy is a successful but unfulfilled manufacturer of advanced brake systems for prams (wonderfully Freudian, since David would leave his wife and three small children a couple of years after the affair). Cassidy encounters the uncompromising iconoclastic writer Shamus and his beautiful wife Helen as squatters in a dilapidated country 'pile' which Cassidy has designs to buy. The names of all three main characters are freighted with meaning. Shamus – the pulp-fiction moniker for a private detective – leads the hero on a riotous journey of self-discovery, helping him sleuth out the secrets of his desires. The name goes to 'sham' too; is he a true artist or just a convincing con-man, the book seems to ask. The mythically named Helen is the wife temporarily stolen from the mighty Agamemnon-Shamus by the young Cassidy-Paris and becomes the *casus belli* between them, when a snowy Swiss rooftop doubles for the gleaming towers of Ilium. Cassidy himself seems to be named for the single purpose of attaching the prefix of his Wild West namesake – Butch. Shamus makes the connection suggestively, calling Cassidy 'lover' and drunkenly claiming them to be 'a pair of pooves' in their new friendship. But there is the hero's first name, too – Aldo. Did David want us to hear 'All-dough' for the rich businessman? Or just 'all dough', no hyphen, because Cassidy is still unbaked, soft in the middle, and in need of the leavening belief that Shamus – not to mention the mysterious Flaherty – will provide?

There are always so many possible interpretations with everything David wrote and even now, I still find myself trying to catch them all. Later in their Quixotic adventures – with Cassidy hopping along as the faithful Sancho Panza beside Shamus's delusional Don – the new friends register in a Parisian hotel under the names of two actual spook 'pooves', Burgess and Maclean. Despite the absolute straightness of both characters, it *is* a love affair. Cassidy loves Shamus with a kind of febrile schoolboy passion, as an idolised older chap in a senior year who models all the dash and daring and iron-clad certainties that he himself has yet to embrace. Next to this, his relationship with Helen barely registers. It was as though David had embarked on the affair with Susan as a proxy for her husband; not in any suppressed homosexual way, despite the jokes, but in order to please his idolised 'lover', James, who simply dared him to do it. It became my view that, when Kennaway died, David subsumed certain aspects of his freer, bolder friend, who had shown him how to live on a different level, how to loosen the shackles of a system run by the Gerrards Crossers of the world.

While David never attempted his late friend's level of womanis-ing – at least no more than briefly after his divorce – it was really only after *l'affaire Kennaway* that he began to allow himself 'other Susans' (in Sisman's cute phrase). In his biography *James and Jim*, Trevor Royle claims Kennaway had a 'violent hatred of reviews and critics'. David adopted this attitude himself. Kennaway claimed a German soul, a Recording Angel and called his children his 'babies', no matter their age. David made these, and many other Jim-isms, his own. And finally, just as Kennaway had always done, he learned to put his writing first and foremost, above all other considerations, no matter the damage and disappointment this caused to others. It was as if there had been a psychological estate sale after the Scottish writer's death – subliminally suggested by the old house in the opening scene of *The Navy and Sentimental* – and David bought up the heritage pieces. Kennaway seems prescient of this, too, in *Some Gorgeous Accident*, calling his own character Link; a man who connects his David character, the faithful and socially obedient Richard David Fiddes (so – *Dick*), to his undiscovered freer self. Kennaway's Fiddes is a doctor in a maternity hospital, what's more, delivering babies for what, in David's book, will be the accessorised prams of Cassidy's business success. Their shared woman is called simply Susie.

Did David adopt these aspects of Kennaway's character deliberately, consciously? Or was it rather an organic assimilation for survival, the way a foetus will sometimes absorb the material of its less viable twin *in utero*? Something of the unconscious rebirthing process is indicated when Cassidy first arrives at the ancient pile, along a dark narrow lane – in the 'businessman's womb' of his Bentley! – mistakenly believing it to be Shamus's ancestral home and wanting to make its history his own, which, at the close of his expansive adventures with Shamus, he actually does. Again, I wonder how conscious David was of his own imagery. I only wish I'd seen all this at the time and had been able to ask him.

If Ronnie's criminality had frightened David into becoming a dutiful servant of the system, albeit the clandestine section of it, then Kennaway's own lawless example showed him how he could escape the whole thing, break all the rules and still stay legit – as an artist, who only ever had to be true to himself. *The Navy and Sentimental* was a tribute to the man who not only loaned him his wife for a few months, but threw in a fresh lease on life for his 'lover' as part of the deal.

I came to see that the success of *Tinker Tailor* was also due, indirectly, to Kennaway's influence. David must have realised that he had followed Kennaway's literary example too closely in *The Naïve and Sentimental Lover*. His embrace of the Scotsman's impressionistic, at times phantasmagorical, style, while producing 'a pretty little book', had fallen largely flat with readers and critics alike. In the face of his first public thrashing, he reined himself in, harnessed the best of his own native powers and finally wrote a book that fulfilled and even exceeded the literary promise of *The Spy Who Came in from the Cold*.

'Jim always claimed he wouldn't live past forty,' David continued as we lay there. 'Six months after his fortieth he was driving home and had a head-on collision with another vehicle. They found him dead at the wheel.'

'Was it suicide?'

'They thought so, of course. But the post-mortem showed he'd had a massive heart attack. He was dead before impact. But I just wasn't supposed to change tack like that.' He'd gone back to his own book of the affair. 'The critics had a field day. I think my readers felt a little lost, too, at the sudden shift in direction.'

I asked if that was feedback from fan mail and book signings.

'I don't do signings,' he said flatly.

'Why not? Your readers love you, don't they?'

'They do. In great numbers. Sodders are always trying to get me to do them. Press the flesh. Talk.'

'So why don't you?'

'It's just not me.'

Like a knighthood. Or the Nobel.

'They write to me, though, my readers. And I reply if I can.'

'Do you get a lot of letters?'

'Mmm. Quite a lot. Sackfuls sometimes.'

That tone of *Weltschmerz* I hadn't heard for a while had crept back into his voice. The demands of others weighing on him.

'Do you like getting the letters,' I asked, 'or would you rather do without?'

'Well, some of them can lift your heart, it's true.' He launched into his Essex housewife voice, a prim nasal pitch with estuary vowels. *Dear Mr le Carré, I just had to write and tell you that I consider you to be one of the finest authors of the twentieth century …*

'That must be gratifying,' I said. But it wasn't his voice for unqualified praise; something dismissive was coming.

'Oh, yes,' he conceded. 'Until they go on to say,' reverting to the voice, *and I put you right up there with that other great English writer, Frederick Forswyth.*

'I take your point,' I said, chuckling at the deft insult and another little twist in a name. 'Do you know him?'

'Who, Forswyth? No. Can't say I've had that pleasure.'

After that, David declared we needed to get some air and so we went for an 'explore' of the new neighbourhood while it was still daylight.

'Everything your Jewish mother's heart could desire,' he commented, as we passed the delis, bakeries, *chocolatiers*, florists, jewellers and beauty salons that lined St John's Wood High Street. There was a French restaurant called Au Bois and a Chinese one called The Fortuna, both within crawling distance of the flat.

'I think we'll make the Chinese our new local,' David said.

And so, that evening – after we'd returned to the flat to anoint the new and, I trusted, newly Scotchgarded sofa, then bathed and dressed – we did.

'It's really The Nova Fortuna,' he told me as we went inside. 'For us, anyway.'

Considering the neighbourhood, it turned out to be a pleasantly unassuming place, quietly busy, with nice lighting and lots of plants. As we sat with our menus, David said how wonderful it was to be free, to have finally escaped.

'No one knows us here,' he said with a sigh of real relief. 'It feels like sanctuary at last.'

I was happy, of course – happy that he was happy and that *we* were, too, which wasn't always the same thing. But I was sorry as well, that this wonderful man could only see freedom in the qualified terms of escaping without detection. The schoolboy revelling in sneaking out of the boarding school dorm at night, as long as he knew he could make it back before register in the morning. I hoped in time – after more times like these – that he'd be able to come to a different understanding. That he'd see being free as simply that – an essential state of *being*.

But he ought to have known he was tempting Fortuna herself with that last statement about no one knowing us. Like a fast sketch Jeremy might have written for *Laugh-In*, our New Fortune turned into the Fickle Finger of Fate before we'd had time to give our orders. David had been doing his usual room-scanning over the top of his menu when he suddenly gave a whispered exclamation.

'*Christ— it's Freddie!*'

I looked up and, sure enough, there was Frederick Forsyth. (It was a couple of years before they made *Beetlejuice*, so David wasn't to know, but I think he'd said his name too many times at the flat.) He and his wife Carrie had just walked in and were being warmly greeted by the smiling Chinese maître d'.

'And he's just clocked me,' David added, setting down his menu. 'This should be interesting—'

(Before I label this Exhibit C in the case for cover, I feel I should point out that if David hadn't been sitting so that he could scan the entrance, Freddie would probably never have noticed him. There was a self-perpetuating component to his paranoia.)

'*Good Lord!!*' boomed the unmistakable phoney-colonel voice across the restaurant, as the author of *The Day of the Jackal* (and the rest) made a beeline for our table. 'David, old man – we meet at *last!*'

A general stir rose up in the restaurant. Forswyth – as he shall forever be known – was making such a big thing of the encounter that other diners were turning to stare. The previously imperturbable proprietor clearly had no idea who David was, but, because he knew who Freddie was and Freddie obviously knew who David was, he was getting himself into a flap. He had his entire staff hovering around in case the flag should go up for a table for four, which would have taken some serious manoeuvring since their table for two was on the other side of the dining room from ours and there wasn't another bigger one that was free.

Somewhere in the midst of it all I wasn't quite introduced, but it didn't appear to matter. Freddie was all for David and Carrie was all for me, saying that she was *so* pleased to meet me and *whatever* brought us *here* to *their* local?

Eventually they moved to their own table and things settled down. David picked up his menu again – we still hadn't ordered – and whispered to me around one corner.

'What's the betting they ask us over to their table for coffee and then back to their *Schloss* for brandy and liqueurs afterwards?'

Chez Forswyth was a Spanish-style villa in one of the lusher St John's Wood avenues and Freddie and Carrie were very proud of it. They hadn't had the house for very long and were thrilled to ribbons to be entertaining the Great Man within its white stuccoed walls. They seemed pretty thrilled to be entertaining me, too, which didn't make sense at first, but after a few minutes the reason became clear.

'Brandy, David?' Freddie asked at the drinks trolley.

'Thanks,' he said.

'What about you, Jane?'

'Just a small one,' I replied.

Freddie declared he wanted to pump David on his views regarding the state of the world's secret services, though from the way their conversation progressed it was apparent that what he actually wanted was to expatiate on his own views now that he had the acknowledged master of the field cornered in his living room. David paid out his subtle give-them-what-they-eat line, tossing in the occasional 'oh, yes' and 'well, quite' to chum the water and keep Forswyth thrashing around. From the passionate flush on Freddie's face and the intense animation in his manner, it was clear this was the best audience – in almost the Papal sense – that he'd ever had.

Carrie, meanwhile, wanted me to tell her *everything about your lovely house in Cornwall*. It was all I could do to stop myself from inviting them down.

We stayed about three-quarters of an hour. David had it nicely timed; long enough to be sociable, but not so long as to induce the belief that he wanted to become pals. Before we left, Freddie presented him with a spiffy edition of his latest tome, which he signed specially. It was then I noticed that the only books in evidence anywhere in the house were those written by its owner. On our way out, the happy couple gave us a tour of their wintry garden, making sure that we noticed the kidney-shaped outdoor pool.

Next morning as we were leaving the flat, David told me how pleased he was that I'd decided to do the research on his father.

'It'll be wonderful having you on the inside of the book with me,' he said.

Things had been going so well since the second Cornish visit – there had even been a third good one over the New Year – that I was beginning to agree. He seemed to have found the right arrangement of things in his head. A new and better balance of all the warring parts.

'I want you to have these too,' he said, and handed me a set of keys.

I wasn't expecting that – the handing-over of access to the new place – and his lack of ceremony as he did it was very telling. I understood instantly that it wasn't the practical gesture that was of consequence. He was making a symbolic gesture to show how much he trusted me; how much he trusted me not to betray his trust. And it was as if he might be beginning to see the logic of meeting in the middle instead of planning a great escape, with each of us just keeping mostly to our own corners while enjoying the good times in some clear space between.

As he walked me down the High Street for a cab, David pulled us into one of the shops – Georgie's, a *chocolatier*-cum-florist – saying that a girl needed some provisions to take home with her. When we came out I was carrying a vast bunch of freesias and a large beribboned box of fresh-cream truffles.

'I've been thinking,' he said, as we walked along again. 'Would a girl like a little cottage in Cornwall so as to be handy for her lover? And maybe a starter-kit car to get her there? A *deux chevaux*, perhaps, and driving lessons to go with it? Think about it, my darling – I'll call you.'

He hailed a cab, kissed me deeply as it drew up, put me and my goodies inside and prepaid the driver excessively for the journey ahead.

Going home, with my flowers in my arms and my truffles on my knee and the keys to the new flat in my pocket, I did think about it. But not for long. David was always generous with his money, as I hope I've shown. I loved him for it and for thinking about me in that way. But frankly, sometimes he didn't have a single wire earthing him to the ground. I was all for meeting in the fresh territory of St John's Wood. But adding another bolthole in Cornwall was an unnecessary complication. That he'd be able to slip away to see me when he was down there would have been fine – *when* he was down there. But in the few months we'd been conducting our affair I'd already seen how erratic David's comings and goings were. I should forever have been trailing up and down the motorway in his tracks, arriving at one end only to find his plans had changed and he was heading off to the other. He would probably have turned it into my fault too, however sweetly he might have phrased the rebuke, if I wasn't in the right place at the right time. It wasn't as though I liked the area or relished the idea of getting to know the natives in St Buryan, who had made such excellent extras in *Straw Dogs* … How long did he think it would be before the beady-eyed locals caught on and realised where their famous neighbour had stashed his bit on the side? How long before someone told someone who told his wife?

Oh, and – Christ Almighty – just imagine if I were ever stuck down there by myself and Tangye got wind of it!

Thinking it through further, as the cab carried me home, I also began to be a tiny bit peeved that David could picture me in a Citroën *deux chevaux*. I was no longer a student, when that type of car might have been acceptable. All I'd had at Oxford was my old sit-up-and-beg pushbike, with a wicker basket in front and no gears. Having one of those motorised sardine-cans then might have been pretty neat. But a 2CV now? Really? How did that fit into the fantasy of his dream girl on the beach? Smiley's Ann wouldn't have been seen dead in one.

By the time I got home I knew I was going to decline David's generous but nonetheless looney-tunes offer. I only wished I could have been enough of a tart to ask for a Chelsea flat and a Golf GTI instead.

AUDIENCE OF ONE

'This is our place, my darling,' David told me on virtually every occasion we were at the flat. I wasn't going to commit the folly of believing there was any true substance to the claim; I'd already seen how mutable the definition of 'his place' was and doubted 'our place' was a declaration of any firmer conviction. But I liked to hear him say it, all the same. I saw it as a sign he was still taking steps towards a freer, easier and less encumbered existence than the one in which he was currently, by his own phrase, 'banged up'. Whether he managed to achieve it by staying married or getting divorced didn't matter to me, I just wanted him to find a way. Not that the problem was a quadratic equation or three-dimensional chess, but the straightforward approach seemed to escape him, even though he'd availed himself of the solution once before.

Nevertheless, the encounters at 'our place' began to develop a sort of regularised irregularity. We would meet often, but almost never without one or two dates being cancelled or re-arranged before we got one that stuck. Could I make it for a late lunch tomorrow? he would call to ask, after saying the day before that he couldn't see me again for the rest of the week. Next morning there'd be a courier at my door bearing a big bouquet from Georgie's with a tender handwritten note cancelling. Then I'd get a phone call the same evening, telling me how wonderful I was and how about an overnight the day after that? Sometimes, with no notice at all, flowers would arrive first thing with a card that read, *Fancy caviar and a fuck at 12.30?*

This erratic on-off-on scheduling caused me a kind of semi-permanent background anxiety as I grew to anticipate it. *Would* I be seeing him on the next date he'd given me? Would it *hurt* as much as last time if, at the very last minute, I didn't? Would I still believe him the next time and could I stand the disappointment *again*? This teetering on the edge of things was counterweighted by the wonderfully restorative order of events whenever we did meet. One thing fed energy into the other. David made every bottle of perfectly chilled Krug and every tin of caviar seem like a first, for him as much as for me. Our on-the-rug picnics were a smorgasbord of deli delights. Then there were the surprise trinkets – invariably period pieces, though not always from Phillips – and so many other gifts besides, each ascribed a special significance and each presented with a sort of worshipful awe that I should keep offering myself to him as much as I did and permit him to love me as much as he did and let him spoil me absolutely as much as he wanted. And over everything was the ever-flowing wellspring of intoxicating, head-turning blandishments and praise, followed by the limitless desire driving the overwhelming sex. I loved and adored David completely and utterly, ached for him whenever he was away. Yet somehow he was always able to find ways to make me love and adore him even more when I was with him, to build me up again after he had previously let me down.

If you remove the element of sex (perhaps, in certain cases, even if you don't), this may also have been how an agent, a Joe, was run. Normalising the otherwise irregular meetings of the covert relationship. Ensuring the continued acceptance of uncertain terms and clandestine conditions by offering treats and praise and the promise of great future reward, creating dependency along the way, instilling the belief that such means were the only way to the glorious ends. In short, by turning the hazardous secret meetings into encounters of irresistible seduction. It became my lingering suspicion that David was running me. Even when I wasn't physically with him, I could still feel his control.

With the book fully underway, there was always also his reading me his latest pages after sex – or, more often than not, between bouts. Lying in bed or on the rug, my head on the crook of his arm, I would listen to his voice as he made me his audience of one – and the seduction would be complete. I knew there were only two other people in the world – his best friend Miller and his wife – who were given access to these early pages, who had the extraordinary privilege of knowing what the next le Carré novel was about. But David read the pages he wrote here to me first, before anybody, with the pale blue ink of his handwriting barely dry on the paper. His own satisfaction after he finished reading was much the same as after sex. He would lie back, replete and spent, his arms flung out, his ankles elegantly crossed. Only David could relax so contentedly in a pose of crucifixion.

Giving me the keys to the flat as a gesture of trust didn't mean he left it at that. He started testing me, fine-tuning the level of trust. If I arrived while he'd stepped out to get something from the High Street, as sometimes happened, he would have left his papers turned face-down on his table and arranged in such a way – only seemingly at random – so that he would know instantly if I'd turned them over to look at them. I wonder now whether he left the flat deliberately on those occasions, in order to expose me to the temptation. He would have Pym do the same thing in the novel, to catch his wife out when they're staying in their little brown house in Plomari (which of course was ours). But it wasn't any temptation since I knew David would read me whatever he wrote. (He'd already shown me the next most interesting items he kept in the flat: his collection of current passports, two dark blue British ones and three or four others in different colours, all in his own name.) But he couldn't seem to resist setting the trap, as if checking to see what bits of his own tradecraft I'd acquired in the course of our association. Perhaps too, since I had the keys and he was so often away, he hunted for traces of my 'other, far inferior lover' there, the one who nagged at his suspicions while existing purely in his imagination. That guy was always 'far older' in David's only half-joking remarks. I think the spectre of a younger competitor was too real for him to articulate. *I'd know if you ever took anyone else while you're with me,* he'd assured me in a smiling, sweet-spoken warning over a restaurant table on our last Swiss trip.

Being the secret mistress of the world's foremost espionage novelist and former spy may naturally have coloured my vision in all this. Perhaps my imagination outran the facts. Perhaps, back at my own flat, I was only imagining the strange new buzz on my telephone line whenever I picked up the receiver. But if it wasn't my imagination then it was something more serious than another test from David. It would be Special Branch with a Home Office warrant authorising a wire-tap.

We talked about a lot of stuff at the flat, nearly all David stuff, naturally, which meant Ronnie stuff too. He gave me pointers about where to look as I embarked on the research, though sometimes they were just random moments from his father's life, whatever rackety episode was uppermost in his mind as he reincarnated the relentless conman who had so dominated his life – even ten years after his death from a heart attack while watching a cricket match on television – as the central rogue in his autobiographical novel.

I'd already brought him a selection of father–son memoirs, titles he hadn't read and said were helpful. The Gosse was chief among them, of course, and the Ackerley. An American one, *The Duke of Deception*, also went down well and he even liked Susan Cheever's father-daughter *Home Before Dark*. Now I set out to find everything I could about Ronnie and brought each new discovery to the flat. There were the court proceedings and convictions, the bogus companies and the bankruptcies. There were the wartime by-elections where Ronnie agented for candidates, his 'wheeze', as David called it, to get out of the army – William Douglas Home, the playwright and brother of the former PM, was one of them – and there was the 1950 general election where Ronnie had stood as a candidate himself in Yarmouth. There were the neverwozzers whose every race entry was helpfully recorded at the Jockey Club, along with Ronnie's racing colours and occasional prize money. There were the bulging files neatly stacked and available for photocopying in the cuttings libraries at the *Mirror* and *Evening Standard* and *Express*, and there were the chilly neglected vaults of local newspapers in Bournemouth and Yarmouth and Poole, with no photocopiers and hardly even chairs, where I had to pore over fusty old bound broadsheets to find glimpses of Ronnie's name and make endless longhand copy.

I wrote letters to anyone who might have tales to tell. Two cricketers from the Australian touring team that Ronnie had entertained at the house, Donald Bradman and Keith Miller, were among my respondents. Bradman — the Don – replied in a courteous letter that he remembered the garden party, while Miller, to whom Ronnie had lent money, left a hasty message on my answering machine to say that he had nothing to tell me. Gordon Richards, the Queen Mother's favourite jockey, who'd advised Ronnie on the purchase of a questionable nag, didn't reply at all. There were mentions of Ronnie in various old celebrity memoirs. One was by Douglas Home, who invited me to talk to him at his London flat. 'Honest as the day', was how Ronnie had seemed to him and he said his agenting efforts were wholly responsible for how well he'd done in his losing campaign against a fellow Old Etonian army officer. 'I shouldn't have got ten votes without him,' he told me cheerily at the recollection. 'As it was, it was nearer ten thousand.' Joe Davis, the snooker champion, had written about Ronnie's legendary ski-season parties in the Swiss Alps and the Cornwell Cup he donated for curling. Ronnie's old school in Dorset regretfully informed me that, between a fire and relocation to new premises, all their records for the years of his attendance had been lost. It crossed my mind that Ronnie had started the fire himself. Finally, there were the records of his birth, his marriages – to Olive, Jean and Joy – his divorces and his death. The only details that completely evaded me were of his service record during the war. Ronnie's 'wheeze', of by-election agenting to get out of basic training, had served him well. The Army Records Office said they were unable to find any listing for an R. T. A. Cornwell in their files. David was thrilled with every item I brought him. Howard Carter could not have taken more delight in the treasures of the pharaoh's tomb. Ronnie was coming to life again before his eyes, his life story playing out like a movie in his son's head. But considering how much damage and mayhem he'd caused, the Ronnie movie didn't appear to be a serious drama, rather a mash-up of old British comedies and crime capers. Ronnie might have been the hapless Will Hay, falling foul of the law but intending no harm; or Alec Guinness in *The Card*, a clever deceiver climbing the social scale on the gullibility of others. (David called the town Gulsworth where Rick stands for election.) Once Ronnie was established in top-notch Mayfair, he seemed to become an amalgam of well-spoken schemers like Jack Hawkins and Nigel Patrick in *The League of Gentlemen*. And when he was banged up to do his time, with his adoring 'lovelies' and devoted old mother waiting for him on the outside, he morphed into Peter Sellers' irrepressible Dodger Lane, driving Lionel Jeffries' Prison Officer Crout into teeth-gnashing comic fury. David's face would light up as he read the material, sometimes even laughing out loud. In the Ronnie movie it didn't seem to matter how many pratfalls the supporting cast had to take, though in real life they frequently sustained lasting financial injury; Ronnie was his son's indefatigable leading man, who always managed to carry on regardless to the next reel. I knew there were other episodes that played in David's mind, he'd told me of some of them – dark haunting scenes from his childhood, of abuse and depravity and torment from the truly appalling man who was his father. But for his present need to turn that monster into Rick Pym, the terrible but lovable rogue of his new book, David had to summon up all the smiles and laughs he could.

Soon after bringing him these files, sometimes only the next day, I'd hear the old details revivified on the new pages as David applied the subtle alchemy of his craft to the historical evidence. It had taken him his whole lifetime to reach the point where he could use it to safely transform Ronnie into Rick.

Raymond Chandler once wrote of wife-murdering physician Hawley Crippen that even after reading all about the case he somehow couldn't help liking the guy. It seemed to be that way with Ronnie. But for all that his powerful bully-boy charm had a half-life glow that still radiated through the tales, he was a terrible man nonetheless.

As the material began to mount up, files and files of it, David surprised me with another suggestion: *Why didn't I go the whole hog and write his father's biography?* He said he would ensure I had free access to everyone who could help me get the full picture of Ronnie. He said he believed I could do it and that he thought it would be a really good idea. It sounded at first like a big leap, but I gradually began to wonder whether I might be up to it. Ronnie was already an inescapable presence, not just in the research but also in the singular experience of being so close to David as he spun his new fiction around him. I would have David himself, of course – not to say le Carré – to guide me through the process, the sort of one-to-one support a first-time writer could only dream of. It was a unique, once-in-a-lifetime opportunity and I agreed to give it some serious consideration. I came up with a title, *Hitch Your Wagon to This Star: The Riotous Life & Ruinous Times of Ronald Cornwell* – sometimes the life was ruinous and the times riotous, I could never quite decide – and set about drawing up an outline, to try and nail all the angles. The main one that gave me pause was how to acquire so much of the lives of both Cornwells, *père et fils*, in my head – with the *fils* also in my heart – and not obliterate my own existence in the process. But I was going to try and nail that angle too.

*   *   *

David must genuinely have felt what he claimed about the flat, that it was a sanctuary, because he began to talk more freely than ever when we were there. The current book required him to revisit his childhood, though the memories were so seared into him that I began to think it had never been very far from his thoughts. But he'd made his hero an only child and couldn't include some of the most poignant tales he told me. How his brother Tony, who was only two years older, had tried to look after him when they were both motherless little boys. How Tony had actually told him that he would be his mother, to try and make things better. How they were first sent away together to pre-prep boarding school, but Tony soon had to go to another school for older boys, some small distance away. How they would write to each other and arrange to meet at a place halfway between.

'We'd each cycle there,' David said to me, 'just to meet up in a field to hug each other and cry …'

He also spoke about his past loves. I'd wondered before if there was anyone else he'd opened up to on this subject. I hoped there had been, most likely someone in the inner circle he'd introduced me to. But since he was lying naked with me in his own private safe house, I think David may yet have been most open with me, there. It was in one of these moments that he asked me if it was safe to love me, because he'd never before let anyone '*this far in*'. It was undeniable in so many ways, but it still didn't mean he ever gave me the full story, about anyone or anything.

With the publication of the paperback edition of *The Little Drummer Girl* and the first anniversary of the Beirut embassy bombing both approaching, he spoke again about Janet Stevens. George Roy Hill was talking about dedicating the film to her, which David found exasperating, not least when Jane got wind of it.

'George Roy hadn't considered the larger problem, you see. Jane assumed there had to be a reason beyond the book. *Were you her lover?* she asked me.'

'What did you say?'

'I denied her utterly, of course.'

But he couldn't deny the relationship to himself. He told me again how he'd gone to the States for her funeral, how wretched it had been. What wasn't clear to me was how he'd presented himself there at the time. I couldn't think he'd told her family the truth of their relationship. It would most likely have distressed them more if he had, and it wasn't in his nature to do so anyway. He must have passed himself off as someone who'd known Janet as a friend, a colleague in the field, one among several who were lost in the bombing. But even though I knew he had genuinely mourned her, it seemed to me rather indulgent of him, even a little selfish, to have attended the funeral dishonestly – as it were, under a false flag. Once again, it didn't seem the moment to ask for clarification and it was almost another quarter century before I discovered the true reason behind his needing to be there and what really made the months afterwards such a 'rough summer' for him.

In 2007, after reading a news item marking the twenty-fifth anniversary of the Sabra and Shatila massacre, I googled Janet Stevens. I hadn't thought of her name since last seeing David a few years previously and wondered idly whether anything had emerged to link her story to him. It appeared that something had, just one small detail.

The first result to come up was an open letter from an American academic and civil rights lawyer named Franklin Lamb. It was posted on the Palestinian Chronicle website and was written as if to Janet herself. Lamb recalled her life, work and death and – so it seemed to me – was using the letter to set the record straight. A fellow Palestinian rights activist, he had apparently been on his way to join Janet in Beirut when the explosion occurred. They had last spoken when he'd called her the night before and were looking forward to seeing each other. They were very evidently a couple; other articles gave Lamb as her husband, though he didn't explicitly say. But he did say that Janet was pregnant when she died, with a son. Lamb named him Clyde Chester Lamb III.

David must have known these details. How could he not? But he didn't tell me. And it wasn't like him to miss the chance to talk about the poignancy of things, to say what a wonderful mother she would have been, how her family suffered two losses in one, compounding their grief at the funeral. Yet he didn't say a word – and his silence on the subject was the dog that didn't bark in the night. David knew, I think, or sincerely believed, that it wasn't Lamb's son who had died with her. That was why he'd attended the funeral. He was being a good soldier under his false flag.

It seemed that Lamb had been on his way to see Janet in Beirut while David was waiting for her in Larnaca. Exactly how Janet had been running her two lovers for those last few months of her life was lost to the explosion. Neither man saw her alive again – though Lamb had to identify her body in the hospital morgue – but they would meet each other at her funeral, when she was buried with her unborn son. It was a storyline that John le Carré himself might have devised and yet another fractal episode in David's life. It illustrated in the most terrible way how all the layers of secrecy and duplicity were the only way for him to maintain all the moving parts within himself, the self that from his earliest years and ever afterwards had to be divided between competing loyalties and hidden loves.

That small connecting detail: Lamb wrote at the end of his letter that he'd recently spoken with some Palestinian refugees who had known Janet. He said they remembered her dearly and still called her 'our little drummer girl'. I'd always understood that David's title was chosen before he went back to Lebanon at the end of '82, before he met Janet, but Lamb made it sound as if the soubriquet had originated in the camps, among the refugees who knew and loved her. Whichever was the case, the novel had no particular currency by that time, so I was left to wonder why Lamb had revived the title, with its implicit association, for the whole world of online readers and possibly David himself to see. Was it to finally claim back the twice-promised girl from her famous lover? Or was it a nod of acknowledgement to him and to his secret relationship with Janet, as she herself might have wished to make?

Life imitating Art – Art imitating Life. With David, there was simply no other reality.

He also told me about Yvette Pierpaoli. She was a French aid worker he met in Phnom Penh in 1974, when he was undertaking research for *The Honourable Schoolboy* (and while Jane, whom he'd recently married, was in England with their infant son.) David told me what the sex had been like with Yvette, though I hadn't indicated I wanted to know. His account came with a French accent.

'Eet was vey queek wiz 'ehr, n'est ce pas? Just go, do, oui? *Va, va, va – ooof!!*'

He couldn't have realised it, but for emphasis he made the same '*Boom*' gesture with his hands that he'd used when he first told me about Janet being killed in the embassy bombing.

He told me how he admired Yvette for her ceaseless work with refugees, children for the most part, in conflict zones around the world.

'She needs to be needed, you see.'

She was still a good friend now, he said, adding the surprising detail – surprising to me, at least; David seemed to see it as quite natural – that she often visited him and Jane and particularly liked to go down to Tregiffian. I thought instantly of our last night on the island, when he'd suggested we call it a day and just stay friends. I'd stood my ground and refused, but it must have been what he'd done successfully with Yvette; 'turned her', to apply the spook term.

'Does Jane know?' I asked. 'About you and Yvette?'

'No, naturally,' he replied, as though it were a perfectly brainless question, which I suppose it was. I already knew the First Rule of

Spy Club: *DENY EVERYTHING*. By this point in our relationship I'd already asked him what he would do if Jane ever found out about us and he'd replied with exactly the same formula he'd used when she actually had challenged him about Janet: 'I'd deny you – I'd deny you utterly.' But he added pleasantly, 'I might introduce you to Yvette next time she's over.'

I nodded vaguely, wondering how he'd react if I declined the introduction. Much as it seemed to have given my ex-spook lover great satisfaction to relate intimate details of his prior secret love life as we lay there in his new safe house, I wasn't sure how he thought I benefitted from the intelligence briefing. But aside from his two wives – of whom he never spoke in such terms – Janet, Yvette before her and Susan Kennaway before either of them, had been the most important past loves of his life. I was the current one and David had already told me I was the last.

I'd imagined we would have wide-ranging conversations about other writers, about literature and writing in general, as we'd begun to do in Greece, but David never really ventured beyond a few general observations. I understood that he didn't read other fiction while he was writing, but he didn't seem to want to say much on the topic at all. When I asked his views on contemporary authors, he responded with a mildly despairing shrug.

'There's just nobody out there. That's why this book has to be my best, you see. I've only my own act to beat.'

I felt I had to single out Greene, the senior ex-spook novelist who was still writing and who also had a multi-layered love life. Surely David had views on him?

'Well, one reads him, of course,' he said. 'But the thing one finds is that no single work really deserves the praise heaped upon the canon. But he speaks of the chip of ice in every writer's heart. He got that right.'

He evidently didn't want to discuss the Greene mistresses, the Greene affairs, or even the Greene novel that was about one of them. But then he hadn't wanted to discuss *Zelig* either. He didn't seem to see – or didn't want to see – reflections of himself and his concerns in other men's work. He hadn't even mentioned Kennaway's novel about their own conjoined affair.

But I wasn't ready to give up. With living writers regretfully but nevertheless summarily dismissed, I asked which ones he admired from history. His reply was only a little less measured, though when the select few names emerged – Ford, Conrad, Mann, Schiller – it was my turn to exit the subject. Mann to me was only the Visconti film of *Death in Venice* and a vague memory of reading an English translation. For Schiller, though I could have offered the *University Challenge* clever-clogs answer of 'chief figure in the *Sturm-und-Drang* movement of German Lit.', his works too were completely unknown to me. If only we could have talked about his *Über naive und sentimentalische Dichtung*. If only I'd known to ask. I had read Conrad of course, extensively for Moderations, but unfortunately still loathed him (*the horror, the horror*) and my only Ford was *The Good Soldier*. It was a novel I'd come to love and David had called it the book of his life, but now that he was writing his own, I knew he didn't want to be drawn on what he saw of himself in the earlier work. In any case, exactly *how* close Ford's character Edward Ashburnham was to David I had yet to fully understand.

'And of course, there's Johann Wolfgang von,' he added. 'Have you read any of him?'

Only translated extracts from *Faust*, I answered – at this point feeling I barely deserved my second – for essays on Marlowe.

'You should try him again,' David advised. 'Even in translation there's a lot to be had. You might like his *Elective Affinities*.'

Hearing the tone of high seriousness when he said the name, I took Goethe to be his literary Supreme Being. Something of the same tone generally coloured his voice when he spoke about anything German. Earlier that day, in response to a news item, he'd proclaimed how loathsome the East German regime was, how it couldn't last and how the reunification of Germany was inevitable. How right he was, though it didn't seem that he could be at the time. Maintaining the tone, David next declared that he believed he had a German soul. I didn't know then that he had this idea directly from Kennaway – indirectly from Mann – and would give it to Pym later in the book. But I was coming to notice in the general way how he would say these notions aloud and then work them into the new novel. He also freely recycled some of his earlier usages. I don't mean the bigger themes that were the mainstay of all his work, but little things, short phrases, passing ideas, often paradoxical ones, that must have mattered to him enough to give them another airing. The notion of spies doing the dirty work while the masses sleep peacefully, which occurs in *The Spy Who Came in from the Cold* (and which had come down, variously expressed, through Kipling, Churchill and Orwell), was something he reworked for *A Perfect Spy*. He once remarked that George Greenfield had a smile like an iron bar and I subsequently found the exact simile describing Haldane in *The Looking Glass War*. He didn't re-work that into the new book, but I think he was trying it out to see if he could. He'd done this recycling in earlier books, too. Connie Sachs' 'God bless all who sail in you' greeting to George Smiley when he unexpectedly visits her at her Oxford flat in *Tinker Tailor* is an echo of a toast Shamus and Cassidy make in *The Naïve and Sentimental Lover*. The indistinct cry Cassidy later hears Shamus utter in his sleep – Cassidy can't decide whether it's *No!* or *Go!* – recurs in *A Perfect Spy*, after already being reused in *The Little Drummer Girl*. At the end of his long confessional letter to his son, Pym makes the claim that he is the bridge Tom has to walk over to escape from Rick. David recycled that line in an interview decades later about his own sons and Ronnie. I could give hundreds more examples, but it would only be to say again that David's life and art really were all one to him. I could never clearly identify where one ended and the other began, though it might have brought me less heartache if I hadn't kept trying so hard to do just that.

'Did you do any languages at school, my love?' he asked me next.

'Latin and Greek.'

'No Moderns?'

'Only French. I gave it up the moment they let me.'

'So no German?'

'It was either German or Greek. I really wanted to do Greek.'

'Ah, well—' He paused and I half-guessed what was coming. 'You're no use to me if you don't speak German.'

He wrote a one-act, one-man play for Guinness that year and read that to me at the flat too. Titled *Before you go out into the world*, it was Smiley addressing the graduation class of new young spooks at Sarratt. Guinness later went off the idea, having initially sounded keen, so it was never performed. But listening then, with my eyes closed, it was as if Guinness were performing it anyway. David's capture of the actor's lugubrious timbre was quite uncanny.

There's a grainy video – now on YouTube – where the elderly Kim Philby can be seen addressing an audience of Stasi officers in East Germany in 1981. He's wearing heavy-rimmed thick-lensed glasses and looks really rather Smiley-ish. Seeing it recently made me wonder whether David saw it too, prior to writing the play, and if the sight of his ageing nemesis lecturing to a room full of younger operatives provoked him into reclaiming the role of wise elder from the traitor, to return it to his own elderly spycatcher. Philby, almost as much as Ronnie, was never very far from his creative thinking, never closer than at that time. I only wish I could have made the connection then myself. But much as I knew how autobiographical David's new novel was, I still didn't realise that only half of the book was written to exorcise the ghost of his father. I didn't yet understand how the other half was an attempt to excise the contamination of Philby.

The never-performed play would also be recycled and become the framing device for his portmanteau book of short stories, *The Secret Pilgrim*. David actually pinched one of the stories in it from me, something I'd told him from my time at Asprey, when the wives of various London-based sheikhs would come in with their well-muscled, well-armed bodyguards and just take – actually shoplift – whatever they fancied, hiding their loot under their burkas, while the staff had to hastily but discreetly keep count of all the items for later billing.

When Graham came back from skiing in Wengen it seemed the right time to tell him about us. David invited him to lunch and we broke the news at La Capannina.

'That explains something,' Graham said when he heard, grinning at me.

'What's that then, Gooders?' I asked.

'Why you've been turning up at the studios in the morning all bright-eyed and bandy-legged.'

Well, I did give him the feed-line. I think he may have sussed us all along.

'I'm happy for you both,' he said and I knew he meant it. 'Sounds like a good match, too,' he added, after a moment of looking at each of us, and I knew he meant that too.

It was a sublimely lovely lunch and I could only marvel at the fact that I was sitting there in Soho's finest staff canteen with these two wonderful men whom I loved dearly and who in their different ways both loved me back and seemed to have become such great chums with each other. I waxed lyrical about it in the taxi going up to St John's Wood afterwards, with the mellow buzz of the lunch still in my head. In smooth reply, almost as though he couldn't help himself, David shifted his voice into donnish-observation mode.

'Yes, of course,' he concurred with a faint smile. 'But the thing about Graham, one always feels, is that there's somehow less to him than the sum of his parts.'

It was the lofty oh-so-reasonable tone, as much as the gratuitous comment itself, which made me fly at him. How could he speak so dismissively of Graham, when he knew how I felt about him? Who the hell did he think he was anyway? Which part of the fucking universe did he think he ruled to make such a high and mighty pronouncement on anyone, let alone *my* great friend? Did he want to hear *my* pronouncements on his po-faced gagging-for-his-cock sister? Or on those revolting lunatic misers he'd made me sit down and eat with in Cornwall? Did he want me to start adding up the sum of *those* parts?

The cab was in the middle of traffic so he had to sit there and hear it. I knew I was going too far, but he'd crossed the line about Graham – and done it so casually, as if it had been nothing more than the obvious next thing to say. It was intolerable.

After I'd said my piece, the force of which astonished even me, we sat in palpable silence the rest of the way up to the flat. When he got out, I quite expected him to tell me to take the cab back to Chelsea and never darken his bulletproof door again, but he paid the driver so I got out too.

It was remarkable really, but he seemed to take it. He didn't apologise – I'd come to understand he never did, under any circumstances, to anyone – but I knew he'd taken it, all the same. David lived in a world – had actually created a world around himself – where his opinions, no matter how absurd or ill-founded, were simply accepted. Save for George and Miller, and certainly Rainer, who I'm sure each chose their words carefully, there was no push-back – only a full-time paid-up Greek chorus chanting, *Of course, David, of course.* I think it likely that no one in his life had ever gone full fishwife on him until then.

We spent the rest of the afternoon in bed, with no further reference to the episode, and had a surprisingly good time.

My birthday fell a couple of weeks later. It wasn't a significant one, just a middling twenty-something, but David was intent on making a great fuss about it. He'd cleared the whole day, he told me a couple of days in advance, so put on a really posh frock and come round to the flat. And get there early. Then we can have a party.

I followed his instructions and when he opened the door his arousal was so great it was all he could do to let me in without ripping my clothes off. We made love urgently and fully clothed on his big writing table. He'd already cleared it, so I didn't get the dramatic sweeping-everything-aside gesture first, but I considered it a literary milestone nonetheless. I must have worn the right dress. When we'd put ourselves back together again he gave me a gold wristwatch, with a note tucked into the box. *For time present and time past and time forever – Happy Birthday my darling, darling girl.*

The intercom buzzer sounded and David gave a conspiratorial giggle as he went to answer it.

'Come on up!' he said into the speaker.

'Who's that?' I asked.

'You'll see – I promised you a party! We'll have drinks here first and then I thought we'd all go off to the Connaught for a birthday bash.'

He threw open the door and, as I peered eagerly over his shoulder, I saw George and Gigi coming up the stairs. George was carrying a brace of Dom Perignon and Gigi a chic little present wrapped with a bow. It was so lovely to see them again; we instantly hugged and talked and laughed like four great friends. It

all made for a wonderful, perfect day, full of the special excitement, the extraordinary sense of occasion, the sheer bubbling *joie
de vivre* that it was David's unique talent to be able to conjure up.
And when he did, when he made the magic happen, it was impossible to remember that things had ever been any other way, or to
imagine that things could ever be any other way again. There were
simply too many rabbits coming out of the hat.

We said goodbye to George and Gigi – after a lunch of legendary proportion and expense – and headed back to the flat. We only
stopped making love when David had to leave for Paddington to
catch the midnight sleeper to Penzance. I took the taxi with him
and saw him onto the train. He said he'd be at Tregiffian alone and
would miss me madly, but he needed to throw himself into his
work.

Then, just as the flat seemed to have become a safe haven for him,
a point of constancy and creativity and love and trust, David
suddenly defected. He rang from Tregiffian early one morning a
couple of days later.

He couldn't go on, he told me. He couldn't work at the flat any
more. It was too close to Hampstead, too accessible. He knew he
could always see me there and he wanted to see me too much.
There were too many good times. He needed to stay away. He
didn't think he could go on, he said finally, and rang off.

The fright response from the awful adrenalin jolt this shot
through me was so disabling that I stood rooted to the spot,
holding the dead telephone receiver to my ear for several pointless
moments afterwards. Then, without giving it a moment's coherent
thought, I grabbed my bag and coat and raced to Paddington. I
caught the next train to Penzance after first telephoning a girlfriend from the station – in those pre-mobile-phone days – and
giving her David's number to call once I was on my way, to tell
him when I'd arrive. There was no point in calling him myself. I

knew I had to see him to stand a chance of bringing him back in from the cold. The long hateful journey was like waiting for a bad diagnosis.

He was at the station, looking pained but tolerant, and drove us back to the house, where we got into hacking jackets and walked and walked and talked and talked. It was an amplified, extra-band-width version of our conversation after the storm in Plomari, with David saying it was impossible for him to continue, for the reasons he'd already given me, and with me saying his reasons made no sense and I wouldn't let him – each of us trying every permutation in our considerable joint-and-several command of the English language to make our case. I remember that the wind prevented my tears from falling by driving them sideways across my cheeks. I *hated* that damned cliff. In one of the milder moments, when the wind stopped howling, or when I did, I likened him to Tigger – a less damning character than the equally inconstant but self-pitying Toad of Toad Hall (*Poop-poop!*), whom at times he more closely resembled. Tigger enthusiastically declaring what he liked best, then defecting from it as if it were suddenly the worst. When we got back inside, he took the waxed coat from me delicately, as if I'd had the bad diagnosis after all, telling me, 'I can't disagree with anything you say.'

I doubted there were too many people who'd ever had quite that kind of acknowledgement from him after an argument, but it was small consolation. He finally stopped my tears with the most glorious fuck either of us had ever had in our joint-and-several lives.

Next day we drove back to London, stopping for lunch at a pub on the way. The journey was quiet and a little polite, but at least it wasn't the train. We agreed – i.e. David insisted, I acquiesced – to maintain 'radio silence' for three weeks until, appropriately enough, 1 April, All Fools' Day. By then he'd have hacked something out, he said, because he didn't want to lose me. He'd be in London, but not at the flat. It would be all right if I wrote to him. *Poste restante* Hampstead.

> **Friday 9th March** [my diary entry reads] – Sent D a Tigger card with a note.
> **Tuesday 13th March** – D called, got my card. Loved it. Loves me. 'I'll call you every day.' (No more radio silence?) Then sent me a vast bunch of flowers and called twice more.
> **Wednesday 14th March** – D rang. Said he just had lunch w. Charlotte, who has a new man. She still thinks I'm wonderful. Told him so. 'You <u>got</u> to get out, David,' she told him too, meaning his marriage.
> **Thursday 15th March** – 9.45am at St John's Wood for the day.
> **Friday 16th March** – More flowers.
> **Tuesday 20th March** – 12.30 at St John's Wood. Lunch, then D read me all his latest pages. 'I've so been wanting to do this. I so want to read it to you.'
> **Wednesday 21st March** – D rang to say meet him by the Round Pond in Kensington Gdns. Fed the ducks. Said he'd just had lunch with Jean & asked her to come & meet me in the park but she declined.
> **Thursday 22nd March** – D rang. Would I like to go with him to Vienna on Sunday for a few days, then on to Munich?

I've let these entries stand to try and convey how frangible, how transmutable and almost entirely quotidian David's personality was. When the disparate parts of him coalesced he could fill your heart with his song – but then he would suddenly take flight at nothing, whirl in the air and vanish, like a startled flock of birds. And just when you thought the best of him was gone forever, you'd hear him singing in the trees again. Beyond sharing a capacity for ever-shifting certainty with Tigger and Toad, there was another childhood character he resembled: the Little Prince, who kept moving his chair so that he wouldn't miss the sinking sunset on his own little planet, when, if he'd only sat down in one clear spot and faced the other way, the rising dawn would have come to him time and time again.

FURTHER ADVENTURES IN THE GERMAN-SPEAKING WORLD

He wanted to be looked upon as a sort of Lohengrin.
Ford Madox Ford, *The Good Soldier*

So, at the start of what would have been week three of the reissued and almost immediately abandoned 'radio silence' directive, we went to Vienna. It was where the Pyms were based in the new book and, David told me, where he'd once before thought of setting a novel, the story of resurgent fascism that he ultimately moved to Bonn for his fifth novel, *A Small Town in Germany*.

'I was advised that Vienna was a fruitful location for the phenomenon at the time,' he said. 'Some might tell you it still is.'

We stayed at a boutique hotel a little out of the way. The Sacher, he told me when we later took coffee and *Torte* there, was a little too famous for cover. David had lived in the city with Ann for a spell in the early sixties, but had first known it when it was divided into sectors between the Allies immediately after the war. I'd never been before. Having forgotten anything I may have learned about the Hapsburgs in school, my main association was with *The Third Man*. Echoes of the film were everywhere in the cobbled streets and squares, aided by an old accordion player sitting on a stool in Stephansplatz, his cap on the ground in front of him as he squeezed out a passable version of the Anton Karas theme. As we set out on the first morning, I assumed we were heading to the diplomatic quarter to case a suitable official residence for the Pyms, with David jotting down promising details of the architecture, but we went directly to the Viennese equivalent of Bond Street.

'I think a girl needs to inspect some serious shops, don't you?' he announced. 'Since we're here, it's got to be leather.'

We spent the entire morning in various select establishments, where I happily tried on any number of garments and David happily waited and watched and offered thoughts on what suited me best – finally settling on a beautifully fitted suede coat, as soft and smooth as butter, and a sleek and sturdy weekend bag.

David was pleased with my choices and especially approved of the bag. 'You'll have that for the rest of your life,' he told me. 'It's the real thing here.'

(In the end, the bag lasted nearly thirty years. But since I used it almost every day, not just at weekends, his estimation wasn't too far off the mark.)

It was only when we chose a restaurant for lunch and David was in the men's room that I had the chance to open the store carriers and look at the receipts that had been discreetly folded over and slipped between the layers of tissue paper. After doing the calculation from schillings to sterling, I realised he had just spent something like £3,000 on me, with an understated elegance about his manner as he did so, as if it were as natural as our taking a cab or checking into a hotel or any other relatively unremarkable expenditure. I so hope that he knew how well he carried his wealth, how utterly faultless and fluent and light of touch he was with his generosity.

He took me on a cultural tour the next day and was a most eloquent guide. (I wonder now whether he had any remembrance of this when he made Ted Mundy assume the same occupation in *Absolute Friends* a few years later.) We went inside the cathedral, with its soaring Gothic architecture, to marvel – as every visitor must – at the glories that were achieved before the advent of power tools. But as we approached the aisle David did a very strange thing. He dipped his fingers in the shallow font of holy water. Then he genuflected while crossing himself. He performed the act so smoothly that anyone watching would have taken him for a born-and-raised Catholic. Yet he was a man of no religion; in fact, I was fairly sure he had no belief in any deity at all. Were we at Fakhreldine again, only with David's concern now being for the sensibilities of the priests instead of the Lebanese waiters? It was the most extraordinary thing.

On our way out, I glanced through a rack of educational pamphlets while David found some large notes in his wallet for the donation box. On a list of famous *Kapellmeister* I smiled to see that one of them had been called Johann Joseph Fux.

Munich was for an award presentation. David underplayed the event, not going into any detail about what exactly he was being awarded or why or by whom. Naturally, I wasn't to accompany him to the ceremony, but I liked seeing him get into his best bib and tucker in the hotel room and took photos of him before he put on his pants and when he was tying his black tie. I took myself down to the hotel bar after he'd left, to have a drink and a light meal by myself. Two young fellows started to chat me up as soon as I sat down and insisted on buying me a drink. Between their halting English and my guesswork German we managed a happy chatty hour or so. But their easy company brought me a sad pang of understanding, too, of how relationships between the sexes didn't need to be beset by such seemingly insuperable problems as being with David entailed.

After bidding my two new friends *gute Nacht*, I returned to the room and switched on the television set – to find that David was on every channel. One station had live coverage of the award ceremony, three more were showing le Carré documentaries of varying vintages and yet another ran a long segment about the event on the main evening news. He wasn't carrying a statuette or the keys to the city when he came in, so I still wasn't clear what he'd been awarded and he still didn't seem inclined to tell me. Whatever it was it must have been pretty significant, at least to the Germans, but David didn't seem especially concerned to have received it. When I told him how extensive his television coverage had been, he only replied, 'Yes, I know. The Krauts love me.'

*   *   *

After seeing once again how the German-speaking world brought David's best self out of him, I enrolled on a four-week *intensiv Sprachkurs* at the Goethe-Institut in South Kensington. Our *Lehrerin* was a German woman with a delightfully wry sense of humour. The first thing she told us was her name, explaining that she was married to a New Zealander, so that it was Frau *Cole* as in Old King, not Frau *Kohl* as in cabbage or the wife of the German chancellor. The second thing she told us was that we should forget any German accent we'd ever heard in films or TV shows, especially those set in the last war. Illustrating the kind of accent she meant, she explained, *Zis iz because, here et zee Goethe-Institut, vee have better vayz of making you talk.*

Herr Flick would have been proud. I liked her straight away.

I made a new girlfriend on the course, Sascha, and every morning we claimed our preferred seats in the classroom *an der Wand, in die Ecke,* as we were soon able to say. The course was planned with Teutonic efficiency and soon the basic elements of the language started to become a joined-up understanding in our heads. Frau Cole's witty touches made it a really fun course.

'I can tell you did English,' Sascha said to me at one point. She was a recent History graduate herself. 'You ask about subjunctives.'

When I told David about the course at the flat – only after I'd got a good half of it under my belt – he was thrilled. He was always a big talker during sex, which was already erotic enough, but that day he switched to German and suddenly everything was off even his previous charts.

Over lunch afterwards, he wanted to hear more about it. Did I find the accent easy? Was I enjoying the grammar? Did I have a good tutor?

Yes to all, I said, telling him how our tutor, Frau Cole, had told me I had a very good accent.

But Herr Professor Higgins immediately stepped in with a correction.

'*Ach, nein! Nicht Frau <u>Coal</u> – sondern Frau <u>Kohl</u>.*'

'*Ja doch!*' I had the immeasurable pleasure of being able to answer back from the minuscule amount of German vocab at my disposal. '*Sie heißt <u>Cole</u> – C-O-L-E. Wirklich. Ihr Mann ist Neuseeländer!*'

The Great German Soul didn't care for a correction himself, it seemed, so couldn't leave it at that, though he might have seemed a somewhat bigger soul if he had.

'Oaaoh,' he said, assuming my tutor must therefore have been English and employing the mealy mouthed Essex accent that was his go-to voice for a put-down. 'You mean *Frow Cole.*'

Later on there was a photography exhibition at the Goethe and I asked David if he'd care to see it with me. Against my expectation he said he would and so we went along. By then we'd been all over London together and no one who hadn't met him before – save for Freddie – had so much as raised an eyebrow in his direction. In those days, it was the name that carried all the recognition, not the face behind it. But all that changed the second we walked into the Institut. It was quite, *quite* astonishing. The sudden arrival of royalty – I could say of *deity* – wouldn't have produced such a moment. The usually *über-höflich* staff all stopped whatever they were doing to stand and stare. They began to gather at a discreet distance as we moved towards the exhibition, watching us as we took ourselves through it. Somebody must have got word to the director of the place, because he suddenly appeared and presented himself, addressing David in German in what even I could tell was a tone of worshipful awe. I think he may even have bowed. Other staff members had scurried away, only to scurry back with their copies of his books for him to sign – which, even more amazingly, *they evidently had to hand.* I introduced Frau Cole, who looked at me fondly, as though I'd achieved the highest application of the foundation course she'd taken me through. We spent no more than forty minutes there, but I was left with the clear impression that it was an event each of those present would tell their grandchildren about in years to come. The director asked David if he would do them the honour of signing their *Gästebuch* before we left, which of course he did. I didn't doubt they would have it framed.

'The Krauts love me,' David said again, quite as straightforwardly as before, as he hailed a taxi to take us up to St John's Wood.

It wasn't long before he returned to Munich, without me this time, for a meeting with film director Wim Wenders – whose *Alice in the Cities* I'd always liked – to discuss a project. Wenders wanted him to play the German sea captain, Dollmann, in a TV film of Erskine Childers' 1903 espionage novel, *The Riddle of the Sands*. David clearly liked the idea of acting – I'd already seen his Strasberg technique in spontaneous action at Athens airport – and his success with his own audiobooks may have encouraged him to indulge Wenders' suggestion. He declined the part, however, though not after reflecting that it was yet another flaky idea from the *Meryl-Streep-Is-too-Icebergy* movie-production handbook, but only, as he told me when he returned, because he didn't have the time.

RETURN TO THE LAND OF THE POD-PEOPLE

David wanted me to go down to Tregiffian again for a few days. I'd privately forsworn the place, but since we appeared to be in a period where no decision of his stuck for longer than it took for a letter of repeal to reach me in the post, or the time one of mine could withstand a seductive phone call to change my mind, I agreed to go. It was the middle of May and technically spring – though someone should have told the weather – so perhaps for once the end of the country wouldn't feel quite so much like the end of the world. David must have registered how much I disliked the long train journey and this time suggested I fly down.

He was waiting for me at Newquay airport and seemed really pleased that I'd made the effort. For the rest of that day, that evening and overnight, things were perfectly fine between us. Really good, in fact. There was even a blue sky over the ocean the following morning, which stayed there throughout the whole weekend, demonstrating once and for all how aptly the pathetic *fallacy* was named.

We were talking easily over mid-morning coffee when the phone rang. The phone was to hand and David answered it where we were sitting. I soon gathered it was Jane, ringing about some matter of concern in Hampstead. His voice acquired a tone of pained endurance and they seemed stuck in for a long exchange. I didn't like the thought of hearing what was going on between them and so I took myself out of earshot into the sitting room, getting comfortable on the big red sofa in front of the fire that was still burning to keep the background chill at bay.

The call ended after a few minutes and David came through to where I was sitting. I suppose I was anticipating a few words of appreciation for not hanging around to fag-end on their conversation, prior to picking up our own conversation where we'd left off. Or we might have started to make love on the sofa, as we had on every occasion I'd been at the house before. But instead of moving in like a lover, David suddenly sprang on to me like an assailant. He thrust me against the cushions, pinning me down with his whole body, his forearm pressing hard and rigid just underneath my throat.

'You did that *deliberately*, didn't you?' he hissed in icy fury, his face close and savage, his eyes piercing.

I had no idea what he thought I'd done or what he thought he was doing. He had me so I couldn't move. I couldn't respond for shock.

'She *heard* you!' he continued through bared teeth. 'She heard your *footsteps* across the floor. "You've got someone *with* you," she said. "I can hear her *heels* on the *flagstones*—"' His breathing came fast and shallow as he snarled out his wife's accusation. 'You *knew* she'd *hear* you if you walked away—!'

I genuinely hadn't given the possibility a thought. I'd been sure I was quiet. But in the insanity of the moment I was too stunned – and fearful – to be sure of anything. *Had* my heels made a noise? Or was it simply that after a generous decade of David's infidelity and denials Jane had developed bat-like sonar to detect frequency changes at her husband's end of a telephone line? That seemed to make as much sense as anything right then, because nothing made any sense at all. I was out of my depth. I had no comprehension of the world he and his wife lived in. It wasn't just the damn awful house and the damn awful cliff; their whole damn awful existence was an alien planet to me.

I still hadn't answered him and in a quick expert shift of his body David inched his forearm up to my throat. I could feel him willing me to say something that would make things worse, to give him licence to escalate to his next trained move.

I could only tell him the truth.

'I was just trying to give you some privacy,' was all I managed to say.

He continued to rake his eyes over mine. I hadn't realised how their colouring was so feral, almost wolven it seemed to me then, with bright streaks of amber and hazel and green and grey narrowing to the deadly black pin-points of his pupils.

'Your credibility hangs by a *thread*,' he said at last, and let me go.

I can't explain how we got through the rest of that day and the night that followed, or why I didn't call for a taxi to take me to the airport or station or all the way back to London by road. I suppose I could even have called the police. I don't know now why I stayed on and I absolutely didn't know then. If there is any explanation then it's another iteration of what I've written before, that David's hold over any situation was so absolute that it was as if he could bend reality, and one's own reactions within the distortion, to his will.

Not that it would have mattered if things hadn't gone to such hell that morning, because they were going to go to hell anyway the following day.

By the time I dressed and came down next morning, David was in his workroom. Or so I thought. I poured myself a mug of coffee in the kitchen and took it back upstairs – I don't know why I did that, either; that vast hard bed was hardly a refuge – only to find David coming out of the bedroom carrying my belongings, including my spongebag and the bath towel I'd just used. He must have waited upstairs somewhere till I was downstairs myself, or perhaps there was a second staircase I hadn't yet seen. He didn't explain what he was doing. He had no words for me. I followed him mutely, assuming he'd called a taxi for me after all, though why he'd taken the towel just then was puzzling, not to say demeaning. But when he went into the guest bedroom I realised he wasn't removing my belongings, only transferring them. He ruffled the bedclothes as he dumped my things on the bed, then laid out my toiletries in the adjacent bathroom as though I'd used them there, complete with the damp towel tossed casually over the edge of the bath.

Then I remembered what he'd told me when I first arrived, when he was still my lover and not a wild-eyed ninja. (Not that he hadn't converted to being my lover again as recently as last night.) Someone was coming to lunch. His accountant, or money adviser, or some such; a man called Hale Crosse. This was for his benefit. David was setting the scene for his own method acting before the cameras started to roll.

Just why he'd arranged for this man to come down while I was there remained a mystery. It might have been simply for cover, to discourage his wife from joining him. Or I suppose he may have wanted us both there together to brush up his Strasberg technique. Or just as possibly, it seemed to me then, since we were already so far down the rabbit-hole, it was so we could all play croquet with flamingos in the garden after lunch.

I remember nothing about Hale Crosse except that he had a voice a little like the actor Richard Bebb, though even that may be an *ex post facto* addition to back-fill the blank in my mind. David introduced me as his researcher, in an offhand way that translated to 'minion'. I took my cue, removed a book at random from a shelf and sat with it outside – under what should have been the cheering blue spring sky, but was quite as depressing to me then as the previous winter grey – leaving David to talk to his man in the kitchen as he prepared lunch. I trusted that he would see I was doing all I could to play along, though I knew he would give me no sign that he too was playing a part. I could easily have burst his play-acting bubble altogether and told his money man what was really going on between us in the most graphic terms, just to be done with the whole lunatic charade. David could hardly have pounced on me again in company. But I think he knew I wasn't up to it. He'd beaten me down, psychologically if not physically too, so wasn't taking much of a risk.

After a little while, David came outside and crouched down over a patch of the garden by the kitchen. I walked over and saw he was cutting sprigs of mint.

'Hello there,' I said. 'Need a hand with anything?'

But he still had no communication for me. He didn't even look up, just tossed out a cool 'No, thanks.'

'Are we having lamb?' I asked, still trying to make contact.

'No. This is for the new potatoes.'

'Oh dear,' I said, momentarily forgetting my reduced role in the movie that was playing; the Saturday twelve noon first show. 'I don't like mint in new potatoes.'

He offered no reply and went back inside, leaving me standing there abjectly. The kitchen window was open and I caught what he said to Hale Crosse, as I was probably meant to.

'Huh! Sue *Dawson* doesn't like *mint* in her *new* potatoes.'

His intonation was masterful, the exact pitch to carry the scene. Perhaps Wenders had known what he was after.

Leaving by train next morning, I came to two conclusions. The first was that David didn't like being at Land's End much more than I did. It was a surprise revelation, but I was pretty sure it was correct. I've read acres of interviews with him over the years, as well as almost everything he ever wrote as a personal account, and though journalists refer to it as *his beloved Cornwall*, I've yet to find one truly fond sentiment for the place from David himself. From everything I witnessed, it brought out the very worst in him, which I somehow think he knew. I believe he tolerated it as a kind of *ultima Thule*; the farthest he could be from Hampstead, which he seemed to hate most of all, without leaving England. (He died with an Eire passport, claimed through his descent from Ronnie's Irish mother, Bessie, and obtained as a reaction to Brexit. I rather think now that if Brexit had happened twenty years earlier he would have used it to leverage a permanent move and found himself another *Schloss* facing the Atlantic there. Not because he had any love for Ireland either, but because of his constant drive to escape from whichever slammer he'd last built for himself and find a new location to build the next one. The only country which did have a *locus* in his heart, I believe, was Switzerland, and I dare say 'the Swissers' would have happily had him. But it wouldn't have suited David to move there. Firstly, it would have associated him with the Roger Moore-type UK tax exiles, which he couldn't have endured, but, far more importantly, having his domestic set-up transplanted there would have invaded the life-long personal secrecy the place preserved for him.)

My second conclusion was that I was never going to set foot on that damn cliff of his ever again.

WIMBLEDON AND BEYOND

Why can't people have what they want? The things were all there to content everybody; yet everybody has the wrong thing!

Ford Madox Ford, *The Good Soldier*

It was hands down the most depressing summer of my life. Not that I didn't see David; in fact, I saw him quite often. He would call me to St John's Wood or visit me on the King's Road. There were still the restaurants and a movie or two – *Silkwood* was one of them, which I think made him regret not agreeing to Meryl when they were casting for Charlie – and more flowers and gifts and expressions of love and praise. And there was still the endlessly astonishing and inexhaustible sex. All that, *per se*, was as fine as ever. But now there was all that went with it – the constant threnody about the book, how everything and everyone was taking him away from it, including the time he spent with me. There were unceasing complaints about his wife, his family and whomever else he felt encumbered by, which appeared to be everybody. When he was back in Cornwall there were also his letters, which would either freely and sometimes nastily blame me, or 'us', for what he believed he was enduring, or prove encouraging and loving, if he decided once again that I was his last great hope. There was no way to tell which sort they were until I opened them, unless he'd added a smiley or frownie face on the outside of the envelope, which he didn't always do and, anyway, sometimes they were both.

David was in a howling state, that was certain, and had arrogated the right to put me in a state too, as though I were some sort of safety valve for him, a means of EQ-ing all the discordant levels in his head. You would have thought he had survived prolonged torture in some heartless regime … Well, there was Ronnie originally, I suppose, who had done something of the sort to his son's psyche. Yet it was also a more general malaise which afflicted him, as much for what he was as who. I'd finished Susan Kennaway's book by then and read other accounts of literary love stories – Sheilah Graham on her time with Scott Fitzgerald, Pamela Hansford Johnson on Dylan Thomas, Anaïs Nin on Henry Miller, Martha Gellhorn and Mary Welsh Hemingway on Ernest (and years later, Joyce Maynard on Salinger, Carole Mallory on Mailer and Emma Tennant on Ted Hughes). A common pathogen was evident. The same high pitch of often thuggish self-indulgence in whatever form it took – drink, sex, emotional turmoil, violence, manipulation, on and on, in any combination – was what each writer believed necessary, if not vital, to release his creativity. It was the self-indulgence that Kennaway had demonstrated and the self-indulgence David subsequently allowed himself, in his own particular combination, after the Scottish writer's death. (Though I would still have to say, in fairness, that after reading all these other women's accounts, David wasn't even close to being the worst.)

It boiled down to the basic premise of great artists suffering for their art. Art – as Shamus puts it in *The Naïve and Sentimental Lover*, probably in a phrase of Kennaway's, via Petrarch – being a kind of lovely agony. The only problem I ever had with that concept was the co-factor that their women – the writers' molls – had to suffer for it too.

Next time Graham called round for a Famous Grouse he told me I was getting thin. He gave me a long straight look and declared I needed a day out. The next day we were sitting under a grey sky in Centre Court, Wimbledon, on debenture seats courtesy of Audrey's late father, watching an early round men's singles match as dull as the weather.

'Great match for radio, isn't it?' Graham remarked with a sniff, as the pair of baseline players relentlessly pounded the ball back and forth like metronomes. 'It's the cure for insomnia if the Beeb ever release it on tape.'

With the tennis providing little diversion, we started to talk. Graham said he could see I wasn't a happy bunny at the moment and that I hadn't been one for a while. I could only agree, telling him it was David's here again/gone again, come here/leave me alone, I can't do it/I can only do it with you behaviour that had me down. Saying this to Graham – who was so constant, so stalwart, always so very much the full sum of all his parts – I suddenly felt ashamed for letting myself be reduced to this condition. I was always bright and quick and funny and capable before David, at least before the worst of how he could be. Now I was the kind of woman I despised, the kind who moped around complaining how her man had done her wrong.

'Well, them's the rules of the game, honey,' Graham replied. 'You're a rich man's mistress now.'

Christ – I wished! I countered instantly, saying that was all I wanted from the start. Just the good times together, like George and Gigi, and the rest of our lives in our own corners. It was David who couldn't stick by the rules. He was the one who insisted he had to get out of his marriage, insisted I had to help him do it, be there for him, be inside the book with him, then be banished when he didn't like having me so close. There were all the broken dates, all the doubled-down promises that followed to patch things up, then those were broken too, with the implication it was somehow all my fault for believing anything he said. Now he was insisting on 'radio silence' – again – right through the rest of the summer, while he worked on the book and 'hacked out' a way to get himself out, the never-to-be-resolved plan that was nobody's idea but his own.

'Nah,' Graham said dismissively after patiently hearing me out. 'He's got you snowed. The bloke's terminally married. He's never gonna leave his wife, so don't believe him if he swears different on his mother's grave. Anyway, why should he get out? He's got you in a nice convenient box, all hot and lovely and waiting to pop out and entertain him whenever he lifts your lid. He's got the wife in another one, doing whatever she does for him – don't ask me what – keeping house, typing his deathless prose, making sure his socks match, like he's still living at home with his ma or else she's the nanny a bloke like him never had. So what've you got to offer that he isn't getting now? You spread your legs whenever he's got the urge, listen to his moans about how much he suffers to earn a fortune, and he never has to take any earache from you because he's got 'er indoors to run back to if you try and dish him any. Bet *she* never gives him earache, or she'd've been traded in for a quieter model a long time ago.'

The match reached set point in the second set and still wasn't worth watching. Graham had put it all horribly well, but I still tried to make my case.

'Then why does he keep saying he wants to get out? Why all the bloody aggro? I don't care if he stays married or not.'

'You're not listening, honey. You just said it yourself. If the man *persists* in going around with his arse in a sling about the way his life is, you can bet the farm it's because he *likes* it that way – either for some miserable reason best known to himself or so that he can moan about it and get special consideration from lovely sympathetic girls like you. If he really wanted out of his marriage, he's got all the money and lawyers in the western hemisphere to throw at it to make it go away. If he didn't like it, he would've left her for whoever he was screwing before you, or the one before that. Don't tell me there weren't others, though probably none with an Oxbridge degree and your legs. It's obvious it's the *tension* he likes – creative or otherwise – the ducking and diving between all the moving parts. That's what races his motor.'

Graham saw how his words were hitting home and planted a big kiss on my forehead.

'Sorry, sweetheart. He's just got you believing a rather literary version of the old my-wife-doesn't-understand-me line, that's all. You fell for it because you fell for him and he's got your number. It's shitty, I know, but that's the way the guy is.'

'I thought you liked him,' I objected pathetically.

'I do, honey – I think he's great. But then, I ain't sleeping with him, am I?'

The next afternoon I had an unexpected visitor for tea. My great friend and ex-beau Jeremy Lloyd, as slim and elegant and idioti-cally handsome as ever, paid me a call at my flat. We quite often saw each other, but hadn't for a while. I hadn't really seen anyone for a while. David had me too wrapped up in coping with what-ever it was he was doing, or going to do, or not going to do next.

I made a pot of tea, found some biscuits and we were soon laughing away like old times. Graham had probably told him how miserable I was and they'd decided he should call round to cheer me up. It would be like them to do that.

As he left, Jeremy gave me a long, rather sexy hug.

'We have to do this more often, darling,' he declared. 'I'd forgot-ten how funny you are.'

Darling JL. Before he called round, I'd forgotten too.

A couple of days later, I decided to make an unannounced visit myself – to St John's Wood, to see if David was at the flat. He'd said he wouldn't be, but I had the strongest feeling that he was. He always unplugged the phone when he was working there – and whenever we were there together – so I knew there was no point in calling him first and, anyway, I didn't want to give him the chance to say no. Revived by the combined efforts of Graham and Jeremy to buoy my spirits, I'd come to a decision about doing the Ronnie biog and wanted to tell David in person before the nebulous end to the current radio silence. For some reason, I'd thought it would help.

I let myself into the stairwell, but knocked first before I opened the bulletproof door. He was there; surprised to see me, but neither smiling nor frowning at my arrival. It was awkward between us – I hadn't quite timed it so that he'd finished his morning's work, though if I had he would probably have already left – so we stopped attempting conversation and went to bed. Afterwards, I told him that after a lot of careful thought I'd decided to do the biography of his father as he'd suggested. Now that I'd finished all the research he needed for his novel, I felt it was a good time to take the material forward into a full project of its own. I was sure that with his—

But David cut me off. He said he didn't think my doing the Ronnie book was a good idea anymore. It could be difficult, there'd be problems. He no longer wanted me to do it.

I think something close to hysteria hit me then. Was there any rug he would place me on without pulling it out from under me? Was there another way I could possibly stand on my head for him – or balance on any other body part for that matter – that would be enough? Was he *ever* going to stay true to his own words on *anything*?

After I'd levelled these fresh accusations at him – I may have screamed some of them – David looked as if I'd scalped him alive. It was his particular talent to drive you to the very edge and then appear shocked when you finally flung yourself into the abyss. But I suddenly didn't care what his reaction was. I couldn't have said another word or listened to one more from him. I dressed and left.

David sent me a letter in reply. It was quasi-apologetic but fully self-justifying; understanding but unaccommodating; he said he believed in our love but doubted his own faith; he claimed I wanted a structure from him (when I didn't), said he had no excuse for his 'zigzagging' and then proceeded to make several excuses and zigzag some more. He put everything down to his not having taken on a relationship like ours before, never any at all while writing a book, though he added that it was the book I'd breathed life into him to write. He ended by declaring another arbitrary deadline for his decision – now it was 1 October – though I'd already lost all track of what it was he was aiming to decide. If he still knew himself, he didn't elaborate. Meanwhile, he intended to go 'hellbent' with the book and would stay at Tregiffian.

Suddenly, 1 October didn't seem at all too long to be away from him. Right then I'd had – as he wrote – far more words from him than I could eat.

After Wimbledon and sending Jeremy round, Graham thought of another antidote for my condition; some recordings for me to do in New York. I packed my new Viennese weekend bag – I'd be hitting the stores between studio sessions, so didn't need more – and flew out. I spent the next two and a half wonderfully David-free weeks recording at Celebration Studios, enjoying the city with Barbara and staying in a little basement apartment on West 12th in the Village, a direct equivalent of my own studio on the King's Road, cat-sitting for a journalist friend of hers who was away.

I hadn't told David I was going. It shouldn't have mattered, if he'd meant what he said about this latest radio silence, but he'd called Graham when he couldn't raise me at my flat and rang me as soon as I was home. He told me he would be in London in a few days and wanted to see me very much. Would I be able to meet him at St John's Wood and stay overnight? He'd be so pleased if I said I would …

And so it went. After barely a month of summer *en famille* in Cornwellshire, David had re-certified the St John's Wood flat as a sanctuary and wanted to see me there all the time. He managed to make things lovely again – so lovely that I once turned up at the flat wearing nothing but my Burberry raincoat and high heels, to make it as lovely back for him.

'And you really came all the way on the tube like that?' David repeated in awe after I'd told him, as if it were the most wondrous erotic notion ever.

He visited at my flat too. But he let me know that, while radio silence was suspended, his 'decision date' of early October still stood. Meanwhile, the show was back on the road.

We went to Dawlish, the rather twee coastal town in Devon that David said he needed to get the feel of for the book. He met me off the train at Exeter St David's and we drove the rest of the way, finding a room in one of the less *jejune* B&Bs. We fell straight on to the bed for an Olympian session, the intensity of which surprised even David, then went out for 'a small wet', as he called it, using Ronnie lingo almost compulsively now. It was mid-afternoon and the pubs were about to shut so we went to the local Co-op and bought a bottle of Smirnoff, a carton of made-from-concentrate orange juice and a pack of paper cups. Suitably *declassé* for the area, we walked down to the front and sat on a bench under the wooden arcade, knocking back the British-made voddie like a pair of derelicts sharing meths. When the evening opening-hour came around, we had an early pub supper of scampi and chips and went back to the B&B for further acrobatics.

'If you ever take another lover, you'd better not let me find out about it,' David told me as we finally turned out the light. 'I'd know, anyway.'

He slept peacefully, his ghosts for once slaked, and woke me at dawn for round three. When we checked out – we may have been the only guests – I was puzzled to see the proprietor look sheepish and red-faced behind the front desk. David saw it too.

'Do you know what, my darling?' he said as we walked to the car. 'I reckon that fellow had a spyhole in the wall and was watching us. That's why he couldn't look me in the eye when I paid the bill. I think he rather felt he should be paying *us*.'

Apparently we'd just spent the night at the Bates Motel, Dawlish.

On the drive to Teignmouth station, where I was to catch the train back to London, David said how amazed he was by the amount of seminal fluid he produced with me.

'It's just so different with you, my darling. Everything about the sex is so different, so much freer and truer. Everything in me is so much more willing. When you get a rotten little duty fuck, you surrender very little ...'

I'd never thought about it till then, but now my latest worry was that he was still availing himself of these when he wasn't with me. I asked him later why he still shared a bed with his wife, hoping he might take the hint. He sounded puzzled by my question and his answer – because I misunderstood it, because he made it deliberately oblique – only made my worry worse.

'Then there really would be no point to the marriage ...'

When the projected 'decision date' arrived there was – axiomatically, at this stage – no decision. I didn't even have to ask when I got to the flat; David was primed and ready with his rationalisations. How could he possibly be held to a date? He couldn't run his life by anything so arbitrary. What did I expect from him?

I reminded him, perhaps not so gently, that it was his date, not mine, and that if I was expecting anything at all, it was only what he'd told me to expect, whatever that may have been when he'd last articulated it, since I was no longer clear on the matter.

Faced with the internal illogic of his own contrivance, he started to sidle around the subject, saying a move now was impossible, but that once the book was in, he definitely meant to move out, just for weekdays to begin with – maybe Oxford, maybe Berlin. That would be doable, wouldn't it?

That he could contemplate adding yet another point on the compass for himself – after Hampstead, Cornwall, Wengen, Zurich, LA for the movies, and anywhere else for everything else – showed how unmoored he was in his present frame of mind. I couldn't let myself be lured down a new rabbit-hole, so I said that I just wanted to see him, however he managed it, but couldn't cope with the unnecessary *Sturm-und-Drang* he attached to the process.

But he didn't like to hear that either. It was too straightforward. I don't think the German phrase troubled him; it was 'unnecessary' that jarred his sensibilities. He'd detected a small rise in my voice – nothing approaching my more full-throated level – but it was enough to hang his self-righteous hat on. He said he didn't need anyone upsetting his equilibrium at this stage of the book; 'anyone', as I understood it in the present context, meaning just *me*, not the whole besetting regiment of *them*, and 'equilibrium' being the turmoil I now knew he created around himself so that he could charge his own system from the swirling emotional chaos, like the dynamo on a bicycle wheel.

I surprised both of us by taking him at his word and leaving. I still had Graham's voice in my ears saying *it's the tension he likes* and knew I couldn't keep draining my own batteries to generate it for him. When I got home I parcelled up all the jewellery he'd given me and sent it by courier to the flat.

David's birthday was coming up. I sent a card to the flat a few days early, so that he'd get it somewhere in the vicinity of the occasion. I didn't know when or if he'd be there and, the way things had been going, didn't expect to see him for a celebration lunch this time round. But it seemed churlish not to send anything. It wasn't actually a birthday card, just a neutral one with a drawing of a dog in a garden. I couldn't think of anything to say that would make any difference to the state of play currently between us, so I sello-taped the slip of paper that was printed with *This card has been left blank for your own message* to the inside and signed my name below. It seemed to say it all.

For all the baffling inconsistencies and contradictions of his behaviour and the murderous drama he generated, on some never-to-be-expressed level I realised it all made a dreadful kind of sense. The central essence of the man was that he had once been a terribly hurt and fearful little boy who never had his tears kissed better. His mother walked out when he was five – or six, or seven, it varied with the telling – and he was left with Ronnie, who was living proof that the Very Bad Man of the scariest-worst childhood tales really existed. As an adult David had spent his life searching for a love that wouldn't let him down, as each of his parents had done in their different terrible ways. But when he did find love he couldn't let himself trust to it, in case it let him down again. So he tried to banish it, break it, make it leave, anything to deprive it of the chance to let him down first, even if – as in our case – it never would. He had to make it hurt first, before he was hurt again. I believe shrinks call this 'anxious attachment'. It's not something you just get over.

He surprised me by calling the next day.

'Hello, my darling. Thank you for your lovely card. How are you? It's lovely, did I tell you? I'm all right between my ears now. I wanted to tell you that. We could make it twelve o'clock at the flat the day before my birthday, couldn't we?'

And because it was impossible to hold out on David when he was looking for love, and asking for it so sweetly, I said we could. An enormous bouquet from Georgie's arrived at my flat by motor-bike despatch rider later that afternoon.

When I arrived at the flat at 11.45, David wasn't there. But he'd laid out a caviar picnic for two on the rug and put a present that I assumed was for me, another red jeweller's box, on one of the plates. I'd brought a present for him and wanted to hide it first, so I'd timed it well – or perhaps he had. He might have been some-where in the street watching me arrive, waiting for me to go up first – how to ever know? I put a little gift tag on the other plate, then hid the present, which was large and flat, in the only place that would take it – under the bed.

Then I heard him pound up the stairs in threes, his huge feet slamming the treads. He burst in carrying chocolates and more flowers from Georgie's.

'I knew you were here,' he said, inhaling deeply, as though he hadn't breathed fresh air for weeks. 'I could smell that delicious light scent you wear the moment I was in the stairwell. Oh, do come here, I want my skin on you—'

David was so, so lovely when he was like this, all right between his ears and trusting to love – if only in the moment – and giving so much more back than he took.

When we finally disengaged from that initial long embrace, he wanted me to open my present. He'd bought me an art nouveau bracelet, silver with a leaf detail and set with amethysts and aquamarines for berries. He wrapped it round my wrist and closed the fastening, his big fingers delicate as lace.

'Please don't throw it back at me,' he said softly, holding my wrist as if to seal the piece there forever. 'It's my love and I do love you so. And do take all the other stuff with you when you go this time, because that's my love too and I don't give it to everybody.'

Then he picked up the gift tag from his own plate. It was attached to nothing, but he studied it solemnly.

'It's more than I deserve,' he said at last.

When I told him that his present was hidden his face lit up.

'On your person, I hope!'

'Wrong dimensions!' I answered. 'Find it—'

The hunt took five seconds. Under the bed was the first place he looked.

'Oh, it's a picture!' he exclaimed, tearing at the wrapping round the frame. 'It's not of a girl on the beach, is it?'

It was, of course. I'd had a poster-sized blow-up made of his favourite naked holiday shot of me.

'Oh, look. Just look—'

The bed took us directly, with the picture of me now hanging on the wall over our heads.

For the rest of the year, David was extraordinarily attentive. We saw ourselves all the time, frequently spending nights together at the flat. He couldn't keep me far enough away over the summer; now it was as if he couldn't keep me sufficiently close or ever get his fill. He was so concerned not to lose me, he said, though now there seemed no possibility that he ever would. Everything was easy between us again, fresh and flowing. No more radio silence. David said it was a new beginning, a new way forward.

'Wait until the spring,' he said. 'That's all. I'll have done the book and then we can sort ourselves out. It's not long, is it?'

He went on to say that I'd opened a door for him and, if I was clever, it might be that he could go through it.

'So shut up,' he said. 'I love you.'

He bought a new item for the flat – a cheval glass – and put it in the bedroom, strategically positioned by the bed. It was just what we needed to be even more narcissistic in our lovemaking – and for me finally to become his looking-glass whore.

In the middle of November, Graham, David and I were back at John Wood to record *The Spy Who Came in from the Cold*. There was a lovely mellow feel to the session, right from the start. We were all on form and no one had anything to prove. Lunch at the staff canteen was a nice easy schmooze.

'He's mad,' Graham declared as we lined up for the afternoon session. David was already in the sound booth and couldn't hear. 'You're obviously good for him and great together. Any village idiot can see it. I want you to know, honey – I've changed my mind on the subject. He bloody well *should* leave his wife.'

* * *

At the end of the month David gave me an early Christmas present at the flat. He wanted to offer me a prepared speech first. He'd evidently made notes.

'Darling, my darling—' he began, standing in the centre of the little living room as I sat on the sofa, his audience of one in the front row. 'When I loved you, I showed you how I loved you. When I desired you so much that my whole body wanted to live inside you and around you forever, I showed you that too. When I despaired, I made you share my misery with me and punished you for sharing. When I wanted to retreat to the confines of an empty relationship, I pushed you away so that I could do so, and expected you to be there when I wanted to bounce back …'

There was more in the same beautifully paradoxical vein. It was lovely and sad by turn, always poignant either way, but, as I listened, I realised that David was always coming full circle in his thinking, arriving where he started and – to invert the Eliot – *not* knowing the place for the first time. Not even recognising the recursion. He knew himself so well. But it didn't seem to matter, because he just couldn't progress *from* himself at all. It was round and round in circles all the time.

That was what the books were always about, I'd read them all by then; saying everything so beautifully but getting nowhere, his heroes always baffled by their own perceptions of paradox, turning and turning – to invert the Yeats now – in the *narrowing* gyre, making the ineluctable recursion to their starting condition. Leamas never does come in from the cold, though it was David's most famous title ever. Given the chance to climb back over the Wall, he deliberately drops back down to his death on the Iron Curtain side. In the next book, Turner – the perfect name – keeps revisiting tired old-war techniques that fail time and again in the new conflict, refusing to learn. Cassidy banishes all remembrance of the liberating bohemian love he experienced with Shamus and

Helen in order to return to the confines of his conventional bourgeois home. Even when Smiley achieves the crowning success of
his career, he can barely bring himself to acknowledge it as a final
concrete fact.

Circular images reinforce this inescapable mechanism of rinse
and repeat; the Circus, Moscow Centre, the nursery round embedded in the *Tinker Tailor* title and Smiley making his rounds of the
suspects. Guillam, David's younger-self character, actually says
about George at one point that the paradox might kill him, but in
le Carré *knowing* the problem doesn't mean *doing* anything about
it. The centre holds because the paradox pins it there. That poor
Pym was doomed to repeat this recursive pattern – fleeing *the
Ring* in Vienna, but only returning to the sad little corner of
England where he originally started, with not an inch of progress
made – was as frustrating as any of it. This was David's great *autobiographical* novel, and yet still no birds sang. There was to be no
progress, no epiphany, no resolution at the end save for death; in
Pym's case, David's case in fictive form, taking Kim Philby, his
internalised double, with him when he blows his brains out
looking at himself in the bathroom mirror. If David's 'going south,
tell them north' rule applied to how he chose his pen name, then I
had come to think that le Carré – the square – was really cover for
le Cercle.

But when David was so lovely and so loving like this, I could
only love him back, without thought of the circle returning. Love
him because of everything he was and in spite of everything else.
The gift he'd bought me was circular, too – did he see the irony? –
an antique eternity ring, of platinum set with diamonds.

'From your eternal lover,' he said, as he took my hand and
gently eased up my ring finger to receive it. 'For the eternity of
pain I've caused you and the eternal future that we may or may
not have.'

The metaphor continued. When he slipped the ring on my finger, it didn't quite fit.

David wanted one last getaway for us before resigning himself to the family holiday in Wengen. In the middle of December we went back to Zurich for four nights, staying at our usual hotel, the Dolder Grand.

ZURICH NOCHMAL – UND SCHLIESSLICH

We arrived at the hilltop hotel in the last of the afternoon light and for once didn't go straight to bed when we went up to our room – not from any faltering desire, but because the view of the city in the gathering winter evening as the lights began to sparkle below was so crisp and dark and enticing that it drew us out into itself. Of all the travelling I did with David, somehow Zurich always felt like 'our place'. We dumped our bags, found gloves and mufflers and grabbed a waiting cab. We got out at the Altstadt and walked along the winding lanes together in the inky frozen night, David's arm snaking through mine as he clutched me to his side.

We soon found a *Bierkeller* and went in, through heavy felt blankets drawn on brass rails across the inside of the door against the cold. The log fire that was blazing in a great sooty hearth gave off enough heat to warm a stadium. The patrons sat at small tables, their hats and heavy coats hanging on racks between. A conversational burr of local dialect filled the room, with occasional bursts of low congenial laughter breaking through, and there was hazy lambent light all round. We sat at a little corner table, holding hands, watching and listening and just soaking it all up. Before long we both had tears in our eyes. We'd reached a new level that was beyond lovely, beyond love, beyond anything we'd experienced together before; some plane of being that was even beyond perfect.

Back at the hotel that night we shared the most tender and truest lovemaking either of us had known in our lives.

Next morning I woke early – very early for me, on the cusp of first light. David was lying beside me on his back, completely still, and I knew instantly that something wasn't right. There was a rigidity to how he lay, I could feel a strange tension across the mattress. It must have been what had woken me. In the semi-darkness I could see that his eyes were open and staring blankly at the ceiling. For one terrible moment I thought he was dead. I reached out and laid my hand on his chest and, to my relief, felt the warmth of his skin and his heart beating underneath. But he gave no response to my touch. He didn't move. He didn't even blink. In a flash of dreadful intuition I knew that he had lain like that for hours, unmoving in the dark. I couldn't begin to guess what was so wrong, but something had to be – badly, badly wrong. I didn't have to ask him what it was, because as soon as he knew that I was awake and had seen that he was too, he told me, as though he'd waited all that time just to speak.

He was still unmoving, still staring at the ceiling. His voice was flat and empty, a terrible void.

'You have to go back,' he said. 'I can't be this happy.'

I didn't – go back – but I only know this because my diary entry gives the date of my return to London, alone, three days later. We must have done things together in that time, walked around together, had meals and drinks together. We must have had sex. But I have no recollection. I've written the same words before, so it must have been how I coped in those never-anticipated moments when he said something I had no means of processing, that left me too shocked or numbed to retain what followed immediately afterwards. I only know that for the first time in my life I experienced a state of absolute despair.

1985

BUT STILL

For pervasive unreason has its own logical processes.
Joseph Conrad, Author's Note, *The Secret Agent*

As soon as he returned to London in the new year, David told me that Yvette was coming over and he wanted us to meet. I think he may have summoned her specially, for an attempt at damage control. I was resistant to meeting her. It felt like the last thing I needed at that time, but David presented it as a special request, something he wanted me to do for him, as though there were something to be achieved by it, so I agreed. He must have thought that the woman he'd successfully 'turned' from lover into platonic friend – I always suspected against her wishes – could persuade me that what had happened in Zurich really wasn't so bad and that she'd survived worse from him in Phnom Penh. Or perhaps he didn't have even that improbable rationale. Perhaps he knew he was flailing and was just trying to come up with anything to explain or justify himself.

We met at Au Bois in St John's Wood. David took me there and introduced us – Yvette was already at the table – then left us to our lunch *à deux*. Seeing her, small and dark with huge brown eyes, I realised for the first time that all David's most significant loves before me had been dark and petite – Ann, Susan, Janet, Yvette herself. My dimensions, I suddenly saw, were closer to the fantasy eight-foot-tall blonde that Cassidy makes a joke about meeting to his dark petite wife.

227

Yvette asked me how I was and how it had been, but she didn't say it in a particularly inviting manner and I wasn't particularly forthcoming in return. She was David's agent on this mission and presumably had been briefed. She may have been as reluctant to meet as I was. She may even have wished that she was still his lover herself and not a platonic family friend at all. I told her some of what had been happening, when she pressed me, but withheld the worst. I wasn't remotely interested in asking how it had been for her. We weren't two girlfriends sharing our problems over salad and spritzers. We were – well, it felt to me then as though we were two characters in search of an author.

He was how he was, she told me finally with a quick resigned shrug, that Gallic purse of the lips. He would never change. I didn't recall asking her if she thought he would. I went back to my own flat afterwards, no happier and no more encouraged.

Yvette must have recognised the signs anyway. She was supposed to be staying in London for another few days, but that evening David rang to tell me she was suddenly going back to France.

'She told me she doesn't like the idea of seeing me at the moment,' he said. 'She doesn't want me to contact her for a while.'

Her reaction had clearly surprised him, but I couldn't tell if he was acknowledging its validity in response to his recidivism with me, or blaming me for enabling her to see it.

I had another birthday. Barbara, who is just three days older than me, came over for a visit. I introduced her to David – they'd previously only spoken on the phone when I was skiing last year – and he was very sweet to her. Barbara's younger sister, Julie, was also over and David was very sweet to her, too. He was just very sweet all the time now. Whenever he and I were together over the next few months, which was often, either at his flat or mine, he was loving and caring and solicitous and kind. He gave me more flowers and gifts. He gave me some manuscript pages from the novel. I'm not sure too many people got those. He was still the most wonderful lover. And he talked about himself more than ever, as if desperate for me to understand him – not recognising that the problem was I finally did. However hard he tried to present the best of himself, after Zurich he just couldn't revive the part of me he had shot out of the sky. Turning the happiest time ever into the absolute worst, simply because it *was* the happiest time ever, was a paradox too far. He'd hung a sword of Damocles over our being that happy again and I didn't think I'd survive it, if it ever fell.

We made it through to the summer. The book was finished and who knows what David may have had in mind for us next. I never found out.

I took no conscious decision to end things. I still loved him as much as ever, still wanted to go on loving him and knew he still loved me, perhaps even more than ever. But when we were at the flat one time, my body took the decision for me. I couldn't hack the sex. It had always been the most extraordinary union, right from the first night. Now it made me feel as if I were one of those unlucky addresses that keep getting burgled. Only there was nothing left to steal. That was when I knew I couldn't go on.

It was over. Or, as I remembered Graham saying with such wonderful unintended irony immediately before it all began – *fin d'histoire.*

Leaving David wasn't easy, coming up from the depths, forfeiting the chance of regaining the heights. Had I missed the best of him by not staying longer, to see if he really could sort himself out 'after the book', after all we'd been through together? Or had I only narrowly escaped with my faculties and my emotional resources intact? My survival instinct at the time – battered and disoriented though it was – persuaded me that if I'd stayed, I should only have proved how completely *The Good Soldier* was the book of David's life, by turning into the girl who loses her wits after falling in love with Edward and ends up almost catatonic, saying 'Shuttlecocks!' spasmodically. But I suppose I could have been wrong.

Either way, it took me a long time to recover. Therapy helped. I found a wonderful therapist, Elizabeth, who diagnosed me as being 'borderline clinically depressed'. Well – at least I could still use the personal pronoun. Long talks and guided hypnotherapy with her gradually restored me back to my better self.

I continued working with Graham and acquired audio publishing clients of my own. Audiobooks were bigger business than ever and when we weren't running back-to-back sessions in London one or other of us would be flying out to record on the continent or in the States. There were more le Carré titles to record and I still did the abridgements, but I didn't attend David's readings. Graham would tell me how they went – which was invariably fine – and pass on David's best wishes.

'He always asks me how you are. Tells me to tell you he'd be happy to take you to lunch. You know, honey, I think he carries a bit of a candle for you.'

I didn't take David up on his offer, though he made it every time. There was only one way it would turn out if I did and I had only just managed to recover from the last time. We were over, but at the same time we'd never really finished, only stopped. Like the first time we parted, in front of Eros, it was a not-continuing, rather than an end.

Gigi and I saw a lot of each other and became firm friends. Of all the people I could talk to about David, she and Graham were the only two who actually knew him themselves. Like Graham, she was always enormously supportive of my side of things.

'I really don't know how you managed it, darling,' she told me, meaning two years with David and only requiring therapy afterwards, not a straitjacket or a padded cell. 'All that *Sturm-und-Drang*.'

That did seem to be the phrase.

'I think you were very lucky to have the strength to get out when you did,' she added, 'before he used you up completely.'

She'd already told me how George described Jane as being 'hoovered up' since her marriage. George had known her before, of course, and had even arranged the introduction. Another of Gigi's admirers had also known Jane – BC, as it were – though just as a pal. He too described someone who had formerly been sparky and adventurous, who loved hitting the road for fast driving; a far cry from what appeared to be her AD – After David – self. Gigi had noted the pattern of progression and was glad I'd escaped.

'I think he gave the best of himself to you, all the same. I think you brought it out in him. It was just a pity he couldn't live up to it. But then, if he'd finally escaped with you, he wouldn't have been able to complain about it all the time, would he?!'

The three of us met up in New York one time, when George and Gigi were on a trip together and I was over there recording. George invited me to dine with them at the Royalton, where they were staying. I was downtown at Morgans.

George had just retired after a long and illustrious career, but the story he told over cocktails was that David had not been best pleased at his electing to leave before he was finished with his services. We shared a hard-won chuckle of mutual experience and further tales of our respective times with the Great Man. George confessed his pet name for David was 'the monster' and called me his comrade-in-arms. It was how he saw it: that we'd both survived close combat with the many-headed hydra.

We recalled the time we'd first met, on my maiden stay at Tregiffian.

'It was such a disappointment when you had to go so soon after we arrived,' Gigi said, speaking for them both. 'David arranged it that way, I suppose.'

'For no good reason, either,' I replied. 'I could have stayed on another day, but he decided I had to go back out into the cold.'

'Yes, of course,' George concurred sagely. 'Having the three of us there together, getting on so well, would have tipped the balance too far away from his control. He would have felt outnumbered, with both flanks exposed.'

'We told him how terrific we thought you were, after you'd gone,' Gigi went on. 'I'm sorry to say, he showed his true colours there too.'

My ears pricked up at this. It was a part of the story I hadn't heard before.

'How so?' I asked. 'What did he say?'

I caught a cautionary look passing to her from George.

'No, George, I think she has a right to know,' Gigi insisted, reading his expression. 'It was hateful then, but it can't hurt her now.'

George shrugged, conceding to her judgement on the matter. 'Well, if you think so, darling—'

'D'you know, it quite shocked me,' Gigi continued. 'It really did. We'd had that lovely supper together and next day, when you'd gone, George and I were extolling your virtues, saying how bright and funny we thought you were.'

Ah, my *levitas* undid me again, I thought to myself – but it wasn't that.

'Then George remarked that you'd obviously got a first-rate Oxbridge mind and David absolutely pounced on him. Do you know what he said, darling? I'm sure you'd never be able to guess—'

I bet I can, I thought, as my mind flashed back to my debriefing from David over our very first lunch. But I let Gigi finish her tale.

'He said, *Oh, come off it, George – she only got a 2:1!* It was so mean of him, so petty. *Can* you believe it?'

I said I could believe it, quite easily. And it was even pettier than she thought, because David knew very well that what I got was a second. You can only get a 2:1 – the equivalent – at Cambridge. George was a Cambridge man himself and had taken a first; in English, no less. So David hadn't just put me down in front of him, he'd deliberately switched terminology to make sure the point was driven home. I don't know why he couldn't simply concur with a simple *Yeah, she's great*, as another man in love might have. Pick a reason, any reason.

'You should consider writing a book about it,' George urged. 'One of your predecessors did, after all. Did you ever read *The Kennaway Papers?*'

I said I had. 'But wouldn't you say,' I asked George, 'that he was really only a little baby monster-in-the-making in those days? He comes off quite well in comparison to Kennaway. I'd be revealing much more about him than she did.'

'All the same,' George replied, not disagreeing, but quietly pressing, 'I think you should try.'

'Wouldn't he just throw his legal team at me?'

'He might. He wanted to injunct Susan Kennaway at first, but I talked him out of it. I would expect any successor of mine to do the same. You might think about it one day.'

With George's advice in my ears, I did start to write. Or rather, it was as Dennis Potter once put it in an interview, that you don't *start* to write, you simply find that you *are* writing. But knowing that George's advice was no longer in David's ears, I didn't attempt *The Dawson Papers*. Not at first. Instead, I tried turning the story into a novel, making the man a playwright. Then I tried a screenplay, making him a world-renowned espionage writer, but one who was German-born. But whichever way I wrote the story out, I knew I hadn't done it justice. I could never find an ending that really worked. In the exercise of trying to nail it down, however, I found that I actually did want to write. And then I had a really odd dream.

Ever since watching and falling in love with the BBC's monumental dramatisation of *The Forsyte Saga* when I was at school, I had adored the Galsworthy novels, re-reading them many times. Once, when I was staying in a country hotel in Ireland with another lover after David, I even made a start on a German edition of *Die Forsyte-Saga*, for want of finding anything more enticing on its reading-room shelves. Over the years I must have read the whole *roman-fleuve* more than a dozen times, and some individual books more often than that. So when I woke up one morning from a dream in which an entire page from the *Saga* appeared in front of me – not unlike the scroll that moves up the screen at the start of *Star Wars* – my initial thought was that I'd finally read it once too often.

The page of writing wouldn't leave me, so I wrote it down just as I remembered it from the dream and, out of idle curiosity, went looking to find it in the originals. But it wasn't there, though it seemed so authentic that I'd been certain it was. Which was when the penny dropped. Sequels to classic novels had been something of a vogue at that time, with the stories of *Gone with the Wind* and *Rebecca* both being successfully continued into new fiction. It was suddenly clear to me that I could write a sequel to the Forsyte books. I'd always thought that Galsworthy must have intended to produce more of the story himself, the mechanisms and themes were all in place, but had died before he could introduce another generation. I told Graham about my idea one night over supper and he was enthralled. He also threatened never to take me out for a meal again if I didn't do something about it, since it was, as he put it, *yet another of your great ideas.*

'*My* great ideas?'

'Yeah. See, you don't even hear yourself. You tell me at least a couple every time we sit down over a bottle together, then I never hear anything about them again. This one's the best so far.'

Not that I could recall any others, which was perhaps Graham's point, but I did have a particularly good feeling about this one.

'What should I do about it, then?' I asked him. I didn't particularly like the idea of just writing it 'on spec', but then I really didn't like the idea of not having another meal with Graham. 'What you need to do,' Graham decided, 'is write up an outline and send it straight to Uncle George. He'll know what to do with it.'

So that's what I did. George wrote straight back, calling my thirty-page proposal 'a very commercial project' – high praise from George – and suggesting a literary agent who might be interested. This happened to be Ed Victor, whom George had first taken on at Farquharson's years before, and who was now one of the top literary agents anywhere in the world. Ed saw me – I could never thank George enough for his referral – but told me straight up that he'd never liked Galsworthy, so wasn't going to take me on. He added, however, that he knew a man who did and probably would – his partner at the agency, Graham C. Greene. I saw him the following week. He was very enthusiastic about my proposal and did, in fact, take me on. A former publisher himself, he was the son of Hugh Carlton Greene, who had been Director-General at the Beeb when they made *The Forsyte Saga*, and the nephew and namesake of the 'senior spook-turned-novelist' of my discussions with David. Sometimes things just seem meant to happen.

Through my new agent's sterling offices, I received permission from the Galsworthy estate to proceed with my sequel and soon had a contract with a publisher.

'They paid you *how* much?!' my original Graham exclaimed when I told him the great news. 'And you haven't even written the bleeding thing yet! Well, *mazel tov*, honey. I always said you could do it.'

It was true. He always had.

It was getting towards the very end of 1991 and Graham was in the studio with David again, with one of the earlier titles, either *A Small Town in Germany* or *The Looking Glass War*, I don't recall which. He called me after the session, with the usual update.

'So how was the reading?' I asked.

'Word perfect, as per. Not that it oughtn't to be, it's not like he doesn't know the script. But I did think he was getting decidedly prissy on the esses this time. He sounded quite camp in places. Maybe he's gone the other way since he stopped nailing you.'

'Well,' I said. '*Après moi …*'

'Yeah, I dare say,' Graham remarked dryly. In all the years of knowing each other and working together, and even with me in my contact lenses, we'd still managed to keep it clean. 'But you know, honey – looking back – you got out at the right time.' It was only what Gigi had said, but Graham was about to add his own take. 'I mean, let's face it – you wouldn't want to be going down on him in his Bath chair in twenty years' time, would you?'

I heard a snorting chuckle at the other end of the line. Graham could never resist corpsing at his own gags.

'But he was very pleased for you when I told him about your book deal.'

'You didn't tell him how much, did you?'

'Of course I did. Why shouldn't I?'

Graham hadn't heard George and Gigi's tale from Cornwall, or the Great Man's reckoning of the sum of his own parts – I'd kept both stories from him. He didn't know what was likely to follow once he inadvertently offered that detail up for sacrifice.

'He actually said you'd done very well,' Graham went on. 'Though he did make a point to say you'd've got a *lot* bigger deal if you'd written the whole thing first.'

There it was. For whatever reason, David hadn't been able to be just plain nice about it; he had to offer the rebuke and send it back to me, soft-route via Graham.

I was suddenly cross with Graham for telling him and Graham was cross back with me for suggesting he'd betrayed a confidence, which in fairness he hadn't, and it led to our very first row. Even at this remove, David had managed to transfer some of the old poison. I began to see how he must never have liked my loving Graham so much, right from the start. *I thought you were his bird at first—*

After the Christmas holidays I knew I had to patch things up with Gooders. I loved him too dearly to let any third-party crap – especially from Cornwell with an e – drive a wedge between us. But he called me first, to say Happy New Year. He sounded all revved up about a multi-voice recording that he'd just booked for later in January. He'd forgotten all about the spat on the phone. That was so like him.

'We've got Baddeley and the gang coming back for the next *Winnie-the-Pooh*,' he told me cheerily. 'Four actors for the voice track at Woodsie's, then full sound effects and music mix for you to do afterwards at Silk Sound. It should be a blast. I'll call round at yours next week and give you all the gen. Get the Famous Grouse in. Love you, honey. *Byee—*'

Graham never did call round. The following week I had a horrible dream about him. I spotted him walking ahead of me in a crowded street – his silver hair was impossible to miss – and called out to him. I knew he'd heard me, but for some reason he didn't turn around and kept walking away. An overwhelming panic seized me then and I knew I had to *make* him hear me. I'd never had a dream come so alive before. I only knew one thing – *I had to make him stop*. I shouted and shouted till I was hoarse, but he just kept walking away from me until I lost sight of him in the crowd.

I woke immediately with a pounding head and sore throat. I must actually have been shouting out in my sleep. I concluded that our brief row on the phone had upset me more than I knew and decided that when he called round I'd have to explain more fully what had bugged me about what David said, to make sure he knew I didn't hold anything against him. I got up, put the kettle on for coffee and began my day.

An hour later my phone rang. It was a former colleague of Graham's, someone we both knew but who had no good reason to be calling me. As soon as I heard her voice I knew what she was going to say. The dream suddenly made the most terrible sense.

'Are you sitting down, Sue? I'm afraid I've got some bad news about Graham—'

He'd had a massive heart attack that morning. He had died an hour earlier, exactly when I'd woken up from my dream.

I'd never shed more tears before in my life than when I saw Graham's flower-laden casket carried past me down the aisle. The little country church in Wiltshire was packed for the service and even the churchyard seemed crowded as we all left afterwards. Everyone who'd ever known Graham – which seemed like half the world – had made a point of being there if they could. I saw Jeremy outside but he couldn't speak to me. A glance and a nod were the most he could manage as he hurriedly left with his friend John Chapman, the playwright. Jeremy had driven every fast car ever built, some of them at breakneck speed across Belgravia after a night at Annabel's with me holding tightly to my seat belt in the passenger seat. He'd once held the lap record for a saloon model at Brands Hatch. Yet he'd asked Chapman to take him to the funeral, because he was so distraught at Graham's death he couldn't trust himself behind the wheel. They'd been best friends for more than thirty years. I saw Frenchie in the churchyard too. He gave me the same smile as always and the look that said *I'm ahead of you,* which even then he was. I threw my arms round his neck and fell completely to pieces. Good old Frenchie, who hugged me hard and mopped me up and was dead himself all too soon afterwards.

David wasn't there, but sent me a letter, saying how, after Audrey, he felt Graham's loss most for me. When his next novel, *The Night Manager*, was published, he sent me a copy with a little note. I saw that he'd dedicated the book to Graham, which more than redeemed him for not attending the funeral.

When my own novel, *The Forsytes*, came out, I returned the favour and sent David a copy. He wrote back sweetly with his congratulations, calling it *the only first novel you will ever write*, though I somehow doubted it would find a place on any of his bookshelves. He had already given me a rare quote for the cover – *'What she doesn't know about the Forsytes nobody does'* – the compliment couched in a characteristic double negative, but a generous endorsement all the same. My book was also dedicated to Graham and it was my greatest regret that he wasn't around to see it published. He would have been so delighted. He was the one who had encouraged me to write the proposal and send it to George, which began my writing career. Before that he had taken me into the sound studios with him and given me my audiobook career. Before that his good offices got me into television as a programme researcher. Since the wintry Saturday lunchtime at San Frediano in Knightsbridge twelve years earlier, when Jeremy had introduced me to him on our third date – *You must meet my best friend, darling* – Graham had been my great friend too. In fact, he was the *sine qua non* of my adult life. He was also the first – and last – conduit between David and me. Now that he was gone, I fully expected never to have any further contact with the Great Man again.

A PERFECT SPY

*— you have all, I dare say, heard of the animal spirits, as how they are
transfused from father to son*

Laurence Sterne, *The Life & Opinions of Tristram Shandy, Gentleman*

There is so much to say about *A Perfect Spy*, the book I witnessed
David write, up close and in real time. But saying anything about
one of his books is to say something else about every other one of
them and then something again about the man who wrote them
all. Art and Life were always indivisible with him and it can all
appear somewhat of a conundrum, as I think David wanted his
creative processes to seem, as I believe he was to himself much of
the time. But there are trails that can be followed into the magical
forest of his fables, ways of decoding at least some of the secrets of
his own *Märchenland*.

The essential premise of this novel is that Magnus Pym is a
perfect spy because, as a double agent, he serves both sides of the
Cold War loyally. This is, of course, an impossibility in the real
world. A double agent might well end up betraying both opposing
sides, but it defies logic that he could remain loyal to both. But in
the world of le Carré the paradox stands. Just as Leamas is the spy
who comes in from the cold by doing the exact opposite, so Pym is
a perfect spy by being a perfect traitor. Magnus is indeed perfect in
his chosen role: perfect in his deceptions as he rises to prominence
in his field, perfect in his urbanity, his charm, his native capacity
for the work, perfect in his clever-clever dance of all-round betrayal
masquerading as unimpeachable loyalty, and latterly even perfect
in maintaining his cover in the face of growing suspicion until the
very last moment when he disappears, just before the game is up.

The hero's career closely mirrors that of Britain's infamous
traitor, Kim Philby, the Third Man in the Burgess–Maclean affair

and a member of the notorious Cambridge spy ring. It's the book's central parallel. Mary Pym believes she has the perfect marriage, with a husband who is attentive, thoughtful, dazzling, a constant lover and companion – until he disappears at the start of the novel. Until the stormy night her own equally uxorious husband suddenly disappeared in Beirut, Eleanor Philby believed exactly the same thing. Wind and rain lash the modest fictional seafront on the night of Pym's arrival at his safe house hideaway, just as they did the grand international waterfront on the night of Philby's departure. Pym's spook career ends in Vienna, where Philby's began. Philby disappeared shortly after the death of his father and Pym disappears shortly after the death of his. Mary Pym herself is a former 'Martha', recruited to the British secret services in her youth. So was Eleanor Philby, in America. Pym's Soviet recruiter and handler, Axel, is a 'charismatic cripple' beloved by the hero, just as Dieter was before him in *Call for the Dead* and as Sasha would be in *Absolute Friends* – as was Gábor Péter, a Hungarian refugee with a hunchback and limp, a high-ranking member of the Communist Party in pre-war Vienna and the man generally credited with being Kim Philby's recruiter. Axel and Sasha, written in more permissive times than Dieter, can also satisfy an endless line of women in bed, despite their disablement. This was supposed to be Gábor Péter's forte, too.

But this is David's autobiographical novel, surely? This is the book about his monstrous father, about his harrowing early life with Ronnie, living through all the conning and double-dealing that led to his becoming a spy. Where does Philby come into the story?

Well, Ronnie was always there in the books, right from the start. Something of his ruthlessness first appears in Scarr, the crooked garage owner in *Call for the Dead*. The phoney grandeur of his business dealings shows through in Old Hugo in *The Naïve and Sentimental Lover*. Jerry Westerby's father in *The Honourable*

Schoolboy is yet another sketch of him and his financial ruin plays into Charlie's childhood background in *The Little Drummer Girl*. Patricide was a persistent fantasy of David's in his youth, but it seemed he could never truly lay his father's ghost to rest in these minor characters, even after Ronnie died. Perhaps bringing him fully to life, as he finally did in *A Perfect Spy*, was the only way to kill him off properly. I trust I've shown some of the alchemy whereby David turned the base metal of his father's life into narrative gold, how Ronnie's rackety dishonest escapades and the apprenticeship in deceit he afforded his son became the backstory to the novel and the genesis of Pym the boy and youth.

But for the top story of Pym the man, the all-betraying double agent, David naturally needed to look elsewhere, beyond his own life. But with all his capacity for invention, why appropriate Philby? It took me a while to see it, to follow the grains of rice into the forest, but Philby too was always there. *He haunted my entire career*, David has said of him. In writing *A Perfect Spy*, he was drawing on all his considerable powers as a storyteller – as the premier fabulist of the Cold War – to slay not just one double-dealing monster, but two.

Tinker Tailor Soldier Spy is generally recognised as David's first exposition of the Philby *débâcle*. George Smiley is brought out of retirement to flush out the long-term Soviet double agent – the mole – whose treachery has turned the Service inside-out. The book was written in the seventies, but has its sentiments in the fifties, where so many of David's own sensibilities always seemed caught. Inevitably so, since it was the decade where it all went down. Burgess and Maclean defected in 1951 and Philby was immediately suspected of tipping them off. He might have been exposed then and there, but Kim – Harold Adrian Russell Philby, born in the Punjab and so nicknamed after Kipling's child spy – was by then too valuable to lose. He was the acknowledged golden boy of the Service and had risen to the heights in the secret world. Institutional denial instantly set in and saved him. If he could be suspected of being a 'double' then perhaps he was really a 'triple', insiders told themselves, and was playing the most dangerous loyalty game of all. (Graham Greene, who had known Philby during the war, believed this to his dying day.) So much belief had been invested in him by his British colleagues and masters that if Philby really was the Third Man then, as David said at that long-ago lunch, *there was no Tooth Fairy, no Santa Claus and Dumbo never could fly.* There was a mock trial, ostensibly to get at the truth, but where all the rules of interrogation were allowed to slide and the interrogator who was most likely to crack him – William Skardon, who had successfully cracked nuclear spy Klaus Fuchs and who himself was probably a partial model for Smiley – wasn't allowed a shot. By mid-decade, Philby was exonerated.

The fifties was also the period of David's early career as a spy and this is where I believe the fusion begins that would lead to their separate legends becoming so inescapably entwined. The two men never met. At least, David always claimed they didn't and Philby never counter-claimed that they did; beyond that, I suppose we can never know. But it is my own belief that David was always seen by his 'fathers' in the Service as their potential next 'golden boy', the most likely candidate among the new post-war genera-tion of recruits to be their future 'Kim', never more so than in those troubling, doubt-ridden years when Philby's own stellar career had begun to wobble. Nothing much less than that can account for David's own drastic, almost visceral response to Phil-by's sudden defection in '63 and the way he sought for years afterwards to mask its importance. First, there is the *Christ, it's Kim!* tale he told to Graham and me, when he took the coded wire that winter's night in Bonn. He probably told it many times and no doubt always, as then, as though it were a special confidence imparted to just a very few. But what did it really show? Young

Cornwell of the FO, the modest spook diplomat with a rising career, by chance the peripheral witness to a crucial moment of British espionage history – the 'Fall', as he would later term it, with Miltonic gravity, in *Tinker Tailor* – but only as other equally modest duty officers would have been when the same message came through to other spook stations at our embassies and consulates around the world. Though imparted as a secret specially shared, how David told the tale of this glancing intersection between himself and the double agent by whose level of treachery all other double agents would be measured seems to me now, paradoxically, to be a distancing device. David's true reaction was far more dramatic. The impact of the revelation hit him hard.

By that time he had already written two novels, effective and well-crafted but modest stories, one involving the world of espionage and both involving Smiley. There was nothing ground-breaking or earth-shattering about either; both if anything were rather old-fashioned. He had also written a partial story, not yet enough for a whole novel, centring around a mock trial to save a double agent. This was the first trace of Philby in his writing and who knows how long it would have lain dormant among his papers had David kept both careers going. But then Philby disappeared and David's third novel, *The Spy Who Came in from the Cold*, was the massive worldwide bestseller that rocketed him to fame and fortune. The mock trial becomes the very culmination of the story, as Leamas realises how he has been used as a pawn by his masters in the devilish plot to save the killer Mundt, a high-placed East German operative whom they've successfully 'turned' into a double to serve the West. Appropriating the key phrase of its title from Fleming's last bestseller – *The Spy Who Loved Me* – the novel was as far away from Bond's world of girls and gadgets and glamour as could be imagined. Overnight, it seemed, David had changed the landscape of espionage fiction forever. But the writer made no acknowledgement of the 'Philby factor' in his success. In fact, he took every care to cover its traces.

David claimed that he wrote *The Spy* in as little as five weeks, in a *state of fugue* in his shock at seeing the Berlin Wall go up, and knew when it was finished *that it was very good … that it worked.* This account of the novel's writing is nonsense, of course. The first barbed wire and breeze blocks that became the Wall went up in the summer of 1961 which, if we are to believe his account, would have meant that David inexplicably kept his 'very good' manu-script for a year and a half before handing it to Victor Gollancz early in 1963 for publication that autumn. But he gave this expla-nation of the book's genesis with a straight face for years afterwards and no one questioned its authenticity. By then he was John le Carré and authenticity was his special domain. (By the time inter-net searches offered historical verification at the click of a mouse, both the Berlin Wall and the Cold War were long gone and David had stopped offering this account.)

So no, the desperate and desperately creative 'fugue state' which birthed the real le Carré must surely have overcome him when he realised whose name was on the coded wire in Bonn. Find a word of six letters – first letter, P. It was the moment of absolute betrayal, when David must have understood that he was 'blown'. And in the very next moment, he must have understood that he always had been. Years later, David's first wife Ann, speaking more candidly than she was perhaps cleared to in a BBC documentary, would reveal that his bosses in MI6 'thought they really had someone special in David …'. Now, at a stroke on that dark night in West Germany in 1963, it was all gone. His life had changed forever. Suddenly, he no longer had a future in the Service. Given the long scope of Philby's treachery, he may not even have had a past. Or am I being fanciful here? Have I bought into the le Carré mythos myself? Perhaps David's Service career really was quite modest and his first wife was simply speaking on cue when she said that *'they thought they really had someone special'* in him. The comparison between Philby and himself may only ever have been an internal fantasy of David's own. But whether it was real or imagined was immaterial to the process of Art-Life fusion by which he turned himself into le Carré. Either way, David never forgave this betrayal and ever afterwards spoke of Philby in terms of loathing and contempt, flatly refusing the offer of a meeting with the old traitor when he was in Moscow years later, shortly before Philby's death.

But – but. What exactly *was* Philby's betrayal as David saw it? Was part it, for him, the fact that Kim had lost his nerve and defected? That he had finally surrendered the Great Double-Double Game? Was that really what made him the fallen idol? I think it may have been. Philby's absolute Miltonic Fall seems to have left David with a quantum of baffled leftover love – not unlike the young boy in Greene's story of the same name – that he needed to pour into all the fallen idols he would create in his books. Dieter was Smiley's discovery first, his own Caliban, before he crossed to the dark side. Even then, to Peter Guillam – forever David's younger-self character – Dieter stands as a heroic and all-but-epic figure of romantic manhood, more Byronic because of his crippled legs than despite them. Axel is never anything but an agent of the darkness that was Stalin's Communism, but Magnus loves him deeply, more than he loves his own father, more than he loves any woman. And Bill Haydon, the most Byronic figure of them all, is beloved by all to the end and suspected by none until the very last minute, not even by Smiley, whose own wife had loved Bill too. When Bill is unmasked as the traitor, poor Peter Guillam is so heart-stricken he sits at his desk the following morning with his tears pouring down onto his blotter.

This was all Philby's doing, I believe, the most despised figure in David's life, but the most beloved idol also, I would argue, before his Fall, and the *sine qua non* of the very best of the le Carré canon. Art and Life for David were always cut from one cloth and Kim Philby, no less than Ronnie, was inextricably part of the weave. Ronnie, as Rick Pym, is already securely laid to rest before *A Perfect Spy* opens, to be revivified only in the safe confines of flashback. But David still had to rid himself of the other haunting presence of his life. As the novel closes, in a final act of exorcism, Pym calmly wraps a towel around his head and, looking at his reflection in a mirror, puts a gun to his temple and dispassionately pulls the trigger. After internalising Philby in his hero, awarding him the 'quasi-homophonic' name Pym and fusing his own past life with the traitor's in his great autobiographical novel, David finally watches himself kill the turbaned Punjabi-born Kim.

THIRD TIME A BLESSING

March 1999

THEATRELAND

I had never dreamed about Graham before having that terrible vision of him walking away from me. It seemed to have been some sort of telepathy occurring at the moment of his death, though I can't say I really know. If it was that, then it must have come from the strength of the emotional bond that was between us. When I'd dreamed a new page of *The Forsyte Saga*, there was a strong emotional connection there too. As for David, I'd never had any dreams of him; not while we were together and not after we parted. I wasn't aware of harbouring any conscious desire to see him again, and if I had an unconscious one – well, I didn't know anything about it. But there must still have been a bond, because fourteen years after we parted for what I'd believed was the final time, I had the most vivid sleeping vision yet.

The living image of David's face appeared to me one night as I was sleeping. It approached suddenly out of the darkness and hovered lover-close above mine, with an expression of gentle anticipation in the eyes.

I think we should see ourselves again, he said softly.

I woke up immediately, to find I was standing shakily in the middle of the room. I had leaped right out of bed with the shock.

I thought about nothing else for the rest of the day. The last contact I'd had with David was the letter he sent to congratulate me on the publication of my Galsworthy sequel almost five years earlier. Since then – and without Graham as our go-between – nothing. But now this.

A few days later my friend Peter called. Peter knew all about my association with the Great Man and my failed attempts to write the story down. A writer himself, he well understood the process of grappling with a reluctant narrative. What he didn't know about was my dream. I hadn't mentioned it to him or to anyone else.

'Are you going to the le Carré lecture?' he asked straight away.

'Who's lecturing on le Carré?' I asked back.

'He is.'

I automatically rejected the information. David had always said he didn't care to 'press the flesh'.

'Can't be,' I said. 'He never did that kind of thing.'

'Well, he does now.'

He'd just read a piece in *The Times* about The Word, the new London literary festival, something I probably wouldn't have seen for myself. The lecture was billed as a headline event, to be held at the Peacock Theatre. It made me think that if Graham had been alive to see the article, he would have rung me too, but just to chuckle irreverently over the well-worn line about ageing actors: *Once a tour de force, now forced to tour!*

'I think you should go,' Peter suggested. 'It might give you an ending for your book. It might even be fun. You can sit in the back row and heckle.'

He gave me the details and left it at that.

The odd coincidence of the call following so quickly after my dream stayed in my mind overnight and in the morning I rang the ticket office. Not because I particularly wanted to go to the lecture, but rather to confirm, as much to Peter as to myself, that I couldn't go anyway. I was certain the event would be sold out – and it was.

There you go, I thought. Que sera.

But it didn't quite set my mind at rest. I was in the West End the next day and decided to go just a little bit out of my way to call in at the theatre box office. (The Peacock, in Portugal Street, belongs to the London School of Economics.) I still had no intention of going to the lecture, but told myself I needed to double-check that it wasn't possible. Graham might have commented that I had myself snowed.

'I expect the le Carré lecture's still sold out?' I asked the young guy sitting behind the ticket window reading a textbook. He looked like a postgrad from the LSE.

'Completely,' he answered without consulting his screen. He must have already fielded the same enquiry multiple times.

There you go, I thought again. Que sera, sera. Cue Doris Day.

Then something prompted him to set aside his book and check.

'How many tickets did you want, though?' he asked. 'Because there's just been one return ...'

I doubt I'd have heckled from the back row, but I didn't have the opportunity. The returned ticket was for Row 2. That would be close to the action in any theatre, but when I took my seat on the evening of the lecture I discovered there was no orchestra pit ahead of me, just the front row and then the stage. Had it been the venue for a Faces concert twenty-five years earlier, I should have been able to throw my knickers at Rod Stewart and probably not miss. Not that this situation was comparable (I didn't think), but I wasn't sure I wanted to see David quite that close up.

The auditorium was packed to the rafters, though with an oddly disparate crowd. There were the usual theatre-and-arts-going professionals – the Sunday supplement crowd – but also a lot of bright-eyed students from the university, many clutching notebooks and pens. And there was a surprisingly large contingent of less home-grown types; elderly men in heavy overcoats and elderly women in equally elderly furs. Émigrés, I realised; le Carré devotees who had come in from the cold of the Eastern Bloc and saw him as the literary Moses who had led them out. David had once told me how his fans from these countries would come up to him, with tears in their eyes, and produce dog-eared mimeograph copies of his novels that they'd passed around in the years when they were forbidden texts. I thought at the time that he was exaggerating for dramatic effect. Now I began to think he had played it down.

But it wasn't only they who had come to touch the hem. There was an air of communion across the whole auditorium, an almost evangelical emanation, filling the social and cultural spaces between the groups as thoroughly as smoke from an Odeon circle. I recognised it for what it was – the dangerous leaven of belief – and wasn't allowing myself to inhale. Fate may have delivered me the last seat in the house, but I was not of this congregation. I was determined to maintain my apostasy.

The house lights continued to stay up as we – the congregants and I – were kept waiting. That was the one thing that was familiar to me in this strange setting, the Great Man making us wait. The lone lectern standing centre stage made me recall seeing the one in his workroom at Tregiffian. The huge video screen behind it made me recall seeing Fleetwood Mac at the Empire Pool, Wembley. Somewhat belatedly, I began to realise that even when they finally cut the house lights I would still be visible in the overspill from the lights on the stage. Not only would I be seeing David close up – if he happened to look down and a little way across he might well also see *me*. I felt uncomfortably exposed. My only hope of cover, very literally, was from an evil-smelling man-mountain occupying the seat in front of me, the rolls of fat on the back of his neck sweating like gelignite, who was another reason I'd been trying not to inhale. What was I doing there? I wasn't a student or a Cold War émigré. I never read the Sunday supplements and I hadn't even read a le Carré for years. I was no longer a believer. I didn't belong in this place. I wondered whether I should just get up and leave.

Before I could come to a decision, a church-like hush fell over the auditorium as the house lights suddenly dimmed.

But even then – exactly as the first time, after that long wait at the studios – the moment of arrival still managed to take me unawares. I'd expected some sort of introduction; not a drum roll necessarily, but at least a few words from one of the festival organisers. But with no fanfare at all, the writer simply appeared stage left and headed towards the lectern.

There were two of him as he walked out; the real one on the stage and the much larger double on the screen. (The metaphors, it appeared, were still writing themselves.) The two versions walked warily in step, soft-footed, as if between the cover of the wings and the sanctuary of the lectern lay a no-man's land that might be mined. The two pairs of eyes swiftly scanned the audience; perhaps, as ever, the exits too. Three paces out and a measured smile to the middle stalls brought thunderous applause. Three more paces and a nod of acknowledgement to the dress circle raised further tumultuous clapping and cheers. Then the last few steps, almost to the lectern, and time for a close reconnaissance of the front rows—

On the screen, the eyes of the enlarged public face, aware of their many watchers, appeared momentarily distracted by something off-camera. But the real eyes – the private ones, visibly worn and older than when I last looked into them – had received a shock. Just perceptibly – against all training and lifelong practice – they gave the tiniest start.

David had seen me.

And when I *saw* him see me, something inside me lurched towards him in response. Only a second earlier it was an impossible notion, not to say an altogether preposterous one, but now – more than anyone present – I *belonged*. My long-lapsed belief had been miraculously reborn in that startled half-second look. Once again, even in an auditorium of a thousand people, I was David's audience of one.

As he took his place at the lectern, with applause continuing all around, I could barely process the enormity of the moment and the sudden certainty of what it meant. It was going to happen again. Every last wonderful, dreadful part of it was going to happen all over again.

FAMILIAR TERRITORY

For every man there comes at last a time of life when the woman who sets her seal upon his imagination has set her seal for good. He will travel over no more horizons … he will retire from those scenes.

Ford Madox Ford, *The Good Soldier*

I returned home that night in a state of – well, I had no idea. Shock? Disbelief? Exhilaration? Whatever it was, I was reeling from it. An extraordinary feeling of familiarity had flooded my senses as David walked out onto the stage. I *know* this man, I was thinking as I watched him; the way he carries himself when he walks, the way he tilts his head when he speaks, his every point of articulation when he makes the slightest gesture. And the voice. It was such an intense and immediate *knowing*.

I saw him at the book signing after the lecture. *Of course I did.* After that startling dream and Peter's uncanny phone call and the very last ticket seating me exactly where David couldn't fail to see me, it was clear we were meant to meet. I bought a copy of the latest le Carré hardback, *Single & Single,* from the display and waited in line.

'I know this lady!' David announced to his small army of female minders from Hodder, who were perplexed to see their VIP leave his signing table and advance towards me as I reached the head of the queue. Back at my flat over an hour later, I still had the sensation of being held hard in his big arms, could still feel the urgent press of him against me and the warm damp of the performance sweat that had soaked through the fabric of his suit.

Hello you, he whispered in my ear.

You were wonderful, I whispered back.

He led me back to the table, and as he signed my copy of his book I slipped him my address and phone number, like the tart I may well always have been, and, like the other tart that he always was too, he pocketed it in one deft move.

David's timing was always idiosyncratic, of his own crazy making, though he could never see that it was so, and was no different now. I could only wait for him to get in touch. But *would* he get in touch? Would he call? Would he write? It was the gorilla joke again. This time I had to remember to let him tell it.

I had only a few days to wait. The lecture was on the last Sunday in March. David rang the following Thursday morning. *Of course he did.* Thursday was 1 April, All Fools' Day, and we were two of them.

'My darling girl,' he began. He sounded breathless, as though I'd been the one calling and he'd been running to the phone. He was actually on Hampstead Heath, on his mobile. 'Phew,' he said, exhaling audibly. 'Is it really you? Are we still us?'

I was as dazed as he sounded. The utter strangeness of the situation came from the fact that it didn't feel strange at all. We hadn't spoken in almost fourteen years and yet the words simply flowed between us. The receptors must always have been there, just waiting to be reactivated.

'I'm sixty-seven, my darling,' he said soon into the call. 'Do you realise? In thirteen years, I'll be eighty.'

How funny. He had made exactly the same calculation about how he was going to be sixty-five when he was fifty-two. I didn't make the same remark about coming to see me on his concessionary bus pass. It wasn't funny now that he qualified for one.

'Don't worry about it, David,' I told him. 'You've aged very well. Really.'

'Thanks for saying so. But *you* don't age. I couldn't believe it was you sitting there, so close—'

'I didn't mean to sit so close,' I said quickly, in case he thought I'd planned it. 'I got the last ticket, the only return. I saw how you didn't believe it at first. You did the world's most covert double-take.'

'Well, you *did* give a chap a *turn*.'

He explained how he'd quickly had to hustle his group of guests out of the theatre after the lecture, drawing on all his powers of persuasion to urge them to go on ahead to the restaurant without him, to keep them clear of the signing. I pictured him doing it. Perhaps his performance sweat hadn't just come from the lecture.

'And yet at the same time I believed it utterly,' he went on. 'That you'd simply appeared. It seemed impossible *and* inevitable at a stroke.'

I told him about my dream and what he'd said in it.

'Well, that was very prescient of you. And of me, to appear in it. I think I like us being predestined. Perhaps we always were. Listen, my love, I have to be away for the next couple of weeks or so. They're making final decisions on the new movie, of *The Tailor of Panama*. John Madden thinks he wants to direct. Did you see his *Shakespeare in Love*? No? So I may have to go over to LA. There are other places too. Our timing's only as good as it ever was, I'm afraid. But when I get back, will you let me take you to the world's best ever lunch? Some establishment where I can spend an inordinate amount of money on you?'

That too was as good as it ever was. Going out on our first date those years ago was delicious, delightful and de-lovely, but only a way to delay the inevitable moment when we jumped each other's bones. It was no different now. The same intense vibe I'd felt at the signing transmitted itself over the phone. *All* the receptors were still there.

'I will,' I replied.

'How wonderful,' he said, and paused, letting it sink in. 'Meanwhile, I'll write to you. I haven't yet, but I will. You will be there, won't you? My darling girl.'

An envelope soon fell onto my doormat, the so-familiar blue handwriting delivering my name to me again, but for the first time at this particular address. I didn't open it immediately. At the theatre, I'd first walked around the block before going in – hesitating between the idea and the reality, to see if there was going to be a shadow. But there wasn't. Not then. There would be a shadow – this was David, who always brought his own – but not for a while.

The letter was as enchanting and loving and even chatty as any he had ever written to me. He called me his *most amazing and peerless Our Sue*, telling me again how astonishing it was to see me appear like an apparition in the theatre and how it had not only made his day, but his year so far, as well as all the years in between. He went into further detail about his schedule: first Amsterdam, then Kenya for his new novel, then LA for the movie, which was now going ahead. Ian McKellen had called him at midnight, apparently, and was mad keen to play Pendel, the tailor, though less keen on Madden. He didn't say why Amsterdam, so I guessed it was for an award; those were usually what he made least mention of. He said his plans were ridiculously fluid, but that he looked forward so much to seeing me again and would propose something as soon as he could see the mists clear.

He ended by underlining that I simply wasn't to go away.

His schedule had always been a maze of criss-crossing vapour trails, a many-partnered dance between competing loyalties and obligations, but now it seemed to demonstrate an extra measure of *Hast*. For all that he'd calculated how many years he had left until he was eighty, I imagined there was very likely a nearer number hanging over him. Ronnie died only months before his *seventieth* birthday, and though David had spent his life trying to escape his father that wasn't to say, even a quarter century after his death, he didn't still feel doomed by him. So I didn't expect to hear from him until the mists did clear, supposing with David they ever really could. But then, late one midweek morning towards the end of that month, he called unexpectedly from Hampstead Heath. Over the background chatter of birds and passers-by, his voice sounded unnaturally light, as it always did when something was wrong.

'Hullo, Sue. I just got back from Nairobi.'

He'd been there only a few days, after Amsterdam and LA. I wondered what had brought him back so soon.

'You remember my friend Yvette?' he asked in the same light tone.

I did, of course. His French former lover, whom he'd turned into a family friend, who he'd arranged for me to meet in the hope that she could explain him to me…

Quite suddenly, I knew why he'd called. I absolutely *knew* – not from any leap of guesswork, but from my heart. It was in his voice. He was even going to tell me while he was standing on the Heath perhaps staring out at the distant view of London, just like the first time. Something as singular and dreadful as that had somehow happened all over again, sixteen years later, even in the very same month.

I waited for the old echo, which came as he told me.

'She's dead.'

Boom—

'She went to Albania to help the refugees from Kosovo,' he continued in that same passive tone, 'and died in a car crash with three other people. On Sunday. It was raining heavily and their vehicle went over a ravine.'

Sunday had been the eighteenth. It didn't seem possible, but Yvette hadn't just died sixteen years to the month that Janet had been killed – she had died sixteen years to the very day.

I began to offer my condolences, but David spoke over me.

'Listen,' he said, 'will you have lunch with me tomorrow?'

I said of course I would.

'Good,' he said, cutting me off again. 'I'll call you then.'

He rang off.

Next morning he rang first thing to check where best to take me for lunch.

'Would a girl like to go somewhere for some caviar?' he asked.

'Why don't you bring some round?' I suggested.

'I'll be there at twelve.'

I spent all morning getting ready. I showered, then washed my hair again with a different shampoo. I tried on three or four outfits. I changed my lipstick twice. This was ridiculous. Why was I so nervous? It wasn't a new lover who would be arriving at my flat, it was David. *My* David, coming to see *his* Sue. We already knew each other inside out. He wouldn't have cared if I greeted him wearing a burlap sack or, indeed, wearing nothing at all. As I almost finished closing the zip on a fifth and final combo, just a soft blouse and skirt, but with lace-topped hold-up stockings – *and the rest* – underneath, the intercom buzzer sounded. He was there, a quarter of an hour early. Despite his face appearing on the little monochrome screen of the video entry panel, I couldn't believe it. I couldn't believe any of it.

'I'm here,' he said. 'Where do I go to find you?'

'Top floor,' I told him.

I didn't add that it was five flights up; he'd managed seven quite readily at John Wood. The flat was in a grand old Victorian mansion block in North Kensington that had nowhere to install a lift, but the huge roof terrace and the view more than compensated for the hike up the stairs. I gave myself another check in a full-length mirror, slipped on an earlier choice of shoes and retouched my lipstick. By the time I opened the front door he was approaching along the terrace, laden with bags and flowers. He let everything tumble to the ground as I rushed out to wrap myself around him. It was two or three wordless minutes before we let go and went inside.

David promptly took off his suit jacket and hung it on the back of a dining chair, then laid out what he'd brought with him on the kitchen counter, after first putting the flowers – an armful of freesias, which he'd remembered I liked – into the sink, running some water for them and stowing a bottle of vodka in the freezer. Thirty-five seconds inside the flat and it was already as if he lived there. Then he embraced me and kissed me again. I was mildly flustered when his hand went straight to the three inches of still-open zipper below the closed back button on the waistband of my skirt, which for all my double- and treble-checking I'd still managed to overlook.

'You were helping a chap out,' he said sweetly, closing the zip.

Keeping his hand on the small of my back, he showed me what he'd brought. In addition to the Stolichnaya now in the freezer, there was a perfectly chilled bottle of Krug, three types of gourmet cheese, some water biscuits, a baguette, a tin of *paté de foie gras aux truffes*, a tin of caviar and – for a reason known only to himself – a large pork pie.

'I didn't know what a girl likes to eat nowadays,' he explained, opening the champagne as I found a pair of glass flutes.

We sat on the sofa, or rather, he sat and I lay, *maja*-not-yet-*desnuda* style, with my legs across his lap. I held both glasses while David poured and we took in the new-old look of ourselves. He set the bottle aside, but before taking his glass from me he undid his shirt cuff and rolled back his sleeve. He drew back the hem of my skirt and laid the underside of his forearm against my thigh.

'Look,' he said. 'Our skin's still the same. Still the same grain, cut from the same bale.'

He restored my skirt to its former position, primly straightening the hem closer to my knees, as though it were altogether too soon for him to have seen the tops of my stockings. Then he took his glass from me, took a first mouthful of champagne and passed it back to me in a tender, careful kiss.

Plus ça change … Except that when he tried the same move again, we weren't quite co-ordinated and some of his next mouthful of Krug went on my hair.

'My darling—' he said, slipstreaming smoothly into a perfect Noël Coward impersonation. 'Your hair smells of Krug. Strange, since we only drink Dom Pérignon …'

But not everything was quite *la même chose*. David's own hair, which previously had been sandy and only speckled with grey, was fully grey now, pure white in places. His face didn't look too much older overall, but was every year older and then some around his eyes. It was the strain of all that time spent scanning entrances and exits, I seemed to know. The constant vigilance, both inside and outside of his own head, had created a network of permanent creases as his gaze narrowed too many times ever to relax. Whatever the source of that drive in him, the thing that sustained his perpetual surveillance, it was still what made David run.

His mouth had altered a little bit. His top lip seemed to have drawn back, giving the appearance of a slight fixed smile. But it wasn't a smile of contentment, I seemed to know that too, more a rictus of resignation, from having to sip too frequently from the poisoned chalice in a life that still wasn't how he wanted it to be. After all the Round Table references he had put into his earlier books – especially in *Tinker Tailor*, with Merlin, Witchcraft and the Lancelot and Guinevere subplot of Bill and Ann – he was almost Arthurian himself now. The questing knight, still strong, still valiant, but ageing; weary from seeking his elusive, perhaps illusory, personal grail and knowing his time to find it, if he ever could, was running out.

Halfway through the Krug we took our glasses to the bedroom.

'You're a phenomenon,' he told me as we undressed. 'You really *don't* age. There's not a line on you and you still have the breasts of a seventeen-year-old. I can't believe it – you're just a wondrous impossibility. You always were.'

David's admiration sang in my ears. It always did.

'I've become quite fat, as you can see,' he added. 'But I'm determined to lose it now, for a girl.'

He overstated the case, but he'd definitely put on weight. In fact, I thought he'd looked quite Smiley-ish at the lecture, especially when he put on a pair of heavy-rimmed glasses to read from his notes. Or even a little Philby-like, from that old video. Art and Life – Life and Art. With David, there was never a clean sheet of A4 space between the two.

I reassured him that he wasn't fat. 'You've just got a belly on you, that's all.' I ran my hand across it, then down. 'I don't mind a bit, except it rather spoils the view—'

Here was something else that hadn't changed. All my nerves that morning had disappeared the moment I saw David walking towards me and they didn't return now. I *knew* this man and he knew *me*. Our appetite for one another was as insatiable as ever, perhaps even more so now it was unleashed to take its fill after a fourteen-year famine.

Afterwards we lay in bed just looking at each other, David framing my hair around my face with his feather-soft touch. Then tears began to flow from his eyes, though his face remained composed.

'No one will ever love you as I do,' he said solemnly. 'That's my vanity.'

I made no reply, just kissed his tears. He had spoken for both of us.

We made a picnic for ourselves on the living-room rug.

'I remembered you liked big balls,' David remarked with a chuckle as we dug into the golden caviar. The conversation went on happily while we ate and drank and looked at each other some more, but then ebbed strangely. It wasn't awkwardness that was the bar to fluency, it was something else. My new-old renewed-restored lover quickly discerned what it was.

'We need new terms,' he declared.

'Agreed,' I seconded. 'What do you suggest?'

'I think we should just make it easy on ourselves. No more big promises. No more great escapes. Just see ourselves and enjoy the good stuff and get away when we can.'

Again, how funny. That was all I'd ever wanted right from the start, the time-honoured married-man-and-mistress template so exemplified by George and Gigi. It was David who wouldn't take the easy route, who made the ever-escalating promises and needed the ever-greater escapes. Did this mean he'd changed? Had he finally learned to stop overloading and over-complicating everything? I told him it sounded like a good way forward; a little late in the day, I didn't add, but better than never.

'But what about a girl? What are her terms? What does she want out of this?'

Hmm. He had just offered my preferred terms as his own, as though I'd been the one originally wanting something else. It took me a moment to think of an additional clause to the new compact. Then the exact thing came to me. David raised his eyebrows expectantly.

'No more talk about your family.'

Meaning; no more minutely parsed critiques of his marriage, no more stories about his endless sons and how *wonderful* they were and, presumably by now, how wonderful *their* families were too. No more tales at all from the domestic areas of his life, in which I had and wanted no part. Meaning also; no more of the inevitable corollary, the lamentations over how he didn't need all their woes and worries loaded on to him, or even the good things with them very much, and how it all took time away from his writing. I'd never wanted to know any of it and it only ate into our time together to have him tell me about it. But I didn't elaborate, I let my statement stand.

'All right,' he said after a moment. 'Absolutely.'

He nodded affirmatively, rather as though he were committing one further item to memory in an advanced round of 'I-packed-my-bag'.

Now we had terms, we could schmooze properly. The Krug was finished, but David retrieved the Stoly from the freezer and picked up two fresh glasses from a drinks tray on the sideboard by the dining table on his way back. He was my room-mate once again and we settled back on the sofa, resuming our former positions, to talk.

He told me about his new book that was 'just on the go'. It was set in Africa, hence the trip to Nairobi, where he intended to return shortly. He was tackling Big Pharma – the multi-national pharmaceutical companies – and how they were unloading bad drugs on patients there, using them as unwitting guinea-pigs for clinical trials. 'My heroine discovers what's happening,' he explained. 'She's killed because of it at the start of the book and her husband sets out to track down her murderers. It's called *The Mad Gardener*,' he concluded happily.

He didn't talk about Yvette and I had the sense that he wanted to keep his thoughts and feelings about her at bay, at least for the duration of his visit to me. We talked instead about our loves in the intervening years. David didn't seem to have had too many. One that was quite fun and lasted a little bit, with a well-regarded photo-journalist who'd approached him at a publicity event in Washington.

'"Is Mrs Cornwell here for a photograph," she asks enthusiastically, looking all around. "Is Mrs Cornwell here?"' David was smiling as he recalled the scene, acting out her gestures with her camera. 'It was quite a good stunt,' he said admiringly, 'establishing I was on my own. I liked that. We used to talk a lot on the phone—' He drank some vodka from the glass he held cradled to his chest, his other hand resting on my thigh. Then the smile slipped away. 'Jane handles all the household accounts now that she doesn't have Nick to see to anymore. She came to me with a phone bill,' he went on without affect, the way he always spoke about his wife to me. '"I think BT have made a mistake," she said. "We don't know anyone with this number, do we?" It was the photo-journalist's, of course. I looked at her and replied, "I don't think I am accountable to you for the phone calls I make." Well, it was frosty for a few days.'

He took another sip of vodka and his face opened again, while his hand closed more tightly on my thigh.

'But it wasn't a great love, for either of us. The last time we met up, nothing happened – we just agreed to lie in bed together and talk.'

There were some other minor encounters, he added, only a few and all *en passant*.

'But nothing like us,' he concluded. 'No one like Our Sue.'

He paused to drain his glass, then grew quite solemn again.

'I said you were my last love and I meant it. I knew it, you see, even then. I'm deathly sure of it now.'

I believed him without question. The two women who had been his most significant loves before me had now both died, each in the most terrible and sudden of circumstances and one just before we began our relationship *each time*. It wasn't anything even he could write. I could feel David consciously summoning the last of his belief in love to seize this un-looked-for second chance with me.

He set his glass down and took my hand in an oddly chaste gesture.

'Were there any writers amongst yours?' he asked.

No, I told him, and he looked relieved. I didn't say that I'd shared Jeremy's Belgravia mews house for a period only a couple of years back. Cohabiting quite happily and platonically with an ex would have taken far too much explaining for David, who had only ever cohabited platonically with his wives, though never, I think, quite happily. My guess was that he meant *his* kind of writer. He was worried there'd been a successor *of rank.*

I listed my intervening lovers for him by occupation, giving no names: one TV guy (Peter), one Old Etonian City headhunter, and the rest were actors (one of whom, I also omitted to tell him, wrote very good plays for stage and screen). They were all lovely men. (There'd also been one diagnosable psychopath, a mercifully brief rebound relationship I'd had immediately after leaving David, but I didn't want to sully the moment, so didn't mention him at all.)

And there was a mad weekend I'd spent with a reader at the Magic Hotel in Hollywood. David laughed when I told him how 'the Hamlet of his generation' had enacted scenes from his recently failed second marriage, playing all the parts in an impromptu one-man show in his hotel room while completely naked. The actor claimed he'd never told anyone those things before, so I suppose I was briefly his audience of one, too. I mentioned that he'd later published a novel with all the same scenes in it.

'I got a mention in it as "a willowy blonde",' I said, 'though only to say that he never went for that type. I think he meant me, anyway.'

Finally, I gave David one name. A big movie star whose go-to girl in London I'd been for several years. I felt I had to name him since he unquestionably had rank.

'Really?' he said in surprise. 'Well – all I can say is that you have very good taste. And so, of course, does he.'

He considered something for a moment.

'Tell me, my darling, does he know about me?'

Yes, I said; in the same way that he and I were talking now. 'Why? Do you mind?'

'No. Not a bit. But it explains something. I encountered him not so long ago in LA, in the elevator of my hotel. I introduced

269

myself and said how much I admired his work and he gave me this frozen look. He was perfectly courteous, but he got out at the next available floor. I wonder now whether he was afraid I was going to ask him to compare notes!'

I pictured the scene and was sorry for my lovely movie star's discomfort. He was such a le Carré fan too. Perhaps his wife was with him in the lift, which might have accounted for his deer-in-headlights response. But David didn't say and the world's worst investigative reporter didn't ask. I was just exceptionally pleased to learn that something from *my* life had slipped through the impenetrable Cornwell surveillance net into *his*.

'Do you still see Gigi?' he asked next. He hadn't mentioned George's retirement or the fall-out from it. He probably wanted to know if I knew about it from her, which of course I did and which he would assume I did once he established we'd kept in touch. I was familiar with David's interrogation technique this time around.

'Yes, I do,' I replied. 'I'm going down to visit her in her weekend cottage in a couple of weeks.'

'I expect she's still vivacious?'

'She is.'

'I always mistrusted that in her. But if you're friends—'

That was rather sly of him, I thought. Since George and he were no longer on terms, I suppose he felt free to take the shot. (He'd felt free to take a shot at me with them, after all, after I left Tregiffian that first time.) But I didn't let it bother me. I knew how David was, how he could be, and none of it was going to bother me this time around. No doubt Graham would have told me one last time that I had myself snowed.

'I don't think we'll miss the St John's Wood flat, do you?' he asked, casting ahead. He already looked as if he lived here with me now. 'I sold it to Willie Shawcross.'

'Yes,' I said. 'I know.'

'*Do* you? That's very clever of you, then. How did you find out?'

The apprehension on his face indicated he was trying to guess how I'd come by that piece of information prior to his disclosing it. I offered a sphinx-like smile but no explanation. It was more therapeutic to let him sweat through all the paranoid possibilities than reveal the mundane truth, which was that I'd phoned the flat a couple of months after we'd last seen each other there, to see if he was still using it as an escape hatch from his marriage. It was in one of those moments of burning post-break-up curiosity and I'd intended to hang up once I heard him answer. (This was still before caller ID, but did I honestly think he wouldn't have known it was me?) But no one picked up. Instead, the out-going message on an answering machine announced – *This is William Shawcross. Please leave a message.*

'I sold it with all the furniture, by the way,' David said finally, when he saw he wasn't getting the story out of me. 'And with that naked picture of you still hanging over the bed.'

David was still averse to taking showers and so we took a bath together before he left, lest he transfer evidence of *that delicious light scent you still wear* back to Hampstead. I asked him if he ever wore cologne himself; he'd just made me realise I'd never noticed any on him. He told me no, he didn't, and I asked him why not. Wouldn't it have been a useful layer of cover for tell-tale traces of perfume? But he only repeated that he didn't use cologne, confirming that even if I *did* think to ask a follow-up question, I seldom received an answer. But in any case, I'd been coming at the subject the wrong way. He would never have *needed* a scent of his own for *domestic* cover. After his disastrous relationship with Susan Kennaway during his first marriage – possibly as a result of it – David only ever had girlfriends *abroad*. Ours was the only other love affair he ever conducted on home turf – the first since 1965.

'I think we need a trip together sometime soon, don't you?' he said from the tap end as we bathed. 'Switzerland, I think. How does Geneva sound to a girl? That would be fun, wouldn't it?'

Switzerland. Where we had taken our very first clandestine trip together and so many others afterwards. Where David always looked so handsome and relaxed and at one with himself and his surroundings. Where his private company and his head man had been based for so many years and where he still kept a chalet, 'his place', in the mountains. Where he'd first escaped from England to become a fledgling spook. If we were going to have trips to Switzerland again then of course we wouldn't miss the St John's Wood flat. That entire country was David's safe house.

I said Geneva sounded terrific – especially, I thought privately, because he hadn't called it a 'second honeymoon'. I was relieved, too, that he didn't suggest Cornwall. I never wanted to go down to Tregiffian again, though I suspected he wasn't going to ask.

'Excellent!' he said happily. 'I'll make some plans and let you know.'

Before he went, he asked to see my copy of *Single & Single*. He gave the title one of his little twists, calling it *Sniggle & Sniggle*. He opened it at the title page, took a pen from inside his jacket and swiftly added something to his signature and date, which was all he'd managed to produce after our hot clinch at the signing. He snapped the cover shut, set the book down on the table, kissed me as urgently as ever and left.

I opened a front window and leaned out. After a few moments I saw him cross from the building and begin to walk up the street towards the main road for a taxi. I knew he'd look back. That was why he'd crossed the road, so that he could.

When he saw me at the high window, he paused to twinkle up a little wave. I'd dressed again after our bath, and before he turned away, in a sudden recollection of our seeing *Silkwood* together, I opened my blouse and flashed one of my breasts at him in reply. It's what Meryl Streep does to Kurt Russell, before she gets into her vehicle and drives off at the end of the film. With a little more reflection, given what had just happened to Yvette, I wouldn't have risked reminding him of a film in which the crusading heroine meets a vehicular death, though it was perhaps what had put it in my mind. But he only saw the gesture for what it was, a spontaneous invitation to come back soon, and blew a kiss up to me in reply. Then I went to see what he'd written in the book.

David had drawn a line from his signature to the nearest bit of space on the title page to record a personal literary addendum.

John le Carré ———— was born again soon after this predestined encounter, following fourteen years solitary, loyally served.

He surprised me ten minutes later with a phone call from the taxi to tell me how much he loved me – 'The technology's moved on since we originally did this,' he noted – and then again later, to say the same thing from Hampstead Heath.

I didn't hear from David again until he rang late morning the following Wednesday.

'I just got back last night,' he said, and drew a great breath. Back from Yvette's funeral, he meant, held at her farmhouse in southern France. He had taken Jane, he said, and confessed to me how he had simply wept throughout the whole thing. He ended the brief call saying, 'I adore you. Your body is exactly as I remember it. So beautiful. I'll call you tomorrow with some proposals.'

But he didn't call the next day. Instead, a letter arrived the day after that, the last day of April. It had two little faces drawn on the envelope, though only one of them was a smiley. The other looked more like its elderly namesake. I'd forgotten how he used to do that with his envelopes, signalling the tone of their contents with a variety of cartoon expressions on little round faces, though usually only one at a time. Seeing the un-smiley one now, I began to wish I'd added a second condition to my side of our new terms – <u>No more bloody letters</u>.

Inside the envelope the smiling face was repeated on what he called letter one, the frown face on letter two. Both parts were written on yellow copy paper instead of his usual white A4.

I was still his darling Sue, it seemed, and what he wrote on all of the first page and most of the second was a memorialisation of our most recent sexual encounter that was so extraordinarily graphic I was almost shocked to read it. But after that he began to cast ahead. We needed a vision that was large enough to allow for our shared life and our separate ones, something that enabled us to feel happy and lucky and free, never caged. This, I already sensed, was his own lifelong fear of a new escape route just leading him to another confinement. He went on to tell me that he loved me and that he had always loved me, but then reminded me how, towards the end of our last relationship, I had thrown some things back at him. He quoted my saying *never do it to anybody else*, meaning, never indulge the worst of himself in another relationship, as he had with me. (I might add that I believe he never did. As his last love, which he always insisted I was, I should have known it was axiomatic that there wouldn't *be* anyone else of consequence for him to do it *to*. From this distance, I can see how the hurt he inflicted was simply concomitant to his letting me so far into his life that he couldn't protect me from the worst of himself. As he told me right from the start in Greece, *It's a rocky path you've chosen, you can't know …*) He went on in the letter to make the nicely ironic point that now 'anybody else' was me. But he acknowledged that we were both possibly wiser and would probably know better.

He claimed to be *very* old, with what he called 'injury time' fast approaching. There were all his commitments – the new book, the movies of old ones, travelling everywhere for everything, including one trip to Panama already made that year with the original director on *The Tailor*, and a second likely to be required now a new director, John Boorman, had been brought in. Of the rapidly diminishing time he felt he had left to him, he feared there would be very little free to spend on us. He wanted to get ahead of the disappointment he saw coming.

He seemed also to be saying, elliptically as ever, that he no longer aimed to get out of what he'd previously called the slammer of his domestic life. From what he wrote, if it had ever been a prison before, it now seemed to be a practical try-out for what would shortly become Guantanamo Bay. He described himself as living in a closely monitored enclave under what seemed to be quasi-carceral conditions, since he appeared to have no friends and neither did Jane, who he claimed never left the house. I had thought our new terms made it clear that I didn't want him to do anything he didn't want to do – 'just make it easy on ourselves', as we'd agreed – but his present frame of mind wouldn't permit that take-it-as-it-comes approach any traction.

He told me again how he'd wept at Yvette's funeral, seeing traces of their old love everywhere in her house and with everyone taking him aside to commiserate with him. But he managed to end the long first section of the letter with something closer to hope: he claimed that love was what would rescue it all and that having gained back in his life what he had lost any hope of recapturing was nothing short of an unimagined blessing. The shorter second section indulged his darkest thoughts and gave further black moments from the funeral, most despairingly when Yvette's closest friends and even her daughter had each told him privately that he was the love of her life.

He ended by saying that he'd be away over the weekend and would ring me once he returned. He didn't explicitly ask me to write back, but said he would call in at Hampstead Post Office before he rang again.

This wasn't unfamiliar territory. After recent events, David appeared to be on the wrong side of his head again. As it happened, I understood better than he knew how he was feeling about Yvette. A former lover and close friend of mine – the big TV exec I'd surrendered to be with David the first time – had died only four months earlier, following eight weeks in intensive care across two hospitals after catastrophic aortic-valve failure. I'd sat next to his bed in the final ICU with my arms around him as he died. He was only sixty-one, the same age as Yvette. There had been a memorial 'do' for him at BAFTA earlier that month, where Barry Took, Bill Cotton and other old friends of his from the Beeb each told me that I'd been – yes – the love of his life. So we'd both recently experienced these terrible too-soon losses and other people's too-well-meaning commiserations. Yet now there was this unexpected second chance for ourselves, this blessing, as he wrote. But so soon after readily seizing both it and me with his two great hands, David was claiming he couldn't see a way to run with the heaven-sent opportunity.

It may seem obvious that it was Yvette's death which had put him into such a tailspin. But I don't believe it was, at least not directly. It may sound brutal, but I'd come to understand that David almost liked to have a quotient of death around him. I don't for a moment mean that he wished it to happen to anyone, least of all to anyone he loved, or that he didn't grieve when it did – only that, should it happen, it was something he could roll with quite comfortably. I think the ultimate loss rendered by death served to validate his belief in the other losses he made himself have in his life – freedom and lasting love, to name only two.

So, as my thesis goes, it wasn't Yvette's death which had so confounded him. It was a different loss altogether, of something he valued above all else, something which, in his whole life, he hadn't believed he would *ever* lose – namely, his *nerve*. It was when he said he'd taken Jane to the funeral that something clicked in my head and made me see it, as though my internal camera had suddenly pulled the focus on the scene David was framing up till then.

I will try and show it here, but the exposition – peeling back the layers – will take a page or two.

David had previously told me that he'd never confessed the affair with Yvette to his wife. The one time I'd asked him what he would do if Jane found out about *us*, he answered flatly, *I'd deny you – I'd deny you utterly*. It was what he'd done when she actually did confront him about Janet Stevens. It was the First Rule of Spy Club: DENY EVERYTHING. All spooks knew it. Until his Fall, Philby was the all-time exemplar. Second Rule of Spy Club was: DENY. EVERYTHING. ALWAYS. Meaning that even two years after Yvette's death, after dedicating *The Constant Gardener* to her and revealing how her tireless aid work had helped inspire the novel, David would still be claiming she was only ever a friend, so thoroughly persuading one interviewer that she wrote how he had only just remarried and started a new family when he met her in '74. As though that confirmed his fidelity! *Sixteen* years after her death, David still barred his biographer from writing about their true relationship. (With the exception of Susan Kennaway, whose story was already in the public sphere, Sisman couldn't write about *any* of his subject's 'other women', including me. More on that later.)

But David had 'turned' Yvette from lover to friend fairly soon into their affair. He had tried to do the same with me, if you recall, though the record shows that a platonic friendship would have been impossible to sustain in our case. Yvette, however, agreed to take the deal. Better to have David in her life somehow, she must have thought, than not at all. Why he pressed for this conversion with each of us goes, I believe, to the notion of imprisonment and escape that had been indelibly imprinted on him, so deeply and from so far back as to be part of the fabric of his soul. His first marriage was an escape from a life of psychological and emotional imprisonment with his father; his second marriage was an escape from the psychological and emotional imprisonment of the first, and then the second marriage – the escape from which he attempted once with me, but never again – finally became Gitmo. David felt constantly that he wasn't free, yet couldn't see it was all his own doing in submitting to his inner demons and letting them run him. He once declared to me that he was *a born architect of slammers*, but even that was an understatement. David carried his own personal slammer around with him, like a snail with its shell on its back. Graham said exactly this in his cut-to-the-chase way on that gloomy day at Wimbledon, after he'd heard all my rationalisations about David's behaviour: *Nah – he's got you snowed. If he's miserable in his marriage it's because he likes it that way – for some miserable reason in himself.* I hadn't liked hearing it at the time, but Graham was right. He so often was. I rather think now that David had himself snowed most of all.

So it was for this reason, I believe, that he so quickly turned Yvette from a lover into a friend – *We'll always have Phnom Penh* – to block his own escape route from leading him to further incarceration. But here's the bigger question: why go the extra step and turn her into a *family* friend?

It was for cover. All his instinct, training and lifelong practice necessitated it. Cover for David, as for any spy, was vital. Without cover there was no deniability. Without deniability he would risk exposure. He could be 'blown'. What better way to dispel any doubts his wife may have harboured about his fidelity, therefore, than to bring the woman he'd betrayed her with into the family fold? To have both women smile and laugh together while he buttled around them – *Fancy a snoot?* – or played *mein Host* so charmingly in restaurants? It was all for cover, of course.

This is the extra quality that made David who he was, that made him *le Carré*. He needed the experience of acting out his fiction for himself so that he could convince other people it was living fact. Because if he could convince others of it, then *it must be true*. I came to understand that this was what all the research trips were really about. Capturing the exact way the sun slipped behind the mountains at a certain location, or the precise flavours of any distant purlieus, was never his primary motivation. Nor was his lead character truly his 'secret sharer', the expression he stole from Conrad and made his own. This commonly held misunderstanding of his creative method has it entirely backwards – as should be clear from the fact that David so often explained it that way himself. *If you're going south, tell them north.* David's secret sharer was always and only *himself.* He needed a lead character for cover, as an adopted persona, a new skin, in order to live through him – through her, once, with Charlie – while he was out in the field. He no longer had the original spook field he was trained for – born for, even – with its high buzz of operational excitement and peril. Philby's personal betrayal – as I believe David always saw his defection, spoiling forever his chance for adventures in the double-double game – had seen to that. So he recreated the tensions, the daring, the deceptions in his fiction and in his personal life.

When David told me he was going out for a walk in Plomari and took a day-old newspaper with him, he transformed his voice and manner to become his character. It was extraordinary to see the whole scene appear in *A Perfect Spy.* But it was a tortuous piece of pretence if you parse it down to its constituent parts. The former real-life spy and current premier spy novelist deceives his secret girl-friend, with whom he is already deceiving his wife, in order to play out a fictional scene wherein his spy hero deceives his wife to meet the secret contact with whom he is deceiving his masters in the Secret Intelligence Service. He did all that just to ginger up the scene. But he *needed* to do it – to create the edge in the experience so that he could recreate it in his writing. I wonder now what would have happened if I'd seen what he was doing and simply asked, *Are you being Pym?* I can't really imagine.

There was a later point too, in our first relationship, when he suggested I join him on research trips to meet people from his father's life with us *both* behaving as though we shared nothing but a work relationship. It was a test of my capacity to take his direction, no doubt a replaying of some erstwhile trick with his Joes, and I declined. Even if I'd wanted to join him in the exercise, there would have been no point in attempting it. His most cloistered maiden aunt wouldn't have been fooled into thinking our relationship was platonic, let alone Ronnie's old lags. But the sheer bravura of David's performance in these deceptions presented a kind of challenge to those who witnessed them. I'd lived through a couple of them myself, after all. It was all about instilling belief, making his fiction, whether lived or written, seem so authentic that it was accepted as the truth – as much in his lies on the phone to his wife while I was in the hotel bed beside him as in his worldwide bestsellers. He had it from Ronnie, who made so many believe in his cons, and from his pulpit-thumping, lay-preaching family on both sides when he was growing up. He was trained to it for years as a spy.

When David channelled all his considerable conjuring powers into *making* people believe him, most were happy to let him pull off the trick, to have him suspend their disbelief. For the longest time, I was one of them. And even if, sometimes, the belief he wanted seemed to strain credulity, who was going to call him out? He was *John le Carré*, for God's sake. Which of us, among the chosen few ever admitted to his world on any level, would want to be the equivalent of the lone kid in the *Peter Pan* audience who refuses to clap to keep Tinkerbell alive? Compelling performance achieved cover and David's instinct for cover overrode all other considerations. Performative control of the narrative in his external life was what took the pressure off his inner dramas, upon which he never succeeded in bringing down the curtain in his head. Had he ever been forced to confess – about something of consequence or of no significance at all – it would have been the end of the entire show.

So Yvette *had* to become a family friend, or else there was no theatre of the real to prove he could still pull off a cover story. Keeping their affair secret from his wife wasn't enough. Keeping it secret while selling her the false narrative of a friendship which had only ever been platonic was what hit the spot. It was a mark of his great regard for Yvette that he included her in his conspiratorial charade. (His estimation of my performance capacity, on the other hand, was entirely misplaced. I would have blown our cover the moment I failed to resist a *double entendre* about 'deep penetration agents' …) And all the while we may imagine that Yvette was silent in her longing to have her lover back – the love of her life – just as Jane would have been silent in what was either her new understanding or the bitter confirmation of an old one, that she didn't possess her husband's heart. The ex-lover was deceiving the wife to please the man she loved, and the wife, if she knew she was being deceived, tolerated the deception for the same reason. And David, who arranged it all that way, had scripted every scene, down to the last unspoken word.

It was a most amazing business, and I think that it would have been better in the eyes of God if they had all attempted to gouge out each other's eyes with carving knives. But they were 'good people'.

No wonder he claimed *The Good Soldier* was the book of his life. I hadn't understood the full degree of parallel until then.

I should add that when Yvette was in London the time I met her, David took to visiting me at my own flat. He'd also asked me for my keys to St John's Wood, saying he was having some work done there. I believed him, of course, though it's quite obvious to me now that he wanted them for Yvette, to put her up at the flat rather than risk her staying at Hampstead. Having his ex-lover maintain the joint fiction of their always-platonic friendship in front of his wife was by then a well-practised show. But expecting her to carry off the same performance after he had just sent her to have a heart-to-heart lunch with his current girlfriend might have called upon levels of dissembling that were beyond David's estimation of Yvette's capacity. That scenario wouldn't have resembled anything from Ford Madox Ford, or even from le Carré – it would have been pure Iris Murdoch.

Again, this must all be understood in light of the fact that maintaining cover was more important to David than anything – *anything in the world*. Maintaining his cover meant maintaining his nerve and he lived constantly in a state of all-points nervous alert lest he ever be *un*covered in any of his deceptions. Eleanor Philby called it *the most tireless watchfulness* in her husband and it was exactly what I saw in David. It never left him, only ever altering as to degree. Even in his sleep, his indistinct mumblings had a fretful, anticipatory edge.

I don't for a moment mean to suggest that he contrived the situation with his wife and Yvette cynically, or did any of it unfeelingly. David felt *everything*, quite as keenly as those poor babies who are born sometimes without a proper top layer of skin. (To pursue the metaphor, Ronnie had flayed David's off him virtually from birth.) I know very well that he was plagued by guilt, not for every hurtful thing he had done in his life by any means and sometimes for that which hurt only himself, but, amortised across the board, there was more than enough to go around. But he could handle guilt. Like death, it was something he could roll with. He was perversely comfortable with both the secret betrayals *and* the secret guilt they engendered in him. One reinforced the need for the other and David needed both. He had never known anything else. Or so my thesis goes. He was simply a perfect spy, always and forever. He had been one long before the British Secret Services harnessed his native capacity for the benefit of Queen and Country and remained one, I dare guess, to the last. An infiltration agent in his own life.

So back now – albeit some few pages later – to his current tail-spin in the letter.

When Yvette died, David took his wife to her funeral. Quite properly; for, despite the initial contrivance, there can be no doubt that Yvette *was* a very sincere friend to both of them for all those years. She had a huge heart inside that tiny little French body and I'm sure she would have made an especially sincere effort with Jane, as reparations for the never-to-be-disclosed original affair. But at the funeral, when David was suddenly confronted with every sad reminder of what Yvette had *truly* once been to him and he to her, he simply couldn't maintain his own fiction any longer. Overwhelmed by the undeniable evidence of their old love, *he lost his nerve.* He 'wept and wept' for her, as he told me, and his tears were his confession of the truth. Even with Jane at his side, for whose continued deception the whole quarter century of dissembling had been undertaken, he couldn't stop himself from revealing that long-held secret of his heart, in a manner that must have been obvious to all, not least to Jane herself. It might have been an extraordinary catharsis for him, as funerals can so often be, if only his wife hadn't been there. But she *had* to be there – to maintain his twenty-five-year fiction that Yvette was only ever a friend. And his wife's presence was the very thing that blew him. Then the other mourners, thinking they were helping to keep his secret for him, only continued to drive the private reckoning home by drawing him aside – *from his wife* – to tell him the very last thing he needed to hear, that he had been the love of his former lover's life. David must have felt the whole house of cards come tumbling down over Yvette's grave.

He returned from France bone-weary from the massive effort that had kept the performance going for so long, drained by the *débâcle* of the final act and shaken to the core by the private mortal shame of losing his nerve – that cardinal failing for any spy – thereby bringing himself to the very brink, if not actually over the edge, of exposure. For all the explaining and justifying in his letter, it was simply to say he felt he had no strength remaining to him to pick up where he had left things with me. No reserves left to maintain his cover for yet another secret love affair, even if it was the continuation of ours.

Long into his retirement, Smiley's tradecraft was as sharp and subtle as ever. It never failed him. Still younger than his aged hero had been at the height of his powers, David had just witnessed the last of his own tradecraft crumble beneath him. He had experienced the sensation of that degree of exposure only once before, when he learned of Philby's defection and believed it had effectively blown his cover as a spy. But he came back from that. The 'fugue state' the experience generated was what drew *The Spy Who Came In from the Cold* out of him and created the nuclear fusion of his past life in espionage with his future life as a world-class writer. Now it had happened again, but this time the exposure was in his personal life, his one remaining area of covert activity. If David couldn't come back from this – if I couldn't bring him back – there was no hope for our relationship to continue.

Schliesse mir die Augen beide
mit den lieben Händen zu!
Geht doch alles, was ich leide,
unter deiner Hand zur Ruh.
Theodor Storm

Once again, I have absolutely no recollection of what I wrote back, *post restante* Hampstead. My only point of true recall is the determination I felt to give it my all. It was a reprise of the situation after my first visit to Tregiffian. David had wanted me to pull him back from the brink of his own apostasy then and he needed me to repeat the manoeuvre now. So, once again, I gave him the sincerest form I could of whatever I thought it was he would eat. Once again, I was relieved to find he ate up every word. It's possible to infer some of what I must have written from his reply, which he sent by special delivery. He even began with the same line he had praised me with before: *That one doesn't go into the shredder, my girl, I can tell you.* (If in fact it didn't, then I suppose there's an outside chance it's still sitting in one of the multiple hundreds of boxes of papers in the le Carré archive at the Bodleian.)

There was another smiley face grinning on the seal of the envelope, this one replete with stick-out ears and stand-up hair. Inside, a much bigger one was positively beaming from the top of the first page above a banner headline that proclaimed all the notes I'd struck were perfect and was signed:– W. A. Mozart

He wrote that my letter was delightful, marvellous, generous and had ended the great battle he realised he had been waging with no one but himself. I had helped persuade him, he said, that it was time to embrace a newer, freer way forward. I must have written in some detail about my former lover, because he asserted that it

285

would be a lucky man who died in my arms and added that he was glad that I too still loved my former lovers. I must have written about Graham as well, because he said he remembered him with a smile. He said again that he would love me always and always had, so much and so constantly that he loved me across rooms where I wasn't present and in restaurants where I wasn't sitting. I believed him too. Only David could have turned such a plangent and paradoxical claim into such a tribute to the power of his love. He declared he couldn't write that morning, but didn't mind, because though nothing moved through his pen, so much was moving in his heart. He quoted the poem by Storm in German. It translates:

> *Close both my eyes*
> *with your beloved hands!*
> *Let all my suffering*
> *gain rest beneath your hand.*

It wasn't possible *not* to love David, you see.

He then explained his immediate itinerary – Ireland first to see Boorman, to discuss the script David had written to replace the one neither of them liked by Andrew Davies, then ten days in the Atlas Mountains on a long-delayed holiday. (He meant with his wife, but knew it would be discordant to say.) But we'd go away together soon, he said finally, and joked that he promised to choose somewhere 'really unpleasant' so that we'd have to spend the whole time in bed. Meanwhile he'd call whenever he could.

He called – and called and called. It was as if there had never been a problem and as if there never would be one again. Right then, he was full of the new movie, which, for his sake, I hoped was going to be an improvement on its predecessors. During the Q&A after the lecture, David was asked to opine about why his films generally failed to set cinema box-office sales on fire. Regarding the failure of the most recent – *The Russia House*, which had Sean Connery in the lead, Michelle Pfeiffer as the love interest, a stellar supporting cast, screenplay by Tom Stoppard, and Fred Schepisi directing – I wondered whether he might be at a loss for an explanation. But I should have had more faith.

'The thing is,' he said sagely to the audience, with a donnish lift of his chin as he prepared to impart a hitherto unremarked detail, 'you can't imperil Bond.'

The quality of voice and the skill in the delivery was still what David's fiction-spinning was all about and the audience bought his entirely specious piece of reasoning with a general murmur of assent. Think about it for a moment. If this were true, then not just Connery but every other action-movie leading man would never have a career beyond his first hit. *We can't cast that guy as the hero again – the audience already knows he's gonna win!* Did I say specious? I meant bonkers. But now the hunt was on for somebody new to imperil. David told me McKellen wasn't in the running for Pendel, which I said was a great shame.

'Do you have any ideas yourself, then, my love?' he asked me. 'Any likely actors? Casting is your field too.'

I said I would let him know if I came up with any candidates.

(At David's urging, Geoffrey Rush would get the part in the end, opposite Pierce Brosnan – not just another peril-proof Bond, in case he hadn't noticed, but actually the current one at the time. And sadly, the film would be another failure-to-launch.)

I went down to see Gigi in her cottage. On my way to the station a charity collector rattled his tin at me.

'Help the Aged?' he asked cheerily.

Lost in thought about my self-described 'very old' lover, I brushed past, telling him emphatically, 'I already gave!'

I hadn't yet told Gigi about this second time around with David. I didn't quite know what was stopping me, except for a mildly shamefaced awareness that she was the friend who had most helped me get over him the first time.

We sat in the riverside garden of her pretty Berkshire cottage, drinking wine in the spring afternoon sunshine and watching the ducks and swans paddle by on the water. She pointed out a clump of bluest blue forget-me-nots from George that were thriving in one corner. She told me I was looking well, then gave me a more sizing glance.

'I know that look!' she exclaimed. 'You've got a new man!'

I didn't confirm or deny her declaration, but I'm sure my face gave me away.

'Come on, Dawson – tell me who he is.'

Can I not, I asked her sheepishly, not just yet? It wasn't that I didn't want to tell her, I said, only that it was all rather new and uncertain at the moment; I was sure she would understand.

'Of course I do, darling. No problem.' She sipped her wine and I thought the subject had passed. But then I saw a sudden thought cross her brow. 'Don't tell me—!' she exclaimed, as her face lit up with a new possibility. 'It's not another impossible famous writer, is it?'

Dearest Gigi. How unconsciously wonderful of her to put it that way. I hadn't wanted to deceive her about what was happening with David and now I wouldn't have to.

'No,' I told her with complete honesty. 'It's not another impossible famous writer.'

I only omitted to say that it was exactly the same one.

On his next visit to my flat, David said he would arrive at ten in the morning but turned up even earlier. I had barely bathed and dressed.

'I haven't put my make-up on yet,' I told him as I let him in.

'No, I thought I wouldn't bother either,' he said sweetly. None of that mattered to him, I'd honestly forgotten.

He was wearing a very spiffy new suit in a fine dark blue cloth. I said it looked very good on him, thinking that even Graham might have approved. He had 'a new suiter', he explained – Douglas Hayward, the man who famously tailored sharp-suited British movie icons such as Terence Stamp and Michael Caine. I'd read that Hayward was the model for Pendel. When I hugged David this time, I could feel a hard shape across the middle of his back under his new suit and for a brief moment I concluded he'd surrendered to the worst of his paranoia – it seemed no more than an inevitability – and was finally packing. But when the jacket came off it wasn't a gun-holster I'd felt, but the leather cross piece on a pair of new braces. He'd already lost enough weight, as he said he would 'for a girl', that he needed them to keep his spiffy new pants from falling down.

He brought an equally snazzy briefcase with him, which must have fitted his cover story, along with the suit, since he intended to spend the whole day with me. There had been a distinct evolution in David's cases since I'd known him, starting with the dull and dated tan briefcase for the *Smiley's People* recording, progressing to a cool black international-traveller-style pilot's case once he acquired the St John's Wood flat, and now there was this ultra-smart flat attaché case, with a very distinctive dark brown covering. I had a suspicion I knew what it was.

'Two-hundred-year-old Russian reindeer hide,' David announced as he saw me admire it. 'They brought up bales of the stuff with an old shipwreck off the Cornish coast and the Duchy awarded licences to local artisans. They've made it into everything possible.'

'Yes,' I said, pleased to have my guess confirmed. 'I know someone who re-upholstered an old Lagonda with it.'

'You know people in Cornwall?' He looked a little startled.

'Yes,' I said again. 'All sorts. I spent six months down there a couple of years ago.'

'You didn't tell me.'

'You didn't ask.'

'Well, that's true.'

'I rented a cottage from some friends,' I told him, not offering the explanation I knew he wanted to dispel his immediate suspicion that I'd had a lover in his own county besides himself. I could see him picturing me riding shotgun in the Lagonda, or something more graphic over the hood. Not that anything close had been the case. I'd simply wanted to be away from my London flat when the outside of the building was being renovated and the offer of the cottage happened to come up. Once again, I didn't want to interfere with the potential therapeutic benefits of leaving him guessing.

'But it was in the habitable part, where trees grow and birds sing and they don't bury cows with their hooves sticking up out of the ground,' I explained, relenting a little, but wishing to make the point about Tregiffian, which I hadn't before. 'So not near your end.'

'Ah.'

I don't think this entirely dispelled his fear of there having been another tall man from Cornwall in my past, but he seemed relieved that he still retained exclusive territorial rights at the *Straw Dogs* end of the county. He was less relieved when I told him I'd picked up some gossip about him while I was there.

'What was that?' he asked gingerly.

I named a local painter, a man with a modest national profile, someone I knew he would have encountered. The mother of the friend I'd rented the cottage from was a painter herself and Cornwall, in terms of social circles, particularly artistic ones, was a very small place. It was she who'd told me the rumour.

'It was believed,' I said, 'that you'd had an affair with his wife.'

'God,' David said quietly. His shoulders rose defensively and he offered a small involuntary gagging sound from the back of his throat.

'So you're saying it was just a groundless rumour, then,' I asked. 'You didn't have a fling with her?'

'Under *no* circumstances.' He looked genuinely appalled.

I believed him, but couldn't resist the tease.

'You were kind to call him a painter, though,' he said to conclude the matter. 'I shouldn't put him above a dauber.'

I hadn't given credence to the story, though it was strenuously urged upon me as being true. I knew David wouldn't so much as flirt with anyone so close to home, particularly in such a socially incestuous place as that county. But it made me wonder, as I hadn't at the time, how he might have responded if I'd contacted him myself while I was down there.

The attaché case contained a copy of his script for *The Tailor*, which he wanted me to have. I noticed a large, leather-bound desk diary in there too, though it wasn't clear why he would want to carry one around. It was a gift from his publisher, apparently, with a literary quotation for each day.

'And not one from me,' David said pointedly.

Though ostensibly bound by our new terms, wherein he'd agreed not to talk about his family, David nevertheless appeared to feel free to talk at length about his wife. Things that didn't start off being about her often devolved into sidelong complaints. He told me he'd started a charity, to return a portion of his own good financial fortune to those less well off.

'It's called the David and Jane Cornwell Charitable Trust. It's a way of paying back, you see. Tithing.'

I asked what sort of aid the charity was set up to offer.

'Small things for now, mostly local. But where it's needed most. Helping a young mother with the train fare to take the kids to see their dad in jail. That sort of thing.'

I imagined David felt for that kind of need very keenly, given Ronnie's incarceration during his own childhood.

'Jane's quite involved with it,' he continued. 'I started it in part to give her something to do. She can patronise them all there to her heart's content.'

I recalled how she had tried her hand with me when she rang about the *Drummer Girl* abridgement.

'I've given her the house in Hampstead,' he went on, warming to his theme. 'And I've made her a millionaire in her own right. But she doesn't *do* anything with it. She came to me recently to ask whether I thought it permissible for her to arrange to have something funded. From the uncertain way she was approaching the possibility, I thought she meant by the Trust. Then I realised she meant the money *I'd* given her.' David raised his eyebrows, to reflect his astonishment at her diffidence. '"My dear woman," I told her, "it's *your* money to do with *as you wish*."'

I suppose he couldn't see it. George had, when he remarked to Gigi how Jane seemed 'hoovered up' since her marriage. I'd heard it for myself, on that call, when she said 'we' so often and never once said 'I'. But David couldn't see it at all. He'd made his wife's every thought and deed subservient to his own for nearly three decades and yet still felt free to be critical of her when she demonstrated uncertainty over acting on her own initiative. Not that he said absolutely nothing in Jane's favour. Before, he'd said that she was a devoted mother. Now, with their son grown and living away, David insisted that she was 'a very fine editor'. But that was about it. As before, I don't believe it was out of any consideration for my sensibilities that he held back on her praise. In a wry aside at the lecture, he'd said that he deliberately put a new generation of heroes into his novels nowadays, because he wanted to 'write about younger men who had sex lives'. This drew a titillated laugh from the audience, as well as a knowing smile from me. But now he told me quite frankly that his marriage had been sexless since *before* we met the *first* time. Well. I only wish he'd told me then, when it would torture me to think of him still having what he'd made a point of calling 'rotten little duty fucks' in those intervals when I couldn't see him.

'We should have just moved in together, you and I,' he said, smiling distantly, 'and fuck the lot of them.'

There was no point in asking him who had stopped us from doing just that – supposing I'd wanted to in the first place.

'You were my best shot at it, Our Sue – getting out of the slammer. But I can't leave a sixty-two-year-old woman now.'

Again – was that anything I'd ever yet asked him to do?

We had a happy early lunch at a local Lebanese restaurant, where David either forbore or forgot to correct me about raising food to my mouth with my left hand. But he made another observation in its place. Reaching out to hold my hand, he looked at my wrist and asked, 'What's the story with your watch?'

There wasn't one. I'd simply liked the look of it in Bloomingdale's on a recent trip to New York. Then I realised what he was really asking. It was a man's watch – probably unisex – and he suspected it had come from the wrist of a lover.

'It's just a watch,' I said. 'No story.'

He tilted his head a little as he continued to look at my wrist. The story for David was that it wasn't the gold watch he'd given me.

'Perhaps you'll let me buy you jewellery again,' he said unassumingly. 'This time, some pieces that you'll actually like to wear.'

It must have hurt him, that I hadn't kept his original pieces. He didn't need to ask if I still had them. He would know I'd have worn them for him if I did. I had kept them for a while, but then it had begun to hurt *me* to see them. I should have said something to this effect by way of gentle explanation at the time – it needn't have been anything more than I've written here – but for some reason I didn't. It's these little moments, not the bigger scenarios, that I so wish I could replay differently now.

We returned to the flat and went straight to bed, taking a pair of tumblers and the Stoly I now always kept in the freezer. Prompted by our conversation, I noticed that when David removed his own watch it wasn't the lovely flat white gold Rolex he had always worn before. I asked him what the story was there and he told me how he had given it to a jeweller to clean, to be told that it subsequently 'disappeared' from the premises.

'Did you sue?' I asked. I imagined him getting Special Branch on the case.

'No,' David replied, with that *Weltschmerz* sigh I hadn't heard in a long while. 'They gave me this one in its place.'

It was funny, mystifying in fact, how he let some slights slide and took other ones to task. Even if we'd ever taken that mythical extra step of moving in together, I should still never have been able to guess which way he would land on things.

He declared our trip to Geneva was on at the end of the month and I asked if the spook travel agents were arranging it.

'No,' he said. 'I've no spooks left anywhere. I'm completely out of tradecraft, my darling. It's all gone. Everything's got to be strictly cash-cash now.'

It was how he'd described Pym's under-the-counter payments for the room at Miss Dubber's, his autobiographical hero's final safe house. Art/Life was with us again, though time had moved inexorably on. Rainer was dead, George was retired and the spook travel agent in the City, like the Cold War and the Berlin Wall, was no more. David took a thick envelope from his attaché case. It contained far more than enough Swiss francs for my plane ticket and instructions as to which flight to book myself on. But it surprised me that he hadn't kept even one covert line open in the whole vast economic enterprise that was John le Carré. He must have believed he'd never need one again.

He'd already be in Switzerland and would meet me at the airport. He would try and call me before then, but it was only two weeks away. It was going to be wonderful, he said, kissing me before he went. Really wonderful. I waved to him again from the bedroom window and he blew up another kiss to my naked breast.

My diary entry for the day has David arriving at my flat at 9.45 am and leaving at 4 pm. It ends with his telling me as he left, *We're married, you and I. So that's it.*

Late afternoon a couple of days later, the face of a uniformed policeman appeared in the little video-entry panel at the flat and asked for me over the intercom. I had a minute or so while he climbed the stairs to wonder what I'd done to put myself on the Met's radar, but I came up clean. Apart from revisiting the married-man's-mistress thing, hardly illegal, I was a model citizen. When I opened the front door and saw that there were actually two uniforms approaching along the terrace, one of them a woman, I began to suspect something else. The policewoman was already giving me *that look* as they asked to come inside.

They'd come to tell me that my mother had died and that my father had collapsed and been taken to the nearest hospital. They were unable to tell me his condition, or indeed anything more. They said how sorry they were to have to bring me this news and, once they were satisfied that I wasn't going to collapse myself, they left.

I rang the hospital immediately, to learn my mother had probably died of a heart attack and there would need to be a post-mortem. My father had been sedated and was resting as comfortably as could be expected. It was only an hour's journey to get there by train (I still didn't drive), just over two hours door to door, but it was still too late to visit him that evening. I said I'd be there the following morning and left my phone number in case anything happened overnight.

I was left to contemplate the sudden news and the complete turn-around it brought with it. It had been the unquestioned assumption throughout my parents' marriage and for my entire life that my father, who was fourteen years older than my mother, would die first. He had been showing mild but increasing signs of dementia for the past few years. He was still lovely, still good humoured and kind, still very much himself, but was growing increasingly forgetful and very unsteady on his feet. My mother needed to watch him like a hawk in case he injured himself if he fell over, or endangered them both if he left an electrical appliance to overheat or put something on the stove and forgot about it. The constant worry of it all – which she insisted on carrying by herself, refusing almost all offers of help from me and from friends who lived nearby – seemed finally to have put too much strain on her heart.

I began to make a list of everything I would need to do. Take an early train down next morning; see my father in hospital; find out what condition he was in; hope I could console him just a little bit. Find out when my mother's post-mortem would happen. Find out how to register her death. Find a funeral home and arrange her cremation. Find a nursing home for my father. Obtain power of attorney for my father's affairs. Sort out their finances. Sort out their papers. Sort out their stuff. Call their friends, most of whom lived nearby, and remaining family members, all of whom did not. I was sure there was more than that to do, but my mind was a blur. I'd never wished for siblings before, but now wished for half a dozen, all married to obliging spouses, with some helpful young adult offspring between them, so that I wouldn't have to do it all by myself. I had no head space left to register that I had just lost my mum.

When my father saw me at the hospital he held out his arms in a dreadful gesture of helplessness mixed with abject relief. I sat on his bed and held him while he wept and wept. My mother and father were in love with each other from the moment their eyes met across a crowded dance floor back in the fifties and they stayed in love throughout the whole of their long marriage. Now my father was still in love, but suddenly bereft and overwhelmed by his loss. The hospital doctor said he hadn't been injured when he collapsed, but they would keep him on the ward for observation till the end of the week, just to be sure. That seemed more than reasonable. Whatever else they might be able to do for him, they couldn't mend his broken heart.

In the ensuing days I managed to get through everything on my list, plus further additional tasks that cropped up in the process. I was operating in a kind of automated blur, a strangely efficient state of mind that lasted right into the day of the funeral, because there were so many people to greet and my father to look after and the flowers and messages to acknowledge. It lasted right up until the moment I saw my darling dad silently raise his hand to wave goodbye to my mother's casket as it rolled behind the curtains at the crematorium. Then I was lost.

There was no alternative to a nursing home for my father and with the invaluable help of my mother's best friend I found a wonderful place for him. They advised me to admit him directly after the funeral and then leave him in their care. I said I'd come back and spend time with him over the next few days, but was told it was better if I didn't. The manager, a kind and capable women whom I would get to know well – whose name happened to be Jane – explained that this was the kindest thing to do. Residents settled in much faster if they were left to adjust to their new surroundings by themselves for a while, not unlike children starting at boarding school. I saw my father into his new accommodation, where I'd already sent some of his belongings so that he'd have familiar things around him, made certain he understood I'd be back to see him in a few days and told him that I was sure everyone would look after him. Then I sat with him until he fell asleep in his new bed and left. It was a strange new reality for us both.

I was back in London the next morning with two days to go before leaving for Geneva. David had left a reel of messages on the answering machine (I hadn't yet acquired my first mobile), wondering with increasing urgency where I'd gone. It was strange – and two weeks ago I wouldn't have believed it possible – but I hadn't thought of him once since the police arrived at my door. He was a huge figure in my life, but he didn't have a presence in this part of my world.

I was there next time he called. He sounded relieved to hear my voice. I was out of town for a few days, I told him, but for some reason didn't tell him why. I knew I would tell him, at some point, just not yet. A problem shared with David wasn't necessarily a problem halved; not this one, anyway. He would be kind, I was sure, but I wasn't ready to handle even the most delicate response from him. When I'd come closer to understanding how I felt myself, I'd feel more prepared to let him that far in.

A Canadian girlfriend was passing through London just then and came to stay for those last two nights. I was running on ghost energy and wasn't sure I could cope with seeing anybody else, let alone having a house guest, but Kate was just the restorative I needed. Over a meal and wine at the Lebanese restaurant and more wine back at the flat, we exchanged all our news, mine being the lion's share. Kate was sorry to hear about my mother's passing, but it was when I told her the story of how David and I had met again after all those years that the tears began to well in her eyes. Well, it *was* one of *those* stories. We talked till the small hours and next morning hit the stores in the West End.

I'd told her how David said he hoped I'd let him buy me jewellery again.

'He's rich, right?' she said, before she pulled me into Cartier in Bond Street, where we looked at some 'Tank' pieces; the watches, but the rings too, a variety of which I tried on. 'Let him know you've been here and checked your ring size,' she told me on our way out.

In another store I bought a simple dark blue linen shift to fly out in, and some ultra-sheer hold-ups and a lace teddy to complete the package when I arrived.

LAUSANNE

I had dropped several pounds dealing with the events of the last fortnight and hadn't been overweight to begin with, so right then I was essentially all leg. David was waiting for me at Geneva airport and the expression on his face when he saw me was entirely composed of wonderment. He was looking his handsome best Swiss self and every lovely thing he had ever said to me was locked into his expression. I don't know whether other travellers stared at us as we stood wrapped around ourselves for what seemed timeless minutes, but it didn't matter. It was just so perfect to be there in his arms.

'Hello, my darling,' he said into my ear. 'You're here. We made it.'

He'd already raided the airport concessions for provisions. Wedged between his suitcase and another black leather bag on his trolley was a paper carrier with caviar and champagne.

'So we can go straight to bed when we get to our hotel,' he explained. 'Just enough to tide us over until we go out to supper later. Come on, we've got a train to catch.'

He put my bag on the trolley and led the way, announcing that we were going to Lausanne; the train we wanted ran directly from the airport. I'd assumed a weekend in Geneva, but David still liked to move on from first places, that old but still very active instinct to present a moving target.

'Come on, this way,' he urged, not understanding my hesitation as he awkwardly forced the trolley down a short escalator ramp clearly marked UP ONLY. 'This way to the train, quick, quick.'

As the train slipped smoothly along, I realised again how much I liked being in Switzerland. It was true that I had only known the country with David, under the easy affluence and familiarity he always provided, with everything always seeming to be of the most effortless quality. But then it was also true that the effortlessly perfect mountains and lakes and sky were all entirely free.

David ordered champagne and we talked happily – about how good the train was, clean, comfortable and stylish – about how good the champagne was, too, available by the glass and perfectly chilled – how everything was, well, Swiss.

About two-thirds of the way through the first glass, just enough to soften the edge of things, David asked me how I was. He knew I'd been away but he also knew something had happened. I knew he knew because it wasn't his habit to ask me how I was. Over the phone, yes, but not in person. It was axiomatic we'd be naked together at some point on every occasion we met, which would tell him how I was more intimately and exactly than any answer I might give. He clearly had his suspicions that there'd been something since he saw me last.

I was fine, I told him. Wonderful.

And it *was* wonderful, just sitting there across the little table from him, with the champagne gently flowing and the scenery whisking by. It would have been wonderful under any circumstances, but especially so after recent events, about which I was determined still to say nothing.

'Well, you *look* wonderful, too, my love,' he said. 'But there's a particular gloss to you. You've been through something and it's left its mark.'

'I've been busy,' I answered. 'I'm just a bit tired, that's all.'

It was lame, of course, but there was no point in attempting a more elaborate cover story. I was with the Master! I began to wonder whether he thought I'd been with another man.

We talked some more, about nothing in particular, but if it had been one exercise not to say anything on the phone at my flat, it was another altogether to withstand David's interrogation face to face, even though I knew the trick of it perfectly well. *Talk to your subject as though you already know everything, thereby rendering any resistance pointless.* And he wasn't even asking questions, just looking at me as though his private guess was quite good enough.

'You'll tell me,' he said gently, just when I was hopeful we'd moved the conversation along. 'I'll get it out of you, I know I shall.'

I continued to resist right through most of another glass of champagne. But then I folded – I didn't want to wait for the thumbscrews – and told him without elaboration that my mother had died.

'Wow,' he said quietly. 'That's big stuff, Our Sue. Crikey. When exactly did this happen?'

I told him when the police had called at the flat.

'Wow,' he said again, looking at me steadily. 'That's nearly two weeks ago.' He took a large mouthful of champagne, as though he needed it after the impact of my answer. 'Well, all I can say is, I admire you for that. I admire you *so* for that, my love – more than you can ever know.'

I was happy to hear him say this – I could always soak up David's compliments like a sponge – but couldn't quite see what it was he found so admirable. Other than the fact I'd handled everything myself and was still standing, which spoke to a certain capacity for endurance, I'd only done what I'd had to.

David stared silently out of the window for another long minute, holding his glass but not drinking. Then he looked back at me again. It was clear I'd impressed him quite substantially and in a way that he was taking his time to formulate. But I might never have guessed how if he hadn't just then explained.

'I think you're astonishing for not telling me. Simply marvellous. *I* shouldn't have been able to do it. I should've *had* to tell you, straight away. But if I hadn't pressed a girl, I don't think you would have told me at all. You're an amazing woman, Sue – I always knew it – but now you've earned my admiration for life.'

So that was it. My perfect spy admired me most for not telling him my 'own' secret. I suppose I should have known.

*　　*　　*

Our hotel was a red-roofed neo-gothic lakeside château and our room was at the very top of the building in its own separate turret, with a private elevator to take us there. With Swiss efficiency and dispatch, our bags were sent up ahead of us as David signed us in. As we stepped into our own lift together, I noticed how David held his breath when the door slid to.

'I don't care for lifts,' he said with a dry swallow.

After seventeen years of occasionally wondering, I finally had the answer to why he'd taken the stairs up to the studios that first day. It wasn't to make a silent entrance. He was claustrophobic.

Our room was decorated in the luscious but slightly faded fin-de-siècle style that David had seemed to favour in the past. It was a lot like our first hotel in Vitznau, except that it was Lake Lucerne then and Lake Geneva now, but with the view still stretching for miles and the placid water still sparkling gently in the late afternoon sun. When I opened the window and leaned out, the air carried the sound of the mast ropes on all the little sail boats moored below us clacking like busy waterfowl in the breeze.

The bed took us almost immediately as we shut ourselves into our private tower and then once again, after we'd assailed the caviar and champagne that David had thoughtfully stowed in the ice bucket. Then he made me a present of the black leather bag I'd seen on the trolley; a Tumi weekend bag that he'd bought with our comestibles at the airport. I'd brought presents for him too, obtained on my West End excursion with Kate. The first was a silk tie from Hardy Amies; it had an abstract pattern that contained all the colours in his eyes.

'I love it,' he told me. 'I really do. How clever of you to choose it.'

'You can say you bought it at the airport,' I said, thinking of when he took it home. 'They have a concession, I checked.'

'Listen. So I bought a tie – so what? The less attention you bring to anything the less anyone else notices. I shall wear it whenever I choose, whenever the colours work. It looks like they always will.'

The second present was a black pinseal notepad with gold corners, from Asprey.

'Oh, how perfect,' he said sweetly. And whether or not he had a drawer full of them at home, he made me feel as if it actually was.

After that we bathed and dressed, David wearing a fresh shirt with his new tie and his notepad slipped inside his jacket, myself in a different shift, this one with pale stripes and slightly translucent, and ventured outside again, into one of those sweet-scented, mauve-tinted evenings to which Switzerland seemed to own the eternal copyright. We sat out at a lakeside restaurant and both marvelled how anybody, including either of us, could freely choose ever to be anywhere else in the world.

My heart had gone back to David completely. His, apparently, had never left me. Just being there with him on that balmy silvered evening absorbed all my senses, all my understanding. He had cast his magic spell again and this time what he conjured seemed more real than ever. But for all the loveliness we had so suddenly regained – all the love that must always have been there – some small watchful part of me was trying so hard not to be fearful that at some point it would have to hurt. David didn't know any other way.

Back in our turret-room that night we made love again, this time with an accompaniment to the proceedings that David had never suggested before. It took him a few moments to figure out the remote control for the television, but eventually he found the channel he wanted and we continued with blue movies playing silently on the screen.

Next morning we had an early al fresco breakfast at the end of the hotel's jetty. The people at the next table clocked David as soon as we sat down, I could tell from the startled expressions of recognition they quickly wiped from their faces. But they didn't approach. This was Switzerland, where even bank accounts had the right to remain anonymous.

Then we set out for an explore. The sun was more intense than I'd anticipated and to save me from burning in what I was wearing – a mid-length unbleached linen skirt and a favourite khaki T-shirt – David offered me one of his shirts to wear as well. It was pale tan and, with the cuffs turned back and unbuttoned, made a nice combo, so he decided I should also wear the cream-coloured Augustus John-looking hat he'd brought with him. David said he didn't have a head for hats, but once I put it on at a rakish angle declared that I did. The hatband matched the colour of my T-shirt, so quite by chance it all looked deliberately styled; Banana Republic meets Calvin Klein meets Herbert Johnson. David told me I looked like Karen Blixen as we set out.

We took the ferry across to Évian-les-Bains on the French side of the lake and had a glass of champagne at each of three separate places along the front. Then we took a taxi inland to David's restaurant of choice for our lunch, Le Relais de la Chevrette, where we ate outside at a rustic table. Afterwards we went for a stroll through the nearby countryside. David had a lovely calm about him that day. It was the effect this part of the world always had on him – the mountains, the altitude, the air. My effect – *our* effect – on him too. I never went with him to his chalet, but would guess that he was a lot like this whenever he went skiing in Wengen, where the exhilarating exercise would help to further tone him down. Though I think I have to say, because it strikes me as being as true as anything else about him, that he'd also had the benefit of exhilarating exercise here. We'd already had five bouts of extraordinarily intense sex, including once in the middle of the night and once again before breakfast that morning, and had only arrived at the hotel late yesterday afternoon.

We found an old tree in a lovely meadow and sat down by it. I kept in its shade with my back against the trunk and David sat in the sun with his arms around his knees. The grass was lush and deep and dotted with yellow and purple flowers. White flowers growing on taller stems above them seemed to catch the sunlight in a haze. High on the horizon, the snow-capped mountains were like clouds and the clouds above them were like more snow-capped mountains and the gentian-blue sky sat atop it all. It was so perfectly Alpine that I wouldn't have raised an eyebrow if Heidi and the Grandfather had appeared on the spot. Or perhaps that was us.

As we sat in comfortable silence in the meadow I began to think how much my mother would have enjoyed this place, on this timelessly lovely day. But now, suddenly, there were no more sunny days for her. I had simply assumed, as I think the adult children of elderly parents too often do, that there were always going to be other summers ahead for her to enjoy.

David must have been operating his uncanny mind-radar again, because without leading up to the subject he asked me, 'What are your thoughts on the Big Moo, my darling? I've never asked you before.'

'The big what?'

'Moo. God. It was Kennaway's expression. Do you think there's anything out there?'

He was right that we'd never ventured onto the topic before. I hadn't ventured onto it for a while with anyone. My parents had always been 'no sale' about religion and I was enormously grateful for it. But David had been raised in the pulpit-thumping West Country and as a child he'd frequently been left by Ronnie in the care of relatives who took it all very seriously indeed. They may even have bashed their Bibles with particular vigour on those occasions, to atone for the fact that they were enabling his godless narcissistic psychopath father to run his ruthless scams by providing childcare.

'Not in the way that any of the religions would have us believe,' I said, after I'd thought about my answer for a moment. 'So, no.'

'Well, I agree with you there, my love,' he replied. 'Religion is one of the institutions I've failed to penetrate in my life, though not for the want of trying at one time.'

I recalled he'd once had a very brief flirtation with joining Miller and Michael in their 'lay brotherhood' in Cornwall. Not that I could ever recall that episode without going for the obvious gag. David had been taking himself way too seriously to see the idiocy of it at the time. It had been another abortive attempt to get out of the 'slammer' at Hampstead and I made no reference to it now.

'But about God Himself,' he persisted gently. 'Or Herself? No?'

I shook my head. 'No. Not the imaginary one we were required to sing praises to every morning in school assembly, nor any of the imaginary others that we weren't.'

'So you don't believe we go on in any way?'

'Actually, I do. I just don't think there's any invoking or worshipping or obeying required for it to happen.'

David cocked his head. 'How so, then?' he asked.

'I think we recycle,' I said. 'Everything else does – matter, light, energy, so I don't see why one's soul or spirit shouldn't recycle somehow too. Just as a basic principle of the way things go.'

I didn't consider this to be a terribly advanced theory – more akin to dinosaurs being thin at one end, fat in the middle and thin at the other – but David listened with great attention.

After a thoughtful pause he said, 'That's a very elegant belief, my darling.'

'But it's *not* a belief,' I corrected him. 'That's the point. It doesn't require any faith. In fact, it's pretty much inductive reasoning. You know – Smiley stuff.'

That drew a wry smile.

'How about you?' I asked in return.

Now it was David's turn to shake his head.

'No,' he said flatly.

'So nothing? Nothing beyond at all?'

'I think we die and that's it. I don't think I know what spirit is. Beyond life, anyway.'

I wasn't particularly surprised to hear him say this. David was very cerebral; the cessation of brain activity and consciousness must have seemed particularly absolute to him. Having been raised in such a harsh religious environment and consciously rejecting all traces of it, he had then failed to find any more sympathetic substitute. I'd already seen how seriously he took his age, how little time he felt he had left. Nearer my God to Thee must have seemed a very bleak proposition to him, with no Thou out there.

'So are your books going to be your immortality?' I asked. 'Is that how you see things?'

'Some of them, yes,' he replied, nodding as he looked out at the mountains. 'I think some will last. But who knows? This new one feels wonderful, full of all sorts of life.'

He would be going back to Africa soon, he said, to continue his interrupted research. The story was shaping up; he was beginning to see how his hero, Justin Quayle, would set about his journey to track down his wife's killers.

'Another chap on his personal odyssey,' I suggested.

'Yes, that's exactly it. Now, tell me, Sue – because you'll know – why was it that Odysseus went on his odyssey in the first place? What was he doing all that travelling for?'

I hesitated before answering. I was waiting for a knowing grin, to show me he was aware of asking the exact same question, in almost those exact words, on our Greek beach all those years before. But David was quite serious in his enquiry. He'd already told me how 'great swathes, whole chapters' of his life were closed to him and, though he may have believed it, I didn't quite believe they were. Some were selectively dormant, perhaps; others lying doggo, waiting for their master's whistle; but none were permanently closed. David remembered everything. Now, quite suddenly, I understood that this was how he kept going, by processing the same things over and over again – the same desires, the same fears, the same concerns, even the same loves – generating ever more layers of complication for himself and everyone around him, while obscuring anything that might lead him to reach resolution. He *was* Odysseus, in a way, as he'd claimed once before. Travelling and travelling, each adventure taking him on to another, but in his case every time ending up back on the same shore where he'd started, yet never really knowing it for the first time. Perhaps, I thought a little sadly in the end, he wasn't really Tigger after all, as he'd liked me to say, bounding enthusiastically from one thing to the next until he found what he liked best. Perhaps he was really poor old Pooh Bear, walking round and round the tree in the snow, getting more and more alarmed as he saw more and more footprints appearing ahead of him, fearing they were made by unknown beasts in the forest, not realising that he had made them all himself.

'Odysseus didn't mean to go anywhere,' I said at last, hearing my own words echo in my ears. 'He was only trying to get home.'

We took a taxi back to Évian. Before taking the return ferry we stopped to have more champagne and a double sugar cone each at an ice-cream parlour by the lake. After our conversation about the Hereafter, I now had something of an existential epiphany myself, which was that if anything came close to manifesting the concept of Eternal Bliss for me, it was a lakeside ice-cream parlour – with an Alpine view – that also served champagne. As we were only a few yards onto French soil, I credited my private revelation to the Swiss, thinking it was no wonder they stayed neutral in wars. They didn't need to fight anyone for anything. They already had the best of everything life could offer right where they were.

My new family situation returned with a bump once I was back in London after our four days *en Suisse*. Thereafter, I was constantly dividing my time between my parents' place, to look after the house and sort their stuff and see my dad, and London, for work and David, and meantime living on the trains that took me to and fro. It was like existing inside a split-screen film with two complex storylines running concurrently and no easy way to completely follow either. Now it appeared to be my turn to keep all the plates spinning on top of all the poles. To keep sane, I purchased my first mobile phone the moment I was back. It and my new Tumi bag were my constant companions as I shuttled between my two lives.

I'd always kept some of my past belongings at my parents' house, but as I went through everything I soon discovered that my mother had kept so much more. My scholar's gown from Oxford; my school uniform blazer; my christening gown she made from the satin of her wedding dress; the miniature cardigan she knitted for my favourite doll to match one she'd made for me. She had kept the first Mother's Day card I'd made for her, aged six, and all my earliest school exercise books with the clumsy printing in pencil and the eager pictures in crayon. She'd kept postcards from me from everywhere. And, in a little blue Tiffany's box that originally contained some earrings I'd bought her on a trip to New York, she'd kept a lock of my baby hair, transferred from its first home in an old blue envelope. It was strawberry blonde and still tightly curled. It broke me to see it and, finally, I wept for my mother from the bottom of my heart.

I always knew what a lovely man my father was, but every time I visited him in his nursing home I learned it anew. He was born just before the First World War and because his own father was serving in France throughout his infancy I always imagined him as a version of the little boy in the Belloc poem who took very great care of his mother though he was only three. Once he met my mother, his one ambition was to take very great care of her and then, when I came along, of us both. Which he did – and always with a smile, good humour and simply endless love. I took him flowers and chocolates and books whenever I visited and sat with him in the quiet sitting room that overlooked the garden, or sometimes in the garden when the weather was fine. He'd been a keen gardener and still liked to name all the flowers – aubretia, chionodoxa, alstroemeria and all the different roses. It was strange but not entirely discouraging to see what remained in his memory and what had slipped away. While he would tell me tale after tale from his childhood, his unmarried youth and the war, all of which remained with him in living detail, losing my mother already seemed to have become a distant event. The sadness hadn't left him, but the immediacy of his grief had gone, as if he'd already been widowed for many years when it wasn't even many weeks. It made me think that his form of dementia, the gently increasing time and memory slippage of old age, was actually rather a merciful condition, something provided by Nature to cushion the emotional blow. The manager at the home told me he might forget my mother altogether one day, but I knew that would never happen – though I could imagine a time when he might altogether forget that she was gone.

When we couldn't see ourselves, David continued to call and call and call, to my new mobile, to the number at my parents' house and to the landline at the flat, leaving long messages when he didn't get through and talking for what seemed like hours when he did. If I didn't manage to pick up before the answering machine clicked on in London, some of the calls were recorded. I kept notebooks through this period, and one of them has verbatim transcripts of his messages and the taped calls. In my diary there's a note that suggests I intended to have the recordings copied by an audio engineer friend, but it didn't happen. I suppose I couldn't find the time. But the transcripts survive. This one is dated three days after we returned from Geneva. David is speaking first.

9.36 am, Thursday 3/6/99

- Hello, my darling. How are you?
- I'm still wonderful. How are you?
- OK. OK. I'm all right.
- Oh. How was it going back? Was it awful?
- Mmm. Pretty awful. Just very sad.
- How was Jane?
- Mmm. She was in a bad way. Thought I'd gone off for less than a good reason. You know.
- What did you say to that?
- Oh, nothing. Never excuse, never explain, of course. But I think she just got it through instinct. So. We just had to go through it. Accusing glances from across the room. You know … So we'll just have to be careful. Talk and write and see ourselves pragmatically … We'll just have to be a bit nimble about it.
- When weren't we?
- Quite so. When weren't we? How is it with your people, your dad?
- Oh, I went down yesterday, planning to stay till Sunday. I got to the station and phoned a local cab driver I'd used for years to pick me up. When he pulled up outside the house I realised I hadn't brought my keys.
- Oh, no!
- Yes. So I said 'fuck' about seventeen times in the back of the cab and cast around for alternatives – getting a locksmith, breaking a window. The nice cab driver was very helpful. 'Can I help you break in?' he said to me.
- I'll bet. Can I help you break in? Can I look after you—?
- I decided the easiest thing to do was just to come back. So I took the taxi to see my dad and came back here afterwards. I'm going back there later this morning, *avec mes clefs*.
- Poor love.

– My head just isn't in the right place at the right time always.
– No. Of course. And how is your dad?
– Oh, doing well, I suppose. They all think the world of him at the home. They tell me he's trying to get on with everyone, trying to laugh and smile and talk a bit, trying to appreciate everything they do for him.
– And they're all making a tremendous fuss of him.
– Yes. They love him. I don't know which is worse really, which is saddest – that he's trying to adjust or if he weren't. Anyway – I'll be there till the weekend. Sunday probably. How was Boorman?
– Oh, really very good. I like him a lot, I think. I really do.
– I've got an actor for you, by the way. But go on—
– Have you? Well, he likes the script. Likes it very much. The book was written to end with—
– With the handover of the Canal in the year 2000, yes—
– Which will be a historic event by the time this film is made. So we've decided to start with the handover ceremony and take the story back from there. So Boorman wants me to write twenty minutes to start the film, using documentary footage they'll have from the handover. Then he'll take my script as written and work on it himself. He likes to write his own stuff, but he'll have a hotline to me and the chance to make further use of my services. It's a good deal and it means I can be free to get on with the new book.
– Wonderful. Do you want to hear my actor?
– Yes.
– OK. Don't react straight away, because it's going to sound like a crazy idea, but I know he'd be perfect.
– All right.
– Michael Caine …
– Ha-ha-ha-*ha*. That's very good and very funny. So Boorman says to me, 'I've got the perfect actor in mind. You'll think it's a crazy suggestion at first, but I know he's right and he's even

Jewish.' So I said, 'Michael Caine,' and he said, 'Absolutely. Michael Caine.' So you're bang on the money, Our Sue. How clever.
- He'd be brilliant.
- Ever since *Little Voice* – he was supposed to be so good in it. Have you seen it?
- No. Just the trailers. But I think he was probably extraordinary in it.
- I'm chipping away at that idea. I'm saying Geoffrey Rush or Tom Wilkinson.
- Hmm. Istanbul Productions. [i.e. a turkey]
- You think so? [laughs]
- Go with Caine.
- You may be right, Our Sue. [I was. He should have.]
- I love you.
- And I love you, enormously. I'll call you tomorrow night, my darling. When I'm back from Scotland seeing my man. [ex-MI6, someone who had worked in Africa]
- Fine. I love you. Travel safely.
- I will. I love you, my darling.
- I love you.
- Bye.

I next saw David later the following week. He called me at about nine thirty in the morning.

'I've just put Jane on the train. Can I come round?'

He arrived at ten forty-five and was hardly inside the flat before he fell on me, fired with a pent-up urgency that was off even his own intense scale, saying my name over and over and over.

'I had to have you,' he told me afterwards.

We stayed in bed, helping ourselves to the goodies he'd brought with him. (I found a yellowed receipt from Selfridges Food Hall inside one of the notebooks, time-stamped 10.17 am and listing

313

exactly what he'd bought: vodka, caviar and a carton of white and green asparagus spears from the deli counter. He was definitely in a hurry to see me!) Two vodkas down, David began to talk of what it would be like to be together all the time.

'The floodgates would open,' he said. 'I'd write all the time. We'd fuck all the time too. I'd write in my room and you'd write in yours and I'd come and take you and fuck you and then go back to work.'

(What was it that Judy Garland is supposed to have said to the Munchkin actor on *The Wizard of Oz*, who claimed he could show her a really good time? 'Well, if you do and I find out about it …')

Whole-cloth fantasy though the vision seemed to be, I believe for David, in that moment, it was very, *very* real. And he was very nearly making *me* think it could be real, too. In another life we'd have to try it, like Daisy Gamble and Dr Marc. Perhaps, on a clear day on a distant time-line, we already had.

Then, out of nowhere, David asked me if I wanted a child.

The straight answer to that question was *no*. But a flat no to anything, particularly something you resolutely wish to avoid, tends to send a challenge out into the ether to deliver the exact thing back to you, to test your resolve. After recently coming off the pill I was a little twitchy about the contraception I was using, so, not wanting to challenge the Universe on that subject, I gave my all-purpose non-denial denial.

'Well – never say never.'

'How marvellous!' he exclaimed.

Funny. He seemed to have heard me say yes anyway.

'I think you'd make a marvellous mother,' he went on. 'Especially if you had a boy. And if it had something wrong with it, you'd be superb. It would be simply marvellous.'

'What would you do if I *were* pregnant?' I asked after a few moments.

'Leave,' he answered without hesitation. I assumed at first he meant leave me, but he went on. 'Get out. Of Hampstead. Join you to look after the nipper.'

To this day, I don't know if he was actually making the offer. It certainly seemed as though he might have been floating the possibility. Perhaps it was some sort of unconscious projection of the child – the damaged one, at that – he saw in himself. Perhaps for some reason – even that one – he needed to have the women with whom he had serious relationships either become or already be mothers. Not to start on the Oedipal thing, since David had been so motherless himself, but Susan Kennaway had a small brood at the time of their affair, Yvette had a natural daughter and an adopted son and went around the globe saving children (the title of her biography was *Femme aux mille enfants*), and Janet Stevens was pregnant when she was killed, possibly with his own child. Then there were his four sons by his two wives.

Perhaps, though, it was something with even more of a David spin to it. Because now there was Dawson – again – to whom no man in his right mind would have attributed the desire for motherhood. But David's right mind was only ever the one that he was in at any given period and served – indeed created – his quotidian reality. I'd seen how hard he was endeavouring to maintain his belief in our renewed us-ness this time around, to make his belief stick. So – *was* it an offer? Did he see it as his last chance to leave the 'slammer' in Hampstead? The one undeniable reason and the unshakable cover it would give him for finally 'getting out'?

Lady Ann Smiley was childless and expressed no desire to be otherwise. It wasn't a question in any of the books. The monkish Smiley kept that slate clean and there was never a whisper that any of her 'First Eleven' succeeded where he failed. When she left him – which occurred in the very first paragraph of the very first book – her name remained behind, turning her into the besetting indefinite article of Smiley's life. *I think Smiley's Ann may be you,*

David had said to me all those years before. It was an extraordinary statement, one he didn't make lightly and which he never rescinded. I wonder now whether he was trying to get me to defect from it myself, so that he could fuse together the two warring elements of escape and imprisonment and finally bring the fantasy home.

Well, the wonderings over David, I've found, can go on forever. Whatever the impulse that made him say this, it clearly suited his vision of me then and that was always what reality was for him, his inner persuasion at any one time. It wasn't always momentary, not all of it was fleeting. That he loved me as truly as he did for as long as he did – over decades, in fact, and, as he wrote, across rooms where I wasn't even present – spoke to the constancy he could bring to his inner reality where it ran deep. But when his own extraordinary power of conjuring made the inner reality start to take hold in the external world, it was usually his cue to defect. The only thing he would never have defected from was another child. It was what Miller had told me right at the very start. David always had to have a reason for leaving …

He stayed until late afternoon, then said he would go home, pack his things and pick me up again for an early supper before he went to the airport to go back to Nairobi.

That evening we went to The Brasserie in South Ken and sat at a table outside for an early supper. While we were deciding what to order, David asked me if I liked Schnitzler.

For a half-second, I swear I looked for it on the menu: *Wiener Schnitzler*, my brain had told me, which wasn't so off the mark, since that writer was actually from Vienna. Then the name clicked in connection with something I'd read about the next and probably last film starring Tom Cruise and Nicole Kidman.

'*Eyes Wide Shut*, you mean?'

'Mmm. *Traumnovelle*. Have you read it?'

Of course not.

'No.'

'Kubrick asked me to write the screenplay.'

I'd read that Kubrick had asked just about everybody to write it at one time or another. But I hadn't come across David's name in the throng.

'Why didn't you? Frederic Raphael did in the end, so I read.'

'I went down to his place in Hertfordshire for the day. I don't think we see this movie the same way, Stanley, I told him in the end. He was really quite mad, I decided. He had all these videos sent in by film students. Hundreds, if not thousands. He never looked at them, just kept them and had them wiped, then sold the tapes off second hand.'

David's mood began to slip before we finished the meal. I'd forgotten that it was never a good idea to see him so close to when his head had either been somewhere else – as on that first trip to Cornwall – or, as now, was about to be somewhere else. He always seemed to need a pause between courses when I was on the menu. I should have just let him leave the flat and wend his way to the airport by himself.

The moody letter I anticipated arrived a couple of days later. He must have delayed his departure, or else given me a fictive date for it in the first place, because I wrote back to the Hampstead dead letterbox, with more of my usual soft-soap reassurances that seemed always to work on him (I don't write that cynically, but he was sometimes so much like a little boy wanting someone to check under the bed for monsters), and he wrote straight back again, sending me a parcel of books, non-fiction titles, *The Surgeon of Crowthorne* and *Nathaniel's Nutmeg* among them. He enclosed a note saying that these were the kinds of books he imagined me writing. I'd told him I was happy ghost-writing at the present time, but he didn't seem to like the idea of it. Beginning with the Ronnie biog, he'd always wanted me to write non-fiction. He also

317

enclosed a picture postcard of a couple on the deck of the *Titanic*. He'd drawn arrows to each of them with captions. The woman's was TOO GOOD FOR HIM and the man's was DOESN'T KNOW HIS LUCK. On the back of the card he'd written simply *Then yes*. He let the subtext of the photograph speak for itself.

TOTAL ECLIPSE

Once David was back from Kenya in early July – after 'a pretty heavy mugging' in Nairobi, a city he detested – it was as if he couldn't tell me enough about absolutely everything else in his life. For the next few weeks, whenever I saw him or we spoke on the phone, he seemed to want to cram in everything he hadn't yet told me, as though he somehow had to shore himself up with me, before his time to tell me all of it ran out.

The mugging, he said, was a natural consequence of his 'white colonial guilt'. Some guy had approached pleasantly, asked David to go with him on some ruse and he'd fallen for it. Then his accomplice appeared with a knife. They'd only taken what cash he had on him, not even his credit cards, and hadn't used the knife, but he'd clearly been shaken by the experience. Then he spoke about talking to the Médecins Sans Frontières doctors who treated the boy soldiers from the various militias, out in the farther reaches of the country.

'They told me that the most disheartening thing was you knew you were only patching the kids up so they could go out and fight again and maybe get permanently maimed or killed the next time.'

The movie was progressing with Boorman and David hoped he wouldn't have to go back to LA for a while.

'Charlotte's out there,' he said. 'She's got a new man. She told me his name, so I decided to get my friend John Calley to check him out.'

Calley was a big-time studio exec.

'He rang me back after he'd asked around. *One word*, he said to me. *Hustler.*'

He told me of his rebarbative falling-out with Hollywood producer Sydney Pollack. Pollack had bought the rights to *The Night Manager* for an exorbitant sum, but then messed him around over how and when to make the film, which ultimately didn't happen. David said he'd felt himself to be just the latest blue-eyed blond boy Pollack had taken up, referencing Robert Redford.

'I simply couldn't stand for it any more. There were never any straight answers. *I think, Sidney,* I told him on our last call, *that you and I should never speak again.*'

David said he'd also had to dispense with the services of his long-time representative in New York, Georges Borchardt, and told me why.

'He used to bring his *wife* to our meetings.'

He didn't see fit to mention – I only discovered it later – that Borchardt's wife was also his partner in his business. He didn't say anything at all, good or bad, about his present UK agent, Bruce Hunter, whom he'd gone to after leaving Farquharson's, or say why he'd left his former agency, though George had already told me that after he retired, Farquharson's had substituted a woman in his place. David asked me how I got along with Ed Victor. I'd been telling him how Graham C. Greene had got me into ghost-writing when I hadn't known what to write after my Galsworthy sequel, how I found I enjoyed it, though I knew David didn't really approve. Graham was someone I liked tremendously, a man of impeccable courtesy and twinkly good humour. David inferred from this that I didn't harbour the same sentiments towards Ed. I answered by relaying something Ed had said to me one time, not long after Graham signed me on.

'*When I get to know you better, Sue*, he said, *Carol and I will have you over to the house.* I was tempted to reply that when I got to know *him* better, I might not want to accept. I think he didn't hear himself.'

'No,' David said, agreeing. 'Ed's a joke. He came to me years ago, when he was still working for George at Farquharson's. He took me to lunch and made his pitch. *Let's you and I go it alone, David*, he said to me. *We'll make millions*. Well, it wasn't pretty.'

'What did you say?'

'I told him I was George's man and that was it. But he didn't seem to think he'd done anything wrong.'

David asked me what I'd thought of the BBC's production of *A Perfect Spy*. Sadly, I said, not a lot.

'Nor I,' David concurred. 'It was astonishing to me how they'd taken this Swiss roll I'd made of my story and managed to flatten out every bit of it. What did you make of Egan?'

'Literally nothing,' I said.

'Nor I,' David said again, and we agreed that the part of Pym had somehow become a cipher in the production. I told him I'd worked with the actor in the studio.

'What was he reading for you?'

I found I couldn't recall – rather underscoring the point – but remembered that the client had been very pleased with the finished recording. (A few years later, I saw Egan in the West End in *Art*, playing opposite my great chum Anthony Valentine, and he was really good. Casting is everything.)

David had got to know Peter Cook in his final years.

'I used to go round to his place and drink vodka with him. He had porn videos playing silently on multiple TV screens around the room while we talked.'

That explained the episode at the Château d'Ouchy. Cook was another inveterate rulebreaker and iconoclast, much like Kennaway, who might well have done the same had he lived into the age of VCRs. David still liked the type, evidently, and still liked to try out some of their native ways for himself. The idea of porn movies playing silently in the background would recur in *The Tailor of Panama* film, in a scene with Geoffrey Rush and Pierce Brosnan.

And when we were lying together in bed he read me pages from the new book, just as he had before. His voice still had the same magical power to transport, to conjure up the characters as if they were with us in the room. But I couldn't help thinking that Gooders had been right when he remarked on David's esses all those years ago. There were moments when Justin Quayle sounded completely 'Brideshead' and very prissy indeed.

I was beginning to see some of the characteristic tropes appear in the new novel. First, the almost Dickensian naming of his characters. After giving us the un-smiling Smiley, the recursive Turner, all-dough Aldo, Magnus Pym's minuscule mother, Dot, and so many others, David was now giving us Quayle, the timid desk-bound husband who nevertheless finds the courage to seek out his wife's killers, only to be hunted down and killed like a game bird himself. And there was the fact that Tessa Quayle was dead at the start of the book, her throat slashed for knowing too much about what the bad guys were doing, for not knowing her place in the male system. Stella Rode meets with a similar fate for similar reasons at the start of *A Murder of Quality*; Elsa Fennan has her neck broken in *Call for the Dead*. The women die by injury to their throats, the female organ of reproach. I can't say how much of this he recognised in his writing. I rather think it hovered just below the surface of his conscious use, the way a great chef reaches for and uses a certain knife without really looking, his thoughts already several stages ahead in the feast he's preparing. He'd previously told me that, until it was pointed out to him, he hadn't realised how often he included 'the watching child' in his books – Roach, the new-bug with another Dickensian name in *Tinker Tailor*, being the best-known example.

'"Her cat-like grace",' David repeated from a passage about Tessa Quayle, stroking my thigh. 'Who's that, then, do you think?' he asked me.

He had Justin growing cacti at the start of the book, a detail he decided to modify when I told him I'd read that in feng shui they were supposed to be bad *chi*.

And just in passing, he mentioned he'd turned down another K that year. Still no Sir David, then, though it might have quite suited the Arthurian touches I'd noticed in him now, which he seemed not to see in himself.

There was going to be a total solar eclipse on 11 August, and the press and media were all over it throughout the summer. David was planning a big gathering of the Cornwell clan at Tregiffian for the occasion, but seemed to be dreading it. He had to go down there at the beginning of August and planned to stay the whole month. He made me promise to write, saying he'd be desperate to hear from me in all the madness of the massing throng. He made it sound as though Land's End would resemble the Gaza Strip.

I checked that I was still to send my letters to Sancreed.

'No,' he said, a little quizzically, as if his own answer puzzled him. 'No, my love. Miller's no good now.'

I gathered from this that they'd had a falling-out of some sort, but he didn't choose to elaborate. He gave me a different address for a new friend, Dave Humphries, another writer who lived down there. His recent credit was the LWT fire-station drama series, *London's Burning*.

Hearing what sounded like his estrangement from Miller made me think of Tangye, who had died in '96. I'd seen David's obituary piece on him. My mother had cut it out of the newspaper and sent it to me. It was something she'd always done since I first left home for college and was one of the thousand things I would miss about her. (It was such a shame that she didn't live to enjoy the full internet age, when she could and surely would have sent me links to everything going.)

'Yes,' David said, his voice growing sombre at the recollection of a man he had sincerely considered a friend. 'He lived for ten years without Jeannie. At first, when she died, if he saw a bird at the window he'd say, *That's Jeannie! There she is – her spirit's come back!* By the end he was pissing and shitting in containers and keeping it all round the house. Jane used to go over to help clean him out.'

For all those years I'd been certain there couldn't be a more revolting image of the man than the one I already had, but David had just proved me wrong. My mother never read his books again after I'd told her about the lunch. She'd believed what she read about their Cornish idyll at Minack and afterwards thought them both frauds. I wondered what she'd have made of Tangye's final chapter. But then, she died before I'd told her about my own latest chapter with David.

The last time I saw him before he had to go down to Cornwall, for what by then had become 'the bloody eclipse', he sounded truly pained at the thought of the big family event.

'But at least they'll make use of the place for once. I've spent half a million there and it really looks like it's had the money spent on it, too. It's just amazing. But it's like *Elective Affinities* or *The Forsyte Saga* – they should never have finished the fucking house and garden …'

His voice tapered off with one of his desolate smiles.

'I thought it was always full of family and friends?' I queried.

'No, not at all. Just the two of us. We don't even have the dogs now. It's deadly.'

Before he left that time, he made a point of saying how easy it was to talk to me, how much he appreciated being able to talk to me as he had.

'We live complete lives when we're together, Our Sue.'

The letters he sent me were all really good, the envelopes sporting beaming smiley faces again. They were so uniformly good, in fact, that I teased him in one of mine that the Nairobi mugging must have involved a substantial blow to the head. He wrote of the sex, very extensively, and of what he considered my elegance, and of our love. He said how I'd made him recall the interconnectedness of fucking and writing. He said he'd make every excuse possible to get away as soon as the eclipse was over and come and see me again.

He was in the papers quite a bit at this time and sent me cuttings. He was in a dispute with the farmer who had sold him the land and cottages thirty years ago. The farmer had applied for planning permission for outbuildings and David had lodged an objection with the local authorities. He had his reasons – suspecting that it was the first step towards a separate more substantial dwelling – but was inevitably tagged with nimbyism in the press. He gave me an account of a local meeting he'd had to attend. His mobile had rung before it convened and David had explained it was an important call from LA that he had to take and excused himself. Twenty minutes later, having concluded the call, he rejoined the locals.

'Ere, David told me that one of them asked him, *'owever much did that cost you then?* To which he replied stony-faced, *The other end pays ...*

Peckinpah had evidently been onto something.

It sounded like a tiresome battle and possibly one that David thought he might not win. Next time he called he said he'd come up with a devilish plan.

'I'm giving my whole fucking mile of cliff to the National Trust! They can fight the farmer now. Stuff him!'

He wrote a piece in the *Observer* to mark Al Alvarez's seventieth birthday. He was the one member of the inner circle I never met. I never found out why, but put it down to some more delicate sensibility on the part of the academic, poet and poker player than had been the case with the others. (I learned subsequently from Sisman that David had once asked Alvarez if he would receive letters for him, as Miller originally did, but Alvarez refused.) He wrote in the article that Alvarez was one of only two people who were permitted to disturb him while he was working. I hadn't heard this rather precious diktat from David himself and concluded the other of the two was his wife, meaning that even his sons weren't allowed that level of access. I had a vision of Jane (only it was Terry Jones in drag) warning one of his sons (played by Eric Idle), *Don't disturb your father – you know what he's like after a few novels* ...

Mobile telephones weren't such an asset in Cornwall at that time. David's next call was from a tor. He said he'd had to walk miles to get to a high point for a signal and even then he sounded as if he were speaking under six feet of water. But he just had to hear my voice.

'I've rewritten the bit about feng shui and bad *chi* from cactus,' he told me, 'and now it really works.'

He called me very early on the morning of the eclipse. He'd walked to a different place and found better reception.

'I'm just going to say quickly that I love you and I'm *surrounded* by people and it's *pissing* with rain. I've got your lovely letters, though, my darling, and cor, you can't half write a letter.'

He rang again the day after the eclipse, another very brief call. It sounded as if this time he was calling from the house.

'It really *was* like a rebirth, just as it was supposed to be,' he said, sounding invigorated by the experience, a renewed energy in his voice. 'Your whole life really does march before you – and who was leading the procession? You, my darling. You.'

He rang again later, when I was expecting a call from my friend Emily, who was just over from the States.

'Hi!' I said.

'*Hi*,' David said back deliberately. 'I'm not even going to ask who *that* was for.'

He asked if I'd got his latest package of non-fiction books, more titles of the sort he was gently suggesting I might write. Because of this persistent suggestion, gentle though it was, I said I wondered whether he'd perhaps found my first attempt at fiction a little hard going.

'Now, listen,' he responded sternly. 'The only fiction we must cease here is about your somehow sucking on the hind teat of literary talent. I have read your book, Our Sue, and it *simply* isn't *true*. And in that I am your staunchest supporter.'

I had to re-run the convolutions of this for a second or two before deciding it was a fairly major compliment from the Great Man.

He'd arranged our trip, he said excitedly, when he rang again the next day. We were on for the start of September, Bern and then Elba.

Bern, I thought when he rang off. Not just Switzerland this time, but *Bern*. For David, there was no place where he could take me further 'in'.

He called again later with explicit travel details. It was Elba first now, Bern after.

'I want you to travel out on Wednesday 1st on Air Engiadina from London City Airport. I'll spell it for you—' He did. I'd never heard of the airline and never flown from the new City Airport. 'I just can't manage any time for us before then, but we'll have a lot of time together once we're away.'

'That's all right,' I said. He sounded worried whether I'd make it there. 'I love you, David. It's all fine.'

'And I love you too. Very much. I'll call you later tonight. And I'm sending you a little letter. Maybe a long letter. And the money for your ticket.'

He was always so concerned that I shouldn't spend a penny of my own money on anything to do with him. But without the Authors Workshop as a cut-out and with his wife now handling the household accounts directly, he couldn't write a cheque. This time the cash came inside a French paperback novel. Its spine wasn't cracked, so he hadn't read it before packing the money inside. There was a lovely letter with it and a back copy of *Granta* where an essay of his, *The Unbearable Peace*, had appeared. It all arrived in a padded envelope he'd addressed to a P. Drax Esq., at my flat, so it must have gone with his wife to the post office in Cornwall.

The next time he called I was out with Emily and hadn't taken my mobile with me. When I told her about being back with David, how it had happened, Emily – like my friend Kate before her – had tears in her eyes. Well, it just *was* one of those stories. I came back to a message on my answering machine.

'I'm just calling again to tell you I love you and I dream of you and I am <u>surrounded</u> by people, but I had to call you. I've sent you a fat letter. And I adore you. I wanted to tell you, but you aren't there.'

I kept my mobile with me at all times after that and the next time he caught me while I was trying on a Jaeger dress in Kensington.

'Guess where I am,' I said.

'The sauna! The bath! Anywhere naked!'

It was another of his uncanny guesses, since I very nearly was.

'I'm trying on something to wear for you,' I told him, naming the store, 'but I think it's the wrong colour. Or I am.'

'So are you standing there bollock-naked, Our Sue? That's really what I was asking.'

'Pretty much,' I said. 'Only without the bollocks.'

'Cor,' he purred. 'But me on my knees with my head between your legs, all right?!'

I looked at myself in the long mirror in the changing cubicle and saw that David had just made me blush.

So how did it end, and why, when everything was going so well?

As always with David, the answer was in the question. Just as there ought to have been a word, solely for him, to mean a man who was so especially and so magically attentive to his mistress, there ought to have been another adjective with his name on it offering some brain-spinning hybrid of axiomatically paradoxical and paradoxically axiomatic. (It wouldn't surprise me if there is such a word in German.) It had to go wrong because it *was* going so right.

I was still visiting my father as often as possible and, much as he never gave anyone a moment's unnecessary trouble in his life (unlike some, as Graham might have observed), there were still all the attendant issues for me to deal with. And seeing him meant that I was still living part-time on the train, my Tumi bag slung permanently over my shoulder as I shuttled between my two realities. I don't think I fully realised the strain I was under, but I was beginning to realise that while I'd heard all of David's problems, he really didn't try to elicit mine. He occasionally asked me how my father was, but didn't ever prompt me to say more, about how the situation was affecting me. But it was. And though I was looking forward to going away with him again – it had been more than a couple of months since Lausanne – something was bugging me about this trip. When I worked out what it was, it seemed so obvious. It was one thing to once again be a married rich guy's secret girlfriend – I trust I've shown I was always fine with that – and to be whisked away on fabulous trips. I liked the whisking; it compensated for the other restrictions in the relationship and was especially welcome now, given what I'd had on my plate all that summer and would continue to have for as long as my father was alive. But somehow, being sent a bundle of cash and told to make my own arrangements wasn't whisking. I realised I wasn't OK with it. I was quite capable of making travel arrangements for myself, of course, but the point was, these were not my arrangements. They were David's. And much as I was happy to accompany him and very much wanted to be with him on his travels, there was something that didn't sit right with me about having to go about things this way. It seemed demeaning somehow, to us both. More so because he was a multimillionaire ex-spy who couldn't find a more elegant way to manage the issue and didn't seem to be looking for one either. It was too close to leaving money on the dresser.

I decided I would find a way to put this to David when we were in Elba. A gentle – *careful* – suggestion that he might think of making a separate arrangement somewhere, as he had before with Rainer; just one credit card that his wife didn't see, to facilitate things for us. I hoped he'd see the nuance in what I felt. But David rang me before I'd had the chance to properly formulate what I would say, how I'd put it to him. He asked if I'd got my ticket to Elba and I told him that I hadn't yet. And then I made the cardinal mistake of just asking him straight. Not unpleasantly, certainly not whiningly – just straight. As if that had *ever* been the way with him.

'Do you think, David, that you could maybe arrange just one credit card your wife doesn't know about to use on these trips?'

I knew the second the words were out of my mouth that I shouldn't have said them. I felt a bristling silence at the other end of the line. It was axiomatic – *of course* – that if he *could* have done that, he *would* have. If Hampstead was practice for Guantanamo Bay then Tregiffian was a revival of Alcatraz, and I'd just reminded him that he was only ever out on licence from either one.

'I think that's a bit stiff—' he said at last.

I tried to explain, I even began to back-pedal – not a thing I was good at because it wasn't a thing I ever did – but I knew it was no use. David half-mumbled some excuses and quickly rang off. I called him back, but got no answer. I didn't stop calling him back for several days. I wrote too – to our latest dead letterbox in Cornwall and to the first one, *poste restante* Hampstead – but nothing elicited a response. I couldn't bring him back from the edge this time. That dated, pink-gin expression – *a bit stiff* – was the last thing he ever said to me. And when he said it, it was as if a light had gone out in his voice.

David wrote to me eventually, but only to underline what I already knew. He claimed I'd 'bawled him out', which I hadn't at all. Not even the tiniest bit. I'd only thought to suggest that it really wasn't too much to ask my ex-spook secret lover to facilitate our secret trips with just one secret account. After I'd spent the previous three months dealing with everything to do with my parents' lives and mother's death; after I'd travelled so frequently on the same train line, back and forth between London and their place, that the train company should have named a carriage after me; after I'd run out of resilience to the slightest challenge myself; after I'd got David back as my lover and all *that* entailed – I hadn't thought it was so much to ask. But after he'd put almost thirty years of his life into what he'd already called a sexless empty marriage, I suppose it was. Though the flesh had still been extraordinarily willing to continue with 'us', his spirit was weak – just about beaten down, I reckon – and so that tiny bit of oh-so-gentle reproach from me had been enough. And far, far too much. My tentative request had confirmed that John le Carré had finally run out of tradecraft.

But then he went on to say that he was grateful I'd done it, because now he knew he had to settle for the life he had, which he described only as 'not the worst'. It was the saddest phrase. If I understood one new thing about David then, it was that the only close relationships he had that didn't end miserably were the ones that continued so.

It was over. *Fin d'histoire*, as Graham always used to say.

But really, this time.

LE FIN DE L'HISTOIRE

I seem to see poor Edward, naked and reclining amid darkness, upon cold rocks, like one of the ancient Greek damned …

Ford Madox Ford, *The Good Soldier*

I immediately went back to Elizabeth, expecting to cry uncontrollably in her consulting room. But as I told her how David and I had met again, had fallen in love again and now it was over – again – the tears were in her eyes, not mine. Well, it just *was* one of *those* stories. And as Elizabeth helped me realise, the story finally had its right and proper ending.

After a long session with her, I returned home and wrote David one last letter, not even covering a full page, just saying I love you and thank you and goodbye. We didn't see each other or speak or write to each other ever again.

Over the years, David had seen off many would-be biographers, scaring them with lawyers or seeming to offer openings that he later blocked, even agreeing to a posthumous publication; anything to stop his life becoming anyone's material save his own. But as he neared the rise to eighty he gave up trying to be King Cnut holding back the tide of his own life story and finally let another writer 'that far in'.

Adam Sisman's biography was published in 2015. But while his extraordinarily comprehensive six-hundred-page book gives the tangled relationship with Susan Kennaway and her husband in some detail, it barely touches on the rest of David's extra-marital life. The whole topic is covered in just a few lines, describing 'impulsive, driven, short-lived affairs', words David supplied himself, Adam told me. For the sake of concluding the project smoothly, they had come to an agreement not to include any specific mention of his sexual relationships, with Yvette, with Janet or with me, or with any of his hitherto nameless second XI, several of whom Sisman had also tracked down. Having at first said publicly that he had no time for 'authorised biographies', David evidently decided he still didn't want the whole truth to come out. The biographer's free hand seemed to be rather more like Bosinney's in the matter of finishing Soames Forsyte's house; 'a free hand in the terms of the correspondence'. Perhaps David had originally assumed he wouldn't be quite so thorough in finding all the women, including me.

Adam and I had quite become chums by then, rather in the way that George Greenfield and I had been, as mutually regarding DC comrades-in-arms. He had initially sent me a charming 'to whom it may concern' email via my former agent, who had told him of my existence but not my name. He would never have found me otherwise. I always intended to write my own memoir of my time with David and had even completed an early first draft. But the combination of UK libel laws, EU privacy laws and, for a period, a legal gagging device called a super-injunction – which errant celebrities were readily using to keep their sexual indiscretions hidden – would have all weighed disproportionately on David's side of the scales of justice, had he ever chosen to avail himself of them against me or any publisher who took the manuscript on. It had made me see that any publication of mine would probably have to wait until he was dead. Since it looked as if our mutual subject was going to live to be a hundred and ten in the shade, I agreed to tell the biographer the key elements of my story, only to have it come to nothing when David insisted that part of his life still shouldn't be told.

'I told him I'd spoken to you, though,' Adam said to me after he'd published.

'What did he say?' I asked, all ears to know what the response had been.

Adam replied simply, 'He said – *Oh, God.*'

I confess I found the Great Man's reaction strangely gratifying.

And oddly enough, for all his intention to mask the topic, David had composed an almost entirely truthful description of his love encounters for the biography. They really weren't much more than brief affairs – the longest of them, with Susan Kennaway and Janet Stevens, not lasting more than a few months in each case and with Yvette even more swiftly converted to a family friend. The one exception was the relationship he had with me. If you were to calculate the combined time David spent with all his 'other women' it still wouldn't amount to as long as we had together. Not even close.

My phone rang around 10 pm on 13 December 2020. It was my friend Peter's ringtone. Over the years that we've known each other, it's become his way often to dispense with any greeting and go straight to the subject he's calling about. This time he was more direct than ever.

'He's dead.'

I thought at first he meant Biden. The election result had only recently been called and the gathering alt-right storm in the States made it seem a horrible possibility.

But it was David. He had died from pneumonia after a fall. It was only a few weeks after his eighty-ninth birthday. *Flights of angels* was the phrase that ran through my mind when Peter said his name.

At the start of the new year, raiding old files for earlier drafts and notes, rounding up the letters and my diaries, I began to write. And I rather think I fell in love with David for the third time as I did. Never more so than when I re-read his letters, and saw again how very much he had opened his heart and his life to me.

So this is it – the story of my time with le Carré the writer and with David the man. I hope I've made him seem as lovely as he was and as loving. I hope I've shown the magic. I trust I've helped elucidate the rest. Did I crack the code? Did I discover what made David run? Perhaps a little. But life – any life – isn't about finding the answers so much as it's about uncovering the clues.

His wife, who died only a short while later, is supposed to have said of him, *No one can have all of David.* I tend to think she had his affairs in mind when she said this and I find myself wanting to say in reply – Well, who can? Even supposing such a thing were possible, who would want the *all* of anyone? But it seems to me now that the exact opposite is what was true of David; that, in fact, there was no 'all' to be had. I think he was entirely fractal. Every piece of him felt like the whole, because he always presented it as if it were, and to him, in each moment, it was the truth. What all the pieces added up to, I rather think that he himself was the very last to know. He once wrote to me that there were at least ten thousand versions of himself, so perhaps, in the end, there are only clues to be had. Lovely, fascinating, baffling, infuriating clues about the essential enigma of him, the puzzle that I think he always wanted me to try and solve. It's what I've tried to do here. He once told me that I was part of the best thing he had so far written. He is the entirety of mine.

The first dream I ever had about David – when his face suddenly appeared, telling me so sweetly that he thought 'we should see ourselves again' – was what led this story to have its final ending. But I had a second dream about him in the course of writing the story down.

I arrived alone at a supper party for ten or a dozen people and was surprised to find myself seated opposite him. I was further surprised when he called me *my darling*, just as he ever had, as I sat down at the table.

'*Am* I still your darling?' I asked him.

'Yes,' he replied, as paradoxical as ever. 'Always.'

GLOSSARY

The Circus – the 'in-house' name for le Carré's fictional Intelligence Service, his MI6, taken from the location of its London headquarters in Cambridge Circus.

dead letterbox – secure temporary hiding place for the exchange of written information; a drop-box.

fallback – agreed alternative arrangements to a plan, in case of emergency.

Joes – agents operating in the field, working to an agent-runner.

lamplighters – surveillance agents, also responsible for clearing drop-boxes and mail intercepts.

legend – cover story involving false biographical details.

Martha – a female recruit to the Intelligence Service.

mole – deep-penetration agent; a long-term 'double'.

Moscow Rules – strictest levels of secrecy and security for operating safely in enemy territory.

mothers – female ancillary staff working for the senior men in the Circus.

Reptile Fund – untraceable money available to fund covert operations.

safe houses – secure premises for clandestine meetings.

Sarratt – le Carré's fictional training school for spooks.

soft-route – the least traceable or accountable way into a country or region.

ACKNOWLEDGEMENTS

Those name-checked so far are Barbara Rudolph, Peter Delaunay, Emily Altman, Sascha Dutton-Forshaw, Elizabeth McKinstry and Kate Sherry. They have seen me through all the various stages of this story, either as it was happening or as I was writing it down. Some were there throughout. At no time did any one of them, say, 'Can we talk about something else?' My love and thanks go to each of them for their friendship and forbearance along the way. Andrew Lownie and Adam Sisman helped me refine my approach to the telling of the story by generously sharing their own encounters and views. The route from manuscript to book deal was expertly navigated by my agent, Jane Graham-Maw, who found the story its safe berth at Mudlark. Stellar work, Jane! And finally I owe more thanks than I can properly express to the extraordinary team at Mudlark and HarperNonFiction; Joel Simons, Jessica Jackson and Fionnuala Barrett (and through Fionnuala, the audio dream team of Lydia Thomson and Rowan Laxton for the sessions at Chatterbox Studios); Mark Bolland, Ameena Ghori-Khan, Imogen Gordon Clark, Zoe Shine, Hannah Sawyer, Oliver Malcolm and Steve Burdett; Holly Macdonald, Claire Ward and Dean Russell – an incomplete list, I'm sure. I could never have imagined – or wanted – a more welcoming reception of my memoir and me. Their careful, thoughtful and appreciative handling of every aspect of this book and its publication has touched me to my heart.

The Evolution
of Human Sexuality

The Evolution
of Human Sexuality

DONALD SYMONS

New York   Oxford
OXFORD UNIVERSITY PRESS
1979

Library of Congress Cataloging in Publication Data

Symons, Donald, 1942–
The evolution of human sexuality.

Bibliography: p.
Includes index.
1. Sex (Psychology) 2. Sex differences (Psychology)
3. Genetic psychology. I. Title.
BF692.S9   155.3'3   78-23361
ISBN 0-19-502535-0

Printed in the United States of America

Acknowledgment is given for permission to quote from the following works:

Combat in the Erogenous Zone by Ingrid Bengis. Copyright 1972 by Ingrid Bengis. Reprinted by permission of Alfred A. Knopf, Inc., and Wildwood House Ltd.

The Vagabond by Colette. Translated by Enid McLeod. Copyright © 1955 by Farrar, Straus and Young. Reprinted by permission of Farrar, Straus & Giroux, Inc., and Martin Secker and Warburg Ltd.

"Sex in Cross-Cultural Perspective" by William Davenport. In *Human Sexuality in Four Perspectives*, edited by Frank A. Beach. Copyright 1976, 1977 by The Johns Hopkins University Press. Reprinted by permission of The Johns Hopkins University Press.

The Kingdom of the Young by Verrier Elwin. Copyright 1968 by Oxford University Press. Reprinted by permission of Oxford University Press (New Delhi).

Sexual Behavior in the Human Male by Alfred C. Kinsey, Wardell B. Pomeroy, and Clyde E. Martin, and *Sexual Behavior in the Human Female* by A. C. Kinsey, W. B. Pomeroy, C. E. Martin, and P. H. Gebhard. Copyright 1948 and 1953, respectively, by W. B. Saunders Co. Reprinted by permission of the Institute for Sex Research, Inc.

The Politics of Rape by Diana E. H. Russell. Copyright © 1974 by Diana E. H. Russell. Reprinted by permission of Stein and Day Publishers.

Married Life in an African Tribe by I. Schapera. Reprinted by permission of Faber and Faber Ltd. and Northwestern University Press.

The Homosexual Matrix by C. A. Tripp. Copyright © 1975 by Sociological Research Associates, Inc. Reprinted by permission of McGraw-Hill Book Company.

Preface

PSYCHIATRIST DAVID HAMBURG once remarked that one of the relics of early man is modern man. Besides the obvious fact of genetic continuity, Hamburg meant that humans have a nature as well as a history. This point of view was not especially controversial in the 1960s, when the chimpanzee (the customary model for early man) was a peace-loving, promiscuous, Rousseauian ape, and students of human evolution emphasized tool-use, cooperation, hunting, language, and "innate" needs for long-lasting, intimate relationships. Today, however, the chimpanzee is a murderous, cannibalistic, territorial, sexually jealous, Hobbesian ape; sociobiologists promote a cynical view of human social life; and an evolutionary perspective on human beings as well as the concept of human nature are intensely controversial. A central theme of this book is that, with respect to sexuality, there is a female human nature and a male human nature, and these natures are extraordinarily different, though the differences are to some extent masked by the compromises heterosexual relations entail and by moral injunctions. Men and women differ in their sexual natures because throughout the immensely long hunting and gathering phase of human evolutionary history the sexual desires and dispositions that were adaptive for either sex were for the other tickets to reproductive oblivion.

The seeds from which this book grew are lost to my memory. My first pertinent recollection is a conversation with Richard Dawkins, which must have taken place in 1968 when Dawkins was an Assistant Professor of Zoology, and I was a graduate student in anthropology, at the University of California, Berkeley. It had occurred to me that men tend to want a variety of sexual partners and women tend not to because this desire always was adaptive for ancestral males and never was adaptive for ancestral females. Dawkins said he had reached the same conclusion by the same line of reasoning, which buoyed me up considerably. This simple notion seemed to explain so much that as my knowledge of the literature on human sexuality grew I continued to ask myself whether new information made adaptive sense. In 1974 a much shorter and, I trust, more naïve version of this book became the basis for my lectures in a course (ostensibly in primate behavior) at the University of California, Santa Barbara. Nothing in my 300 students' responses to these lectures (including anonymous, written responses) prepared me for the difficulties that lay ahead. Without those difficulties, however, the present volume never would have been written.

Although this book is about sex and about sex differences, it is not about sex roles. By this I mean several things. First, I suspect "sex role" of being a concept that obscures more often than it enlightens and, in Veronica Geng's words, makes it impossible to think. Second, I am only peripherally concerned with matters such as the division of labor by sex and the possibility of sex differences in cognition which loom so large in the literature on sex roles, and I assume that men and women do not differ in their capacities to perform almost any job in the modern world. Third, although discussions of sex roles unaccompanied by normative and prescriptive rhetoric may exist, I have yet to run across them, whereas my discussion of sex differences in sexuality is not intended to have social policy implications.

This book is organized as follows: Chapter One introduces basic evolutionary concepts, and Chapter Two considers the special difficulties in applying these concepts to human beings. Since evolutionary analyses of human sexuality traditionally emphasize changes that occurred in the female—the capacity for orgasm and the loss of estrus—Chapters Three and Four respectively deal with these matters. The basic components of sexual selection—intrasexual competition and sexual choice—are taken up in Chapters Five and Six. Chapter Seven, about the desire for sexual variety, emphasizes male sexuality, and Chapter Eight integrates much of the earlier material in arguing that among all peoples sexual intercourse is understood to be a service or favor that females render to males. In Chapter Nine, the hypothesis that male sexuality and female sexuality differ by nature is tested with two independent kinds of evidence. Chapter Ten recapitulates the book's major themes. References to nonobservable entities—desires, dispositions, minds, and the like—crop up throughout these chapters since, to my mind, limiting oneself to behavior when one is really interested in psyche is like the drunk looking for his lost car keys under the streetlamp: he knows he lost them somewhere in the dark, but under the streetlamp the light is better. I hope to persuade the reader that an evolutionary view of life can shed light on psyche, which eludes us because it is us.

I am deeply grateful to many individuals for their help during the writing of this book. Charles Akemann, Owen Aldis, Paul Bohannan, Miriam Caldwell, Miriam Chaiken, Charles Erasmus, Geri-Ann Galanti, Patricia Gibson, Raymond Hames, Thomas Harding, Elvin Hatch, Elizabeth Holbrook, Cyd Hunt, James M. B. Keyser, Elaine Koss, Russell Ludeke, Laurence Mamlet, Paul Mattson, Mattison Mines, John Platt, Barbara Sacharow, Elman Service, Shirley Strum, John Townsend, Barbara Voorhies, and Phillip Walker were kind enough to read and comment on various parts of various drafts of this work. Priscilla Robertson introduced me to the history of feminist movements. Paul Heuston, Pattilee Patterson, and Albert Spaulding prepared Figures 3.1 and 8.1. Margaret Ehmann, Deborah Reinke, and Patricia Sanderson provided research assistance far beyond the call of duty. Heidi Pitts, Mary Shannon, and Jeanette Woodward typed the manuscript.

I owe a special debt of gratitude to two people, without whom this book probably would not exist. Robert J. Tilley of Oxford University Press found merit in the original manuscript and maintained this opinion throughout the book's evolutionary history. His encouragement and support are, in large part, responsible for my persistence. Finally, my friend and colleague D. E. Brown patiently read more drafts of this work than either of us cares to remember, called attention to many lapses in logic and continuity, and offered consistently sound advice. My thinking about human sexuality owes a great deal to years of exchanging ideas with Brown and to his remarkable analytic abilities.

D.S.

Santa Barbara
June 1978

To D. E. Brown

Contents

What I shall try to show, without carping, will be that there is a very good reason why the erotic side of Man has called forth so much more discussion lately than has his appetite for food. The reason is this: that while the urge to eat is a personal matter which concerns no one but the person hungry (or, as the German has it, der hungrig Mensch), *the sex urge involves, for its true expression, another individual. It is this "other individual" that causes all the trouble.*

JAMES THURBER and E. B. WHITE,
Is Sex Necessary?

The Evolution
of Human Sexuality

Introduction

It is an unsafe assumption, born of anthropomorphic generalizations about animal behaviour and vague thought about evolution, that if human behaviour itself will not reveal those "basic instincts and impulses," comparison with the lives of other organisms will.

SOLLY ZUCKERMAN

To UNDERSTAND THE HEAD, said the Yellow Emperor, Huang-Ti, investigate well the tail. Forty-five hundred years later Darwin's theory of evolution by natural selection provided an intellectual basis for Huang-Ti's belief that sexuality informs the human psyche; but the implications of the Darwinian revolution in biology for understanding human psychology remain largely unexplored. Darwin argued that living organisms evolved from one or a few simple forms of life through the process of natural selection. The essence of this process is that the individuals that comprise a population differ in the number of viable offspring they produce during their lifetimes, the more fecund individuals owing their relative reproductive success to features of structure, behavior, or psyche not possessed, or possessed in differing degree, by the less fecund members. Since progeny tend to resemble their parents, there is constant and inevitable selection for characteristics that result in successful reproduction. Natural selection is not necessarily for complexity or simplicity, altruism or selfishness, pugnacity or timidity, cooperation or conflict, survival or death: it is simply for reproductive success.

This book is about the evolution of human sexuality and, more particularly, the evolution of typical differences between men and women in sexual behaviors, attitudes, and feelings. Sex differences are emphasized because each sex provides a perspective or vantage point from which to view the other. The comparison of males and females is perhaps the most powerful available means of ordering the bewildering diversity of data on human sexuality. Furthermore, an evolutionary approach to sexuality may counteract the frequently stated or implied notion that a difference between human males and females inevitably indicates that one sex is inferior or defective.[1] For example, since it is commonly assumed to be "natural" for humans to be sexually aroused by viewing an attractive, unclothed member of the opposite sex, the evidence that women are less likely to be sexually aroused by the sight of naked men than men are by the sight of naked women often is attributed to systematic early repression of female sexuality, and women thus are seen as inhibited or defective. On the other hand, Shulasmith Firestone (1970) argues that, unlike women, men are not able to love. She implies that although the sexes are identical at birth, males are crippled emotionally by early Oedipal experiences that females escape; hence, insofar as they differ from women in their romantic feelings, men are seen as defective. But the view advanced in this book—that selection has produced marked sex differences in sexuality—implies that neither sex can be usefully considered to be merely a defective version of the other.

In the present chapter I introduce basic evolutionary concepts and in the next chapter consider the special difficulties encountered in applying these concepts to humans. The actual evidence on human sexuality—which is the subject of the remaining chapters—is in some respects less difficult and convoluted than are the theoretical issues involved in interpreting this evidence. The origins of problems discussed in the first two chapters often are not scientific, in the usual sense of the word, but conceptual, historical, and emotional. Semantic confusions, non sequiturs, false dichotomies, and arguments at cross purposes must be identified and disentangled.

Chapter One can be outlined as follows: (1) Modern understandings of "natural selection" and "fitness" are value-free. "Natural selection is the differential reproductive success of individuals within a population that occurs because of genetic differences among them" (Alcock

---

[1] This opinion is widespread in part because most of the sex differences studied by psychologists are, in fact, skills or abilities—such as verbal proficiency and perception of spatial relations—that can be measured on a scale of competence. Male-female differences in sexual behavior *per se* usually are omitted (see, for example, a review of the literature by Maccoby and Jacklin 1974).

1975:7). "Fitness" is a measure of relative reproductive success and does not refer to human value judgments. (2) Species-typical behavior in a natural habitat is subject to two kinds of causal analysis: proximate (immediate) analysis and ultimate (evolutionary) analysis. The failure to distinguish between them results in confusion and sterile debate. Proximate causal analyses are attempts to explain *how* animals come to develop and exhibit behavior patterns; ultimate causal analyses are attempts to explain *why* animals exhibit behavior patterns. In a proximate sense, an animal exhibits a given behavior pattern because it possesses a particular complement of genes, has encountered particular environmental circumstances during its lifetime, and is in the presence of particular stimuli. In an ultimate sense, an animal exhibits a given behavior pattern because its ancestors promoted their reproductive success in specific ways by exhibiting that behavior pattern in similar circumstances. (3) A feature of structure, behavior, or psyche may have a variety of effects on an animal's survival and reproduction, but it is not useful to consider all beneficial effects to be "functions." Function refers to the purpose for which a character was designed by natural selection. Other consequences, even beneficial ones, are best referred to simply as "effects." (4) In historical perspective, the persistence of the nature-nurture controversy can be seen in part as the consequence of failing to distinguish between proximate and ultimate causation. Species-typical behavior observed in a natural environment can be expected to have an ultimate explanation; that is, it was designed by natural selection to serve a particular function or functions. To provide an ultimate explanation for a given pattern, however, is not to imply that the behavior is "innate" or unlearned. (5) Learning abilities rarely are general capacities. They are designed to solve the specific problems that have been important in the evolutionary history of a species. Our human bias that the ability to learn necessarily represents evolutionary "advance" or "progress" has distorted our understanding of nonhuman animals and of ourselves. Learning often has disadvantages compared with "innate" development, and even human beings possess "innate" psychic and behavioral predispositions, not because such predispositions are residues of our animal past, but because they regularly resulted in adaptive behavior. (6) Although males and females of most animal species have evolved secondary sex differences in structure and behavior, these differences are not necessary concomitants of sexuality. Ultimately, they are the consequences of males and females pursuing different reproductive "strategies."

Natural selection and fitness

The modern theory of evolution synthesizes Darwinian selection and Gregor Mendel's discovery that inheritance is based on the transfer from parent to offspring of particulate units, or genes, which generally remain unchanged though they are shuffled and reshuffled in the course of successive generations. In the language of evolutionary biology an organism's "fitness" is a measure of the extent to which it succeeds, compared with other members of the population, in passing on its genes to the next generation. An organism is reproductively successful or unsuccessful only compared with other members of the population, and in this sense reproductive "competition" is inevitable (Williams 1966). If we are told that a given female wolf produced three viable offspring during her lifetime we cannot describe her as successful or unsuccessful, as fit or unfit, until we are told the average number of viable offspring produced by female wolves in the population. If the average is one offspring per female, our female is highly successful and fit; her genes (and hence wolves that physically and behaviorally resemble her) will increase in frequency in the next generation. If the average is six offspring per female, our female is highly unsuccessful and unfit; her genes will decrease in frequency in the next generation. Nutritional "competition," for example, is not inevitable in this sense because it is possible to specify the degree to which an organism succeeds in meeting certain absolute nutritional requirements without reference to the nutritional success of other members of the population. That reproductive "competition" is inevitable in the genetic sense does not imply that organisms themselves necessarily will engage in overt reproductive conflict, although it does imply that sexual intercourse normally will not be random. In Darwin's words (1871:362): "promiscuous intercourse in a state of nature is extremely improbable."

Natural selection is thus for organisms that maximize the representation of their own genes in the next generation. But an individual's genes are carried by members of the population in addition to the individual's direct descendants, hence selection can favor organisms who promote not only their own individual fitness but also the fitnesses of individuals with whom they share genes by common descent. That is, selection is for the maximization of "inclusive fitness" (Hamilton 1964), which is the sum of an individual's own fitness plus its influence on the fitnesses of organisms, other than its direct descendants, with whom it shares genes by common descent. Hamilton (1975) points out that the argument is the same for nonrelatives in whom genetic affinity can be recognized.

Inclusive fitness theory represents a major conceptual advance and has provided satisfying ultimate causal explanations of such apparent anomalies as the existence of sterile insect castes. But the importance of precise fractions of relatedness—halves, quarters, eighths—in inclusive fitness theory has perhaps given it the misleading impression of making far more precise predictions than classical Darwinian theory. Inclusive fitness theory does, in fact, provide better explanations than Darwinian theory. It better accounts, for example, for the substantial body of evidence that "Human beings, wherever we meet them, display an almost obsessional interest in matters of sex and kinship" (Leach 1966). Inclusive fitness theory may become a powerful predictive tool, but, at present, the implication that it makes specific predictions about what will evolve is likely to foster only misunderstandings, such as Sahlins's (1976) misguided attack on sociobiology.

For two reasons, inclusive fitness theory, like classical Darwinian theory, does not predict that specific behaviors will evolve: the contingencies affecting selection are too complex to be predicted; and mutations—the raw materials on which selection acts—occur randomly with respect to fitness. Inclusive fitness theory predicts that the species-typical behavior of an animal in a natural habitat will not be found to promote the inclusive fitness of another animal, or group of animals, at the expense of the behaver's own inclusive fitness. So-called "altruistic" behaviors *can* evolve when the positive effects on the fitnesses of kin outweigh the negative effects on personal fitness, but there is no guarantee that such behaviors *will* evolve. (In the following chapter I discuss the semantics of "altruism.") Lemuel Gulliver wrote in his journal: "Alliance by blood or marriage is a frequent cause of war between Princes, and the nearer the kindred is, the greater is their disposition to quarrel." Nothing in inclusive fitness theory implies that selection will not sometimes favor maximum violence toward the closest kin.

Proximate and ultimate causation

Two fundamentally different kinds of questions can be asked about the causation of species-typical behavior in a natural habitat: one can inquire into proximate and ultimate causes (Mayr 1961). Proximate, or immediate, causal analyses consider *how* the behavior came to exist. The answers to questions about proximate causation will be that the animal possesses a particular given complement of genes, that it has encountered a particular set of environmental conditions during the course of its lifetime which resulted in its developing particular features of structure and physiology, and that it is in the presence of particular stimuli. In other words, questions about the proximate causes of behavior deal with development, physiology, and immediate stimulus: they consider the individual animal's history and present circumstances. In theory it is possible to provide a complete proximate explanation of a behavior pattern without reference to, or knowledge of, evolution and evolutionary processes.

Ultimate, or evolutionary, causal analyses consider *why* the behavior exists. The answers to questions about ultimate causation will be that the behavior functions in specific ways to maximize the animal's inclusive fitness. Functions result from the operation of natural selection in the populations from which the animal is descended: members of ancestral populations who exhibited that behavior in similar circumstances were more fit than were conspecifics who exhibited some other behavior. Questions about the ultimate causes of behavior thus consider primarily the species's history, and, for this reason, they are more difficult to answer than questions about proximate causes. The ancestral populations in which the behavior evolved are gone and cannot be studied. The behavior itself may have many effects, beneficial, neutral, and harmful, on the animal's survival and reproduction, and often it is difficult to determine which beneficial effects are the functions that the behavior evolved to serve (this point is pursued below). Nonetheless, in theory it is possible to provide a complete ultimate explanation of a behavior pattern without reference to proximate matters of physiology and development.

Although proximate and ultimate causations are separate—and equal in the sense that each provides challenging scientific problems—they are not equal in their potential for providing a general theory of behavior: no theory of behavior even remotely compares in usefulness or generality to evolutionary theory (Alexander 1975).

While natural selection may occur at the level of the group or population, selection at these levels almost always is negligible compared with selection at the level of the individual organism (Williams 1966, Alexander 1974). But just as selection is weak at levels above the individual, so it is weak at levels below the individual; that is, at the levels of the structural, physiological, and neural components that constitute the damp machinery of behavior. It is the organism as a whole that reproduces or fails to reproduce, not any of its components or attributes. The maximization of inclusive fitness necessarily entails selective compromises within the organism itself, so that no single one of its attributes ever is likely to be maximized or optimized (Alexander 1975). During the course of evolutionary history a diverse array of nervous and hormonal structures and processes has arisen that functions to produce reproductively successful behavior. Even outwardly similar behaviors, or behavioral processes, are not necessarily produced by similar internal machinery. For example, we may refer to behavioral modification in two different species as "learning," but the neural underpinnings of these modifications may be different. There is no reason to anticipate the discovery of universal proximate causes of behavior.

The simple process of evolution, on the other hand, is the central explanatory principle of biology. Alexander (1975) argues that, unlike any known proximate mechanism, differential reproduction is in two senses the most basic unit in the study of life. First, differential reproduction is both common to all life and unique to life. Second, differential reproduction is only one of several evolutionary mechanisms (other mechanisms include, for example, the chance events of mutation and genetic drift), but it is by far the most important determinant of the course of evolution. Natural selection can, for example, alter the rate at which mutations occur (mutability), but the mutations themselves occur randomly with respect to fitness. Mutation thus provides the raw material for the evolutionary process but it is not a guiding force. Differential reproduction occurs continuously in all lineages and at all times; but its effects are cumulative and it can change direction at any time. Many and various effects are thus produced in different times and places by this basic, unitary process.

In considering the arguments put forward in this book, the distinction between ultimate and proximate causation must be borne in mind. That a given behavior, or behavioral predisposition, has an ultimate explanation does not imply that the behavior has a particular proximate explanation; specifically, it does not imply that the behavior is unlearned or "innate." Among rhesus monkeys, for example, invariant, species-typical patterns of copulation are the products of natural selection and have obvious adaptive significance, yet deprivation experiments reveal that in both sexes these patterns are partly learned.

Effect and function

Species-typical behavior in a natural habitat can be expected to be adaptive; that is, it can be expected to serve a particular function, or functions, in maximizing reproductive success, since "Only characters which confer a positive biological advantage can survive for long against the forces of mutation and selection" (Hinde 1975:7). Hinde suggests three possible explanations for the existence of a species-typical character that appears not to be adaptive: it may be the by-product of an adaptive character; although its normal use is adaptive, it may appear occasionally in nonadaptive contexts; it may be a relic of a formerly adaptive character in the process of being lost. Although behavior generally can be expected to serve at least one function, functional hypotheses are difficult to test and therefore tend to be speculative to a degree that would not be tolerated in hypotheses about proximate causation (Hinde 1975).

Williams (1966) points out that principles and procedures for answering the question "What is function?" are not highly developed in biology; that is, there are no generally agreed-upon criteria for identifying the functional significance of characteristics of plants and animals. As a guide to the development of such criteria, Williams (1966) advocates that the doctrine of parsimony be applied to the study of adaptation: "adaptation is a special and onerous concept that should be used only where it is really necessary. When it must be recognized, it should be attributed to no higher a level of organization than is demanded by the evidence" (pp. 4-5).

The crucial point in Williams's approach to the study of adaptation is that *function* must be distinguished from *beneficial effect*. Williams argues that of all the effects produced by a biological mechanism, at least one may correctly be called its function, or goal, or purpose; but not all beneficial effects may correctly be called functions. Ultimately, function refers to the basis of differential reproduction in ancestral populations. To say that a given beneficial effect of a character is the function, or a function, of that character is to say that the character was molded by natural selection to produce that effect.

Four kinds of evidence have been considered relevant to determining function (see Symons 1978b). One approach is to correlate individual variation in the expression of a character with variation in reproductive success. There are, however, several difficulties with this approach:

individual variation in the expression of a character may not have a genetic basis; variation in reproductive success may actually be caused by variation in some other character with which the character being observed is correlated; variations of major evolutionary significance may be too small to be detected; and the selection pressures that *maintain* a character in the population may not be the pressures that *molded* the character. A second approach to function, which sometimes can circumvent the difficulties presented by minimal naturally occurring variation in a character and unsuspected covariation among characters, is experiment. As noted above, however, even when natural selection presently is maintaining a character through an experimentally demonstrated effect, different selection pressures may have molded the character.

A third approach to function is to compare distantly related species that have independently evolved similar characters (convergence) or to contrast closely related species that have evolved different characters (divergence). Finally, according to Williams, evidence that a character evolved through the process of natural selection to serve a particular function is to be found in the *design* of that character: "The demonstration of a benefit is neither necessary nor sufficient in the demonstration of function, although it may sometimes provide insight not otherwise obtainable. It is both necessary and sufficient to show that the process is designed to serve the function" (1966:209). A function can be distinguished from an incidental effect insofar as it is produced with sufficient precision, economy, and efficiency to rule out chance as an adequate explanation of its existence. The detailed structure of the vertebrate eye, for example, provides overwhelming evidence of functional design for effective vision, and indicates continued selection for this purpose throughout the evolutionary history of the vertebrates. But if an effect can be explained adequately as the result of physical laws or as the fortuitous byproduct of an adaptation, it should not be called a function. Function implies design: "The decision as to the purpose of a mechanism must be based on an examination of the machinery and an argument as to the appropriateness of the means to the end. It cannot be based on value judgments of actual or probable consequences" (Williams 1966:12).

As a presumably noncontroversial illustration of the distinction between effect and function, Williams imagines a fox that makes its way laboriously through heavy midwinter snow to a henhouse, steals a hen, and departs. On subsequent visits to the henhouse the fox follows the path it has already tramped down through the snow, thereby conserving energy and reducing hen-stealing time. Williams argues that, despite the benefits and possible increase in fitness accruing to the fox as a result of its having tramped down the snow with its feet, nothing in the structure of fox feet or legs suggests that they are designed for snow packing or removal. The structural features of fox feet and legs can be explained adequately as adaptations for running and walking. No anatomical evidence exists that natural selection favored foxes whose feet were more efficient at snow-packing over foxes whose feet were less efficient at snow packing. Walking and running, then, are properly called the functions of fox limbs, while snow packing is simply a fortuitous effect. The capacity of fox brains to detect and make use of the easiest path is, however, an adaptation.

Although evolutionary theorists regularly praise Williams's landmark book *Adaptation and Natural Selection*, some theorists appear to forget that Williams advocated the doctrine of parsimony as a guiding theoretical principle, not just as a reason to reject "group selection," and they treat adaptation as a general and facile concept that should be used wherever possible. This point can be illustrated by considering recent arguments that among human females the menopause is an adaptation.

The menopause is the permanent cessation of menstruation and the beginning of infertility which most commonly occurs in modern populations at forty-eight years of age (Melges and Hamburg 1977) and in medieval human populations at about fifty years of age (Jones 1975). Since natural selection is for reproductive success, it is difficult to account for the evolution of menopause. Using a group selection model, Campbell (1971) suggests two functions for menopause: first, because humans mature so slowly, a postreproductive period is essential to ensure the survival of the last child a woman bears; second, nonreproducing older people contribute knowledge and wisdom to the social group or population and thereby enhance its survival. Alexander (1974) and Dawkins (1976), however, use inclusive fitness theory to explain the evolution of menopause. Since human females become reproductively less efficient with age, at some point in a woman's life her inclusive fitness may be better served by investing time and energy in her existing offspring—by finding them mates, for example—or in her grandchildren than in attempting to bear additional offspring. Dawkins (1976:136) writes:

When a woman reached the age where the average chance of each child reaching adulthood was just less than half the chance of each grandchild of the same age reaching adulthood, any gene for investing in grandchildren in preference to children would tend to prosper. Such a gene is carried by only one in four grandchildren, whereas the rival gene is carried by one in two children, but the greater expectation of life of the grandchildren outweighs this, and the "grandchild altruism" gene prevails in the gene pool. A woman could not invest fully in her grandchildren if she went on having children of her own. Therefore genes for becoming reproductively infertile in middle age became more numerous, since they were carried in the bodies of grandchildren whose survival was assisted by grandmotherly altruism.

This might be called the Jewish Mother Theory of Menopause.

But comparative evidence indicates that, if they live long enough, all female mammals become infertile. Although it is extremely rare for a wild female mammal to reach the age of infertility, many do so in the artificially secure conditions of captivity (Jones 1975). During the third decade of life, captive female rhesus monkeys experience progressive decline and eventual termination of menstruation, changing patterns of hormone production, and termination of fertility that parallel human patterns (Jones 1975, Hodgen *et al.* 1977). Lawick-Goodall (1975) reports that one free-living female chimpanzee reached menopause before she died—in an extremely decrepit state rarely observed in the wild—at an estimated age of fifty, and that one other old female evidenced a spacing out of cycles before her disappearance and presumed death.

Vallois (1961) summarizes the skeletal evidence on the life-span of Pleistocene humans and demonstrates that "few individuals passed forty years, and it is only quite exceptionally that any passed fifty" (p. 222). Until recently, the number of women who lived long enough for infertility resulting from old age to influence reproductive success must have been negligible. Menopause probably is an artifact of recent improvements in the circumstances of human life analogous to the artificially secure conditions of captivity for nonhuman mammals. Dawkins (1976) suggests that the abruptness of menopause, compared with the gradual fading of male fertility, provides evidence that menopause is an adaptation, and he attributes this sex difference to differing patterns of parental investment: it is to a male's advantage to remain fertile into old age because of the possibility of siring offspring in which he will not invest time or energy (presumably he too is investing in grandchildren). But in fact, menopause is not an abrupt event; it is preceded by several years of declining fertility and irregular menstrual cycles (Jones 1975). In any case, if survival beyond fifty years of age for either sex was almost nonexistent throughout most of human evolutionary history, present sex differences among older people are byproducts of something else. The male-female difference in termination of fertility may be a concomitant of the much greater physiological expenditure female fertility entails. Thus the menopause is more parsimoniously interpreted as an artifact than as an adaptation.

The nature-nurture controversy

One of the most persistent controversies in the study of human and animal behavior is whether elements of behavior are "innate" or "acquired"; that is, whether they result from the influences of heredity or environment. Perhaps the most penetrating analysis of this controversy is that of Lehrman (1970), and I rely largely on his paper in the following discussion. An animal's observable structure and behavior (its phenotype) are produced by the interaction of its hereditary endowment (its genotype) and the environments to which it is exposed during the course of its development. At every developmental stage the organism interacts with its environment, and the outcome of this interaction produces the succeeding stage. Hence, as every behavior pattern is the product of both genes and environment, it is misleading to speak of behavior as determined solely by one or the other.

One explanation for the persistence of the nature-nurture controversy is that the word "innate" has two fundamentally different meanings, and yet these two meanings often are confused. The first meaning is strictly comparative: innate refers to *differences* in the behavior of two animals resulting from differences in their genotypes. If two animals are raised in identical environments, any behavioral differences they exhibit must be the consequences of genetic differences, and hence one may speak of these behavioral *differences* as innate.[2] Geneticists use the word "innate" in an analogous way: they describe a character as innate if, under a given set of conditions, its distribution in a

[2] Similarly, if monozygotic twins are raised in different environments, any behavioral differences they exhibit must be the consequences of environmental differences, and these behavioral *differences* may be called "acquired."

population of offspring can be predicted from the knowledge of its distribution in the parent population and the mating patterns of the parent population. The comparative use of the word "innate" implies nothing about development; specifically, it does not imply that behavior is not learned. This use of "innate" apparently is not controversial.

The second, and more problematic, meaning is not comparative but developmental: the behavior of an individual animal is said to be "innate" if it develops in a relatively uniform or fixed way despite normal environmental variation. Specifically, "innate" is used by some scientists to refer to adaptive behavior that is not learned. This use of "innate" is controversial because some students of animal behavior, especially those primarily interested in development, believe that "innate" versus "learned" is not a natural or useful way to classify developmental processes. They point out that to call a behavior pattern "innate" specifies only that certain traditionally recognized processes (Pavlovian conditioning, operant conditioning, observational learning, imprinting, etc.) are *not* required for its development, but does not specify what processes *are* required. The environment influences the development of behavior in many ways, not merely through traditionally recognized learning processes. An organism's "experience" includes "the contribution to development of the effects of stimulation from all available sources (external and internal), including their functional effects surviving from earlier development" (Lehrman 1970:30).

Although a given species-typical behavior pattern ultimately is the outcome of natural selection in ancestral populations, this does not imply that the proximate development of this pattern is "innate," in the sense of being relatively impervious to environmental influences during its development, or that it is not learned. Consider, for example, mate choice among ducks. It is adaptive for both male and female ducks to choose to mate with a conspecific of the opposite sex; any other mate choice clearly is maladaptive. Hence, in ancestral duck populations natural selection favored ducks that chose to mate with conspecifics and disfavored ducks with uncommon sexual proclivities. But when male ducks are raised experimentally with birds of a different species, upon reaching maturity most of the experimental males attempt to mate with females of the species with which they were raised, and they ignore conspecific females. Female ducks, on the other hand, generally choose to mate with conspecific males even when they have been raised experimentally with birds of a different species (Marler and Hamilton 1966). In other words, although natural selection favored intraspecific mating in both male and female ducks, it achieved this end via remarkably different developmental mechanisms in the two sexes: learning (imprinting) plays an important role in the development of male, but not female, mate choice. Lehrman (1970:36) writes: "Nature selects for *outcomes*. Natural selection acts to select genomes that, in a normal environment, will guide development into organisms with the relevant adaptive characteristics. But the path of development from the zygote stage to the phenotypic adult is devious, and includes many developmental processes, including, in some cases, various aspects of experience." A scientist interested primarily in ultimate causation and in adaptation of animals to natural environments might call the choice of conspecific mates by normally reared male ducks "learned" and by female ducks "innate," and believe this to be an important and useful distinction. A scientist interested primarily in behavioral development, on the other hand, might point out that however interesting it may be to know that mate choice among female ducks does not depend on imprinting, this knowledge does not illuminate the proximate mechanisms that *are* responsible for the development of mate choice among females, nor is it enlightening to call the choice "innate."

Lehrman concludes that the nature-nurture controversy has persisted in large part because writers frequently appear to be arguing about the same problem when in fact they are concerned with quite different problems:

> It is clear that at least some of the difficulties in the discussions of the concept of "innateness" arise from the fact that while the various writers believe, and convey to their readers, that they are arguing about matters of fact or interpretation with respect to which one side or the other must be wrong, they are in fact talking about different problems. To some biologists interested primarily in the functions of behavior and in the nature of behavioral adaptations achieved through natural selection, many developmental effects of experience seem trivial and uninteresting, and do not appear to bear upon *their* central question, of the role of natural selection in the establishment of the specific details by which the behavior of specific species is adapted to the necessities of specific environments. To the student of development, however, experiential effects, no matter how diffuse and no matter how remote from the specific details of any particular sensory discrimination or motor act, must be seen as part of the network of causes for the development of any behavior pattern or behavioral capacity to which they are relevant (p. 46).

Although the concept of "innateness" is of little use in the study of behavioral development, it can be useful when one's aim is to call attention to the existence of developmental fixity or to explain, in an ultimate sense, why, or in what circumstances, selection favors particular developmental strategies. Thus, in the course of this book when I wish to emphasize the existence of developmental fixity I shall use the word "innate" and enclose it in apologetic quotation marks.

Learning as a developmental strategy

Since human adaptation depends so profoundly on learning abilities, we sometimes are inclined to imagine that there is an inherent advantage—almost a moral superiority—in such abilities and to forget how rare they are: adaptation in most animal species depends very little on learning abilities. Perhaps this is one reason Darwin reminded himself never to use the words "higher" or "lower" with respect to animal species. Indeed, to an evolutionary biologist it is quite reasonable to ask: "Why learn anything?" (Alcock 1975). A developmental approach to the study of behavior makes it possible to ask whether learning plays a role in the development of a given behavior pattern and, if so, what the role is; but an evolutionary approach makes it possible to ask *why* learning plays a role in the development of some behavior patterns and not others.

Both the sophisticated learning abilities and the sophisticated "innate" responses of living animals must have evolved from the more rudimentary abilities of ancestral animals to respond to their environments in adaptive ways. An animal that learns a particular adaptive response to a given stimulus situation after twenty exposures to that situation (learning trials) will have a reproductive edge on conspecifics that are unable to learn the response at all. Subsequent generations—in which the learner's progeny will be disproportionately represented—may contain individuals capable of learning the response with even fewer learning trials. If invariably it proves adaptive to exhibit the response in that particular situation, natural selection may eventually produce animals that exhibit the response the first time they encounter the situation; that is, with no learning trials. The response has become "innate." A rudimentary learning ability thus may become increasingly refined and specific through the operation of natural selection and terminate in an "innate" response. More rarely rudimentary learning abilities become the basis for the evolution of higher intelligence (Wilson 1975).

There seem to be three general circumstances in which selection favors learning abilities:

(1) According to Wilson (1975), learning processes sometimes become incorporated into the development of a species-typical behavior pattern as an incidental effect, or byproduct, of selection for neural economy. If certain stimuli are reliably present in the environment in which immature animals develop, those immature animals that, as a result of a chance mutation, *require* the stimuli's presence to develop normal behavior will be more fit than those that do not require the stimuli's presence if the neural mechanisms underlying the former type of development are more simple, and hence more energetically economical, than the mechanisms underlying the latter type of development. (In either developmental strategy the behavioral outcome is the same.) Wilson suggests, for example, that some species-typical behavior patterns of Old World monkeys, which at present must be learned, were "innate" in ancestral populations. Certain stimuli—such as those provided by mothers and peers—were present so uniformly and reliably in the environment in which immature monkeys developed that learning processes which depend on the presence of these stimuli could become incorporated into the development of normal behavior as a byproduct of selection for neural economy.

(2) Learning abilities may represent adaptations to make complex discriminations or to develop complex motor skills that are exhibited in species-typical form among adults. The sex difference among ducks in the developmental processes underlying mate choice probably exemplifies the influence of environmental complexity on the evolution of learning abilities. In most duck species, natural selection has favored cryptically colored females; hence females are drab and inconspicuous, and the females of many species resemble one another. Male ducks, on the other hand, are brightly colored, and the males of various species are distinctive (Marler and Hamilton 1966). Since they are conspicuous and distinctive in appearance, it is easy to identify males of various species, and "innate" recognition of an appropriate mate may be genetically economical for females; but learning (imprinting) may be the genetically economical solution to the far more difficult discrimination problem facing males.

Learning also seems to be especially important in the development of behavior patterns exhibited in "antagonistic" interactions, such as intraspecific fighting, predation, and predator avoidance (Symons 1978a). In antagonistic interactions one interactant succeeds in achieving its goal only to the extent that the other fails, resulting in the evolution of strategies and counter-strategies of extraordinary complexity. Probably it is far more genetically economical to construct an animal with a relatively small set of rules or criteria by which such behaviors can be learned than it is to construct an animal that "innately" discriminates each of the thousands of slight but significant variations in antagonistic interactions and exhibits an appropriate response in each.

(3) Learning abilities may represent adaptations to exhibit behavioral flexibility. According to Alcock (1975), behavioral flexibility requires complex underlying neural mechanisms that are costly to build and maintain; it requires that time and energy be devoted to the learning process itself; and, if the "correct" response to a given situation must be learned, the animal is unlikely to make this response the first time it encounters the situation, which sometimes is disastrous. Furthermore, the greater an animal's flexibility, the more it can learn maladaptive, as well as adaptive behavior. Alcock (1975) argues that the capacity to learn individually flexible behavior can evolve where an animal typically has the time to learn, can afford the consequences of mistakes, and enjoys a significant reproductive advantage from flexibility. Alcock (1975:259) writes that "Learning is adaptive when environmental unpredictability of some biological importance to an individual is RELIABLY present in certain situations. In other words, some animals live in places where they are sure to face variable factors or events that can profoundly affect their fitness." He notes, for example, that the omnivorous toad learns through trial and error which insects are edible. This learning ability is adaptive because the insect species available to individual toads during their lifetime vary, and hence are not "predictable" by the genome. Similarly, the specific characteristics that make a given offspring unique obviously cannot be "known" in advance by the parent's genome. Animals of many species are able to learn to recognize their own offspring because it is adaptive to give aid selectively to offspring rather than to immature conspecifics at random. As these examples illustrate, most behavioral flexibility is based on sensory learning; that is, animals learn to discriminate be-

tween various stimuli, but they act on these discriminations with species-typical motor patterns. In very few species do the motor patterns themselves vary from individual to individual.

When a specific response to a particular stimulus is invariably adaptive, selection can be expected to favor animals who reliably exhibit the response to that stimulus. As outlined above, if the environment is predictable, whether and to what extent learning processes are incorporated into the development of such a response presumably is determined by energetic costs: given two competing developmental strategies that produce the same behavioral outcome, selection favors the more energetically economical one. But the more variable the environment, the less likely to be present are the specific conditions necessary to ensure that a given response will be learned. For example, the development of normal adult rhesus monkey copulation depends on the prior occurrence of copulationlike behavior in the infant and juvenile peer group. If rhesus groups varied in size to such an extent that infants sometimes had no peers during their early years, selection would favor monkeys in whom normal copulation behaviors developed "innately." Thus a kind of paradox can be discerned: depending on the circumstances, environmental variability can favor either learning or "innate" development. Learning is favored when it is adaptive for an animal to exhibit different behavior patterns, or to make different discriminations, in various environments. "Innate" development is favored when it is adaptive for an animal to exhibit the same behavior pattern to a particular stimulus in all environments. In the latter situation, "innateness" constitutes a kind of insurance against environmental exigencies.

So far I have written of learning as if it were a general ability to modify behavior in adaptive ways—the very antithesis of the specificity implied by "innate"—but this is not the case. Natural selection has shaped the capacity to learn just as it has shaped "innate" behavior, and "Animal species differ in what they can learn, when they can learn it, and how easily they can learn different things" (Alcock 1975:235). Constraints on learning and predispositions to learn can be understood only with respect to the specific problems a species has encountered during the course of its evolutionary history. Washburn *et al.* (1965: 1546) write:

> It has become clear that, although learning has great importance in the normal development of nearly all phases of primate behavior, it is not a generalized ability; animals are able to learn some things with

great ease and other things only with the greatest difficulty. Learning is part of the adaptive pattern of a species and can be understood only when it is seen as the process of acquiring skills and attitudes that are of evolutionary significance to a species when living in the environment to which it is adapted.

The toad, which learns in one trial to avoid eating a noxious species of millipede, will continue to consume BBs that are rolled past it until it becomes a living beanbag (Alcock 1975). Ancestral toads never encountered BB-like objects, and toad nervous systems simply are not constructed to permit toads to learn to discriminate, and to avoid eating, BBs with any number of learning trials. The African village weaver bird learns to discriminate its own eggs and ejects eggs placed in its nest by the parasitic cuckoo, but the herring gull, whose ancestors lacked nest parasites, cannot discriminate its own eggs from eggs experimentally introduced into its nest, even if the experimental eggs are the wrong color. Herring gulls do, however, learn to recognize their own chicks after they are five days old, at which age they begin to wander from the nest. Kittiwake gulls, on the other hand, nest on narrow ledges on sheer cliffs and their nestlings do not leave the nest until they are ready to fledge, hence ancestral kittiwakes were never faced with the problem of discriminating their own offspring from other immature kittiwakes. Accordingly, kittiwakes cannot learn to recognize their own young, and will even feed nestlings of other species—of entirely different size and appearance—if they are introduced into the nest by a human experimenter (Alcock 1975). Wilson (1975: 156) writes:

> What evolves is the directedness of learning—the relative ease with which certain associations are made and acts are learned, and others bypassed even in the face of strong reinforcement. Pavlov was simply wrong when he postulated that "any natural phenomena chosen at will may be converted into conditioned stimuli." Only small parts of the brain resemble a tabula rasa; this is true even for human beings. The remainder is more like an exposed negative waiting to be dipped into developer fluid.

The evolution of sex differences

Among nonhermaphroditic, many-celled animals that reproduce sexually there are two and only two sexes, defined on the basis of the sex cells they produce: a female produces eggs, which are large and carry a reserve of food for the embryo; a male produces sperm, which are small and possess a taillike organ to enable them to reach the egg. Some sexually reproducing animals exhibit few additional male-female differences. This is true, for example, of some marine animals, such as starfish and sea urchins, with external fertilization (Maynard Smith 1958). But because a female invests far more energy in an egg cell than a male invests in a sperm cell, in most species selection has favored females who sequester and protect this investment, leading to the evolution of internal fertilization and primary sex differences in reproductive anatomy, which, in a sense, parallel the differences between egg and sperm: females have evolved structures to nourish the embryo, such as the placenta among mammals, while males have evolved structures to introduce sperm into the female's body (Maynard Smith 1958). The high initial female investment also explains why females rather than males generally provide parental care (Wilson 1975).

In addition to primary sex differences in gonads and reproductive organs, most animal species also have evolved secondary sex differences in structure, physiology, and behavior. Darwin (1871) attributed secondary sex differences primarily to the operation of "sexual selection." He distinguished sexual from natural selection in that the latter results from the differential abilities of individuals to adapt to their "environments" while the former results specifically from the differential abilities of individuals to acquire mates. Darwin identified two types of sexual selection: intersexual selection, based on female choice of males ("the power to charm the females"), and intrasexual selection, based on male-male competition ("the power to conquer other males in battle"). The first results in the evolution of bright color and ornamentation, the second in large body size, natural weapons, and pugnacity, though both types of sexual selection can occur simultaneously (Ralls 1977).

That sexual selection is far more common among males than females ultimately can be traced to the differences between sperm and egg cells. Even among animals with few sex differences and no parental behavior, the females' eggs represent a greater initial investment in each offspring than the males' sperm cells do. For a male, eggs thus are a limiting resource; that is, his reproductive success is determined by the number of eggs he fertilizes, not by the amount of sperm he produces. But a female offers a greater energetic investment with each fertile mating and hence is much more likely to have each egg fertilized. Because males invest relatively little with each mating "it is to their advantage to tie up as many of the female investments as they can" (Wilson 1975:325). "Active competition for a limiting resource tends to increase the variance in the apportionment of the resource. Some individuals are likely to get multiple shares, others none at all. The resulting differential in reproductive success leads to evolution in secondary sexual characteristics within the more competitive sex" (Wilson 1975:325).

Trivers (1972) proposes that the occurrence and intensity of sexual selection are determined by the "parental investment" each sex typically makes in its offspring. Parental investment is "any investment by the parent in an individual offspring that increases the offspring's chance of surviving (and hence reproductive success) at the cost of the parent's ability to invest in other offspring" (Trivers 1972:139). Such investment may be in the form of time, energy, or risk. In this view, the more the males and females of a species differ in their typical parental investments the more intense is the reproductive competition among members of the sex with the lesser investment, the greater is the variance in reproductive success among members of the competitive sex, and the more intensely sexual selection favors structures and behaviors of use in the competition. Since female parental investment usually is substantially beyond the minimum, and males often invest only a trivial amount of time and sperm in each offspring, in most animal species the male-female difference in parental investment is far greater than that entailed by the disparity in the size of sex cells. Thus, "At every moment in its game of life the masculine sex is playing for higher stakes" (Williams 1975:138). The most reproductively successful males are those who gamble and win. Sexual selection favors calculated risk-taking in male-male competition, hence the evolution of large body size, strength, pugnacity, playfighting, weapons, color, ornament, and sexual salesmanship, which often are interrelated in that displays can function both to attract females and to intimidate other males (Wilson 1975). This is why most animal species are "polygynous"/"promiscuous" (more females than males contribute sex cells to the next generation),[3] few are "monogamous" (males and females

---

[3] Emlen and Oring (1977) identify three forms of "polygyny": resource defense "polygyny," in which males compete among themselves for access to resources that are essential to females; female (or harem) "polygyny," in which males aggressively herd females and exclude other males from the area; male dominance "polygyny," in which males compete among themselves for rank and females choose mates primarily on the basis of status.

contribute sex cells to the next generation in equal numbers), and still fewer are "polyandrous" (more males than females contribute sex cells to the next generation) (classification follows Ralls 1977).

Females rarely can increase their reproductive success by copulating with many males, but they have a great deal to gain by copulating with fit males and a great deal to lose by copulating with unfit males. If a male is unsuccessful in a mating encounter he has lost almost nothing, even if he has inadvertently mated with a female of a different species, whereas a female often risks months of time and a great amount of energy in attempting reproduction; a reproductive failure is much more costly for her than it is for a male (Williams 1966). Since it is adaptive for a male to pretend to fitness whether or not he is fit, it is adaptive for a female to be resistant to courtship—thereby evoking further and stronger displays—in order to discriminate genuinely fit males and perhaps to incite male-male competition (Cox and Le Boeuf 1977). "Consequently, there will be a strong tendency for the courted sex to develop coyness" (Wilson 1975:320). Females tend to be more cryptically colored than males, smaller in body size, less pugnacious, and equipped with less formidable weapons, since they seldom need to compete for, or advertise for, males.

One test of the hypothesis that patterns of parental investment influence sexual selection is to consider species in which the male's typical parental investment substantially exceeds the female's. If the hypothesis is correct, in these species sexual selection should operate among females, and females should exhibit structural and behavioral characteristics useful in reproductive competition. The available evidence confirms this prediction (references in Wilson 1975). Among pipefish and sea horses, for example, the female transfers eggs to the male's broodpouch where they develop, making placental connection to the male's bloodstream. In the pipefish-sea horse species for which there is information, females show aggressive courtship and willingness to mate with any male, and males show caution and selectiveness (Williams 1966). Among birds, because much of the development of the young takes place outside the female's body, and because, unlike mammals, the mother does not suckle her young, a male can make a substantial parental investment very early in the life of its offspring, and the great majority of bird species are "monogamous" (Selander 1972). It is even possible for the male to assume the entire burden of incubation and provisioning of the young, in which case the female can invest her time and energy laying additional clutches for other males, resulting in "polyandry." In the few known cases of avian "polyandry" there is intense female-female competition for males, and females are the larger and more aggressive sex (Jenni 1974). "The evidence strongly supports the conclusion that promiscuity, active courtship, and belligerence toward rivals are not inherent aspects of maleness" (Williams 1966:186). Male-female secondary sex differences are not natural or necessary concomitants of sexuality but the results of sex differences in reproductive "strategies."

Because young mammals develop within their mother's bodies and are nursed after birth, the female's initial investment in each offspring is very large compared with the male's; hence among nonhuman mammals the mother-family is the basic social unit, "monogamy" is rare, and "polyandry" is absent: the great majority of mammals are "promiscuous"/"polygynous" (Eisenberg 1966). Elephant seals, described by Le Boeuf (1974), are an extreme case. Among these annual breeders the male's entire parental investment is the insemination of the female, and a male attempts to inseminate as many females as possible. A successful female can produce about ten pups in her lifetime, but an outstanding male can sire at least twenty times this number. In Le Boeuf's study, one male dominated breeding for four consecutive years and inseminated more than 200 females. Most males do not breed at all, or breed very little, because they die before reaching maturity or are prevented from breeding by other males. Male reproductive success is extremely variable, but female reproductive success is not, and there is intense sexual selection among males for size, fighting ability, long life, and the capacity to fast throughout the breeding season so that a harem is never left unguarded, hence the extreme divergence in structure and behavior between male and female elephant seals.

Although parental investment clearly is an important determinant of sexual selection, it is not the whole story. In species where one sex is freed from parental care, members of this sex potentially can expend more time and energy and take greater risks competing with one another for mates or for scarce resources, but emancipation from parental care does not necessarily lead to intense sexual selection: sexual selection also is a function of the extent to which the particular ecological/environmental circumstances make it economically feasible for an individual to monopolize multiple mates or the resources critical to gaining multiple mates (Emlen and Oring 1977, Ralls 1977). The intensity of sexual selection among male elephant seals, for example, results not only from the minimal male parental investment but also from the fact that elephant seals copulate on land. Aquatic mammals that copulate in the water are less "polygynous" and exhibit fewer sex differences because in the water it is more difficult for a male to control females or to prevent other males from copulating. Thus, while "monogamous" mammals typically exhibit few secondary sex differences, and extremely "polygynous" mammals typically exhibit extreme sex differences (as parental investment theory predicts), small male parental investment is a poor predictor of extreme "polygyny" and extreme sex differences: among mammals, environmental circumstances may be more important determinants of the intensity of sexual selection than parental investment is (Ralls 1977).

While most sex differences in color, ornamentation, and weapons probably are the products of sexual selection, the magnitude of the sex difference in body size in a given species is not necessarily an accurate index of the intensity of male-male competition. Sexual selection may, for example, favor nonfighting competitive strategies among males, such as sequestering females (Ghiselin 1974). Furthermore, secondary sex differences result not only from sexual selection but also from natural selection as, for example, when the males and females of a species typically eat different kinds of food or otherwise occupy different ecological niches (Mayr 1972, Selander 1972). Ralls (1976) reviews the literature on mammalian species in which females are larger than males and concludes that this circumstance never results from more intense sexual competition among females than among males; that is, large females are not produced by sexual selection. Once the mammalian commitment to internal development of the embryo and to lactation was established, the female's parental investment was so great that it was unlikely ever to be exceeded by male investment, hence, it is unlikely that the intensity of female competition for mates ever exceeds the intensity of male competition. Relatively large female mammals are not associated with "polyandry" (which does not exist in nonhuman mammals), greater aggressiveness in females than in males, greater development of weapons in females, female dominance, or matriarchy. Ralls suggests a number of hypotheses that might account for large females, such as differential niche utilization and more intense competition among females than among males for some resource, but finds that no single hypothesis can explain all the cases. She suggests that females will be the larger sex where more than one selective pressure favors large females and where there are not even stronger pressures favoring large males. (Sexual selection may operate among males even in species in which females are the larger sex; without sexual selection, males would be smaller still.) Many of the cases, however, seem to be accounted for best by Ralls's "big mother" hypothesis: sometimes a big mother is a better mother. Ralls reviews evidence that in several mammalian species, including humans, larger females typically have more surviving offspring.

I shall argue that in considering the evolution of human male-female differences in sexual desires and dispositions, the minimum possible parental investments may be more significant than the typical parental investments, and the rare opportunity or danger may be more significant than the typical "mating system." This is because psyche—more than structure or behavior—is adapted to atypical events in the sense that an important function of psyche is to cope with and to bring about such events. The enormous sex differences in minimum parental investment and in reproductive opportunities and constraints explain why *Homo sapiens*, a species with only moderate sex differences in structure, exhibits profound sex differences in psyche.

The primary male-female differences in sexuality among humans discussed in Chapters Three through Ten can be summarized as follows: (1) Intrasexual competition generally is much more intense among males than among females, and in preliterate societies competition over women probably is the single most important cause of violence. (2) Men incline to polygyny, whereas women are more malleable in this respect and, depending on the circumstances, may be equally satisfied in polygynous, monogamous, or polyandrous marriages. (3) Almost universally, men experience sexual jealousy of their mates. Women are more malleable in this respect, but in certain circumstances women's experience of sexual jealousy may be characteristically as intense as men's. (4) Men are much more likely to be sexually aroused by the sight of women and the female genitals than women are by the sight of men and the male genitals. Such arousal must be distinguished from arousal produced by the sight of, or the description of, an actual sexual encounter, since male-female differences in the latter may be minimal. (5) Physical characteristics, especially those that correlate with youth, are by far the most important determinants of women's sexual attractiveness. Physical characteristics are somewhat less important determinants of men's sexual attractiveness; political and economic prowess are more important; and youth is relatively unimportant. (6) Much more than women, men are predisposed to desire a variety of sex partners for the sake of variety. (7) Among all peoples, copulation is considered to be essentially a service or favor that women render to men, and not vice versa, regardless of which sex derives or is thought to derive greater pleasure from sexual intercourse. These propositions by no means constitute an exhaustive analysis of human sexuality, excluding, for example, such topics as incest taboos and female eroticism associated with breast feeding (Newton 1973); nevertheless, the comparison of men and women provides, I believe, the most powerful and coherent available perspective on human sexuality.

Wilson (1975) notes that most theories about human evolution take the form of advocacy, wherein the theorist marshals and integrates all available evidence in support of his view and attempts to render it invulnerable, and as an antidote to this approach Wilson suggests that evolutionary hypotheses be framed in a way that permits falsification. I cannot claim either that the arrangement of data in this book is independent of my theoretical views or that I do not have protective —perhaps paternal—feelings about the book. But I do believe that available data are remarkably consistent in supporting the above propositions and that all the propositions are testable, and hence falsifiable.

TWO

Evolution
and Human Nature

Man's brain, like the rest of him, may be looked upon as a bundle of adaptations. But what it is adapted to has never been self-evident. We are anything but a mechanism set up to perceive the truth for its own sake. Rather, we have evolved a nervous system that acts in the interest of our gonads, and one attuned to the demands of reproductive competition. If fools are more prolific than wise men, then to that degree folly will be favored by selection. And if ignorance aids in obtaining a mate, then men and women will tend to be ignorant. In order for so imperfect an instrument as a human brain to perceive the world as it really is, a great deal of self-discipline must be imposed.

MICHAEL T. GHISELIN

HOWEVER DIFFICULT AN evolutionary perspective on any animal species may be, such a perspective on human beings is fraught with still greater difficulties and with unique problems. Most frequently discussed is the question of the relation of human "culture" and "society" to organic evolution and individual reproductive success. Every possible relation appears to have been conceived by someone. Malinowski (1927) argued that human culture and animal instincts are functionally equivalent: "Thus it can be said without exaggeration that culture in its traditional bidding duplicates the instinctive drive" (pp. 209-10). To Malinowski, instinctive drives function to perpetuate the species to which an animal belongs, and although in a proximate sense human culture and society satisfy the biological and psychological needs of individual human beings, ultimately culture and society function to perpetuate the human species. Whatever truth there may be in Malinowski's views, clearly they are inadequate. Animal "instincts" are shaped by natural selection to maximize inclusive fitness, and any species benefit is an incidental effect, of no functional significance. If human culture and society are species-promoting mechanisms it is not because they duplicate "instinctive drives." Since natural selection appears to operate primarily at the level of the individual organism, Alexander (1975) argues, contrary to Malinowski, that society is founded on lies, by which he apparently means that individuals covertly pursue their own reproductive advantage via the various norms, values, and traditions that collectively constitute society. But Campbell (1975), who assumes the same organic evolutionary mechanisms that Alexander does, arrives at the opposite conclusion, arguing that "sociocultural selection" counters the biologically based, "selfish" impulses of individual human beings. Following a tradition that probably began with Plato's *Republic*, and continued in the writings of Radcliffe-Brown (1935) and later social science functionalists (Jarvie 1964), Campbell assumes that culture and society promote the material well-being of the collective. Durkheim, on the other hand, held that "social facts" do not serve the needs of human beings at all, either as individuals or as groups; rather they make possible "the persistence or existence of the system of collective representations" (Hatch 1973:201). And Dawkins (1976), following F. T. Cloak, proposes a similar notion, except that he does not view society as a system, but instead argues that beliefs, values, ideas, and the like are selected in the same way that genes are, on the basis of their ability to perpetuate themselves. These "memes"— the basic components of culture and society—can best be understood as parasites on human beings. Finally, Sahlins (1976), in criticizing sociobiology, repeatedly refers to human traditions as "arbitrary." Thus human society is variously regarded as: promoting individual interests; promoting the interests of genes; promoting the collective good; promoting its own existence as a "system"; consisting of innumerable discrete "memes," each of which promotes its own existence; or being largely arbitrary. (See Richerson and Boyd 1978 for references to the recent literature on the relationship between genetic and cultural evolution.)

I touch on these questions throughout the book, though, needless to say, I do not resolve them. But the relation of culture and society to individual reproductive success is only one of the problems presented by an evolutionary perspective on human beings. In fact, it may be that the failure to come to grips with other problems has impeded analysis of the culture-and-society issue. In this chapter I shall argue that an evolutionary perspective has both implications and limitations that are not always appreciated. In brief, the arguments are: (1) It is reasonable and parsimonious to expect species-typical behavior in a natural habitat to be subject to ultimate causal analysis, but since natural human habitats probably no longer exist, much human behavior may be inexplicable in terms of ultimate causation. (2) Although some sociobiological writings imply that an evolutionary perspective on humans favors determinism over free will, this implication is without foundation. (3) Since natural languages have been designed to facilitate communication about everyday, proximate matters, the use of ordinary language in discussions of ultimate matters sometimes engenders serious confusion. (4) Modern evolutionary theory implies that a tabula rasa view of the mind is untenable, an implication consistent with the evidence for cognitive and emotional universals. (5) Although some biologists imply that evolutionary theory is unique in seeing human groups as composed of fundamentally self-interested individuals, this implication is incorrect. (6) In Western folk beliefs the creator of life also is the source of morality, hence problems arise when evolution replaces God as the creator. The failure to abandon the belief that morality is to be found in natural creative processes promotes misunderstandings of animals, of humans, and of the creative processes themselves. (7) Although there is an enormous body of information about human sexuality, its evaluation presents a number of special difficulties.

The concept of a natural environment

In Chapter One it was argued that ultimate and proximate explanations of a behavior pattern represent answers to completely different kinds of questions. Specifically, the evolutionist does not necessarily take sides in the nature-nurture controversy, which is a controversy about *how* behavior develops. The evolutionist inquires into the ultimate causes of behavior observed in natural environments. As a result of learning, behavior often varies markedly with environmental variation, and evolutionary theory is as concerned with providing ultimate explanations for these variable, or "facultative," adaptations as it is with providing ultimate explanations for "obligate" adaptations such as relatively invariant, "innate" behaviors (Emlen 1976). The learning abilities upon which behavioral variability is based are themselves the products of natural selection: these abilities evolved because, on the average, they resulted in adaptive behavior in the range of environments typically encountered during the evolutionary history of the species. But the issue of "natural environments" has especially far-reaching implications for an evolutionary perspective on human beings because natural human environments may no longer exist.

During the evolutionary history of any species, natural selection operates only within a limited range of environmental conditions. Evolutionary theory predicts that an animal's behavior, whether or not it is learned, typically will be adaptive when the animal develops in an environment that is within the range to which its ancestors were regularly exposed. When an animal develops in an unnatural environment its behavior may be maladaptive.

An organism's phenotype—its observable structure and behavior—is the product of the interaction of its genotype and the environment in which it developed and exists. Different phenotypes are regularly observed when a given genotype develops in different environments. Behavior geneticists use the phrase "norm of reaction" to refer to the total range of phenotypes that can develop from a given genotype in all the environments in which the genotype can develop at all. For species with relatively plastic behavior patterns, the norm of reaction is effectively infinite. In a strict sense, ultimate explanations are possible only for the relatively narrow portion of the norm of reaction that develops in environments to which a species is regularly exposed during the course of its evolutionary history.

Figure 2.1 outlines possible relationships between environments and phenotypes for a given genotype. Environments E_1 through E_4 represent four different natural environments; that is, environments to which ancestral populations were exposed for sufficient lengths of time to become adapted to them. In each of these four environments a different phenotype (P_1-P_4) develops, and each phenotype represents an adaptation to that environment. Environments E_5 through E_8 represent four environments to which the species has not been regularly exposed during the course of its evolutionary history, but in which the genotype can nonetheless develop.

In E_5 the organism exhibits P_1, a phenotype typical of E_1 but which in E_5 is maladaptive. This circumstance is perhaps most likely with "innate" behavior patterns. If a given response to a particular stimulus

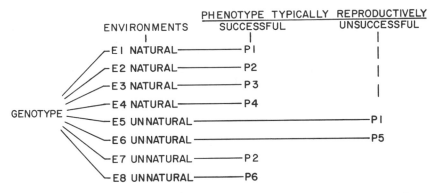

FIGURE 2.1. Different phenotypes can result from a single genotype in different environments. See text.

has been adaptive over a wide range of environmental conditions that response is likely to develop in a relatively fixed and invariant manner and hence to be exhibited in most environments in which the organism can survive at all. The toad that becomes a living beanbag as it consumes BBs rolled past it by the human experimenter provides an example. Toad nervous systems are not adapted to discriminate moving BBs from insects.

In E6 the organism exhibits a new phenotype, one that never occurs in a natural environment, and which does not promote reproductive success. Rhesus monkeys raised by human experimenters in conditions of total social deprivation, for example, develop a variety of aberrant behavior patterns, such as self-mutilation.

In E7 the organism exhibits P2, a phenotype typical of E2, but which also is adaptive in E7. When rabbits were introduced into Australia by humans, for example, many environmental features were different from those that any rabbit ancestor had encountered, but the Australian environment was in many respects so similar to a natural environment that rabbit behavior was exceedingly adaptive, and rabbits flourished.

In E8 the organism exhibits a phenotype never observed in a natural environment, but which, fortuitously, is reproductively successful; nevertheless, the behavior cannot be considered an adaption in the strict sense because it was not shaped by natural selection. This possibility can be illustrated with an imaginary example. Consider a population of humans, living in an unnatural environment, in which a family's youngest son usually becomes an exclusive homosexual and hence does not sire any offspring. Imagine further that in this society there is sufficient variability in sexual orientation of youngest sons so that it is possible to compare the total reproductive success of exclusively heterosexual and exclusively homosexual youngest sons. Through genealogical analysis it is demonstrated that youngest sons who become homosexuals typically provide so much aid to their siblings' offspring that their inclusive fitness actually is higher than that of heterosexual youngest sons who marry and have children. Now this fact alone is not sufficient evidence that homosexuality is an adaptation. An adaptation is the result of the operation of natural selection in ancestral populations; to demonstrate adaptation it is necessary either to show that youngest sons frequently are homosexual in certain natural environments, which this unnatural environment resembles, or at least to provide a convincing argument that homosexuality could be functional under similar natural conditions. If, under natural conditions, exclusive homosexuality does not occur, or if it is always maladaptive when it does occur, or if it does not operate to favor youngest sons who aid their nephews and nieces, even if it is adaptive for some other reason, then although the behavior has a reproductively beneficial effect, it has no function (see Chapter One).

These issues are crucial to an evolutionary appraisal of human sexual behavior in unnatural environments, such as industrial societies. In the study of function, the situations exemplified by E_5 and E_7 are relevant, despite the maladaptiveness of P_1 in E_5, since they represent behavior that has been shaped by natural selection, and the situations exemplified by $E6$ and $E8$ are irrelevant, despite the fortuitous benefit of $P6$ in $E8$, since they represent behavior that has not been shaped by natural selection. For example, a modern American husband may experience sexual jealousy of his wife, who is taking birth control pills. This jealousy may have no effect on fitness in the unnatural circumstances in which it occurs, but it almost certainly represents adaptation to natural environments in which birth control pills did not exist. On the other hand, a medical student may achieve enormous reproductive success by contributing to sperm banks, but this is not evidence that human males are adapted to contribute to sperm banks.

Obviously the distinctions I have drawn will not be so clear-cut in any real situation. An environment is not a global entity, but the sum of innumerable particulars. An environment is not really natural or unnatural, but rather each of its aspects varies along a continuum of naturalness. Some environmental features which, strictly speaking, are unnatural may resemble natural features so closely that the difference is irrelevant. On the other hand, the introduction of even one unnatural feature—say vasectomy—might have a profound effect on ultimate explanations of human behavior in a given population.

All behavior that occurs in a natural environment is not adaptive—animals can and do exhibit maladaptive behavior under natural conditions. But behavior can be expected to be adaptive on the average in natural environments, and the hypothesis that behavior is adaptive is a reasonable and parsimonious working assumption. It is equally obvious that all behavior in an unnatural environment cannot possibly be maladaptive, since the organism at least survives and perhaps also reproduces. It is no longer necessarily reasonable or parsimonious, however, to assume adaptiveness as a working hypothesis. In considering behavior in environments known to be unnatural, an ultimate explanation of a given behavior pattern should be accompanied by an attempt to show that the pattern also occurs, or would be likely to occur, in more natural circumstances and that the pattern can be expected to have the proposed function in these natural circumstances. If the concept of a natural environment is ignored, and evolution is imagined to be an omnipotent entity that has created organisms which miraculously display uniformly adaptive behavior in all possible environments, then "evolution" becomes, in S. L. Washburn's phrase, only a "magic word."

Large-brained hominids with advanced tool technologies have existed for more than one million years (Clark 1976). For over 99 percent of this period humans lived in small nomadic groups without domesticated plants or animals. This hunting and gathering way of life is the only stable, persistent adaptation humans have ever achieved. While opinion is not unanimous (see Wilson 1975), it is generally agreed that insufficient time has elapsed since the invention of agriculture 10,000 years ago for significant changes to have occurred in human gene pools. Certainly there is no evidence that living hunter/gatherer peoples—whose ancestors presumably were all hunter/gatherers—are less well adapted genetically to agricultural or to modern technological societies than are peoples whose ancestors lived in such societies since their inception. In other words, I see no reason to believe that a group of infants born to hunter/gatherer peoples and a corresponding group of infants born to Western peoples would succeed differentially if raised in a Western society (unless, of course, the former were subject to discrimination and exploitation). Humans can thus be said to be genetically adapted to a hunting and gathering way of life, a way of life characterized by small groups, low population densities, division of labor by sex, infanticide, and nomadism. It was in such environments that selection molded human sexuality.

We do not know how diverse human societies were during the Pleistocene, but in many respects they were certainly far less diverse than the range of post-Pleistocene societies. This raises the possibility that the plasticity underlying human behavioral variability is, at least in part, an adaptation to something else. That "something else" may be the complexities of a human way of life. I have argued elsewhere (Symons 1978a) that the function of many animal learning abilities is not the production of variable behavior patterns in response to variable environmental conditions but rather the production of complex, learned, species-typical behavior patterns which are responses to complex, but relatively uniform environmental conditions (see Chapter One).

These considerations grew out of a study of the function of aggressive play among rhesus monkeys, but may have general applicability. I argued that the primary function of aggressive play is the practice and perfection of extremely complex and fast-paced species-typical motor skills useful in predator avoidance and in intraspecific fighting. The learning potential that underlies the monkeys' abilities to improve their fighting performances is not an adaptation designed by natural selection to permit them to develop individual differences in behavior; that is, in a natural environment it may well be that all monkeys learn the same or very similar fighting skills. But any learning ability makes possible—as an incidental effect, or byproduct—the development of behaviors other than those for which it was designed by natural selection. The plasticity of rhesus nervous systems that underlies their ability to learn through play to fight skillfully also permits them to learn many other behaviors, and they do so if rearing conditions are abnormal. In captivity, for example, rhesus monkeys go through a stage of play in which they aggress against inanimate objects, a stage which is absent in a natural environment. Thus, even if someone were to demonstrate a reproductive advantage to object-aggression in captivity, it is nonetheless an artifact; that is, it has no function. Rhesus monkeys have far less potential for variability in their repertoire of communicatory postures, gestures, and vocalizations than they have in their aggressive play: their communicative signals develop very similarly in almost every environmental condition in which rhesus can survive at all. And yet it is possible that the learning abilities that underlie aggressive play have not been designed by natural selection to produce behaviors that vary among individuals any more than do their "innate" communicative signals.

Unlike behavioral development in rhesus monkeys and almost all other animals, learning is important in the development of most human behaviors, and humans can thus develop a wide array of behavioral phenotypes in different environmental conditions. But this is not conclusive evidence that the function of all, or even most, human learning abilities is to permit behavioral variability. It may be that the plasticity which makes human diversity possible is in large measure an adaptation to the complexities of a human way of life. If this view is correct, a great deal of observed human behavioral variability is an artifact of the unnatural habitats in which all humans live today, or simply random "noise."

Much of the human cerebral cortex is devoted to the complexities of language and tool-use. Humans are genetically adapted to learn to speak a natural language, but the *differences* among natural languages apparently are trivial compared with their fundamental similarities in structure and ontogeny. There is no evidence that variations in natural languages have any adaptive significance, hence the human capacity to learn a variety of languages is best considered an incidental byproduct of linguistic ability. Similarly, while human societies today exhibit major differences in tool traditions, during the Pleistocene there was frequently continuity in tool traditions over huge areas and hundreds of thousands of years (Clark 1976). The human ability to learn to use and to manufacture tools may be best considered to be an adaptation to the complexity and difficulty of mastery of these tasks; the ability to master a wide variety of tool traditions may be largely an incidental effect. Finally, much of the human cortex makes possible the intricacies of social life but, again, one need not postulate that human societies exhibited great differences during the Pleistocene to account for a human brain that makes possible the present variety of societies. The complexity of human interaction and the subtleties of judgment and calculation required to achieve reproductive success in any given society may be sufficient to account for the evolution of learning potentials that make possible—as an incidental effect—human social variability.

I believe that this possibility should receive serious consideration especially since it is in many ways uncongenial. It is uncongenial, for example, because we value creativity and do not value Machiavellian intrigue, and to propose that intrigue is a function of the human brain and creativity is an incidental effect may seem to elevate and justify the former and to denigrate and trivialize the latter; but this is true only to the extent that natural is equated with good. This point of view is also uncongenial because it implies that a great deal of human variability observed today probably is not explicable by any general scheme but is largely a product of unique historical circumstances. If this is true, it seriously compromises the possibility of finding general explanations for human behavior. But however uncongenial this may be to our satisfaction in intellectual generalization, it may be true nonetheless. The recent stunning successes in teaching chimpanzees to communicate using various kinds of sign language—behavior which, for chimpanzees, is completely unnatural—should give us pause for thought. The enormous diversity of unnatural play activities exhibited by domesticated and captive animals indicates that the ability to learn —even when its function is not the production of variable behavior— makes possible a great deal of behavioral variability, variability which will be expressed in unnatural environments.

The problem of free will

The problem of free will (and determinism) is how to reconcile our subjective impression that we can choose to act or not to act with the scientific assumption that everything—including mental events—is subject to necessity. While evolutionary theory sometimes appears to contribute to this problem's solution, I believe that this appearance is largely illusory.

The August 1, 1977, issue of *Time* magazine carried a feature article on sociobiology accompanied by a cover photograph of a young man and woman in awkward embrace: their expressions are fixed and wooden; they do not meet each other's eyes, but stare vacantly into space; and their limbs are being manipulated by strings, though the puppet master is not visible. The message is clear: human beings are marionettes, and genes—the puppet masters—pull the strings. This photograph was not just a device to sell magazines but an accurate reflection of some recent writings on the implications of evolutionary theory. For example, in *The Selfish Gene*—a book highly praised by W. D. Hamilton (1977), with a foreword by Robert L. Trivers— Richard Dawkins writes: "We are survival machines—robot vehicles blindly programmed to preserve the selfish molecules known as genes"

(p. ix). In the following section I shall consider the semantics of this statement. Here I simply wish to point out that Dawkins's implication —through the use of words like "robot" and "blindly"—that evolutionary theory favors determinism is utterly without foundation.

Theories about ultimate causation can and do vary independently of positions on the problem of free will. Thus it is possible for two people who agree that a deity is ultimately responsible for the creation and preservation of everything that exists to disagree about whether that deity has endowed humans with a free will. Similarly, the theory that organic entities have been designed by natural selection does not favor determinism over free will: answers to "why" questions do not necessarily constrain answers to "how" questions. This is not to say that ultimate causal analyses have no potential implications for the problem of free will. If the ultimate causal analysis in the Judeo-Christian Bible had included a clearer statement of God's views on the problem of human free will, for example, a great deal of theological debate would have been avoided. And—ironically, in light of determinist sociobiological rhetoric—the theory of evolution has been said to favor the free will position to the extent that it disfavors an epiphenomenal view of mind. The view that only physical events can cause other physical events, and that mind is mere epiphenomenon of brain activity, appears untenable if natural selection is the primary creative force in nature. An omnipotent deity presumably could, if it wished, create mind as a functionless epiphenomenon, but natural selection implies (at least to some scientists and philosophers) that were mind functionless it would long ago have withered away, not become more elaborate, as it obviously has.

The problem of free will is bound up with the general problem of mind. Perhaps the solutions to these problems await the formulation of better questions, the discovery of new analytic techniques, or the advent of another Newton, Darwin, or Einstein; or perhaps the problems of mind and free will are inherently refractory to the scientific method. But determinist rhetoric notwithstanding, sociobiology has contributed nothing to the solution of these problems.

The semantics of ultimate causation

Language is a tool. Its function is to facilitate communication about matters of daily life, not to permit insights into ultimate causation or to promote scientific progress. Science, by definition, expands knowledge, but it does not necessarily expand language. Indeed, the constant creation of new terms may raise suspicions that a lack of content is being concealed with a smoke screen of jargon. But ordinary words used in new scientific ways come trailing clouds of ordinary meanings, hence the possibility of confusion, especially when the old associations are strongly emotional. MacLean (1970:346) writes that "The self-oriented nature of affect is . . . relevant to man's proclivity to choose familiar, workaday models for scientific explanations," and he cites examples from molecular and genetic biology such as "messengers," "operators," "promoters," "master genes," and "slave genes." MacLean cautions that "It is important to keep asking how such anthropomorphic modeling may interfere with detached thinking and thereby limit our intellectual horizons" (p. 347).

Natural languages are ill-designed for thinking about and communicating about ultimate causation because the meanings of ordinary words have to do almost entirely with proximate matters. Our tendencies to reify and to anthropomorphize—to imagine gods, cultures, or genes in our image—may be at least partly the result of the limitations that natural languages place on our thinking. I believe that the proclivity of some evolutionary theorists for using ordinary language uncritically in discussing ultimate causation has engendered serious confusion. I shall limit my criticism to *The Selfish Gene* because Dawkins's popularization of recent evolutionary theory is exceptionally lucid and powerful, and makes explicit what is often only implicit in the more technical literature.

To set the stage for a discussion of the language of ultimate causation I would like first to consider L. Susan Stebbing's (1937) semantic analysis of the language used by certain physicists and astronomers in popularizing their sciences. In a popular exposition of the principles of modern physics Sir Arthur Eddington described the difficulties faced by a physicist about to enter a room, difficulties of which the layman is unaware: the layman believes that the plank on which he is about to step is solid, but the physicist knows that the appearance of solidity is illusory. To the physicist, said Eddington, the plank "has no solidity of substance. To step on it is like stepping on a swarm of flies" (Stebbing 1937:48). Stebbing, however, points out that stepping on a plank is nothing at all like stepping on a swarm of flies: we know what it is like to step on a solid plank, we can imagine what it would be like to step on a swarm of flies, and the two experiences are different. The plank appears to be solid, and, in fact, it is solid. "Solid" can be opposed to "empty," "hollow," or "porous," or it can be used figuratively, "but there is no common usage of language that provides a meaning for the word 'solid' that would make sense to say that the plank on which I stand is not *solid*" (p. 52). If the plank is not solid, "solid" has no meaning; that is, if the plank is not solid, there are no examples of things that are. "The pairs of words, 'solid'–'empty,' 'solid'–'hollow,' 'solid'–'porous,' belong to the vocabulary of common-sense language; in the case of each pair, if one of the two is without sense, so is the other" (p. 53). And "Nothing but confusion can result if in one and the same sentence, we mix up language used appropriately for the furniture of earth and our daily dealings with it with language used for the purposes of philosophical and scientific discussion" (p. 47).

With Stebbing's caveat in mind, consider again the word "robot" in Dawkins's (1976) statement, "We are survival machines—robot [later (p. 21) qualified as "lumbering" robot] vehicles blindly programmed to preserve the selfish molecules known as genes." A robot is a mindless automaton. Perhaps some animals are robots (we have no way of knowing); however, Dawkins is not referring to *some* animals, but to *all* animals and in this case specifically to human beings. Now, to paraphrase Stebbing, "robot" can be opposed to "thinking being," or it can be used figuratively to indicate a person who seems to act mechanically, but there is no common usage of language that provides a meaning for the word "robot" in which it would make sense to say that all living things are robots. If humans are robots, "robot" has no meaning. Similarly, "lumbering" can be opposed to "graceful," but there is no common usage of language in which it would make sense to say that all living things lumber.

It should not be supposed that Dawkins is merely employing colorful language in order to emphasize nature over nurture; on the contrary, he is not concerned with proximate causation at all. Presumably Dawkins intends to contrast dramatically the theory of evolution with (unspecified) competing theories of ultimate causation. The sense of his statement is that organisms have been designed by natural selection; the purpose of the "robot" metaphor is to communicate astonishment at this fact to the reader, as his subsequent sentences make clear: "This is a truth which still fills me with astonishment. Though I have known it for years, I never seem to get fully used to it. One of my hopes is that I may have some success in astonishing others" (p. ix). The reader is indeed astonished to learn that he is a robot, for the same reason he is astonished to learn that his floor is not solid: neither claim is true.

The concept of natural selection is astonishing, but so are all theories of ultimate causation. Since human intuition apparently has not been designed to perceive ultimate causes, any conceivable ultimate explanation of life is bound to be astonishing if it is really thought about, just as the idea of an infinite universe and the idea of a finite universe are equally astonishing. Dawkins's rhetoric in *The Selfish Gene* might actually promote such competing theories of ultimate causation as the one advanced in Genesis, since, whatever its shortcomings, Genesis at least has the virtue of not claiming that humans are robots or that gazelles lumber. In summary, the rhetoric of *The Selfish Gene* exactly reverses the real situation: through metaphor genes are endowed with properties only sentient beings can possess, such as selfishness, while sentient beings are stripped of these properties and called machines. Had Dawkins intended to convey the message that behavior is more "innate" than is commonly supposed these metaphors might have some utility, but since he intended only to contrast a particular theory of ultimate causation with competing theories, any pedagogical gains are, in my opinion, more than offset by semantic and conceptual losses. Furthermore, the anthropomorphization of genes, like the creation of anthropomorphic deities and the reification of societies, obscures the deepest mystery in the life sciences: the origin and nature of mind.

The evolution of mind

In his review of Edward O. Wilson's *Sociobiology*, C. H. Waddington (1976) argues that the most fundamental and far-reaching issue in biology is the evolution of mind. Surely the mental aspects of sexuality, not observable behavior or physiology, make the study of human sexuality so compelling to so many people. It is, for example, the quality and intensity of human experience, and not the physiological complexity, that accounts for the existence of a 533-page book entitled *The Female Orgasm* (Fisher 1973) and the nonexistence (to my knowledge) of even a small pamphlet entitled *The Female Sneeze*.

If Gazzaniga (1970:vii) is correct in stating that "The mysteries of the mind remain as elusive today as ever before" because researchers do not know "the proper and most important questions to ask," the evolutionist has a contribution to make to the study of mind. Darwin was aware of the significance of the theory of evolution to understanding psyche: "To study metaphysics [psychology] as they have been studied appears to me like struggling at astronomy without mechanics.—Experience shows the problem of the mind cannot be solved by attacking the citadel itself.—the mind is function of body.—we must find some *stabile* foundation to argue from" (notebook N, Barrett 1974). The proper and most important ultimate question is: How did mental events function in maximizing reproductive success in ancestral populations?

Natural selection clearly shaped mind via mind's effects on behavior. This view rests on the commonsense interactionist position, also held by some students of brain function (Sperry 1969, Popper and Eccles 1977), that mental events may both cause and be caused by physical events: the visual stimulus of a beautiful woman may cause a man to experience lust; the experience of lust, independent of any outside stimulus, may cause various behaviors.

One of the central concerns of this book is the degree to which sexual experiences vary among individual humans and the "distances" of these experiences from the genes. Wilson (1975) and others use the concept of distance as an analogy for the degree to which particular characteristics of organisms and the societies they comprise are independent of gene action. Protein synthesis, for example, is very "close" to the genes in that the genotype is highly predictive of protein synthesis. Gross morphology is farther from the genes, and behavior is farther still; that is, a given genotype is usually more predictive of morphology than of behavior. (In fact, among some animal species the behavioral phenotypes that can develop from a given genotype are so varied that some scholars believe that it is misleading to speak of the evolution of behavior: what evolves, they argue, are behavioral capacities.) Social organization is still farther from the genes: the behavior patterns of most animal species are relatively fixed, but in many cases differing social organizations arise as a consequence of differing frequencies or intensities of the same behaviors. Some primate species, for example, exhibit one-male groups in some environmental conditions and multimale groups in other conditions, presumably as a result of differing frequencies or intensities of male-male aggression.

One approach to mind from an evolutionary perspective then, may be to inquire into the relative distances from the genes of the various events to experience or awareness—in William James's words, "sensations, mental images, thoughts, desires, emotions, volitions and the like." It seems likely that some mental events are closer to the genes, and less variable, than observable behavior, while others are more distant from the genes, and more variable than behavior. Surely visual sensations, for example, are very much alike among individuals and close to the genes; even minor perturbations, such as red-green color blindness, are of major interest. The experiences underlying great scientific achievements, on the other hand, are perhaps more distant from the genes than any other biological phenomenon. Einstein's thoughts about relativity were singular events. But the basic structure of human cognitive and emotional experience may not vary substantially from person to person or from culture to culture.

The notion of a human nature, a psychic unity of mankind, a shared substratum of experience underlying the diversity of human behaviors is more a matter of inference than observation. Geertz (1965) points out that this notion is an old one: it characterized Enlightenment thought and it "has been present in some form or another in all ages and climes. It is one of those ideas that occur to almost anyone sooner or later" (p. 100). But Geertz argues to the contrary, that "humanity is as various in its essence as in its expression" (p. 97). Of course no one has ever seen a desire or a cognition, nor has any of us experienced an emotion or a thought other than his own; rather, we infer the existence and the nature of other minds from what people say and write and do. Geertz's views seem to reflect in part his own experiences in Java and his conviction that the Javanese feel distinctive, essentially untranslatable, emotions.

Our ideas about the nature of other minds can be characterized as hypotheses, hypotheses which are constantly being unconsciously scrutinized and revised when necessary. The propensity to conceive other minds in the image of one's own very likely is a fundamental human skill, a genuine adaptation, largely "innate," but capable of refinement and modification through experience. That is, we are disposed both by nature and experience to imagine that other minds are much like our own because, in fact, they are.

Maurice Bloch (1977) criticizes the notion, which apparently originated with Durkheim and is accepted by most anthropologists, that society determines human cognition. Why this notion has gone largely unchallenged is not clear, but, according to Bloch, it is partly because most anthropologists believe that different cultures or societies have fundamentally different systems of thought, and he notes that it is a "professional malpractice of anthropologists to exaggerate the exotic character of other cultures" (p. 285). Calling attention to research that demonstrates that, universally, "colour, plant, animal and even human classifications are based on identical criteria and produce identical classes and subclasses varying only in degree of elaboration" (p. 282), Bloch argues that the basic structure of human cognition, the structure that typically is used in the "practical" matters of daily life, is the product of human interaction with nature, rather than culture, and is everywhere the same. He analyzes in detail the cultural relativists' claim that concepts of time vary from society to society and argues that culturally variable concepts of time are used only in ritual communication. According to Bloch, humans also have an invariant, universal concept of time which is used in practical, nonritual activities. Once an anthropologist learns a people's language he can communicate not only *with* them but *about* them and make their thoughts and activities intelligible to his readers. Bloch writes:

> . . . if other people really had different concepts of time we could not do what we patently do, that is communicate with them. Evidence for such a conclusion also comes from a completely different source, and that is the mass of recent studies of syntax and semantics of different languages that have been carried out by American linguists. Disagreements and polemics in this field are many, but at least consensus seems to be emerging on one point, and that is that the fundamental logic employed in the syntax of all languages is, Whorf notwithstanding, the same. The implications of this for notions of time are clear. The logic of languages implies a notion of temporality and sequence and so if all syntax is based on the same logic, all speakers must at a fundamental level apprehend time in the same way (p. 233).

However universal human cognition may be, I believe that human emotion is still more basic, older, and universal, and that "emotion has taught mankind to reason" (Marquis de Vauvenargues). Discussions of the evolution of the human brain tend to emphasize the enormous expansion of the cerebral cortex and the functional significance of this expanded cortex for language, tool-use, planning, memory, sustained attention, and complex social life. But the "lower-centers" also have expanded, and they function in close reciprocal collaboration with the cortex; the limbic system, for example, functions to mediate sensory input and motor output in a manner subjectively recognized as emotional (Campbell 1974). The human thalamus, a major component of the limbic system, is about twelve times as large, and the chimpanzee thalamus is about five times as large, as the thalamus of a monkey. These thalamic disparities are about the same as the disparities in the size of the cerebral cortex among humans, chimpanzees, and monkeys (Washburn and Strum 1972). Thus while humans undoubtedly exhibit unprecedented potential for "cool reasonableness" (Campbell 1974), we probably also exhibit unprecedented emotional complexity. Emotional capacities may exemplify human universals of mind and represent experiences closer to the genes than observable behavior.

It cannot be accidental that during the course of evolutionary history "higher" and "lower" brain mechanisms expanded together. No matter how plastic an organism's mind or behavior may be the function of mind and behavior remains the same, the perpetuation of DNA molecules. Since mental plasticity increases the number of maladaptive, as well as adaptive, behaviors that can be learned, it can only evolve along with concomitant mechanisms that evaluate stimuli and motivate the seeking of stimuli, thereby making likely the development of adaptive behaviors. These mechanisms of evaluation and motivation must be closer to the genes than are the behaviors they produce. Emotions might be considered to be the genes' closest representatives in the mental processes of learning and decision making: they constitute evaluations of stimuli, whether these stimuli originate outside the organism (sensation) or in the brain itself (memory, fantasy), and motivate the seeking of particular stimuli.

The *Oxford English Dictionary* identifies "emotions" as feelings, to be distinguished from other mental events such as cognitions, but the obsolete meaning—to move from place to place—clearly remains alive, since we are moved by emotions, both figuratively and literally. "Motive" and "emotion" are very close in derivation and in meaning. This was Shand's (1914:67) point of view: "All intellectual and voluntary processes are elicited by the system of some impulse, emotion, or sentiment, and are subordinate to its end." And this view is also apparent in recent behavioristic analyses of observable behaviors and physiological processes associated with emotion: "Howsoever obvious the differences between such affective ('feelings') and effective ('emotional behavior') response patterns, the evident interrelationships between the two in complex interactional situations can not be ignored" (Brady 1975:20). In *The World of Sex* Henry Miller points out that "desire is paramount and ineradicable, even when, as Buddhists express it, it passes over into its opposite. To free oneself from desire one has to *desire* to do so."

Perhaps every evolutionary step taken in the direction of increased behavioral plasticity—which presumably is reflected in certain kinds of increased mental plasticity—entails a step in the direction of increased experiential capacities that are relatively invariant among individuals. This point can be illustrated by considering some features of behavioral development among chimpanzees. Chimpanzees probably are exceeded in behavioral plasticity only by humans. Infant chimpanzees that were separated from their mothers shortly after birth and reared for two years in impoverished, monotonous, and asocial environments developed striking individual differences in behavior (Rogers 1973). These individual differences undoubtedly are far greater than those developed by similarly deprived monkeys, but this behavioral plasticity does not indicate that chimpanzees are adapted to exhibit idiosyncratic behaviors: neither in captive social groups nor in free-ranging populations do chimpanzees exhibit such striking individual differences. Rather, chimpanzee plasticity represents an adaptation to learn adaptive behaviors from other chimpanzees. When the deprived chimpanzees mentioned above were given social experience with more normally reared chimpanzees "A large part of their eventual socialization was the elimination of idiosyncratic behaviors and the learning of patterns more typical of the species" (Rogers 1973:191).

In the laboratory (Menzel *et al.* 1972) and in the wild (Lawick-Goodall 1973, Teleki 1974), chimpanzee groups exhibit "cultural" differences in motor patterns probably unmatched by other nonhuman primate species, and these group differences are primarily ones of technology and tool traditions. Chimpanzees, then, have relatively "open" motor patterns, made possible by complex cortical structures mediating tool-use that monkeys and other nonhuman mammals do not possess. When a chimpanzee falls into human hands at an impressionable age it can learn American Sign Language, to smoke cigars, to ride a unicycle, and many other unchimpanzeelike behaviors.

In natural environments chimpanzees learn adaptive tool-using patterns from careful observation of other chimpanzees, especially their mothers, from imitating these activities, and from practicing them—often for years—to attain complete mastery (Lawick-Goodall 1973, Teleki 1974). Goodall (1976:88) writes that "in the wild, young chimpanzees do spend much time watching others intently, particularly their mothers. Often, after watching some activity such as a male charging display or a complex tool-using performance, an infant may then try to perform the same actions. Subsequently he may practice the behavior time and again." The evolution of relatively plastic abilities in tool using and tool making in ancestral chimpanzee populations must have been accompanied by increasing differentiation and elaboration of invariant brain mechanisms that underlie pleasure or satisfaction in observing other chimpanzees, in imitating, and in practicing. In summary, one might speculate that chimpanzees have experiences associated with the actual mechanics of skilled tool-use (experiences of which monkeys are incapable), that these experiences are far from the genes in the sense that they cannot be predicted from knowledge of the genotype, and that they vary among individual chimpanzees. But presumably chimpanzees also have emotional experiences (of which monkeys are equally incapable) that represent pleasures or satisfactions in observation, mimicry, and practice, and which motivate these behaviors. These experiences are close to the genes and do not vary substantially among individuals.

Humans are so much more complex and flexible than chimpanzees that there are no scales on which the intelligence of the two species can be usefully compared (Wilson 1975). But intelligence is a two-edged sword. While chimpanzee "cultural" behavior depends on learning, but not on teaching, humans actively teach each other. The more teachable an organism is, the more fully it can profit from the experiences of its ancestors and associates, but the more it risks being exploited by its ancestors and associates. The more an animal "goes in for ethicizing" (Waddington 1960), the more it can acquire traditions of social wisdom that are too complex or subtle to be learned through individual experience, and the more it can acquire worthless and destructive superstitions. The more cooperatively interdependent the members of a group become, the greater is their collective power, the more fulsome are the opportunities for individuals to manipulate one another for their own ends, and "the more scope there is for the inconspicuous idler" (Hamilton 1975:145). "As language becomes more sophisticated there is also more opportunity to pervert its use for selfish ends: fluency is an aid to persuasive lying as well as to conveying complex truths that are socially useful" (Hamilton 1975:135). In short, human variability and human vulnerability are inseparable.

If a simple, unitary continuum of emotional experience, from strong pleasure to strong displeasure, were effective in shaping human learning and in motivating human behavior, greater emotional complexity presumably would not have evolved. The range of human emotional experience must be the result of natural selection. I propose that selection favors the elaboration of invariant motivational/emotional neural systems as a direct function of: (1) the degree of behavioral plasticity exhibited by a species, which makes maladaptive learned behaviors possible; and (2) the extent to which the environment actually encourages the learning of maladaptive behaviors.

Humans possess far more plasticity and skill in tool-use and manufacture than chimpanzees do—skill that is reflected in major elaboration of human motor and sensory cortices. Such human skill is perhaps also reflected in the elaboration of neural mechanisms that underlie specific emotions: uniquely human aesthetic experiences may function to motivate the painstaking effort required to manufacture tools, such as the Acheulian hand-axe, of exceptional precision and elegance (Washburn 1970). But it seems unlikely that environmental forces existed during the course of human evolution that actually encouraged maladaptive tool production, and hence one need not posit brain mechanisms to counter such forces. The learning of object-related skills does not seem to be an area in which manipulation or exploitation is problematical. Children learn such skills largely from their peers and parents, and it seems unlikely that circumstances arise frequently in which one individual can profit from inculcating maladaptive tool-using behaviors in a second individual. Indeed, with the exception of college laboratory classes composed primarily of undergraduate pre-med majors, manipulation and deceit in the teaching of physical skills is probably rare among human beings.

In contrast to the uncompetitive circumstances surrounding tool-use and manufacture, however, opportunities for people to profit genetically from controlling, manipulating, and exploiting each other sexually are ever-present features of human existence. As discussed in Chapter One, reproductive competition is inevitable in the sense that success or failure is always relative, and among organisms that reproduce by internal fertilization the sine qua non of reproduction is copulation. Without copulation parental behavior is impossible and survival is irrelevant. In part, an animal maximizes its reproductive success by controlling its own copulations and those of others. If there is any validity in the argument I have presented, the features of the human brain that make possible variable and complex sexual behaviors and experiences entail a concomitant evolutionary elaboration of relatively inflexible sex-related emotional/motivational neural mechanisms designed to insure against the development of maladaptive sexual behavior in natural environments.

An evolutionary perspective implies that as long as selection is potent at the level of the individual a tabula rasa view of the human mind is untenable, even in theory. The argument can be presented as follows: (1) The only known circumstance in which selection favors substantial behavioral plasticity is when "cultural" knowledge replaces "innate" knowledge. The human cerebral cortex that makes possible language and skilled tool-use implies natural environments containing language speakers and skilled tool-users as surely as the vertebrate eye implies natural environments containing specific frequencies of electromagnetic radiation. (2) Cultural knowledge is transmitted nongenetically from one individual to another. (3) Among sexually reproducing organisms, no two individuals (except monozygotic twins) have the same genotype, hence no two individuals have identical reproductive "interests." (4) Therefore an individual must have mechanisms —and I assume these are best described as emotional/motivational mechanisms—to recognize and look after its own "interests." If it lacked such mechanisms, it would be vulnerable to random environmental influences and to exploitation. I am arguing, in effect, that just as the members of a species may exhibit a variety of behaviors but similar anatomy, so the variability in human sexual behavior and custom may be underlaid by certain uniformities of mind. From this point of view emotions and intellect are not opposites: emotions by definition are nonrational, but they are not irrational. In psychic life the intellect is how, the emotions why.[1]

Evolution and self-interest

While natural selection may operate at the level of a social group or even a population, selection at these levels almost always is negligible

---

[1] Whether human action is "basically" rational or "basically" emotional has been a major issue in the history of anthropological theory (Hatch 1973). This issue has again arisen in the debate surrounding *Sociobiology*, Wilson's critics arguing that he overemphasizes human emotions (Gurin 1976). I believe that such debates are futile. According to Webster, "rational implies the ability to reason logically, as by drawing conclusions from inferences, and often connotes absence of emotionalism." But there is no such thing as a rational goal: rational and irrational refer to processes, not end states. Difficulties arise when "rational" is used metaphorically to refer to long-term, complex goals and "emotion" to immediate, simple goals. The persistent belief that some goals are more rational than others appears to be a misguided secular effort to find meaning and purpose apart from the human mind, to find nontheistic justification for moral feelings.

compared with selection at the level of the individual organism (Williams 1966, Alexander 1975), and Wilson (1975) therefore argues that the central problem in sociobiology is to explain how "altruism" could evolve. I enclose "altruism" in quotation marks because the sociobiological meaning of this word differs from its ordinary meaning and I wish to contrast sociobiological "altruism" with ordinary altruism. Wilson defines "altruism" as "self destructive behavior performed for the benefit of others." But nearly all the words in this definition are meant in nonordinary senses: "self destructive" refers to the reduction of personal fitness; "the benefit of others" refers to the enhancement of the fitnesses of other organisms; "performed for" refers to typical effects on the fitnesses of other organisms, not to intention or motive, and is as applicable to mindless organisms as it is to organisms that are capable of having intentions. In ordinary usage, however, altruism means "Devotion to the welfare of others, regard for others, as a principle of action; opposed to egoism or selfishness" (*Oxford English Dictionary*). Altruism refers primarily to intent or motive ("devotion to," "regard for"), hence a mindless organism could be neither altruistic nor selfish; furthermore, the effects of an organism's activities on its own fitness or that of others has nothing whatever to do with altruism. Welfare is not synonymous with fitness. In short, Wilson's "altruism" has *only* to do with the survival of genes, while altruism in the ordinary sense has *nothing* to do with the survival of genes.

Eddington was in no danger of sowing confusion among physicists in writing popularly of nonsolid planks; his error was in believing that laymen could understand the concepts of modern physics without understanding the language—mathematics—in which these concepts have meaning. But, I believe, sociobiological rhetoric about "altruism" and "selfishness" misleads laymen and scientists alike. Consider Dawkins's explanation for the title of his book, *The Selfish Gene:*

> The argument of this book is that we, and all other animals, are machines created by our genes. Like successful Chicago gangsters, our genes have survived, in some cases for millions of years, in a highly competitive world. This entitles us to expect certain qualities in our genes. I shall argue that a predominant quality to be expected in a successful gene is ruthless selfishness. This gene selfishness will usually give rise to selfishness in individual behaviour. However, as we shall see, there are special circumstances in which a gene can achieve its own selfish goals best by fostering a limited form of altruism at the level of individual animals. "Special" and "limited" are important words in the last sentence. Much as we might wish to believe otherwise,

universal love and the welfare of the species as a whole are concepts which simply do not make evolutionary sense (pp. 2-3).

Genes are "selected" on the basis of their ability to survive. For this reason Dawkins calls them selfish, but since molecular survival has nothing to do with ordinary usages of selfish (we do not consider radioactive elements to be altruistic because they decay into other elements), we are entitled to ask why the word "selfish" entered the picture in the first place; why, that is, was Dawkins's book not called *The Surviving Gene?* The notion of the selfish gene derives, I believe, not from the nature or activities of genes, but from a particular view of life—a view that can be characterized as mechanistic, utilitarian, unsentimental, tough-minded, and cynical. The sense of the last-quoted passage from *The Selfish Gene* is that the theory of evolution by natural selection has very different scientific implications from, say, the theory of Genesis or the theory that organisms have been designed to promote the survival of their species.

With respect to "selfishness" and "altruism," sociobiologists have partitioned species-typical behaviors into three types:

(1) Behaviors that promote individual fitness.

(2) Behaviors that promote individual fitness in a special way: the behaver incurs an immediate cost (in the currencies of time, energy, or risk), and a function (not just an effect) of the behavior is to promote the inclusive fitness of another (not necessarily related) animal. Such behaviors evolve, in theory, if the recipient of the "altruistic" act typically repays it sometime in the future, and if animals that establish relationships in which "altruistic" acts are reciprocated enjoy greater than average reproductive success. The emphasis here is not so much on the immediate cost and delayed payoff, since all behaviors have immediate costs, and almost all payoffs are delayed, but rather on the fact that the behavior is designed to "benefit" another animal, and on the fact of reciprocity.

(3) Behaviors that reduce personal fitness. As discussed in Chapter One, such behaviors evolve, in theory, if they sufficiently "benefit" the behaver's kin (or unrelated animals in whom genetic affinity can be recognized by the behaver).

Sociobiological usages of "selfishness" and "altruism" thus differ from ordinary usages of these words. First, in sociobiology *all* species-typical behaviors are either "selfish" or "altruistic": category (1) behaviors are "selfish"; category (2) behaviors are "reciprocally altruistic" (Trivers 1971); category (3) behaviors are "altruistic" (Hamilton 1964). But in ordinary parlance, most behaviors are *neither* selfish nor altruistic; a monkey scratching itself is behaving "selfishly," but few of us would wish to call its behavior selfish.[2] Second, in sociobiology "selfish" and "altruistic" are defined entirely on the basis of the effects the behavior has on the fitness of the behaver and other animals. But there is no common usage of selfish and altruistic that partitions behavior this way: there may well be examples of both selfish and altruistic behaviors in each of the three sociobiological categories. And while there undoubtedly are statistical correlations between "altruism" and altruism, and between "selfishness" and selfishness, in the absence of perfect correspondence these correlations simply make the semantic confusion worse. Third, as noted above, sociobiological usages have nothing to do with the behaver's intent, while ordinary usages are defined on the basis of intent. Sociobiologists themselves emphasize this contrast; but to emphasize that "altruism" and "selfishness" refer only to effects of behavior and not to intentions conveys the impression that this is the *only* important peculiarity in the sociobiological use of these words, and diverts attention from the facts that ordinary usages of altruism and selfishness also have implications about the effects of behavior and that these effects have nothing to do with inclusive fitness.

Inclusive fitness theory has provided satisfying ultimate causal explanations of many nonhuman animal behaviors; since in everyday life we almost never use the words "altruistic" and "selfish" to refer to nonhuman animals, sociobiologists can define these words almost any way they wish, in referring to nonhuman animals, without causing too much confusion. And if nonhuman animal "altruism" can be explained sociobiologically, is it not reasonable to expect that human altruism will yield its mysteries to the same analytic techniques? This depends on, among other things, how close "altruism" and altruism really are;

[2] The present discussion assumes, for the sake of clarity, that people generally agree in classifying everyday acts as selfish or altruistic. Often, however, this is not the case. For example, a couple's decision to remain childless might be called selfish by the potential grandparents and by boosters of family life; altruistic by sociobiologists and by those who, like the poet Heinrich Heine, believe that not to have been born is a miracle; and neither selfish nor altruistic by most disinterested observers. Indeed, a dichotomy as vague and essentially prescriptive and exhortatory as selfish/altruistic seems most unlikely to be a productive approach to the study of human social life.

we do not, after all, consider that a physicist's understanding of "charm" among subatomic particles qualifies him to teach in a charm school.

The hypothesis that a human group is essentially a collection of selfish individuals who cooperate among themselves, when they do, in order to further their own individual interests has seemed to some biologists to be a view of human society that is at odds with nonevolutionary views. Indeed, some recent applications of evolutionary theory to human behavior emphasize individual self-interest as if it were the unique and most important discovery of such theory, implying that all social science theories consider human behavior to promote group interests at the expense of the interests of the constituent members. Alexander (1975:90), for example, writes: ". . . the basic conflict in the conduct of a group-living organism is not 'How can I help myself?' versus 'How can I help the group as a whole?' It is 'How can I help myself directly in the competition with others?' and 'How can I help myself indirectly by helping my kin and cooperating in the social group in which I am forced to live if I am to reproduce at all—and upon the success and persistence of which my own persistence and reproductive success are therefore predicated?'" Alexander implies in this passage that previous approaches to group-living organisms have assumed, incorrectly, that although individuals do act selfishly at times, they also act selflessly to help the group as a whole at their own expense. Such approaches, he argues, have characterized students of human culture: "Unlike the modern evolutionary biologist, students of culture still see the benefits of systems of altruism or reciprocity as being chiefly applicable at the group level. Their concepts of function or adaptiveness usually involve the maintenance of the group as a whole, with little emphasis upon variations in the reproductive success of individuals" (p. 90).

But in fact, the view that societies are best conceived as consequences of the behavior of self-interested individuals is held by many social scientists (especially economists), and human conflict in some form is the theme of all great works of literature. Sociobiologists seem to have a rather Machiavellian view of human social life, but so did Machiavelli. Sociobiologists argue that natural selection has produced individuals who put their own welfare above that of society, but long ago Thomas Huxley (1897) reached a similar conclusion: ". . . with all their enormous differences in natural endowment, men agree to one thing, and that is their innate desire to enjoy the pleasures and to escape the pains of life; and, in short, to do nothing but that which it pleases them to do, without the least reference to the welfare of the society into which they are born. That is their inheritance . . ." (p. 27).

The sociobiological view of life is mechanistic, utilitarian, unsentimental, tough-minded, and cynical. This view of life, however, is not unique to sociobiology, and by writing as if evolutionary theory provided insights into the dark corners of human psyche that the human psyche itself does not provide, sociobiology, like Henry James, chews more than it bites off. By stressing that "altruistic" and "selfish" do not refer to people's conscious motives, sociobiologists often seem to imply that ultimate causal analyses shed light on unconscious motives; but contributions to a cynical view of human motivation must go beyond the insights of Montaigne, La Rochefoucauld, Mark Twain, Bierce, and Freud. Although sociobiological theory may yet achieve such insights, at present La Rochefoucauld's maxims appear to be in little danger of being superseded.

Evolutionary theory thus is by no means uniquely responsible for the notions that human societies are composed of self-interested individuals, that humans dissimulate to achieve their goals, and that sociality is a two-edged sword. Economists such as McKenzie and Tullock (1975) maintain that all human behavior can be understood as attempts to maximize individual self-interest (utility) and that groups must be considered to be merely collections of selfish individuals. The writings of sociologists such as Goffman (1969) continually emphasize that humans communicate and dissimulate to promote their own interests. The anthropologist Charles Erasmus (1977) addresses himself to the question: How and why do men provision collective good? He reviews the results of his own research, spanning nearly thirty years, in Mexico, South America, Africa, Israel, and Western Europe on cooperation in agriculture, as well as the evidence on 19th-century communes and the recent social experiments in Russia and China, and concludes: "Nowhere do we find a collective good maintained without self-interest. Nowhere, in other words, do we find 'altruism' without some form of individual reinforcement." A recent best-selling book on how to succeed in business makes a point very similar to Alexander's: "In business, no one ever does anything for anybody else without expecting to gain something in return. A person may say that he's doing something just to be nice—and he may even believe it—but don't *you* believe it. In the final analysis, his non-altruistic subconscious mind will automatically regulate his actions" (Ringer 1976).

The self-interested nature of animals looms large in the writings of many evolutionary biologists. Here, for example, is Alcock's (1975) description of the motivation of subordinate individuals in a dominance hierarchy:

> Subordinate individuals do not persist in accepting their status, giving up food, mates, and space to others, because they are altruistic and intend to sacrifice themselves for the benefit of the group. They do so because of the realities of the situation in which they find themselves. They do not contest their low status because they have in their contacts with others judged that they are incapable of physically defeating the higher-ranking members of the group. They remain in the group because of the benefits this brings (protection from predators, increased probability of finding or capturing food, etc.). By conserving their resources, by not wasting them in a constant struggle to improve their status, subordinate animals have a better chance of living to compete for higher status (and all that goes with it) another day when the odds in their favor are improved (pp. 301-2).

But in a remarkably similar passage Hatch (1973) suggests that to Malinowski, moral traditions constrain the pursuit of individual interests in the same way that Alcock envisages dominance relations constraining individual nonhuman animals:

> Malinowski tended to view human behavior in terms of individual incentives, not social morals. The implication is that social equilibrium consists in a delicate balancing of actual and potential interests, advantages, and opportunities. Each individual is engaged in pursuing his interests, and the structural relations which result are a type of stalemate. The commoner in Trobriand society would like to press himself forward and assume the prerogatives and fame of a wealthy chief, but he does not have the resources to do so. On the other hand, the system offers him sufficient advantages and potential opportunities that it pays him to accept his position, at least for the moment. The Trobriand chief would like to improve his position also, but like everyone else he is caught in a web of duties and obligations which he cannot avoid if he is to maintain the benefits he already enjoys. Malinowski's focus on the individual was leading him to the view that social equilibrium or stability is the outcome of competitive self-interests, not jural rules or disinterested morality (pp. 312-13).[3]

The belief that reciprocity and altruism function primarily to maintain the group as a whole is not universal among social scientists; and

[3] Malinowski appears to have held conflicting opinions about the relationship between individual and collective interests. In *Sex and Repression in Savage Society* (1927) he expresses substantially different views.

ethnographic evidence suggests that this belief may not be widespread among humans in general. The Gahuku-Gama, a people of the Eastern Highlands of New Guinea, for example, whose moral code is described by Read (1955), do not appeal to abstract principles, but emphasize the practical consequences of moral deviation. Although they believe that some things are intrinsically right or wrong, they do not say it is good or right to help others but rather, "if you don't help others, others won't help you" (p. 255), or "give food to those who visit you so they will think well of you" (p. 256). Even when the practical rider is omitted, it is implicit: ". . . disrespect for elders, lack of regard for age mates, failure to support fellow clansmen, incest or breaking the rules of clan exogamy all involve practical penalties, not explicitly stated in each case but undoubtedly understood by the individuals who assert that the norms concerned are right" (pp. 255-56). Moral rules are not universally applicable but are specific to certain situations and certain individuals: ". . . it is wrong for an individual to kill a member of his own tribe, but it is commendable to kill members of opposed tribes, always provided that they are not related to him" (p. 262). Similarly there is no general injunction against lying. "The prudent individual is truthful, because 'lying makes people angry; it causes trouble,' and most people wish to retain the good opinion of those with whom they are in close daily association" (p. 263). But no one expects an individual to tell the truth if he is charged with theft by a member of another clan, and no one expects a member of another group to tell the truth if he can gain advantage by lying.

Colson (1974) reviews a great deal of literature on the problem of order among peoples not controlled by a state power. The significance of social action and belief to these people seems consistent with Gahuku-Gama morality. Preliterate peoples apparently possess as detailed an understanding of the social terms of their existence as they do of the local flora and fauna, and for the same reason: their survival and reproduction depend on it. They are aware, for example, that their safety depends on alliances with neighbors whom they cannot afford to antagonize: "The communities in which all these people lived were governed by a delicate balance of power, always endangered and never to be taken for granted: each person was constantly involved in securing his own position in situations where he had to show his good intentions" (Colson 1974:59). In summary, although evolutionary theory indicates that humans can generally be expected to promote their own "interests" when these conflict with the "interests" of larger entities, such as groups or societies, evolutionary theory is not unique in this respect: many social scientists hold these views, and it is conceivable that most human beings throughout most of human history have implicitly held them.

But evolutionary theory, in which human action is seen as *ultimately* "self-interested," has one significant advantage over theories in which human action is seen as *proximately* self-interested: predictions based on evolutionary theory can be falsified, although the absence of natural human environments considerably erodes this advantage. Concepts developed to provide general proximate explanations of behavior—utility, reinforcement, self-interest, and the like—either are defined circularly, and thus represent elaborate, although often useful, tautologies, or rely on intuition. These concepts, and the theories of human behavior based on them, are therefore difficult to disprove. (That intuition-based concepts have as widespread explanatory power as they do is testament to a certain psychic unity of mankind, and even of animalkind.) The exceptions are theories which apply only to a narrow range of activities in which operational measures of self-interest can be defined: in business, for example, self-interest is defined as maximizing money (Ringer 1976). Theories intended to apply only to a limited range of human activities may be testable but cannot provide a general theory of behavior. Evolutionary theory, on the other hand, is both general and testable—and hence disprovable—because it specifies that something external to the organism is being maximized: reproduction. The testability of evolutionary theory was noted by Darwin (1859:201): "If it could be proved that any part of the structure of any one species had been formed for the exclusive good of another species, it would annihilate my theory, for such could not have been produced by natural selection." And Alexander (1975) points out that "To find an adaptation in an individual that evolved because its sole or net effect is to assist a reproductive competitor within the same species, would also annihilate Darwin's entire theory" (p. 82).

Is and ought

If evolutionary biology is far from unique in considering individual organisms to be in some sense self-interested competitors, one might ask: Why so much fuss over sociobiology? (See, for example, Allen *et al.* 1975, Wade 1976, and Gurin 1976.) The answer may be, at least in part, that sociobiology sees humans not just as self-interested, but as self-interested by nature. The emphases in evolutionary biology on individuals as the primary units of selection and on the likelihood of, and empirical evidence for, competition among individual animals for food, space, and mates are profoundly at odds with the idea of a unity and harmony in nature. This idea is as old as Western history: it was explicit in Sumerian, Greek, and Judeo-Christian cosmologies (Glacken 1967), and it is implicit today in some biology and social science. No doubt much of the reaction against sociobiology stems from the threat sociobiology constitutes to the myth of the peaceable kingdom. It is easier to abandon an anthropomorphic deity than the emotional underpinnings of a folk cosmology. In Joseph Heller's *Catch-22*, Lieutenant Scheisskopf's wife says tearfully to Yossarian: "I don't [believe in God]. . . . But the God I don't believe in is a good God, a just God, a merciful God. He's not the mean and stupid God you make Him out to be."

Indeed, traditional Western views of nature may have impeded progress in the natural and social sciences. Williams (1966), for example, speculates that "biology would have been able to mature more rapidly in a culture not dominated by Judeo-Christian theology and the Romantic tradition. It might have been well served by the First Holy Truth [attributed to the Buddha] from tl ₂ Sermon at Benares: 'Birth is painful, old age is painful, sickness is painful, death is painful' " (p. 255). And Ghiselin (1973) suggests that Darwinian theory did not become a dominant force in psychology owing to "the radical departure from the Western intellectual tradition that was implicit in Darwin's new cosmology. A world populated by organisms striving to no end but rather playing ridiculous sexual games, a world in which the brain is an extension of the gonads . . . sin ply cannot be reconciled with the old way of thinking" (p. 968).

More is at stake, however, than conflicting cosmologies. For one thing, ultimate and proximate causation frequently are confounded: "produced by natural selection" is equated with "innate," and an evolutionary view of humans is thought, erroneously, to imply that attempts at social reform are doomed. But perhaps a more serious problem is that in folk tradition the creator of organic entities also is the source of morality, hence difficulties arise when natural selection replaces God as the creator.

Scientifically acceptable views of ultimate causation have existed for a relatively brief period of time, and have not superseded older theories of ultimate causation to the extent that science has superseded mythology in matters of proximate causation. (It is not unknown today for a scientist not directly involved with evolutionary biology to hold essentially the same views on ultimate causation that were held by desert nomads 3000 years ago.) Perhaps because of its recent origin, the limitations of evolutionary theory are not always recognized, and it is often treated as if it has the same sorts of implications about proximate matters that traditional myths of ultimate causation have. In Judeo-Christian theology, unlike evolutionary biology, there is no disjunction between ultimate and proximate; on the contrary, ultimate and proximate are intimately and immediately related. What one ought to do, for example, is a direct function of God's will. Despite the absence of God in most scientific writing, the implicit belief that nature constitutes a moral order frequently persists. Thus writers with tolerant or positive views about homosexuality often begin their discussions by emphasizing the frequency with which nonhuman animals and preliterate peoples engage in homosexual activities, implying that homosexuality is natural and hence acceptable. Writers with less sanguine views of homosexuality point out that a great deal of mounting among nonhuman animals is not sexually motivated, that homosexual behavior is more frequent among captive than among free-ranging animals, and that exclusive homosexuality is rare among preliterate peoples, implying that homosexuality is unnatural and hence unacceptable.

When evolution replaces God as the creator of organic entities, how does one deal with the belief that the creator is the source of morality? There seem to be three possible solutions to this problem, and each has its advocates.

(1) One can deny that the guiding evolutionary force is natural selection and substitute a more acceptable mechanism. Marx and Engels, for example, enthusiastically supported the idea of evolution and its materialistic implications, believing that their analysis of human society paralleled Darwin's analysis in biology, but they explicitly rejected Darwin's major discovery, natural selection, in favor of a Lamarckian mechanism. Natural selection seemed to them to justify immorality (Venable 1966). Venable summarizes Engels's views thus: "In short, far from supporting Marxism, this theory [natural selection] merely serves, if transferred back from natural history into the society from which it was originally borrowed, to eternalize and justify as though grounded in nature itself, the barbarous economic relations of the particular historical epoch of bourgeois capitalism" (p. 64).

(2) One can define "good" as that which is produced by natural selection. An individual thus would be acting ethically as long as it was maximizing its inclusive fitness. Probably no one has seriously maintained that whatever an individual does to further its reproductive interests is right, although DeVore (1977) comes close when he remarks that sociobiology "ultimately lends a certain dignity to behaviors that one might otherwise consider aberrant or animalistic" (p. 87). Rather, this strategy of reconciling "good" and "natural" usually is pursued by altering the meaning of "natural selection," and differs from the first strategy in that the alterations tend to be implicit and unconscious. Sperry (1977), for example, writes that "what is good, right, or to be valued is defined very broadly to be that which accords with, sustains, and enhances the orderly design of evolving nature. Conversely, whatever is out of line, degrades, or destroys nature's grand design is wrong or bad" (p. 243). Williams (1966:255) notes that "There is a rather steady production of books and essays that attempt to show that Nature is, in the long run and on the average, benevolent and acceptable to some unquestionable ethical and moral point of view. By implication, she must be an appropriate guide for devising ethical systems and for judging human behavior."

The search for morality in nature has led to sentimentalizing and romanticizing nonhuman animals and preliterate peoples, to unsupported implications that selection favors groups, populations, cultures, societies, and ecosystems at the expense of the constituent individuals, to fantasies of ancestral utopias and matriarchies, and to various kinds of functionalism. Some anthropologists imply that anything that occurs in a preliterate society—infanticide, geronticide, warfare, mutilation—is "good" because it "functions" to promote stability in a culture, society, or ecosystem. It is sometimes said to be "good" that mountain lions tear deer to pieces, as this is nature's way of preventing deer from starving to death. Lack (1969) notes that the world of birds often strikes us as idyllic, a model for human societies to emulate. But this view of birds results from anthropomorphism and ignorance: "We would not enjoy a society in which one-third of our adult friends and over four-fifths of the teenagers die of starvation each year" (p. 21).

(3) One can deny the equation of natural and good; that is, deny that morality is to be found in the operation of natural selection. Thomas Huxley (1897) pointed out that from a wholly intellectual point of view, nature appears to be beautiful and harmonious, but if we allow moral sympathies to influence our judgment, our view of na-

ture is a darker one: "In sober truth, to those who have made a study of the phenomena of life as they are exhibited by the higher forms of the animal world, the optimistic dogma, that this is the best of all possible worlds, will seem little better than libel upon possibility" (p. 196). Huxley contrasted the state of nature, and the cosmic process (evolution by natural selection) of which it is the outcome, with the state of art, produced by human intelligence, exemplified by a garden. The garden can be maintained only by counteracting the forces of nature, creating an artificial environment in which Malthusian reproductive competition is restrained and hence the struggle for existence is largely arrested. Like the garden, the kind of society in which most of us would like to live can exist only by virtue of "artificial" ethics, in opposition to the cosmic process.

I believe that Huxley's is the only tenable position. More than two hundred years ago David Hume demonstrated the fallacy in deducing normative conclusions from descriptive premises: *is* and *is not* specify fundamentally different kinds of relations from those specified by *ought* and *ought not*. Values are not properties of things or events but are the projections of human needs and desires (see Flew 1967). Reasonably unbiased scientific inquiry probably is impossible unless this distinction is maintained: if investigators believe that scientific research can shed light on right and wrong it is virtually certain that their findings will "support" their preconceived ethical positions.

But even if there is no necessary relation between the *is* of natural selection and the *ought* of morality, it is nonetheless conceivable that the promulgation of evolutionary biology could have evil consequences. Some critics of sociobiology (for example, Sahlins 1976) argue that regardless of the personal beliefs of scientists who attempt to see human behavior and psyche as the products of natural selection, such attempts inevitably have reactionary political consequences. This hypothesis presumably is testable, and the history of Social Darwinism certainly provides food for thought. But evolutionary biology is not the only perspective on human nature and human social life that has been said to have reactionary political consequences. The doctrine that human societies are integrated, harmonious systems, for example, has been said to justify social inequities by promoting the view that inequities exist for the benefit of the "social system" or for the larger good (Martindale 1965). Indeed, such social science doctrines are suspiciously reminiscent of the traditional Western religious tenets that Marx called the opium of the people.

Maurice Bloch (in his 1977 article discussed above) argues that cognition of society is double: one cognitive system, which is used primarily in everyday activities, is a human universal; but a second system, which Bloch calls "social structure," and which is used almost exclusively in ritual activities, is culturally specific. Bloch proposes that the "amount" of social structure a people possesses is correlated

> with the amount of institutionalised hierarchy and *that is what it is about*. Please note, however, that I am not proposing a simple connection with the degree of inequality. Some inequality is often manifested as unadorned oppression, but, as Weber pointed out, it is then highly unstable, and only becomes stable when its origins are hidden and when it transforms itself into hierarchy: a legitimate order of inequality in an imaginary world which we call social structure. This is done by the creation of a mystified "nature" and consisting of concepts and categories of time and persons divorced from everyday experience, and where inequality takes on the appearance of an inevitable part of an ordered system (p. 289).

D. E. Brown (n.d.) has recently collected evidence of quite another kind that fits well with Bloch's conclusion. Using data on nineteen societies in Asia, the Near East, and Europe, Brown shows that *"the quality of historiography varies directly with the openness of social stratification."* He implies that in societies with hereditary ranking those in power suppress sound historiography because an accurate historical record would conflict with, and hence undermine, the mythology that justifies their hereditary position. Sound historiography develops in societies with vertical mobility because an accurate historical record is useful to, and does not threaten, those in power. In their different ways, then, Bloch and Brown suggest that although accurate notions of time, society, and history can be useful tools, the promulgation of inaccurate notions also can be useful in justifying and perpetuating inequalities. In Bloch's words, we have cognitive systems "by which we know the world" and "systems by which we hide it" (p. 290).

That humans have the capacity to learn the ideology of "social structure" and mythology raises fascinating evolutionary questions. Is this capacity simply a functionless effect of human mental plasticity? Is it an adaptation which gives evidence for the occurrence of group selection during human evolutionary history? Is it an adaptation whose function is to permit humans to play nonzero sum games? A question of more immediate concern, however, is: To what extent is the idea of social structure *itself* social structure in Bloch's sense of that phrase? That is, to what extent are certain social science concepts mythology rather than science. Consider the following passage from George Peter Murdock (1972):

> It now seems to me distressingly obvious that culture, social system, and all comparable supra-individual concepts, such as collective representations, group mind, and social organism, are illusory conceptual abstractions inferred from observations of the very real phenomena of individuals interacting with one another and with their natural environments. . . . they resemble the illusory constructs so prevalent in the early days of the natural sciences, such as those of phlogiston and the luminiferous ether in physics, and systems of theory based upon them have no greater validity or utility.

> *   *   *

> They are, in short, mythology, not science, and are to be rejected in their entirety—not revised or modified.

Now Murdock is not arguing for nature over nurture. On the contrary, he is an "environmentalist" and an advocate of behaviorism. Neither is he objecting to the use of "culture" and "social system" as convenient ways of summarizing observations of human behavior; rather, he is objecting to their reification as entities that cause human behavior.

I raise this issue here for two reasons. The first is that throughout this book I maintain a sort of commonsense, everyday perspective on human sexuality which often contrasts with certain social science perspectives and with folk standards of what constitutes acceptable public pronouncements. For example, there is now good evidence, which corroborates everyday experience, that physical attractiveness is an extremely important determinant of heterosexual relationships. Yet until very recently, this was not the dominant opinion in social psychology, and if young people are asked what they seek in a partner of the other sex they generally emphasize personality, character, and the like. In an unimaginably vast universe containing objects as unlikely as black holes and quasars, it may seem preposterous to advocate a commonsense approach to *any* scientific question; I have discussed the views of Bloch, Brown, and Murdock because I hope the reader will consider whether everyday experience sometimes is a better guide to the truth than social science or folk theory. To paraphrase Bloch, social science theory may be an amalgam of efforts to know the world and efforts to hide it. The second reason I raise this issue is that I believe the assumption of a self-interested human nature—whether or not this assumption purports to be derived from evolutionary theory—can have socially and politically desirable consequences.

In *Civilization and Its Discontents* Freud wrote that "men are not gentle creatures who want to be loved, and who at the most can defend themselves if they are attacked. . . . their neighbor is for them not only a potential helper or sexual object, but also someone who tempts them to satisfy their aggressiveness on him, to exploit his capacity for work without compensation, to use him sexually without his consent, to seize his possessions, to humiliate him, to cause him pain, to torture and to kill him." We may safely assume that these observations were derived, not from psychoanalytic theory, but from Freud's experiences and his reading of history. This view of life does not indicate that social reform is impossible. It does indicate that reform is unlikely to come about via the promulgation of doctrines that humans have no nature. It is a dangerous fantasy to imagine that there are naturally limited, or reasonable, human "needs": as Durkheim saw, human desires are limitless, constrained only by the bounds of human imagination. The fulfillment of desire is primarily a function of opportunity. Nor will egalitarian societies be promoted by "authorities" and "experts" who reinforce good behavior. History shows that authorities will use whatever means are available to pursue their own interests. Given sufficient power over the socialization of children, authorities and experts will attempt to create human beings who are tools or extremities of those in power. As Noam Chomsky has pointed out, a tabula rasa view of the human mind is the totalitarian's dream. An egalitarian social order can arise only through collective efforts to limit and check the political and economic power that can be obtained by any individual or group.

The belief that women's rights rest on scientific evidence that men and women are naturally or potentially very similar is understandable in light of the history of sexism and the repression of women. Martin and Voorhies (1975) and Fee (1976), for example, show that 19th-century views of human sex differences were intimately associated with doctrines of male superiority and were alleged to have normative implications. But the notion that women's rights can or must be justified by particular views of history or biology is both philosophically untenable and strategically misguided, in that social and political positions become vulnerable to scientific disproof. That men and women differ by nature has no necessary implications whatsoever for normative questions: it is frequently the case that individuals hold similar scientific views and opposed political views, or vice versa.

It is, of course, true that scientific writings can have unintended impact. Mead (1967), for example, castigates Kinsey for "allowing" his studies of sexual behavior to become best sellers. Mead believes that Kinsey acted unethically in that, by revealing how frequently behavior fails to conform to cultural norms, he undermined those norms and interfered with young people's efforts to resist their nonconforming impulses. I believe, perhaps naïvely, that the benefits of scientific inquiry into human behavior almost always outweigh the deficits, and that, in any case, accurate knowledge is itself an acceptable goal. Furthermore, social action is most likely to succeed if it is based on a realistic appraisal of the human condition. In my view, part of such an appraisal is an understanding of the sexual differences between men and women. Veronica Geng (1976:68) writes: "Men lie to women. In trying to fight free of those lies, women are now lying to women, and their lies are as poisonous as the original ones. Alibis are traps. Vague language about roles or militant pluralism or social forces makes it impossible to think." To "roles," "militant pluralism," and "social forces" one might add "culture," "society," "system," and "nature," insofar as these notions are reified as explanatory causal agents. These too make it impossible to think and conceal the sources of oppression.

The data on human sexuality

Information about human sexuality comes from anthropology, sociology, psychology, economics, biology, medicine, psychiatry, history, fiction, autobiography, and personal experience; each source has its own strengths and limitations. How this enormous, heterogeneous, and profoundly uneven body of data can best be evaluated is by no means self-evident. One difficulty is that reports and discussions of sexuality often are permeated with their authors' normative and prescriptive biases. Some feminist writers, for example, persistently attempt to minimize sex differences in sexuality, and in doing so seem to imply that males and females *ought* to have equal social and political rights because they *are* (naturally, or potentially) very similar. The scientific literature on human sexuality probably is unmatched in the extent to which descriptive statements are intertwined with advice-giving and unabashed moralizing. Robinson (1976) points out that even such pioneering works as those of Kinsey and Masters and Johnson, which explicitly lay claim to scientific impartiality, are thoroughly saturated with their authors' normative biases. This by no means renders such reports useless, or even necessarily diminishes their value, but it does suggest that they must be read with a critical eye.

Excellent discussions of some of the problems associated with field studies of sexuality among non-Western peoples can be found in Mead (1961) and Suggs and Marshall (1971). Some of the major difficulties are: (1) Human beings almost always seek whatever privacy is available to engage in sexual activities.[4] Thus investigators must rely on reported, not observed, sexual behavior (Mead 1961, Suggs and Marshall 1971). When information is collected from one or a few informants, descriptions of behavior, attitudes, beliefs, and desires tend to be highly idiosyncratic (Suggs 1971a, 1971b). (2) Sexual data are extremely likely to be distorted as a result of fear of disclosure or a desire to picture oneself or one's group favorably (Mead 1961, Suggs and Marshall 1971). Mead emphasizes that most preliterate peoples do not consider giving factual accounts to be a moral obligation; on the contrary, many peoples believe that courtesy demands the questioner to be told what it is thought he wants to hear. Even when informants do attempt to provide factual accounts, retrospective falsification is inevitable in recollections of emotional matters, especially with the passage of time (Mead 1961). Moreover, it is not always clear whether informants are reporting actual or ideal behavior (Mead 1961, Neubeck 1969). (3) European and American investigators often are hampered by their own antisexual biases (Suggs and Marshall 1971).

Furthermore, anthropologists traditionally have been more interested in differences among peoples than in similarities, and they may be emotionally committed to cultural relativism. Ethnographies should be evaluated with this in mind, especially when generalizations are not supported, or are actually contradicted, by specific examples. Holmberg's (1950) description of the Siriono, a semi-nomadic people living

---

[4] Ultimately, this probably is the outcome of reproductive competition. Where food is scarce, and the sight of people eating produces envy in the unfed, eating is often conducted in private. While there are many societies in which everyone normally has enough to eat, there are no societies in which everyone can copulate with all the partners he or she desires. Furthermore, humans are unprecedented among animals in the subtlety with which they control and manipulate each other's sexuality, and it is often adaptive to keep sexual activities secret. The seeking of privacy for sex probably has been uniformly adaptive and hence is virtually universal among humans.

in the tropical forests of northern and eastern Bolivia, provides an example of conflict between generalization and example. According to Holmberg, the Siriono enjoy substantial sexual freedom; that is, a man is said to be "permitted" to have intercourse not only with his wives, but also with their real and classificatory sisters, while a woman may have intercourse with her husband, his real and classificatory brothers, and with the potential husbands of her real and classificatory sisters. Nevertheless, quarrels and fights over sex are common.

Although the Siriono understand the role of the father in conception, Holmberg (p. 73) writes: "considering the sexual freedom allowed by the Siriono, the true paternity of a child would be difficult to determine, but, as far as the group is concerned, it is only the social role of the father that is important." In "only" one of the eight births Holmberg witnessed was there a question of paternity, or a reluctance of the woman's husband to accept the infant, but Holmberg's vivid account of this singular instance is worth careful consideration. One of the wives of a man named Eoko went into labor in the early morning, but Eoko left to hunt knowing the birth was imminent. The mother gave birth about 8 A.M. and spent the day waiting for Eoko to return and cut the cord, an act that symbolizes that the child is accepted by the father. By 5 P.M. Eoko had not returned, and Holmberg, fearing the infant would die from infection of the cord and placenta which had been exposed to flies all day, urged that the cord be cut, but was told that it was necessary to await Eoko. Eoko returned at sunset, threw down his catch by the hammock of his first wife, and did not so much as glance at the mother and her infant.

> Meanwhile, the mother took out a piece of bamboo and sat patiently on the ground waiting for Eoko to cut the cord. Instead of so doing, he lay down in his hammock and ordered his first wife to extract the thorns from his hands and feet. This operation took approximately half an hour, by which time it was fairly obvious to all present that Eoko had no intention of cutting the cord. Women began to gather. Seaci, who was Eoko's niece, came up to me and said softly: "You speak to Eoko; tell him to cut the cord." I replied: "No, you speak to him." She was afraid to do so. Then one of Eoko's relatives remarked that Eoko claimed the child was not his, that he had "divorced" this woman some time before. Following this declaration, one of the mother's female relatives came forward and publicly demanded that Eoko cut the cord. He paid no attention whatsoever to her but continued to lie in his hammock and smoke his pipe. The mother of the infant took no part in the proceedings but continued to sit quietly on the ground with the child. Darkness set in. The mother's female rela-

tives continued to put pressure on Eoko to cut the cord. Finally, after about an hour, he got up from his hammock, called for a calabash of water, and took a hasty bath. He then stooped down, took the bamboo knife from the mother, and severed the cord, thereby recognizing the child as his. Before doing so, however, he emphatically stated that the child was not his and that he was only cutting the cord to prevent the death of the child.

Eoko's reluctance to accept the infant as his was clearly reflected in his behavior during the period of couvade. He acted as if he did not care whether the infant lived or died. He paid no attention whatsoever to the mother, and although he was decorated with feathers like every father of a newborn child, he underwent few of the other observances designed to protect and insure the life and health of the infant. He was not scarified on the legs, for instance, nor did he observe the rules of staying close to the house. He paid no attention to the food taboos and took no part in the rites terminating the couvade. He repeatedly told me that he had "divorced" this woman and that he would have nothing more to do with her. This was borne out by subsequent events (pp. 73-74).

If one were to accept at face value Holmberg's general statements about sexual freedom and the resulting uncertainty and unimportance of biological paternity, one would be left with the impression that the Siriono are emotionally very different from most Western peoples. On the other hand, the reader has little difficulty empathizing with all the participants in the events Holmberg describes in detail. It is perhaps reasonable to hypothesize that if biochemical paternity eliminations had been performed on the Siriono infants that were accepted by their social fathers, social and biological paternity would have been found to correspond more frequently than Holmberg implies. If Holmberg had failed to provide such a vivid account of this incident, or if, by chance, he had witnessed only the seven unproblematical births, generalizations about Siriono sexual freedom and lack of concern with biological paternity would have been far more compelling. When detailed accounts are not provided, or when the accounts contradict generalizations, it seems reasonable to question whether preliterate peoples really are as emotionally diverse as they are sometimes pictured in ethnographies.

Readers who are not anthropologists may be unaware of the existence of fundamental differences of professional opinion about the merits of some ethnographic works. Suggs (1971a), for example, critically discusses the description of Marquesan culture and sexual behavior published in 1939 by Ralph Linton and subsequently used by Abram

Kardiner as the basis for theories of personality development. The Linton report has become an anthropological classic, cited in general textbooks and in texts on culture and personality, and has been influential in psychology and sociology as well. Suggs points out that Linton spoke neither the native language nor French, did not live among the Marquesans, based many of his conclusions on single informants and observations of single cases, and was ignorant of the historical literature on the Marquesas. As a result, Linton was wrong about major and minor facts as revealed by Suggs's fieldwork and that of all other students of Marquesan life. Linton was wrong, for example, about orthography, basic environmental data, socionomic sex ratios, subsistence patterns, history, marriage forms, child-rearing practices, and the influence of these factors on sexual practices, feelings, and folklore. Linton claimed that historically the Marquesan sex ratio was 2 ½ males : 1 female, which in turn was related to the practice of polyandry, to a lack of male sexual jealousy, and to various other beliefs and practices. Suggs shows that as long as censuses have been made in the Marquesas the sex ratio has been almost exactly 1 : 1, that there is no evidence that polyandry was ever practiced, and that male sexual jealousy was and is pronounced. Suggs cites an unpublished paper by Sheahan which states, in short, that the Linton report describes a culture that never existed. Suggs concludes:

> One final, profoundly disturbing question remains: what is the state of a scientific discipline that permits an undocumented, internally inconsistent report such as Linton's not only to go unchallenged but be accepted, praised—and even protected—for thirty years, as though a body of contradictory evidence did not exist? This question deserves the careful consideration of all anthropologists. In their answers will be found clues to the many obstacles which anthropology has to overcome if the field is to gain acceptance as a science (p. 185).

Even the works of anthropologists who have specialized in the cross-cultural analysis of sexuality are not invariably free from controversy. For example, any list of ethnographers who have made major contributions to the study of human sexuality would include, near the top, Margaret Mead. And yet Mead's best-known and most widely cited fieldwork on this topic (Mead 1935) has been severely criticized by social scientists not merely on minor technical matters but on whether the reported observations support the conclusions or, in fact, are sufficient to support any conclusions (for example, Thurnwald 1936, Bernard 1945). Malinowski (1962:172) deplores theories that "reduce anthropology to a purely subjective interpretation of each culture in terms of figurative speech, of pathological simile, of mythological parallel, and other more or less literary or artistic ways of intuition." He goes on to note that "Many of the younger generation are drifting into mystical pronouncements, avoiding the difficult and painstaking search for principles; they are cultivating rapid cursory field-work, and developing their impressionistic results into brilliantly dramatized film effects, such as the New Guinea pictures of Dr. Margaret Mead in her *Sex and Temperament* (1935)." And if the reliability of some ethnographic reports is controversial, it is still more difficult to evaluate summaries of ethnographic data, such as those compiled by Ford and Beach (1951) from the Human Relations Area Files.

Reports that a society "permits" this and "discourages" that tell little about the behavior and feelings of individuals and less about individual differences. As Sagarin (1971) has pointed out, the studies conducted by the Institute for Sex Research have shown that there is great diversity in sexual behavior among Americans, and that behavior commonly said to be deviant is in fact widespread. Probably the best available evidence on cross-cultural variation in human sexual behavior is found in the writing of field workers characterized by Gebhard (1971a) as "progressives": anthropologists who have recognized the importance of sexual activity in human life and who have attempted to examine and record it as objectively as possible (see, for example, Marshall and Suggs, eds., 1971:244-49). Cross-cultural evidence is most useful for an evolutionary perspective when it indicates major regularities in human sexuality. If humans exhibit relatively uniform dispositions under a wide range of environmental conditions, these dispositions probably were uniformly adaptive among our Pleistocene ancestors and hence develop in a relatively stereotyped manner. (This does not mean that they will develop identically in every environment in which humans can survive, but simply that they are likely to develop and that they probably represent adaptations to conditions of times past.) Cross-cultural data also indicate aspects of human sexuality that are highly plastic.[5]

---

[5] As discussed in Chapter One, plasticity may be an adaptation; that is, it may exist because individuals in ancestral populations who were capable of developing varied responses to variable environmental conditions enjoyed greater reproductive success than did less flexible individuals. On the other hand, observed behavioral variability may have no adaptive significance, being simply an artifact of development in unnatural environments.

Data on the sexual behavior, attitudes, and feelings of contemporary Western peoples are orders of magnitude better than data on non-Western peoples. These include massive and detailed surveys, such as those of Kinsey and his associates, as well as complex and extensive introspective reports. Unlike most anthropological research, studies of human sexuality in the West often represent samples so large that individual differences become apparent and quantification is meaningful. Interviewers do not have social relationships with informants, and interviews are usually long and thorough with internal checks for consistency. These studies reveal great variation in sexual behaviors and attitudes with nationality, geographic region, religion, race, social class, age, and educational level (Kinsey *et al.* 1948, 1953; Christensen 1960; Peretti 1969; Shiloh, ed. 1970). Contemporary Western societies comprise enormously heterogeneous and rapidly changing circumstances of life: the variety of sexual practices in the United States today may well exceed those of all preliterate societies combined.

Autobiographical accounts, such as *My Secret Life*, the anonymous sexual history of a Victorian gentleman, and the verbatim reports of women's sexual feelings and experiences compiled by Hite (1974, 1976) are—with the exception of a few fictional works—as close as we are likely to get to accurate descriptions of human sexuality. Unlike ethnographic reports, these accounts were written anonymously, which probably is important in minimizing distortion; many of the women quoted in Hite (1976), for example, remarked that they could never have told anyone the facts that they were willing to describe anonymously. Moreover, in many cases it is clear that these women believed, as did the author of *My Secret Life*, that by being as accurate as possible they were performing a valuable public service.

But what significance can evidence about humans living in unnatural environments have for an evolutionary perspective? (That these data are abundant does not guarantee their usefulness.) If one's goal is to explain human behavior as adaptation to the environment in which the behavior occurs, if, that is, one is disposed to see behavior as maximizing inclusive fitness, data on peoples living in unnatural environments are of limited value. As discussed above, even where individuals achieve extremes of reproductive success (contributing to sperm banks, for example), such behavior and its underlying motivation may not represent adaptation. I have argued, however, that a great deal of the variability in human behavior results from a diversity of compromises among universally experienced emotions, and that these emotions can be considered to be "closer to" the genes than behavior is. If fulfillment of desire is largely a function of opportunity, the circumstances of modern industrial societies may comprise an unprecedented series of experiments on human sexuality insofar as these environments provide unprecedented sexual opportunities and insofar as they sometimes reduce the necessity to make various kinds of compromise. For example: (1) the author of *My Secret Life* was independently wealthy, lived in a social environment in which a great degree of anonymity was possible, and thus had the time, resources, and opportunity to pursue sexual gratification; (2) the existence of large communities of homosexuals provides a context in which individuals can express behaviorally their desires and dispositions without having to compromise with the desires and dispositions of the other sex; (3) freedom from many constraints occurs during warfare, and evidence about sexual behavior during war may be instructive, if unpalatable.

Thus, although behavior cannot be expected to be adaptive in modern Western societies, paradoxically, the least natural environments may sometimes provide the best evidence about human nature. This point may be clarified by an analogy with the consumption of refined sugar. Western peoples consume enormous per capita quantities of refined sugar because, to most people, very sweet foods taste very good. The existence of the human sweet tooth can be explained, ultimately, as an adaptation of ancestral populations to favor the ripest—and hence the sweetest—fruit. In other words, the selective pressures of times past are most strikingly revealed by the artificial, supernormal stimulus of refined sugar, despite the evidence that eating refined sugar is maladaptive.

The most promising approach to understanding the evolution of human sexuality probably is to consider the evidence as widely as possible and to focus especially on those aspects that seem to be relatively universal, as universals are most likely to indicate adaptation. My approach to the data on human sexuality is catholic, but I rely most frequently on the works of those scholars who have made the study of sexuality their special concern. Where necessary, I attempt to elucidate possible biases. Reports in which generalizations are supported by specific examples are considered most reliable. Since summaries of the cross-cultural literature combine data of various degrees of reliability, they are considered most useful when major regularities are demonstrated. To some extent, however, my selection of data is a matter of hunches and taste. For example, I use *The Hite Report* because my hunch is that it contains accounts actually written by women, though nothing in Hite's methodology guarantees this. And I use *My Secret Life,* but not Frank Harris's autobiography, because I believe that the latter is unreliable, almost unreadable, braggadocio and the former is both reliable and a literary masterpiece (see Marcus 1966).

In appraising the evidence on the evolution of human sexuality Williams's doctrine that "adaptation is a special and onerous concept that should be used only where it is really necessary" is a valuable guide. This doctrine implies neither that nature is simple nor that explanatory accuracy is to be sacrificed on the altar of parsimony. The principle of parsimony is a scientific tool, useful not only in studying adaptation but also in determining whether adaptation exists at all. In the study of a subject as emotionally volatile as sexuality, it provides additional benefit in mitigating biased interpretation of the evidence.

THREE

The Female Orgasm: Adaptation or Artifact?

The expense of spirit in a waste of shame
Is lust in action; and till action, lust
Is perjur'd, murderous, bloody, full of blame,
Savage, extreme, rude, cruel, not to trust;
Enjoy'd no sooner but despised straight;
Past reason hunted; and no sooner had,
Past reason hated, as a swallow'd bait,
On purpose laid to make the taker mad:
Mad in pursuit, and in possession so;
Had, having, and in quest to have, extreme;
A bliss in proof—and prov'd a very woe;
Before, a joy propos'd; behind, a dream.
All this the world well knows; yet none knows well
To shun the heaven that leads men to this hell.
WILLIAM SHAKESPEARE

ORGASM IN THE HUMAN female is a highly variable peak sexual experience accompanying involuntary, rhythmic contractions of the outer third of the vagina—and frequently of the uterus, rectal sphincter, and urethral sphincter as well—and the concomitant release of vasocongestion and muscular tension associated with intense sexual arousal (Masters and Johnson 1966). Two fundamentally different theories have been proposed to account for the evolution of the female orgasm.

One theory holds that orgasm is an adaptation unique to the human female and thus is to be explained by selective forces operating exclusively in the human lineage. According to most versions of this theory, human beings are basically monogamous, the relationship between wife and husband can be described as a "pair-bond," and female orgasm is one of several adaptations whose function is to enhance the pair-bond, making family life more rewarding. Morris (1967:67) writes: "with both appetitive and consummatory behaviour, everything possible has been done to increase the sexuality of the naked ape and to ensure the successful evolution of a pattern as basic as pair-formation. . . ." Beach (1974:361) writes: "Since copulation tends to result in mutual physical gratification and since simple learning promotes association of positive values with perceived sources of reward, intrafamilial copulation provides one source of reinforcement of emotional bonding between males and females. In other words, sexual behavior reinforces family structure, and family structure reinforces sexual behavior." Eibl-Eibesfeldt (1975:503) suggests that orgasm in the human female "increases her readiness to submit and, in addition, strengthens her emotional bond to the partner." Barash (1977a:296-97) argues that selection favored mechanisms to keep husband and wife together: "Sex may be such a device, selected to be pleasurable for its own sake, in addition to its procreative function. This would help explain why the female orgasm seems to be unique to humans. . . ." Hamburg (1978:163) writes: "The ability of the human female to experience orgasm comparable to the male enhances the reward value for both. It maximizes the utility of sexual behavior as a potent form of interpersonal bonding." The similarity of these views is remarkable considering the diversity of their authors' perspectives and professional backgrounds: Morris and Eibl-Eibesfeldt are ethologists, Beach is a psychologist, Barash is a sociobiologist, and Hamburg is a psychiatrist; the majority implicitly assume group selection, but Barash's views are based on inclusive fitness theory.

At the opposite pole are theories that assume orgasm to be normal—or at least not uncommon—among female mammals, and the frequent nonoccurrence of orgasm among modern women to be abnormal and to require explanation. The most extreme form of this position is Sherfey's (1972), which integrates Freudianism and Masters and Johnson's work on orgasmic physiology. Masters and Johnson (1966) showed that, unlike males, females do not necessarily experience a refractory period following orgasm during which they are resistant to sexual stimulation; if stimulation continues, females may experience multiple orgasms. Sherfey (1972:4-5) considers this physiology to constitute evidence for "the existence of the universal and physically normal condition of women's inability ever to reach complete sexual satiation in the presence of the most intense, repetitive orgasmic experiences, no matter how produced. . . ." In contrast to proponents of the pair-bond theory of female orgasm, Sherfey contends that monogamy is unnatural and that the orgasmic capacity of the human female is an adaptation to a lascivious, preagricultural past: "Primitive woman's sexual drive was too strong, too susceptible to the fluctuating extremes of an impelling, aggressive eroticism to withstand the disciplined requirements of a settled family life . . ." (p. 138). Like Wilhelm Reich, Geza Roheim, Herbert Marcuse, and Norman O. Brown, who regard sexual repression as a principal mechanism of political domination in Western societies (Robinson 1969), Sherfey concludes that the rise of patriarchy and "civilization" in postagricultural times required the ruthless subjugation of female sexuality. In order to evaluate these disparate views, it is necessary to consider the available evidence on nonhuman and human female orgasm in some detail.

Nonhuman females

The use of the word "receptive" to describe the sexual behavior of nonhuman female mammals has generated the misleading impression that females are sexually passive and merely submit to the advances of sexually aggressive males. Beach (1976b) clarifies this matter by discriminating three characteristics of estrous female mammals: attractivity, proceptivity, and receptivity. Attractivity refers to the extent to which the female is sexually stimulating to males; it is powerfully enhanced by high levels of estrogen. Proceptivity connotes the extent to which the female actively solicits and initiates copulation; it too varies directly with estrogen levels, though androgens also appear to play a role (Baum *et al.* 1977). Receptivity consists of the female's reactions that are "necessary and sufficient for fertile copulation with a potent male" (p. 125). Although details vary among mammalian species, receptivity always includes the adoption of a posture appropriate for insertion and the maintenance of this posture long enough to permit intravaginal ejaculation. There is abundant evidence that receptivity generally depends on estrogen levels, but Beach notes that among some species of primates receptivity sometimes is independent of hormones, especially in captivity; receptivity and proceptivity may, according to Beach, depend on different neural mechanisms. The possibility of orgasm among nonhuman female mammals must be distinguished from the fact of proceptivity: there is no question that estrous females often actively seek, and presumably enjoy, copulation; the question is whether they experience orgasm in the human sense.

Fox and Fox (1971) summarize four kinds of evidence for the existence of orgasm among nonprimate female mammals. (1) In bitches, peaks in blood pressure, respiration, and heart rate during copulation resemble peaks in human females during orgasm. (2) In females of a number of species, changes in muscular tension (including vaginal and uterine contractions) during copulation "may or may not indicate a sudden climactic event in the female, but they do suggest that the female is not completely passive during coitus" (p. 327). (3) In females of several species, hormonal changes during copulation are similar to hormonal changes in women. (4) In some species, females emit sounds during copulation. Evidence of this kind has not convinced most students of mammalian sexual behavior. Beach (1974:359) writes: "behavior indicating the occurrence of sexual climax in copulating females is extremely rare. One or two species may be excepted, and individual members of still other species may not conform to the general rule; but the weight of available evidence favors the theory that female orgasm is a characteristic essentially restricted to our own species."

Several primatologists recently have reported evidence that nonhuman primate females may experience orgasm. Zumpe and Michael (1968) describe a female "clutching reaction" during heterosexual copulation among captive rhesus monkeys that they believe may indicate female orgasm. The reaction was highly variable: some females only turned their heads to look back at their partner; others also reached back with one hand and grasped the male; a few reacted more vigorously, twisting their heads and shoulders from side to side, clutching the male with alternate hands, and sometimes biting him. Rhesus copulations consist of a series of mountings, each comprising about two to eight thrusts, with ejaculation on the last mount; the clutching reaction almost invariably was confined to the ejaculatory mount.[1] Zumpe and Michael note that it remains to be determined whether the clutching reaction indicates an orgasm homologous with that of the human fe-

---

[1] Eric Phoebus (personal communication) recently discovered a characteristic cardiovascular response on ejaculatory mounts in two older-dominant rhesus females which differed both from their responses on nonejaculatory mounts and from the responses of two younger-subordinate females.

male. They appear to favor this interpretation, however, for two reasons: first, frame by frame analysis of motion picture film of two females showed that the females began to turn while the male was thrusting, and that ejaculation occurred a moment later, suggesting that the clutching reaction might be associated with an ejaculation-triggering vaginal spasm; second, the clutching reaction varied with experimentally induced hormone changes.

Hanby (1976), however, notes that among Japanese monkeys, males and females of all ages often turn and reach back during mounting—even mounting that occurs in play—and that this gesture could not be reliably associated with the end of a series of mounts or with male ejaculation. Fox and Fox (1971) point out that among women, clutching during intercourse often occurs independently of orgasm. Michael (1971) admits that evidence associating the clutching reaction with orgasm is tenuous; he suggests that this association would be strengthened if it could be shown that clutching is accompanied by muscular spasms similar to those that occur during human female orgasm. Telemetric recordings of uterine electrical activity in female rhesus showed a characteristic increase during copulation (a pattern that differed from the electrical activity recorded during artificial vaginal stimulation) but no evidence of a specific activity pattern accompanying clutching (Michael 1971). Michael's published recordings indicate a uterine response to every thrust by the male, rather than the autonomous, circumscribed, rhythmic contractions that Masters and Johnson (1966) recorded during human female orgasm. Michael cites a paper by Serr et al. (1968) which reports increased cervical electrical activity in women as a result of clitoral stimulation similar to the uterine electrical activity Michael recorded during rhesus copulation; but since Serr et al. recorded increased electrical activity during stimulation, not orgasm, their paper seems to me to constitute further evidence that the electrical activity Michael recorded in rhesus monkeys represents sexual excitement, not orgasm.

Recently Zumpe and Michael (1977) experimentally manipulated the attractivity of female rhesus by administering and withdrawing intravaginal estrogen (which does not affect receptivity or proceptivity) while maintaining proceptivity via subcutaneous implants of testosterone (which does not affect attractivity) over a series of heterosexual test-pairings. For a given pair of monkeys, ejaculation in one test and its nonoccurrence in the following test was associated with more frequent female sexual invitations in the latter test. Although ejaculation is known to suppress female invitations for a short time, Zumpe and Michael show that this cannot fully account for their data. Therefore, they conclude "that invitations can be regarded as appetitive behaviour for the consummatory stimulus provided by the male's ejaculation" (p. 274). Since ejaculation is temporally associated with the clutching reaction—which Zumpe and Michael believe may represent female orgasm, "the consummatory event in the female that reinforces her sexual invitations" (p. 274)—some readers may conclude that these new data lend support to the hypothesis that rhesus females experience orgasm. Zumpe and Michael do not report the frequencies of male mounting, intromission, and thrusting; these behaviors presumably were correlated with ejaculation, hence a conservative interpretation of these data is that the relatively high frequency of female invitations in tests following tests in which ejaculation occurred might represent appetitive behavior for the stimuli provided by mounting, penetrating, and/or thrusting, not ejaculation. Thus the temporal association of ejaculation and the clutching reaction may be irrelevant in assessing the significance of these data for the question of female orgasm. In short, the results both of this experiment and Michael's (1971) experiment demonstrating uterine electrical activity during copulation may reasonably be interpreted as evidence that female rhesus monkeys are sexually stimulated by copulating; but these experiments do not provide compelling evidence for orgasm.

Female orgasm during copulation has been posited for several other species of nonhuman primates. After a number of thrusts by the male, free-ranging chacma baboon females often emit a characteristic vocalization and then leap away when the male stops thrusting (Saayman 1970). As with rhesus monkeys, chacma baboon copulations consist of a series of mountings, with ejaculation occurring on the final mount, but female vocalization and withdrawal occurred throughout the series. Saayman suggests that these female reactions may indicate orgasm because: "Both the copulation call and the withdrawal reaction . . . resemble involuntary responses" (p. 85); the reactions occurred most frequently among females with inflating or swollen sex skins (indicating high levels of estrogen); and the reactions were more likely to occur when females were mounted by adult males than when they were mounted by subadult or juvenile males, suggesting "that adequate physical stimulation from a fully developed mature male was necessary for the full expression of this consummatory response" (p. 107).[2] In at least 14 percent of the heterosexual copulations observed among captive stumptail monkeys, the female partner reached back with one hand, grasped the male, and looked at him with a "positive emotional expression," which Chevalier-Skolnikoff (1974) believes indicates female orgasm. McGinnis (cited in Hanby 1976) reports that free-ranging female chimpanzees often emit a distinctive vocalization during copulation "which may indicate at least extreme sexual excitement if not actual orgasm" (p. 49). Like the female rhesus clutching reaction, these observations on chacma baboons, stumptail monkeys, and chimpanzees are perhaps most prudently interpreted as evidencing female sexual excitement, not orgasm. This interpretation becomes especially compelling when these observations are compared with the following three reports.

(1) Burton (1971) attempted to determine experimentally whether female rhesus monkeys can experience orgasm. The subjects were three estrous adult females; during experimental trials a subject was held on a wooden counter in an apparatus consisting of a metal framework, ropes, and harnesses. Each trial proceeded thus: the subject was fed and groomed until her heartbeat was close to the resting state; this was followed by three minutes of sacral grooming (to induce her to present), five minutes of clitoral stimulation, five minutes of vaginal stimulation with an artificial penis, four minutes of rest, and five more minutes of vaginal stimulation. Although all three subjects reacted negatively on at least one trial, on other trials animals responded to sacral grooming by assuming the full lordosis posture. One of the subjects "had a series of intense vaginal spasms, to a maximum of 5 contractions which also involved the anus on 4 occasions" (p. 185), and one other subject had less intense vaginal spasms on two occasions. Burton suggests that the experience of orgasm accompanied these vaginal spasms and, in light of Masters and Johnson's data on human female orgasm, this seems to be a reasonable supposition. Burton notes that since the usual duration of intromission during rhesus copulation is three or four seconds, female orgasm is extremely unlikely to occur in nature.

[2] But Saayman's actual data indicate only minor differences: for example, among swollen females the withdrawal reaction was observed in 89 percent of the copulations with adult males, 86 percent of the copulations with subadult males, and 78 percent of the copulations with juvenile males; copulation calls were recorded in 98 percent of the copulations with adult males, 98 percent of the copulations with subadult males, and 86 percent of the copulations with juvenile males.

(2) Michael *et al.* (1974) paired forty wild-captured adult female rhesus with adult males in hour-long tests. Fifteen of these females mounted, or attempted to mount, their male partners—using a variety of postures—at some time during the tests; during mountings, females frequently made pelvic thrusts against the male's back or shoulders. Female mountings tended to occur near ovulation, were reduced in frequency by ovariectomy, and were restored by subcutaneous administration of estradiol benzoate, suggesting that mountings were sexually motivated. On six occasions one female appeared to orgasm,[3] "showing small but obvious rhythmic contractions of the thigh muscles and around the base of the tail . . . after a mean of 16.3 mounts and 102.3 thrusts, 27.5 minutes from the start of the female's mounting series" (p. 404).

(3) In her captive group of stumptail monkeys, Chevalier-Skolnikoff (1974) observed twenty-three mountings of one female by another: the mounter climbed on top of the mountee and rubbed her genitals on the mountee's rump, making approximately sixty pelvic thrusts in the course of a minute. On three occasions the mounter exhibited the same behavior patterns that a male stumptail exhibits as he ejaculates; that is, "a pause followed by muscular body spasms accompanied by the characteristic frowning round-mouthed stare expression and the rhythmic expiration vocalization. The mountee never made the characteristic orgasmic facial expressions or vocalizations" (p. 109). Chevalier-Skolnikoff's suggestion that these behaviors indicate female orgasm seems reasonable; but, at the same time, these observations make her hypothesis that female stumptails experience orgasm during heterosexual copulation even less reasonable, since none of the masculine orgasmic patterns are exhibited by females during heterosexual copulation.

In conclusion: (1) While the possibility that nonhuman female mammals experience orgasm during heterosexual copulation remains open, there is no compelling evidence that they do. On the other hand, there is abundant evidence that female mammals are not sexually passive: they actively solicit and initiate copulation, which they presumably enjoy. (2) Compelling evidence of nonhuman female primate orgasm has been obtained only among captive animals. More intense and varied sexual behavior than occurs in natural circumstances is commonly observed among animals in zoos and laboratories (Ford and Beach 1951); probably all mammals, of both sexes, have the capacity

---

[3] Following Hite (1976), I shall use "orgasm" as a verb as well as a noun.

for far more varied and intense erotic experiences than ever occur in nature. (3) Even where the evidence for its existence is strongest, the occurrence of female orgasm appears to have been highly variable: not all individuals experienced orgasm, and those that did experience orgasm did not do so consistently. (4) In each case in which there was compelling evidence for female orgasm, the orgasmic female obtained direct and prolonged stimulation of her clitoris or clitoral area, either by experimental design or by rubbing against another animal.

Human females

In a predominantly upper-middle-class sample of 800 married couples, Terman (1938) reported the following frequencies of female orgasm during sexual intercourse: always 22.1 percent; usually 44.5 percent; sometimes 25.1 percent; never 8.3 percent. In every sample of the almost 8000 American women interviwed by Kinsey et al. (1953), fewer than half the women orgasmed during intercourse 90 to 100 percent of the time. Chesser (1956) reported the following frequencies of orgasm among 2000 married English women: always 24 percent; frequently 35 percent; sometimes 26 percent; rarely 10 percent; never 5 percent. Hunt (1974) reported that 53 percent of approximately 700 married white American women orgasm all or almost all of the time, and only 7 percent almost none or none of the time. And recently, Tavris and Sadd (1977) reported that in a sample of 100,000 American women who responded to a Redbook magazine questionnaire, 15 percent always orgasm during coitus, 48 percent orgasm most of the time, 19 percent sometimes, 11 percent once in a while, and 7 percent never.

Two recent studies have investigated the circumstances of female orgasm in greater detail, and both have shown the importance of clitoral stimulation. In Fisher's (1973) study of 300 married American women, most of whom were in their early or middle twenties, 38 percent always or nearly always orgasm during intercourse, 5 percent never do, and the majority do so "frequently." Of the women who do orgasm during intercourse, about 63 percent orgasm by clitoral stimulation followed by intromission and about 35 percent orgasm by direct clitoral stimulation either before or after their husband's ejaculation. About 30 percent of the time the average woman in Fisher's sample requires manual clitoral stimulation to orgasm: "35% of the women said they require such final direct manual stimulation 50 or more percent of the time to attain orgasm. Only 20% of the women said they never require a final push from manual stimulation to reach orgasm" (p. 193). The average woman reported that her husband's penis is still inserted in her vagina 57 percent of the time she orgasms; 33 percent of the women said the penis is inserted half the time they orgasm, and only 33 percent reported that the penis always is inserted at orgasm.

Summarizing responses to about 3000 very detailed questionnaires about female sexuality—excluding the 12 percent of the sample who have never experienced orgasm and the 3 percent who have never had intercourse—Hite (1976) reported that 30 percent orgasm regularly during intercourse without manual stimulation of the clitoris; 19 percent orgasm regularly from simultaneous intercourse and manual stimulation; 22 percent rarely orgasm during intercourse; and 29 percent do not orgasm during intercourse. Furthermore, Hite noted that those women who do orgasm regularly during intercourse without manual stimulation of the clitoris generally use positions and techniques that provide clitoral stimulation (for example, from their partner's pubic area) in addition to the stimulation provided by penile thrusting.

Sexual intercourse among Western peoples normally is preceded by a substantial amount of foreplay which usually includes clitoral stimulation: Kinsey *et al.* (1953) reported that 89 percent of their sample typically engaged in more than 3 minutes of foreplay and 22 percent typically engaged in more than 20 minutes; the median duration of foreplay in Fisher's (1973) sample was 12.5 minutes and in Hunt's (1974) sample it was 15 minutes. Fisher (1973) also noted that to most women, stimulation of the clitoris during foreplay was more exciting than stimulation of any other part of the body. Although Kinsey (cited by Hunt 1974) believed that, at the time of his studies, the average duration of intercourse was about 2 minutes, Hunt (1974) reported a median duration of 10 minutes, and Fisher (1973) noted that the average woman in his sample required about 8 minutes of sexual intercourse to orgasm, the range being 1 to 30 minutes. Although there may not be a statistically significant correlation between duration of foreplay or intercourse and the occurrence of female orgasm (Kinsey *et al.* 1953, Fisher 1973), it is nonetheless clear that in order to orgasm most human females require sustained sexual stimulation, especially stimulation of the clitoris.

Cross-cultural variability in the occurrence of female orgasm is astonishing: among a few peoples, all women are said to experience orgasm, and to expect it during sexual intercourse (Marshall 1971,

Davenport 1977); but among many peoples, women do not experience orgasm, and even the concept of female orgasm is absent (Mead 1967, Messenger 1971). The absence of severe sexual repression appears to be a necessary but not sufficient condition for the occurrence of regular female orgasm during intercourse: also required is male interest and skill. Consider Marshall's data on sexual behavior on Mangaia, a southern Cook Island in central Polynesia, where all women are said to orgasm during intercourse. At the age of 13 or 14 Mangaian boys undergo superincision, and at this time are instructed in sexual matters by the superincision expert. The expert emphasizes techniques of coitus, cunnilingus, kissing and sucking the breasts, and bringing the partner to several orgasms before the male allows himself to ejaculate. According to Marshall, Mangaian knowledge of sexual anatomy probably is more extensive than that of most European physicians. Two weeks after superincision there is a "practical exercise" in intercourse with an older, experienced woman. She coaches the neophyte in applying the information he has acquired from the superincision expert, especially the techniques of delaying and timing ejaculation so that he orgasms simultaneously with his partner.

Girls of the same age are instructed in sexual matters by older women. Although sexual intercourse in Mangaia typically is preceded by only about 5 minutes of foreplay, Marshall emphasizes that considerable skill is applied during these 5 minutes; Mangaians are not interested in foreplay for its own sake, and the only goal is to arouse the female sufficiently for intercourse. To Mangaians, extended foreplay detracts from their primary goal which is 15 to 30 minutes of intercourse with continuous thrusting and active female participation, during which the female orgasms two or three times, her final orgasm occurring simultaneously with her partner's. Mangaians state that "orgasm must be 'learned' by a woman and that this learning process is achieved through the efforts of a good man" (p. 122). If a man fails to bring his partner to orgasm, she is likely to leave him for someone else, and she may ruin his reputation with other women. At "East Bay," a Melanesian island in the southwest Pacific, female orgasm is regularly achieved by extended mutual heterosexual masturbation, with insertion just before mutual orgasm (Davenport 1977), a technique reminiscent of descriptions in Fisher's (1973) and Hite's (1976) reports.

From a cross-cultural perspective, however, these Pacific peoples are the exception, not the rule. Davenport (1977:149) summarizes the ethnographic literature thus:

In most of the societies for which there are data, it is reported that men take the initiative and, without extended foreplay, proceed vigorously toward climax without much regard for achieving synchrony with the woman's orgasm. Again and again, there are reports that coitus is primarily completed in terms of the man's passions and pleasures, with scant attention paid to the woman's response. If women do experience orgasm, they do so passively.

Is female orgasm an adaptation?

Unlike the unicorn, which is specially interesting precisely because it does not exist, or extrasensory perception, which probably does not exist but is interesting because of the possibility that it might, or the male orgasm, which exists with monotonous regularity and for the most part is interesting only to people directly involved in one, the female orgasm definitely exists and yet inspires interest, debate, polemics, ideology, technical manuals, and scientific and popular literatures solely because it so often is absent. Orgasm almost certainly is far more common among human than among nonhuman primate females, if, indeed, it exists among the latter at all. But even among humans there is enormous variability; female orgasm is normal among some peoples and unknown among other peoples. Where it is normal, the female orgasm does not emerge on its own, like breasts or pubic hair, but is consciously cultivated. Among Western peoples, some women orgasm every time they have intercourse, others never orgasm, and most fall somewhere in between. When women's own statements are reported verbatim, as in Fisher (1973) and Hite (1974, 1976), still more variation appears; some women consider intercourse without orgasm to be worthless, others value intercourse but place little importance on orgasm. Hite (1976) found that, whether or not they regularly orgasm during intercourse, the overwhelming majority of the women who responded to her questionnaire cited affection, intimacy, and love—not orgasm—as the primary reasons for liking sexual intercourse. Neither did most women consider orgasm to be the most important physical sensation during intercourse: the favorite physical sensation by far was the moment of penetration.

The question of the adaptive significance of female orgasm requires further consideration of the role of the clitoris. Masters and Johnson concluded that, however they are caused, all female orgasms are physiologically identical and essentially clitoral, and that during intercourse clitoral stimulation almost invariably is indirect: "Clitoral stimulation during coitus . . . develops indirectly from penile-shaft distention of the minor labia at the vaginal vestibule. A mechanical traction develops on both sides of the clitoral hood of the minor labia subsequent to penile distention of the vaginal outlet. With active penile thrusting, the clitoral body is pulled downward toward the pudendum by traction exerted on the wings of the clitoral hood" (1966:59). The implication frequently drawn from Masters and Johnson's writing, an implication that I believe was intended, is that the female genitals are designed (presumably by natural selection) to generate orgasm during hetero-sexual copulation. To evaluate this notion it is helpful to consider two biases in Masters and Johnson's work to which Robinson (1976) has called attention. First, since Masters and Johnson required orgasmic ability of their female subjects, and since the most common motive women gave for participating in the reseach was the desire for sexual activity, it is reasonable to suspect that the sample was biased toward libidinousness. Since all the participating women orgasmed during in-tercourse, orgasm was made to seem a "natural" concomitant of inter-course. Second, Robinson (1976:158-59) notes that Masters and John-son's "enthusiasm for marriage is reflected both in direct statements on the subject and in their elaborate and often strained attempts to demonstrate the complementary nature of male and female sexuality." I believe that one result of Masters and Johnson's marital bias is their implication that male and female genitals are not only complementary in their proportions but equally adapted to orgasm production during (marital) intercourse.

Kinsey et al. (1953) point out that the human female's ability to respond rapidly to sexual stimulation and to reach orgasm is not intrin-sically inferior to the male's: without foreplay, most females can mas-turbate to orgasm in about four minutes. Hite (1976) notes that almost all women who masturbate orgasm easily in this way, whether or not they typically orgasm during intercourse. Kinsey et al. and Hite sug-gest that many women do not orgasm during intercourse, or do so sporadically, simply because sexual intercourse is an extremely ineffi-cient way to stimulate the clitoris. These authors describe a variety of female masturbatory techniques, almost all of which are clearly de-signed to provide clitoral stimulation; but conspicuous by their absence are techniques that simulate sexual intercourse: women almost never masturbate by inserting something in the vagina. According to Kinsey et al. (1953), in many cases a female who inserted objects in her vagina during masturbation did so out of ignorance, and stopped once she "had acquired a better understanding of her own anatomy and sexual capabilities" (p. 163). Masters and Johnson (1966) found that the most intense female orgasms—whether measured subjectively or by the number and strength of contractions—occurred during masturbation, not intercourse.

Males, on the other hand, do mimic the sensations of intercourse when they masturbate, and recent developments in masturbation technology vividly emphasize male-female differences: the clitoral stimulation women obtain from electric vibrators is quite unlike anything that is likely to occur during sexual intercourse, but men can now masturbate in the operational genitalia of inflatable "female" dolls, thereby simulating intercourse as closely as possible given the present state of the art. Hite (1976) suggests that the Masters and Johnson theory of indirect clitoral stimulation during intercourse is more like a Rube Goldberg scheme than a reliable way to orgasm; as one of her informants wrote (p. 133): "Sex in the best of all possible worlds? My clitoris would be in my vagina, for Christ's sake, so I could come when I fuck!" Hite (1976:168) quotes Alex Shulman: "Masters and Johnson observe that the clitoris is automatically 'stimulated' in intercourse since the hood covering the clitoris is pulled over the clitoris with each thrust of the penis in the vagina—much, I suppose, as a penis is automatically 'stimulated' by a man's underwear whenever he takes a step." But the target of Shulman's irony might better have been "stimulated to orgasm" than "stimulated": female genitals in fact may be efficiently designed to produce pleasurable stimulation during sexual intercourse without necessarily being designed to produce orgasm.

The only known function of the clitoris in the great majority of mammalian species is to generate sensation—presumably pleasurable—during copulation. While among nonhuman mammals there is little or no direct clitoral stimulation during copulation (Ford and Beach 1951), very likely there is indirect stimulation, and female mammals are far from sexually passive; they are proceptive during estrus and become more so with sexual experience (Diakow 1974). But, although there are some striking exceptions, most mammals mate very quickly; it is generally adaptive for males to ejaculate as soon as possible after penetrating (Ford and Beach 1951). Sexually experienced male mammals require less stimulation, and ejaculate more quickly, than naïve males do (Diakow 1974), and there is no compelling evidence that nonhuman female mammals orgasm during heterosexual copulation.

Human females are extremely variable in this respect: among some peoples female orgasm is unknown; where it is known, its occurrence usually is sporadic; in the few societies where all females are said to orgasm, substantial clitoral stimulation occurs during foreplay or during consciously and deliberately prolonged intercourse; orgasm never is considered to be a spontaneous and inevitable occurrence for females as it always is for males. Women's statements about their sensations during intercourse, and the data on masturbation, further undermine the view that women's genitals are designed to generate orgasm during intercourse. On the other hand, abundant evidence exists that—like other female mammals—women usually enjoy sexual intercourse. Hite (1976), for example, reports that the women in her sample uniformly find sexual arousal to be pleasurable and almost invariably enjoy sexual intercourse.

As discussed in Chapter One, "adaptation" is an aspect of structure, behavior, or psyche that has been produced by the operation of natural selection. Female orgasm is an adaptation only if in ancestral populations orgasmic females enjoyed greater average reproductive success than nonorgasmic females. If one accepts Williams's (1966) arguments that adaptation should be posited only where it is really necessary and that adaptive design can be recognized in such features as precision, economy, and efficiency, it seems to me that available evidence is, by a wide margin, insufficient to warrant the conclusion that female orgasm is an adaptation. When nonhuman primate females receive prolonged clitoral stimulation they apparently can orgasm (Burton 1971, Michael et al. 1974, Chevalier-Skolnikoff 1974), and the same seems to be true of human females. Although there is, and probably always has been, enormous variation in the ease with which individuals can orgasm—and hence ample grist for the evolutionary mill—there is no compelling evidence that natural selection favored females that were capable of orgasm, either in the evolution of mammals or specifically in the human lineage; nor is there evidence that the female genitals of any mammalian species have been designed by natural selection for efficiency in orgasm production. Orgasm is most parsimoniously interpreted as a potential all female mammals possess. Humans differ from other mammals primarily in that, among some peoples, techniques of foreplay and intercourse provide sufficiently intense and uninterrupted stimulation for females to orgasm.

The view that human female orgasm is best regarded as a potential has been elegantly expressed by Margaret Mead (1967):

There are many primitive societies in which women's receptivity is all that is required or expected, in which little girls learn from their mothers, and from the way their fathers pat their heads or hold them, unworriedly, close to their bodies, that women are expected to be receptive, not actively or assertively sexed. That whole societies can ignore climax as an aspect of female sexuality must be related to a very much lesser biological basis for such climax (p. 214).

        *   *   *

Societies like Samoa that emphasize a highly varied and diffuse type of foreplay will include in the repertoire of the male acts that will effectively awaken almost all women, however differently constituted they may be. But in cultures in which many forms of foreplay are forbidden, or simply ruled out by social arrangements that insist on both partners being clothed, or on the absence of lights, or on the muffling of all body odours by scented deodorants, this potentiality, which all women can develop under sufficiently favorable circumstances, may be ignored for a large proportion or for almost all of them. It is important also to realize that such an unrealized potentiality is not necessarily felt as frustration (pp. 218-19).

        *   *   *

Comparative cultural material gives no grounds for assuming that an orgasm is an integral and unlearned part of women's sexual response, as it is of men's sexual response, and strongly suggests that a greater part of women's copulatory behaviour is learned (p. 222).

Some investigators find a correlation between the frequency with which women experience orgasm and their satisfaction with sexual relations (for example, Chesser 1956, Hunt 1974), while others find no such correlation (for example, Terman 1938, Hite 1976). Surely there can be little doubt that women who have orgasmed, or who are aware of the possibility of orgasm, may experience its nonoccurrence as a loss, especially if they are aroused so intensely during intercourse that they experience physical discomfort without orgasm. But if sexual intercourse in most societies is, and always has been, "primarily completed in terms of the man's passions and pleasures," female arousal intense enough to produce physical discomfort in the absence of orgasm may be of relatively recent origin.

To Sherfey (1972), adaptation is revealed not only in the existence of female orgasm but in the possibility of multiple orgasms: "That the female could have the same orgasmic anatomy (all of which is female to begin with) and not be expected to use it simply defies the very nature of biological properties of evolutionary and morphogenetic processes" (p. 113), and the female's theoretical capacity to experience an indefinite number of successive orgasms without being satiated indicates an erotic adaptation so deeply rooted, so potent, and so anarchic as to constitute the primary impediment to the development and continuity of civilization. To my knowledge, Sherfey's argument has not been taken seriously by evolutionary biologists, but her work is cited so frequently by scholars unacquainted with evolutionary theory that a brief consideration of it may be of some use.

(1) As noted above, ethnographies of preliterate peoples provide scant evidence of preagricultural, sexually insatiable females. In Western societies, multiple orgasm is the exception, not the rule (for example, Kinsey *et al.* 1953, Hite 1976), and Fisher's (1973) data fail to confirm Sherfey's (1972) prediction that, owing to increased pelvic vascularization, the probability of multiple orgasm increases after each pregnancy. Puzzling over the fact that the great majority of the women in her sample desire only one orgasm during intercourse, Hite (1976) concludes—as do Sherfey (1972) and (apparently) Masters and Johnson (1970)—that women only imagine themselves to be satisfied owing to their ignorance of the theory of insatiability. But even on Mangaia, where multiple orgasms appear to be the rule, there is no mention of insatiability, and Marshall (1971) notes that men are considered to be more desirous of intercourse than women are. Masters and Johnson (1966) discuss the case histories of five married men who were unable to ejaculate intravaginally and typically continued sexual intercourse for thirty to sixty minutes, a circumstance that might be thought to approximate a Sherfeyian paradise for their wives. Of the five wives, three were multiorgasmic, and intercourse was "terminated by the female partner's admission of sexual satiation" (p. 219).

(2) The evidence from living hunter/gatherer peoples indicates that a woman cannot rear more than one child every third or fourth year. It is difficult to see how expending time and energy pursuing the will-o'-the-wisp of sexual satiation, endlessly and fruitlessly attempting to make a bottomless cup run over, could conceivably contribute to a female's reproductive success. On the contrary, insatiability would markedly interfere with the adaptively significant activities of food gathering and preparing and child care. Moreover, to the extent that insatiability promoted random matings, it would further reduce female reproductive success by subverting female choice; as discussed above, no female mammal experiences difficulty finding applicants to fertilize her, and females of species such as the mountain gorilla give birth at predictable intervals with—from the human perspective—almost no

copulation. Any psychological disposition that interferes with a female's being fertilized by the fittest available males or obtaining male assistance in rearing offspring is virtually certain to prove maladaptive, and insatiability very likely would constitute such a disposition.

(3) Perhaps the strongest evidence against the existence of the lascivious preagricultural past that Sherfey imagines is the sexual capacity of the human male. In a milieu of sexually aggressive and insatiable females, the reproductive edge would go to the males who were the most potent and indefatigable. Sherfeyian human females imply human males beside whom bulls, rams, and stallions pale to sexual insignificance. The sexually insatiable woman is to be found primarily, if not exclusively, in the ideology of feminism, the hopes of boys, and the fears of men.

For at least two reasons, female orgasm might actually be dysfunctional. While I do not take either of them very seriously, they are perhaps worth mentioning since they are not obviously inferior to the arguments others have advanced in support of the view that female orgasm is an adaptation. First, female orgasm might reduce the probability of conception. According to Masters and Johnson (1966), during intense sexual arousal vasocongestion constricts the outer third of the vagina, producing a stopperlike effect that helps to retain the semen. Since the vasocongestion is dissipated by orgasm, Masters and Johnson advise women attempting to conceive not to orgasm during intercourse. Second, if orgasm were so rewarding an experience that it became an autonomous need, it might conceivably undermine a woman's efficient management of sexuality. Throughout evolutionary history, perhaps nothing was more critical to a female's reproductive success than the circumstances surrounding copulation and conception. A woman's reproductive success is jeopardized by anything that interferes with her ability: to conceive no children that cannot be raised; to choose the best available father for her children; to induce males to aid her and her children; to maximize the return on sexual favors she bestows; and to minimize the risk of violence or withdrawal of support by her husband and kinsmen. This view of female sexuality is a major theme of this book; it is the biological reality that underlies W. H. Auden's observation that "men are playboys, women realists."

The female orgasm may be a byproduct of mammalian bisexual potential: orgasm may be possible for female mammals because it is adaptive for males. Beach (1976a) notes that the existence of neural mechanisms mediating sexual behaviors typical of one sex does not necessarily entail the suppression of mechanisms mediating sexual behaviors typical of the other sex: "The same individual cannot develop both a penis and a vagina, but the same brain can contain mechanisms for both male and female behavior" (p. 480). Males and females do not usually exhibit the same behaviors owing to "*sex-linked prepotency* of integrative brain mechanisms and sex differences in secretion of and sensitivity to gonadal hormones" (p. 481). Sex-linked prepotencies may be the result of male-female differences in the prenatal hormones that control the sexual differentiation of the brain. Kinsey *et al.* (1953) call attention to the fundamental similarity of the male and female orgasm, and Masters and Johnson (1966) refine this view, establishing the remarkable fact that the initial orgasmic contractions occur at intervals of 0.8 seconds in both sexes.

The ability of females to experience multiple orgasms may be an incidental effect of their inability to ejaculate. Ejaculation "is unique in the entire cycle of sexual response and is the essence of the male orgasmic experience" (Masters and Johnson 1966:282). Kinsey *et al.* (1948) recorded orgasm in boys of every age from five months to adolescence. Except for ejaculation, these orgasms duplicate those of sexually mature males, and "The most remarkable aspect of the preadolescent population is its capacity to achieve repeated orgasm in limited periods of time. This capacity definitely exceeds the ability of teen-age boys who, in turn, are much more capable than older males" (Kinsey *et al.* 1948:179). Approximately a third of the orgasmic boys remained in erection and proceeded directly to a second orgasm, another third remained in erection but experienced "some physical and erotic let-down before trying to achieve a second orgasm" (p. 180), and the rest experienced complete loss of arousal immediately following orgasm; this range of variation is perhaps similar to that of orgasmic women. The female orgasm may be homologous with the orgasm of the preadolescent male, which occurs before the capacity for successive orgasms—among a minority of individuals—is eliminated by the development of ejaculatory ability.[4] That orgasmic abilities could exist among boys and women (and, for that matter, girls) and not have adaptive significance is no more an occasion for astonishment or dis-

---

[4] Similarly, I would speculate that the capacity of the female nipples to generate pleasurable, erotic sensation is an adaptation designed to promote breast feeding, not foreplay, and that the erotic potential of the male nipples—indeed, the very existence of male nipples—is a functionless artifact of the mammalian bisexual potential.

belief—and is no more contradictory of evolutionary or morphogenetic principles—than is the existence of the human ability to learn to read and write, for which there is absolutely no evidence to suggest adaptation.

On the surface, the insatiable-female and the pair-bond theories of the evolution of female orgasm are opposites, but closer examination reveals fundamental similarities. Both, of course, consider female orgasm to be an adaptation. For the most part, both ignore reproductive competition—the basis of evolution—and view natural selection as a more or less beneficent creative process that has designed human beings to live in harmony and happiness. The theories differ primarily in their conceptions of Eden: Sherfey is a sexual radical for whom paradise is endless, orgiastic sexual indulgence, while Morris *et al.* are sexual conservatives who favor a paradise of intimate, sexually intense monogamy. Both theories posit an underlying reality that differs radically from the reality we experience in daily life, in scientific studies of Western peoples, in the ethnographic record, and in major literary works. Sexually insatiable females and people who pair-bond like gibbons (an issue I shall examine in the following section) appear to exist in substantial numbers only in the human imagination.

To say that female orgasm *per se* is not an adaptation is not to say that nothing of adaptive significance can be recognized in the circumstances of its occurrence. On the contrary, the brain and body that make the female orgasm possible are an amalgam of adaptive compromises reflecting specific—and at least theoretically identifiable—selective forces that operated during evolutionary history. Any activity or experience of which an organism is capable in some sense reflects its adaptive history. But the fact that in certain circumstances bears ride unicycles and dolphins never do is not evidence that unicycle riding was adaptive among bear ancestors and unadaptive among dolphin ancestors, nor is it evidence that bears in a natural habitat necessarily do anything that is analogous to unicycle riding. Nevertheless, the ability of bears to ride unicycles, and the inability of dolphins to do so, obviously results from the different ways of life to which these mammals are adapted.

I have already suggested that the potential for female orgasm can be understood as a byproduct of selection for male orgasm. Whenever the human female orgasm is discovered (which may be more likely among humans than among nonhuman mammals because of the greater clitoral stimulation produced by face-to-face copulation and perhaps other human peculiarities), like agriculture, the wheel, and indoor plumbing, the female orgasm will come to play a role in human affairs, and adaptations are likely to be revealed in the ways in which humans deal with it. A woman who has experienced orgasm is likely to want to do so again. A male might want his partner to orgasm for many of the same reasons he might want to give her a gift or an affectionate touch or glance: to be gratified by evidences of her pleasure or happiness; to announce his concern for her feelings; to increase his value to her; to make her think well of him; to create an obligation. A Mangaian male who risks losing not only his partner but his reputation—and hence future partners—through mediocre sexual performances is likely to be especially diligent in matters relating to his partners' orgasms. A male's concern with female orgasm (perhaps based on the misconception that it plays the same role in her sexual experience that it does in his own) might inadvertently lead him to discover heretofore latent erotic possibilities in himself and hence to modify further his behavior to increase his own sensual pleasures. In certain circumstances individuals of either sex might gain status and self-esteem via reputations as skilled lovers; in other circumstances they might gain status through a show of sexual indifference. A female might have or pretend to have orgasms to enhance her partner's self-esteem, to increase his sexual pleasures as they reverberate with his imaginings of her pleasures, to increase her value to him, or to indicate that she cares for him; on the other hand, she might avoid having or pretending to have orgasms to communicate anger or indifference.

In an exceedingly simple-minded way, then, one senses in human behaviors and feelings about female orgasm the basic adaptations that seem to inform most human social life: the seeking of sensual pleasures, self-esteem, and status; the desire to obtain and to hold on to sexual partners and other useful persons, and to increase one's value to others; the ability to empathize and sympathize—to imagine the existence of other minds almost as real as one's own—and to use empathy and sympathy to manipulate effectively social intercourse; the ability to profit from experience; the ability to make extraordinarily complex and subtle social observations and calculations, to manage effectively the innumerable interactions of daily life, and to imagine alternate futures and to plan for them; in short, the ability to transact favorable compromises in the economy of the emotions.

FOUR

Pair-Bonds, Marriage, and the Loss of Estrus

Sex is an antisocial force in evolution. Bonds are formed between individuals in spite of sex and not because of it.

EDWARD O. WILSON

BEACH'S (1976a) SUMMARY OF the patterns of sexual behavior found among nonhuman mammals provides a useful perspective from which to view human sexual patterns.

> The vast majority of all animals engage in no sexual behavior at all during most of the year, and for all nonhuman species copulatory activity is periodic rather than continuous. This is because mating is closely tied to reproduction, generally occurring only when a male and female are fertile and copulation can lead to pregnancy. At those times when they normally are infertile, adult males and females are unresponsive to sexual stimulation. The timing of sexual receptivity in females and potency in males is determined by ovarian and testicular hormones, secretion of which is controlled by the same pituitary hormones that govern production of eggs and sperm.
>
> Perhaps 90% of all mammals are seasonal breeders, but some tropical species normally reproduce throughout the year and still others do so under domestication. In these cases, males are more or less constantly fertile and potent whereas the female's periods of sexual receptivity and attractiveness are synchronized with the cyclic maturation of egg cells in her ovaries, and mating therefore occurs only when copulation can result in impregnation (p. 471).

Beach notes that chimpanzees and monkeys appear to deviate from this pattern in that they sometimes copulate when the female is infertile, but he also points out that these deviations from the rule generally occur among captive animals, an issue to which I shall return later in this chapter.

Against the mammalian background, humans stand out in the degree to which sexual behavior is independent of hormonal control: "Production of sperm and eggs and secretion of sex hormones are determined by pituitary hormones just as in other mammals; but the effects of testosterone, estrogen, and progesterone on the brain and thus on psychological functions are much less obvious and obligatory" (Beach 1976a:471). Humans regularly copulate at times when conception is not possible, hence human sexual behavior is commonly said to serve nonreproductive functions. Insofar as they are more or less constantly fertile and potent, adult human males are typical of species that breed throughout the year, but human females appear to be in some respects sexually unique. Therefore most evolutionary hypotheses have centered on changes that occurred in female sexuality during the course of human evolution, especially on the loss of estrus.

Estrus is a relatively brief period of proceptivity, receptivity, and attractivity in female mammals which usually, but not invariably, coincides with their brief period of fertility. Human females do not experience estrus. Since the widespread occurrence of estrus leaves no doubt that it represents the primitive mammalian condition, estrus must have been lost at some point in human ancestry. In considering the question, Why did the loss of estrus occur? it may be useful to consider as well: What is the human condition with respect to proceptivity, receptivity, and attractivity? Are human females always in estrus? Never in estrus? How does the human condition compare with that of other higher primates? Are humans unique? Can comparisons with other primates suggest functional interpretations and historical reconstructions of the loss of estrus?

Mammalian sex cycles

Butler's (1974) review of evolutionary trends in primate sex cycles provides standard definitions of terms used to describe sex cycles in mammals. The "sexual season" is the time of year during which mating occurs, but most female mammals copulate only during periods of estrus, which in some species occur only once and in others at regular intervals during the sexual season. Estrus is preceded by the growth of the uterine lining under the influence of estrogen which is secreted by the developing ovarian follicle (the follicular phase). The close association of estrus and the rupture of the ovarian follicle (ovulation) in most mammals is clear evidence of an adaptation to maximize the likelihood that copulation will result in fertilization. After the egg is released the follicle is re-formed into a progesterone-secreting corpus luteum. If fertilization occurs, estrus and ovulation usually are suppressed until some time after the birth of the infant; if fertilization does not occur, the uterine lining undergoes a second growth phase under the influence of progesterone secreted by the corpus luteum (the luteal phase). The nonfertile cycle ends with the degeneration of the corpus luteum and the return of the uterus to its resting state. Menstruation in human females results from the periodic destruction of the uterine lining at the end of a nonpregnant cycle. Since human females do not exhibit estrus and do menstruate, their cycles are referred to as menstrual cycles. Many higher primate females also menstruate, however, and some scholars (for example, Rowell 1972a, 1972b) use the term menstrual cycle to refer to the sex cycles of all higher primate females, whereas other scholars (for example, Butler 1974) restrict the term menstrual cycle to humans. Disagreement in terminology reflects different interpretations of the data with respect to the uniqueness of humans: Rowell emphasizes the lack of distinct estrous periods among some nonhuman primate females and their similarity to human females, while Butler emphasizes that, although nonreproductive copulation does occur among many Old World monkeys and apes, the human female nonetheless is unique in that menstruation is the only observable event that marks her reproductive cycle. I shall follow Rowell's usage with the understanding that most nonhuman primate females that menstruate also show clearly defined estrous periods.

Sex and society

Zuckerman (1932) proposed that the social relations of all mammals are determined primarily by the physiology of reproduction. Vast breeding schools of seals, a horde of monkeys, and a pair of foxes during the mating season are equally the product of sexuality: "the framework of mammalian society is determined by physiological mechanisms. Reproductive physiology is the fundamental mechanism of society" (p. 30). In this view, groups of monkeys, apes, and humans, unlike groups of other mammals, are permanent because higher primates, unlike other mammals, are continuously sexual. Nonprimate mammals have a yearly season of anestrus in which sexual activities are completely absent, but, according to Zuckerman, monkeys, apes, and humans "experience a smooth and uninterrupted sexual and reproductive life" (p. 51). Zuckerman acknowledged that many higher primates may exhibit seasonal variation in the frequency of mating and that female attractiveness is not constant through the menstrual cycle but is much higher in the middle; nevertheless, "there is no implication that the sexual stimulus holding individuals together is ever totally absent" (p. 57).

Although Zuckerman argued that continuous sexuality *causes* primate societies he definitely did not argue that the production of societies is a *function* of continuous sexuality. On the contrary, Zuckerman clearly had little interest in questions of ultimate causation; he acknowledged that natural selection may have favored social life, but he considered such functional speculation to be teleological and probably untestable, and he confined his analysis to proximate mechanisms.

Given the evidence available at the time, Zuckerman's conclusions were reasonable, but later field studies reviewed by Lancaster and Lee (1965) revealed that many groups of macaque have sexual seasons and in the rest of the year exhibit complete cessation of true copulation. Lancaster and Lee concluded:

> It is clear that constant sexual attraction cannot be the basis for the persistent social groupings of primates. Despite the absence of primary sexual behavior in the Japanese macaque for a period of from four to nine months each year, stable group organization is maintained without interruption or change. . . .
>
> The human pattern of reproduction does not resemble reproduction of any other primate. The human system is characterized by the absence of estrous cycles in the female and of the marked seasonal variations that appear to characterize reproduction in nonhuman primates. The reproductive systems of man and the monkeys and apes are closely related in respect to the evolutionary development of the one from the other—but they are qualitatively different in the behavior they produce. The important similarities in the social lives of higher primates, such as living in year-round bisexual groups, cannot be attributed to nonexistent similarities in mating systems (p. 513).

Primatological thinking about sexuality seems to have cycles of its own. A recent trend is to emphasize the existence of nonreproductive mating among some species of nonhuman primates and to revive some of Zuckerman's ideas concerning the differences between primates and nonprimate mammals, the similarities of human and nonhuman primates, and the relations of sex and society. Some recent reviews go beyond Zuckerman and suggest not only that nonreproductive sexuality is a cause of primate society but that it is an adaptation whose function is to maintain troop cohesion and reinforce social bonds (for example, Rowell 1972b, Saayman 1975). It is not necessary to review the recent evidence in detail as a number of relevant reviews are available (Rowell 1972a, 1972b, Eaton 1973, Butler 1974, Saayman 1975, Beach 1976b, Baum *et al.* 1977, Lancaster in press), but the following brief summary of the nonhuman primate evidence may be a useful perspective from which to view human sexuality.

(1) In some populations of free-ranging nonhuman primates matings are confined to a discrete season, in others matings occur year-round but peak at certain seasons, and in a few matings are nonseasonal. Primates are not, however, unique in this respect. In habitats with marked seasonal climatic changes selection favors female mammals who give birth at the time of year that is optimal for the survival of their young, thus favoring matings that produce births at the appropriate time. Where environmental pressures are relatively constant throughout the year, newborns may be equally viable in any season. Many species breed seasonally in the wild but nonseasonally in the constant conditions of captivity. In a frequently cited paper, Loy (1971) reported that some free-ranging female rhesus monkeys that do not become pregnant during the sexual season continue to exhibit estrus during the birth season. Loy used grooming as an index of estrus, however, and the frequencies of actual matings during the birth season were extremely low. Certainly his data do not invalidate the findings of many field workers that free-ranging rhesus breed seasonally.

(2) Pregnancy generally suppresses estrus, although postconception estrous periods have been reported in a number of primate species.

(3) Lactation suppresses estrus for a time in all primate species, although females resume cycling before their offspring are fully weaned.

(4) In the wild, estrous periods of some species are substantially longer than seems necessary for fertilization. Females of a few species are reported to copulate throughout the menstrual cycle with no midcycle peak that might be termed "estrus," but these findings are almost all from captive groups, and it is possible that they are captivity artifacts. Butler (1974:30) notes that "there are very remarkable differ-

ences between the sexual behavior of wild and captive animals. The continuous erotic behavior seen in captive gorillas and orangutans must be regarded as a deviation resulting from the boredom of captivity. . . . It is comparable to the stereotyped pacing back and forth along the same track seen in captive hunting mammals." Butler points out that "Numerous observations on the sexual behavior of captive chimpanzees show that copulation can occur at any time during the sex cycle. Sexual receptivity parallels the amount of sex skin swelling, increasing during the period of swelling, reaching a climax at maximum swelling, and diminishing with detumescence. However, the occurrence of copulation does not necessarily imply sexual receptivity, and the female may solicit a hostile male as an apparently placatory gesture or may submit to his advances at a time during her cycle when she normally would not do so" (p. 23). In an eighteen-month study of free-living chimpanzees, McGinnis (cited in Beach 1976b) never saw an adult male mount a female with unswollen sex skin.

(5) In all nonhuman primate species that have been studied, hormonal fluctuations during the menstrual cycle have been shown to affect profoundly sexual interactions. Female attractivity is markedly enhanced by estrogen and diminished by progesterone; the effect on attractivity of fluctuating levels of these hormones during the menstrual cycle probably is the primary cause of observed fluctuations in sexual interactions (Beach 1976b, Baum et al. 1977). Proceptivity is enhanced both by estrogen and androgen, which are maximal at midcycle; Beach (1976b) suggests that estrogen has the greater effect while Baum et al. (1977) favor androgen. Receptivity among captive female primates, in contrast to that among nonprimate mammals, has not been shown either to fluctuate markedly during the menstrual cycle or to depend on estrogen. Baum et al. (1977) argue that proceptivity and receptivity are both largely dependent on androgen and, contrary to Beach (1976b), find no evidence to indicate that proceptivity and receptivity depend on different neural mechanisms.

The primate order as a whole, then, does appear to exceed most mammalian orders in nonreproductive sexual activity; that is, in the length of estrous periods and in the frequency of postconception estrus. But there are marked species differences in this respect and substantial individual differences as well. For example, Kaufmann (1965) reports that during a three-year study of a group of free-ranging rhesus monkeys the three most sexually active females averaged three times as many estrous periods, fifteen times as many days of estrous activity, and three times as many male partners as the three least active females.

Nonreproductive mating among nonhuman primates may be functionally significant or it may be the byproduct of some other adaptation. Since sexuality entails considerable expenditures of time, energy, and risk, however, it seems likely that nonreproductive sexuality is functional, but to my knowledge no one has explained species or individual differences in nonreproductive sexuality in terms of ultimate causation. Rowell (1972a), who favors the hypothesis that nonreproductive sexuality functions to maintain primate societies, nonetheless calls attention to the "paradox" that "some of the most highly developed social organizations yet described, also have some of the most clearly identified, short, and precisely timed estrous periods known" (p. 100). There is no apparent trend toward increasing sexuality among our closest living relatives: free-living gibbons, orangutans, gorillas, and chimpanzees exhibit totally different patterns of social life and mating, but are alike in exhibiting infrequent and clearly defined periods of sexual activity. Kleiman (1977) reviews the literature on mammals in which heterosexual pairs mate exclusively ("monogamy") and finds that, except during the early stages of pair formation, sexual activity is very infrequent.

In summary, permanent groups are the rule among higher primates, permanent sexual activity is not the rule, and functional explanations for variations in nonreproductive sexuality are lacking. As discussed above, Zuckerman attempted to account for the permanency of primate social life in proximate terms; he did not view group-living as an adaptation, and it was natural to expect that permanent groups would result if an activity, like sex, that is intuitively understood to be rewarding became permanent instead of episodic. But if one views the matter in terms of ultimate causation, and assumes that permanent group-living is adaptive for some reason, then, all other things being equal, selection can be expected to favor the most economical of the available mechanisms that result in permanent sociality. One possible mechanism is for a formerly episodic reward to become permanent, but in terms of time, energy, and risk this seems to be a very expensive solution if the reward is sexual activity. It is much more economical to alter the reward mechanism of the brain itself, so that the sight, sound, or smell of familiar conspecifics comes to be experienced as pleasurable. The existence of such a mechanism was demonstrated long ago by Butler (1954), who showed that rhesus monkeys will learn an operant task for the reward of seeing a conspecific, and human children clearly find social stimuli "reinforcing" (Stevenson 1972). Williams (1966:266) notes that "One of the chief goals of establishing a hierarchical organization of adaptations is to distinguish between the forces that initiated the development of an adaptation and the secondary degenerations that the adaptation, once developed, permitted." Permanent social life almost certainly represents a basic adaptation evolved very early in primate history. Once developed, it may have permitted the occasional decoupling of sexual activity and ovulation without lessening the probability of conception.

While it has yet to be shown what benefits accrue from extended periods of sexual activity, progress is most likely to be made if the sexual behaviors and nonbehavioral signals emitted by an individual are interpreted only with respect to that individual's fitness. An interaction between two animals is not necessarily of benefit to each interactant and may be disadvantageous to one and sometimes to both (as in a fight ending in a Pyrrhic victory); any benefits accruing to the group probably are evolutionarily irrelevant, and still less relevant are benefits accruing to noncorporeal entities or systems like "societies" and "social organizations." I have argued elsewhere (Symons 1978b) that the study of function in primatology has been impeded in part by the influence of social science concepts of function. In social science functionalism, the behavior of individuals is thought to function to promote the welfare of a superindividual entity or system with needs of its own. This view has been remarkably unproductive in the social sciences, and when applied to nonhuman primates it is disastrous. As long as "society" is thought to be the beneficiary of animal behavior, the ultimate causes of nonreproductive sexuality will remain obscure.

Hints about possible benefits to individuals of nonreproductive sexuality already exist in the nonhuman primate literature. For example, as mentioned above by Butler (1974), there are indications that females of some species may solicit a hostile male to avoid being attacked. Among free-ranging langurs, males sometimes enter a troop from outside, displace the resident males, and kill the infants in the group; according to Hrdy (1974), it is possible that a usurping male will not kill infants born subsequent to his takeover if he has consorted with the infants' mothers during pregnancy. Hrdy suggests that "one of the most effective counter-infanticide tactics may be post-conception estrous behavior. That is, if males are actually able to evaluate past consort relationships . . . a pregnant female may induce a male to tolerate her subsequent infant (not necessarily his) by soliciting this male in the months before her infant is born" (p. 51). These suggestions are highly speculative and rather Machiavellian, but cynicism may be a useful antidote to current tendencies in primatology to explain non-reproductive sexuality as functioning to cement social bonds and maintain troop cohesion. The ultimate goal for which selection molds behavior is reproductive success not, as is so often implied in primatology, social integration.

That primatologists so often accept the birth-season estrous periods exhibited by some nonpregnant rhesus females (Loy 1971) as evidence of an adaptation to promote troop cohesion—despite the infrequency of birth-season matings and the obvious unadaptiveness of failing to become pregnant in the first place—leads me to suspect that primatological thinking about sex is not formed entirely by the primate behavior literature. Perhaps primatology has been influenced by changing intellectual perspectives on human sexuality. During the last decade sexuality has been gradually, if unevenly and inconsistently, politicized. The vaginal orgasm was shown by Masters and Johnson to be a myth, and the penis-Goliath was slain by the clitoris-David; female sexual insatiability was found to be restrained only by the veneer of civilization, yet at the same time males were discovered to be basically monogamous (although frequently prone to compensate for sexual insecurities with extramarital adventures) and to be so vulnerable that only the greatest female understanding, patience, and tact could achieve potency; rape was revealed to be a political act that indicated nothing about male sexuality; and the sexual revolution foundered when it was exposed (somewhat inconsistently) as a revolution by and for males. To some extent the other recent influential academic view—that sexuality does not exist except insofar as it is arbitrarily scripted by societies and cultures (Gagnon 1973, 1977, Simon 1973)—has been eclipsed by the view that sexuality does exist sui generis and is important, not in the sense of an anarchic Freudian "id," or a libertine Kinseyian "outlet," but a cozy Masters-and-Johnsonian "marital unit." I shall return to these issues, but raise them now to call attention to the possibility that primatological thinking is swept along with strong intellectual currents when it implies that cohesive, intimate, intense, orgasmic, noncompetitive sexuality is fundamental to primate nature.

The relations between hormonal fluctuations and sexuality obviously cannot be studied among humans in the same way that they are studied among other primates, and in human studies receptivity and proceptivity rarely are distinguished; hence it is difficult to compare the human and nonhuman primate data (Beach 1976b, Baum *et al.* 1977). Udry and Morris (1968) report a mid-cycle peak in copulation and orgasm in women, but there were substantial variations both among samples and individuals, and in any case the peaks did not constitute anything remotely like discrete estrous periods. Several other investigators have not found rhythmic changes in human sexual interactions during the menstrual cycle (references in Baum *et al.* 1977). Most women report retrospectively that they are most sexually responsive just before and just after menstruation (for example, Fisher 1973). Neither ovariectomy nor menopause (which reduce estrogen levels) appear to decrease women's libido; but adrenalectomy (which reduces androgen levels) promptly diminishes libido, and giving testosterone to intact women often increases libido, suggesting that, as in nonhuman primates, adrenal androgens play a role in human female sexuality (Baum *et al.* 1977). Beach (1976b) and Baum *et al.* (1977) emphasize that present techniques of investigating human sexuality leave open the question of cyclic hormonal influences; however, their intuitions appear to be somewhat different. Beach (1976b:133) concludes: "Experience, conditioning, and individual differences have such profound effects upon human sexual life that potential hormonal influences are masked or modulated to such an extent that they will remain virtually unassessable until their behavioral correlates are more effectively conceptualized and measured." But Baum *et al.* (1977:189) conclude that future investigations "may confirm that the hormonal modulation of the human female's sexual activity is similar in many ways to that of the monkey."

Whatever future research may disclose, however, it seems reasonably certain that human females do not experience estrus, and it seems especially likely that human female attractivity does not fluctuate to any significant degree with levels of estrogen. Beach (1974:356) notes that few basic changes in women's reproductive physiology have occurred since humans last shared a common ancestor with a living ape: "Her monthly rhythm of ovogenesis, ovulation, estrogen and progesterone secretion, uterine stimulation, and menstrual bleeding follows the basic primate pattern." Human females deviate from this pattern in that the preovulatory rise in estrogen is accompanied neither by increased desire and responsiveness to sexual stimulation nor increased attractiveness to males. Vaginal lubrication occurs during sexual excitement and does not require the presence of high levels of estrogen. But Beach takes issue with the usual statement that the loss of estrus means that women are "constantly receptive": "No human female is 'constantly receptive.' (Any male who entertains this illusion must be a very old man with a short memory or a very young man due for a bitter disappointment)" (pp. 354-55). Beach goes on to say that "Although human females definitely are not continuously sexually 'receptive,' they are continuously 'copulable'; and their sexual *arousability* does not depend on ovarian hormones. This relaxation of endocrine control contributes to the occurrence of coitus at any stage of the menstrual cycle" (pp. 357-58). I believe that this is the clearest available statement about what the "loss of estrus" means. In summary: (1) recent research has not endangered Lancaster and Lee's (1965) conclusion that patterns of sexuality among free-ranging monkeys and apes differ markedly from human patterns; (2) sex is not the basis of primate society; (3) during the course of human evolution estrus disappeared.

Pair-bonds and marriage

Recent attempts to account for the loss of estrus are much alike in suggesting that continual sexual activity functions to cement the male-female pair-bond which, it is said, is the basis of marriage and the human family. "Pair-bond" is an ethological term defined by Barash (1977a:330) as "A behavioral affiliation between an adult male and an adult female associated with reproduction and especially characteristic of monogamous species." Fairbanks (1977) argues that the independent evolution of adult male-female pair-bonds in fish, birds, and primates results from functionally similar reproductive strategies. Within the primates, "The nuclear family as a social unit appears only in man, the lesser apes (gibbon and siamang), and the distantly related South American marmoset. The similarity of the human nuclear family to that of these other species is a result of convergence toward a similar solution to a similar problem" (Fairbanks 1977:100).

Morris (1967) writes that among humans sexual behavior occurs almost exclusively in a pair-bonded state, which he equates with marriage; adultery reflects an imperfection in the pair-bonding mechanism. According to Morris, "sexual imprinting . . . produces the all-important long-term mateship so vital to the prolonged parental demands" (p. 79), and the loss of estrus is an adaptation to maintain the pair-bond in order to rear the children: "The vast bulk of copulation in our species is obviously concerned, not with producing offspring, but with cementing the pair-bond by providing mutual rewards for the sexual partners" (p. 55). Campbell (1971:260) writes: "more permanent sexual ties underlie the structure of the family." Beach (1974) suggests that the loss of estrus antedated the family, and that the family evolved to ensure that intercourse was frequent enough to guarantee fertilization once ovulation and copulation had become desynchronized: "It is a reasonable assumption that existence of the family with the associated intensification and prolongation of interpersonal bonds and dependencies would promote more frequent intercourse than would be likely to occur in the absence of family structure" (p. 360). Eibl-Eibesfeldt (1975) argues that the slow development of the human child necessitated the permanent association of its parents, resulting in the evolution of a "sexual bond." The loss of estrus enables a woman "to maintain a tie with the man on the basis of a sexual reward, and that is probably the function of this unique physiological adaptation" (p. 502). Barash (1977a:297) writes that the "loss of estrus among humans contributes to sexual consistency that may in turn help to maintain a stable pair-bond." Hamburg (1978:163) writes: "Stable adult human male-female pair-bonds . . . may be facilitated by the absence of estrus. . . ." As with theories about the evolution of female orgasm, the similarity of these theories is especially remarkable considering that their authors represent traditional ethology, anthropology, psychology, sociobiology, and psychiatry and have totally different understandings of the nature of the evolutionary process. Although pair-bonded "monogamous" mammals are characteristically hyposexual (Kleiman 1977), none of the scholars quoted above calls attention to the special pleading implicit in the view that the human "pair-bond" is associated with hypersexuality.

The gibbon is a classic example of primate "monogamy." Gibbons are highly territorial and typically live in groups composed of a mated pair and their immature offspring (Carpenter 1940, Ellefson 1968). The male regularly invests substantial time and energy defending the boundaries of his small territory against incursions by neighboring males, and females also repulse each other, although apparently they are somewhat less combative than males are (Brockelman et al. 1974, Tenaza 1975). Successful reproduction occurs only after pair-bonds and territories are well established (Brockelman et al. 1973, 1974). A male gibbon's belligerence toward neighboring adult males can be considered mostly parental investment: a male normally has only one mate, so his belligerence does not deprive other males of mates. The substantial male parental investment and "monogamy" apparently are responsible for the lack of male-female differences, the adult female being, in various gibbon species, 93 to 103 percent the size of the adult male (Schultz 1969).

Talk of why (or whether) humans pair-bond like gibbons strikes me as belonging to the same realm of discourse as talk of why the sea is boiling hot and whether pigs have wings. Since intelligent, responsible, and experienced scholars seem to believe that humans are gibbonlike and that marriage is based on a sexual tie, I assume that this way of describing human relationships in some measure reflects their personal and professional experiences; but their belief is the only evidence I know of in favor of these views. The lexicon of the English language is woefully inadequate to reflect accurately the texture of human experience; for example, even to refer directly to the common and interesting phenomenon of déjà vu necessitates borrowing from another language, and there is no word for the emotional conflict between getting up to urinate and going back to sleep. English does, however, contain hundreds of words that are useful in describing the thoughts, feelings, and behaviors associated with marriage and with other relations among men and women, and written communication consists not of single words but of sentences, paragraphs, articles, and books. The nature of marriage and the family has been described at length in the works of artists and social scientists: while the range of feeling and the diversity of traditional practices recorded in these works is far greater than any one person could experience, no doubt complexity and subtlety of thought, feeling, and action inevitably must be sacrificed if a written record is to be made at all. It is quite conceivable that progress in the study of marriage will entail expanding the lexicon used to describe human experiences and relationships; but to shrink the present vocabulary to one phrase—pair-bond—and to imagine that in so doing one is being scientific—subsuming humans under principles that account for the data on nonhuman animals—is simply to delude oneself.

The nature and origin of the human family have always been central concerns of anthropology. Controversies still exist about such matters as the universality of the family, whether it has changed since its inception, the correct definition of "family," and so forth, but technical disagreements among specialists are largely irrelevant to the present discussion of the evolution of human sexuality and the loss of estrus; what is relevant, however, is the fact that no anthropological specialist maintains that the human family is analogous to the gibbon "family" or that marriage is a pair-bond, cemented by sexual imprinting. To clarify this point, I shall briefly review two recent discussions of marriage and the family, that of Stephens (1963) and of Gough (1971).

Stephens defines the family as "a social arrangement based on marriage and the marriage contract, including recognition of the rights and duties of parenthood, common residence for husband, wife, and children, and reciprocal economic obligations between husband and wife" (p. 8). Marriage is "a socially legitimate sexual union, begun with a public announcement and undertaken with some idea of permanence; it is assumed with a more or less explicit marriage contract, which entails reciprocal rights and obligations between spouses, and between the spouses and their future children" (p. 5). Stephens discusses a number of problems in applying these definitions: the vagueness of some of the terms; the difficulty in assessing whether there is intent to marry permanently in societies with very high divorce rates; the inadequate data provided by many ethnographers; the existence of societies in which the nuclear family is not a distinct economic entity but is embedded in an extended-family economic unit; the frequent economic division of families in societies with unilineal kin groups; the fact that wives are often partially or wholly self-supporting; the arbitrariness inherent in deciding how far from the mother and children a father can live and still be considered to be in common residence with them; the frequency with which boys do not live with their parents; and the attenuated rights of a father over his children in some matrilineal societies. Stephens concludes that the family is universal, or at least almost universal, and that "everywhere, or almost everywhere, these three elements—nuclear family, extended kinship, and incest taboos—run through human societies like a scarlet thread, giving some degree of sameness, everywhere, to the conditions of mating, child rearing, and social placement" (p. 30). The family unquestionably is universal among living hunter/gatherers, and almost certainly existed among our ancestors for a very long time.

Gough (1971) defines the family—which she believes exists in all societies—as "a married couple or other group of adult kinsfolk who cooperate economically and in the upbringing of children, and all or most of whom share a common dwelling" (p. 760). Gough notes that the family implies four other universals: incest taboos; a division of labor based on gender; socially recognized marriage from which springs social fatherhood; and the higher status of men and their "authority over the women of their families, although older women may have influence, even some authority, over junior men" (p. 761).

Needless to say, debates about the relations between sexuality and marriage have a long history. Elwin (1968) reviews the disagreements on this matter in the early 20th century between Ellis and Westermarck, on the one hand, and Briffault, on the other. Ellis and Westermarck argued that boys and girls who are brought up together from infancy develop feelings of affection for one another that inhibit sexual arousal, hence the failure of the "pairing instinct" to manifest itself in these circumstances. Briffault did not deny that familiarity dulls the edge of lust, but he contended that to believe that marriage is founded on sexual feelings is to confound the "mating instinct" with the sexual impulse: "it is on companionship and affection, and not on sexual desire, that the success of permanent sexual association depends" (cited in Elwin 1968:196). Both sides found support for their views in the available literature on preliterate peoples, but Elwin notes that "their arguments are weightier than their authorities." To analyze the effects of childhood association on later feelings and on marriage would entail distinguishing the effects of various kinds of "association" at different ages; recent evidence from kibbutzes and elsewhere indicates that marriages are unlikely to occur—or, if they occur, to succeed—between people who have had certain kinds of intense childhood associations; but these data are not necessarily pertinent to the general question of the relationship between sexuality and marriage, nor do they necessarily refute Briffault's position. A glimpse of the variety of possible relationships among sex, affection, and marriage can be obtained by considering four cases from the ethnographic record: the Mangaians, the Trobrianders, the Muria, and the Kgatla. These were selected because they are among the few well-documented studies of human sexuality, they illustrate diversity, and the ethnographers explicitly deal with the matters at hand.

Mangaian attitudes about these matters are extensively discussed by Marshall (1971). Mangaians, it will be recalled, begin at puberty to have frequent sexual intercourse with a variety of partners. There is no connection between willingness to copulate with a person and affection, and the degree of passion a couple experiences is related to competence in sexual techniques, not emotional involvement. Boys compete with one another to copulate with the greatest number of girls and to induce the greatest number of female orgasms. Marriages arranged by parents without consulting the principals are infrequent today, although they were common in the past, but parents are involved nonetheless, and their considerations are perhaps much like parents' considerations elsewhere; for example, "Complicating kinship considerations in arranging marriages are questions of land ownership and land tenure. Parents weigh advantages of the consolidation of property against disadvantages of distant kin connections" (p. 137).

Given the extreme emphasis that Mangaians place on sexual intercourse, sexual compatibility naturally is a factor—although by no means overriding—in a young person's choice of a marriage partner, but it is never problematical since compatibility always has been tested before marriage. Other considerations are a girl's facial beauty, money, social standing, and evidences of industry. A boy may try to make himself attractive as a potential husband by such means as planting a great many taro stalks, and a girl may attempt to win a reputation as a mat maker and hard worker around the house. Marshall quotes a middle-aged Mangaian school teacher's advice to a younger colleague on the desirability of marriage:

. . . "marriage is a good thing. A young man spends his time going about doing nothing during the day. When he comes home there is nothing waiting for him to eat. But when you are married the wife has food for you whatever the time of day you get home. Also, as an unmarried man you can't study, as your mind is on the girls all the time." The variation in motives for marriage is summed up by the Mangaian who said, "Some Māori marry only to get a pretty face; some want only a sexual partner and care nothing for cooking ability; some want to get the girl's salary—and some marry to get into a good family and to get a smart wife" (p. 135).

Sexual intercourse remains frequent after marriage but is no longer a central focus of life:

As a rite of passage, marriage brings social recognition of a significant change—the termination of that major stage in the male life cycle which was initiated by the superincision rite of passage. That high period is, in later years, recalled by the reflective phrase *I toku tuatau* . . . "In my time . . ."—referring back to a time when a man was both "strongest for work" and "strongest for chasing women." The one strength is diminished by aging and the loss of physical powers; the latter is cut off by marriage (p. 142).

The married man no longer emphasizes the number of times he can bring his partner to orgasm, but instead whether he can copulate every night of the week. Men say that they want to have intercourse more frequently than women do, and they believe that marriage gives them the right to copulate whenever they want to; they may badger or even beat their wives for failure to comply. Marshall notes, however, that "marriage and the concomitant presence of children, and the increasing need for continuous physical exertion of work, reduce the number of climactic acts. There is also a decrease in the talk, stroking, and (for today's younger couples) the kissing between partners" (p. 121).

Little affection apparently exists between young married couples, but this does not prevent the husband and wife from becoming effective economic partners, or from cooperating in decision making. Mangaians do not have the European concept of love: "The components of affection and companionship, which may characterize the European use of the term [love], puzzled the Mangaians when we discussed the term. Informants state that 'when the Māori gets old, that's the time to "get close" to his wife; but this is when they are over fifty years of age.' And some Māori have 'no good feeling between husband and wife' even then, for they feel only *wareae*—sexual jealousy" (pp. 158-59). Thus a deep emotional attachment may or may not develop among long-married couples (when the frequency of intercourse has markedly waned), but sexual jealousy is a prominent marital emotion. In summary, regular sexual activity and sexual compatibility are important to married Mangaians, as they are to unmarried Mangaians, but sex is not associated with affection, and neither sex nor affection is the basis of marriage. Fundamental to Mangaian marriage is economic cooperation between the partners and mutual sexual jealousy.

Malinowski (1929) discusses the relations between sex and marriage in the Trobriand Islands, a coral archipelago in Melanesia. Trobriand boys and girls spend most of their time playing, without adult supervision or interference, and are unrestricted in sexual activity. Girls begin copulating between the ages of six and eight, boys between ten and twelve. Malinowski comments that "everyone has a great deal of freedom and many opportunities for sexual experience. Not only need no one live with impulses unsatisfied, but there is also a wide range of choice and opportunity" (p. 236). As boys and girls grow older, sexual liaisons tend to become more intense and to last longer; personal preferences "may be based on true sexual passion or else on an affinity of characters" (p. 67). Sooner or later the man decides to stabilize one of his liaisons by marriage. Malinowski notes that, although they already possess each other sexually, individuals spontaneously desire marriage, and he also notes that there is a customary pressure toward marriage. But why, asks Malinowski, "in a society where marriage adds nothing to sexual freedom, and, indeed, takes a great deal away from it, where two lovers can possess each other as long as they like without legal obligation, [do] they still wish to be bound in marriage" (p. 78)?

The motives of the man and the woman differ. A man does not have full status in social life until he is married: he has no household of his own, and he is debarred from many privileges; hence, except for the physically and mentally handicapped, all mature Trobrianders marry. Second, the wife's family provides her husband with a dowry and a yearly tribute in staple food; if a man is of high rank, he requires this tribute to finance ceremonial enterprises and festivities. "Thus a man, especially if he be of rank and importance, is compelled to marry, for, apart from the fact that his economic position is strengthened by the income received from his wife's family, he obtains full social status only by entering the group of *tovavaygile* [married men]" (p. 81). Third, a man gains the services of a wife and the satisfactions of having his own children (although in the Trobriand Islands biological paternity is not acknowledged, and his wife's children will not continue his line). Fourth, the Trobriand man is personally devoted to his future wife, which prompts him "to make certain of her by means of a permanent tie, which shall be binding under tribal law" (p. 82). Even by early adolescence, the boy has developed "a desire to retain the fidelity and exclusive affection of the loved one, at least for a time," although he "does not feel obliged to reciprocate this fidelity" (p. 63). Trobriand males are extremely sexually jealous of their mates; a man may kill his wife for adultery, but more commonly he thrashes her, or sulks. Marriage provides public support for the man's desire that his wife remain faithful to him. The woman, on the other hand, has no economic inducement to marry; her motives are mainly "personal affection and the desire to have children in wedlock" (p. 82).

In contrast to Mangaian marriages, then, mutual love is a major determinant of the choice of a mate and the decision to marry in the Trobriand Islands (although marriage can occur only with the consent of the girl's family). As in Mangaia, however, wealth and social status are often important determinants of mate choice, sexual activity tends to be reduced by marriage, and sexual jealousy—especially male jealousy—plays a significant role in marital relations.

Elwin's (1968) classic study of the *ghotul* (village dormitory) of the Muria, a people living in Bastar, central India, provides another well-documented example of the possible relations among sex, affection, and marriage. Muria boys and girls live in the ghotul from six or seven years of age until they are married. There are two types of ghotul: in the older type, boys and girls pair off and are more or less sexually faithful to one another; in the newer type, sleeping partners rotate, and a boy is fined if he sleeps with the same girl for more than three nights in succession. Elwin suggests that from the parents' standpoint, the ghotul exists to prevent children from seeing their parents copulating and to enlist the older children in the task of educating the younger children. He also notes that the ghotul

> fits in too with what seems to be a genuine psychological discovery of primitive peoples, that the less you see of people the better you get on with them. So, normally, a bride should be brought from another village; so, betrothed couples should have nothing to do with each other; so, if boys and girls are not shut up with their parents all the time, especially in the evenings when the father may be drunk and the mother tired and both ill-tempered, family life runs more smoothly and is more permanent (p. 23).

Elwin characterizes the Muria attitude toward sex as simple, innocent, and natural:

> In the ghotul this is strengthened by the absence of any sense of guilt and the general freedom from external interference. The Muria believe that sexual congress is a good thing; it does you good; it is healthy and beautiful; when performed by the right people (such as a [boy] and [girl] who are not taboo to one another), at the right time (outside the menstrual period and avoiding forbidden days), and in the right place (within the ghotul walls where no sin can be committed), it is the happiest and best thing in life (p. 97).

Some boys and girls pass through the ghotul period without ever having a passionate love affair, others may have one or two, and some are always falling in and out of love. Yet "the boys and girls form a compact, loyal, friendly little republic; they are all evidently very fond of each other; there is a large, generous, corporate romance uniting them. They do really seem to live in a sort of glow; the superb light of cleopatrine passion is absent, but so is the harsher glare of excited grasping lust" (p. 118).

The great majority of Muria marriages are arranged by parents, primarily on the basis of family and economic considerations. Parents take into account whether potential spouses and their families are hard workers, free of scandal and the taint of witchcraft, and obedient to Muria traditions. An engagement is not simply a contract between individuals, but an alliance of families and clans. Sexual romance is not considered to be good preparation for marriage: in the older type of ghotul, a boy and girl who are betrothed to one another are never permitted to be ghotul partners; in the newer type of ghotul, an engaged couple must practice mutual avoidance and must never have intercourse with one another. Marriages that do occur between ghotul partners who elope are more likely to end in divorce than are arranged marriages.

The Muria marriage ceremony is extraordinarily complex and extravagant in order to impress on the couple the importance of the step they are taking: "Marriage here does not, as in so many other cultures, mark an initiation into the mysteries of sex. It is not, usually, the binding together of two people who have fallen in love with each other. It represents instead the end of a life of sexual and domestic freedom and the companionship of young people. It marks the beginning of economic responsibility, a change of residence, a transformation of the whole way of life" (p. 182). Marriage rites and songs stress the parting of the couple from their ghotul friends, and the new social and sexual union of the bride and groom; but in contrast to ghotul sexual relations, where pregnancy is a disaster, the marriage rites attempt to ensure that marital sexual relations will be fertile.

A husband will not permit his wife ever again to enter the ghotul, but he may continue to visit it for some time after the marriage; nevertheless, "his sex life is undoubtedly curtailed" (p. 193). As with the Mangaians and Trobrianders, the Muria desire for marriage is not based on sex.

> For a Muria the sexual side of marriage is comparatively unimportant; he marries because he wants to have children whom he can call his own, so that he can have a home of his own, and so that he can have a partner whom he can regard as his own, over whom he has authority and a right, with whom relationship will be permanent and recognized.
> This is not mere individualism; it is part of the process of growing up. It is the discovery that sexual excitement is not enough; it is often . . . the still deeper discovery that romantic attachment is not always the best foundation for a lifelong union (p. 187).

*   *   *

> Every Muria contrasts the free happy life in the ghotul with the eco-
> nomic drudgery of marriage. "The ghotul is for happiness," they say at
> Nayanar. "The home is for work" (p. 188).

Marriage satisfies the longing for security, permanence, and children.
Although a married man must eventually stop visiting the ghotul, by
this time his "married life has become established and serene. Happiness has begun to illuminate the hard tasks of home and field. That is
why the Muria regard marriage of such supreme importance; everyone
must pass through its gate to the fulfilment of tribal and social life"
(p. 193). Muria wives are said to desire sexual intercourse daily until
the first child is born, after which twice a week is enough; nevertheless, when a husband is more ardent it gives his wife great satisfaction,
and she may brag of this to her friends.

With respect to the debate discussed above between Ellis and Westermarck, on the one hand, and Briffault, on the other, the Muria provide
some support for both sides. Marriage does not seem to be threatened
by childhood association *per se*, since divorce is very rare among couples who have lived in the same ghotul without being sexual partners,
but marriage does seem to be threatened by childhood romance, as at-
tested by the high divorce rate among former ghotul partners. The
Muria are sexually excited by unfamiliar members of the opposite sex,
"But this is nothing to do with the mating impulse which, for the
Muria, is normally divorced from sexual desire. . . . Westermarck's
contentions explain the popularity of the modern ghotul where partners must frequently be changed; Briffault's, explain the success and
stability of Muria marriage" (p. 197).

As among the Mangaians and Trobrianders, the primary sexual significance of marriage is that spouses obtain sexual rights over each
other. Elwin emphasizes the lack of sexual jealousy as a ruling marital
passion among the Muria, but this is not because Muria are indifferent
to adultery; on the contrary, adultery is regarded as a great evil, and
social tradition and religious belief render it so difficult and dangerous
that sexual rights are rarely threatened, making constant sexual jealousy
unnecessary. The Muria recognize jealousy as a problem and a threat
to marital happiness, and they direct the education of the children to
eliminate it:

> After marriage, the fellowship of the ghotul widens out into the fel-
> lowship of the tribe. Sexual communism is no longer practised, but a
> great deal of the fear that Descartes noticed as a root of jealousy is
> eliminated by the strong social feeling against adultery; Muria simply

do not commit this crime just as they do not commit the crime of theft, and therefore there is no need to fill one's mind with fears about the safety of one's possessions. Since love is not afraid, it is not possessive. Adultery is not only socially condemned, it is very dangerous; it casts a blight on the village, it ruins the ritual hunt, it diverts the fisherman from his catch, it brings wild beasts upon the cattle, and it causes the offenders to swell all over and perhaps even die. Social and supernatural sanctions alike make it unnecessary to be jealous (p. 217).

When Elwin writes that Muria do not commit adultery he means, of course, that they do not do so frequently, and he is not referring to male behavior in the period immediately following marriage. Wives are never happy about their husbands' visits to the ghotul in the early months of marriage, and may insist on having intercourse before their husbands leave the house, hoping to reduce the temptations that the ghotul offers. Marital quarrels and wife-beating occur primarily over domestic chores, not sex, but Elwin reports one case in which a husband beat, and eventually killed, his wife because of her infidelity.

Schapera's (1940) report on marriage and family life among the Kgatla, a South African Bantu tribe, provides some instructive contrasts with the Mangaians, Trobrianders, and Muria. At the time of Schapera's writing, the Kgatla had been influenced by Western civilization for a little over a century. Christianity and a European colonial administration have substantially changed traditional Kgatla practices: for example, parents have decreasing control and authority over their children; polygamy is becoming less common and concubinage more common; infant betrothal, once frequent, has almost disappeared; and premarital sexual intercourse is now the norm, whereas in times past it was severely condemned.

The Kgatla consider marriage to be essential for every normal person, and no one deliberately chooses to remain single. Schapera characterizes their motives for marriage as follows:

> Unmarried people are in tribal law always subject to the guardianship of their father, and are less highly respected than husbands and wives. Through marriage, therefore, they acquire enhanced social status. Marriage also enables them to indulge freely in sexual relations, undisturbed by fear of the trouble sometimes resulting from premarital intrigues. It permits a woman to bear children, without involving her in the disgrace that would ensue if she were unmarried; it entitles her husband to claim these children as his own, and so to rely upon them for support in his old age. It provides him also with a helpmate whose labour at home and in the fields is economically advantageous. The

woman, again, will in time become the mistress of her own household, a position that she values highly. Finally marriage, through the comprehensive daily intimacy it permits, affords both husband and wife personal companionship of a kind otherwise unobtainable in Kgatla society (pp. 38-39).

For the Kgatla, then, sexual opportunity is one motive for marrying, and it may have been a more important motive in the past, when boys and girls were rigorously separated at puberty and premarital intercourse was far less common.

In the old days, all marriages were arranged by the parents without consulting the principals, but now it is more common for a boy to court a girl first, and for his parents to open formal negotiations at his request; similarly, a girl's parents now normally consult her when a proposal of marriage is received. In arranging a marriage, parents take into account a potential spouse's capacity for work—rather than physical beauty—and also inquire into the character of the potential spouse's parents, especially with respect to ancestry and freedom from suspicion of practicing sorcery. Since marriage binds two families, not just two individuals, parents attempt to arrange marriages that increase harmony and cooperation between the families. While modern Kgatla boys may emphasize the sexual attractiveness of a potential spouse more than their parents do, "The Kgatla youth prefers sexually attractive girls for his mistresses, but demands additional qualities in his future wife" (p. 48). He considers a girl's behavior, character, cleanliness, industry, temperament, and so forth, and similarly, girls consider a boy's industry, ability, and the wealth or prominence of his father.

"When discussing with Kgatla the relations between husband and wife," writes Schapera, "I was continually struck by the open importance they attached to the sexual aspect" (p. 180). Although almost all Kgatla are sexually active before marriage, marital sex assumes a different character: "Coitus is no longer merely the closest form of intimacy in which two lovers can indulge, and the highest favour a girl can bestow upon a boy. With marriage it becomes also a duty that husband and wife owe to each other . . . since marriage is regarded primarily as a union for the production of children, husband and wife are expected to sleep together so that she may fulfill her destiny of becoming a mother" (p. 181).

Husbands believe that they have the right to have sexual intercourse with their wives whenever they want to, and many women complain "bitterly that however tired they were they received little consideration, and that if they refused or resisted they were usually beaten into submission. One, only recently married, said that if she had known what was before her she would rather have remained single, for then she could at least have chosen her own times for sexual intercourse, instead of having to yield to her husband every night" (p. 182). On the other hand, many women complain that they do not receive as much sexual attention as they want from their husbands: "Adultery is so commonly practised by men after a few years of marriage, when the novelty of perpetual access to the wife's body has faded, that women frequently find themselves neglected, and in sheer desperation may take lovers of their own, or resort to masturbation" (p. 183). Men pay little attention to female orgasm, and many are unaware of its existence or confuse orgasm with vaginal lubrication. Schapera notes that the frequency of masturbation among married women, and its absence among married men, indicates that wives often are not sexually satisfied by their husbands. Women complain that "men do not stay on them long enough, but quickly ejaculate, 'and then want to rest and sleep, while you are still feeling excited'" (p. 190). Schapera quotes a middle-aged husband who complains that his wife frequently awakens him at night, allegedly to talk, but actually to induce him to make love to her: ". . . when you married her you married her for sexual intercourse, and now she wants you to keep on fulfilling the promise you made to her through marriage" (p. 184).

Adultery is common among the Kgatla but is, of course, a breach of marital rights. Men are thought to be naturally promiscuous, and a wife has no legal remedy against her husband's infidelity unless it is accompanied by other forms of neglect or mistreatment. Men sometimes consort openly with older unmarried girls or with widows, but if a woman's husband is living, an affair is kept as secret as possible. A man may thrash his wife for infidelity or send her away or divorce her. He may thrash her lover if he catches them red-handed, but more commonly, he claims damages in cattle, which are paid by the adulterer. Kgatla adultery will be discussed more fully in Chapter Seven.

Schapera concludes:

> If we now review generally the sexual relationship between husband and wife, it is, I think, evident that there is a good deal of maladjustment, to which labour migration has obviously contributed greatly. If I appear to have stressed the unhappy marriages too much, and to have paid little attention to the happy ones that do also exist, it is because the latter, so far as I could judge, are comparatively rare. Few of the

women I got to know well enough to talk on this topic pretended to be living harmoniously with their husbands. Almost always there were complaints of sexual ill-treatment or of infidelity, and the character-istic female attitude was one of resignation rather than of happiness. Newly-married couples are often very much in love with each other, and the wives will speak most affectionately of their husbands, but after a few years little of this remains except in isolated instances. Many women grow reconciled and manage to lead a tolerable existence with husbands who are not unduly inconsiderate, others find some sort of relief by being unfaithful themselves, and some are acutely miserable. The men are not always to blame, for the wanton wife is common enough, and the jealous shrew is by no means unknown. Many men, too, are by Kgatla standards fairly considerate, and live peacefully enough with their wives. But the polygamous ideal still prevails and the virtually enforced monogamy of to-day has not been accompanied by the true companionship upon which a successful union should rest (p. 212).

In summary, unlike the Mangaians, Trobrianders, or Muria, the Kgatla do marry in part for sexual gratification, yet sex clearly constitutes the major source of marital misery.

In their review of the sociological literature on sex in marriage, Bur-gess and Wallin (1953) write:

The unique personal consequence of marriage in our society is the fact that it affords men and women a socially approved relationship within which they can attempt to satisfy their sexual desires. In the United States, as in most of the Western world, persons reach full sexual maturity several years before they marry. In the intervening time they may have had heterosexual intercourse more or less sporadi-cally or they may have engaged in petting, masturbation, or homo-sexual relations. But it is only with marriage that virtually all men and women can look forward to the possible fulfillment of sexual desire with some regularity and convenience and with complete respectabil-ity. Consequently, for the majority of men and women—and more particularly for the latter—this feature of marriage marks a radical change in a fundamental area of their lives. It is, therefore, under-standable why the sexual component should loom so large in many persons' conception of marriage (p. 656).

And yet,

. . . the evidence indicates that marriage is to some extent a failure in this respect for a large proportion of husbands and wives (p. 657).

Similarly, Robinson (1976) notes that Kinsey often seemed to sug-gest "that marriage succeeded, when it did, not because of but in spite of the sexual obligations it entailed" (p. 163). On the other hand, on the basis of a more recent survey, Hunt (1974:218) reports "a generally high level of interest in, enjoyment of and satisfaction with marital sex on the part of contemporary husbands and wives."

A few examples cannot convey the variability of human marriages, but perhaps they are sufficient to illustrate that marriage is not remotely adequately described as a pair-bond, that human beings are not monogamous in the sense that gibbons are, and that the human family and the gibbon "family" are not convergent adaptations. The issue is not that animal behavior is based on "instinct" and human behavior on "culture," although there is probably much truth in the argument that classifying together "men, parrots, penguins, and ducks . . . as illustrating the institution of permanent monogamy . . . only tends to mask the important fact that animal behaviour is almost entirely on a physiological plane, while almost all human behaviour is conditioned by culture" (Zuckerman 1932:222). Nor is the issue a cynical versus a romantic view of marriage, although it is very likely true that "the ongoing, sexually vivid, delicately intimate monogamous tie . . . exists—like mermaids, perpetual motion, and heaven itself—in the human imagination" (Tripp 1975:61). Rather, the issue is that in important respects the gibbon "family" and the human family are almost exact opposites: the gibbon "family" exists because mated adult males and females repulse from their territory same-sex adult conspecifics, and the "family" is both the smallest and the largest gibbon social group; the human family, on the other hand, does not really exist apart from the larger social matrix that defines, creates, and maintains it. For the great majority of humanity—and possibly for all of it before modern times—marriage is not so much an alliance of two people but rather an alliance of families and larger networks of people; among most nonmodern peoples marriages are negotiated and arranged by elders, not by the principals, although the latter may have a say in the matter; in some cases a girl is betrothed before she is born. Marriage begins with a public announcement—and usually a ceremony—and can be said to exist only insofar as it is recognized by the community at large. Obligations and rights entailed by marriage vary among societies, but marriage is fundamentally a political, economic, and child-raising institution, based on a division of labor by sex and on economic cooperation between the spouses and among larger networks of kin.

Ironically, the gibbon pair-bond and human marriage are alike in that neither is founded in any primary sense on sexuality. When Stephens (1963) writes that marriage is "a socially legitimate sexual union" he is referring to sexual rights and obligations, not to lust. Sexual attractiveness is rarely a more important consideration in choosing a spouse than are such matters as industry, ability, temperament, character, adherence to custom, freedom from suspicion of witchcraft, and so forth. Elwin (1968) reports that the Muria actually consider a person's work habits to be one determinant of physical attractiveness. Stephens points out that in many societies there are times when sex between husband and wife is taboo. The post-partum taboo on sex may last several years, and Stephens speculates "that in the 'average' primitive society (if there is such a thing), sexual intercourse between husband and wife is socially legitimate *less than half the time*" (pp. 10-11). While sterility is a personal tragedy among preliterate peoples (and perhaps most literate peoples), a much more common problem is the birth of infants who cannot be reared; a hunter/gatherer woman cannot rear more than one child every third or fourth year, and all known aboriginal hunter/gatherer peoples practice systematic infanticide. Since lactation does not suppress ovulation completely, and sexual intercourse can lead to impregnation, the post-partum sex taboo makes a good deal of adaptive sense. The very existence of the taboo implies that a husband is likely to experience lust for his wife (which may be reciprocated), and yet—since a hunter/gatherer woman spends most of her adult life nursing infants—his wife is one of the few women it is usually maladaptive for a husband to impregnate, since he ultimately shares to some extent the risks to fitness entailed by her pregnancies, abortions, and infanticides. Hence it may generally be adaptive for a man to harbor substantially less lust for his wife than for other women (other reasons why this may be so are discussed in Chapter Seven).

Human females are, in Beach's phrase, constantly copulable, and human males are more or less constantly potent and are sexually attracted to females without respect to the phase of their menstrual cycles. Thus it is not surprising that where people must marry to obtain a sexual partner sex is often one motive for getting married; but this does not mean that the primary basis of marriage is a "sexual tie," a "sexual bond," or "sexual imprinting." In most preliterate societies, marriage is "not erotic, but economic" (Lévi-Strauss 1969:38). As Kgatla and many Western marriages illustrate, marrying for sexual gratification is no guarantee that the union will be successful. Where premarital sexual intercourse prevails, as among Mangaians, Trobrianders, and the Muria, marriage is accompanied by a substantial reduction in the frequency of, and the importance of, sexual intercourse (providing no support for Beach's [1974] assumption that the evolution of the family would promote more frequent intercourse), nor is it sex that motivates these peoples to marry. Most often, marriage is motivated by the desire to attain adult status and recognition in the community, to have a household of one's own, to have children, to gain an economic partner, and to acquire exclusive sexual rights. Marriages may be based on love or affection, as is frequently the case in the Trobriand Islands and in Western societies, or not, as among Mangaians and the Muria; in the latter cases there is no indication that marriage—as an economic and child-rearing institution—suffers in comparison with the former. There is no cross-cultural evidence to suggest that sexual intercourse necessarily produces affectionate relationships (although it may), or even that sex is an especially effective means to this end;[1] nor is there evidence to suggest that the development of strong mutual attachments among human beings requires sexual intercourse, much less fellatio and cunnilingus, which Weinrich (1977) argues are adaptations to promote pair-bonding in circumstances where income is predictable. Rossi (1973) notes that women who have undergone adrenalectomy and ovariectomy, and who thus have been deprived of almost all androgens, exhibit "an impairment of the purely erotic component of sexuality but no impairment of the affectionate, anaclitic component. This is an important reminder that the affectionate component of sexuality is not physiologically dependent upon the erotic component" (p. 159).

Although marriage is not founded on lust, it does entail sexual rights and duties, the most important of which probably is the husband's right to exclusive sexual access to his wife, a right respected and perhaps enforced by the community at large, if not by the occasional male adventurer. To the extent that marriage has emotional sexual underpinnings, the most relevant emotion is not lust but jealousy, especially male jealousy.

The view that estrus was lost to promote marital stability is widespread in part, I believe, because it is often assumed implicitly that natural selection is for human happiness. Yet the relationships between selection and happiness seem to have been largely unexplored, and

[1] Even when sexual intercourse does appear to promote friendship, affection, or love, this may sometimes result more from the elimination of sexual tension and gamesmanship, which were inhibiting the expression of affectionate feelings already present, than from any simple process of association. Such cases would provide more evidence for the divisive effects of sexuality than for a "bonding" function.

where the subject has been touched on explicitly, opposite conclusions apparently have been reached. In his discussion of adaptive human aggression, for example, Wilson (1975:255) writes: "The lesson for man is that personal happiness has very little to do with all this. It is possible to be unhappy and very adaptive." Trivers (1974), on the other hand, implies that happiness is a direct function of the adaptiveness of behavior:

> Two kinds of nonreproductives are expected: those who are thereby increasing their own inclusive fitness and those who are thereby lowering their own inclusive fitness but increasing that of their parents. The first kind is expected to be as happy and content as living creatures ever are, but the second is expected to show internal conflict over its adult role and to express ambivalence over the past, particularly over the behavior and influence of its parents (p. 261).

It is tempting to conclude from this that ultimate causal analyses shed no light on questions of human happiness. But clearly this is not the case. It is a reasonably safe prediction, for example, that the great majority of men would be happier making love with a beautiful woman than being poked in the eye with a sharp stick, and, presumably, none of us doubts that this has something to do with the way selection operated in times past, and with the probable effects on fitness of these activities. And yet this is a rather trivial prediction, one that could have been made on the basis of classical Darwinian theory, inclusive fitness theory, species selection theory, or, indeed, the theory of creation advanced in Genesis. To make a more profound contribution to the understanding of human happiness, evolutionary analyses will have to consider seriously: the relevant data on mental events; the function of these events; and the nature of natural environments.

Consider first some actual reports of mental events. Here are James Harvey Robinson's (1921) thoughts on thinking:

> We do not think enough about thinking, and much of our confusion is the result of current illusions in regard to it. Let us forget for the moment any impressions we may have derived from the philosophers, and see what seems to happen in ourselves. The first thing that we notice is that our thought moves with such incredible rapidity that it is almost impossible to arrest any specimen of it long enough to have a look at it. When we are offered a penny for our thoughts we always find that we have recently had so many things in mind that we can easily make a selection which will not compromise us too nakedly. On inspection we shall find that even if we are not downright ashamed of

a great part of our spontaneous thinking it is far too intimate, personal, ignoble or trivial to permit us to reveal more than a small part of it. I believe this must be true of everyone (p. 37).

In this passage Robinson calls attention not only to the bewildering complexity of mental events but also to our reluctance to reveal more than a few of them. Why should this be? Perhaps a general proximate answer is supplied by Montaigne (*Essays* I:22): "let each man sound himself within, and he will find that our private wishes are for the most part born and nourished at the expense of others." Similarly, La Rochefoucauld notes that "In the misfortune of our best friends we often find something that is not displeasing." Our happiness appears to be predicated in part on the unhappiness—or at least the lesser happiness—of others: I want my wives to be beautiful, hence, since beauty is largely relative, other men's wives must be less beautiful. Indeed, "happiness" is defined by the *Oxford English Dictionary* as "The state of pleasurable content of mind, which results from success or the attainment of what is considered good," which implies that if "success" is relative, happiness also must be relative.

Now in a gross fashion these data are illuminated by modern evolutionary theory: happiness is relative because reproductive success is relative and selection has always been potent at the level of the individual. Neither species selection nor Genesis can so successfully account for the competitive aspects of human happiness. But the insights of Robinson, Montaigne, and La Rochefoucauld were not derived from evolutionary theory, nor does the presently available theory appear to take us beyond them. The evidence is primary, the theory is secondary; were the evidence different, a different ultimate causal analysis would be required.

Trivers writes that an organism promoting its own inclusive fitness is expected to be happy, while an organism promoting its parents' fitness is expected to experience conflict and to express ambivalence; but nowhere does he state how he derived these expectations. Trivers appears to believe that happiness is somehow doled out by natural selection as a direct and immediate reward for maximizing inclusive fitness. But predictions about the relationship between fitness and happiness must be based on an evolutionary explanation of mind and, more specifically, on an argument about the functions of happiness. Trivers provides neither, nor does he indicate how showing "internal conflict" and expressing "ambivalence over the past" have been shaped by natural selection to promote reproductive success. Durkheim observed that "man aspires to everything and is satisfied with nothing," which, insofar as it implies motivation for constant striving, seems to make more adaptive sense than Trivers's views. In any case, in the absence of a convincing argument about the functions of happiness, Wilson's claim that fitness and happiness are almost unrelated appears to be as tenable as Trivers's claim that the latter is a direct function of the former.

The issue of natural environments makes the relevance of evolutionary theory to human happiness still more obscure. Human nature evolved in a world without agriculture, cities, industry, writing, mathematics, science, medicine, or effective contraception. Is a contemporary person who devotes his life to maximizing his reproductive success likely to be happier than a person who neglects reproduction entirely in order to study and perform the works of Beethoven? Perhaps so, but certainly nothing in evolutionary theory forces this conclusion, since neither Beethoven nor most of the activities that are likely to promote reproductive success in a modern environment have existed for an evolutionarily significant length of time. On the other hand, some of the competitive aspects of happiness most likely are "innate": people everywhere consciously and unconsciously compare their lot in life with that of others.

Adult humans are more or less prerennially sexual and more or less perennially married, but this by no means constitutes evidence that the former evolved to promote the latter. In fact, many features of human sexuality suggest that it is ill-adapted to ensure marital happiness. Where human females are taught to view sexuality with disgust, the sexual duties marriage imposes are an unwelcome burden (see, for example, Messenger 1971); where females are more open to sexual feelings, their interest in, and desire for, sexual intercourse are likely to increase with age, whereas male interest and capacity decrease with age (Kinsey, *et al.* 1953). Furthermore, the existence of adultery in all human societies—despite the extreme risks that adulterous women may face—suggests that women are often sexually attracted to men other than their husbands. Finally, there is the human male's desire for sexual variety; in her review of the sociological literature on marriage, Bernard (1972) identifies the provision of opportunities to satisfy this desire as one of the two fundamental social changes required in Western societies to promote marital happiness. The existence of this male disposition cannot be readily interpreted as a marriage-maintaining mechanism, although it may motivate the accumulation of wives.

If natural selection is considered to be a benevolent force that operates to promote human happiness, the disparity between human impulses and the sexual exigencies of marriage is difficult to explain. If society is considered to be the source of human feeling, thought, and action, it is not clear why society does not create human dispositions in harmony with human institutions. But if natural selection is for reproductive success, not happiness, and society ultimately is a human product, human sexuality may be adapted, not to promote marriage, but to promote reproductive success in a marital environment. Perhaps the affection that sometimes develops among older, long-married couples in Mangaia and in the West requires so many years to ripen because it is made possible by the waning of sexual conflict.

Evolutionary games: ground rules

An evolutionary appraisal of human sexuality entails reconstructing the changes in behavior and psyche that occurred in the course of human evolution and analyzing the causes of these changes. In other words, we wish to know how our ancestors behaved and felt and the bases of differential reproduction in ancestral populations. The time span involved is so great it has no intuitive meaning. Furthermore, our ancient ancestors are gone for good; they have left relics—fossilized bones and teeth, tools, and ourselves—but they can never be studied in the field or brought into the laboratory, and even if they could be, the selective pressures responsible for evolutionary changes might remain obscure. For these reasons, Washburn (1973) suggests that the reconstruction of evolutionary history is better regarded as a game than as a science, and he recommends that evolutionary hypotheses be stated with varying degrees of confidence, as warranted by the supporting evidence, always keeping in mind that certainty cannot be achieved.

With respect to the loss of estrus, considerations to this point can be summarized thus: estrus was lost some time after humans last shared a common ancestor with any living nonhuman primate, and pair-bond theories are not notably successful in accounting for this loss. I shall propose two alternate historical reconstructions of the loss of estrus in the spirit, advocated by Washburn, that evolutionary speculations should be regarded, not as a science, but as a game. On the basis of current evolutionary theory, I propose to play according to the following ground rules: (1) Teleological explanations are not permitted;

evolutionary changes are not to be explained by the action of future circumstances or preordained goals. Evolution occurs in response to circumstances in the environment that result in differential reproduction; evolutionary change is constrained by the specific history of the lineage, by the randomness of mutation with respect to fitness, by opposing selection pressures, and by the necessity to compromise the demands of various adaptations. (2) No superorganic force is to be invoked to explain evolutionary change, explicitly or implicity, benevolent or otherwise. (3) Behavior and psyche are to be explained as adaptations to promote the inclusive fitness of the individual, not to promote the interests of another individual, groups of individuals, or abstractions like society.

A commitment to playing the loss-of-estrus game nonteleologically has a number of implications. Evolutionary changes occurred in response to conditions that existed at any given time; there was no inherent tendency for a chimpanzeelike ancestor to become human, and given different circumstances ancestral apes would have remained apes or become something else. Evolutionary change need not have proceeded continuously and uninterruptedly from an apish condition to a human condition: in some respects intermediate forms may have been less like either chimpanzees or humans than the latter species are like each other. Throughout evolutionary history one of the most important environmental features affecting selective pressures on hominid sexuality was the sexual nature of conspecifics: to some extent the evolution of human sexuality can be considered to be a continuous dialogue between males and females, a change in the nature of one sex producing an adaptive reaction in the other. Furthermore, the evolution of sexuality influences and is influenced by nonsexual aspects of the social and physical environment.

The problems involved in reconstructing the evolution of humans from a chimpanzeelike ancestor are far greater than the problems involved in, say, deriving gorillas from a chimpanzeelike ancestor. It is not clear how meaningful comparisons are to be made between humans and other animals, and seemingly straightforward comparisons may mislead more often than they enlighten; many times biology not only fails to increase our understanding of human beings but seems to have the magical power to make us forget what we already know. Words that originally referred to human social life often are applied to nonhuman animals; for example, "monogamy" referred to a kind of human marriage for over 150 years before it became a zoological term. There is no harm in such borrowings unless they are taken seriously and imagined to reveal deep biological truths.

Marriage and the loss of estrus

The failure to play the loss-of-estrus game according to the suggested ground rules invites the production of evolutionary scenarios such as the following one. Five or six million years ago chimpanzeelike ancestral hominids began to invade the savannah, and cooperative hunting by males became frequent and intense enough to produce substantial surpluses of meat, which set up the following selection pressures: to facilitate cooperation in the hunt, males had to reduce their sexual rivalries and to develop strong tendencies to bond with one another; at the same time, individual male-female pairs had to develop bonding tendencies in order to become effective economic and child-rearing partners—the female gathering, the male hunting, the proceeds shared with each other and with their children. Since chimpanzee females can rear a maximum of one child every fourth year, this can be presumed to have been the case with early hominid females as well, hence they had to evolve the most rigidly circumscribed estrus of any higher primate. Hominid females came into estrus about every fourth year, as chimpanzee females do, but unlike chimpanzees they did not experience postconception estrus, and their estrous periods lasted only a day or so, coinciding precisely with ovulation. This had a number of selective advantages: it permitted the mated pair to seclude themselves in recurrent honeymoons for a couple of days every fourth year during the female's estrous period; thus the male could be certain of paternity, which further reinforced the pair-bond and motivated him to great enterprise in the hunt, confident that his efforts would contribute to the welfare of his own offspring. Since a female was sexually attractive and active for an insignificant portion of her life, she wasted no time and energy in fruitless copulation, and hence maximized the time and energy she could devote to gathering and to mothering; similarly, males were freed to focus their energies on hunting and on teaching their sons to hunt, as they were not engaged in superfluous sexual activity with their mates. Neither were males spending time lusting after and plotting to seduce their neighbors' mates, since the latter were almost never sexually attractive and, when they were attractive during their rare estrous periods, had their husbands' undivided attention;

sexual rivalries thus were eliminated and male-male bonding was facilitated, rendering the hunting band a still more tightly knit, cooperative unit.

Finally, the male-female pair-bond was not sundered by the suspicions, jealousies, resentments, fears, anxieties, compromises, deceptions, disappointments, failures, nameless longings, named longings, misunderstandings, recriminations, divergent impulses, disparate fantasies, and conflicting moods—in short, the quiet desperation—that might have occurred in a more sexually active species. At the end of the day, when dinner was over and the children were asleep, the mated pair generally groomed one another for twenty or thirty minutes, and eventually fell asleep in each other's arms. It is this evolutionary background that explains why all human societies provide some means of seclusion for a pair-bonded (married) couple during the woman's estrous period—whether one considers the simple estrous huts of preliterate peoples or the elaborate estrous palaces maintained by wealthy Europeans. It also explains why even the most outspoken critics of capital punishment find it "natural" to make an exception of the crime of copulating with another man's wife during her estrous period.

The point of this exercise is to suggest that if the outlined ground rules are not followed, one can begin an evolutionary scenario at a plausible starting point (chimpanzeelike ancestors), add a plausible environmental change (increasing importance of hunting), and explain something that didn't happen as easily as something that did. As in the preceding scenario, in my loss-of-estrus game humans are derived from a chimpanzeelike ancestor, and the increasing importance of cooperative male hunting is considered to be the key to the loss. Like many anthropologists, I consider chimpanzees to be by far the best available model for a human ancestor of six million years ago, both because the biochemical data indicate that humans and chimpanzees are very closely related (King and Wilson 1975), and because recent field studies demonstrate marked behavioral similarities between chimpanzees and human hunter/gatherers.

The basic social unit of human hunter/gatherers is the nuclear family in which men hunt, women gather vegetable foods, and the results are shared and given to their offspring. No nonhuman primate regularly provisions another weaned animal; among mammals, systematic male provisioning of females is found only in *Homo sapiens* and in group-hunting canids (Eisenberg 1966). While the social behavior of social carnivores varies from species to species, it frequently shows conver-

gence—in food sharing, cooperation in hunting, division of labor, reduced dominance, and large home ranges—with that of human hunter/
gatherers, which suggests that hunting played an important role in
the evolution of human social life (Eisenberg 1966, Schaller and
Lowther 1969). Washburn and Lancaster (1968) suggest that the
nuclear family is a result of intensive hunting by males and the consequent sharing of meat. McGrew (in press) argues that since vegetables are much more reliable than prey animals, female gathering and
sharing may have made it possible for males to gamble on the hunt.
Lévi-Strauss (1969:39) describes the plight of the human bachelor
thus: "Denied food after bad hunting or fishing expeditions when the
fruits of the women's collecting and gathering, and sometimes their
gardening, provide the only meal there is, the wretched bachelor is a
characteristic sight in native society. But the actual victim is not the
only person involved in this scarcely tolerable situation. The relatives
or friends on whom he depends in such cases for his subsistence are
testy in suffering his mute anxiety. . . ." The persistence of marriage
and the family implies that they were adaptive for both sexes.

Although the evolution of human sexuality must have been affected
by the development of marriage, it seems unlikely that females became
continuously attractive in order to lure males into marriage. There is
no reason to expect selection to have favored hominid males or their
marriage-arranging relatives who chose as mates females with extended
estrous periods over females with more discrete periods. Extended estrous periods are likely to reduce a male's confidence in paternity and
to entail greater expenditures of time and energy copulating and sequestering. The human male's intuitive assumption that constant copu-
lability and attractivity are desirable in a wife is the result of a male
psyche that is adapted to an environment in which ovulation is not
advertised; ancestral male hominids, before the loss of estrus, would not
necessarily have shared this assumption. If marriage did develop while
estrus was being lost, young males may have pined for an old-fashioned
girl who was not in estrus all the time. Wifely virtues—overlapping
only partially with indices of sexual attractiveness—might have included evidence of sexual fidelity, youth, health, industry in gathering,
and skill in mothering. As discussed above, marriage is not in essence a
sexually based behavioral association between a male and a female, but
rather an economic and child-rearing partnership, embedded in networks of kin, and entailing sexual rights and duties. To the extent that
marriage is founded on sexual emotions, the most relevant emotion

probably is sexual jealousy; to the extent that marriage is founded on sexual behaviors, the most relevant behaviors probably are agreements among groups of males about sexual rights over females.

The chimpanzee as a model hominid ancestor

As a background for my evolutionary reconstructions, I shall briefly review the pertinent data on chimpanzee social behavior in the wild, stressing the evidence for reproductive competition.

(1) *Dispersion.* Very similar patterns of chimpanzee dispersion have been reported in the Gombe Stream National Park (Lawick-Goodall 1975, Goodall *et al.* in press, Halperin in press, Pusey in press, Wrangham in press) and in the Mahali Mountains of Tanzania (Nishida in press). A stable "community" of related adult males maintains a large territory with well-defined boundaries against other such communities. These large territories overlap a number of smaller adult female ranges; adult females are far less social than adult males, associate mostly with their own offspring, and do not participate in defending the males' territory. Males thus maintain sexual access to females by cooperating in holding a female-containing tract of land, a pattern that has been favored by selection presumably because the males can control collectively a larger area than the sum of the areas they could control individually (Bygott in press, Wrangham in press).

Interactions between males of different communities are hostile. Patrolling parties of two or more prime males travel together along territorial boundaries—silently and alertly, stopping from time to time to scan and to listen—apparently seeking interactions with their neighbors. If members of neighboring communities encounter one another, small parties retreat from larger ones; if two patrols are of approximately equal size, they aggressively display at one another until one or both retreat. The data "suggest that parties of adult males are motivated to approach individuals of other communities, even if they subsequently retreat upon finding themselves outnumbered or faced with more formidable opponents" (Goodall *et al.* in press). Patrolling parties attack isolated individual males of neighboring communities and apparently attempt to kill them. Goodall *et al.* describe three such attacks in detail, commenting that they were "characterized by extreme violence and brutality shocking to observers." Males also were observed attacking and threatening females of neighboring communities, and the females responded by following the males. In one case, the males threatened the female whenever she hesitated, indicating that she was forced against her will to travel with them, and Goodall *et al.* suggest that one purpose of these male excursions is to recruit females.

(2) *Female reproductive development.* Free-ranging chimpanzees may have birth peaks, but they do not have sexual seasons, and estrous females may be observed at any time of the year (Goodall 1965, Nishida 1968, Sugiyama 1969). According to Lawick-Goodall (1975), menstrual cycles last 37 or 38 days and are characterized by menstrual bleeding and periodic swelling and deflating of the anogenital region. Most matings occur during a period of maximal swelling which lasts about 16 days. Females exhibit small swellings at 9 to 10 years of age, and menarche occurs at 11 to 12 years, but females are sterile until they are 13 or 14 years old. Since observations began at the Gombe Stream National Park, 7 females have each produced 2 live infants, second conceptions occurring when the females' offspring were between 4 and 6 years old.

Copulation may be initiated by either sex, but generally the female presents in response to a male's display; the female crouches close to the ground and the male squats behind her, ejaculation occurring after a few thrusts during which the female usually utters short, high-pitched screams. The female then darts forward, away from the male, and the male remounts only if he has not ejaculated (Nishida 1968, Sugiyama 1969, Lawick-Goodall 1975). Adolescent estrous females travel widely, sometimes to neighboring communities where they mate with the resident males; although migrating females may be attacked by resident females, some apparently transfer permanently (Lawick-Goodall 1975, Bygott in press, Goodall *et al.* in press, Halperin in press, Nishida in press, Pusey in press).

(3) *Male reproductive development.* Males experience a growth spurt and begin sperm production at about 9 to 10 years of age, but "It is unlikely that young adolescent males play a significant role in the reproductive rate of their community for at least three or four years after puberty since they typically occupy a peripheral position in any association where there are older males, and are usually inhibited from mating a sexually popular female when superior males are nearby" (Lawick-Goodall 1975:86). By the time he is 11 or 12 years old a male

dominates most adult females, but at the same time becomes cautious around adult males, who are increasingly likely to threaten or attack him. The adolescent male is attracted to adult male groups, but remains on their periphery and seldom attempts to copulate when adult males are nearby (Lawick-Goodall 1973, 1975). Adolescent males engage in status contests with other males of similar age and rank, which usually are limited to threat but sometimes involve considerable fighting (Hamburg 1971, 1973, 1974, Lawick-Goodall 1973, 1975). During the final years of adolescence, between 13 and 15 years of age, males begin to attack or threaten lower-ranking males in the adult hierarchy (Lawick-Goodall 1973, 1975, Nishida in press). According to Lawick-Goodall (1975) and Riss and Goodall (1977), the following appear to be important determinants of a male's rank: (a) size; (b) the formation of coalitions with other males, which are especially common between adult male siblings; (c) the requisite intelligence to display effectively and to time challenges skillfully in order to take advantage of the presence of one's own allies, the absence of a rival's allies, or a rival's illness or injury; (d) since adult males may fight over rank (Lawick-Goodall 1968, 1971, 1973, Hamburg 1971, 1974, Riss and Goodall 1977, Nishida in press), and since Lawick-Goodall (1975:118) indicates that "when combat does occur it may be extremely violent and may result in injury to one or both of the chimpanzees," it may be surmised that fighting skill also plays a role in the acquisition of status.

(4) *"Promiscuous" matings.* Females with large estrous swellings may be followed and mated by a number of adult males with little overt aggression. The infrequency of male fighting in these circumstances has often been cited as evidence that chimpanzee males are not sexually competitive, but a more likely explanation is that "the more competitors present the sooner male combat will experience diminishing returns" (Ghiselin 1974:146). McGinnis (in press) found that the frequency of fighting in groups of males surrounding an estrous female was inversely related to group size; in one case, while the highest-ranking male was attacking another male, three other males managed to copulate.

Bygott (in press) suggests that among chimpanzees "competition for females is between communities of males rather than between individual males; within a community, mating is more or less promiscuous, and the larger an area that a group of males can control, the more females will be available to them." Bygott argues that collective defense of the territory is advantageous to individuals because a border-patrolling group of males is a powerful deterrent to males of neighboring communities and yet each individual incurs only slight risk: "Thus by merely accompanying other males on border patrols (which can be combined with foraging) an individual male can help to maintain his continued access to a large number of females." Excessive intracommunity aggression over access to females will be penalized, according to Bygott, because selfish males will be unable to enlist aid; intracommunity competition is to be expected only insofar as it does not jeopardize the stability of the coalition. Bygott suggests that the much greater testes/body ratio of chimpanzee males compared with males of other primate species indicates that males compete via "sperm competition," the reproductive edge going to the male who deposits the greatest number of sperm in the female's vagina during promiscuous mating.

Nevertheless, there is substantial evidence for intracommunity reproductive competition. As mentioned above, adolescent males—who copulate with an estrous female whenever they get the chance—can be easily intimidated, and are threatened by adult males and physically prevented from mating (Lawick-Goodall 1968, 1973, 1975, McGinnis in press). Moreover, there is also evidence of aggression among adult males over sexual access to an estrous female, including attacks by dominant males on subordinates attempting to mate (Lawick-Goodall 1968, 1975, Nishida 1968, in press, Tutin 1975, Riss and Goodall 1977); Tutin notes that in every case she witnessed in which a male successfully interfered with another male's copulation, the interfering male was the higher ranking. But the relationship between male dominance and mating success is not clear. Bygott (in press) did not find a significant correlation between dominance and copulation frequency, but he notes that low-ranking males tended to copulate infrequently and that in some cases high-ranking males monopolized an estrous female by aggressive displays at rivals (of the 6 male "courtship" displays described by Lawick-Goodall [1968], 5 also are threat displays). Nishida (in press) found that in one group in the Mahali mountains, containing 6 adult males, the alpha male accounted for 46.2 percent of the 383 observed copulations, and male copulation frequencies were directly related to rank. In two other groups, however, alpha males may not have copulated especially frequently, but Nishida notes that both males were past prime and may have copulated more frequently during their prime. Males also have been observed to disrupt copulations by attacking the female member of the pair (Sugiyama 1969,

McGinnis in press), a tactic occasionally employed by male rhesus monkeys (Symons 1978a).

(5) *Consortships*. Adult males have been observed to form exclusive consortships with estrous females, frequently traveling to a peripheral part of the range where other adult males are unlikely to be encountered (Lawick-Goodall 1968, 1971, 1973, 1975, Goodall *et al.* in press, Tutin 1975, McGinnis in press). Tutin reports the existence of "sexual partner preferences," and suggests that, in fact, most chimpanzee matings are not promiscuous. Tutin argues that the formation of a consortship requires the female's cooperation; she found no correlation between the frequency with which males formed consortships and either their dominance rank or the amount of agonistic behavior they directed at females, but male courtship frequency did correlate both with the amount of time they spent grooming swollen females and the frequency with which they shared food with females. Tutin hypothesizes that female choice is the basis of consortships, and adds that "If female choice is involved, it is of interest to note that the selection criteria appear to be social and caretaking abilities of the males and not their dominance status" (p. 448). But it is not clear that consortships depend on female choice. As Lawick-Goodall (1968, 1973, 1975) and McGinnis (in press) point out, males often herd females away from other males and force females to follow them to remote parts of the range by severely attacking them if they fail to follow or attempt to escape; that the female eventually follows without hesitation is hardly evidence for female choice, and McGinnis points out that it is often difficult for an observer to determine whether the female is following of her own accord. Neither is it clear that male rank is unrelated to reproductively significant consortship. McGinnis (in press) writes: "While the frequencies of inferred consortships do not show significant correlations with agonistic rank, there is a tendency for certain high-ranking males to begin consortships significantly more often during tumescence and maximal swelling than during detumescence or no swelling phases of the female's sexual cycles." Males in consort do not vocalize loudly and they threaten or attack the female if she vocalizes: "on occasions when the female's vocalizations attracted another male of higher rank, the consort attempt was usually terminated. On two occasions when a higher ranking male came upon a would-be consort in the act of intimidating the female, the high-ranking male attacked the suitor. On other occasions when a higher ranking male came upon a would-be

consort between bouts of intimidation of the female, the suitor failed to repeat the displays as long as the higher ranking male was present" (McGinnis, in press).

Thus, in addition to whatever sperm competition there may be, there is substantial evidence for aggressive reproductive competition among free-ranging male chimpanzees, including intercommunity aggression over territories, aggression during promiscuous matings, and aggression during the formation and maintenance of consortships. Bygott (in press) found that 90 percent of all agonistic interactions he observed involved at least one adult male. There is also evidence, both from the Mahali mountains and the Gombe Stream National Park, that dominant males are often more reproductively successful than lower-ranking males. This is precisely what evolutionary theory predicts: since males expend considerable time and energy and incur significant risks in status contests with other males, high rank can be expected to pay off in fitness; otherwise selection would have favored males who economized on time and energy and did not incur the risks of fighting. The effects of male-male aggression are reflected in socionomic sex ratios: although the male/female ratio is 1:1 at birth, the ratio of mature males to females in one community was 9:16 in 1972 and 9:15 in 1973 (Lawick-Goodall 1975), and Lawick-Goodall notes that because adult females are more solitary than adult males, their numbers may have been underestimated. There is no evidence that sex differences in survivorship result from anything other than male-male aggressive competition.

(6) *Hunting and meat sharing.* The hunting of small mammals by adult male chimpanzees has been described by a number of investigators; it is especially frequent among roaming male groups who cooperatively stalk, pursue, capture, divide, and distribute the prey (McGrew in press). One male may, for example, climb a tree in which a monkey is sitting while other males station themselves at the bases of nearby trees, thus blocking the monkey's escape routes (Lawick-Goodall 1975). There may be a partial suspension of dominance during hunts, in that a subordinate male may lead the hunt (Teleki 1973). The males divide the carcass and hence consume more meat than any other class of chimpanzee; but although females and subadults do not participate in the hunt, they do often receive meat from adult males (Teleki 1973, Lawick-Goodall 1975, McGrew in press). McGrew found that 80 percent of the instances of meat sharing consisted either

of males distributing meat among themselves or of males giving meat to adult females. Episodes of sharing generally are peaceful, but are not always so, and intense bursts of competition may occur (McGrew in press). Age and kinship appear to be associated with success in obtaining meat from males, but the effects of these variables are not yet clear; what is clear, however, is that estrous females are more likely to participate in meat eating episodes than nonestrous females are, and estrous female participants are more likely to receive meat from males than nonestrous participants are (Teleki 1973, McGrew in press).

Two scenarios

Female mammals become sexually attractive to males near ovulation because it is to the females' reproductive advantage to copulate at this time, and hence they advertise. It is difficult to imagine circumstances in which selection would favor males who lacked the ability to detect and to respond sexually to female ovulation announcements. Ancestral male hominids lost the ability to detect ovulation, not because the loss was to their advantage, but because it was to the females' advantage to conceal ovulation. It seems likely that selection would penalize a female who stopped advertising altogether, and, therefore, I assume that initially estrus was "lost" when females began to advertise continuously. Perhaps female sexual attractivity was based on the production of a pheromone under the influence of estrogen, as it seems to be in rhesus monkeys and perhaps in other nonhuman primates. If so, the loss of estrus may have begun with the continuous production of this pheromone. Once males were no longer able to detect ovulation by smell, selection would have favored males who were able to discriminate and to be sexually aroused by other indices of female reproductive value, an assessment males almost certainly made visually. In the absence of selection pressure to maintain it, the old, olfactory signaling system would have degenerated. Recent in vitro experiments demonstrate the existence of detectable changes in the odor of vaginal secretions during the menstrual cycles of some (but not all) women (Michael and Bonsall 1977), but there is little evidence that such changes have behavioral significance.

Scenario A. The most straightforward interpretation of the loss of estrus is suggested by the data on chimpanzee hunting. Estrous female chimpanzees are more successful than nonestrous females in obtaining meat from males. When hunting became a dominant male economic activity, as it did during human evolution, perhaps the costs (in terms of fitness) to females of constant sexual activity were outweighed by the benefits of receiving meat, hence selection favored females who advertised continuously and thus were continuously attractive to males. It must be emphasized that continuous attractivity is as important as receptivity, since the latter is relevant only if males first are sexually motivated. Proceptivity among constantly attractive ancestral females may have been a function of, among other things, male physical and behavioral characteristics associated with fitness; but perhaps receptivity had more to do with day-to-day fluctuations in male hunting success, as is the case in some human societies (Siskind 1973a), and female sexual overtures may have been motivated more often by pragmatism about protein than by sexual emotion. In evolutionary perspective, the possession of surplus meat by males is in some respects analogous to an emergency, such as in intraspecific fight or an attack by a predator, in that meat possession creates intense selective pressures. Natural selection for hominid male hunting abilities has been discussed by many scholars (for example, Laughlin 1968, Washburn and Lancaster 1968); but given males of equal hunting prowess, selection would have strongly favored those who distributed their surplus meat to promote most effectively their inclusive fitness. Effective use might have included sharing with kin and using meat to obtain sexual partners or wives. Optimal male strategies in distributing meat may depend in part on whether they were able to detect ovulation. If hominid males regularly possessed meat surpluses before estrus was lost, a good hunter might do best reproductively by exchanging meat for copulations with estrous females. If ovulation could not be detected, however, a successful male might be better off acquiring permanent sexual rights to a female or females, resulting in relatively high confidence in paternity, male provisioning of his mate's offspring, and the evolution of other kinds of paternal behaviors and dispositions. In this scenario the loss of estrus is a precipitating cause of the evolution of marriage and the family.

Scenario B. In another scenario, the family evolved before the loss of estrus, because of the advantages to both males and females in the division of labor once intensive male hunting was established. As I have already suggested, in choosing a wife extended estrous periods are not necessarily a desirable quality; but estrus may have been lost anyway, after the evolution of the family, because the loss was advantageous to females in an environment in which physical and political power was wielded by males.

Lawick-Goodall (1973:1) writes that "In the wild, chimpanzees probably always live in male-dominated societies," and in all known human societies political power is normally wielded by adult males (Gough 1971, Martin and Voorhies 1975). Chimpanzee male dominance is clearly a function of size, strength, and aggressiveness; the same probably is true of humans, but one can ignore the issue of aggressiveness and still explain human male dominance. As Hamburg (1978) points out, the importance of physical strength in human affairs should not be underestimated. Men are much stronger and are much better fighters than women, and among preliterate peoples men are regularly reported to use their strength in disputes with women. To explain male political dominance, all one needs to assume is that individuals tend to use the most effective tools they have at their disposal to get what they want, and that males choose other males rather than females as political allies because males make more effective allies. Bygott (in press) writes: "Male chimpanzees, perhaps more than males of any other primate species, have developed the ability to spend long periods in peaceful proximity to one another, to take collective action against intruders, and even to cooperate in the hunting of mammalian prey." Hominid males refined these abilities. As Lévi-Strauss (1969) has discussed at length, among preliterate peoples marriages result from reciprocal exchanges of women among groups of men (never the other way around): "the woman herself is nothing other than . . . the supreme gift among those that can only be obtained in the form of reciprocal gifts" (Lévi-Strauss 1969:65).

Most women will be married to other than their ideal husband, both because marriages are made and enforced largely by networks of males and because the most desirable males will be able to obtain and support only a very few wives. Thus selection favored females who made the most of such circumstances. Even if a female had little power to choose her husband, since humans do not live as gibbons do in small defended territories where a mate's activities can be continuously monitored, human females always had some power to choose their sexual partners. Continuous attractivity may have evolved in a "marital environment"— where a female could not often choose the social father of her children—as a female "strategy" for occasionally choosing her children's biological father. Although the fittest males are sharply limited in the number of wives they can obtain, given the opportunity they can fertilize an indefinite number of females. By not advertising ovulation, females may have minimized their husbands' abilities to monitor and to sequester them, and maximized their own abilities to be fertilized by males other than their husbands. To be adaptive, this advantage would have had to more than offset the increased expenditures of time, energy, and risk continuous attractivity entailed.

Thus, in Scenario A the loss of estrus is in part a cause of marriage, in Scenario B it is in part a result of marriage. I have little confidence in these scenarios; probably both are wrong, but they need not be right to be useful or interesting, they need only be as good as, or better than, competing explanations. These scenarios have the advantage of explaining why, although most adult humans are, and probably always have been, married to only one person at a time, human sexuality is in many respects the opposite of that of "monogamous" mammals. Human sexual peculiarities are less likely to be accounted for in terms of characteristics that humans share with many mammals—such as forming durable, affectionate relationships—than in terms of other human peculiarities. I have called attention to two such peculiarities: division of labor by sex, and marriage. There are other peculiarities and other ways to play the loss-of-estrus game.

Not infrequently ethnographers report that husbands and wives are genuinely fond of each other, and there may well have been selection during human evolution for the capacity to develop tender, specifically marital emotions. But intuitions about marriage based on the extremely artificial circumstances of modern industrial societies may be somewhat misleading, since in industrial societies, unlike the face-to-face, kin-based societies in which the overwhelming majority of human evolution occurred, one's mate is often one's only hope for establishing an intimate, durable relationship with another adult. Whatever their shortcomings, the scenarios I have presented are compatible with a good deal of evidence about human behavior and do not require the leap of faith that sexually insatiable females or gibbonlike pair-bonds require, nor do the proposed scenarios require the belief that natural selection acts to promote human happiness.

FIVE

Reproductive Competition

It seems odd, considering the acknowledged fact that so much of human behavior is sexual behavior, that psychologists have virtually ignored Darwin's theory of reproductive competition.

MICHAEL T. GHISELIN

THE AVERAGE ADULT human female's body weight is 80 to 89 percent of the weight of the average adult human male (Crook 1972, Schultz 1969). This disparity is much less than that of some primates, such as the gorilla, orangutan, and baboon—in which females are about half the size of males—is slightly greater than that of the chimpanzee—in which female weight is 89 to 90 percent that of the male (Schultz 1969, Crook 1972)—and is far greater than that of the gibbon. But Washburn (cited in Tiger 1975) points out that the convention of expressing physical sex differences among primates in male-centered terms—for example, the female's body weight is a given percentage of the male's—is misleading in that it ignores function. The female, according to Washburn, should be considered to represent the basic size of the species, adaptation to diet, and so forth, and the male a deviation from the female norm. Apart from primary sex differences in reproductive anatomy, a male differs from a female by possessing anatomical apparatus for bluff and fighting. To state that the human female is 85 percent of the weight of the human male is to average features in which the sexes differ and features in which they are the same. If one focuses on the anatomy that is primarily responsible for sex differences, it becomes clear, according to Washburn, that human males have evolved roughly *twice* the aggressive apparatus of females.

Darwin (1871) believed human secondary sex differences to be largely the product of sexual selection:

There can be little doubt that the greater size and strength of man, in comparison with woman, together with his broader shoulders, more developed muscles, rugged outline of body, his greater courage and pugnacity, are all due in chief part to inheritance from his half-human male ancestors. These characters would, however, have been preserved or even augmented during the long ages of man's savagery, by the success of the strongest and boldest men, both in the general struggle for life and in their contest for wives; a success which would have ensured their leaving a more numerous progeny than their less favoured brethren (p. 325).

Darwin also believed that women would have tended to choose mates who could best defend and support them, that men would have tended to choose the most beautiful women, and that structure, behavior, and psyche are, like the dancer and the dance, inseparable: males are not more pugnacious than females because they are larger, but rather pugnacity and size are consequences of the same evolutionary process.

While de facto monogamy is the general rule among humans, the overwhelming majority of human societies are classified as "polygynous" because some men have more than one wife (Ford and Beach 1951); there can be little doubt that among preliterate humans the male variance in reproductive success is greater than the female variance. A well-documented case is that of the Xavante of the Brazilian Mato Grosso (Neel et al. 1964), who subsist mostly by hunting and gathering but who also practice some rudimentary agriculture. Of 37 Xavante adult males, 16 had more than one wife. The chief had 5 wives, more than any other man. He produced 23 surviving offspring who constituted about 25 percent of the surviving offspring in that generation. The mean number of live births for women who had completed reproduction was about 7. Since women spaced children, mainly through infanticide, to 1 child every 4 to 5 years, and female sterility was very rare, the variance in live births per female was low (Neel 1970). Even more startling data on male-female differences in reproductive variability are provided by Chagnon (in press) for the Yanomamö of southern Venezuela. Shinbone, the most reproductively successful male, had 43 children, while the most successful female had only 14. Shinbone's brothers also were highly successful, and, thus, Shinbone's father had 14 children, 143 grandchildren, 335 great-grandchildren, and, at the time of Chagnon's study, 401 great-great-grandchildren. The Xavante and Yanomamö male-female disparity in variability of reproductive success may be more extreme than the disparity that obtained throughout most of human evolutionary history, but the fact of disparity is more important than its magnitude; clearly it has always been possible for some males to produce more offspring than any female, and these males succeeded at the expense of other males who produced fewer offspring than most females. Humans, then, are typical mammals in that selection has favored greater male-male reproductive competition; but humans are unique in the complexity and subtlety of this competition and hence in the male characteristics that selection has produced.

While competition does not necessarily entail violence, the existence of systematic violence is unambiguous evidence for competition. A brief consideration of the nature and circumstances of violence among preliterate peoples may provide a perspective on the competitive milieu in which human sexual dispositions evolved.

Violence among preliterate peoples

Four important conclusions about the nature of aggression can be drawn from recent progress in evolutionary theory and field studies of nonhuman animals: (1) The ultimate cause of intraspecific aggression is competition for scarce resources (Lack 1969, Marler 1976). (2) Selection among alternate alleles in Mendelian populations very likely can account for naturally occurring patterns of aggression (Maynard Smith 1972, 1976, Maynard Smith and Price 1973, Parker 1974, Dawkins 1976). (3) There is no "aggressive drive" or accumulation of aggressive energy that must be discharged. Fighting entails risk and even when successful can sometimes be an ineffective competitive strategy. Natural selection favors willingness or desire to fight only when benefits typically exceed costs in the currency of reproductive success, and in the absence of such circumstances, even a member of a typically aggressive species could live out its life-span in peace (for discussions of nonhuman primate aggression and dominance from this perspective see Clutton-Brock and Harvey 1976, Symons 1978a, Popp and DeVore in press). (4) Aggression is a much more important cause of mortality among free-ranging animals than has generally been believed; mortality results both from fights and from the withholding of resources critical to survival by territoriality and dominance, which Marler (1976) calls "quiet violence."

The great majority of ethnographies describe peoples who have been profoundly influenced by state powers. Since such powers eventually attempt to eliminate fighting among indigenous males, Service

(1967:166) writes that "for evolutionary purposes of the comparative method, travelers' and missionaries' accounts are still useful, whereas our modern dissertations by trained anthropologists are not, except for such rare cases as Chagnon's study of the savage Yanomamö." Relatively peaceful modern hunter/gatherers, such as the Bushmen and Hadza, are known to have engaged in intergroup combat when they were not surrounded by stronger peoples (Livingstone 1967, Eibl-Eibesfeldt 1974). Eskimos killed each other at the rate of about one person per thousand per year (Graburn 1968, personal communication). In his study of Eskimo life, Rasmussen (1931) reports that he never met a grown man who had not been involved in a killing. Studies of preliterate peoples who practice some agriculture but who have not been influenced by state powers reveal a similar pattern. Chagnon (1968a) estimates that at least 24 percent of Yanomamö males die in warfare. In his report on the previously uncontacted Hewa of highland New Guinea, Steadman (1971) states that he never encountered a male over sixteen years old who had not participated in a killing; he estimates the Hewa killing rate to be at least 7.78 per thousand per year. On the basis of archaeological evidence and the record of living hunter/gatherers and preliterate agriculturalists not under the control of a national power, Livingstone (1967) estimates that in a state of nature approximately 25 percent of human males die in fighting, and he concludes that human warfare has been a major agent of natural selection. Even among free-ranging chimpanzees intelligence appears to be an important determinant of male success in achieving high rank and, hence, reproductive success (Riss and Goodall 1977), and a number of scholars have argued that selection for skills in cooperative male violence has played an important role in the evolution of human intelligence (Alexander 1971, 1974, 1975, Bigelow 1973, Alcock 1975, Hamilton 1975).

In her review of the literature on the problem of order among peoples not controlled by a state power, Colson (1974) concludes that the lives of these peoples are dominated by the possibility of violence. Among all people living in proximity for long periods of time there are many accumulated grievances, grudges, and reasons for conflict. When fighting does break out, informants can always cite a number of precipitating historical causes. In nonstate societies people clearly recognize the danger of quarrels and feuds. They attempt to prevent them, and to avoid becoming involved in them when they do occur, because of conscious recognition of personal danger. Parents tell their children about the consequences of improper behavior: social control rests on the fear of violence. Colson suggests that whether or not folk beliefs about past violence are true, they are thought to be true and are repeated as cautionary tales. The anthropologist may see "people apparently behaving with kindness, generosity, and forbearance, avoiding disputes and sharing resources, tolerant of each other's foibles," but this is the result of fear: "Anthropologists have a liking for paradoxes and it should therefore be no surprise to us if some people live in what appears to be a Rousseauian paradise because they take a Hobbesian view of their situation: they walk softly because they believe it necessary not to offend others whom they regard as dangerous" (p. 37).

The purposes of violence

The sociologist H. T. Groat (1976) makes the following points in his discussion of violence among Western peoples: individuals compete for goods, services, prestige, and status; the need for "rewards" is not an absolute but a state of mind, and results in part from comparing oneself with others, hence the demand for rewards is limitless; power, which ultimately is based on force, determines how rewards are distributed, and the rules of reward distribution are the products of past violence; force is perceived as authority, and power as legitimate, primarily by those who profit from the existing system of distribution; even the definition of "violence" can be manipulated to advantage by those in power; and after formerly disadvantaged groups have secured power, they use this power to repress presently disadvantaged groups. Now if this perspective is not especially controversial in sociology, one might ask why, until very recently, it has not informed studies of nonhuman animals and preliterate peoples. (For example, in primatology fighting has been said to maintain the fabric of primate society, playfighting has been said to constitute the mechanism whereby monkeys learn how to avoid harming each other, and harassment of copulators has been said to function to direct the copulating male's aggression away from his partner and thereby assist him in fertilizing her.) The answer, I believe, is that a folk cosmology is at stake in studies of nonhuman animals and preliterate peoples. Everyone knows that Westerners often are motivated by envy, ambition, lust, malice, and so forth, but if animals and preliterate peoples are similarly motivated, traditional conceptions of the basic creative process in nature are jeopardized.

In Judeo-Christian tradition the creator is a fundamentally benign entity, the living world was created as peaceable kingdom (a kingdom lost to humans through weakness and error), and the good consists in adhering to the will of the creator which is manifest in nature. The influences of this tradition are evident even in apparently simple and straightforward statements about human behavior. For example, it is well known that wherever serious, organized human combat occurs it is the adult males, not the females, who fight. But consider the following statement, some variant of which is to be found in many discussions of human sex differences and their evolution: "In all known societies, the defensive role is assigned to adult males." In at least three respects, this statement implies far more than the original observations—males fight and females do not—that it purports to summarize. I believe that in each case, the deviation from simple description is aided and abetted by folk cosmology.

(1) The passive construction conceals the subject, the agent who did the assigning. When the subject does materialize in such statements, almost invariably it turns out to be "society." Perhaps we are predisposed to assume that human behavior is caused by, and serves the needs of, a beneficent, superindividual, noncorporeal entity or system which may be called variously God, nature, society, culture, species, or ecosystem.

(2) The way in which "role" is used in such statements frequently implies an organismic view of society, in which individuals are functional components of a more encompassing entity, much as the heart is a functional component of the body. Although this position has been steadily attacked in recent years, and organismic functionalism is an embattled, if not yet an endangered, species in social science theory, the literature on human sexuality and sex differences appears to constitute something of a functionalist refuge. I suspect that such statements remain acceptable in the study of sexuality and sex differences because of their latent ideological content. If defense is a "role" that men are assigned, the implication is that differences between men and women are to be explained by the apparently arbitrary process of assignment; hence women would be as likely to be assigned this role if, for example, it did not interfere with their performance of the maternal role (which has been assigned by nature, not society) or, perhaps, with their fetuses' performance of the fetal role. Thus statements that appear to be simply descriptive may conceal in their manner of phrasing far-reaching theoretical conclusions—which may or may not be

correct—but which do not follow of necessity from the observations they summarize.

(3) Finally, only the defensive role is mentioned, the offensive role remains unassigned. This curious imbalance is apparent in much of the literature on human evolution, living preliterate peoples, and nonhuman primates. Once again, I suspect that the source of this imbalance is ideological, and that by illuminating its causes light will be shed on major stumbling blocks in the study of human evolution. Consider two other circumstances in which offense is played down: in newspaper accounts of armed clashes in various parts of the world, almost invariably each side claims to have acted defensively; modern nations have enormous defense budgets and no offense budgets. In matters of combat and preparation for combat, humans attempt to present their actions in a favorable light, hence, in the modern world, there is an emphasis on morally irreproachable defensive activities. Probably defense is emphasized with respect to human ancestors, preliterate peoples, and nonhuman primates for precisely the same reason.

But why should we wish to inflect our prose with political rhetoric to portray imagined ancestors, preliterate peoples, and nonhuman primates in a favorable light? I suggest two motives. First, the behavior of our ancestors, preliterate peoples, and nonhuman primates often is treated as a metaphor for our own propensities. As Flew (1967) points out, if A evolved from B, A cannot be B; yet often the past becomes a metaphor for unconscious or repressed impulses, the dimension of time standing for depth in the human psyche: if our ancestors were apes, we must be latent apes. We do not wish to believe that our ancestors were pragmatic men who defended and attacked whenever the payoffs were likely to repay the risks, but rather to believe that they were peace-loving men who defended their families and homelands from the unprovoked attacks of predatory humans bent on conquest, rape, and pillage, because that is what we wish to believe about our own nature. Second, our ancestors, preliterate peoples, and nonhuman primates often are considered to represent the "natural," and it is impossible to reconcile traditional concepts of an essentially benevolent creative force in nature with the concept that the force that drives the flower operates solely upon the principle of expediency. But by permitting ourselves the intellectual sleight of hand of imagining a nature with defense but no offense, we sacrifice the possibility of understanding nonhuman animals, our own history, and our own nature.

Durham (1976) argues that warfare among preliterate peoples can be explained ultimately by the same reproductive cost/benefit analysis that accounts for violence among nonhuman animals. While traditional patterns of violence are learned, the ability to learn—to acquire culture—is the product of natural selection; hence, according to Durham, it is reasonable to assume that culture "evolves" by the selective retention of patterns that promote individual inclusive fitness in a given environment. In this view, intergroup aggression arises from competition over scarce resources that promote fitness, and warfare is prevalent among human societies because of the prevalence of circumstances in which the benefits of initiating violence outweigh the costs, not because humans are "innately" aggressive. Where the costs of initiating violence outweigh the benefits, violence is expected to be absent, as, in fact, is sometimes the case among living preliterate peoples. Similarly, Dyson-Hudson and Smith (1978) argue that humans defend territories only in circumstances in which critical resources are so abundant and predictable that the costs of exclusive use and defense are outweighed by the benefits of controlling the resources. In this view, the question is less, "Must children be taught violence?" than, "In what circumstances is violence likely to be taught?" Elsewhere (Symons 1978a) I call attention to certain limits of this perspective; but with respect to humans living in natural habitats, this model may well account for most intergroup violence.

Violent intergroup competition may occur over any scarce resource affecting reproductive success—land, animals, metals, and so forth—but often it appears to occur over women, and even where women are not directly at issue, the combatants may recognize that women are at stake indirectly (although obviously men cannot be aware of abstract scientific notions of inclusive fitness). For example, in discussing warfare to gain and hold arable land among the Mae Enga of the New Guinea highlands, Meggitt (1977) notes that Mae Enga men explain why they are willing to go to painful lengths to defend and appropriate land thus:

> We must have the land, they say, to feed our people and our pigs. The land is the basis (root, cause) of everything important in our lives. A clan whose territory is too small cannot expect to survive. It is not simply that its members may go hungry in bad seasons; they will also be vulnerable to the pressures of neighboring groups. A clan that lacks sufficient land cannot produce enough of the crops and the pigs needed to obtain the wives who are to bear future warriors to guard its domains and daughters whose brideprice will secure mates for their "brothers." Other groups do not dispose of their women simply to

establish affinal connections of dubious worth; they seek a more rewarding investment. And without wives, how can this clan tend its
gardens and pigs? How can we contribute to exchanges of pigs to attract military and economic support in times of trouble? Therefore,
men say, a clan has no choice but to use all means at its command to
acquire more land as quickly as possible, or it will have a short life
(pp. 182-83).

In Chapter One I contrasted "nutritional competition" with reproductive competition, noting that the former is not inevitable, since
nutritional adequacy can be specified in absolute terms, but that the
latter is inevitable, since reproductive success exists only in comparison. This contrast must be taken into account to understand the evolution of the psychological mechanisms that determine both what constitutes a "resource" and when a resource is felt to be "scarce." Since
it is necessary to life, food always is a resource, but it is not always
scarce, and hunger can be fully satisfied. Male-male competition for
wives, on the other hand, while undoubtedly exacerbated by anything
that reduces the number of available women, is the result, not of
skewed sex ratios or polygyny, but a male psyche that makes women
always a resource and always in short supply. Lévi-Strauss (1969:37)
writes: "Social and biological observation combine to suggest that, in
man, these tendencies [toward a multiplicity of wives] are natural and
universal, and that only limitations born of the environment and culture are responsible for their suppression." Among polygynous peoples
some men will be unable to obtain wives,

> But even in a strictly monogamous society . . . This deep polygamous
> tendency, which exists among all men, always makes the number of
> available women seem insufficient. Let us add that, even if there were
> as many women as men, these women would not all be equally desir-
> able—giving this term a broader meaning than its usual erotic connota-
> tion—and that, by definition . . . the most desirable women must form
> a minority. Hence, the demand for women is in actual fact, or to all
> intents and purposes, always in a state of disequilibrium and tension
> (Lévi-Strauss 1969:38).

Lévi-Strauss does not consider the male desire for many wives to be
primarily sexual. He points out that marriage is economic, not erotic,
that wives provide many nonsexual services, and that an adolescent's
sexual "discomfort" while waiting for a wife can be assuaged by such
practices as homosexuality, polyandry, wife-lending, and premarital
sexual freedom. Nevertheless, I shall suggest that the human male's desire for sexual variety also is "natural and universal," and may in part

motivate the accumulation of wives. Lévi-Strauss' argument—that the apparent insufficiency of wives is largely the product of the male psyche, not the number of available women—is equally potent when turned against his own contention that sexual gratification is not at issue: the male desire for sexual variety may make the number of available partners always seem insufficient and male "discomfort" inevitable.

If reproductive success is always directly at stake in male combat, in a sense women are always at least indirectly at stake, and ethnographic evidence indicates that women often are the proximate cause of fighting. A clearly documented case of male competition for women is that of the Yanomamö, described by Chagnon (1968a, b). Although the Yanomamö are not hunter/gatherers (the bulk of their diet is derived from gardening), they have been almost completely uninfluenced by national powers. Intervillage raiding is an established pattern among the Yanomamö. Raids are not initiated solely to obtain women, but this is always seen as a desired side effect, and "The Yanomamö themselves regard fights over women as the primary cause of their wars" (Chagnon 1968b:123). When Chagnon (in press) explained to the Yanomamö that some of his colleagues refuse to believe that the Yanomamö fight over women and believe instead that they really are fighting over high-quality protein, the Yanomamö laughed and said: "Even though we enjoy eating meat, we like women a whole lot more!" Villages regularly enter into alliances against other villages, and each partner in the alliance expects to profit by acquiring women. It is to a village's advantage to be large in order to raid other villages successfully and to protect itself from raids; villages of fewer than forty people cannot survive because they are so vulnerable to attack. As villages increase in size, however, male-male fighting and killing over extramarital affairs within the village becomes so frequent that the village must split, despite the resulting increase in vulnerability. If a group becomes too small to survive, it seeks refuge with another group, but refuge is never given without expectation of gain: women are always demanded in payment.

Hunter/gatherer populations probably are rarely as dense as the Yanomamö; nevertheless, there is substantial evidence among hunter/gatherer peoples of fighting over women. Mass combat among Australians of northern Queensland was described by Lumholtz (1889), who noted that "Many a one changes husbands on that night. As the natives frequently rob each other of their wives, the conflicts arising from this cause are settled by borbory [combat], the victor retaining the women"

(p. 124). "As a result of the borbory several family revolutions had already taken place, men had lost their wives and women had acquired new husbands" (p. 127). Among the Tiwi of north Australia, there was an "enormous frequency of disputes, fights, duels, and war parties arising directly or indirectly out of cases of seduction. If we may call this area of life the legal area, then over 90 percent of legal affairs were matters in which women were in some way involved" (Hart and Pilling 1960:80).

Among aboriginal Eskimos, competition for women was a major cause of fighting (Rasmussen 1931, Graburn 1968, Balikci 1970). Rasmussen (1931:199) writes: "men fight among themselves for a wife, for a simple consequence of the shortage of women is that young strong men must take women by force if their parents have not been so prudent as to betroth them to an infant girl." Wife-stealing was common, and men sometimes murdered in order to obtain their victims' wives (Rasmussen 1931, Balikci 1970). Fighting among Eskimos, as among the Yanomamö, often was cooperative, but cooperation seems to have been based on individual advantage. Rasmussen (1931: 205) writes: "The Eskimo . . . is ready to fight for his woman, the greatest and most indispensable possession of all, and every time he takes sides in a dispute he does so with the greatest risk a man can expose himself to." Among the Bushmen of the Kalahari desert, adultery frequently results in males killing other males (Lee 1969, Eibl-Eibesfeldt 1974).

Among preliterate peoples male competition for females is a major theme of life; nowhere are the relations between male and female reversed. Mead's (1935) description of three New Guinea peoples, *Sex and Temperament in Three Primitive Societies,* is regularly cited as evidence for unlimited human plasticity, although Mead herself makes no such claim.[1] Even this work, however, does not contradict the notion that women are universally a scarce resource. For example, both Arapesh men and women are said to have a "maternal" temperament, "But although actual warfare—organized expeditions to plunder, conquer, kill, or attain glory—is absent, brawls and clashes between villages do occur, mainly over women" (p. 23). The fierce, cannibalistic Mundugumor, among whom girls are said to grow up as aggressive as boys, "quarrel principally over women" (p. 186). Among the Tchambuli, former head hunters, where the temperaments of men and women

[1] Mead's findings have frequently been called into question (for example, Thurnwald 1936, Bernard 1945, Malinowski 1962, Blurton-Jones and Konner 1973).

are said to be the reverse of those considered to be normal among Western peoples, "young men and old struggle stealthily for the possession of women's favors—but the struggle is for the most part an underground one" (p. 262). Sustained fighting and killing are everywhere exclusively male activities, and "Quarrels over women are the key-note of the New Guinea primitive world" (p. 78). In summary, the evidence supports Berndt and Berndt's (1951:22) view that "the majority of arguments in an aboriginal society are directly or indirectly brought about through trouble over women."

Since it is possible for a man to impregnate a woman at little cost to himself in terms of time and energy, women need never compete among themselves to be fertilized; a woman is more likely to be prevented from copulating with the man of her choice by the threat her husband and/or male kinsmen pose to herself and to her intended partner than by competing women. Neither need women in preliterate societies compete to obtain a husband. Wives are always in short supply among preliterate peoples, and although some males may never acquire a wife, girls will almost always be married by the time they become fertile (Evans-Pritchard 1965, Mead 1967). Of course males are not all equally desirable as husbands, hence there may be female-female competition for the most desirable mates, but the intensity of such competition is limited for a number of reasons. First, aggressive competition entails risks to fitness. Second, among preliterate peoples marriages are made and enforced largely by male political networks, hence there is diminished scope for females to compete directly with one another for mates. Third, there is no reason to believe that men find a woman's ability to compete successfully with other women a particularly desirable characteristic in a wife, and an unaided woman cannot force marriage on a reluctant man.

A woman is most likely to compete by promoting her image as a desirable mate, enhancing her physical attractiveness, or advertising her wifely skills. A Mangaian girl who tries to acquire a reputation as a mat maker and hard worker around the house (Marshall 1971) is competing in that she is attempting to appear to be superior to other girls in these respects. Although ethnographic reports may sometimes have an androcentric bias that obscures the subtleties of female-female competition, it is certain that intense competition evidenced by organized fighting and killing—as is common among men—occurs nowhere among women.

When women do compete for a man it is not to acquire sexual ac-

cess, or even a husband, but to protect a substantial and probably irre-
placeable investment in a man. In an autobiographical short story, "The
Kepi," the twenty-five-year-old Colette suggests to a forty-six-year-
old female friend that she (the friend) bring her lover the next time
she comes to visit. The friend declines. "I remained appalled," writes
Colette, "at having caught, in one look, a glimpse of a primitive female
animal, black with suspicion, hostility and possessive passion. For the
first time, we were both aware of the difference in our ages as something sharp, cruel and irremediable." Married Bushmen women may
fight over sexual jealousies (Eibl-Eibesfeldt 1974), and Schapera (1940)
writes that a really jealous and angry Kgatla wife, whose husband is
having an affair, "may deliberately seek out and fight with her rival.
Village life is often enough enlivened by squabbles of this kind, in
which obscene abuse is freely bandied about, and actual scratching and
biting may occur . . ." (p. 208). Berndt (1962) notes that among New
Guinea peoples an established wife may fight a new wife introduced
into the household by her husband. But even in such circumstances,
female-female competition may be indirect: an established Yanomamö
wife may insist that her husband get rid of a newly introduced, younger,
more attractive wife (Chagnon 1968a), and according to Rasmussen
(1931), Eskimo wives sometimes hit their husbands if the husbands
were discovered in adultery. A woman's desire or willingness to fight
a co-wife or a woman with whom her husband is having an affair can
be expected to be largely a function of the degree of perceived threat.
As discussed below, it is not always to a woman's disadvantage to have
co-wives, and female sexual jealousy is not inevitable.

What is selected for in a milieu of violence?

Available data on preliterate peoples strongly suggest that during the
course of human evolution males regularly fought over females and
other fitness-promoting resources. In such a milieu selection is extremely unlikely to favor simple male belligerence, aggressive drives,
or territorial imperatives. Human violence usually is a complex group
activity. Even among baboons and some species of macaque, the ability
to participate in male coalitions may be as important as individual
fighting skills in achieving reproductive success, and, as discussed above,
among chimpanzees a great deal of reproductive competition seems to
occur between mutually hostile communities of males. The extraordi-

nary development of cooperation among human males reflects the historical success of cooperation as a competitive strategy: male reproductive success depends on social and political skills in planning, controlling, and managing aggression (see Chance and Mead 1953, Fox 1967, Tiger 1969, Caspari 1972, Bigelow 1973). Chagnon (in press) notes that among the Yanomamö a major portion of the variation in male reproductive success results from differential success in the political maneuverings and machinations associated with male competition for mates.

The literature on preliterate peoples indicates that headmen tend on the average to have a disproportionate number of wives, hence clues as to how selection operated in the course of human evolutionary history may be found in ethnographic descriptions of headmen. To become a big man with many wives among the Tiwi, for example, required years of maneuvering and increasing prestige. A man's assets were "friendship, 'help,' goodwill, respect of others, control over others, importance and influence" (Hart and Pilling 1960:52).

Among bands of Nambikuara Indians of the Brazilian Mato Grosso, chiefs are characterized by Lévi-Strauss (1944) as ingenious, generous, and good humored, and almost single-handedly responsible for group leadership:

> [The chief] must have a perfect knowledge of the territories haunted by his and other groups, be familiar with the hunting grounds, the location of fruit-bearing trees and the time of their ripening, have some idea of the itineraries followed by other bands, whether hostile or friendly. Therefore, he must travel more, and more quickly, than his people, have a good memory, and sometimes gamble his prestige on hazardous contacts with foreign and dangerous people. He is constantly engaged in some task of reconnoitering and exploring, and seems to flutter around his band rather than to lead it (p. 25).

During the dry season the chief orders the start of the wanderings, selects routes, chooses stopping places, organizes hunting, fishing, and gathering expeditions, determines relations with neighboring bands, and leads war parties. The chief has no means of coercion at his disposal; he governs only by consent. If he is less successful in fulfilling his duties than the chiefs of other bands are, members of his band may leave to join bands with more effective leadership. A band must be large enough to protect its women from theft; if it falls below this minimum size the chief will be forced to give up his command. The arrangement between the chief and his band is reciprocal: the chief provides security in exchange for wives. Normally only the chief and the sorcerer (if these are not the same man) have more than one wife, and the chief selects from among the prettiest and healthiest available girls.

Chagnon (1968a) describes the headman of the Yanomamö village in which he lived as the most astute man in village politics. The headman exercises his influence diplomatically, leading by example, not by coercion. If an enterprise is being considered, he may point out attendant dangers. The headman has high status in part because of kin ties and in part because of the loyalty of the villagers; he is a wise leader. Chagnon describes this man as unobtrusive, calm, modest, and perceptive. He contrasts the headman with an unsuccessful challenger for this position, who is characterized as belligerent, aggressive, ostentatious, and rash. The contrasting dispositions of these two men may, in part, indicate that the qualities of character useful in gaining rank are different from those that are useful in holding rank; nevertheless, if people admire calm, intelligent political perception and judgment in leaders they will look for some evidence of these qualities in evaluating potential leaders. Yanomamö raiding patterns require complex cooperation among men, and Chagnon notes that raiders may concentrate on killing especially "fierce" males. Good judgment, not simple belligerence, seems to be adaptive in a state of chronic violence.

Neel et al. (1964) describe the power struggles over chieftainships among the Xavante. Success in these struggles is heavily dependent on the abilities to cooperate and to take calculated risks, and a Xavante chief obtains wives as a result of his status. Neel et al. (1964:127) write: "The evidence suggests that fertility differentials have far more genetic significance in the Xavantes than is true for civilized man today. The position of chief or head of clan is not inherited but won on the basis of a combination of attributes (prowess in hunting and war, oratory, skill in wrestling, etc.). The greater fertility of these leaders must have genetic implications." Service (1975) characterizes male qualities generally associated with positions of power among preliterate peoples:

> Sometimes a person combines high degrees of skill, courage, good judgment, and experience so that his very versatility in a variety of contexts might give the appearance of authority of full chiefship. But even in such a case, this is not an *office*, a permanent position in the society. Rather, it depends entirely on his personal qualities, real and ascribed—power of the sort usually called *charismatic*. But just because

this position is personal rather than a post, he cannot truly command. He can only hold the position so long as people respect him and listen to him; it is a kind of moral influence that he wields (p. 52).

Judgment and intelligence are necessary not only in acquiring wives but probably also in the successful conduct of adultery. According to Balikci (1970), some Eskimo men were famous for their sexual enterprise including seduction, affairs, and rape. One such Eskimo frequently got into fights with the husbands of women he seduced, ". . . but he was prudent and avoided getting involved with stronger men" (Balikci 1970:161).

If the evidence of living peoples can illuminate human evolution, it suggests that during the Pleistocene sexual access to women was in part dependent on achieving positions of leadership. Selection probably favored political abilities, such as judgment, oratory, and persuasion, abilities to conceive and carry out complex plans, and skills in cooperative violence, including the evaluation of violent situations and the taking of calculated risks. It seems likely as well that in a milieu of complex, cooperative violence, selection would favor a male who was able to induce other males to take risks for his benefit.

Now the foregoing analysis may be correct without necessarily having much to do with male sexuality. Lévi-Strauss (1944) suggests that men are motivated to become chiefs not by their desire for wives but by their desire for prestige. But as noted above, Lévi-Strauss (1969) also has called attention to the human male's desire for a multiplicity of wives, and it is hard to imagine that during the course of human history men failed to notice that positions of leadership were rewarded with women. This is not to deny that status is valued in its own right or that prestige and access to women interact: women are both a reward and a sign of status. But the correlation of women and status cannot be arbitrary; the Nambikuara chief selects from among the prettiest and healthiest available girls, not because beautiful young women have been arbitrarily singled out by Nambikuara culture or society as symbols of status, but because men universally value them. For prestige to have evolved as an autonomous human motive—which it undoubtedly has—the effort and risk that achieving high status entails must have been recompensed with reproductive success. Hominid males who were satisfied with tokens of prestige that were arbitrary with respect to fitness must always have been less successful reproductively than males who "innately" preferred to receive attractive young wives. Environmental circumstances in which males pursue positions of status that are not, on the average, recompensed with women probably came into existence only very recently, in "artificial" state societies. The desire for a multiplicity of wives does not necessarily entail the desire for a variety of sexual partners, but I shall argue that, in fact, the desire for sexual variety almost surely is an important underpinning of the desire to accumulate wives.

In *Letters from the Earth* Mark Twain chronicles archangel Satan's reports to his colleagues Gabriel and Michael about how the human experiment is coming along. (Owing to his too flexible tongue, Satan has been banished from heaven for one celestial day—a thousand earth years—and he has decided to spend the day on earth.) Satan, a sort of celestial 18th-century rationalist, is continually astonished at the unreasoning perversity of human nature. For example, he writes:

> Now there you have a sample of man's "reasoning powers," as he calls them. He observes certain facts. For instance, that in all his life he never sees the day that he can satisfy one woman; also, that no woman ever sees the day that she can't overwork, and defeat, and put out of commission any ten masculine plants that can be put to bed to her. He puts those strikingly suggestive and luminous facts together, and from them draws this astonishing conclusion: The Creator intended the woman to be restricted to one man.

> *   *   *

> Now if you or any other really intelligent person were arranging the fairnesses and justices between man and woman, you would give the man a one-fiftieth interest in one woman, and the woman a harem. Now wouldn't you? Necessarily. I give you my word, this creature with the decrepit candle has arranged it exactly the other way.

But the ultimate logic of the emotions that underpin human behavior is a Darwinian bio-logic—the calculus of reproductive success—not an arbitrary logic of capacity: the reward mechanisms of the human brain are products of natural selection.

Hunting and sex

Among all hunter/gatherers, as well as among many other peoples, the primary economic activity of adult males is hunting, and nowhere do men hunt only for themselves; the fruits of the hunt are always shared with women and children. Lee (1968) points out that vegetables generally are available far more routinely and reliably than animals are, hence, except where the environment offers them no choice, hunter/ gatherers eat as much meat as they can but rely on vegetables gathered by women. Vegetable foods are abundant, sedentary, and predictable while game animals are scarce, mobile, unpredictable, and difficult to catch. There is, however, substantial evidence that meat is considered— sometimes obsessively—to be the most desirable food, and many peoples have a distinct word meaning "meat hunger" (see Gross 1975).

Men are often urged to hunt by meat-hungry women (Holmberg 1950, Maybury-Lewis 1967, Gross 1975, Marks 1977, Hames personal communication), and among the Eskimo (Rasmussen 1931, Balikci 1970), the Tiwi (Hart and Pilling 1960), and the Xavante (Neel *et al.* 1964) a man's hunting prowess is directly related to the number of wives he can obtain. Holmberg (1950) writes that among the Siriono

> Food is one of the best lures for obtaining extramarital sex partners, and a man often uses game as a means of seducing a potential wife. Failures in this respect result not so much from a reluctance on the part of a woman to yield to a potential husband who will give her game, but more from an unwillingness on the part of the man's own wife or wives to part with any of the meat that he has acquired, least of all to one of his potential wives. In general, the wife supervises the distribution of meat, so that if any part of her husband's catch is missing she suspects him of carrying on an affair on the outside, which is grounds for dispute. Hence, instead of attempting to distribute meat to a potential wife after game has already been brought in from the forest, a man may send in some small animal or a piece of game to the woman through an intermediary, and thus reward her for the favors he has already received or expects to receive in the future.
>
>   *   *   *
>
> However much men are chided by their wives for deceiving them, this seems to have little effect on their behavior, for they are constantly on the alert for a chance to approach a potential wife, or to carry on an affair with a yukwáki (young girl) who has passed through the rites of puberty (p. 64).

Holmberg notes that one Siriono man who was an unsuccessful hunter "had lost at least one wife to better men. His status was low; his anxiety about hunting high" (p. 58), although he attempted to compensate for his inability to hunt by planting more crops and collecting more forest products than anyone else and trading vegetables for meat. Holmberg began to go hunting with this man and to give him game, which the other Siriono were told the man had shot, and eventually Holmberg taught him to use a shotgun to kill his own game. By the time Holmberg left, this man "was enjoying the highest status, had acquired several new sex partners, and was insulting others, instead of being insulted by them" (p. 58).

Woodburn (1968) notes that among the Hadza of Tanzania a man "may find it more difficult to marry a wife, or, once married, to keep a wife, if he is unsuccessful in hunting big game" (p. 54). In his description of the Guayaki of southern Paraguay, Clastres (1972:264) records a conversation with an old man about a time fifty years in the past: "Quand on est de très grandes chasseurs, alors on peut avoir beaucoup de femmes et les nourrir toutes" (When one is one of the great hunters, then one can have many women [probably as wives] and feed them all). Among the Mehinacu of central Brazil, men engaging in extramarital sex "are expected to provide their mistresses with regular gifts of food" (Gregor 1973:245), which invariably include meat. Siskind (1973a, b) reports that Sharanahua women of eastern Peru goad men to hunt and reward successful hunters with sex. She writes that the prestige of hunting is not a vague goal; hunting "brings a definite reward, the possibility of gaining women as lovers and/or wives. It is a common feature that the Sharanahua share with all tropical forest hunters: The successful hunter is usually the winner in the competition for women" (1973a:95-96).

On the basis of an eighteen-month study of a Siona-Secoya village in eastern Ecuador, Vickers (1975) disputes Siskind's claim that in tropical environments hunting prowess is universally rewarded with sexual favors. While a single negative instance is, of course, largely irrelevant to evolutionary considerations, Vickers's argument raises some interesting issues. The Siona-Secoya Vickers studied had recently moved from a village where game was scarce to a new village where hunting generated the highest yields of meat ever reported in Amazonia, and Vickers notes that these yields could not be expected to continue for long. Although individual hunters varied from an average of 13.08 kg. of meat per hunt to an average of 46.83 kg. per hunt, an analysis of variance could not reject the null hypothesis that these differences in hunting success resulted from sampling error; a second statistic attributed 11 percent of the variance to differences in male hunting abilities. But informants did not report that extramarital sex was obtained with meat. Siona-Secoya men hunt so that their families will eat well: "For them meat is meat, not sex." Vickers concludes that his data do not disprove the observations of other investigators that meat is exchanged for sex, but do show that the practice is not universal.

In considering Vickers's conclusion that there is little difference among men in hunting abilities, the following may be relevant: (1) The most successful hunter averaged more than three times as much meat per hunt as the least successful hunter did. That an analysis of variance could not reject the null hypothesis may simply reflect the sample size, since short-term, "lucky" variation in hunting success is substantial (Hames personal communication). For a human to be a successful hunter requires years of training and experience (Laughlin 1968); if obvious individual differences in hunting ability do not exist, hunting is in this respect unique among human skills. Vickers does not report the amount of time hunts lasted, but in an area unusually rich in game, men may hunt until they kill something, thus tending to reduce variability in yield per hunt (Vickers reports no unsuccessful hunts). (2) Even if only 11 percent of the variance can be attributed to individual differences in hunting skills, in evolutionary perspective 11 percent is a major difference, and in any competitive activity small differences can be crucial (Symons 1978a). One would like to know whether differences among men were apparent to the Siona-Secoya themselves. (3) In considering exchanges of meat for sex (or anything else) the most important statistic is the amount of meat a man has to exchange, not his average yield per hunt (Hames personal communication). Vickers did not, apparently, sample all men equally, hence the total yields per man that he reports cannot be evaluated, nor does he discuss polygyny.

Raymond Hames (n.d.) has kindly allowed me to cite data, which bear on these issues, from his sixteen-month study of a Ye'kwana village and a neighboring Yanomamö village in Venezuela. Hames weighed all kills made by all hunters in the two villages for 215 days (a 100 percent sample). Hunting success varied among the men from an average of .45 kg. per hour to an average of 7.2 kg. per hour; the total yields for individual men during this period ranged from 22.5 kg. to 1004.9 kg., which in large part reflects enormous differences in the frequencies with which the men hunted. Informants agreed closely with one another in their estimates of the hunting prowess of individual men, and these assessments were generally in agreement with Hames's own quantitative record. With respect to the relation between hunting and sex, the following anecdote may be of interest. A young Yanomamö couple with one child who had lived in a Ye'kwana household for one and one-half years were asked to leave by the head of the household because the eighteen-year-old husband was a poor hunter and did not contribute enough meat. As in the Siriono case discussed above, this boy attempted to enhance his economic value by working hard at gardening, canoe making, fishing, and various household tasks, but in the eyes of the head of the household these efforts could not compensate for the boy's failure to bring in meat. A twenty-year-old, unmarried male Yanomamö, an excellent young hunter, told Hames that he was going to take the boy's wife away from him. He said: "He's not even a man [referring to his lack of hunting prowess, not his age]. She will leave him and come to me because he can't hunt and I can." The best hunter in the villages was the only man to have two wives; a second man, who had had two wives but who had been persuaded by a missionary to give one to his brother, was regarded as having been a great hunter in his prime.

Conclusions

The evidence suggests that in hunting, as in fighting, human males are effectively in competition for females, and that often there are substantial differences among males in competitive abilities. For an evolutionary perspective the fundamental issue is not the relative contributions vegetables and meat make in the diets of hunter/gatherer peoples: evolution results from individual differences. Skill plays a far greater role in hunting than in gathering, and skill plays an important role in fighting as well. Sex differences in the significance of skill for reproductive success are apparent in children's play (Symons 1978a): among hunter/gatherer peoples, boys spend an enormous amount of time playing at hunting and fighting and thereby perfect skills in these activities. But because women's activities typically require less skill than men's activities do, they do not need as much prior play, and most ethnographers report that boys play more than girls do (in this respect humans are typical primates). Girls can begin to make a significant economic contribution much earlier in life than boys can, so while boys play at hunting and fighting, girls assist their mothers in gathering, infant care, and other domestic tasks. Available evidence suggests that men vary much more in hunting abilities than women do in gathering abilities, hence, as with violence, selection acts far more intensely among males than among females. Thus, as with most animal species, "At every moment in its game of life the masculine sex is playing for higher stakes" (Williams 1975:138). Mead (1967) writes:

. . . the small girl learns that she is a female and that if she simply waits, she will some day be a mother. The small boy learns that he is a male and that if he is successful in manly deeds some day he will be a man . . . (p. 80).

*   *   *

[He] has to face the need to grow, to learn, to master a great variety of skills and strengths, before he can compete with grown males. . . . Growing-up may be phrased in terms of physical growth, or taking a head, or having collected enough property to purchase a wife. But almost always the attainment of the full rights of a male to the favours of women becomes conditional on his learning to act in specified ways, some of which will seem difficult . . . he is taught, sometimes explicitly, sometimes implicitly, that there is a long, long road between the lusty, exhibitionistic self-confidence of the five-year-old and the man who can win and keep a woman in a world filled with other men (pp. 156-67).

*   *   *

But the little girl meets no such challenge. The taboos and the etiquette enjoined upon her are ways of protecting her already budding feminity from adult males. . . . Upon the initial uncertainty of her final maternal rôle is built a rising curve of sureness, which is finally crowned—in primitive and simple societies, in which every woman marries—with childbearing (pp. 157-58).

The evidence suggests, then, that for millions of years hominid males and females pursued substantially different reproductive "strategies" and typically exhibited very different behaviors: throughout most of human evolutionary history, hunting, fighting, and that elusive activity, "politics," were highly competitive, largely male domains. It is not a simple question of high female parental investment and male competition for females: males and females invested in different ways. Not only did males hunt while females gathered, but, if warfare was often over land and other scarce resources from which the winning males' offspring benefited, male fighting was in part parental investment; that is, like hunting and gathering, fighting and nurturing were part of the human division of labor by sex. Far more than in any other animal species, natural, sexual, and artificial selection were intertwined and perhaps inseparable during the course of human evolution. Does the Nambikuara chief who is given extra wives by his group in exchange for his leadership (partly in hunting and warfare) provide evidence about natural, sexual, or artificial selection?

Even accepting Washburn's assessment that human males possess roughly twice the fighting anatomy that females possess, the degree of sexual dimorphism in modern human populations seems intuitively to be rather small relative to that of many animal species, especially considering that human males and females differed in patterns of parental investment as well as in the intensity of intrasexual competition. Given the nature of male investment, one might expect that increasing male parental investment in the hominid lineage would have increased, rather than decreased, sexual dimorphism. (In fact, human male parental investment undoubtedly exceeds male chimpanzee investment, and humans are more sexually dimorphic than chimpanzees in body size.) One interpretation of the apparently slight extent of human sexual dimorphism is simply that I have overestimated the disparity between male and female variability in reproductive success and/or the differences between typical male and female activities. Another possibility is that selection for efficiency in bearing and in caring for infants favored large females (Ralls 1976), and thus sex differences in body size substantially underestimate the intensity of male reproductive competition during the course of human evolutionary history. But there are at least two other interpretations.

(1) Some selection pressures on males may not have resulted in the evolution of physical sex differences. Human patterns of hunting and fighting are unique in the complexity of social cooperation they entail, in the degree to which these complexities must be learned, and in their dependence on tool traditions. In most animal species, intrasexual competition or sex differences in foraging patterns result in selection for characteristics whose utility is largely specific to intrasexual competition or to a particular foraging pattern, and hence in the evolution of physical sex differences; but many of the abilities that selection favored in human hunting, fighting, and politics may be adaptive for typical female activities as well, even though it is rarely adaptive for females to incur the risks of hunting or intrasexual competition. Every individual has both a male and a female parent, and many of the effects of intrasexual competition and hunting among males may have been manifested equally in male and female offspring.

(2) Some effects of intrasexual selection among males may be "invisible." For example, the selective pressures of hunting may in some respects have countered the selective pressures of fighting. Washburn and Lancaster (1968) suggest that the very narrow range of stature seen in the fossil record of Pleistocene humans reflects the demands of hunting; if so, this may limit the sex differences in body size that would have resulted from male fighting alone. But perhaps more important,

the unique nature of human male competition may have promoted sex differences not in the size of anatomical structures, but in the brain, which, with present techniques of analysis, are "invisible." For example, all nonhuman primate species with large sex differences in body size also exhibit major male-female differences in the size of the canine teeth; the absence of this sex difference among humans does not indicate that ancestral human males did not fight more than ancestral human females did, but simply that males did not fight with their teeth. There may be substantial sex differences in the human brain associated with violence. If men who have been differentially reproductively successful throughout human evolutionary history owed their success more to their brains than to their body size, the nonhuman animal perspective—which suggests that the intensity of intrasexual competition will be reflected in the magnitude of sex differences in body size and natural weapons—is likely to be misleading when applied to humans. With respect to sexual behaviors and dispositions, I shall argue that in some ways selection acted oppositely on human males and females, and that these differing selective pressures are evidenced in sex differences in the brain and are reflected in behavior and psyche but not so much in easily observed and measured anatomy.

SIX

Sexual Choice

. . . many men are goats and can't help committing adultery when they get a chance; whereas there are numbers of men who, by temperament, can keep their purity and let an opportunity go by if the woman lacks in attractiveness.

MARK TWAIN

SELECTION CAN BE EXPECTED to favor humans who prefer to copulate with and to marry the fittest members of the opposite sex, and since human female parental investment may typically exceed male investment, females might be expected to be choosier than males. By and large, these expectations probably are fulfilled, but the matter is more involved than it may at first appear. Crook (1972) argues that among preliterate peoples, and by inference among our Pleistocene ancestors, the constraints of marriage rules and restrictions leave little room for mate selection based on personal choice. Indeed, the fact that marriages normally are negotiated by elder kinsmen narrows the scope for personal choice of spouses still further, and especially narrows the scope for female choice. Thus, one might argue, as Crook seems to do, that during the course of human evolution opportunities in which individuals could make their own choices were encountered so infrequently that selection favored sexual indifference and complete acquiescence to the decisions of elders or to the dictates of culture and society. To explain why this did not occur, it is necessary to distinguish the outward behaviors associated with marriage and copulation from the underlying psychology of sexual choice; to distinguish, that is, between action and desire.

Because sexual emotions are closer to the genes than sexual behaviors are, emotions are central to an evolutionary perspective on sexuality. The organism—at least the human organism—is neither a passive mediator between stimulus and response nor a mindless vehicle of culture, but an active assessor and planner. Psyche becomes important precisely where the external environment is unpredictable or complex. The overwhelming majority of an organism's biological processes and energetic transactions with the external world are unconscious; in fact, it appears that every process—digestion, oxygen transport, breathing, reflex blinking—that can be carried out unconsciously is more efficiently carried out this way, and conscious processes seem to become unconscious whenever possible. In the learning of a complex skill, for example, component movements are practiced until they no longer require attention—until they become automatic, or reflexlike—and consciousness then is freed to monitor larger groupings of components and to plan future strategies (see Symons 1978a). In short, mind is usually about the rare, the difficult, and the future; the everyday becomes unconscious habit. Proust remarked that love, "ever unsatisfied, lives always in the moment that is about to come," and Montaigne observed that "Nature makes us live in the future, not the present." It is the "us," which is living in the future, rather than the observable body, which is behaving in the present, that is of primary importance in understanding human sexuality. Sexual experience is largely adapted to the exceptional. We react consciously to the rare opportunity or threat, and we fantasize about desired and feared states of affairs, imagining how the former might be realized, the latter coped with or avoided.

The primary issue with respect to sexual choice, then, is not whether our ancestors usually were able to choose their own mates, but whether they sometimes had a voice in mate choice, and, still more important, whether they were occasionally able to choose their sexual partners. All available evidence points to the conclusion that everywhere the complexities of human social life provide scope for the occasional satisfaction of desires, hence selection can be expected to favor the existence of desires, though they may rarely be translated into behavior. In this regard it is crucial to distinguish between sex and marriage. Although the opportunities for individuals to arrange their own marriages—at least their initial marriages—may have been slight, there must have been much more scope for individuals of both sexes to arrange their own copulations. As argued in Chapter Four, human sexual dispositions should be considered not so much adaptations to strengthen marriage as adaptations to maximize reproductive success in an environment in which marriage is ubiquitous. Although individual humans constrain one another's sexual activities to an unprecedented degree, the complexities of human social life everywhere provide opportunities for occasionally evading such constraints. One's own evasions must be planned for, the evasions of others guarded against.

If modern ethnographies are reliable guides to the past, in ancestral populations a young person's initial marriage probably was arranged by elders, especially male elders. Now the *ultimate* basis for the decisions that elders made was their own genetic "interests," which could not have been identical with the genetic "interests" of the principals. Trivers (1974) calls attention to the existence of inevitable "conflicts" between parent and offspring owing to the fact that they are imperfectly related genetically. Choice of spouse may constitute one such conflict. Indeed, the literature on preliterate peoples suggests that all the individuals involved in a marriage arrangement attempt to influence the marriage for their own ends. Usually, this means that men use women for barter to get other women, but women themselves exercise whatever influence they can. This point is clearly illustrated in Hart and Pilling's (1960) account of sex and marriage among the Tiwi. Although a Tiwi woman had no power to choose her first mate, after her husband's death she sometimes exercised considerable influence in making subsequent marriages (also see Goodale 1971). A young Tiwi male could not exercise control over his mother and sisters because a female was controlled by her husband or father. Later in life, however, a man with power and influence might gain some control over the remarriages of his elderly sisters and mother. Hart and Pilling (1960:24) write: "Whenever this occurred, although the resulting situation might have the superficial appearance of clan solidarity—with sons, mothers, brothers, and sisters all acting and planning together as a partnership—such surface appearance was illusory. The motivations involved in it were scarcely altruistic desires on the part of the brothers to look after their mothers and elderly sisters, but rather efforts by the brothers to use to advantage, in their intricate political schemes, some women of their own clan. . . ." But when Hart and Pilling write "altruistic desires" and "use to advantage" they are referring to proximate human motives; the relationship of these motives to fitness and ultimate causation is an open question (see Chapter Two).

Offspring receive many benefits from their parents, and it is possible that in some parent-offspring conflicts there is not, in fact, a great deal of "conflict" in terms of fitness. Adults' far greater knowledge and experience may result, on the average, in a better choice of spouse than an offspring would be likely to make on its own. Williams (1966) has even suggested that the hypertrophy of the human cerebral cortex is not the result of selection for adult intelligence but rather is a by-product of selection for the abilities to understand and to respond to parental verbal commands in childhood. Whether or not this hypothesis is correct (I doubt that it is), it provides a useful corrective to excessive emphasis on parent-offspring conflict. If a child wants to play with the saber-toothed tiger and the child's parent has a different view of the matter, the parent may be 100 percent right and the child 100 percent wrong, even though they share only 50 percent of their genes. Yet it is the existence of an environment containing watchful parents that permitted the evolution of juvenile desires to experiment with playmates.

Until very recently, selection occurred within a fairly narrow range of environments, and impulses selected in one set of circumstances may be maladaptive in others. Consider, for example, the potential parent-offspring conflict Trivers (1974) outlines over weaning. Mothers may be selected to want to wean an offspring when it is X months old, whereas offspring may be selected to want to nurse beyond X months. But if offspring are, in fact, *always* weaned before the theoretical "ideal" age—from their genetic point of view—selection would have no way of "knowing" what the ideal age is, and it might favor the relatively simple infant disposition *always* to resist weaning. If such an infant were raised in an artificial environment in which it was allowed to nurse as long as it liked, its disposition always to resist weaning would certainly prove maladaptive. Similarly, in an environment in which young people have relatively little say in spouse choice, selection might favor strong adolescent emotions about members of the opposite sex, emotions that have been designed by selection specifically to function in a milieu in which an adolescent's actual behavior will be constrained by the necessity to compromise with elders. Just as a child's desire to play with the saber-toothed tiger or always to resist weaning might be adaptive precisely because social constraints and safeguards exist in a natural environment, so an adolescent's desire to marry person A rather than person B (whom the elders favor) might be adaptive even if B is, in many cases, the better mate choice. An adolescent's desires may be designed to function primarily as one important item of information that the elders will consider in reaching their decision. These emotions may prove to be poor guides when adolescents are free to choose their own mates. Elwin's data, discussed in Chapter Four, for example, indicate that arranged Muria marriages are less likely to end in divorce than elopements are.

In considering the circumstances that promote human sexual arousal it is useful to keep in mind: first, the concept of a natural environment; and second, that arousal is experience as well as behavior.

Sexual arousal

Kinsey *et al.* (1948, 1953) reported that men are sexually aroused far more easily and frequently by visual stimuli than women are, and they pointed out that everywhere and always, pornography is produced for a male audience. Furthermore, Kinsey *et al.* found that males almost universally fantasize visually during masturbation, and require visual fantasy to orgasm, whereas two-thirds of their female informants did not fantasize during masturbation. But recently, a number of investigators have challenged Kinsey's conclusions: the current trend in the literature on human sexuality is to minimize sex differences in visual arousal and to attribute Kinsey's findings to the sexual repression of women in that era and to Kinsey's reliance on retrospective reports instead of immediate reports or physiological measurement.

As with theories of the evolution of female orgasm and the loss of estrus, much of the recent scientific writing about visual arousal implies that underlying the everyday world—in which there appear to be enormous sex differences in sexual response to, and interest in, visual stimuli—is a deeper reality in which males and females are virtually identical. Some insight into this strange state of affairs can be gained from a major American sex researcher's response to recent findings that women are sexually aroused by pornography: he remarked that these new data eliminate the last claim for human female hyposexuality. In my view, as long as the matter is phrased in terms of hyper- versus hyposexuality (with hypersexuality assumed to be good or desirable), and as long as evidence for sex differences in sexuality is felt to be necessarily detrimental to women, experiments will continue to be designed, and their results interpreted, to emphasize similarities between men and women, and the everyday world will continue to suffer neglect.

According to *The Report of the U.S. Commission on Obscenity and Pornography* (1970), the pornography industry in the United

States—including books, periodicals, and motion pictures—grosses between $537 and $574 million annually, almost entirely from men. The Commission characterized patrons of adult bookstores and movie theaters as "predominantly white, middle-class, middle-aged, married males, dressed in business suit or neat casual attire . . ." (p. 21). The male fantasy realm—"pornotopia"—portrayed in Victorian pornography (Marcus 1966) appears to differ little from the realm portrayed in modern pornography (Smith 1976); the major social changes that have occurred during the last century have left pornotopia largely untouched. Written pornography gives scant description of men's bodies (unless, of course, it is aimed at the homosexual market), but describes women's bodies in great detail (Smith 1976). The most striking feature of pornotopia is that sex is sheer lust and physical gratification, devoid of more tender feelings and encumbering relationships, in which women are always aroused, or at least easily arousable, and ultimately are always willing. There is no evidence that a similar female fantasy world exists, and there appears to be little or no female market for pornography.

But although women apparently are rarely motivated to read or to watch pornography, a number of recent studies demonstrate relatively minor sex differences in sexual arousal when subjects are exposed to explicit depictions of sexual activity. The Commission on Obscenity and Pornography sponsored a number of such studies, reviewed in the Commission's report, which found that 60 to 85 percent of males and females experience sexual arousal when reading or viewing erotic material. Similarly, recent studies of West German university students indicate relatively minor male-female differences in sexual arousal to pictures, films, and stories that explicitly depict human sexual activities (Sigusch et al. 1970, Schmidt and Sigusch 1970, 1973). Heiman (1975) measured changes in penile and vaginal blood volume and pressure pulse among forty-two male and seventy-seven female college students as they listened to taped descriptions of human activities. Students were divided into four groups on the basis of the content of the tapes to which they listened: (1) erotic description, with no romantic content; (2) romantic description, without explicit sexual content; (3) combined erotic-romantic description; and (4) control description, neither erotic nor romantic content. Heiman reports that both men and women responded most strongly to the erotic tapes (although the accompanying figure shows little difference between responses to the erotic tapes and responses to the erotic-romantic combinations). Furthermore, both men and women responded most strongly to tapes in which the female was the sexual aggressor and in which description centered on the female's rather than the male's body. The figure accompanying Heiman's article shows that males responded more strongly than females, but Heiman does not discuss this, nor does she mention whether the difference is statistically significant.

In summary, recent studies indicate that both men and women usually experience sexual arousal when they voluntarily expose themselves to erotic stimuli; but for several reasons, this fact may reveal little about sexuality as it exists in ordinary life. First, although men and women respond sexually once they have agreed to view, read, or listen to erotic material for experimental purposes, sex differences in motivation to be exposed to such material in everyday circumstances apparently have not diminished: there is an enormous male market for pornography, and no female market. Second, there may be major sex differences in the psychological processes that produce sexual arousal to pornography. Money and Ehrhardt (1972) suggest that although males and females may respond with equal intensity to erotic pictures, they do so in different ways. To a man, the female in the picture is a sex object, and he imagines taking her out of the picture and copulating with her. A woman is aroused by the same picture because she subjectively identifies with the female as an object to whom men sexually respond, and she becomes, in her imagination, the sexual object. Heiman's data showing that both men and women are aroused most strongly by descriptions that emphasize the female's body provide support for the hypothesis that a basic sex difference exists in the psychology of sexual arousal. Third, pornography is, in a sense, an artificial stimulus, and responses to it may provide little insight into the everyday interactions and experiences of men and women. All peoples seek whatever privacy is available to copulate: the everyday human environment very rarely provides visual stimuli of humans engaged in sexual activity. Experimental data on human responses to more normal stimuli substantially reduce the apparent discrepancies between the evidence of science and the evidence of daily life.

Although Heiman (1975) found few sex differences in sexual responses to erotic tapes, she did find major differences in responses to the "control" tapes, which did not depict explicit sexual or romantic interactions. She notes that "a small proportion of the men and even fewer women" were sexually aroused by control tapes, but, in fact, her published figure shows that in the first session the male change in penile pressure pulse to the control tape was at one point as strong as any male sexual response observed during the entire study (11 mm above baseline), while the maximum female response to a control tape was extremely small (1 mm above baseline). To put the matter another way, the male response to a control tape was stronger than the strongest female response to an erotic tape. Heiman writes: "I have always suspected that men can interpret the most unsexy situations as erotic, and there they were, turned on by a bland narrative of a student couple discussing the relative benefits of an anthropology major over pre-med" (p. 93). She suggests that the male response to the control tape disappeared in the second session because the men had learned that nothing erotic was going to happen. Now in my view, the marked sex difference in responses to control tapes has far more significance for understanding ordinary interactions between men and women than does the lesser sex difference in responses to erotic tapes. I wonder, in fact, whether a male investigator would have been as likely as Heiman to consider a conversation between a young man and woman to be a "control" tape at all.

While a natural human habitat seldom provides pornographylike stimuli, it regularly provides the visual stimulus of members of the opposite sex in varying states of dress. Photographs, drawings, or paintings of nudes approximate normally encountered stimuli far more closely than pornography does, and therefore the responses of men and women to nudes are much more relevant than their responses to pornography in understanding what goes on in everyday life. Kinsey et al. (1953) reported that 54 percent of the men in their sample had been erotically aroused by seeing photographs, drawings, or paintings of nude females, whereas only 12 percent of the women had been erotically aroused by seeing such depictions of nude males or females. (Unfortunately, Kinsey et al. did not distinguish between women who had been aroused by male nudes and women who had been aroused by female nudes; as discussed below, there is reason to suspect that many of the 12 percent may have been aroused by female, but not male, nudes.) Kinsey et al. (1953:652-53) write: "It is difficult for the average female to comprehend why males are aroused by seeing photographs or portrayals of nudes when they cannot possibly have overt sexual relations with them. Males on the other hand, cannot comprehend why females who have had satisfactory sexual relations should not be aroused by nude portrayals of the same person, or of the sort of person with whom they have had sexual relations." Given the apparent changes that have occurred in women's sexual arousal to pornography since Kinsey's investigations, it seems highly significant that recent studies of university students find, just as Kinsey did, that men are far more likely than women to be sexually aroused by depictions of nude members of the opposite sex (Sigusch *et al.* 1970, Steele and Walker 1974); both of these studies report minimal sex differences in sexual arousal to pornography.

Commercial portrayals of nude human figures provide a natural experiment on sex differences. Kinsey *et al.* (1953) noted that enormous numbers of photographs of nude females and magazines exhibiting nude or nearly nude females are produced for heterosexual men; photographs and magazines depicting nude males are produced for homosexual men, not for women. Since Kinsey's time, two nationally distributed women's magazines depicting nude males have appeared in the United States, *Viva* and *Playgirl*. In 1976 *Viva* eliminated male nudes. Editor Kathy Keeton (*Viva*, Aug. 6, 1976:8) listed a number of reasons for this decision: photographs of nude males were distasteful to many potential advertisers as well as to many women; supermarkets and drugstores—where women typically shop for magazines—often would not stock *Viva* because of the photographs; furthermore, Keeton cited an industry poll which showed that women of every age are consistently less approving of nudity in magazines than men are. Keeton also called attention to a study conducted by Stauffer and Frost (1976) of 50 male and 50 female Boston college students, aged 16 to 23 years, which evaluated male reactions to *Playboy* magazine and female reactions to *Playgirl* magazine. Stauffer and Frost reported that 88 percent of the men and 46 percent of the women gave the centerfold and photo essays high ratings for "interest"; no man rated these features low, but 14 percent of the women did. The students were asked to rate on a 10-point scale the degree of sexual stimulation they experienced from the magazine's nude photographs: 74 percent of the women responded on the lower half of the scale, and one-third said male nudity is not sexually stimulating at all; 75 percent of the men responded on the upper half of the scale, and 58 percent reported photographs of nude females to be definitely stimulating. Eighty-four percent of the men said they might buy future issues of *Playboy*, but 80 percent of the women said they would not buy future issues of *Playgirl*. In her *Viva* editorial, Keeton expressed her own opinion—that men look silly posing without clothes—and remarked that the novelty of male nudes had simply worn off. She went on to say, however, that *Viva* would continue to feature occasional female nudity because women are interested in, and are not embarrassed by, other women's bodies.

In 1976 *Playgirl* also considered discontinuing photographs of nude males, and decided to base their action on a privately commissioned survey; 537 urban women aged 18 to 59 were asked to list their reactions to photographs of nude men: 26.1 percent said that they enjoyed looking at them "a great deal," 35.7 percent "somewhat," 22 percent "a little," 11.7 percent "not at all," and about 4 percent were undecided[1] (unfortunately, the question of sexual arousal was not posed). On the basis of this survey, *Playgirl* decided to continue featuring photographs of nude men.

One difficulty with natural experiments is that they are uncontrolled. At this writing, *Playgirl* continues as a viable business enterprise, but there is a serious question of the extent to which its readership actually is composed of women. According to *New York Magazine* (Feb. 14, 1977:57), *Playgirl* is having subscription problems because a large percentage of its readership has always been homosexual men, and these men are shifting to new publications specifically geared to homosexuals (*Playgirl* editors deny that their readers, or viewers, are primarily male). My own modest efforts at assessing *Playgirl*'s readership—interviewing clerks at newsstands—suggest that most *Playgirl* purchasers are men, but perhaps women readers are more likely to subscribe to than to buy the magazine at a newsstand. (According to Keeton, private surveys showed that since *Viva* dropped male nudes a greater proportion of their readership is female.) Another difficulty in evaluating the significance of the existence of *Playgirl* is that, unlike dozens of men's magazines whose sole purpose is the portrayal of nude women, *Playgirl* carries articles and features that are likely to interest young women. My own opinion is that *Playgirl* editors design photograph and comic strip layouts largely, but not exclusively, for homosexual men, and the rest of the magazine largely for young women. In summary, as in Kinsey's era, some women are sexually aroused by photographs of nude men, but it is not clear that even in a country the size of the United States there are enough such women to support a single magazine featuring photographs of nude males, and it is extremely unlikely that such a magazine would have a substantial female market if that were all it featured.

Although inexperienced girls may wish to satisfy their curiosity

---

[1] *Los Angeles Times*, June 16, 1976, Part II:1.

about the nature of the male genitals, cross-cultural evidence suggests that the tendency of human males to be sexually aroused by the sight of females—especially the female genitals—and to make great efforts to see female genitals (and any other part of the female body that is typically concealed), simply has no parallel among human females, and is often intuitively incomprehensible to women. In describing his travels through Europe and parts of Asia and Africa during the latter half of the 19th century, the author of *My Secret Life* ("Walter") notes that wherever possible, men bored holes through thin walls in order to peep at undressed women. At one French railway station, the men's closets adjoined the women's; with the help of the women's closet attendant, Walter spent an entire day peeping through a hole at an endless parade of women. Although the closet attendant was a lusty, nonprudish, working-class woman, she nonetheless "wondered '*pourquoi mon Dieu*,' why they wanted to see women, when they were doing their nastiness."

According to Marshall (1971:117-18), "Little stimulation is required to prepare the Mangaian male for sexual intercourse; custom and habit seem sufficient. However, the Mangaian does admit to increased sexual excitement and desire upon hearing music. Somewhat more exciting is the sight of the nude female body—a knowledge used by Mangaian females to arouse flagging interest in their partners. Perfume, the sight of a woman's well-rounded hips, and the actions of the Polynesian dance also incite the male Mangaian to thought of copulation, as does the sight of female genitalia. . . ." One of Schapera's (1940) Kgatla informants remarked that when girls wear short skirts "you can then easily see the girl's thighs, and so you begin to wish for her" (p. 47). Elwin (1968) described the Lotus Stalk Dance, performed by Muria ghotul girls—but rarely in public as it is considered risqué—in which each girl rests one leg on her neighbor's waist. On one occasion a boy

> sat down near the dancers and tried to peep in a rather unpleasant manner. The girls stopped dancing and took him inside the ghotul. "What were you sitting down for?" "Nothing." "You wanted to look at us, you dirty little beast, so we're going to punish you." They tied his hands together and bound them to the roof for fifteen minutes. When he was released, he had to salute each of the girls in turn and beg forgiveness (pp. 84-85).

Muria boys carve symbols of the vagina, erect penises, and breasts (with details of the areola) on combs, tobacco-pouches, walls or pillars of the ghotul, and tree trunks. Similarly, adolescent Grand Valley Dani boys of West New Guinea make charcoal drawings of vulvas on rock overhangs, or scratch them in sand, or carve them in the bark of trees (Heider 1976). This typically adolescent male behavior is especially interesting because Heider characterizes the Grand Valley Dani as having substantially lower sexual interest and activity than any other known people. The ethnographic literature does not indicate that girls make similar drawings or carvings.

Anthropological discussions of sex differences in dress and posture emphasize the likelihood of male sexual arousal at the sight of the female genitals. Ford and Beach (1951:102) write: "There are no peoples in our sample who generally allow women to expose their genitals under any but the most restricted circumstances. The wearing of clothing by women appears to have as one important function the prevention of accidental exposure under conditions that might provoke sexual advances by men." Davenport (1977) reports that concealment of women's genitals is much more widespread than concealment of men's genitals; in the few instances in which women do go naked, inevitably there are strict rules against males staring at women's genitals (perhaps not unlike Western nudists), and women always sit so that their vaginas are not exposed. Mead (1967) points out that in all societies girls are permanently clothed before boys, and that a little girl is taught to cross her legs, or to tuck her heels under her, or to sit with her legs parallel: "Older boys and men find little girls of four and five definitely female and attractive, and that attractiveness must be masked and guarded just as the male eye must be protected from the attractiveness of their older sisters and mothers" (p. 105).

I interpret the evidence on human sexual arousal as follows: pornotopia is and always has been a male fantasy realm; easy, anonymous, impersonal, unencumbered sex with an endless succession of lustful, beautiful, orgasmic women reflects basic male wishes. Pornography has changed so little in the last century compared with other aspects of social life and relations between men and women because pornotopia lies closer to the genes than behavior does. One of Hite's (1976:199-200) informants writes: "There have been several men who seemed to care whether I was happy, but they wanted to make me happy according to *their* conception of what ought to do it (fucking harder or longer or whatever) and acted as if it was damned impertinent of me to suggest that my responses weren't programmed exactly like those of mythical women in the classics of porn."

That the female nature portrayed in pornography really does exist almost exclusively in the male imagination is perhaps most strikingly revealed in recent novels that are often alleged to constitute evidence for the opposite conclusion. While this is not the place for extended literary exegesis, I believe that an unbiased reading of Erica Jong's *Fear of Flying*, for example, will reveal that although Isadora Wing, the protagonist, and presumably the author, are able to entertain the notion of a "zipless fuck"—intercourse unencumbered by zippers or personal relationships—and to imagine in a rather detached way that such intercourse might eliminate the trauma usually associated with heterosexual relations, the zipless fuck is not primarily an emotionally based fantasy in that it is not what the protagonist really wants, although it is perhaps what she would like to want. Indeed, she does not really feel strongly about this fantasy in the sense, for example, that she obviously feels strongly about Germans. Taken as a whole, *Fear of Flying* reflects fairly typical female sexual desires, not because the protagonist eventually returns to her husband, which is irrelevant, but because strongly felt sexuality always is imagined in the context of relationships with specific men who are more than sex objects. Indeed, Isadora Wing brings to mind the marital restiveness and sexual/romantic longings of 19th-century fictional ladies, such as Emma Bovary and Anna Karenina, much more strongly than she brings to mind, say, the lusts of a Henry Miller.

The intractably male nature of pornography is problematical for those who wish to see men and women as in some fundamental sense sexually identical. Individuals who believe that human sexuality is basically a male sexuality, and thus imagine that sexually liberated women will act and feel as men do, must cope first with the evidence that while many women respond sexually to pornography in an experimental setting, few apparently are motivated to seek it out, and second with the evidence that sex differences in sexual arousal to depictions of nude members of the opposite sex seem to be as substantial as they ever were. On the other hand, individuals like Brownmiller (1975), who imply that human sexuality is basically a female sexuality, and that liberated men will act and feel as women do, generally interpret heterosexual interactions in political rather than in sexual terms; thus Brownmiller avoids directly confronting the challenge pornotopia poses to her theoretical position, yet indirectly acknowledges the difficulties when she states that pornography is *inherently* sexist, and advocates a political solution, viz., the total elimination of pornography.

The recent evidence of women's sexual arousal to pornography has demonstrated, in my view, primarily what was already known: first, that women are capable of being aroused by erotica, mainly via the subjective process of identification with the female participant; and second, that once heterosexual activity is under way, women have the potential to be at least as strongly aroused as men. To the extent that exposure to pornography during scientific experiments simulates anything in a woman's everyday life, it simulates an actual heterosexual interaction to which she has already consented and in which she is a willing and eager participant. I regard a female subject's agreement to participate in an experiment on sexual response as approximately equivalent to her agreement, or decision, to have sexual relations with a man in everyday life; her erotic responses during the experiment simulate her ordinary response during sexual interaction. Men and women differ far less in their potential physiological and psychological responses during sexual activities *per se* than they do in how they negotiate sexual activities and in the kinds of sexual relationships and interactions they are motivated to seek. This may explain the anomaly (from the male point of view) that although women can be strongly aroused by pornography they are unlikely to seek it out. It also may explain women's general lack of sexual response to nude males: a woman may be "interested" in a nude male, in that she evaluates him favorably as a potential sex partner and wishes to become sexually involved with him and to be sexually aroused by him, but a wish for future sex is not the same as immediate arousal.

One observation of the Committee on Obscenity and Pornography may be especially relevant in the present context: "When viewing erotic stimuli, more women report the physiological sensations that are associated with sexual arousal than directly report being sexually aroused" (*Report* 1970:24). Obviously this finding is subject to a number of possible interpretations,[2] but I believe that the most parsimonious interpretation also is the most likely: I suggest that during such experiments some women experience the physiological changes that prepare their bodies for sexual intercourse without, in fact, experiencing emotional sexual arousal, and that this ability is the result of the unprecedented independence of receptivity and proceptivity in the human

[2] The usual, quasi-political, interpretation is that women are sexually aroused but do not recognize their arousal. On the other hand, Rossi (1973), in criticizing studies of women's genital responses to visual stimuli, writes: "many women experience clitoral engorgement in situations of stress and tension without sexual stimuli or association. . . . The physiological manifestation may *appear* sexual, but the emotions associated with it are not" (p. 165).

female (see Mead 1967). This independence is, I believe, a basic human female adaptation to use sexual intercourse and the possibility of sexual intercourse to advantage in an environment in which males wield physical and political power.

Male-female differences in tendencies to be sexually aroused by the visual stimulus of a member of the opposite sex—whether this stimulus is a drawing, painting, photograph, or actual person—can be parsimoniously explained in terms of ultimate causation, although their proximate bases remain obscure. Because a male can potentially impregnate a female at almost no cost to himself in terms of time and energy, selection favored the basic male tendency to become sexually aroused by the sight of females, the strength of such arousal being proportionate to perceived female reproductive value; for a male, any random mating may pay off reproductively.[3] In other mammals, female reproductive value is revealed primarily by the presence or absence of estrus; that is, by ovulation advertisements. But human females do not advertise ovulation, hence selection favored male abilities to "assess" reproductive value largely through visual cues, as discussed below. Human females, on the other hand, invest a substantial amount of energy and incur serious risks by becoming pregnant, hence the circumstances of impregnation are extremely important to female reproductive success. A nubile female virtually never experiences difficulty in finding willing sexual partners, and in a natural habitat nubile females are probably always married. The basic female "strategy" is to obtain the best possible husband, to be fertilized by the fittest available male (always, of course, taking risk into account), and to maximize the returns on sexual favors bestowed: to be sexually aroused by the sight of males would promote random matings, thus undermining all of these aims, and would also waste time and energy that could be spent in economically significant activities and in nurturing children. A female's reproductive success would be seriously compromised by the propensity to be sexually aroused by the sight of males.

[3] The relationship between "girl watching" and sexual intercourse is implicit in Irwin Shaw's classic short story "The Girls in Their Summer Dresses," which may well be the most concise summary of sex differences in sexuality ever written (see *Short Stories from the New Yorker*. New York: Simon and Schuster, 1940). And in *Remembrance of Things Past*, Proust writes: "The men, the youths, the women, old or mature, whose society we suppose that we shall enjoy, are borne by us only on an unsubstantial plane surface, because we are conscious of them only by visual perception restricted to its own limits; whereas it is as delegates from our other senses that our eyes dart towards young girls. . . ."

The male's desire to look at female genitals, especially genitals he has not seen before, and to seek out opportunities to do so, is part of the motivational process that maximizes male reproductive opportunities. There is no corresponding benefit for females in wanting to look at male genitals, hence selection has not favored female impulses to become sexually aroused by the sight of male genitals or to seek out opportunities to look at them. If females tended to be sexually aroused by the sight of male genitals, men would be able to obtain sexual intercourse via genital display; but the deliberate male display of genitals to unfamiliar women is understood to be a kind of threat, whereas a similar female display is understood to be a sexual invitation. Although the practice of covering the genitals with clothing is almost universal, the underlying reasons for concealing male and female genitals probably are different.

While the most significant question for an evolutionary analysis is how human dispositions develop in natural environments, it is likely that selection so consistently favored males who were sexually aroused by the sight of females and the female genitals, and so consistently disfavored females who were aroused by the sight of males and the male genitals, that the resulting male-female differences approach "innateness," and are manifested even in artificial, modern environments. I hasten to add that this does not mean that environments could not be designed in which most females would develop malelike dispositions and vice versa; but such environments probably never existed, nor are they likely to exist in the future. The profoundly different natures of men and women are dramatically illustrated by Bryant and Palmer's (1975) study of masseuses in four "massage parlors." The primary service these women offer their male clients is masturbation, but in the process the clients are allowed to massage or fondle the naked masseuses. The purpose of this is to arouse the clients sexually as quickly as possible and hence to generate maximum business: the masseuses' motto is "get 'em in, get 'em up, get 'em off, and get 'em out" (p. 233). Although masseuses regularly look at, masturbate, and are masturbated by naked men, and although most of the women expressed a positive attitude toward their clients, only one masseuse reported that she herself experienced sexual arousal during her work, and this apparently occurred as a result of being massaged rather than massaging. To overcome her arousal, she would stand up, look at her client, and lose interest. The ability to engage in these activities without being sexually aroused represents a uniquely female adaptation. This adaptation cannot be accurately characterized as "hyposexuality," since the masseuses may be strongly sexually aroused and active with partners of their own choosing; rather, it represents this ability *not* to become sexually aroused simply by the stimuli of male bodies *per se*. Few heterosexual men could massage and masturbate naked women without being themselves sexually aroused, and I suspect that if the women clients also masturbated their masseurs, even many homosexual masseurs would find themselves aroused.

The natural experiment of commercial periodical publishing provides further evidence of human sex differences: attractive women—in varying states of dress and exhibiting varying degrees of sexual provocativeness—are featured not only in men's and in general interest magazines but also in magazines designed exclusively for women. *Viva*'s decision to continue publishing occasional female nudes, but to eliminate male nudes, was based on the editors' understanding that women enjoy looking at other women's bodies. Indeed, women's magazines—especially fashion magazines—are saturated with an eroticism that often seems more genuine than the male fantasy-simulating eroticism of men's magazines. My impression from unsystematic discussions with women (especially during the seminars on primate and human sexual behavior that D. E. Brown and I have taught for a number of years) is that most young women prefer the photographs in *Playboy* to those in *Playgirl*, and that many young women "girl watch" as much as or more than they "boy watch." Parallel male preferences and behaviors would probably indicate homosexuality, and a magazine featuring photographs of men who exude the erotic narcissism of women's fashion magazines almost surely would be intended for a male homosexual market. But women's interest in other women's bodies is not—as a male bias might suggest—evidence for lesbianism. Heterosexual women do not look at other women as sex objects; rather, they *identify* with women in photographs and become, in their imagination, erotically alive and desirable objects (see Money and Ehrhardt 1972).

I believe that women's magazines provide vivid, albeit grossly exaggerated, evidence of a basic human female adaptation, which Colette referred to as women's "instinct for spontaneous comparison": viz., to learn from observing other females how to stimulate, and use to advantage, male desire. This is analogous to the human abilities—which almost surely represent adaptations—to observe another person's skilled tool-using performance, to imagine oneself performing the same activity, and to use this imagined performance as a template with which to compare the sensations of one's own performances. Human females have always been objects of male sexual desire, and it is difficult to believe that a natural environment ever existed in which females did not have some opportunity to increase their reproductive success by learning to manage and manipulate this desire. Learning to be effective as an erotic stimulus is underpinned by the abilities to imagine oneself as a sex object and to discriminate and identify with sexually attractive women. Although female intrasexual competition ultimately underlies women's interest in other women's bodies, competitive emotions apparently do not normally interfere with women's abilities to learn through identification.

Perhaps substantial numbers of women will never be sufficiently interested in magazines whose *raison d'être* is photographs of nude men to make the publishing of such magazines profitable; nevertheless, the hypotheses presented here generate several predictions about how more effective magazines could be designed. First, the notion must be abandoned that women are simply repressed men waiting to be liberated: large numbers of women will not be appealed to by the slavish mimicking of men's magazines. Selection has not only not favored a female propensity to become sexually aroused by the sight of males, but very likely it has disfavored this propensity. Selection has, however, favored female abilities to discriminate visually, and to be sexually interested in, males who evidence fitness. Sexual arousal—primarily via touch (Money and Ehrhardt 1972)—may eventually result from this female interest. To stimulate most effectively female sexual arousal, as opposed to sexual "interest," photographs of males must suggest not just the possibility of a future sexual interaction but rather an actual sexual interaction.

I thus offer the following unsolicited advice to would-be editors of magazines for the sexually liberated woman. (1) Photographs of men with erect penises will be far more effective than photographs of men with flaccid penises in sexually arousing women. The former suggest an actual sexual interaction, not just the possibility of a future interaction. (2) Because female sexual arousal by visual stimuli appears to depend more on subjective identification with females than on objectifying males, photographs in which women appear along with nude men will be more effective than photographs of men alone. The former provide a vehicle with which the observer can project herself into the photograph. (Photographs in which the man and woman touch each other, not necessarily sexually, will be especially effective.) While the presence of women in photographs may also arouse emotions such as competition and jealousy, which conflict with sexual arousal, the net effect for most women will be increased erotic appeal. (3) Few women desire anonymous sexual variety, hence the potential for sexual arousal is unlikely to be maximized by photographic layouts of a series of men. Young women who were exposed to *Playgirl* magazine in Stauffer and Frost's (1976) study reported that they would prefer photographs that depict a believable, developing heterosexual relationship that could reasonably result in nudity and sex. (This female preference is the opposite of pornotopia, which deliberately and consistently excludes believable relationships, reasonable contexts, and, in fact, any intrusion of the realities of sexuality in everyday life.)

The widespread failure to appreciate the extent of sex differences in sexual arousal has a number of possible explanations. One possibility is the (generally adaptive) human tendency to conceive other minds in terms of one's own. For example, although it is regularly alleged that men believe, and propagate the myth, that women are "hyposexual," in fact, men often grossly misunderstand women's experiences because they imagine women to be repressed men waiting to be awakened. Kinsey *et al.* (1953:653) write:

> We have histories of males who have attempted to arouse their female partners by showing them nude photographs or drawings, and most of these males could not comprehend that their female partners were not in actuality being aroused by such material. When a male does realize that his wife or girl friend fails to respond to such stimuli, he may conclude that she no longer loves him and is no longer willing to allow herself to respond in his presence. He fails to comprehend that it is a characteristic of females in general, rather than the reaction of the specific female, which is involved in this lack of response.

Women themselves sometimes imagine that their failure to respond as men do is primarily a matter of repression. As Stauffer and Frost (1976) note, the fact that the editors of *Playgirl* magazine copied *Playboy*'s format so closely reflects the misconception that liberated women will be like men.

Sexual attractiveness

Nowhere are people equally sexually attracted to all members of the opposite sex; everywhere sexual attractiveness varies systematically with observable physical characteristics (Ford and Beach 1951). In their review of the social psychological literature on physical attractiveness, Berscheid and Walster (1974) note that this topic has been neglected in part because appearance is closely tied to the genes, hence the importance of physical attractiveness in everyday life is antagonistic to the optimistic environmentalistic bias of American psychology: it seems undemocratic that hard work cannot compensate for genetic happenstance. Berscheid and Walster argue that nonscientists are more likely than scientists to assess accurately the importance of physical attractiveness because nonscientists have not been misled by social science theories:

> . . . social scientists have taken longer to recognize the social significance of physical appearance than have laymen; the accumulating evidence that physical attractiveness is an important variable to take into account if one is plotting the course and consequences of social interaction may be more startling to social scientists than to those who were never exposed to the strong "environmentalist" tradition of psychology, who did not take at face value beliefs of equal opportunity, and who were not aware that an interest in physical appearance variables relegated one to the dustbin of social science (p. 207).

But even Berscheid and Walster may be guilty of an environmentalistic bias when they state that "culture transmits effectively, and fairly uniformly, criteria for labeling others as physically 'attractive' or 'unattractive'" (p. 186). As discussed below, the extent to which criteria of physical attractiveness are transmitted by culture is debatable.

Berscheid and Walster's review indicates: (1) People generally agree very closely in rating the physical attractiveness of others, regardless of the sex, age, socioeconomic status, or geographical region (within a given country) of the individuals doing the rating. (2) Physical attractiveness greatly influences the formation of heterosexual relationships; as Murstein (1972:11) writes, "physical attractiveness, both as subjectively experienced and objectively measured, operates in accordance with exchange-market rules." Naturalistic studies of heterosexual couples in public places indicate that members of a pair tend to be approximately equal in physical attractiveness. Experimental studies confirm the importance of physical characteristics. For example, men were paired randomly with women (except that the man was always taller than his partner) at a college dance, and subsequently participants were asked how much they liked their partner. Liking proved to be a direct function of the partner's physical attractiveness; every attempt to discover other factors failed. Needless to say, such findings are at variance with young people's statements about what they value most in a member of the opposite sex, which tend to emphasize "personality" and "character."

Berscheid and Walster call attention to the "dazzling variety" of characteristics considered attractive in various societies and in times past and also to the absence of theories capable of bringing order out of this chaos. Although physical attractiveness is both easily assessed and of great importance in everyday life, "an answer to the question of who is physically attractive is neither available currently nor foreseeable on the immediate horizon" (Berscheid and Walster 1974:181). They do note, however, that in the West tallness is considered attractive in men, and that people of high socioeconomic status are judged, on the average, to be more attractive than people of low socioeconomic status. In discussing standards of beauty in cross-cultural perspective, Ford and Beach (1951) also emphasize the diversity of standards, both in what characteristics are admired, and in what parts of the body are considered to be most important.

But standards of physical attractiveness may be neither so variable nor so arbitrary as they seem. I suspect that variability and arbitrariness have been overemphasized for the same historical and ideological reasons that physical attractiveness itself has been ignored in the social sciences: physical characteristics are close to the genes and are distributed undemocratically. If standards of attractiveness can be shown to vary arbitrarily, attractiveness itself is made to seem trivial. Thus Rosenblatt (1974), in reviewing cross-cultural standards of physical attractiveness, describes beauty as an "impractical" criterion on which to base mate choice, whereas economic and political gain are said to represent "practical" criteria. I shall argue that the tendency to discriminate physical attractiveness among members of the opposite sex and to be more sexually attracted to some than to others represents an adaptation whose ultimate basis is that people vary in reproductive value. That humans universally assess one another in terms of physical attractiveness and universally desire attractive partners indicates that these assessments and desires—like economic and political considerations—are "practical" in the sense that they are designed to promote reproductive success.

The perception of physical attractiveness seems to originate in three different kinds of phychological mechanisms. These mechanisms do not, of course, operate independently, but they can be considered separately for analytical purposes. First, some physical characteristics, which can be specified in an *absolute* sense, universally indicate high reproductive value. The ability to discriminate these characteristics and the tendency to desire them in a partner are relatively "innate," in that humans who make these discriminations and experience these desires tend to develop in all natural environments and probably in most unnatural environments as well. Second, some physical characteristics, which can be specified only in a *relative* sense (by comparing individuals in the population with one another), universally indicate high reproductive value. The ability to discriminate these characteristics is acquired through experience, but this does *not* mean that relative standards of physical attractiveness are transmitted from one individual to another, much less from culture to individuals. The mechanisms underlying the learning of these relative standards may be best considered "innate" *rules*, or programs, that specify how standards of physical attractiveness are to be derived from experience; the development of these relative standards may occur completely outside of consciousness, and the standards thus developed may be unavailable to introspection. Third, individuals derive some criteria of physical attractiveness from one another. Whether these "cultural" criteria are systematically related to reproductive value is an open question, but if they are not, selection can be expected to oppose tendencies to adopt other people's standards of physical attractiveness.

Absolute Criteria. Health obviously is very closely associated with reproductive value, and at least some characteristics predictive of good health are universally attractive. As Byron said, "health in the human frame / Is pleasant, besides being true love's essence." Ford and Beach (1951) report that among all peoples good complexion and cleanliness are considered attractive, poor complexion and filthiness unattractive. These characteristics very likely are the most reliable available indices of good health, and tendencies to pay close attention to skin condition and to be attracted by a clear, clean complexion probably are "innate" human dispositions. Furthermore, the ethnographic record suggests that evidences of disease or deformity render individuals less physically attractive. Perhaps many other physical characteristics—clear eyes, firm muscle tone, sound teeth, luxuriant hair, or a firm gait, for example— are reliably associated with health and vigor and are universally attractive, but the topic has yet to be investigated systematically. Social psychologists have not emphasized the importance of indices of health and skin condition on physical attractiveness perhaps in part because their study populations are often middle-class college students who are, on the whole, extremely clean and healthy; the effect of ringworm on physical attractiveness, for example, is unlikely to be disclosed in such a sample. Furthermore, many social psychological studies of physical attractiveness rely on photographs, in which skin condition may be virtually undetectable; in the case of yearbook photographs, blemishes and irregularities may even have been deliberately eliminated.

A human female's age is very closely associated with her reproductive value, and physical characteristics that vary systematically with age appear to be universal criteria of female physical attractiveness; Williams (1975), in fact, remarks that age probably is the most important determinant of human female attractiveness. The correlation of female age and sexual attractiveness is so intuitively obvious that ethnographers apparently take it for granted—as they do the bipedalism of the people they study—and the significance of female age tends to be mentioned only in passing, in discussions of something else. For example, in discussing Kgatla adultery, Shapera (1940:207) describes one embittered woman "whose husband had recently been carrying on with a younger and more prepossessing rival. . . ." Davenport (1977: 142) writes that in modern China, before the revolution, "one of the motivations for taking concubines was to gain young and attractive sex partners." Chagnon (1968a:66) discusses a Yanomamö wife "who is quite jealous of her [younger] co-wives because they can command some of the tasty morsels of food that would otherwise be her own prerogative. And, since the younger wives are more attractive physically, [the husband] does pay considerable attention to them." According to Goodale (1971:227), it is often the fate of a Tiwi woman to outlive several husbands and eventually to become the wife of a younger man: "If this happens, the young man may have several quite young wives whom he prefers as sexual partners." The woman's opportunities to engage in extramarital affairs also diminish at this time, and, in fact, Tiwi women believe that the "stopping of sexual intercourse causes menopause." In discussing human sexual competition in cross-cultural perspective, Mead (1967:198) alludes to "the struggle between stronger older men and weaker younger men or between more attractive younger women and more entrenched older ones. . . ."

Since Western studies of physical attractiveness have focused on people of college age or younger, age is seldom mentioned as an important variable, except incidentally, as in Mathews, Bancroft, and

Slater (1972), but the waning of female attractiveness with age is well known. Social scientists may also have neglected age as a variable influencing female attractiveness because in the artificial environments of modern Western societies women can maintain a youthful appearance far longer than is possible under more natural conditions. Where women begin their reproductive careers at seventeen, spend most of their lives pregnant and nursing, and engage in strenuous gathering and domestic activities in which they are regularly exposed to the elements of nature—especially to the effects of the sun on skin texture—the aging process is manifested dramatically in physical appearance.

How age affects female sexual attractiveness can be expected to depend on whether the male's (unconscious) mechanism for "evaluating" female physical characteristics has been designed by selection primarily for wife-detecting or primarily for sexual partner-detecting (Williams 1975). Montagu (1957) provides data relevant to this question in his discussion of "adolescent sterility": in cross-cultural perspective, menarche, accompanied by anovulatory cycles, occurs at 13–16 ± 1 years of age; nubility, the beginning of fertile, ovulatory cycles, occurs at 17–22 ± 2 years of age and is accompanied by high rates of maternal and infant mortality; maturity, in which full growth is attained, occurs at 23–28 ± 2 years of age. Hence, "the best time for conception, pregnancy, and childbirth in the human female is, on the average, at the age of 23 ± 2 years and for about 5 years thereafter" (p. 193). If males have been designed by selection to "evaluate" females primarily as sex partners, males should be attracted most strongly by females of 23–28 ± 2 years, since they are most likely to produce a viable infant; but if males have been designed by selection to "evaluate" females primarily as wives, males should be attracted most strongly by females who are just about to become nubile, at 17–22 ± 2 years, since a male who marries a female of this age maximizes his chances of tying up her entire reproductive output. In the West, males might be expected to be attracted most strongly by somewhat younger females (depending on what physical characteristics males use to assess age) since the age of menarche (and presumably of nubility and maturity as well) has been steadily dropping for the last century (Melges and Hamburg 1977), hence most of the observable signs of fertility appear earlier among Western females.

Among many higher primate species that do not form harems, adult males are known to prefer older females as sex partners; more dominant rhesus males, for example, tend to copulate with older females (see Symons 1978a). Ultimately, this preference is the result of the relative infertility of the younger estrous females. On the other hand, hamadryas baboons form harems, and a hamadryas male may start his harem by "adopting" permanently a prepubescent, two-year-old female (though his motive may not be sexual). While the relevant data on human male preferences have yet to be collected, it seems very likely that the male "evaluative mechanism" has been designed more for detecting the most reproductively valuable wives than for detecting the most reproductively valuable sex partners. The probabilities that a 30-year-old woman and a 20-year-old woman will produce healthy, viable offspring from a given act of intercourse would seem to be far too similar to explain their differential attractiveness; but, in a natural environment, the 30 year old would have completed perhaps half of her reproductive career and hence, other things being equal, would make a far less valuable wife than the 2c year old. Although I have argued that marriage is not primarily based on lust, marriage may sometimes be motivated by lust, and, more importantly, lust may motivate the male's attempt to accumulate young wives. In *Don Juan*, Byron describes a Turkish sultana who is still an overpowering beauty despite her advanced years: "there are forms which Time to touch forbears / And turns aside his scythe to vulgar things." She is twenty-six years old.

There has recently been a good deal of public discussion of romantic relationships in which the woman is substantially older than the man. With respect to the issue of sexual attractiveness, the following points may be pertinent: (1) Humans are flexible, and individual ontogenetic histories vary enormously in modern societies; no doubt some men are most strongly sexually attracted to older women. (2) The competition for older women is much less keen than the competition for younger women, and, as a group, young men—like most young male mammals—are in a weak competitive position. Among rhesus monkeys, for example, young, low-ranking males tend to mate with the youngest females—who are least likely to produce viable offspring—because the dominant males monopolize the older, more fertile females (see Symons 1978a). (3) Physical sexual attractiveness is only one component of a romantic relationship; older women are likely to be much more interesting intellectually, less inhibited sexually, more highly skilled in lovemaking, and, perhaps, less demanding.

The universal, absolute criteria of physical attractiveness associated with health and female age have been neglected by physical attractiveness theorists perhaps because these criteria are obvious and not very interesting; nevertheless, they may account for much of the variance in physical attractiveness within a given population. Anthropologists may have failed to emphasize these criteria because anthropology takes culture to be its subject matter and universals appear to lie outside the province of culture. But, as argued below, some of the standards of physical attractiveness that do vary cross-culturally probably also lie outside the province of culture.

Relative Criteria. The tendencies to find healthy people and young women attractive are relatively "innate" because they are universally associated with reproductive value[4] and because some indices of health and age (such as unblemished and unwrinkled skin) can be specified in an absolute sense. But the reproductive value of most characteristics can be specified only relatively; hence selection may favor "innate" mechanisms that specify the *rules* by which the individual is to develop standards of attractiveness by comparing members of the population with one another.

The human female tendency to detect and to be attracted by high-status males may constitute one such "innate" rule. When the males of a species regularly compete for status, high rank will, on the average, confer reproductive advantage (Wilson 1975). Females of such species might be expected to prefer dominant males—other things being equal —because such males are more likely than low-ranking males to produce reproductively successful sons. Ford and Beach (1951:94) write that, in cross-cultural perspective, "One very interesting generalization is that in most societies the physical beauty of the female receives more explicit consideration than does the handsomeness of the male. The attractiveness of the man usually depends predominantly upon his skills and prowess rather than upon his physical appearance." Social psychological studies have found that female "popularity" is more closely correlated with physical attractiveness than is male popularity, and that males are more likely than females to report that physical attractiveness is important to them in evaluating a member of the opposite sex (Berscheid and Walster 1974).

[4] Indeed, "innate" development may protect the individual from developing maladaptive sexual preferences owing to random environmental influences or Machiavellian attempts to influence his or her taste. If there were any hope of success, might a man attempt to convince his reproductive competitors that forty-year-old women are much more attractive than twenty years olds? Certainly similar attempts are typical of human economic transactions.

In *Remembrance of Things Past*, Proust writes that the women the aristocratic Charles Swann found to be beautiful and charming

> . . . were, as often as not, women whose beauty was of a distinctly "common" type, for the physical qualities which attracted him instinctively, and without reason, were the direct opposite of those that he admired in the women painted or sculptured by his favourite masters. Depth of character, or a melancholy expression on a woman's face would freeze his senses, which would, however, immediately melt at the sight of healthy, abundant, rosy human flesh.

These sex differences are precisely what evolutionary theory predicts: since, in a natural habitat, females appear to vary relatively little in the number of children they produce during their lifetime, female reproductive value is primarily a function of age and health; but male reproductive value varies substantially with prowess and status, and may increase with age.

Because male reproductive value is not a function of age, the passage of time can have different—even opposite—effects on men's and women's sexual attractiveness. In her novel *The Vagabond*, Colette, that quintessential observer of the aging process, makes the thirty-four-year-old protagonist write to her lover (whom she is about to abandon) as follows:

> Max, my dear love, I asked you yesterday the name of that young girl playing tennis with you. I need not have bothered. As far as I am concerned she is called *a girl, all the girls, all the young women* who will be my rivals a little later on, soon, tomorrow. She is called the unknown, my junior, the one with whom I shall be cruelly and lucidly compared, yet with less cruelty and clearsightedness than I shall use myself.
> Triumph over her? How often? And what is triumph when the struggle is exhausting and never-ending? Understand me, please understand me! It is not suspicion, not your future betrayal, my love, which is devastating me, it is my own inadequacy. We are the same age; I am no longer a young woman. Oh my love, imagine yourself in a few years' time, as a handsome man in the fullness of your age, beside me in mine! Imagine me, still beautiful but desperate, frantic in my armour of corset and frock, under my make-up and powder, in my young, tender colours. Imagine me, beautiful as a full-blown rose which one must not touch. . . .

The attractiveness of high-status males may shed light on the question of whether the female "evaluative mechanism" is designed primarily to detect husbands or primarily to detect sex partners (assuming, of course, that ancestral females sometimes had some say in choosing their husbands). If male A has higher status or greater hunting ability than male B, A's wife or wives can expect, other things being equal, to be better off than B's wife or wives; but if B's wife has an affair with A (assuming that she receives no material compensation), all she has to gain, ultimately, is the possibility of conceiving a child by A instead of by B. Selection can be expected to favor the female desire for high-status sex partners, as distinct from husbands, only to the extent that the variance in male status has a genetic basis.

The situation is not as clear-cut as the previously discussed effect of age on female attractiveness: from the male's point of view, the ideal age for a wife is different from the ideal age for a sex partner; but from the female's point of view, a high-status male is both the best choice for a husband and for a sex partner. Nevertheless, I suspect that the proportion of the variance in male status that is caused by genetic differences among males is far too small to account for the persistent female interest in male status and prowess and therefore speculate that the human female "evaluative mechanism" has been designed by selection more for detecting the most reproductively valuable husbands than for detecting the most reproductively valuable sex partners.

The human female preference for high-status males is rapidly becoming a sociobiological cliché (for example, van den Berghe and Barash 1977) and perhaps is not worth belaboring. Good data are needed on this question. In gathering such data, it will be important (and difficult) to distinguish between intellectual judgments and actual sexual attraction: there is no question that humans of both sexes can calculate rationally that they are likely to benefit materially from marriage—or even from association—with a high-status member of the opposite sex. But the interesting question is the extent to which the emotion of sexual attraction varies with the status of the individual being evaluated. Berscheid and Walster (1974) report that middle-class people are, on the average, perceived as more physically attractive than working-class people; this may result from class differences in nutrition and medical care; genetic differences between classes arising from the tendency of attractive women to marry high-status men; and/or specific cues associated with social class. Possibly the effect of status on male attractiveness is not linear, but instead, only a few males of the highest status benefit substantially from intense female interest. This possibility should be considered in designing experiments to assess the effects of status on attractiveness.

Rosenblatt (1974) argues that Ford and Beach's finding—that cross-culturally, male attractiveness is based more on prowess than on handsomeness, while female attractiveness is based largely on beauty—is an artifact of women's lack of power in most societies to choose their own mates. He predicts that women will be equally concerned with handsomeness, and equally unconcerned with prowess and status, when they have equal power to choose their own mates. The question of whether there are "innate" male-female differences in the importance of status as a criterion of sexual attractiveness may be resolved in the near future as Western women achieve economic and political equality. My own prediction is that even when men become used to women in high-status positions, and are not emasculated by the fear of such women, and women become used to holding high-status positions, status will not substantially affect women's sexual attractiveness but will continue to affect men's attractiveness. (The rise of the 20th-century groupie is food for thought.) It might prove interesting to study individuals who regularly move between environments in which they have high status and environments in which they are unknown. I suspect that many men experience dramatic fluctuations in their attractiveness to the other sex as a result of such transitions, and that women generally experience little or no such fluctuations.

If high status is desirable in a mate or a sex partner, and humans are disposed to detect and to be attracted by such individuals, the next best thing to possessing high status is appearing to possess it, hence people may imitate signs of status in order to enhance their own attractiveness. "Fashion" in Western societies may be largely status-imitation run amok: change for its own sake must occur constantly at the top because signs of status are constantly being imitated at lower levels and thereby rendered useless. Imitation may, of course, be prevented by penalties, such as those for impersonating an officer, but the existence of penalties among many peoples implies the existence of impulses to violate them.

Health and status are unusual in that there is no such thing as being too healthy nor too high ranking. But with respect to most anatomical features, natural selection produces the population mean, either directly, in that individuals exhibiting the mean tend to be the most reproductively successful, or indirectly, in that the extremes of the population distribution tend to be reproductively less successful. Thus sexual selection can be expected to favor an "innate" mechanism to detect the population mean (or other measure of central tendency) of most physical characteristics and to find it attractive. Cross-cultural variation in standards of physical attractiveness must be in part the result of racial variation; *Homo sapiens* is an extremely polytypic species. Darwin (1871) argued that peoples tend to admire characteristics peculiar to their own race, characteristics, that is, which distinguish their race from others, and that sexual selection would therefore tend to exaggerate racial differences; in fact, Darwin believed that sexual, rather than natural, selection is primarily responsible for racial differences. It seems more likely, however, that during most of human evolution individuals rarely encountered members of races very different physically from their own, that racial differences are primarily the result of natural selection, and that any tendency to prefer one's own race is an artifact of the tendency to prefer the norm, a norm which is reinforced rather than exaggerated by sexual selection. That is, sexual selection may simply tend to reduce variability by eliminating the tails of the population distribution.

Almost a century ago, Galton (1883) developed a method of making a composite photograph from many individual photographs of faces, thus generating a kind of pictorial average. He found that "All composites are better looking than their components, because the averaged portrait of many persons is free from the irregularities that variously blemish the looks of each of them" (p. 224). Galton also quotes from a letter (to Charles Darwin) from A. L. Austin of New Zealand, who blended portraits of women in a stereoscope and noted "in every instance, a *decided improvement* in beauty" (p. 226). If the ideal of facial beauty is largely the population average (more likely, the average of individuals of the most desirable age, in the case of adults), individuals *must* possess an unconscious, "innate" mechanism that operates in a manner analogous to composite portraiture and derives a standard of facial attractiveness by averaging observed faces. Individuals—not culture—must possess this mechanism, as it is difficult to see how a cultural tradition of preferring the composite face could originate unless some actual persons could average observed faces, and even if such a tradition somehow got started, the ideal would tend to drift away from the composite unless individuals possessed an average-detecting mechanism which limited drift. Averaging clearly is done unconsciously, although the adjective "regular" does frequently crop up in attempts to describe facial beauty; in fact, the ideal must almost always be a face that no one has ever seen.

The human beauty-detecting mechanism probably evolved to deal with small, relatively homogeneous groups of people. How this mechanism operates in large communities, often of varied racial composition, provides interesting problems for research. In a small, relatively homogeneous population there may be a single ideal face, but if the averaging mechanism is designed to detect *relations* among facial features, rather than absolute dimensions, in a large, heterogeneous population a number of "ideal" faces may exist, each characterized by a different harmony in the relative proportions of its features. Moreover, one wonders whether humans have completely distinct criteria of attractiveness for different racial groups, or whether exposure to a number of races results in a mutual influence of standards. Elwin (1968) found the same Muria attractive that the Muria themselves did, but he had associated with them for many years prior to the time of this writing. Malinowski (1929) makes the intriguing observation that after he had lived in the Trobriand Islands for some time his judgments of Trobriand beauty began to agree with the Trobrianders' judgments. (I see no reason to assume that Malinowski simply adopted Trobriand standards, as he showed little inclination to adopt natives' opinions in other matters.) Perhaps Malinowski initially judged Trobrianders by European standards; if so, one wonders whether his standards of European physical attractiveness were different upon completion of his fieldwork, or whether he had developed entirely separate systems of evaluation, just as he had developed entirely separate languages.

The means of such adaptively significant characteristics as body height and skin color can also be expected to be perceived as most attractive. Relevant data should be fairly easy to gather. My impression from the ethnographic literature is that some peoples prefer lighter than average skin (although albinism, like all deformities, is everywhere considered decidedly unattractive). But in these cases one would like to know whether skin color varies with status, whether colonialism is perhaps implicated, and whether informants attempt to spare the feelings of the light-skinned ethnographers. Although Trobrianders generally found Europeans physically hideous, they graciously emphasized that Malinowski himself was a notable exception to this rule, and, in fact, informants remarked that in many ways Malinowski looked rather more like a Trobriander than a European (Malinowski 1929). (Malinowski also notes that the bearer of such good tidings expected to be recompensed with a gift of tobacco.)

According to Berscheid and Walster's (1974) review, tallness is valued in American men, which appears to contradict the hypothesis that the most attractive height will be the population mean. But the evidence on this question is equivocal, and raises a number of interesting issues. How sexual attractiveness varies with male height has not, in fact, been systematically investigated; furthermore, the data Berscheid and Walster cite have more to do with political success and the hiring practices of American businessmen than with male attractiveness to females. Berscheid and Walster report no evidence that men taller than the mean (about seventy inches) are consistently judged to be more sexually attractive than shorter men; according to their discussion, the male's absolute height does not appear to be as important as his height relative to that of the female doing the evaluating. Women clearly prefer men somewhat taller than themselves, but how much taller is not known.

The following points—which are intended to be hypotheses rather than conclusions—may be worth considering. First, humans are designed by selection to live in small, relatively homogeneous groups in which the variability in body height is far less than the variability existing in the United States today. In a natural human habitat, virtually all adult men will be taller than all adult women, so perhaps it is "natural" for women to prefer men somewhat taller than themselves. The problem of a "restricted field of eligibles" faced by tall women and short men in the United States (Berscheid and Walster 1974) probably is peculiar to modern, heterogeneous societies. Second, although inquiries into the effects on attractiveness of posture, gait, and body carriage have not, to my knowledge, been made, these characteristics probably influence attractiveness and may tend to favor shorter men. Third, although there are no data to show that men taller than seventy inches are considered more attractive than seventy-inch-tall men, it does seem likely that a man whose height is above the mean generally will be considered more attractive than a man who is the same distance from the mean in the other direction. Since at least the beginning of this century, mean body height (for both sexes) in the United States has steadily increased;[5] perhaps it is not too farfetched to imagine that, as a refinement on a mean-detecting mechanism, humans also are able to detect major trends—presumably by comparing members of different generations—and have a tendency to prefer individuals who deviate from the mean in the direction of the trend. Such a mechanism would be adapted to long-term environmental changes; the perceived trend

[5] *Advance Data from Vital and Health Statistics,* No. 3, United States Department of Health, Education, and Welfare, November 19, 1976.

in phenotypes naturally need not be the result of genetic evolution, but a trend-detecting and -preferring mechanism might lead to genetic tracking (Wilson 1975) of facultative responses.

According to Darwin (1871), the human male's preference for physically attractive females resulted in sexual selection for beauty. Crook (1972:248), however, argues that "since in tribal societies virtually all women marry, the case for differential selection is poor because the less beautiful are not known to be less fecund than the more beautiful." But it is also true that the less beautiful are not known *not* to be less fecund than the more beautiful. Data are lacking. If higher-status males were able to obtain a disproportionate share of physically attractive wives, beautiful women may have had a slight reproductive edge. Nevertheless, if for most anatomical characteristics the population mean is considered most attractive, male preference for beauty would have reinforced natural selection and reduced population variability. Indeed, it is difficult to believe that sexual selection acted very strongly among hominid females, nor is there convincing evidence that the function of any human female anatomical characteristic—such as breasts—is to stimulate males visually. Most likely, female anatomy is stimulating to males owing to evolution in male brains, not female bodies. Consider that in cross-cultural perspective the sight of the female genitals, more than any other feature of female anatomy, is consistently reported to stimulate males, yet no one (to my knowledge) has yet suggested that any part of female genital anatomy was designed by selection for the purpose of visually stimulating males (although artificial elongation of the labia minora is sometimes thought to enhance attractiveness).

Much of the cross-cultural variation in standards of physical attractiveness reported by Ford and Beach (1951) is in body build, especially in the amount of body fat that is considered to be ideal. Among most peoples, plump women are considered more attractive than thin women. Rosenblatt (1974:87) remarks that "in a world where food is often scarce and nutritional and digestive-tract illnesses often epidemic, plumpness is an indication of wealth and health." Tobias (1964) suggests that the characteristic steatopygia of Bushmen women is adaptive in an environment of periodic food shortages, and he notes that Bushmen men prefer women with the fattest bottoms. Body fat is one of the most variable physical characteristics: major intra- and inter-population variation occurs, in part owing to differing nutritional opportunities, and the amount of body fat an individual possesses can change noticeably in the course of a few days. Humans do not seem to

have an "innate" preference for a particular body build; rather, individuals learn to associate variation in body build with indices of health
and status. Plumpness has gone out of fashion in Western societies
during the last century, probably as a result of the changing relationship between body fat and status: when food was scarce for many
people, plumpness was a sign of wealth, but as circumstances improved
for the majority, the rich began to distinguish themselves through thin-
ness. (A similar argument sometimes is made with respect to suntans.)[6]
That a preference for plumpness is not "innate" seems to support arguments that hunter/gatherers (and by inference our Pleistocene ancestors) do not exist in a state of perpetual nutritional insufficiency.
Alternatively, humans may have a tendency to prefer plumpness, a
tendency that can be overridden by the enormous influence of health
and status on standards of physical attractiveness.

Ford and Beach (1951) report substantial cross-cultural variability
in the particular anatomical features that are considered to be most
relevant to assessing beauty: this group emphasizes the lips, that group
the nose, another group the ears, and so forth. I confess to a certain
amount of skepticism. Such data are almost always obtained in an unsystematic and haphazard way, and must depend heavily on what features one or a few informants happen to mention. We know from
more careful and systematic studies in the West that physical attractiveness—at least facial beauty—is perceived more as a total Gestalt
than in isolated features (Berscheid and Walster 1974). Neither is the
fact that a people adorn one facial feature and not another convincing
evidence for the overriding importance of the former. It would be incorrect to assume, for example, that because many more Western
women color their lips than their noses that lips are a more important
criterion of beauty than noses are.

None of the foregoing is intended to deny the existence of cultural
traditions of beauty that are unrelated to fitness, or of personal idiosyncrasies that result from unusual learning experiences; rather, it is intended to suggest first, that the ability to detect and to be attracted
by members of the opposite sex who evidence high reproductive value
is an important adaptation, and second, that humans have "innate" pref-

[6] Suntans may, once again, go out of fashion in Western societies. If there are
marked class differences in access to information about the sun's effects on the skin,
upper-class people may tend to avoid the sun, despite some loss of physical attractiveness, both to avoid cancer and to maintain a youthful appearance. And if un-
tanned skin comes to be reliably associated with the upper classes, it may come to
be perceived as attractive.

erences for certain physical characteristics (for example, good skin), and "innate" rules by which other preferences are learned (for example, "prefer characteristics associated with high-status people"). If one argues, as so many people continue to do, that behavior must be caused either by the genes or by the environment, and that any exception to a general rule demonstrates environmental causation (unless the exception can be shown to have a genetic basis), one can deny the existence of any genetic influences on human sexual preferences. But if one acknowledges that behavior and psyche result from the interactions of genes and environments, and that human genes were selected on the basis of their ability to perpetuate themselves within a limited range of environmental circumstances, then, despite exceptions, one can interpret the cross-cultural regularities in standards of physical attractiveness as powerful evidence for "innate" dispositions. There is no a priori reason to doubt that a human child could be taught to be sexually attracted to anyone or anything; but this in no way diminishes the significance of the standards of attractiveness that develop in existing human environments.

Sex Differences in the West. In *The Selfish Gene*, Dawkins (1976) ends the chapter on the "battle of the sexes" as follows:

> One feature of our own society which seems decidedly anomalous is the matter of sexual advertisement. As we have seen, it is strongly to be expected on evolutionary grounds that, where the sexes differ, it should be the males who advertise and the females who are drab. Modern western man is undoubtedly exceptional in this respect. It is of course true that some men dress flamboyantly and some women dress drably but, on average, there can be no doubt that in our society the equivalent of the peacock's tail is exhibited by the female, not by the male. Women paint their faces and glue on false eyelashes. Apart from actors and homosexuals, men do not. Women seem to be interested in their own personal appearance and they are encouraged in this by their magazines and journals. Men's magazines are less preoccupied with male sexual attractiveness, and a man who is unusually interested in his own dress and appearance is apt to arouse suspicion, both among men and among women. When a woman is described in conversation, it is quite likely that her sexual attractiveness, or lack of it, will be prominently mentioned. This is true, whether the speaker is a man or a woman. When a man is described, the adjectives used are much more likely to have nothing to do with sex.
> Faced with these facts, a biologist would be forced to suspect that he was looking at a society in which females compete for males, rather

than vice versa. In the case of birds of paradise, we decided that females are drab because they do not need to compete for males. Males are bright and ostentatious because females are in demand and can afford to be choosy. The reason female birds of paradise are in demand is that eggs are a more scarce resource than sperms. What has happened in modern western man? Has the male really become the sought-after sex, the one that is in demand, the sex that can afford to be choosy? If so, why (pp. 177-78)?

I have tried to show that the ultimate cause of the greater importance of female than of male physical attractiveness is easily explained by the nature of reproductive competition during the course of human evolution: a female's reproductive value can be assessed more accurately from her physical appearance than a male's reproductive value can. Human females compete with one another in the currency of physical attractiveness because that is primarily what males value. (Appearance is enhanced in large measure by making the skin look healthier and younger.) A woman's physical attractiveness is significant not only in heterosexual interactions that may result in sexual intercourse, but in almost any heterosexual interaction in which male sexual interest can be advantageous to the woman or to her employer. Thus women employers are likely to be no less concerned than men about the physical attractiveness of their female employees, since they recognize that beauty is a tangible economic asset. Of course this is true also of male employees, but to a markedly lesser extent.

Furthermore, the fact that most men in modern Western societies wear more drab or conservative clothing than women does not mean that men are uninterested in being sexually attractive to women; on the contrary, this mode of dress is attractive to most women. Drabness connotes a responsible, hard-working family man, and almost all criteria of conservative good taste in men's clothing are simply signs of high status and membership in the upper classes. Men with the most to conserve—that is, those with the most power—tend to be the most conservative and to require conservative appearance of their subordinates. And in any species that typically exhibits both male-male competition and some female choice, visible signs of success in intrasexual competition are also likely to be important determinants of male attractiveness to females. Overt, flamboyant, sexual advertising in male attire is often perceived by women as a sign of promiscuous tendencies, which few women find attractive. As homosexual men are much less likely to be put off by signs of promiscuity in a potential sex partner, they are much freer than heterosexual men to use clothing as sexual advertising.

Dawkins's discussion does, however, raise some interesting questions about the peculiar circumstances of modern societies. Although Western women's concern with physical attractiveness doubtless does in part reflect female intrasexual competition, I trust no one believes that women compete for opportunities to copulate. In the West, as in all human societies, copulation is usually a female service or favor; women compete for husbands and for other relationships with men, not for copulation (when prostitutes compete for customers they are competing for money, not copulation). This competition is artificially magnified in Western societies because, by custom and by law, polygyny has been almost eliminated. Mead (1967:196-97) writes: "In modern societies where polygamy is no longer sanctioned and women are no longer cloistered, there is now a new problem to meet, the competition of females for males. Here we have an example of a problem that is almost entirely socially created, a product of civilization itself imposed upon an older biological one. . . . So in those societies in which there are more women than men—our normal Western sex ratio —and in which monogamy is the rule, we find the struggle of women over men also."

There is a second feature of modern Western societies that may conceivably increase female competition. Mead (1967) maintains, in effect, that the desire to be a mother is more "innate"—that is, develops under a wider range of environmental circumstances—than is the desire to be a father. She argues that "men have to learn to want to provide for others, and this behaviour, being learned, is fragile and can disappear rather easily under social conditions that no longer teach it effectively. Women may be said to be mothers unless they are taught to deny their child-bearing qualities" (p. 192). In modern Western societies not only may males be relatively ineffectively taught to want children, but many of the former economic motives for having children have disappeared. If more women than men do desire to have children (a proposition which has yet to be established), female competition may be rendered more fierce. Finally, modern women's sexual emancipation may have the effect of making some men reluctant to form durable heterosexual relationships (thus exacerbating female competition) not because men desire such relationships less strongly than women do, but because more males than females desire sexual variety for its own sake. The opportunities to satisfy this desire probably are greater, for the majority of men, in modern Western societies than in any other time or place, and the opportunities are greatest for the most desirable men.

The male peacock's tail and the bright, ostentatious plumage of male birds of paradise, to which Dawkins refers, were produced by intersexual selection, which results from the combination of individual differences in the males' "power to charm the females" and female choice. Among species in which females have the power and opportunity to choose their mates, if male fitness happens to be reliably associated with an observable physical characteristic, selection favors females who are predisposed to choose males exhibiting this characteristic. As this female predisposition becomes widespread in the population, selection begins to favor males who manifest this characteristic in the most extreme form—that is, males with the most effective advertising—and females who choose such males, since these females produce sons who are differentially chosen as mates. The resulting "run-away" sexual selection exaggerates the male characteristic until sexual selection is eventually halted by the counter-pressure of natural selection (the more flamboyant the male peacock's tail, for example, the more energy is expended in its development, the more conspicuous the male is to predators, and the more his mobility is limited).

There is no evidence that any features of human anatomy were produced by intersexual selection. Human physical sex differences are explained most parsimoniously as the outcome of intrasexual selection (the result of male-male competition) and perhaps natural and artificial selection, not intersexual selection or female choice. Analogies between humans and birds, and the perspective of modern Western societies, both lead to serious overestimation of the importance of female choice in human evolution. Also, the natural desire to have one's views accepted may—given current standards of acceptability—lead evolutionary theorists to exaggerate the importance of female choice: perhaps it is felt that the often unwelcome messages of an evolutionary view of life—an amoral universe and a creative process that is founded on reproductive competition—can be to some extent ameliorated by the welcome news that in the battle of the sexes nature has given females the upper hand.

Although copulation is, and presumably always has been, in some sense a female service or favor (Chapter Eight), hominid females evolved in a milieu in which physical and political power was wielded by adult males, and the substantial evidence, documented in the ethnographic record, that men will use their power to control women should not be underestimated. A particularly brutal example is provided by Chagnon (in press) from his studies of the Yanomamö: "the wife of one of the village headmen began having a sexual affair with another man. She came from the other large lineage in the village, and her brother, also one of the village headmen, attempted to persuade her to stop the affair. The two headmen were brothers-in-law and had exchanged sisters in marriage. The woman in question refused to follow her brother's advice, so he killed her with an ax." And Steadman (n.d.) writes that among the Hewa "when a married woman runs off with a lover, she is likely to be pursued by her brothers and her husband and, if caught, killed." Women, of course, evolved to use their assets to their own advantage. In modern Western societies males are severely limited in their opportunities to accumulate wives or to capitalize on their greater strength, and male political dominance is being steadily eroded; hence female choice (of mates and sex partners)—the psychological underpinnings of which presumably have always been present— is now manifested to an unprecedented degree in behavior. Ironically, the social, political, and sexual features of modern societies that have increased women's opportunities to chart the course of their own lives and to choose their own sexual partners and mates are the same features that have increased female intrasexual competition.

A final point: Dawkins writes that "a man who is unusually interested in his own dress and appearance is apt to arouse suspicion," which I take to mean "suspicion of being homosexual." Probably many heterosexual men are, in fact, as concerned with dress and appearance as any homosexual man (although heterosexuals may be more reluctant to admit such concern); nevertheless, homosexual men in general undoubtedly are more concerned with their appearance than heterosexual men in general are. As with all behaviors that characterize homosexuals, this emphasis on appearance provides a powerful insight into the nature of human sex differences (Chapter Nine). Homosexual men tend to be interested in dress and appearance not because they are, as a group, effeminate, but simply because they face the same problem that heterosexual women face: they wish to be sexually attractive to males, and males assess sexual attractiveness primarily on the basis of physical appearance.

To some extent the artificiality of modern Western environments can be considered to constitute an unplanned experiment (see Chapter Two). Although most human behavior in such environments is not explicable as adaptation (since the environments have existed for an infinitesimal amount of time), the modern world may dramatically reveal formerly adaptive human dispositions by allowing them, to an unprecedented degree, to be realized in behavior. For example, mate selection tends to be based on physical attractiveness to a much greater extent when young people arrange their own marriages than when marriages are arranged by elders (Rosenblatt 1974). It is a mistake to imagine either, as Rosenblatt does, that beauty is a totally "impractical" criterion, or, as a sociobiological perspective might imply, that young people "know" what is in their reproductive interests, and that elders and principals disagree over mate choice only because elders are "looking out" for their own inclusive fitness at the expense of the principals' inclusive fitness (although this undoubtedly is sometimes the case). Perhaps the typical differences between the criteria of elders and the criteria of the principals in matters of spouse selection can be thought of as a division of labor, elders taking account of factors they are uniquely situated to perceive owing to their age and experience, and principals assessing reproductive value evidenced largely in physical attractiveness, the final choice being a compromise (heavily weighted in favor of the elders).

By the standards of preliterate peoples, modern human communities provide an enormous pool of potential sexual and marital partners, relatively few taboos, unprecedented freedom from parental influences, and thus great scope for personal attraction based on physical appearance. While the choices made under such circumstances perhaps are not often the most adaptive ones possible, the underlying psychological mechanisms that determine physical attractiveness are strikingly illuminated, since they are regularly manifested in behaviors and marriages. These mechanisms represent adaptations to maximize reproductive success in the environments normally encountered during the course of human evolutionary history.

SEVEN

The Desire for Sexual Variety

Woman wants monogamy;
Man delights in novelty.
Love is woman's moon and sun;
Man has other forms of fun.
Woman lives but in her lord;
Count to ten, and man is bored.
With this the gist and sum of it,
What earthly good can come of it?
                                 DOROTHY PARKER,
                              "General Review
                              of the Sex Situation"[1]

IT MAY WELL BE TRUE in general, as Dawkins (1976) writes of modern Western societies in particular, that the typical human male and female parental investments are not too dissimilar, and most human beings throughout most of human evolutionary history probably had only one spouse at a time. But in considering the evolution of sexual desires the most relevant statistics are not typical parental investments but the minimum possible investments, and here the male-female difference is enormous. Scientists' tendencies to emphasize behavior, typical events, and "mating systems" promote neglect of the emotions and cerebration which make human conduct intelligible. I have argued that a human being is a feeler, an assessor, a planner, and a calculator, that the proximate goal of mental activities always is the attainment of emo-

---

[1] From *The Portable Dorothy Parker*. Copyright 1926, 1954 by Dorothy Parker. Reprinted by permission of The Viking Press; also from *Collected Dorothy Parker* (Duckworth 1973).

tional states, and that mind is adapted to cope with the rare, the complex, and the future: what is ordinary, predictable, or simple ceases to take up valuable space in awareness. Jesus said "Whosoever looketh on a woman to lust after her hath committed adultery with her already in his heart" because he understood that the function of mind is to cause behavior; even if only one impulse in a thousand is consummated, the function of lust nonetheless is to motivate sexual intercourse.

A male hunter/gatherer with one wife (who will probably produce four or five children during her lifetime) may increase his reproductive success an enormous 20 to 25 percent if he sires a single child by another woman during his lifetime. If he can obtain (and support) a second wife, he may double his reproductive success. The reproductive realities facing his wife are very different. She will bear four or five children during her lifetime whether she copulates with one, ten, or a thousand men. In general, the more men a married woman copulates with (and in a state of nature almost all fertile women are married) the more likely she is to be abandoned or harmed by a jealous husband or angry brothers, the more time and energy are diverted from reproductively significant activities such as nursing, gathering, arranging her childrens' marriages, etc., and the less likely she is to have an offspring sired in an adulterous liaison with the fittest available man. On the other hand, sexual intercourse with men other than her husband may benefit her in three ways: (1) She may exchange sex for meat or other goods and services. (2) She may, if she mates selectively, be impregnated by a fitter man than her husband. The magnitude of this potential benefit depends on the extent of genetic variation among males in the population and on the woman's ability to detect male fitness. I suggested above that it is unlikely that much of the variance in male status and prowess results from genetic variation; nevertheless, if a woman is married to a man with some obvious physical or mental defect, the time, energy, and risk adultery entails may pay off reproductively. (3) She may be able to use sexual intercourse to divest herself of her present husband and acquire a better one. Since men typically vary much more in their economic and political abilities than they do in their genes, and differences in status and prowess can be detected much more easily and reliably than genetic variation can, the potential reproductive benefits of changing husbands must sometimes be great, much greater than the potential benefits of being impregnated by a man other than one's husband.

Thus selection can be expected to operate in very different ways on human males and females. Since a man may benefit reproductively from copulating with any woman (except his wife) during her fertile years, and since, other things being equal, the greater the number of sexual partners the greater the benefit, selection universally favors the male desire for a variety of partners, although this desire may be satisfied only rarely. The waning of lust for one's wife is adaptive both because it promotes a roving eye and, as discussed in Chapter Three, because it reduces the likelihood of impregnating one's wife at times when an offspring cannot be reared and will have to be aborted or killed at birth. Abortion and infanticide waste energy and incur risk, reducing the husband's fitness along with his wife's.

A woman has nothing to gain reproductively, and a very great deal to lose, by desiring sexual variety *per se;* however, this does not mean that selection necessarily favors lusting after, or being faithful to, one's husband. As outlined above, a woman may benefit from extramarital sexual intercourse in several ways, and it is sometimes adaptive for her to experience sexual desire primarily for a man, or men, to whom she is not married. But this is very different from desiring sexual variety for the sake of variety.

I am suggesting that, in Byron's words, "fresh features" should be added to the list of "innate" criteria of female physical attractiveness, but that fresh features are usually unimportant in determining male attractiveness. Shakespeare wrote of Cleopatra: "Age cannot wither her, nor custom stale / Her infinite variety"; but "other women cloy / The appetites they feed" and their charms, presumably, wither with age. Had Shakespeare added that Cleopatra also suffered from some loathsome skin disease he would have made her triumph over male standards of attractiveness complete. In this section the evidence for variety-seeking is reviewed and evaluated, first with respect to nonhuman mammals, and then with respect to humans, including data on nonmarital, marital, and extramarital sexuality and on spouse exchange.

The Coolidge Effect

Montaigne wrote: "I have put out to stud an old horse who could not be controlled at the scent of mares. Facility presently sated him toward his own mares: but toward strange ones, and the first one that passes by his pasture, he returns to his importunate neighings and his furious heats, as before." In the laboratory, a male of many mammalian species typically copulates and ejaculates several times with an estrous female, but his sexual activity eventually wanes and finally stops. That the cessation of the male's sexual activity is not a result of fatigue is shown by experiments in which the original female is removed as soon as the male has ceased to copulate with her and a new estrous female is provided: the male immediately begins to copulate with the new female and to ejaculate. This renewed sexual activity does not occur if the first female is removed and then reintroduced, and the male's response to a new female is largely independent of whether she has recently been mated by another male. If the original female is removed and placed with a second male, copulation and ejaculation occur, suggesting that copulation *per se* does not render a female less sexually attractive to males in general. The phenomenon of male rearousal by a new female is called the Coolidge Effect.

In cattle and sheep the Coolidge Effect is so strong that the sexual limits of the experimental males have not been discovered. Schein and Hale (1965) report that when, each time a bull ceases to copulate with a cow, that cow is removed and a new cow is substituted, the bull's sexual response to the seventh cow is as strong as his response to the first. If a ram is provided with a single ewe he will not ejaculate more than five times, but if new ewes are substituted each time the ram ceases to copulate his rate of ejaculation is almost the same with the twelfth ewe as the first (Beamer *et al.* 1969, Bermant *et al.* 1969).

When the heads and bodies of ewes were disguised, by being covered with canvas sacks, the Coolidge Effect was undiminished; that is, the ram never was fooled by the reintroduction of the same covered ewe, and never failed to be aroused when a different covered ewe was provided (Beamer *et al.* 1969). In a similar experiment, when cows' hindquarters were smeared with a strong-smelling substance, the bull's behavior was not affected; although all the cows had been smeared with the same substance, the bull always differentiated between females with which he had and had not copulated (Bermant 1976).

The Coolidge Effect apparently is a widespread mammalian phenomenon (Wilson *et al.* 1963, Beach 1965), but its magnitude is variable; laboratory rats, for example, show the effect much less than cattle and sheep do (Wilson *et al.* 1963). Bermant (1976) suggests that the Coolidge Effect is most pronounced in species in which males, in the natural habitat, secure large harems, and he notes that there is little evidence for harem formation in the wild rat. The larger body size, more effective natural weapons, and greater pugnacity of males of many species—which function to make females available to a male—would be reproductively meaningless unless males were also disposed to copulate with a variety of partners.

Whether the Coolidge Effect occurs in females is not known, and data would probably be difficult to obtain. Estrous females of many mammalian species will accept the sexual advances of any male. In species where males compete for females and form harems, females might be expected to exercise minimum choice, both because they will not normally have much opportunity to do so, and because the best choice almost invariably is a male who is successful in intrasexual competition. An estrous female that continued to experience sexual desire after a male had ceased to copulate with her might solicit a second male, not in search of variety *per se* but in search of sexual stimulation. Rowell (1972a) reports such a phenomenon among forest-living baboons: "estrous females were observed to be 'in consort' with each of the five adult males in their group during the course of a single day: as each male tired and became less eager to follow, he was abandoned by the female in favor of the next" (p. 87). A good experimental design for testing the Coolidge Effect in female mammals would discriminate between the tendency to seek copulation and the tendency to seek a variety of partners. On the basis of evolutionary theory, there is no reason to anticipate the existence of the Coolidge Effect among female mammals except, perhaps, as an incidental byproduct of some other adaptation.

In discussions of the evolution of sexual behavior, males often are said to be "indiscriminate" because—having little to lose and a great deal to gain—they will copulate with any female; but experiments on the Coolidge Effect demonstrate that many male mammals are extremely sensitive to differences among females and continue to distinguish one female from another despite systematic experimental efforts to frustrate such discrimination. In this sense, bulls almost certainly are far more discriminating than cows are. "To discriminate" has two meanings: the first, to recognize as being different; the second, to show partiality or prejudice. While males of many species are indiscriminate in that they will copulate with any estrous female of their species, they are extremely discriminating in that they recognize females individually, and they are partial to variety and prejudiced against familiarity. The ability to seek variety depends on the ability to recognize individuals. A male who was indiscriminate in the sense that he could not recognize, or was uninterested in, individual differences would find one female the same as another and would have no motive to seek variety.

Bermant (1976:76-77) recounts the genesis of the term "Coolidge Effect":

> One day the President and Mrs. Coolidge were visiting a government farm. Soon after their arrival they were taken off on separate tours. When Mrs. Coolidge passed the chicken pens she paused to ask the man in charge if the rooster copulates more than once each day. "Dozens of times" was the reply. "Please tell that to the President," Mrs. Coolidge requested. When the President passed the pens and was told about the rooster, he asked "Same hen every-time?" "Oh no, Mr. President, a different one each time." The President nodded slowly, then said "Tell that to Mrs. Coolidge."

Bermant suggests that although laboratory experiments on the Coolidge Effect undoubtedly elucidate mechanisms of animal behavior as they occur in nature, similar experiments on humans—regardless of their outcomes—would shed little light on normal human sexual activity and would not answer questions about possible parallels between the Coolidge Effect in nonhuman animals and human mating patterns in their normal social contexts. By and large, Bermant probably is correct. Perhaps more significant than experiments on humans is the fact that we understand, and may be amused by, the story of President and Mrs. Coolidge. Certainly the human male's sexual capacities provide potent evidence that ancestral males did not normally acquire and rapidly inseminate large harems. Nevertheless, polygyny is and was common throughout the world, and the Coolidge Effect raises some interesting questions about the immediate effects of ejaculation on the human male's desires and perceptions.

My Secret Life, a 2300-page meditation on sexuality, is the most thorough description of the desire for sexual variety that has ever been —or is ever likely to be—written. The primary critical work on this greatly underestimated classic is *The Other Victorians* (Marcus 1966), which examines *My Secret Life* largely in light of its contribution to the study of 19th-century England. Marcus notes that *My Secret Life* is the longest autobiography ever published, is the best source of its kind on Victorian life, and is not pornography. It is also a remarkable and enduring statement about sexuality by a thoughtful, intelligent man—no doubt of somewhat unusual temperament—who was able to realize many of his sexual desires. Walter's passion for sexual variety is a major theme of his autobiography, and his sexual encounters with more than one woman (almost always prostitutes) at the same time, or in rapid succession, allowed him to observe the Coolidge Effect in his own responses. He writes: "fresh cunt, fresh courage always" (p. 1256).

In *The Female Eunuch*, Germaine Greer (1971) quotes the following poem of Charles Baudelaire:

> When she had sucked the marrow from my bones
> And languorously I turned to her with a kiss,
> Beside me suddenly I saw nothing more
> Than a gluey-sided leather bag of pus!

Greer implies that this poem illustrates the depth of men's contempt for, and hatred of, women, an interpretation that strikes me as both wrong and unfair, although the experience recalled in the poem perhaps implies Baudelaire's contempt at least for a particular woman. The poem's general significance may lie in its suggestion that lust and ejaculation can have profound effects on men's perceptions.

If the effort and risk are low enough it is to a man's reproductive advantage to copulate with any woman. Hence, where a fertile woman can be had at little or no effort or risk, it is adaptive for a man to experience lust for her without respect to her physical attractiveness or other personal attributes; that is, it is adaptive for males to be able to be "blinded" by lust. For men, celibacy of relatively brief duration appears to be a powerful aphrodisiac which profoundly affects the perception of female beauty. *My Secret Life* contains a number of pertinent observations; for example: "Then when it left their cunts, how different some ladies looked to me, to what they had before. Surely a prick stiff and throbbing, and a prick flabby, wet, and flopping, affect the powers of imagination very differently" (p. 1194). And again: "Never have I had more completely voluptuous fucking as far as mere cunt was concerned, but that was all; I was sick of the sight of her directly our bodies unjoined" (p. 1683). Contrary to Greer's interpretation, however, Walter makes clear that this change in perception was not inevitable (note that in the first quote he specifies *some* ladies); furthermore, he much preferred to have intercourse with partners he genuinely liked (or loved), and he liked many women.

Malinowski (1929) remarks that some Trobrianders were considered to be so ugly that they were spoken of with repulsion and horror and were left out of all social games and amusements. Informants reported "that all such people are absolutely debarred from sexual intercourse and that they have to resort to solitary means of satisfaction" (p. 292).

That many of the women who were considered thoroughly repulsive had several offspring was cited by Trobriand men as conclusive evidence for virgin birth. Malinowski writes: "This was one more of several cases in which I found how strongly convention (ideals of behaviour) obsesses the mind of the natives, but only on the surface and controlling their statements rather than their behaviour" (p. 294).

It is not to a woman's reproductive advantage to copulate with most men, even if there is little effort or risk (including pregnancy) involved. Hence, it would generally be maladaptive for women to be able to be "blinded" by lust, and it would certainly be maladaptive to lust for men without regard to their attractiveness simply because the effort and risk involved in copulation were slight. Thus one might predict that lust and orgasm may affect female and male perceptions very differently; if so, this would be especially interesting in light of the recent evidence that male and female orgasms are extremely similar physiologically.

Statistics and the desire for sexual variety

Although statistics and statistical trends loom large in many discussions of sex differences in the desire for sexual variety, it is difficult to know what, if anything, these numbers signify about human desires and dispositions. Heterosexual intercourse involves a male and a female, so that the total number of copulations for each sex must be the same; moreover, since each time a man has intercourse with a new partner a woman is doing the same, the total number of copulations with new partners must be identical for each sex.

Almost all studies of Western peoples indicate that males have premarital intercourse more frequently than females do (Kinsey *et al.* 1953, Christensen 1960, Peretti 1969, Hunt 1974), but recent data suggest that this sex difference is likely to disappear in the near future (Vener and Stewart 1974, Udry, Bauman, and Morris 1975). Males are also reported to have a greater variety of premarital sex partners (Kinsey *et al.* 1953, Schofield 1965, James and Pike 1967, Hunt 1974, Vener and Stewart 1974), but this sex difference does not appear to be diminishing (Tavris and Sadd 1977). Even in modern northwestern Europe, where a woman is as likely as a man to engage in premarital intercourse, men appear to have intercourse with a greater number of partners than women do (Schmidt and Sigusch 1973).

Men are also more likely than women to engage in extramarital intercourse (Kinsey *et al.* 1953, James and Pike 1967, Johnson 1970, Hunt 1974), although the most recent national survey indicates that in the youngest age group (under twenty-five) the sex difference is small; 32 percent of the husbands and 24 percent of the wives had engaged in extramarital intercourse (Hunt 1974). Recent evidence implies that this sex difference too will be reduced, although perhaps not eradicated, within a few decades (Bell and Peltz 1974, Bell, Turner, and Rosen 1975, Tavris and Sadd 1977). Of those married people who have had extramarital intercourse, one recent national survey indicates that men average a greater number of extramarital partners than women do (Table 7.1).

The findings that men have a greater variety of sex partners than women do can be explained in three ways: (1) prevarication; (2) male and female samples have not been drawn from the same populations; (3) most females have fewer partners than most males but a few females have a very large number of partners. It is not certain that the last explanation is the correct one, but Ehrmann (1963) suggests that the existence of prostitutes and nonprostitutes with reputations for having sex with many partners makes it likely. If so, are we to conclude that most men have a greater desire for variety than most women do, but that a few women have a stronger desire than any man? I believe that no such conclusion is warranted. Behavior is largely the outcome of opportunity and constraint, and the numerical logic of heterosexual coupling makes substantial male-female differences in these statistics impossible. Given suitable circumstances (which may differ

TABLE 7.1

Number of Extramarital Partners: Percents

	Males*	Females**
1 only	19	40
2 to 5	45	44
6 to 10	17	10
11 to 20	10	4
21 to 30	4	2
31 plus	4	0
Total	99	100

* Joseph S. Ruben, Director of Research, Playboy Enterprises Inc., personal communication.
** Hunt 1974.

for males and females) I would expect almost 100 percent of both sexes to engage in extramarital intercourse. Questions about sexual desires and dispositions cannot be settled by the statistics of copulation; we need evidence about feelings, not just behaviors, about how and why copulations are negotiated.

Nonmarital sex

If in a state of nature fertile human females almost always are married, and their husbands have sexual rights over them (Evans-Pritchard 1965, Mead 1967), the most "natural" subdivisions of human sexual activities might be: (1) the typically infertile activities of unmarried people; (2) the potentially fertile activities of married people. But since there are few data on human sexuality in anything approaching a state of nature, and much of the best data come from societies where women normally become fertile before they marry, the most natural subdivisions are not the most convenient ones. Hence, in this section I shall consider the question of variety-seeking among unmarried people without regard to age.

Although intense adolescent sexual behavior clearly exists among some peoples—the Muria, the Mangaians, and the Trobrianders, for example—the extent of premarital sexual freedom may often be exaggerated by an emphasis on theory over practice. For example, Goodenough (1949) reports that the natives of the Micronesian island Truk allow adolescents great sexual freedom: premarital intercourse carries no stigma of any kind, and no value whatsoever is attributed to virginity in either sex. Girls normally begin to have sexual intercourse at about fourteen years of age, boys at sixteen to seventeen years. Nevertheless,

> Aside from the lack of guilt-feeling, the interests of a number of the young men in sex seemed surprisingly like those of American adolescents, or of men working in lumber camps, or in the Army, or in other places where women are relatively unavailable. The conversation of young men between sixteen and thirty years of age was constantly dwelling on sex, and one heard much good-natured banter about it. The lengths to which an individual might go to achieve intercourse, and the failures which he had suffered, frequently provided the theme of such joking. Some of the young men carried pornographic photographs obtained from the Japanese during the war, while older in-

formants stated that in aboriginal times men used to make pornographic carvings on tree trunks. Masturbation was said to be fairly
common among the younger adolescents (pp. 615-16).

The primary reason for this state of affairs is that while premarital
freedom exists in theory, it is difficult to realize because communities
on Truk are small and girls marry earlier than boys do. In the community Goodenough studied there were only ten women and eleven
men between the ages of fourteen and twenty; only one of the women
was single and only one of the men was married. "Half of the remaining ten adolescents were not in competition because the girls did not
consider them sufficiently mature to take them seriously. The older
lads were forced to compete for the favors of the one girl, or to take
their chances in adulterous affairs with married women" (p. 617), a
situation perhaps not unlike that which existed during most of human
evolutionary history. Goodenough advises anthropologists to pay more
attention to the sociological factors that facilitate or hinder sexual behavior and not to rely solely on culturally patterned attitudes.

The argument that men stand to benefit reproductively in direct
proportion to the number of women with whom they copulate, while
women benefit reproductively, not from multiple partners, but from
copulating with the fittest available man, obviously assumes that copulation may result in impregnation. But human females (like other
higher primate females) normally experience "adolescent sterility,"
which in the human case is several years of anovulatory cycles following menarche, and in cross-cultural perspective, intense adolescent sexual activities seem to be remarkably pregnancy-free. (For discussions
of adolescent sterility see Ford and Beach 1951, Evans-Pritchard 1965,
Mead 1967, Elwin 1968, and especially Montagu 1957). Selection
might therefore be expected to affect adolescent and adult sexual desires and dispositions differently, including the desire for sexual variety.

Elwin (1968) briefly mentions the desire for sexual variety among
Muria boys and girls, and does not indicate the existence of any substantial sex difference, although he does not explicitly discuss sex differences. He writes: "In one ghotul the boys gave as a reason for
changing their partners the very human liking for change, 'love's
sweetest part, variety.' One of them said, 'You don't want to eat the
same vegetable every day.' The change of object undoubtedly stimu-
lates the sexual instinct and makes ghotul life more exciting" (p. 47).
And yet elsewhere Elwin notes that "The Muria, just like the stallion
and the buck-rabbit, and most of us, is excited by a new object of

sexual attraction. A visiting [boy] receives far more attention from the [girls] than any of their regular boys; a new girl in the ghotul may for the time being threaten its solidarity" (p. 197).

Marshall (1971) implies that Mangaian adolescents of both sexes may be interested in sexual variety:

> For many young males, the premarital period becomes a "contest" to see which one of the competing age mates can copulate with the most women and which one can gain the reputation of giving women the most sexual pleasure. If a girl tells her lover that her previous partner came to climax four or five times in one evening, the new boy will do his best to achieve six or seven times—to "win." He may use similar techniques to make a name for himself when he goes to a new island, to "prove" his admiration for a new girl, or to persuade a girl that she should marry him, as "no one else will have taken her in this way before." (The most extensive example of "racing" that I discovered was the Cook Island youth who was reliably reported to have "received" twelve successive girls in one day.) The sexual "racing," moreover, extends to both sexes, with competition among members of each sex to see who will be first to copulate with the newest male or female visitor to the island; competitors then compare notes with one another as to how the newcomer behaved and how he or she achieved orgasm (pp. 125-26).

Yet Marshall's statistics on sexual partnerships during adolescence paint a more conservative picture and imply male-female differences that are difficult to explain: between the ages of thirteen and twenty, girls typically have only three or four sex partners, while boys copulate with ten or more girls, and "some of the strongest contestants in the 'race' (those who have a penis tattooed on their thigh or a vagina tattooed on their penis) will have tested up to sixty or seventy (some of the more sophisticated youths maintain notebook records of their exploits). I am at a loss to fully explain the difference between the figures for the male and the female; that boys travel more to other islands and make extensive use of the looser women of the village is but a partial answer" (p. 126).

That Mangaian boys are clearly in sexual competition for girls more than the other way around implies that Mangaians, like all peoples, consider copulation to be fundamentally a female service or favor—an issue I shall take up in the following chapter—which in turn raises the suspicion that even among Mangaian adolescents the desire for sexual variety may be stronger in the male. In any case, Elwin's and Marshall's statements are the only ethnographic evidence I came across that females, in general rather than as isolated individuals, may typically desire a variety of sexual partners for the sake of variety; in neither case were such copulations likely to result in pregnancy. A few women who copulate with many men have been reported in Western Arnhem Land, Australia (Berndt and Berndt 1951), the Marquesas (Suggs 1966), and Mangaia (Marshall 1971). In each of these cases men give gifts in exchange for sexual intercourse; nevertheless, the desire for a variety of partners sometimes may be a woman's motive. Kinsey *et al.* (1948) interviewed a few women who were as interested in sexual variety as any man.

Studies of nonmarital sexuality in the West support the folk idea that boys typically seek sexual intercourse for its own sake while girls seek it within the context of, or as a means of developing, a relationship. On the basis of interviews with 200 college boys in the United States, Kirkendall (1961:237) writes: "The situation, to put it bluntly, is that the girl wants a boy, and the boy wants sex. So in order to get the boy the girl provides (or offers) him sex hoping that this will entice him into a permanent association, or he seeks it aggressively to prove to himself at least, that he is a man." In his study of 1873 English adolescents Schofield (1965) found that "Girls prefer a more permanent type of relationship in their sexual behaviour. Boys seem to want the opposite; they prefer diversity and so have more casual partners" (p. 92). Of those who had engaged in sexual intercourse, 46 percent of the boys and 16 percent of the girls said it was because of sexual appetite; 10 percent of the boys and 42 percent of the girls said it was because they were in love. In Freedman's (1970) study of the sexual behavior of forty-nine seniors at an eastern U.S. women's college, a number of informants expressed a desire for more frequent sexual intercourse; they were, however, unanimous in stating that they would not seek sex for its own sake, but only in the context of an important relationship. Among the economically secure working-class West Germans studied by Sigusch and Schmidt (1971), both men and women described sexual intercourse as enjoyable and satisfying, women usually expected and had orgasms, and proponents of a double standard were a small minority. But when informants were asked about their ability to remain faithful to their steady partner, 46 percent of the men and only 6 percent of the women said they certainly or probably would engage in intercourse with an attractive person of the opposite sex if the opportunity presented itself; 68 percent of the women and 24 percent of the men were rather sure or very sure they would remain faithful.

Tavris and Sadd (1977) summarize 100,000 responses of *Redbook* magazine readers to a questionnaire on female sexuality. They characterize their sample as "middle American," since it parallels the national distribution very closely in geographical area, religious beliefs, and the percentage who work; however, the sample is younger, better educated, and more affluent than the national profile. Although the great majority of women in the *Redbook* sample had had sexual intercourse before marriage, usually it was with the man they loved and planned to marry. Women who had had sexual intercourse by age fifteen tended to be more sexually experimental and to have had a greater number of partners before marriage, but also to be more unhappy sexually and to orgasm less frequently. Tavris and Sadd write:

> For most women, orgasm depends on being in love and feeling comfortable with their lovers. The *Redbook* women who had had premarital sex on a casual basis—once or a few times with several partners—were apparently not doing so for pure sexual pleasure, as they were the *least* likely to be reaching orgasm. The women who were *most* likely to be orgasmic in their premarital experience were having sex in a regular, stable relationship. Among the women who had had a series of one-night stands, for example, fully 77 percent said they never reached orgasm, compared to 23 percent of the women who had sex frequently with their partners. What matters in premarital responsiveness is not the number of lovers, actually, but the number of times with each one. As it ever was in this society, the great majority of young women need a sustained sense of intimacy, security, and trust from a relationship before they shake off inhibitions and respond sexually (pp. 53-54).

Tavris and Sadd quote Doris Lessing's *The Golden Notebook:* "And what about us? Free, we say, yet the truth is they get erections when they're with a woman they don't give a damn about, but we don't have an orgasm unless we love him. What's free about that?"

That women tend to be choosier than men about their sexual partners is, of course, precisely what is predicted by evolutionary theory; but since romantic love does not appear to be a universal human experience (although surely it must be a universal possibility) one would not expect love to be the basis of female choice everywhere. Among Mangaians, for example, the male's sexual prowess appears to be the primary determinant of his partner's sexual response. Since a male generally incurs far less risk to fitness from a sexual relationship than a female does, and has a great deal to gain from such a relationship, among peoples who do experience romantic love one might expect not only that males would tend to be sexually aroused by females whom they do not love but also that males—since they have less to lose— would tend to fall in love more easily than females; this appears to be the case. In a study of 250 males and 429 females, Kanin, Davidson, and Scheck (1970) found that young men tend to fall in love more easily and earlier in a relationship than women do, but that, once in love, women are more apt to behave in accordance with traditional American romantic stereotypes: "the female demonstrates her 'more romantic' behavior in a somewhat more judicious and rational fashion. She chooses and commits herself more slowly than the male but, once in love, she engages more extravagantly in the euphoric and idealizational dimensions of loving" (p. 70). Kanin, Davidson, and Scheck suggest that heterosexual involvement "connotes a greater investment of self and involves a payment of a greater price" for females, an economic metaphor for proximate psychological processes that could be translated easily into the ultimate economics of genetic fitness.

Perhaps the most impressive recent evidence for pervasive male-female differences in the desire for sexual variety and in the enjoyment of sex for its own sake comes from battle-scarred female veterans of the sexual revolution. Hite's (1974, 1976) publications of women's statements about their sexual feelings and experiences are especially valuable in this respect because her sample of 3000 is heavily biased in favor of single, urban, feminist, sexually liberal women and thus might be expected to detect a trend for sexually emancipated women to act and feel as men often do; however, no such trend is evident. Despite the enormous sexual diversity that is apparent in these lengthy and detailed responses, as Hite notes, almost no woman in the study wanted casual, spontaneous sex very often, although some of the women believed that they ought to want it or that they might be happier if they were able to want it. Some of the women described themselves as ex-"hip chicks"; although they had had extensive sexual experiences with many men, they had found such experiences to be generally unsatisfying. While it seems fairly obvious that Hite's particular feminist perspective informs her selection, arrangement, and interpretation of data, the number of women who reported that they had tried a male pattern of sexuality and found it wanting is nonetheless impressive. One of Hite's informants wrote: "If the Sexual Revolution implies the attitude that now women are 'free' too, and they can fuck strangers and fuck over the opposite sex, just the way men can, I think it's revolting. Women don't want to be 'free' to adopt the male model of sexuality;

they want to be free to find their own" (1976:303). Overwhelmingly, the women Hite quotes want sex with feeling, not sex for its own sake or a variety of partners, just as the 100,000 "middle American" *Redbook* readers do.

The existence of intractable differences between men and women in the desire for sexual variety is the unifying theme of Ingrid Bengis's (1973) remarkable autobiography, *Combat in the Erogenous Zone.* Bengis is less concerned with the question of casual, spontaneous sex than with the male-female differences that become apparent in the course of romantic affairs. She writes:

> There are times when I wonder whether nature isn't really the one to hold responsible. It seems a lot easier to blame nature than to blame men (although blaming society runs a close second), and often I find myself thinking that perhaps the rigors of biology will at least succeed in reducing the pain of the personal. I conclude that the real trouble derives from the fact that men and women are vitally different, not in those ways which provide for an interesting variety, but in ways which make of sexuality a veritable war zone. At moments when I despair, when man-hating fills up the space between me and my opposite number, I conclude that we are up against the barrier reef of an anatomical destiny which yields nothing to sensibility (p. 67).

> *   *   *

> . . . my attachments to men usually deepened the longer I knew them, and the more I shared with them, whereas their attachments seemed to lessen (p. 161).

> *   *   *

> The question then becomes one of: do multiple love affairs satisfy our needs? If they do, fine. I have no doubt that they satisfy the needs of some women, and those women are no better and no worse than I am. There is little point, however, in creating false solutions to real problems, and those of us who are *not* satisfied by multiplicity are still left with the difficulty of adapting ourselves to the fact that men, on the contrary, usually seem more inclined to multiple relationships than we are, to sex for its own sake rather than sex as an expression of more complicated impulses. How do we acknowledge the disparities in our needs, while neither shattering the requirements of intimacy, nor imposing our values on another, nor feeling cheated or betrayed or belittled? How deal with the fact that although "sharing" is theoretically a question of mutual concern, it is more often a question of your willingness to share him, rather than his willingness to share you, since you rarely have much desire for anyone else, and might be able to trump up such a desire only for the sake of the argument, for the sake of not being in a position where his freedom is your bondage. Say to me, "You are free to do as you wish," and I will do what I have done all

along, that is, be inclined toward one man in most situations. Say to him, "You are free to do as you wish," and usually he, too, will do what he has done all along, that is, be inclined toward several women (pp. 195-96).

In evaluating Bengis's experiences it is helpful to consider the ways in which they may be exceptional, both with respect to the cultural milieu in which they occurred and with respect to Bengis as an individual. In some ways her experiences obviously are "artificial": they can exist only where women are free to remain single (Bengis was twenty-nine years old when her autobiography was published) and to choose their own sexual partners, and where modern methods of contraception allow the separation of sexual intercourse and reproduction. It is in just such an environment, however, that women would be expected to be most like men if men and women do, in fact, possess the same basic sexual desires and dispositions. Where reliable contraception is not available, any emotional sex differences would be likely to be masked, since everyone will be cognitively aware that copulation exposes males and females to very different risks. Yet eliminating the risk of pregnancy does not seem to eliminate sex differences in emotions.

Also, it may be significant that Bengis is unusually sophisticated, intelligent, professionally successful, and physically attractive. The men with whom she became romantically involved were a highly selected group, sexually attractive not just to her but to most middle-class women, and therefore her lovers undoubtedly had greater than average sexual opportunities. One is reminded of Madame Bovary's wealthy and handsome lover, Rodolphe Boulanger, to whom "Emma was like any other mistress; and the charm of novelty, gradually slipping away like a garment, laid bare the eternal monotony of passion, whose forms and phrases are for ever the same." Bengis probably could have found men of lower market value who would have been more content to remain faithful to her, but she would have been less likely to want them. One woman in the *Redbook* magazine survey who wished to remain a virgin until marriage deliberately "gained thirty pounds, which made her undesirable to the 'sex-mad' popular boys and within reach of the shyer, less-demanding ones" (Tavris and Sadd 1977:41).

Perhaps the degree of "sex-madness" experienced by human males can, to some extent, be considered a facultative adaptation: a high-ranking or handsome male may tend to desire a multiplicity of sexual partners, a low-ranking or ugly male may be more satisfied with one. Trivers (1972) alludes rather obliquely to such a possibility, and it is difficult to believe that there is not something in it; moreover, one might expect that an individual male's desires would vary over time with variation in his sexual opportunities. (In a sense, this is logically true: to experience a desire for sexual variety one must first experience sex.) On the other hand, as discussed above, opportunities do not just exist in "environments," they are created: while opportunity may to some extent generate desire, surely desire also generates opportunity. Humans have always lived in extraordinarily complex social circumstances in which the possibility of arranging copulation with a fertile woman almost always is present, and hence a male itch (requiring substantially less than seven years to develop) is universally adaptive. Only occasionally does this itch dominate male psychology, resulting in the obsessions documented in *My Secret Life* (despite his lifelong dislike of red hair, Walter once went home with a red-haired prostitute simply because it meant a change) and in Edwards (1976), but the itch generally seems to be present and available to introspection. On the basis of interviews with 5300 American men, Kinsey *et al.* (1948:589) concluded: "There seems to be no question but that the human male would be promiscuous in his choice of sexual partners throughout the whole of his life if there were no social restrictions. . . . The human female is much less interested in a variety of partners."

Marriage forms and sexual jealousy

As noted above, the great majority of human societies are said to be "polygynous" because some successful men have more than one wife and polygny is "permitted." Polygynous marriages may also occur, however, where they are not permitted; for example, Seiler (1976) estimates that there are 25,000 to 35,000 polygynous marriages in the United States, mostly in the western states, and Cuber and Harroff (1965), in their study of sex and marriage among 437 highly successful Americans, interviewed men who maintained two families, each family unknown to the other. The reproductive benefits for men of having several wives are obvious, and the desire for sexual variety may motivate the accumulation of wives. A Kgatla male described his feelings about sexual intercourse with his two wives thus: "I find them both equally desirable, but when I have slept with one for three days, by the fourth day she has wearied me, and when I go to the other I find that I have greater passion, she seems more attractive than the first, but it is not really so, for when I return to the latter again there is the same renewed passion" (Schapera 1940:193).

Variability in economic success among men may be so great that women too can benefit from polygyny. Among some nonhuman animals "polygyny" results from female choice: this occurs when there is enough variation in the quality of male territories that some females can rear more young by choosing an already-mated male with a good territory than by choosing an unmated male with a poor territory (Orians 1969). Rose (1968) suggests that the extreme form of polygyny found in aboriginal Australia resulted from female choice; that is, women tended to aggregate as a collective of co-wives around a man at the peak of his productive and political power since, despite his several wives, such a man was a greater asset to a woman and her children than was a young, wifeless man.

Even if the opportunity for human females to exercise choice was not usually as great as Rose implies, the fact that, in cross-cultural perspective, women often appear to be content to be co-wives (Evans-Pritchard 1965, Mead 1967) suggests that during evolutionary history polygynous marriages frequently were adaptive for human females. Indeed, co-wives often assist one another in child care and in other ways, and the ethnographic literature provides examples of a man taking a second wife to help with household chores at the insistence of his first wife. Co-wives, may, of course, also be mutually hostile, and there are ethnographic examples of a man getting rid of one of his wives at the insistence of another of his wives. Throughout human evolutionary history, circumstances probably existed in which a male could increase his own fitness at the expense of his wife's fitness by obtaining a second wife. Selection may have favored females with the ability to "assess" the effects existing or potential wives on their own fitness and to experience the appropriate emotion; sexual jealousy of co-wives, or potential co-wives, may be one proximate mechanism mediating female-female competition, and marital disagreements over the desirability of adding another wife often may reflect underlying genetic "conflicts of interest." But since polygyny apparently was sometimes adaptive for females as well as for males, the experience of sexual jealousy of one's co-wives can be expected to be a facultative rather than an obligate adaptation. Even where co-wives are in conflict, sexual jealousy may be absent. Examples of conflicts among co-wives over a limited food supply have already been cited, and Elwin (1968) remarks that in polygynous Muria households "It is everywhere said that the wives quarrel, not through sexual jealousy or about prestige, but because each thinks the other shirks her due share of work" (p. 208).

Unlike polygyny, polyandry is extremely rare among human societies, is not common among any known hunter/gatherer peoples, and probably was virtually absent throughout most of human evolutionary history. Prince Peter (1963) reports that polyandry—as a regularly occurring form of marriage—is confined to agriculturalists and pastoralists living under very difficult economic conditions. He writes: "Having appeared as the product of very special economic and social circumstances, it [polyandry] disappears again with great facility when more usual conditions are present" (p. 570) owing to the male's "natural" desire to have exclusive sexual possession of his wife. If polyandry was exceedingly rare throughout human history, one would not expect selection to have favored a female desire for a multiplicity of husbands, even if women would, in theory, benefit reproductively thereby, since, unlike the male desire for variety, a female's desire for polyandry would be very unlikely to bring about the circumstances in which desire could be satisfied. Neither would one expect selection to have favored a facultative male disposition to be content with a polyandrous marriage. In some recent, unnatural environments a man might increase his fitness by participating in a polyandrous marriage (just as a man might increase his fitness by working fourteen hours a day on an assembly line), but this does not necessarily indicate genetic adaptation to polyandry, except perhaps in the general sense that humans can recognize—with respect to any desired object—that half a loaf is better than none. In other words, I am suggesting that although circumstances obviously do exist in which men will become co-husbands, circumstances do not exist in which men will do so as contentedly as women will become co-wives.

Owing to an extremely harsh environment, in which a man could not survive without a woman, Eskimos occasionally practiced polyandry, and the Eskimo data support the hypothesis that it is difficult for men to share a woman sexually. Balikci (1970) contrasts polygynous and polyandrous Eskimo households:

> In the polygynous household, the two wives generally got along quite well, and only rarely were feelings of jealousy expressed overtly. . . . Although desire for sexual enjoyment undoubtedly prompted polygyny, economic factors related to the division of labor within the household contributed as well (p. 156).

*   *   *

While polygynous marriages were relatively stable and provoked little resentment and jealousy, such was not the case with some polyandrous alignments. It seems that co-husbands were frequently jealous of each other concerning sexual prerogatives and had difficulties in concealing their sentiments (p. 157).

Rasmussen (1931) makes clear that these "difficulties" often led to murder. In summary, the experience of sexual jealousy of a co-spouse seems to be a facultative adaptation in the human female but more of an obligate adaptation in the human male. When a wife does experience sexual jealousy, there is no reason to suppose that her feelings are any less intense than a husband's feelings.

Extramarital sex and sexual jealousy

Kinsey et al. (1953) believed the male-female difference in the desire for sexual variety they found among Americans to be a human universal:

> Among all peoples, everywhere in the world, it is understood that the male is more likely than the female to desire sexual relations with a variety of partners. It is pointed out that the female has a greater capacity for being faithful to a single partner, that she is more likely to consider that she has a greater responsibility than the male has in maintaining a home and in caring for the offspring (p. 682).

The sexual "double standard" usually is said to result from society's suppression of women (Harper 1961, Kim 1969, Magar 1972). Ford and Beach (1951) review some of the data in the ethnographic literature on extramarital liaisons, and conclude that observed sex differences may be mostly a product of culture and reflect little about human nature:

> In the light of the cross-cultural evidence which we have presented it seems at least possible that the difference reflects primarily the effects of a lifetime of training under an implicit double standard. It has not been demonstrated that human females are necessarily less inclined toward promiscuity than are males. What the evidence does reveal is that in a great many societies the woman's tendencies to respond to a variety of sexual partners are much more sharply restricted by custom than are comparable tendencies in the man. And most important is the additional fact that in those societies which have no double standard in

sexual matters and in which a variety of liaisons are permitted, the women avail themselves as eagerly of their opportunity as do the men (p. 125).

Ford and Beach do not, however, provide convincing evidence for the existence of societies lacking a double standard. Furthermore, I would like to call attention to two assumptions which, I believe, can be detected between the lines of Ford and Beach's statement, assumptions which seem to underlie most discussions on this topic. First, the phrase "it seems at least possible . . ." seems to imply that it not only is *possible* but *preferable* to attribute a sex difference to culture rather than to human nature, if such an interpretation is not absolutely contradicted by the evidence (which, of course, is unlikely, given the difficulty of absolutely proving *anything*). I argued in Chapter Two that this position is both philosophically and tactically misguided: philosophically, because it confounds "is" and "ought"; tactically, because it leaves moral positions vulnerable to scientific disproof. Second, the tone of Ford and Beach's statement seems to imply that it is somehow "better" to desire sexual variety than not to desire it. If "better" is taken to refer to human happiness, this implication is debatable.

Consider the tendency to be aroused by visual stimuli, which, as Kinsey pointed out, is partly responsible for the male's desire for sexual variety. Although most men no doubt do, in some sense, enjoy "girl watching," this proclivity is no more an unmixed blessing than window-shopping is for most poor people. The protagonist of Peter De Vries's novel *The Tunnel of Love* remarks of an especially "nobly hewn blond": "She made even me salivate; I say even me because I am normally plunged into despair rather than excitement by such presences, which are but part of the world's weary wasted stimuli." In *The Mackerel Plaza,* another De Vries protagonist attempts to make deprivation bearable by compulsively ferreting out flaws in every attractive woman he sees. And Jim Dixon, the hero of Kingsley Amis's *Lucky Jim,* confronted at close quarters by Christine Callaghan, a young woman of exceptional beauty who seemed to be forever beyond his reach,

> studied the Callaghan girl, despite his determination to notice nothing more about her, and saw with fury that she was prettier than he'd thought. . . . He wanted to implode his features, to crush air from his mouth, in a way and to a degree that might be set against the mess of feelings she aroused in him: indignation, grief, resentment, peevishness,

spite, and sterile anger, all the allotropes of pain. The girl was doubly guilty, first of looking like that, secondly of appearing in front of him looking like that.

The desire for sexual variety dooms most human males to a lifetime of unfulfilled longing; when the desire can be satisfied easily, as among many homosexual men, it often frustrates the satisfaction of other desires, such as those for intimacy and security (Chapter Nine). I raise these issues here because I believe that the study of human sexuality has been impeded by the unquestioned, and perhaps unconscious, assumptions that cultural determinism is morally superior to biological determinism and that male sexuality is emotionally superior to female sexuality.

When culture or society are credited with causing and limiting human behavior, with expecting this and allowing that—as is frequently the case in summaries of the ethnographic literature—it becomes difficult to determine who (or what) actually does the causing and the limiting, who expects, and who allows. For example, Ford (1945:29) writes: "After marriage most societies expect the wife to obtain sexual gratification from her husband alone. Men, too, are more often restricted in their sexual promiscuity after marriage than before, although a husband's fidelity is less important than that of his wife in the majority of primitive tribes." One would like to know: less important to whom? Schlegel (1972) attributes more frequent restrictions on female than on male adultery in matrilineal societies to the action of society:

> . . . almost double the percentage [of societies] allow adultery for the husband . . . as allow it for the wife . . . in spite of the fact that children resulting from an adulterous union belong to their mother's descent group and are not, therefore, cuckoos in the father's lineal nest. It is hard to explain why wives should be expected to be sexually faithful so much more often than husbands. I can think of no biological or psychological reason for this, and the usual structural explanation of the child's membership in his father's descent group is not valid for matrilineal societies (p. 88).

The primary difficulty with superindividual concepts is that the interests of individual human beings conflict with one another, whether "interests" are understood in the ultimate genetic sense or in the proximate sense of motives and goals. Even if everyone in a given group were taught, and believed, that society is an entity possessed of a need to perpetuate itself and that humans are simply vehicles by which society survives, conflict would continue because humans satisfy their desires in part at one another's expense. Conflict originates in emotions and cannot be eliminated by beliefs, whether those beliefs are promulgated by social scientists or by more traditional mythmakers. When ethnographers consider the desires of individual human beings, conflict, not cultural uniformity, is usually apparent. Consider the following statements concerning men's feelings about adultery:

(a) "The men believe it is a good thing for them to have many lovers, but bad for women and especially bad for their wives" (Gregor 1973:247, on the Mehinacu of Brazil).

(b) "While men conventionally regard any woman outside the prohibited range, married or not, as a potential sexual partner, their own wives, they consider, should remain faithful to them" (Berndt 1962: 127-28, on New Guinea).

(c) "Men constantly attempt to seduce the wives of their village mates and take extreme offense when their own wives, in turn, are seduced" (Chagnon 1968b:131, on the Yanomamö).

(d) "Even those males who disapprove of extra-marital coitus for their own wives may be interested in securing such contacts for themselves, and this in most instances means securing coitus with the wives of other males" (Kinsey *et al.* 1953:415, on the United States).

While women's views on adultery may typically differ from men's views, I would expect women's feelings to be no less self-interested than men's. These statements suggest that the most fundamental, most universal double standard is not male versus female but each individual human versus everyone else. In a proximate sense, using male adultery as an example, this double standard results from such banal facts as that one's own orgasms feel substantially better to oneself than anyone else's orgasms do, and imagining one's wife copulating with another man in substantially more painful and threatening than imagining someone else's wife committing adultery (if the imagined accessory is oneself, the image may be pleasant rather than painful). In an ultimate sense, this double standard results from the fact that, among sexually reproducing organisms, every conspecific is to a greater or lesser extent one's reproductive competitor.

The word "promiscuous," in the sense of nonselective sexual intercourse, is pejorative in English and generally is applied to women (Huber 1969); this also is true of the equivalent word in the Trobriand Islands (Malinowski 1929), Western Arnhem Land (Berndt and Berndt

1951), and highland New Guinea (Berndt 1962). Similarly, Marshall (1971:150) writes of Mangaia: "Traditionally, a male goes from female to female—leaving one for another when he tires of the first or hears that she has gone with another man. People admire the boy who has had many girls, comparing him to 'a strong man, like a bull, going from woman to woman.' . . . But they do not admire the girl who has many boys, comparing her to a pig." I suggest this represents, not culture causing the sexual double standard, but the cumulative history of individuals attempting to influence one another through language. It seems likely that parents (and perhaps other elder kin) have systematically attempted to inculcate one set of sexual attitudes in their daughters and another in their sons, since copulation exposes males and females to very different risks.

None of the foregoing is intended to deny that human behavior is influenced by traditional values, that values themselves are grounded in emotion, or that values differ among peoples. Why traditions vary is a central problem of social science, but—aside from such matters as the absence of igloo-building traditions among Polynesian peoples— the lack of consensus is remarkable. Given the enormous changes that have occurred in most human environments since the recent origin of agriculture (making it unreasonable to expect self-interest as perceived by individual humans to coincide with genetic fitness), the unique history of each human community, and the fact of human plasticity, perhaps there can never be a substantial science of human society; nevertheless, evolutionary theory implies that everywhere, traditional values represent a history of compromise among competing individual interests.

There is no question that substantial cross-cultural variation exists in the frequency with which extramarital affairs occur; even in North America, sociologists have found that the likelihood of adultery varies with socioeconomic status, religiousness, and community of residence (Edwards 1973). Yet the combined weight of evolutionary theory, specific statements by ethnographers and other social scientists (such as those quoted above on adultery), works of fiction and autobiography, and personal experience makes me doubt the usefulness of such sweeping statements as "society A permits adultery" or "society B does not permit adultery." Even common generalizations about Western values and traditions often seem to be gross oversimplifications; for example, I question the existence of a monolithic double standard in the United States. Sexually active and sophisticated women often are portrayed favorably in literature and films,[2] and men who seek sexual variety often are characterized—especially by social scientists—as immature and irresponsible. Variety-seeking men are said to be avoiding the risks of intimacy or compensating for unconscious fears of sexual inadequacy or homosexuality. In *My Life as a Man*, Philip Roth points out that only a few years ago such a man was likely to be accused of suffering from the dread 1950s emotional malady: "being unable to love."

While it may be comforting to believe that men commit adultery in order to brag of their conquests to other men—since this belief can be taken to imply that adultery will disappear as men become sexually secure—in fact, male sexual braggadocio rarely is about adultery. Sexually adventurous adult men pose a threat to other men, and the fear of discovery generally triumphs over the desire to be envied. Malinowski (1929) speaks to this point in his discussion of Trobriand attitudes:

> . . . too open and too insistent an interest in sex, especially when exhibited by a woman, and too obvious and too general a success in love are both censured; but the kind of censure is entirely different in the two cases. In the latter, it is the male who incurs the disapproval of his less fortunate rivals. The great dancer, the famous love magician or charmer of his own beauty, is exposed to intense distrust and hatred, and to the dangers of sorcery. His conduct is considered "bad," not as "shameful," but rather as enviable and, at the same time, injurious to the interests of others (p. 458).

Goodenough (1949) notes that on Truk "There is little evidence that the motive for young men to commit adultery is a simple competitive one. There seems to be little boasting about successful night excursions. Informants were much more likely to tell of narrow escapes on unsuccessful ventures" (p. 618). Kinsey *et al.* (1948) report that most married men were very interested in knowing how frequently extramarital intercourse occurs, because they themselves desired it, but were reluctant to volunteer their own histories because they feared discovery. Kinsey *et al.* believed that this fear was the major reason that men of high educational or socioeconomic status refused to be interviewed. Many men who finally consented to participate in the survey after months or years of refusal were found to have nothing in their sexual histories that would explain their original hesitation except adultery.

---

[2] Even during Victorian times, most women, including middle- and upper-middle-class women, may not have been hostile to sexual feelings, despite the strong antisexual ideology that was pressed upon them (Degler 1974).

My concern in the remainder of this section is to suggest that the emotional bases of adultery are similar everywhere, and that these emotional bases can be illuminated by considering male-female differences. In brief, I shall suggest that a woman's sexual desire for a man other than her husband results largely from a comparison between the potential partner and her husband, and indicates either that she perceives the potential partner as being in some way superior to her husband, or that she is sexually or emotionally dissatisfied with her husband, or both. While men too make these comparisons, a man's sexual desire for a woman to whom he is not married is largely the result of her not being his wife. In addition, I shall suggest that a wife's experience of sexual jealousy varies with the degree of threat to herself that she perceives in her husband's adultery, whereas a husband's experience of sexual jealousy is relatively invariant, his wife's adultery almost always being perceived as threatening.

In a study of 792 middle- and upper-middle-class California couples, Terman (1938) found that men were more likely than women to report that they very frequently or frequently desired extramarital intercourse (13.3 percent of the men versus 3.5 percent of the women), and women were more likely to report that they never desired it (27.7 percent of the men versus 73.4 percent of the women). More significantly, the relationship between marital happiness and lack of desire for extramarital intercourse was much stronger in women than in men. Terman (1938:337) writes: "a husband ordinarily has to be above average in marital happiness to have as little extramarital desire as is expressed by rarely, while the wife must ordinarily be far below average in happiness before she will express that amount."

Chesser (1956), in his study of 6500 English women, provides similar evidence on the relationships between marital and sexual satisfaction and the desire for extramarital sex. Of those women who rarely or never orgasmed, 10 percent said that they frequently felt that they would like to have intercourse with someone other than their husbands, while only 3 percent of those women who frequently or always orgasmed reported this. Of the former group, 52 percent said they never desired intercourse with men other than their husbands, while 72 percent of the latter said this. Of those women in Chesser's sample who rated their marriages as exceptionally happy, only 2 percent said that they frequently wanted to have intercourse with another man, while 23 percent of the women who rated their marriages as unhappy or very unhappy said this. Of those women who rated their marriages as exceptionally happy, 80 percent reported that they never desired intercourse with another man, but only 32 percent of the women who rated their marriages as unhappy or very unhappy reported this.

Bell and his associates recently investigated the sexual behavior of 2372 married women; compared to the national distribution, these women were better educated and more frequently employed. Bell and Peltz (1974) report that 15 percent of the women who rated their marriages as very good had had extramarital intercourse, compared with 67 percent of the women who rated their marriages as poor or very poor; 18 percent of the women who rated their marital sexual satisfaction as very good had had extramarital intercourse compared with 48 percent of the women who rated marital sexual satisfaction as poor or very poor. Similarly, in the *Redbook* survey 51 percent of the wives with fair to very poor marriages had had extramarital sex compared to 24 percent of the wives with good marriages (Tavris and Sadd 1977). While some women who are happy with their marriages do have extramarital sex (Bell and Peltz 1974, Bell, Turner, and Rosen 1975, Tavris and Sadd 1977), in general, female adultery "seems to be related to both feelings of personal frustration and unhappiness with their husbands. The result often means that women turn to other men to find what they feel is missing with their husbands" (Bell and Peltz 1974:18). Commenting on Bell and Peltz's article, the psychiatrist Bernard L. Green remarks that in his clinical study, as well as in his clinical practice, women's motives for engaging in extramarital sex were primarily sexual frustration, curiosity, and revenge. Schapera (1940) also calls attention to revenge as a motive for adultery among Kgatla women.

Correlations of marital and sexual happiness and the presence or absence of extramarital sexual experience, while interesting, are difficult to interpret. For one thing, cause and effect are obscure; as Tavris and Sadd (1977) note, the experience of extramarital intercourse may cause a woman to perceive her marriage less favorably. For another thing, the experience of extramarital intercourse is not necessarily a good measure of desire: a woman with a good marriage might desire other lovers, yet not have them because of the risk to her marriage, whereas a woman with a poor marriage might feel she has less to lose.

Investigations that sacrifice large and representative samples for thoroughness in interviewing, such as Wolfe's (1975a, b), are helpful in assessing women's motives. Wolfe interviewed at length sixty-six nonreligious, economically secure, highly educated women living in

New York City or its suburbs who had had or were having affairs. The motives, feelings, and attitudes revealed in the interview excerpts (1975a) are so diverse they defy summarizing. Wolfe (1975a) emphasizes that a woman's extramarital activities are not necessarily directed against her husband; some women in her sample did have retaliatory affairs, yet others bore their husbands no grudges. Wolfe (1975a:242-43) writes:

> There were no universals, there was only a wide variety of patterns. I met women who engaged in extramarital activities because they were trying to wend their way out of unhappy marriages and women who engaged in them because they believed such activities would help them hold on, help them preserve their marriages. I met those who followed the romantic tradition and fell in love with their lovers, and others who had sexual relations quite casually, totally in opposition to the myth of the sexually cautious woman. It became clear to me that women are as disparate in their motivations and capacities for extramarital sex as they are in their appearances, and that affairs, like thumbprints, have whorls and markings and histories that are absolutely unique and individual.

Wolfe stresses that, like men, women "feel compelling sexual and emotional drives. We respond as intensely as men do to inadequate marriages, to feeling ignored, to starting to age" (1975a:244).

Yet two trends do emerge in Wolfe's interviews. First, despite their diversity, only one of Wolfe's informants evidenced a generalized desire for sexual variety, and even this woman remarked, "I'm not saying I like promiscuity. I don't. I wouldn't want to go screwing around a lot. It's just something I do when I feel like it and somebody comes along. But those two things don't happen at the same time too often" (1975a:112). Second, female adultery very frequently leads to divorce (1975a, b). Wolfe (1975b:55) concludes:

> . . . once the women were divorced, they usually began to seek to remarry—or at least to live in one-to-one relationships with new men, who were not necessarily their previous lovers. Some of them, remarried after former adulterous marriages, were impeccably faithful, firm believers in the fact that their previous situations had turned them to extramarital sex. To put it more simply, it was the rare woman who expressed the belief that sustained sexual variety was a psychological, biological necessity. It had been a necessity only in certain relationships.
>
> *   *   *
>
> Extramarital sex, at least as I encountered it among an urban and suburban group of well-educated, middle- to upper-class women, was

only minimally the province of sexual radicals. For most of the women I interviewed, it had far more to do with holding on to or obtaining a partner—with living in pairs, albeit sequentially—than with living in threes and fours, and at sixes and sevens.

Male sexuality in general seems to be less interesting and less frequently studied than female sexuality, and motivation for extramarital sex is no exception, yet some studies do exist. Edwards and Booth (1976), in a study of 294 married women and 213 married men in Toronto, found "negative perception" of the marriage and perceived "sexual deprivation" in the marriage to be correlated with the experience of adultery for both sexes. On the other hand, Johnson (1970), in his survey of 100 middle-class, middle-aged, midwestern couples, found that although husbands were more likely than wives to have had extramarital intercourse (20 husbands and 10 wives), were more likely to fantasize about having it, and were far more likely to desire extramarital intercourse if they had not had the opportunity to engage in it, the relationship between "marital adjustment" and the experience of extramarital intercourse was insignificant for both sexes. Johnson also found that although the relationship between reported sexual satisfaction in marriage and the experience of extramarital intercourse was insignificant for wives, husbands who reported low sexual satisfaction in marriage were more likely to have had extramarital intercourse than were those who reported high satisfaction. Pietropinto and Simenauer (1977) report that 629 men in their nationwide (USA) survey said they would not be tempted to cheat on their wives or steady girlfriends and 3614 men said they might be tempted to cheat. Of the latter, 63 percent said they would be most likely to cheat for an explicitly comparative reason ("poor sex at home," "fighting at home," "a woman who understands me better") and 37 percent said they would be most likely to cheat for a noncomparative reason ("exceptionally attractive woman," "available woman at work"). But Kinsey et al. (1948), on the basis of interviews with 5300 American men, conclude that extramarital intercourse results primarily from the male's interest in a variety of sex partners, that it occurs whether or not other "outlets" are available, and that it occurs "without respect to the satisfactory or unsatisfactory nature of the sexual relations at home" (p. 590).

In his report of the results of a recent survey of sexual behavior in the United States, Hunt (1974) advocates an environmentalistic interpretation of sex differences in the desire for extramarital intercourse because, in the under-twenty-five age group, wives were almost as likely as husbands to have had extramarital intercourse. However, Hunt gives twelve verbatim transcripts of interviews with five women and seven men in which they discuss the circumstances of their extramarital affairs. Four of the women and three of the men mention emotional or sexual unhappiness in their marriage; four of the men and none of the women mention the pleasures of variety. Also of interest are the reasons for abstinence given by married people who had not engaged in extramarital intercourse: the greatest sex difference was in the item "no one you wanted," cited by 39 percent of the women but only 16 percent of the men (Joseph S. Ruben, personal communication).

Berndt and Berndt (1951) note that among the Australian aborigines of Western Arnhem Land, extramarital affairs are most likely when a woman's husband is old and not sexually satisfying to her. In Berndt's (1962) report on peoples of highland New Guinea, the desire for extramarital sex is implied to be inevitable in a man, but in a woman it apparently depends on the quality of sexual relations with her husband. Berndt (1962:157) writes: "Complete sexual satisfaction is rarely to be obtained from one legitimate partner. The pleasure a man receives from his wives soon becomes monotonous and devoid of excitement." Although New Guinea men usually initiate extramarital affairs, women sometimes do, and sexual dissatisfaction seems to be their main motive. Men are advised to copulate regularly with their wives to keep them faithful, and, Berndt observes, the evidence bears out this advice.

In a study of the sexual behavior of fifty Canadian couples receiving marriage counseling, James and Pike (1967) found typical sex differences in motivation to engage in extramarital intercourse: "For the husbands, coitus was more likely to be a goal in itself rather than the consequence of a well-developed interpersonal relationship, while the reverse holds true for the wives" (p. 235). And among Cuber's (1969) sample of 437 "distinguished white Americans," a woman who was a married man's lover tended to feel less satisfied with that relationship than did a man who was a married woman's lover.

Among the residents of "East Bay," a large district on an unnamed island in Melanesia studied by Davenport (1965), sexual intercourse is regarded as natural and very pleasurable; all women are orgasmic, a woman often has many orgasms to her partner's one, and East Bay inhabitants believe that no marriage can be happy and stable unless the partners are sexually attracted to each other. Nevertheless, "it is assumed that after a few years of marriage, the husband's interest in his wife will begin to pale, and the frequency of intercourse will drop to once a day or perhaps even to once every five or ten days. Some wives complain bitterly about insufficient sexual attention, and it is regarded as justifiable for a woman to leave her husband when she is not attended at least once every ten days or so" (Davenport 1965:185). Until the practice was forbidden by colonial law, groups of East Bay men acquired young women as concubines. Wives were not jealous of concubines, but rather regarded them as status symbols, and both women and men today consider the loss of concubines to be the worst result of contact with whites. Every older East Bay man reported that he believed his sex life would be much more active if concubines were still permitted. Davenport (1965:190) writes: "Older men often comment today that without young women to excite them and without the variety once provided by changing concubines, they have become sexually inactive long before their time. To them a wife is sexually exciting only for a few years after marriage." Similarly, Masters and Johnson (1966:264) report: "Loss of coital interest engendered by monotony in a sexual relationship is probably the most constant factor in the loss of an aging male's interest in sexual performance with his partner." They note that frequently such a man may be rejuvenated by having sexual intercourse with a younger woman, although the young woman may not be as adept a lover as his wife.

If men and women typically differ in their sexual emotions, these differences may be obscured by the tendency for each individual to conceive other minds by analogy with his or her own, and by the necessity for men and women to express their thoughts and feelings in a common language. It is possible, for example, that questionnaire items have different emotional meanings for men and women, and hence that comparing their responses quantitatively may be somewhat misleading. Then, too, individuals probably do not often conceptualize their emotional life along the lines discussed here. It seems unlikely that a man about to embark on an affair is thinking, "Aha! At last an opportunity to satisfy my desire for sexual variety *per se!*" or that his lover is thinking, "I hope this man, unlike my husband, will satisfy my emotional and/or sexual needs." More likely, each is simply experiencing sexual desire for the other.

To my mind, then, one of the most persuasive evidences of sex differences is the suggestion—albeit vague and difficult to measure—that men and women find it intuitively difficult to understand one another. Although the Kgatla believe that men are naturally inclined to be promiscuous, Kgatla women seem to find it difficult to understand male desires intuitively; as one of Schapera's (1940) female informants remarked, "We wonder what it is that a husband really wants, for his wife's body is there every day for him to use" (p. 207). Similarly, in spite of the importance of sexuality in the lives of Mangaians, and Marshall's suggestion (cited above) that Mangaian girls may be interested in variety, Mangaian women apparently do not comprehend the male desire for variety. A Mangaian wife, upon discovering her husband's adultery, may ask: "Why do you want a whole crate of oranges when I am here?" (1971:148). And Kinsey et al. (1953:409) write:

> Most males can immediately understand why most males want extramarital coitus. Although many of them refrain from engaging in such activity because they consider it morally unacceptable or socially undesirable, even such abstinent individuals can usually understand that sexual variety, new situations, and new partners might provide satisfactions which are no longer found in coitus which has been confined for some period of years to a single sexual partner. . . . On the other hand, many females find it difficult to understand why any male who is happily married should want to have coitus with any female other than his wife. The fact that there are females who ask such questions seems, to most males, the best sort of evidence that there are basic differences between the two sexes.

With respect to the desire for sexual variety, the data on adultery can be interpreted as follows. For both sexes, adultery is without doubt influenced both by ontogenetic experiences and by immediate circumstances: people who have been taught that adultery is bad or dangerous are less likely to engage in it than are people who have been taught differently; adultery is more common when its costs—in terms of time, energy, and risk—are low than it is when its costs are high. But although human beings are complex, the determinants of human behavior various and interacting, and the human condition one of mixed emotion, the persistent hint of male-female differences holds out some promise of regularity within diversity.

Women do not generally seem to experience a pervasive, autonomous sexual desire for men to whom they are not married; a woman is most likely to experience desire for extramarital sex when she perceives another man as somehow superior to her husband or when she is in some way dissatisfied with her marriage (while investigators have most often considered emotional and sexual dissatisfactions, economic dissatisfaction may also be important). A woman about to embark on an affair may not be thinking of her husband or her marriage at all, but simply be experiencing sexual desire for her intended lover; yet from the standpoint of ultimate causation, her sexual desire may function primarily as part of the process by which women trade up in the husband market. Wolfe (1975b) began her investigation of women's extramarital affairs convinced that adultery can be therapeutic and beneficial to marriage, and was surprised to discover that—despite the diversity of motives and circumstances—women's adultery regularly preceded divorce. Adultery may also function to increase the genetic quality of a woman's offspring, but, as suggested above, this probably is a minor (or rare) function, since it seems unlikely that the detectable genetic differences among males are often great enough to repay the investment of time, energy, and risk that adultery entails.

A male obviously stands to benefit genetically from adultery in that he may sire offspring at almost no cost to himself in terms of time and energy, even when he cannot obtain or support additional wives. Males can be expected to experience a persistent, autonomous desire for extramarital sex because this desire functions to create low-cost reproductive opportunities. As suggested above, human communities probably have always been complex enough that reproductive opportunities could occur at almost any time to almost any adult male; if the desire for variety were satisfied even once in a lifetime, it might pay off reproductively. Adultery does, of course, often entail substantial risk, including risk to marital happiness. For males, then, the occurrence of a low-risk opportunity probably is the most important determinant of adultery. A striking, if unusual, example is reported by Hunt (1974): a male informant had his first affair during his honeymoon when his bride was occupied at the hairdresser and a low-risk sexual opportunity presented itself. In the section on nonmarital sex, it was mentioned that on Truk young men have few sexual opportunities because most young women are married. By the time a man is capable of obtaining a wife, usually in his early twenties, he is also becoming attractive to women in general. Goodenough (1949) writes that while these young men "no longer need to resort to such means of sexual gratification as masturbation, it is actually at about the time of marriage, when they have reached an age to be taken seriously by the women, that they become most involved in adulterous affairs and remain so until they are about thirty years of age" (p. 617).

The male desire for sexual variety may also pay off reproductively if it results in obtaining additional wives, especially young wives, and the strength of the sexual desire for young women may vary with male age. It seems likely that throughout human history in early middle age married men often became able to obtain and to support an additional wife or wives, and hence the sexual desire for young women would be especially adaptive at this age. This desire could be adaptive regardless of a male's circumstance if it functioned to motivate the economic and political effort that might make its fulfillment possible. That the desire for prestige, status, and power are autonomous and important male motives and that possession of women is often a sign of status do not negate the importance of sexual motives for economic, political, or sexual behavior. In the West—where polygyny is illegal—affairs involving young women and middle-aged men, which are usually attributed to such factors as "male menopause," and which not infrequently result in a man's divorcing an aging wife and beginning a second family with a young wife, might have resulted in polygyny in times past.

The good-natured and unprincipled Oblonsky, in Tolstoy's *Anna Karenina*, is the classic literary portrait of the philanderer's point of view:

> Oblonsky was honest with himself. He could not deceive himself by telling himself that he repented of his conduct. He could not feel repentant that he, a handsome, amorous man of thirty-four, was not in love with his wife, the mother of five living and two dead children, who was only a year younger than he. He only regretted that he hadn't been able to conceal things from her better. But he felt the full gravity of his position and was sorry for his wife, their children, and himself. He might have been able to hide his misconduct from his wife better if he had expected the news to have such an effect on her. He had never thought the matter over clearly, but had vaguely imagined that she had long since guessed he was unfaithful to her and was shutting her eyes to it. He even thought that a completely undistinguished woman like her, worn out, aging, already plain, just a simple good-hearted mother of a family, ought to have been indulgent, out of a feeling of fairness. What had happened was just the opposite.

Sex differences are also apparent in the occurrence of sexual jealousy over a spouse's adultery. In cross-cultural perspective there is no doubt that husbands typically are more concerned about their wives' fidelity than wives are about their husbands' fidelity (Ford 1945, Kinsey *et al.* 1948, 1953, Safilos-Rothschild 1969). Among the Turu of Tanzania, marriages are made for economic rather than emotional reasons and, since marriage is almost exclusively a business enterprise, women are lonely and may initiate extramarital affairs, although most commonly men initiate them (Schneider 1971). (According to Schneider, women attempt to establish a kind of relationship missing in their marriage and do not appear to seek sexual variety *per se*.) But although extramarital affairs are common, most Turu husbands want their wives to be faithful; the Turu have an extremely high divorce rate and one of the highest assault and murder rates in Tanzania, primarily owing to wives' extramarital affairs. Kinsey *et al.* (1953) note that men, twice as often as women, said that their spouses' extramarital activities was the main factor precipitating divorce. Kinsey *et al.* (1948:592) write: "Wives at every social level, more often accept the non-marital activities of their husbands. Husbands are much less inclined to accept the non-marital activities of their wives. It has been so since the dawn of history. The biology and psychology of this difference need more careful analysis than the available data yet afford."

In Philip Roth's *Portnoy's Complaint*, Alex Portnoy fantasizes giving his father the following pep talk should the latter be discovered in adultery: "What after all does it consist of? You put your dick some place and move it back and forth and stuff came out the front. So, Jake, what's the big deal?" Why adultery so often is a big deal, and why it is especially likely to be a big deal to men, can be explained in a straightforward manner by evolutionary biology. As a man never can be certain of paternity, a cuckold risks investing in the offspring of, and having his wife's reproductive efforts tied up by, a reproductive competitor; as a woman always is certain of maternity, and as her husband's adultery does not diminish his capacity to inseminate her, a wife may risk little if her husband engages in extramarital sex (Barash 1977). This also explains why having an affair is a more effective female than male tactic in marital skirmishing and why even modern, sophisticated males may be ambivalent about the desirability of libidinousness in a wife.

Charlie Citrine, the protagonist of Saul Bellow's novel *Humboldt's Gift*, says of his lover: "as a carnal artist she was disheartening as well as thrilling, because, thinking of her as wife-material, I had to ask myself where she had learned all this and whether she had taken the PhD once and for all." Sex researchers often seem to consider the male tendency to divide women into "whores" and "madonnas" (a tendency which reaches ludicrous extremes in some societies) to constitute a sort of perverse contradiction in the male psyche. From an evolutionary perspective, however, a wife's most important sexual attribute by far is fidelity, and this male tendency is less paradoxical.

Needless to say, the hypothesis that the ultimate function of male sexual jealousy is to increase the probability that one's wife will conceive one's own rather than someone else's child does not imply that this is a conscious male motive, any more than it is a motive of any sexually jealous male animal. The often vitriolic debate in the literature over whether the members of any human group are really ignorant of the male's role in procreation is fascinating; the reader of this debate gradually abandons the naïve notion that a given people either are or are not ignorant of paternity, and ultimately confronts the questions: What constitutes ignorance or awareness of paternity? and, How can ignorance or awareness be determined? (see Leach 1966, Spiro 1968, and *Man* N.S. 3:651-56, 1968). The most likely candidate for a people lacking awareness of paternity are the Trobriand Islanders, among whom male sexual jealousy is pronounced (Malinowski 1929). Indeed, over a very long period of time the existence of reasonably accurate knowledge of the male's role in procreation might actually promote the reduction of male sexual jealousy by natural selection. If the primary function of male jealousy is to reduce the probability that one's wife will be impregnated by another man, and if husbands are able to predict with some accuracy their wives' fertile periods, selection might favor males who are emotionally committed to the goal of siring their wives' offspring (that is, males among whom the ultimate goal had become the proximate, conscious goal) but who rely more on intellect than on "blind" sexual jealousy to achieve this goal. Such men could be more emotionally flexible on the issue of their wives' extramarital activities and hence could more easily engage in adaptive wife exchanges and could profit from gifts bestowed on their wives in exchange for sexual favors.

In modern Western societies it seems fairly clear that some, perhaps even many, married men can learn to overcome sexual jealousy in order to participate in spouse exchanges and group sex. These sexual arrangements are carefully structured to minimize romantic involvements that might disrupt marriages, and the possibility of conception is eliminated by modern contraceptive technology. But in the few non-Western cases in which male sexual jealousy is alleged to be minimal, it is also stated or implied that paternity is uncertain and unproblematic. In Chapter Two, one such example was discussed in detail—the

Siriono of Bolivia (Holmberg 1950)—and it was pointed out that in one of the eight births Holmberg witnessed the woman's husband maintained that the infant was not his; he refused to accept it, and subsequently he would have nothing to do with his wife or her child. Moreover, Holmberg notes that quarrels and fights over sex are common. It was suggested that biological paternity may be more certain, and more important to Siriono males, than Holmberg implies, and that there may be substantially less "sexual freedom" among the Siriono than Holmberg was led to believe.

A second ethnographic example of sexual freedom is that of the Kuikuru of the Brazilian Mato Grosso (Carneiro 1958). According to Carneiro, all adult Kuikuru participate in an elaborate system of extramarital relations: each person has one or more extramarital partners (*ajoi*) who are known to everyone, including spouses, and "adultery, as a crime, cannot be said to exist in Kuikuru society" (p. 137). The number of *ajois* a person has is said to vary with his or her attractiveness. Although Carneiro indicates that extramarital liaisons are conducted clandestinely, and that husbands and wives may quarrel and even scratch and bruise one another in disputes over extramarital adventures, no fights among males are recorded, and only one man is reported to have divorced a wife because of her affairs (he subsequently married a less attractive, but harder working, woman who had only one *ajoi*).

An unmarried Kuikuru woman who becomes pregnant attempts abortion; if this fails, she kills the infant at birth. But

> if a married woman is going to have a child which she believes has been fathered by an *ajoi* rather than by her legal husband, she goes to the village plaza and makes a public declaration of this fact. The men of the village are then supposed to beat the man allegedly responsible for making her pregnant. This, at any rate, is the idealized procedure. We could learn of no instance in which any such public denunciation had actually been made. In practice, of course, the average Kuikuru wife would ordinarily have no way of knowing just who the biological father of her child was. But at least in this way the Kuikuru can preserve the myth that whether he be wise or not, every man knows his own father (pp. 141-42).

Ajoi relationships are the subject of a great deal of gossip, joking, and teasing. Carneiro writes:

> The Kuikuru did not at first reveal to us the existence of their system of extra-marital sex partners. But once they knew that we had become aware of it, they lost no time in trying to bring us into the system, in name if not in fact. This attempt, indeed, became the basis of a good

deal of friendly humor between the tribe and ourselves. They jokingly assigned 5 or 6 *ajois* to my wife and to me, and soon everyone in the village knew the names of our alleged *ajois* as well as they knew the actual tribal ones. They never tired of trying to get us to name our supposed sex partners, and enjoyed it immensely when we counted them off on our fingers, Kuikuru style.

The chief's wife was said to be one of my *ajois*, and one day when I was in her house an elderly man came up to me and with a perfectly straight face asked me for my red plaid shirt in payment for favors purportedly granted to me by this woman. She was his classificatory daughter (p. 140).

Now Carneiro does not claim to have ever witnessed an actual act of extramarital intercourse; like all ethnographers, he inferred their existence from the information provided him, information which apparently seemed to be internally consistent and consonant with other aspects of Kuikuru culture. Yet in the single instance in which he had independent evidence—namely himself—the number of publicly known *ajois* was five or six, but the number of actual *ajois*, according to Carneiro, was zero. In a second instance—Carneiro's wife—the actual number of *ajois* also was believed by Carneiro to be zero. Thus it seems reasonable to entertain some skepticism concerning Carneiro's conclusion that biological paternity among the Kuikuru is essentially unknowable.

Uncertain paternity and lack of male jealousy are easily accounted for sociobiologically: where paternity is uncertain, it need only be assumed that men invest in their sisters', rather than their wives', offspring (although this does not appear to be the case among the Kuikuru). Uncertain paternity and lack of male jealousy can be accounted for even more easily by cultural determinism since, in this view, it is the persistence of social systems that is important, and human emotion is largely the product of these systems, rather than the other way around. Biological paternity eliminations on a series of Kuikuru infants would be helpful in resolving this matter; as things stand, the issue remains an open one. Nevertheless, the evidence presently available seems to me not to rule out the following hypotheses: (1) men everywhere prefer their wives to be sexually faithful; and (2) there is not now, and never has been, a society in which confidence in paternity is so low that men are typically more closely related genetically to their sisters' than to their wives' offspring. Happily promiscuous, nonpossessive, Rousseauian chimpanzees turned out not to exist; I am not convinced by the available evidence that such human beings exist either.

The typical male-female differences in the occurrence of sexual jealousy should not be understood to mean that men in some sense have a larger quantity of, or a greater capacity for, sexual jealousy (although men are more likely to express jealousy in physical violence, hence their feelings are more often visible and less easily overlooked). Rather, jealousy about a spouse's adultery may be a difficult-to-overcome, more or less obligate, response among husbands, but a flexible, facultative response among wives. When wives do experience such jealousy, there is no reason whatever to believe that their experiences are any weaker or stronger than husbands' experiences. Tolstoy makes Oblonsky's wife, Dolly, say of her husband's adultery: "The terrible thing is that my heart has suddenly been transformed, and instead of love and tenderness for him all I have is rage, yes, rage. I could kill him. . . ."

The evidence is substantial, however, that women do not inevitably experience sexual jealousy over a husband's extramarital activities; for example, "East Bay" wives not only were not jealous of their husbands' concubines but regarded concubines as status symbols (Davenport 1965). Yet ethnographic examples have also been cited of jealous and angry wives. Variation exists within a given society and perhaps even within a given woman at different times. Schapera (1940) writes of Kgatla wives:

> Wives vary greatly in their attitude towards an unfaithful husband. Often enough a woman is fairly complaisant, or at least resigned, so long as her husband continues to look after her decently, sleeps with her regularly, and does not obviously favour his concubine. One of my informants said that at his wedding-feast he was greatly attracted by two of the girls present, and asked his wife if he might take them as mistresses. Her reply was in his eyes eminently reasonable. "Well," she said, "you are still a young man, so I suppose that you need more than one woman, but don't make your affairs too public, and remember that we also must have a baby of our own!" This attitude is by no means unusual. Accustomed to a tradition of polygamy, women regard it as natural for a man to distribute his attentions, and many a wife, provided that her husband does not talk of marrying again, and does not humiliate her by openly flaunting his infidelity, judiciously refrains from making it a bone of contention, except when she is thoroughly angry with him over something else as well.
>
> But the wife is not always so accommodating. She may object to being neglected for some one else, she may fear the possibility of her husband's infection by one of the "blood" diseases, she may resent the indignity of not being regarded as sufficiently attractive in herself, and she may simply and furiously be jealous (pp. 206-7).

Although her husband cannot become pregnant with another woman's child, a wife nonetheless can incur other kinds of risks to fitness as a consequence of her husband's adultery, risks which may be quite as serious as those a husband incurs as a consequence of his wife's adultery. A husband's dalliance may have no effect whatsoever on his wife's reproductive success or it may presage a liaison that will entail a reduction in the husband's investment in his wife and her children; furthermore, today's paramour may be tomorrow's co-wife. Selection favored men who kept mistresses, changed wives, and obtained additional wives when these activities increased their own inclusive fitness, regardless of the effects on the fitnesses of the women involved. (Of course, moral traditions can limit male activities, but traditions are part of the environment in which selection occurs.) I suggest that selection has favored the female capacity to learn to distinguish (not necessarily cognitively) threatening from nonthreatening adultery, and to experience jealousy in proportion to the perceived threat. This male-female difference probably is one of the bases of the double standard, but it is unlikely to be the only basis. In *Anna Karenina*, to the liberal Pestov's remark that in his opinion the inequality between husband and wife consists of the fact that a wife's infidelity and a husband's infidelity are punished inequitably, both in law and in public opinion, Karenin replies: "I think the foundations of this attitude are rooted in the very nature of things." But surely an important aspect of the nature of things is the power to make and to enforce the law and to mold public opinion. The double standard is the product not only of sex differences in emotion but also of sex differences in access to power.

Spouse exchange

Married couples who exchange partners for the purpose of sexual intercourse have been reported among the North Alaskan Eskimo (Spencer 1968), the Pagan Gaddang of the Philippine Islands (Wallace 1969), the Qolla Indians of Peru (Bolton 1973), and white, middle-class Americans (Bartell 1971): in each case there is at least a hint that the male's desire for sexual variety is the emotional source of these arrangements, although mate swapping may have other uses as well.

Among the North Alaskan Eskimo, wife exchanges were arranged between the husbands, and the wives were not consulted. Spencer emphasizes that wife exchange was a sexual, not economic, matter in the sense that an Eskimo husband desired another man's wife not because she possessed economic skills his own wife lacked but because she was not his wife. On the other hand, wife exchange also was a means of cementing ties of friendship and mutual aid among men who "sought in every way possible to extend the patterns of economic cooperation" (Spencer 1968:142).

Pagan Gaddang husbands first informally discuss the possibility of exchanging wives, but unlike the Eskimo, the exchange (which is negotiated by the husbands' parents) occurs only if the wives agree to it. Wallace notes that these exchanges may create a basis for future economic cooperation and sometimes are entered into in the hope that a wife who has not produced a child will become pregnant; but the Pagan Gaddang also explain the practice by saying: "another cook another flavor."

As with the Pagan Gaddang, Qolla spouse exchanges are initiated by the husbands but require the consent of the wives. Bolton (1973:149) writes:

> If an agreement is reached by the men, they are then faced with the problem of convincing their wives to accept the arrangement. For the most part it is maintained by the villagers that women do not readily agree to form *tawanku* [spouse exchange] bonds. Consequently, the usual procedure for the men is to settle upon a date when all four persons can get together, to drink and become drunk. After they have gotten the two women completely inebriated they all go to bed in the same room, each man taking the other man's wife to one side of the hut. Following sexual intercourse with the friend's wife they remain together to sleep for the night. In the morning the women discover what has happened. In the ensuing discussion the men convince the women that they should be *tawanku* partners.

Qolla *tawanku* relationships may become the basis for economic cooperation.

A dramatic increase in the frequency of mate swapping and group sex—collectively, "swinging"—occurred in the United States in 1963-64, coinciding with the widespread use of oral contraceptives. While there is a rather large and tedious literature on swinging, I shall rely on Bartell (1971), which strikes me as the most balanced, clear-eyed, and thorough investigation. On the basis of interviews with 350 swingers from the Chicago metropolitan area and other urban centers, firsthand observation at swingers' parties, and analysis of swingers' magazines, Bartell concludes, as did Kinsey *et al.* (1953), that swinging is fundamentally a male device for obtaining extramarital sex:

. . . most male swingers are, in effect, bartering their women. True, these couples do not like the term "wife-swapping." It seems to show that the women are not equal to the men. Nevertheless, the facts are that men almost invariably initiate swinging, they exchange pictures of their nude or seminude women with other couples, and that they circulate such pictures much more readily than pictures of themselves together with their mate (p. 288).

About 80 percent of the ads placed by couples in swingers' magazines are accompanied by a picture of the woman only, and the wife's physical attractiveness is more important than the husband's in determining the couple's success in swinging. Single men sometimes send in a picture of a woman, falsely implying that they have a woman to swap. Women can place ads without charge, and letters from women to men are forwarded without charge. The response a couple's ad receives is a function of the woman's age and physical attractiveness, and the amount of clothes she is wearing in the photograph (usually there is no response to an ad unaccompanied by a photograph). Even when ads specify "no single men," 40 to 75 percent of the responses are from single men. A couple typically receives three or four letters in response to their ad, while a single, twenty-five-year-old woman—who was thirty pounds overweight and not pretty—received 500 responses to her ad. Most couples, in fact, seek a single woman rather than another couple, but single women are difficult to obtain. Some swingers' magazines and organizations are run by single men whose primary aim is to gain sexual access to women, and many magazines are purchased by men who do not have the opportunity to swing but who enjoy fantasizing about it.

The far greater male than female interest in swinging becomes especially significant when one considers sex differences in sexual capacities (to which Mark Twain's Satan called attention), women's increasing dissatisfaction with the frequency of marital intercourse, and the realities of group sex. Since the 1920s the proportion of American wives who say that marital intercourse occurs too frequently has steadily fallen and the proportion who say that it occurs too infrequently has steadily risen; in one recent survey in Philadelphia, 32 percent of the wives reported marital intercourse to be too infrequent and 2 percent reported it to be too frequent (Bell 1974). In the *Redbook* survey, 38 percent of the wives said marital intercourse occurs too infrequently and 4 percent said it occurs too frequently (Tavris and Sadd 1977). Thus one might expect that many married women would welcome the opportunity for more sexual intercourse with men (some of whom may be more attractive than one's husband) who find new women sexually exciting, especially since most women apparently are able to be sexually satiated during group sex, largely owing to sexual involvement with other women. Bartell notes that 92 percent of the women at swingers' parties are sexually active with other women, that the likelihood of such activity is a direct function of the length of time the woman has been swinging, and that such activity is encouraged by husbands, who invariably find watching it to be sexually arousing. Bartell writes: "the fact that women who are not lesbians greatly enjoy sex with other such women was plainly evident at every party we observed. . . . Each would enjoy numerous orgasms, and the activity ceased only when all were exhausted" (pp. 152-53).

In contrast, tension and anxiety may render men impotent in group sex, and in order to satisfy their desire for variety men must husband their semen, moving from woman to woman without ejaculating; in general, men frequently find themselves unable to live up to their own expectations, and may say that swinging is "unfair" to men. Thus if human emotional life operated according to Satan's naïve rationalism, women could be expected to be the driving force behind swinging, but clearly they are not. Furthermore, women's motives for swinging apparently are not the same as men's motives. Bartell notes that although both husbands and wives may be bored with marital sex, men swing for sexual variety while women swing in part to be reassured of their sexual desirability; also, women's satisfaction in group sex seems to have more to do with sexual satiation than with sexual variety.

Spouse exchange seems to engender far less male jealousy than a wife's unilateral adultery does. There are several possible explanations: first, an arrangement the husband himself has contrived presumably constitutes little threat to his marriage; second, although in the course of a spouse exchange his wife may be impregnated by someone else, the husband has an equal chance to impregnate the other woman; third, in a spouse exchange a husband is in a far better position to assess paternity than he is when his wife is secretly adulterous. Spencer (1968) does not discuss the question of pregnancies arising from Eskimo wife exchanges, and modern contraceptive technology has eliminated this problem among swingers in the United States (Bartell 1971). As noted above, a Pagan Gaddang couple may actually enter into a spouse exchange hoping that a barren woman will in this way begin her reproductive career. A child sired by the exchange partner rather than the

woman's husband "is primarily a member of his social family of procreation, and his biological father and the latter's relatives assume little
responsibility for him" (Wallace 1969:185). Among the Qolla, too,
children of couples in *tawanku* are "legitimized" as offspring of the
mother and her husband. Yet according to one informant, "*tawanku*
men sometimes beat their wives when they have been impregnated by
the *tawanku* partner" (Bolton 1973:152).

Conclusions

Presently available evidence supports the view that human males typically experience an autonomous desire for a variety of sex partners and
human females are far less likely to do so. While there is no reason to
doubt that rearing conditions could be devised that would reverse this
sex difference, the appropriate conditions are unlikely ever to have
existed. The fashionable way of expressing such a difference—that
males by nature can learn to desire variety more easily than females can
—does not seem to be particularly helpful in this case, since there is no
evidence that the development of the desire for sexual variety in the
human male depends on the specific kinds of prior circumstances that
normally are considered to be "learning experiences." Neither can the
existence of this desire be usefully considered to be a facultative adaptation (though its strength may be) since it seems most unlikely that
there has ever been an even remotely natural human environment in
which some desire for variety—tempered with appropriate caution and
restraint—would not have been adaptive to males. In fact, human males
appear to be so constituted that they resist learning *not* to desire variety despite impediments such as Christianity and the doctrine of sin;
Judaism and the doctrine of mensch; social science and the doctrines of
repressed homosexuality and psychosexual immaturity; evolutionary
theories of monogamous pair-bonding; cultural and legal traditions that
support and glorify monogamy; the fact that the desire for variety is
virtually impossible to satisfy; the time and energy, and the innumerable kinds of risk—physical and emotional—that variety-seeking entails;
and the obvious potential rewards of learning to be sexually satisfied
with one woman.

Women's motives for adultery are various; but although they often
express sexual desire for men other than their husbands, women rarely
seem to experience a generalized, autonomous desire for sexual variety

per se, and it is hard to conceive of a natural environment in which such a desire would be adaptive. Women appear to seek extramarital sex when they experience some deficit—sexual, emotional, or, perhaps, economic—in their marriage, or perceive another man as being superior to (not merely different from) their husbands. Indeed, wives' adultery may be more often a byproduct of their husbands' desire for variety than their own: a husband's desire may cause him to neglect his wife sexually or emotionally, and his infidelity may trigger a retaliatory affair.

Sex differences in the desire for variety may explain why spouse exchanges are initiated by men. Women do sexually desire other women's husbands, but a woman most likely will want to husband-swap only with women whose husbands are more attractive than her own. But another man's wife—who is no more physically attractive than one's own wife—is perceived as more sexually desirable owing to her "fresh features," hence each man is able to profit emotionally from the transaction.

The existence of a fundamental sex difference in the desire for sexual variety can be accounted for easily in an ultimate sense, since the minimum male and female parental investments are enormously different, hence selection can be expected to act in opposite ways on males and females; but the documentation of this difference is beset with problems. For one thing, the numerical logic of heterosexual copulation means that substantial sex differences in the statistics of sexual intercourse with new partners cannot occur. For another, desires cannot be observed, counted, or measured; they are inferred from what people say and do. If each of us constructs a model of other minds by analogy with his own, it may be easier to imagine that some external force—society, culture, etc.—causes members of the opposite sex to act at variance with their truest impulses than it is to imagine that males and females have different impulses. And of course learning can never be ruled out entirely: if men do desire variety and women do not, this difference will be to some extent apparent in talk and in action which constitute part of the environment in which young people grow up. It is impossible to prove that a sex difference in desire would develop in a nonexistent environment in which knowledge of the difference was absent (indeed, if such an environment could be manufactured for experimental purposes it would be unnatural). Consider that all humans grow up in environments in which everyone believes that men typically are larger and stronger than women, and yet few of us would ascribe this sex difference entirely to tradition. But many of us would ascribe sex differences in desires entirely to tradition; and yet it has not been shown that desires (as opposed to behaviors) are "farther" from the genes than gross morphology is. Finally, the male desire for variety very rarely is an all-consuming passion that dominates the psyche; most men most of the time are, and probably always have been, primarily involved in the day-to-day concerns of making a living and raising a family. Low-risk opportunities for sexual variety are rare for most men, and when a married man does embark on an affair with a married woman it is unlikely that he is thinking of sexual variety or that she is thinking of comparisons between her lover and her husband.

Despite these difficulties, however, better evidence can be gathered than exists at present. For example, married people who are sexually attracted to, and sexually active with, their spouses could be asked the following question: If you had the opportunity to copulate with an anonymous member of the opposite sex who was as physically attractive as your spouse but no more so, and as competent a lover as your spouse but no more so, and there was no risk of discovery, disease, or pregnancy, and no chance of forming a more durable liaison, and the copulation was a substitute for an act of marital intercourse, not an addition, would you do it? I predict that there would be a major and universal sex difference in response to this question. Furthermore, I predict that if the experiment could be conducted in reality rather than in fantasy, and more than one such opportunity were provided, the sex difference would become greater still. Many women who had initially said "yes" out of curiosity would find the experimental intercourse less satisfying than intercourse with their husbands, and would subsequently decline; many men who had initially said "yes" reluctantly, despite serious misgivings, guilt, and anxiety would subsequently assent more easily and with less guilt and anxiety. In Chapter Nine a more realistic test of the hypothesis is presented.

EIGHT

Copulation as a Female Service

I never yet touched a fig leaf that didn't turn into a price tag.
SAUL BELLOW, *Humboldt's Gift*

AMONG ALL PEOPLES it is primarily men who court, woo, proposition, seduce, employ love charms and love magic, give gifts in exchange for sex, and use the services of prostitutes. And only men rape. Everywhere sex is understood to be something females have that males want; it constitutes a service or favor that females in general can bestow on or withhold from males in general, although "favorless" intercourse also occurs, and the exchange may be reversed in certain circumstances. In a sense the whole literature on human sexuality documents this claim, but the issue is explicitly considered by only a few writers.

Blau (1964) describes the economics of love in the United States as a series of transactions between a male and a female in which the male exchanges evidence of "commitment" to the female for sexual access to her. Courting is thus a series of strategies and counter-strategies, with mutual love as the goal, in which sex and commitment are manipulated, each partner attempting to maximize gains and minimize losses: "A woman promotes a man's love by granting him sexual and other favors, as demonstrations of her affection and as means for making associating with her outstandingly rewarding for him, yet if she dispenses such favors readily—to many men or to a given man too soon— she depreciates their value and thus their power to arouse an enduring attachment" (p. 80). Blau assumes that the specific form the exchange takes varies with culturally determined sex roles, yet underlying his analysis is the assumption that sexual access to a woman is a commodity, which she can bestow or withhold to maximize its value, and the ethnographic record shows that this aspect of the relations between men and women is universal.

In Chapter Four it was noted that in the Trobriand Islands "everyone has a great deal of freedom and many opportunities for sexual experience. Not only need no one live with impulses unsatisfied, but there is also a wide range of choice and opportunity" (Malinowski 1929:236). As a result of early and intense sexual activity a Trobriand boy learns from a very early age to accept sexual rejection, and it is he who is accepted or rejected by the girl. Furthermore, it is the male who must give gifts to his lovers:

> In the course of every love affair the man has constantly to give small presents to the woman. To the natives the need of one-sided payment is self-evident. This custom implies that sexual intercourse, even where there is mutual attachment, is a service rendered by the female to the male. . . . This rule is by no means logical or self-evident. Considering the great freedom of women and their equality with men in all matters, especially that of sex, considering also that the natives fully realize that women are as inclined to intercourse as men, one would expect the sexual relation to be regarded as an exchange of services itself reciprocal. But custom, arbitrary and inconsequent here as elsewhere, decrees that it is a service from women to men, and men have to pay (p. 319).

The Trobriand case is especially helpful in clarifying the economics of sex because it discriminates sex and marriage. At marriage the flow of goods is primarily in the opposite direction: "Marriage is meant to confer substantial material benefits on the man" (p. 93). As discussed in Chapter Four, marriage is fundamentally an economic and child-rearing alliance between networks of kin. In most preliterate societies a brideprice must be paid by the husband's family, but in some societies —such as the Trobriand Islands—the wife's family pays a dowry. Yet, even in the Trobriand Islands, in a purely sexual relationship the "dowry" does not exist.

Sharanahua men, it will be recalled, use meat to obtain and to keep wives and lovers, and gaining sexual access to women is one of their main motives for hunting. Siskind (1973b) writes of this arrangement: "Whether men prove their virility by hunting and thus gain wives or offer meat to seduce a woman, the theme is an exchange of meat for sex. This theme is not unusual, but it cannot be understood by a direct appeal either to biology or psychology. That is, I know of no real evidence that women are naturally or universally less interested in sex or more interested in meat than are men" (p. 234).

Whatever the dominant opinion on female sexuality may have been during Victorian times, it is clear that the author of *My Secret Life* believed that lust is as strong in women as it is in men and that both are preoccupied with sex. Walter writes: "What rot then this talk about male seduction, when it is nature which seduces both" (p. 2062). Since Walter was regularly the seducer and rarely, if ever, the seduced, his belief that men and women lust equally for one another had to be squared with sexual reality as he experienced it, which was that "all women are paid for their favours either in meal or malt" (p. 2266). He concluded that from an early age girls are taught to hide their sexual desires in order to increase their economic bargaining position:

> It was a wonder to me that when both sexes feel so much pleasure in looking at each other's genitals—that they should take such extreme pains to hide them, should think it disgraceful to show them without mutual consent, and penal to do so separately or together in public.—I came to the conclusion that in the women it is the result of training, with the cunning intention of selling the view of their privates at the highest price—and inducing men to give them that huge price for it— the marriage ring. Women are all bought in the market—from the whore to the princess. The price alone is different, and the highest price in money or rank obtains the woman (p. 957).

Sexual freedom apparently is not sufficient to neutralize female power in sexual transactions. Like the Trobrianders, Mangaians of both sexes place great stock in sexuality, begin sexual activities in childhood, and cultivate sexual skills (Marshall 1971). All Mangaian women are orgasmic and the great sexual responsiveness of women is taken for granted; it is normal for a woman to have three orgasms to her partner's one. During intercourse a man expects his partner to experience multiple orgasms and all men develop the sexual competence which allows this to occur. Nonetheless, it is clearly the man who is the applicant for the woman's favors, the woman who judges, who tests, who establishes criteria for adequate performance:

> The Mangaian, or Polynesian girl takes an immediate demonstration of sexual virility and masculinity as the first test of her partner's desire for her and as the reflection of her own desirability. (In fact, the Cook Island female may test the male's desire rather severely, as did the Aitutaki girl who went for several days without washing her privates and then insisted that her would-be lover perform cunnilingus upon her before admitting him to more intimate acts of coitus.) One virility test used by Mangaian women is to require a lover to have successful

sexual intercourse without making contact with any part of the partner's body other than the genitalia (Marshall 1971:118-19).

Because the male generally is the petitioner in extramarital sex, he
risks having his petition rejected. In a study of extramarital affairs
among the Mehinacu of Brazil, Gregor (1973) notes that men always
take the initiative in establishing an affair: "A young man who plans to
approach a girl sexually for the first time is highly vulnerable since
rejections are often received as personal humiliations" (p. 251). And if
his petition is accepted, the male risks being judged inadequate. Gladwin and Sarason (1953), for example, write that on Truk men always
take the initiative in forming extramarital liaisons and are accepted or
rejected by the women: "In extramarital affairs it is the woman whose
position is at every turn secure and the man who exposes himself to
hazards. A man has committed himself by writing the first letter; the
woman holds and can expose the incriminating document. With the
entry into the house and his approach to the woman it is again the man
who runs the risk: of being discovered or of being rejected. And finally, during intercourse itself it is the man who stands to 'lose' if he
ejaculates too soon" (p. 113).

Davenport (1977) contrasts Polynesian eroticism with the "surface"
eroticism of the Ibans of Borneo, but the difference seems to lie mainly
in the criteria women use to assess male sexual desirability:

> Great value is placed upon the gratifications obtained in intercourse,
> but, at the same time, women grant their sexual favors to men, with
> parsimony and manipulative skill. Men taunt women with sexual ad-
> vances; women flirt back but stop short of full cooperation. Romantic
> love and the joys of copulation are extolled in song and poetry. How-
> ever, the underlying understanding is that women, even wives, grant
> sexual gratification to men in accordance with how well they fulfill
> their masculine roles. The traditional expression of this is contained in
> many heroic stories and songs in which the vigorous young man pro-
> fesses his love. The girl urges him to go out and demonstrate his cour-
> age and skill in fighting. He returns with trophies that prove his brav-
> ery, and she grants him his desire (p. 130).

Male political dominance does not alter the fundamentals of sexual
economics. Women always are a scarce sexual resource: where women
are free to contract their own relationships, they themselves control
this resource; to the extent that men control women, men control this
resource:

Custodial rights over sex and reproduction in women in some societies may be regarded as forms of capital assets which can be traded and accumulated. This is notably the case in some Australian Aborigine societies. The custodians are always men, and before marriage they are men of senior generations. Wealthy men are those who, in return for services performed, have received these rights from other men. Put simply, custodial rights over sex in women, in effect, mean the power to grant women in marriage, and in these societies which have very few forms of valuable capital, such rights constitute a source of power and influence. Furthermore, sexual rights in females not yet born are also recognized, and these, too, can be traded, accumulated and inherited. Thus, there is such a thing as sexual futures in these societies (Davenport 1977:141).

Prostitution appears to be the least ambiguous example of males receiving a sexual service: prostitutes, whether male or female, almost always service males. The more pleasure a prostitute appears to take in the sexual act the more desirable she is to the male and the more valuable her services are; but it is the prostitute who is paid. Yet Gebhard (1971b) comments on the difficulty of delimiting "prostitution" in cross-cultural perspective: "Gift giving or even cash payment for sexual intercourse cannot be used as criteria to define prostitution, for these occur in courtship or even in marital situations" (pp. 257-58). Junod's (1962) description of the wedding night of a South African Thonga couple provides an extreme example of gift giving in marriage: "The first night when she sleeps in the hut with her husband, she may refuse to allow him his conjugal rights. The bridegroom then goes to his father and asks him what he ought to do under the circumstances. The father says: 'Give her sixpence or a shilling.' Then she consents!" (p. 113).

To gain some cross-cultural perspective on gift giving during sexual relationships between men and women, I surveyed the heading "extramarital sex" in the Human Relations Area Files and considered all accounts of gift giving turned up this way, whether extramarital or not. Gifts given in the contexts of "courting," "wooing," "extramarital affairs," "among lovers," "in exchange for sex," etc., were recorded; gifts given at marriage were not recorded, nor were arrangements that the ethnographer characterized as "prostitution." I intended to divide gift giving into five categories according to who gives to whom and how much: (1) only men give gifts; (2) men and women exchange gifts, but men's gifts are of greater value; (3) men and women exchange gifts and there is no mention of relative value (in no case were men's and women's gifts specifically stated to be of equal value); (4) men and women exchange gifts, but women's gifts are of greater value; (5) only women give gifts. In fact, only three categories had to be used: fifteen societies fell in category 1, one society in category 2, three societies in category 3, and no societies in categories 4 or 5.[1]

According to Webster, "to prostitute" is "to sell the services of (oneself or another) for purposes of sexual intercourse." Whether gift giving in the context of a sexual relationship "essentially" constitutes prostitution thus depends on the principals' motives, and the human condition is often one of mixed motives. Among the Australians of Western Arnhem Land, for example, extramarital intercourse is relatively common, both men and women take great pleasure in copulation, and women are said to have sexual freedom equal to men; yet it is the man who gives gifts to his lover, and "The distribution of gifts in return for sexual favors is an aspect which should not be under-estimated" (Berndt and Berndt 1951:179). Furthermore, the principals may have different understandings of the situation. In *My Secret Life* Walter reports that he kept a supply of cameo brooches to aid in seducing working-class women and cites a friend's advice in these matters: "he said that he did not offer servants and that class of women money, that a bit of jewellery caught them much more readily than gold, and that it was very much cheaper. 'They may refuse a sovereign or two, they may be offended, but jewellery they can't refuse'" (p. 876). It is clear in many cases that women consented to have sexual intercourse with Walter because they wanted the gift, and these situations might best be considered simply prostitution laced with a little hypocrisy; but perhaps in other cases women felt genuine desire for, or attraction to, Walter and considered—or at least tried to consider—the gift evidence of an interest on his part that transcended the lust of the moment.

One-sided gift giving in the context of a sexual relationship thus is not always "essentially" prostitution; nevertheless, it is not a coincidence that males generally are the gift givers as well as the prostitute payers. A woman may desire a gift for its symbolic rather than its material value: the gift indicates the man's willingness to sacrifice and thus can be considered evidence of an interest more enduring than

[1] (1) Bush Negro, Caingang, Delaware, Easter Islanders, Hausa, Iban, Kapauku, Marshalls, Navaho, New Ireland, Nootka, Samoa, Tikopia, Wogeo, Yap; (2) Ojibwa; (3) Bellacoola, Mongo-Nkundu, Nahane.

the moment's passion, having more in common with Hellespont swimming than with prostitution. But the reason that men rather than women need to proffer such symbols in the first place is that men in general wish to have sexual intercourse with many women in whom they have neither a nonsexual interest nor a long-term sexual interest. This fact underlies human sexual arrangements.

How one conceptualizes this situation seems to depend in part on where one's interests lie. The wide range of feminist opinion on the issue of sexual economics is made possible by the fact that proximate economic analyses rest on nonobservable, nonmeasurable, human emotions: reward, reinforcement, satisfaction, benefit, cost, utility, etc., are, in the final analysis, defined by human intuition, and when intuitions differ, so do analyses. Thus women with identical opinions on such matters as equal pay for equal work can nonetheless reach almost any conclusion about payment for sexual services. Consider, for example, one of Wolfe's (1975a) informants, a married university professor, characterized by herself and by Wolfe as a radical feminist heavily involved in women's liberation, who is having a sexually and emotionally satisfying affair with a married man:

> Her new lover is a doctor and has a classy future. Pamela has therefore opened negotiations with him concerning money. She feels this is the one area in which maried women who have lovers are most retrogressive. "They're afraid to ask for money. But why shouldn't they, particularly if the man has it? If they married him, they'd expect some financial sharing. If one conducts an extramarital affair like a half-marriage, then there should be financial arrangements to cover the situation." She is currently looking into legal precedents (p. 212).

Although the financial sharing is intended to be one-sided, there is no suggestion of prostitution or of conflict with feminist principles; on the contrary, Pamela and Wolfe seem to regard the proposed arrangement as evidencing a tough-minded feminism. Indeed, since money is not Pamela's motive for having a lover, the proposed sharing seems to be more opportunism than prostitution.

To the members of the radical prostitutes' union COYOTE, it is self-evident that feminist principles imply that women have the right to use their bodies in any way they wish; but to Brownmiller (1975), the same principles imply that men should not be permitted to purchase sexual access to women. When people reach opposite conclusions from similar premises it is worth looking for emotional self-interests behind ideologies. To the extent that heterosexual men purchase the services of prostitutes and pornographic masturbation aids, the market for the sexual services of nonprostitute women is diminished and their bargaining position vis-à-vis men is weakened. The payment of money and the payment of commitment are not psychologically equivalent, but they may be "economically" equivalent in the heterosexual marketplace. The implicit belief of heterosexual feminists such as Brownmiller that, in the absence of prostitution and pornography, men will come to want the same kinds of heterosexual relationships that women want may be an attempt to underpin morally a political program whose primary goal is to improve the feminists' own bargaining position. This belief—which, in essence, is that men want the service prostitutes provide because prostitutes exist, rather than the other way around—morally underpins political ideology insofar as it implies that men will not be deprived of anything, and that prostitutes too will be better off if prostitution is eliminated. In fact, feminist prostitutes and many nonprostitute, heterosexual feminists are in direct competition, and it should be no surprise that they are often to be found at one another's throats. A final point: some feminists have argued that marriage is "essentially" prostitution; while this undoubtedly is true of some marriages (see, for example, Hite 1976), in cross-cultural perspective it is not true. Among the Trobrianders, the Muria, the Mangaians, and perhaps most modern Western peoples (Pietropinto and Simenauer 1977), for example, men want to, and do, marry in spite of the substantial reduction in sexual opportunity marriage entails. As discussed above, motives for marrying are many, and generally are much more complex than mere sexual opportunity. Where marriages are founded on love, women may give sex for love while men give up sex for love.

Blau (1964), Malinowski (1929), Siskind (1973b), and Walter observe that, in specific societies, copulation is understood to be a female service. According to the last three writers, since women generally derive as much pleasure from sexual intercourse as men do, relative pleasure cannot explain this fact, and a deeper analysis is needed. Their analyses vary according to their theories about the underlying causes of human behavior and psyche: Malinowski believes that "custom, arbitrary and inconsequent" causes behavior; Siskind assumes that behavior functions to promote ecosystem stability; Walter implies that humans act rationally to maximize their financial interests. One difficulty with these analyses is that they do not account for universality.

In addition, Siskind's analysis depends on her assumption that natural selection at the level of the ecosystem is more powerful than natural selection at the level of the organism, an assumption for which there is no supporting evidence.

Copulation as a female service is easily explained in terms of ultimate causation: since the minimum male parental investment is almost zero, males stand to benefit from copulating with any fertile female (if the risk is low enough), whereas females do not stand to benefit reproductively from copulating with many males no matter what the risk is. But few people are aware of "ultimate economics," and humans have not evolved to care about ultimate causes even if they do become aware of them. The most interesting questions thus are ones of proximate sexual economics: the psychological, biological, and social factors that underlie sexual transactions. Interactions of the following factors, several of which have already been discussed, may be important determinants of trading in the heterosexual marketplace: sexual pleasure, sexual capacity, visual arousal, sex drive, ability to abstain, the sex ratio, the desire for sexual variety, sexual attractiveness, sexual sophistication, and marriage. The concept of a heterosexual marketplace implies that a sexual interaction occurs only when everyone involved consents to it; but sexual interactions do occur in which this is not the case, and such interactions—forcible rapes—also will be discussed.

Sexual pleasure

That copulation is considered to be a female service even where women are believed to derive as much pleasure as men do from sexual intercourse does not mean that relative pleasure is irrelevant to sexual economics; it simply means that pleasure is not the whole story. There are actually two interrelated issues here: the pleasure males and females actually experience in sexual intercourse, and the pleasure they are thought to experience. In general, the more pleasure one derives, and the more pleasure one is thought to derive, the weaker one's bargaining position is. This may be the primary message in one account of how Tiresias, the legendary blind Theban seer, lost his sight and gained his wisdom. According to *The Oxford Classical Dictionary* (second edition) Tiresias "one day saw two snakes coupling and struck them with his stick, whereat he became a woman; later the same thing happened again and he turned into a man. Being asked by Zeus and Hera to settle a dispute as to which sex had more pleasure of love, he decided for the female; Hera was angry and blinded him, but Zeus recompensed him by giving him long life and power of prophecy." In an interaction between two people, the relative value of the interaction to each participant determines which, if either, is providing the service; but value and pleasure are nonobservable states of mind, and goods or services are worth whatever one can get for them, hence Hera's anger and Zeus's satisfaction: were Tiresias's decision to become generally known, it would give males added leverage in sexual transactions with women and very likely in nonsexual transactions with women as well.

The gain in power to control heterosexual interactions of all kinds that accompanies the reduction of sexual pleasure probably is one reason (not the only one) that feminism and antisexuality often go together. Writing of the suffragist movement in Edwardian England, Hynes (1968:174) comments that "The woman's revolution is a dramatic demonstration of the truth that all relations between the sexes will sooner or later be treated as sexual." As with some more recent feminist movements, the militant suffrage movement in England before World War I "never made sexual freedom a goal, and indeed the tone of its pronouncements was more likely to be puritanical and censorious on sexual matters than permissive: 'Votes for Women and Chastity for Men' was one of Mrs. Pankhurst's slogans" (p. 201). This "protest against Maleness and even against sex itself" presaged the "man-hating" of feminists such as Bengis (1973); the suffragette beliefs that "Man, on a lower plane, is undeveloped woman" and "Life is feminine" presaged feminists, such as Sherfey (1972), who see profound political significance in the fact that, in the absence of the male hormone testosterone, the mammalian embryo develops a female morphology. In every age the battle of the sexes is largely a battle over sex.

Although most modern feminists do not seem to be antisexual, much recent feminist writing about female sexuality does emphasize masturbation and, not infrequently, lesbianism, which in some respects are politically equivalent to antisexuality. According to the political/economic analysis developed above, writings that call attention to women's enormous capacity to experience sexual pleasure will tend to reduce female power over sexual transactions and hence might be seen as dysfunctional or irrational. But perhaps: (1) women's power over heterosexual transactions is so firmly entrenched that women do not foresee significant loss of power as a result of increased sexual pleasure; (2) many women may be glad to give up some power in exchange for sexual pleasure; (3) as women achieve political and economic equality with men there will be less need for women to wield sexual power, and if—as many women believe—liberated men will act and feel as women do, the marketplace analogy will become less meaningful.

The relative pleasure males and females derive or are thought to derive from sex probably plays a minor role in determining which, if either, provides a service. Furthermore, sexual intercourse is an interaction in which pleasure can reverberate between (or among) the participants, so that the ability to derive pleasure from sex can make an individual more sexually attractive to others; the prostitute who appears to take pleasure in sexual intercourse provides a more valuable service than the prostitute who appears not to take pleasure.

Sexual capacity

While there is little or no evidence for female sexual insatiability, in capacity to have orgasms, as well as in capacity to have sex, the typical human female seems to have a definite edge on the typical human male, hence an economic analysis based solely on orgasm scarcity might predict copulation to be a male service. But, in fact, differential sexual capacities seem to become a significant factor in sexual economics only in unusual circumstances, such as swingers' parties (Bartell 1971); even here, women apparently cope easily with male exhaustion by engaging in sexual activities with other women. On Mangaia, the woman's position is so secure that she can demand sexual satisfaction from her partners, and men must meet this demand lest they lose sexual access to women via gossip (Marshall 1971). Throughout Elwin's (1968) account of the Muria, there are abundant indications that the economics of sex favors the female; for example, Elwin asks rhetorically: How do boys "approach a new girl whom they desire to win? How do they even persuade the girl with whom they regularly sleep to allow them consummation? For in most ghotul, though a girl is bound to sleep with one of the [boys], she need not have congress with him unless she wants to" (p. 123). And again, "None of the evidence suggests that congress in the ghotul is readily achieved. It is not a place where girls are 'easy'; a [boy] has no harder work than this" (pp. 124-25). As with Mangaians, the Muria's knowledge of female sexual capacity does not appear to diminish appreciably female sexual power:

> Woman is indeed regarded as insatiable. "Woman is earth; man cannot plough her." The proverb means that as a single plough cannot break up the universal earth, so no man can really satisfy a woman. Here we have the opposite view to that commonly held in Europe, that sex is the man's privilege and the woman's duty; in aboriginal India, sex is the man's duty and the woman's right. It is her compensation for the embarrassments of menstruation and the pains of child-bearing. She has no more powerful means of dominating and subjugating the male (p. 132).

This proverb almost surely refers to marital, rather than premarital, ghotul sex (an issue I shall take up below), but in neither case is the female a petitioner for male favors. Should sexual relations among men and women in a population come to resemble relations at a swingers' party, perhaps the sexual capacity factor would tip the balance in favor of the male; however, like sexual pleasure, sexual capacity does not appear to be decisive in the sexual economics of any known people.

Visual arousal

As discussed in Chapter Six, available evidence strongly supports the view that human males are more likely to be sexually aroused by the sight of females, clothed or unclothed, than females are by the sight of males. In the course of everyday life, males thus are sexually stimulated much more often and intensely than females are, and this probably tends to give females leverage in heterosexual transactions.

Sex drive

Davenport (1977) writes that it is "widely believed that a man's sexual needs exceed those of a woman, and this opinion persists even in cultures that grant equal sexual privilege to both sexes" (p. 116). It is often said that human males have a higher sex drive than females do (for example, Gebhard 1965, D'Andrade 1966, Tripp 1975), and Weitz (1977) notes that human males are more likely than females to exhibit sexually appetitive behavior. The evidence is impressive that human males are more strongly motivated to seek sexual intercourse *per se* than females are. Scientific insight into these matters will require elucidation of brain mechanisms and the physiology of arousal; at present, literary accounts, interviews, surveys, and ethnographies constitute the best available data. If, as these data seem to suggest, human males are more likely than females to experience an autonomous desire for sexual intercourse and to seek opportunities to have sexual intercourse, this too probably gives females an edge in sexual negotiation.

Abstinence

Closely related to the notion of an autonomous sex drive is the notion of dissatisfaction or discomfort accompanying sexual abstinence and lack of orgasm. Scientists frequently call attention to the fact that many human females tolerate sexual abstinence and lack of orgasm without experiencing significant discomfort (for example, Kinsey *et al*. 1953, Mead 1967, Bernard 1968; and see Hite 1976:336-54). Indeed, as discussed in Chapter Three, in most societies some women never experience orgasm and in some societies probably no women experience orgasm. On the other hand, all physically normal males experience orgasm, and the great majority probably do so regularly for most of their adult lives. Heider (1976) suggests that Grand Valley Dani males may go for years without "sexual outlet"; however, his belief that Dani males do not masturbate strikes me as rather tenuously based, and even if Heider should prove to be correct, as he himself notes, the Dani would be in this respect unique. Kinsey *et al*. (1948) write:

> While all males must have known of the regularity of sexual activity in their own histories, the significance of the fact for the population as a whole has never been fully appreciated. The assumption that the unmarried male has only occasional outlet, or that he may go for long periods of time without any sexual activity, is not in accord with the fact. The assumption that there can be such sublimation of erotic impulse as to allow an appreciable number of males to get along for considerable periods of time without sexual activity is not yet substantiated by specific data. For most males, whether single or married, there are ever-present erotic stimuli, and sexual response is regular and high (p. 217).

To the extent that heterosexual males are less able or willing to tolerate sexual abstinence than females are, males constitute a market for female sexual services.

The sex ratio

The supply of sexually available individuals of each sex—which is determined both by the population sex ratio and by such practices as polygyny—doubtless affects sexual economics and in part determines which, if either, sex provides a service to the other. If the ratio of available men to women were low enough, it seems likely that copulation would become a male service. While this is unlikely to occur in a human population as a whole, certainly copulation can become a male service within polygynous marriages (Mead 1967).

The desire for sexual variety

Lévi-Strauss (1969) suggests that the natural and universal polygamous tendency of the human male makes women always seem to be in short supply, regardless of their actual numbers, and I have suggested that the male's desire for sexual variety makes sexual partners always seem to be in short supply. This is another factor that tends to make copulation a female service. Ironically, some support for this hypothesis comes from a study of pimps and prostitutes, among whom the ordinary sexual economics are reversed: according to Milner and Milner (1973), the pimp provides his women with security—which is the primary source of his attractiveness—and he dominates and controls them by parsimoniously granting and withholding his sexual favors. His control depends, however, on rigid self-discipline, on overcoming his urge to seek variety. The pimp believes that a man's "innate sex urges may drive him to want many women, whereas a woman wants to capture one man with whom she can be secure. However, it is man's duty to conquer and control his sex drive, so that he may channel the energies into directions his controlling mind finds useful and productive" (p. 161). (The pimp's own controlling mind apparently finds it useful and productive to accumulate money, drugs, clothes, cars, women, and the status that goes with them.) As soon as a pimp allows his impulses free rein he ceases to be a pimp and becomes a "trick," controlled by women instead of controlling them. The Milners point out that a pimp's survival depends on understanding his own sexuality and that of others. "Like the sociologist and the anthropologist, pimps and hustlers depend for their livelihood on an awareness of social forces and an understanding of the human psyche. In fact, the social scientist rarely applies his knowledge directly, and so has much more leeway than the hustler or pimp in being wrong before he is out of a job" (p. 242).

Sexual attractiveness

Sexual transactions occur, not between males as a group and females as a group, but between individuals, and the direction of the favor/ service in a sexual transaction is partly a function of the principals' sexual attractiveness. The ultimate reproductive fact—that males stand to benefit from copulating with any fertile female (if the risk is low enough), whereas females do not stand to benefit from copulating with many males (no matter how low the risk)—is most directly expressed in the proximate psychological fact that the typical male is at least slightly sexually attracted to most females, whereas the typical female is not sexually attracted to most males. (This obviously is related to such matters as sex drive, visual arousal, and variety-seeking, but is considered separately here for analytic purposes.) The effect of this sex difference in psychology on sexual economics is outlined in figure 8.1, which illustrates male and female sexual attractiveness to the other sex in an imaginary, ideal population. In constructing figure 8.1, the following assumptions were made: there are equal, and large, numbers of males and females; there is general agreement concerning the ranking of individuals (as discussed above, a female's rank depends largely on physical characteristics, a male's rank largely on physical characteristics plus social/economic/political status); sexual attractiveness is normally distributed; as with reproductive success, there is substantially more variability in male than in female attractiveness; and the upper ends of the male and female distributions coincide. Figure 8.1 does not depict any specific data: it is purely descriptive, intended only to assist the reader in visualizing the analysis.

Given the opportunity, all females in this idealized population would prefer to copulate with the most attractive males and all males would prefer to copulate with the most attractive females; but, in fact, most individuals never have such opportunity. As one moves down the attractiveness scale, female sexual interest in males drops off much faster than male sexual interest in females does: an individual experiences an immediate, "purely" sexual attraction only to those members of the

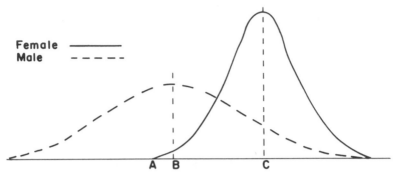

FIGURE 8.1. Sexual attractiveness to members of the other sex in an imaginary population. See text.

opposite sex who fall to the right of, or at the same point as, him- or herself. Consequently, an individual at any point on the scale considers him- or herself to be granting the favor if he or she copulates with any individual of the other sex to the left of that point, and considers him- or herself to be receiving the favor if he or she copulates with any individual to the right of that point. Favorless, purely sexual, encounters occur only between individuals at the same point on the scale. Needless to say, this figure is in many respects inadequate to reflect real sexual relationships; but if it reflects reality sufficiently to advance the present analysis even slightly, it will have fulfilled its purpose.

Figure 8.1 suggests that the average male (B) considers that he is being granted a favor if he copulates with most females, whereas the average female (C) considers that she is granting a favor if she copulates with most males. Further, it suggests that at the bottom of the scale (to the left of A) are males with whom no female considers it a favor to copulate. Recall that in the Trobriand Islands some women were alleged by the natives to be so physically repulsive that no man would copulate with them, hence, it was said, they were absolutely debarred from sexual intercourse and had to resort to solitary means of satisfaction, but that this allegation was called into question by the fact that many of these women had a number of offspring. Some men, however, actually are debarred from sexual intercourse unless they can make some form of payment (or resort to rape). In *Down and Out in Paris and London*, George Orwell describes the life of the English tramp—at the very bottom of English society. Below a certain level,

Orwell points out, society is entirely male, and because tramps generally do not have even enough money for food, they are almost entirely cut off from women:

> . . . any presentable woman can, in the last resort, attach herself to some man. The result, for a tramp, is that he is condemned to perpetual celibacy. For of course it goes without saying that if a tramp finds no women at his own level, those above—even a very little above—are as far out of his reach as the moon. The reasons are not worth discussing, but there is no doubt that women never, or hardly ever, condescend to men who are much poorer than themselves. A tramp, therefore, is a celibate from the moment when he takes to the road. He is absolutely without hope of getting a wife, a mistress, or any kind of woman except—very rarely, when he can raise a few shillings—a prostitute.

Of course, all males to the left of (A) are not deprived of sexual opportunities, but simply of sexual opportunities in which they are the favor-granters.

While enormously oversimplified, the analysis depicted in figure 8.1 may be closer to reality than it appears initially. In the first place, it is customary in our society to pretend not to notice that many forms of informal exchange are, in fact, exchanges; for example, even in straightforward, reciprocal exchanges of dinners between two couples, it would be very poor form for one couple to mention a dinner "debt" to the other couple, and yet the debt might be routinely acknowledged and matter-of-factly discussed (in economic terminology) between a husband and his wife. In the second place, the language of economics—which seems to be necessary to express these concepts—inevitably connotes arid, cold-blooded calculation which, in fact, rarely characterizes psychic life. Probably only in prostitution do the principals actually think in terms of favors or services. Nevertheless, it may be helpful analytically to conceive of money and "commitment" (or gift giving, or wooing, or courting, or precoital conversation) as in some sense economic equivalents, although they may rarely be psychological equivalents. Moreover, there may be sex differences in the extent to which economic metaphors actually reflect psychic life.

In my experience it is commonplace to hear males say, in more jaundiced and despairing moments, "You pay for it one way or another," thereby acknowledging that, for them, the economic analysis does have some psychological significance. The reality behind this comment is that males frequently would not court, woo, make commitments, or engage in extended precoital conversations if they could have sexual

intercourse with desired females without doing so. But for most females, money and commitment are not at all psychologically equivalent: although a direct payment of money is unlikely to make a woman
sexually attracted to a man, a payment of commitment often has this
effect. In terms of figure 8.1, the average man (B) is sexually interested
in the average woman (C), but (C) becomes sexually interested in
(B) only if some prior payment (commitment, etc.) is made (the
greater the disparity in sexual attractiveness, the greater the necessary
payment); otherwise, even should sexual intercourse occur, it might
not be experienced as sexually stimulating to (C) any more than would
prostitution, or even rape. This is one reason why the relative pleasure
males and females experience, or are thought to experience, in sexual
intercourse is not a decisive factor in sexual economics. Most sexual
acts occur only after negotiations have been completed, payment made,
trust established, at least a minimal relationship begun. In these circumstances a female may experience pleasure equal to or greater than her
partner's, but this does not mean that she had the option of experiencing the same pleasure without these preliminaries. That females exist
to whom this does not apply, and that most males prefer to have sex
with someone they like or love, does not substantially diminish the importance of this male-female difference in sexual psychology for an
analysis of sexual economics. Neither does the fact that a sexual interaction is initiated by the female necessarily indicate that copulation is
a male service (a prostitute can, after all, approach a trick). A male
may decline an implied sexual invitation not because he does not want
the sex, but because he does not want it enough to pay the price, or to
incur the debt, that sex entails.

This is but one example of a general, biological Catch-22, a catch
which has its ultimate origin in reproductive competition. One expression of this catch is "Coolidge's Law" (not to be confused with—but
not entirely unrelated to—the Coolidge Effect): "Anytime you don't
want anything, you get it." Now obviously Coolidge's Law does not
apply to all areas of life, and I would amend it thus: "With respect to
those areas of life in which intense reproductive competition has occurred in ancestral populations, it is relatively difficult to get what you
want and relatively easy to get what you don't want." Indeed, it was
the difficulty of "getting" that led to selection for "wanting." There
has been no reproductive competition over access to oxygen, and
hence—although we require it to survive—oxygen is obtained uncon-

sciously: we don't have to want it to get it. But in sexual matters, reproductive competition has been intense. One proximate result is that men frequently want to have sexual intercourse with many women without making any form of nonsexual payment, but it is difficult for them to do so; most women could easily have intercourse with enormous numbers of men, yet they don't want to, not solely because society has taught them not to want to, but because selection did not favor women who found such intercourse to be sexually satisfying.[2] On the other hand, folk wisdom has it that "a good man is hard to find." This is perhaps least true in polygynous societies, but in a monogamous society with a 1 : 1 sex ratio in which most people want to marry—as should be clear from figure 8.1—there will be substantial female-female competition for the most desirable men. As long as men are able to make some form of payment, the great majority of them can obtain a much more desirable wife or long-term sexual partner than they can a "free," short-term partner; but the great majority of women can obtain a much more desirable short-term partner, from whom they demand nothing but sex, than they can a long-term partner or husband. Since most people want the most attractive individuals possible, both as mates and as sex partners, sexual interactions generally occur between heterosexual pairs in which the female is to the right of the male (in terms of figure 8.1), and copulation generally is a female service; when purely sexual (favorless) heterosexual transactions are made, figure 8.1 implies that the male generally will rank higher among males than the female ranks among females.

This analysis may also shed some light on the "sex object" issue: which members of the opposite sex one views as sex objects is partly a function of one's own ranking. Most women are to some extent sex

[2] Difficulty of one sort or another probably is the ultimate source of all emotional capacities (moreover, if "emotion has taught mankind to reason," perhaps all aspects of consciousness originated in the overcoming of obstacles). Tripp (1975) explores at length the notion that high levels of erotic feeling depend on resistance and the overcoming of barriers, particularly for men. If in natural human habitats females almost always were a scarce sexual resource, Tripp's hypothesis makes adaptive sense, since selection favors the experience of pleasure or satisfaction not just in the consummation, but in the effort to consummate as well. Where resources typically can be obtained effortlessly, as in ordinary breathing, there is neither striving nor consummation, only mindless physiology. Difficult though it may often be for us to get what we want, had it not been for the difficulty, there would not be any sentience; that is, there would not be any "us" at all.

objects to most men, but some men are sex objects to some women, and a few men are sex objects to most women.[3] (This assumes a reasonably libidinous female population.) It is not always understood that men too are sex objects because far more women than men are seen as sex objects, men generally are more sexually aggressive than women are, and more nonphysical characteristics influence male than female sexual attractiveness. Furthermore, although men tend to be interested in women's bodies, this does not mean they are interested in other men's minds; men generally are indifferent to most men, just as women generally are indifferent to most women.

An individual's sexual-attractiveness ranking probably is an important determinant of how that individual perceives the economics of sex, and this is especially true for males. The highest-ranking males will perceive few male-female differences because, in fact, at their level there *are* few differences: these males are sex objects to most females, and—although they are not sexually interested in most females—it is relatively easy for them to arrange sexual encounters with females in whom they are interested. On the other hand, even when they are not as unfortunately placed as the English tramps described by Orwell, lower-ranking males will perceive females, especially the more desirable females, as being very difficult to obtain.

While these points perhaps are not especially controversial, the magnitude of the male-female difference, and the sexual scarcity of females to most males, is not always understood, especially by women. Because a male's sexual attractiveness is so heavily dependent on his status, it is possible for a male to enjoy an enormous increase in rank in a very brief period of time, and such males may be best situated to perceive the real magnitude of sex differences in sexual economics. This is made clear, for example, in a recent interview with the actor Henry Winkler.[4] At the time of the interview, Winkler shared top billing on the most popular television series in the United States. His picture could be seen on posters, T-shirts, and in fan magazines; books were written about him; and his likeness appeared in the Hollywood Wax Museum. In short, he had become, in a brief time, one of the most popular, sexually sought-after men in the United States. During the course of the interview Winkler remarked: "In the past, I've always done the

[3] In animal husbandry insemination is said to be a male service, probably because it is provided only by the very best males.

[4] *Playboy* 24:62, August 1977.

asking and women have said yes or no. I now know what it is to be a woman. . . ."

To cite one other example, the American movie star Dustin Hoffman recently was being interviewed in a restaurant; as word of his presence spread throughout the restaurant, young women began to congregate on the other side of the glass partition which enclosed the dining area. At one point during the interview Hoffman suddenly broke off, ran to the partition, and shouted at the crowd of women on the other side: "Where were you when I needed you?" As the typical woman's market value decreases with age, she loses a sexual advantage that few men ever possess.

Sexual sophistication

That sexual sophistication may be a factor in sexual economics is speculation, advanced simply as a hypothesis. For a number of reasons, increasing sophistication may tend to reduce male-female disparities and hence to make the economics of sex more a person-to-person than male-to-female matter. Sexual intercourse is an interaction, and pleasure can reverberate between the participants. If men tend to be especially aroused by novelty, some sexually sophisticated women may learn to enjoy this male response, to learn, in essence, to allow this response to become part of their own pleasure.[5] And if most women become sexually uninhibited primarily in the context of an established relationship, some sexually sophisticated men may learn that—despite the absence of the jolt novelty provides—intercourse with a trusting, familiar partner is potentially the most intense sexual experience possible.

Neither the female ability to learn to enjoy novelty nor the male ability to learn to cultivate sexuality with a single partner is likely to be an adaptation: these possibilities exist in spite of natural selection, not because of it. I see little evidence in the ethnographic or animal

[5] Nevertheless, when one considers (a) how many sexually sophisticated women there are, (b) the relative ease with which many women can obtain new partners, (c) the fact that, if she will settle merely for sex, the typical woman can choose a much more attractive partner than can the typical man, and (d) that women do not risk impotence, premature ejaculation, or other performance hazards, and run a much lower risk of rejection than men do, the number of variety-seeking women seems small indeed.

behavior literatures to suggest that ancestral humans, in a state of nature, were in any modern sense sexually sophisticated; thus natural selection did not have the opportunity to grant to Coolidge's Law complete dominion over human sexuality. Like Huxley's garden, which can be maintained only by counteracting the cosmic processes of reproductive competition and natural selection (Chapter Two), the garden of human sexuality is likely to flourish to the extent that we abandon our folk belief that there is wisdom in nature.

If the process that Paul Robinson calls "the modernization of sex" continues, and if this process is, as I believe, part of a general modernization (denaturalization) of human sensibilities, the marketplace aspects of heterosexual relations may wane, although they are unlikely to disappear. Increased self-knowledge and mutual understanding increase mastery over social transactions, enabling us to exploit one another more effectively for our own ends, or, if "not-exploiting" is itself one of our ends, enabling us to be more considerate of one another. In addition, women's increasing political and economic equality will reduce their sexual vulnerability as well as their need to use sex for economic and political gain or security.[6]

During the years I have taught an undergraduate seminar in primate and human sexual behavior, I have been struck by the regularity with which women students have reported, in anger and bewilderment, that simple, friendly gestures toward men are consistently misinterpreted as sexual invitations. Probably neither female gestures nor male misinterpretations are completely ingenuous; but to some extent they are ingenuous, and result from taking at face value the fashionable academic notion that few basic sex differences exist. Such considerations lead me to believe that an appreciation of sex differences is more likely to promote a cease-fire in the battle of the sexes than are naïve promulgations of the "good news" that there are no important differences.

[6] It seems unlikely that male-female differences in this respect ever will be eliminated entirely. In a bureaucracy in which males and females were represented equally at every level of the hierarchy, "innate" sex differences still would make the "casting couch"—to the extent that it existed at all—more likely to be found in a man's than in a woman's office. Economic equality will not eliminate the tendency for some ambitious females to trade sex for upward mobility simply because economic equality will not eliminate their opportunity to do so. Opportunities for males to trade sex for advancement will, of course, increase when females are as likely as males to occupy high-status positions, but the typical male's opportunities are unlikely ever to approach the typical female's, for reasons outlined in this chapter.

Marriage

Most sexual intercourse occurs between partners who have an established relationship, usually marriage. Between established partners the question of service or favor may become largely meaningless, and to the extent that it does not become meaningless, it is likely to be enmeshed in the idiosyncrasies of particular relationships. Nevertheless, a few generalizations can be hazarded.

Marriage implies a drastic limiting of the market for the principals' sexual services, so to some extent the sexual balance of power depends on the marriage's sex ratio: obviously copulation is more likely to be a male service in a polygynous than in a polyandrous marriage. The effectiveness with which each partner can limit the market for the other's services also may play a role; for example, the young Muria wife, barred forever from the ghotul, is at a clear disadvantage, since her husband continues to visit the ghotul for some time. Further, when partners are unequal in sexual attractiveness, the more attractive partner is in the superior position owing to his or her greater value in the wider marketplace. Although marriages are unlikely to occur between very unequal principals, sexual attractiveness can change through time, usually to the wife's disadvantage, since a woman's market value is more inexorably tied to age than a man's is. On the other hand, if husbands tend to have the greater fear of their spouses' infidelities, this fear operates to the advantage of wives.

In general, marriage probably markedly increases male leverage in sexual economics. Issues of sexual pleasure and sexual capacity—which do not seem to be decisive in the wider marketplace—may assume great importance in the micromarketplace of marriage. To the extent that women come to realize their sexual potential, their sexual bargaining position within marriage worsens. As noted above, the majority of wives in the United States consider the frequency of marital intercourse to be about right—which perhaps implies that in most marriages the issue of service may not arise—but since the 1920s, the proportion of wives who consider marital intercourse to be "too frequent" has steadily fallen and the proportion who consider it to be "too infrequent" has steadily risen, which probably results in part from women's increasing enjoyment of sex and lack of interest in abstinence.

The male's sex drive and tendencies to be visually aroused and to desire variety may tend to make husbands more sexually restive than wives. Flaubert called attention to "that advantage in clarity that belongs to the one who lags behind in any relationship," and it is a sociological truism that the partner with the lesser emotional investment in a relationship controls the relationship. The very qualities of male sexuality that are, in large part, responsible for female dominance in the wider marketplace may typically have the opposite effect within a marriage. Finally, the addition of children may alter sexual economics. Marital sexuality tends to deteriorate following the birth of the first child, and this deterioration becomes greater with the birth of each additional child (Cuber 1975). If children do have a consistent effect on sexual economics, this effect remains to be elucidated.

Forcible rape

The concept of a sexual marketplace implies that a sexual interaction occurs only when everyone involved consents to it; however, sexual interactions between males and females do occur in which this is not the case, and in such circumstances it is always the female who does not consent. "Forcible rape" may be defined as "sexual intercourse accomplished without the consent of the female" (LeGrand 1977:68).

Since males can potentially sire offspring at almost no cost, typical parental investments notwithstanding, selection favors male attempts to copulate with fertile females whenever this potential can be realized. One possible cost to males—in terms of time, energy, and/or risk—is female resistance. But selection favors female resistance to male copulation attempts only when the benefits of resisting typically exceed its costs. Unambiguous instances of forcible rape are relatively uncommon in nature for the same reason that mutual fighting is relatively uncommon (Symons 1978a, b). Like mutual fighting, male attempts to force resisting females to copulate can be expected to occur only in circumstances in which the outcome cannot be "predicted" by the principals: when females are capable of very effective resistance (or are effectively protected by conspecifics), selection will not favor male attempts to copulate with nonconsenting females, and when females are incapable of effective resistance, selection will not favor attempts of nonconsenting females to resist; hence, the human observer of animal behavior normally sees either females declining suitors' advances, and suitors acquiescing, or females accepting suitors' advances without violent protest. In short, in sexual disagreements, as in most circumstances in which interacting animals have conflicting goals, selection favors a willingness or a desire to employ force, offensively or defensively, only if the animal has a fighting chance.

Male rape of females has been reported in a number of invertebrate species (see Abele and Gilchrist 1977) and in several species of North American puddle duck (Barash 1977b). Male homosexual rape also occurs among some invertebrate species: in the anthocorid bug the rapist's sperm enters the victim's vas deferens and is used by the victim during subsequent copulations; in the acanthocephalan worm the rapist seals off the genital region of the victim with cement, thereby effectively removing the victim from the reproductive population (Abele and Gilchrist 1977).

The primary difficulty in deciding whether a given copulation between members of a nonhuman animal species is "really" rape is the same difficulty that jurors in rape trials often face: how can "consent" be determined? Among free-ranging orangutans some copulations are unambiguous rapes, the rapist almost invariably being a subadult male (as with females of most species, orangutan females prefer to copulate with fully adult males): not all attempted rapes are completed, and completed rapes entail severe, obvious struggles in which the female may be struck and bit (Galdikas in press, MacKinnon in press).[7] Yet from our modern perspective, other nonhuman primate copulations probably should be considered rape, and perhaps still more would be so considered if nonhuman primate females could speak of their feelings. Police investigating alleged rapes, and attorneys defending accused rapists, often argue that a given act of intercourse was not really rape because the victim did not physically resist, yet police generally advocate nonresistance—as the most adaptive strategy—for victims of other kinds of violent, or potentially violent, crimes. Nonhuman primate females sometimes may exhibit adaptive, nonresisting behavior while resisting in their hearts. Male chimpanzees who force estrous females to travel with them to the periphery of the group's range might be considered to be committing rape, even though they do not

[7] Galdikas (1978) stresses, however, that males appear to be sexually rather than aggressively motivated, and that no male attacks on females other than rapes were observed. She writes: "males never furiously bit females, or even appeared to be angry, during the actual rapes. Rather, their energies seemed to be concentrated solely on holding the female to prevent her escape. As soon as the raping male stopped thrusting, he invariably released the female."

employ force before each copulation. And among free-ranging Indian rhesus monkeys, Neville (cited in Agar and Mitchell 1975) reports that the alpha male could suppress the sexual activity of any female in the group, and that females rarely rejected the sexual advances of an extremely dominant, aggressive, and feared male. Rhesus males have been observed to attack the female member of a consort pair when the male member was lower-ranking than the attacker (Carpenter 1942, Lindburg 1971, personal observations). Thus among species so closely related to ourselves that some interactional subtleties can be appreciated by the human observer, rape does not appear to be a cut-and-dried, either/or matter, but a continuum: force and the threat of force are tactics which sometimes can be used—directly or deviously—to gain sexual access to fertile females. Most commonly, males use force against other males in competition for females, but force may be used against females as well.

The apparent infrequency of rape among nonhuman primates can be attributed to the following: (1) Mutation—which occurs randomly with respect to fitness—provides the raw material upon which natural selection operates: that, in a given species, the opportunity exists *in theory* for males to increase their reproductive success through rape does not mean that rapists *necessarily* will evolve. (2) A female's "best" choice often is a male who succeeds in intrasexual competition, and these males are most likely to be her suitors. (3) The higher the cost of resistance, the less likely females are to resist. (4) The higher the cost of forcing copulations, the less likely males are to employ force. (5) Other animals may interfere with attempted rapes (the solitary nature of orangutans facilitates rape, and the male chimpanzee's major effort is to separate the female from other males).

There is a large and rapidly growing literature on rape among humans (see Chappell, Geis, and Geis, eds. 1977, for a critical review of, and orientation to, this literature). Analysis of the rape literature is far beyond the scope of this essay; the purpose of this section is simply to place the topic in the framework of the wider discussion and to suggest that some currently fashionable views are, at best, incomplete.

In *Against Our Will*, Susan Brownmiller (1975) popularized the view that rape is not motivated by male sexual desire. Perhaps no major work since Lorenz's *On Aggression* has so inadequately documented its major thesis (see Geis 1977 for references to critical reviews); William Styron (1977) writes that Brownmiller provides no insight into "the tragic complexities of sexuality, power and the human will," and to some extent Styron's criticism applies to much current thinking about rape. In my view, the major scientific contribution of recent feminist investigations of rape has been the thorough documentation of the victim's point of view: women do not want to be raped and almost never experience rape as a sexual act; rape victims' responses are likely to include rage, disgust, self-recrimination, misery, fear, and feelings of helplessness and confusion (see especially the interviews with rape victims in Russell 1975).

The notion that rape is not sexually motivated may have a number of sources. First, part of the modernization of sex is the belief that sex is a good thing; yet almost everyone agrees that rape is a bad thing, and one way of eliminating the threat of cognitive dissonance is to deny that rape is sex. Second, those who write about rapists' motives often appear to equate sexual feelings with "impulsiveness" or even "uncontrollable" lust. Many writers seem to fear that to admit sex as a motive for rape is to risk condoning rape: lust is presumed to be less easily controlled through an act of will than are other possible motives for rape, hence, in this view, if lust motivates rape, the rapist cannot be held fully accountable for his actions. Third, if women do experience the desire for power, but do not experience the desire to employ force to copulate with unwilling partners, the human tendency to conceive other minds by analogy with one's own may frustrate women's attempts to understand rapists. Furthermore, since the great majority of men not only do not rape but do not report having fantasies of rape (Pietropinto and Simenauer 1977), it is probably difficult even for most men to enter the mind of the rapist. Fourth, despite years of criticism of functionalism, naïve functionalist statements remain acceptable in the social sciences, and most nonprofessionals probably are not even aware that these criticisms exist. Brownmiller (1975:15) writes: "From prehistoric times to the present, I believe, rape has played a critical function. It is nothing more or less than a conscious process of intimidation by which *all* men keep *all* women in a state of fear." More than any other statement in *Against Our Will*, the specifics of this statement have been vigorously contested (see Geis 1977); but the more general point should not go unremarked: a creative process that generates such "functions" has yet to be shown to exist.

Brownmiller and others have advanced a number of arguments to support the view that rapists are not motivated by sexual desire, but none of these arguments is watertight. Although most rapes apparently are premeditated, so, surely, are most seductions. That some rape victims are old and unattractive is not evidence that sexual desire is not a motive for rape, any more than the alleged physical repulsiveness of certain Trobriand mothers is evidence that male sexual desire played no part in their impregnation. Recall too that an advertisement in a swingers' magazine placed by a woman who was thirty pounds over-weight and not pretty received 500 responses (Bartell 1971). When convicted rapists at the Atascadero State Hospital were asked what kinds of victims they prefer, they "portrayed the 'American dream ideal'—a nice, friendly, young, pretty, middle-class, white female" (Geis 1977:27). A statistical profile of the age of rape victims (Hinde-lang and Davis 1977) suggests that the probability of being raped varies with physical attractiveness (to the extent that attractiveness corre-lates with female age). The fact that most rapists have available other sexual "outlets" is not evidence that sexual desire is not involved in rape; most patrons of prostitutes, adult bookstores, and adult movie theaters are married men, but this is not considered evidence for lack of sexual motivation in these matters.

The prevalence of rape during war—thoroughly documented by Brownmiller (1975)—is not evidence that "political emotions" *per se* are sufficient to produce erection and ejaculation. As Brownmiller shows, military leaders may, for political purposes, encourage their subordinates to commit rape, but even in these cases lust may, in large part, motivate the rapists. During Victorian times, London prostitutes who worked in parks said that even normally timid men became bold in the fog (*My Secret Life*); during war, many normally risky behav-iors can be performed at little or no risk. In his essay "Looking Back on the Spanish War," George Orwell wrote: "The fact often adduced as a reason for scepticism—that the same horror stories come up in war after war—merely makes it rather more likely that these stories are true. Evidently they are widespread fantasies, and war provides an opportunity of putting them into practice." While in everyday life few men either commit rape or fantasize about committing it, every-day life almost never provides opportunities to rape without risk; if most men desire no-cost copulation, the high rates of rape during war-fare are understandable.

Finally, the use of rape as punishment in a number of societies does not prove that sexual feelings are not also involved, any more than deprivation of property as punishment proves that the property is not valuable to the punisher. On the contrary, rape as punishment implies that some peoples view sexual access as a commodity women have that men want: it can be given freely, bought, or taken by sanctioned or unsanctioned force.

The question of rapists' motives remains an open one. Geis (1977: 30) notes that "The sexual component of rape should not be downplayed in the haste today to accentuate the violent nature of the behavior." In his classic study of rape among the Gusii of southwestern Kenya, LeVine (1977; originally 1959) shows that the frequency of Gusii rape has varied directly with bridewealth rates: when the rates were highest, "Many young men could find no legitimate way of getting married, and they resorted to cattle theft and all types of rape" (pp. 219-20). Among the Gusii almost all sexual intercourse—even marital intercourse—is rather a combative affair, and LeVine points out that the distinction between rape and nonrape is not always clear. Gusii girls traditionally adopt a reluctant pose, and a young man may not recognize when his advances are being genuinely rejected; furthermore, an originally willing girl may pretend she is being raped if caught in the act; and finally, some

> girls who have no desire for sexual relations deliberately encourage young men in the preliminaries of courtship because they enjoy the gifts and attention they receive. Some of them act provocative, thinking they will be able to obtain desired articles and then escape the sexual advances of the young man. Having lavished expense and effort on the seduction of an apparently friendly girl, the youth is not willing to withdraw from the relationship without attempting to obtain sexual favors (p. 215).

LeVine concludes: "Thus, the similarity of Gusii seduction to rape, the communication difficulties arising out of this similarity, the girls' anxiety about their reputations and consequent fear of discovery, and the provocative behavior of girls whose motivations are not primarily sexual—all of these contribute to turning the would-be seducer into a rapist" (p. 216).

In the hundreds of copulations described in *My Secret Life*, money, gifts, force, class differences, persuasion, entreaties, seductive words, and sexual technique were so inextricably intertwined in the author's mind—being merely alternate ways of achieving his aim—that although these copulations might conceivably be arranged along a continuum of willingness to unwillingness, seduction to rape, they cannot be divided into distinct categories. Walter considered only one of these acts to be rape (and even this one only tentatively and after the fact), but to a modern sensibility many more would be so considered, and from certain perspectives most were rapes, since the power of social position almost always played a part in Walter's sexual successes.

Every interview with a rapist that I have seen or read suggests to me that rapists have mixed motives, and that part of the mixture is sex. But since motives are inherently nonobservable, it is always possible to interpret rapists' statements almost any way one chooses. Consider the following excerpts from an interview with a white, forty-nine-year-old male of lower-class Southern background who had committed four rapes (Fremont 1975):

> . . . at that particular time it gave me a sense of power, a sense of accomplishing something that I felt I didn't have the ability to get. You see something or somebody that you want, and you know that under normal circumstances you wouldn't be able to attract this person, so you take her.

> *   *   *

> This was something I wanted, and I felt that I would never be able to make this, and I've always been told that this was the thing to have, you know. I wanted this particular kind of person—she was a college girl—but I felt that my social station would make her reject me. And I just didn't feel that I would be able to make this person. I didn't know how to go about meeting her. Anyway, I waited one night until she had gone to bed. After the lights were out I just went into the window. She was frightened, of course, and I took advantage of her fright and raped her.

> *   *   *

> I wasn't concerned with her fear. I was only concerned with her body and being able to accomplish something that, given my upbringing, I couldn't accomplish any other way. I felt elated that I was able to accomplish what I wanted. It gave me power over her. Her feelings didn't mean anything to me at all. The thing that mattered was the thrill. I wasn't interested in whether someone else felt, or what they felt. I was only interested in a selfish thing. All I wanted was a convenient place to get rid of my thing.

> *   *   *

> . . . some had to be coerced, but I didn't enjoy doing it. It wasn't a turn-on. I wanted things as easy as I could get them. And if they didn't give in, I would threaten, and if I had to go through a big hassle, or exert any kind of violence, well, that was nothing for me then, but I didn't like it (pp. 244-46).

When asked whether there was any difference between sex with a willing and an unwilling woman the rapist replied, "there was no difference at all." Yet, presumably because this man reported experiencing a sense of power during intercourse with women whom he could not have obtained in any other way, Fremont reaches the—to me astonishing—conclusion that "sexual desire was not what motivated him to rape" (p. 244).

Recently I had the opportunity to see the videotape of a panel discussion with four convicted rapists at the Atascadero State Hospital.[8] Habitual sex offenders with psychological problems are committed to this facility for an indefinite period; an inmate is released only when Hospital authorities decide that he has been rehabilitated. In their initial, rather formal, statements, the men stressed power, control, dominance, and violence as motives for rape, played down sexual impulses, implied that the responsibility for their rapes lay not with themselves but with a society that glorifies machismo and objectifies women, and used the past tense when referring to the attitudes toward women which had allowed them to commit rape. Yet as the discussion wore on, sex loomed larger and larger, and it became clear that sexual desire for the victim inevitably preceded rape. While the men expressed anger at a society that had judged them losers, clearly their status as losers entailed a felt deprivation of sexually desirable women. It is difficult to avoid the conclusion that the men's conscious attempts to emphasize their correct attitudes and to minimize their sexual impulsiveness were to some extent calculated to foster the impression that they no longer constituted a threat: attitudes can change, sexual impulses rarely do. Given the extremely high rate of recidivism for men released from the Atascadero State Hospital, fashionable efforts to minimize sexual motives for rape—if taken seriously by Hospital authorities—might actually promote rape.

Sex and power are not antithetic; human motives are complex, intertwined, and often conflicting, and perhaps no human act results from a single, pure impulse. Surely no completed rape has ever occurred in which the rapist did not experience some sexual feeling, and very likely no rape has ever occurred in which this was the only feeling the rapist experienced. Cohen et al. (1977) describe the psychology of a group of rapists committed for an indefinite period to a Massachusetts treatment center because they were considered to be sexually dangerous. The authors emphasize that these men are not typical rapists, but a pathological extreme. Yet even in this group motives for rape were mixed, varying from almost purely sexual to almost purely predatory.

[8] Produced by the Santa Barbara District Attorney, moderated by Rex Komanti of Atascadero State Hospital.

Men and women have many motives for any sexual activity: it has yet to be shown that the ratio of sexual/other motives is lower for men committing rape than it is for men engaging in sexual intercourse with consenting partners. What has, of course, been shown is that rape very rarely is a sexual experience for the victim.

The major interest most of us have in rape is in its total elimination. But rape also is problematical because its existence threatens the foundations of beliefs which many people not only cherish but believe to be integral to the morality which underpins social order. Rape challenges the notion that men and women are fundamentally sexually similar: women not only do not rape but some, apparently, have great difficulty intuitively conceiving that a sexual desire could result in forcible rape. And rape challenges the notion that the living world is naturally harmonious, disrupted only by sin, weakness, or pernicious social systems.

Many feminists call attention to male anger as a motive in some rapes but fail to note what is obvious in many interviews with rapists, that the anger is partly sexual, aimed at women because women incite ungratifiable sexual desire. Deliberately provocative behavior or dress is not the key issue: women inspire male sexual desire simply by existing. In the excerpts, quoted above, from an interview with a rapist, general issues of social class and felt deprivation of power are apparent; but these issues should not obscure the following facts: the rapist wanted to copulate with the most physically attractive women; his victims were attractive not just to him but to most men; one of the perquisites of power, and one of the male motives for obtaining power, is access to scarce, desired commodities which—in our own as in most societies— include sexually desirable women; the rapist's belief that he could not have had sexual intercourse with his victims in any other way probably was correct.

Despite its manifest psychological and sociological complexity, rape constitutes further evidence that among humans copulation is generally a female service, a service which can be given freely, traded, or taken by force. I do not believe that available data are even close to sufficient to warrant the conclusion that rape itself is a facultative adaptation in the human male; but the evidence does appear to support the views—which ultimately are explicable by evolutionary theory— that human males tend to desire no-cost, impersonal copulations, that there is nothing natural about the Golden Rule, and hence that there is a possibility of rape wherever rape entails little or no risk. LeVine's

(1977) general discussion of the control of sexual behavior in human societies strikes me as especially sensible. In his view, control can result either from structural barriers or from socialized inhibitions, or both:

> A *structural barrier*, as I define it for sexual control processes, is a physical or social arrangement in the contemporary environment of the individual which prevents him from obtaining the sexual objective he seeks. A *socialized inhibition* is a learned tendency to avoid performing sexual acts under certain conditions. Structural barriers are part of the settlement pattern and group structure; socialized inhibitions are the products of the socialization process which the individual undergoes in his early years (p. 222).

Control of sexual behavior, as outlined by LeVine, does not require that people learn to value each other's feelings as much as they value their own, nor does LeVine rely on the wishful thought that minor modifications in boys' socialization will produce men who want only the kinds of sexual interactions that women want. LeVine implies that a human being is neither a tabula rasa nor a passive vehicle: socialization toward a gentler, more humane sexuality entails inhibition of impulses that exist sui generis. These impulses are part of human nature because they proved adaptive over millions of years. Sexual customs apparently can change very rapidly, probably because human emotion is especially intense in sexual matters; but much change is merely superficial. Where males can win females' hearts through tears rather than spears, through a show of vulnerability rather than strut and swagger, many will do so, but the desires persist and the game remains essentially the same. Given sufficient control over rearing conditions, no doubt males could be produced who would want only the kinds of sexual interactions that women want; but such rearing conditions might well entail a cure worse than the disease.

NINE

Test Cases:
Hormones and Homosexuals

DIANE KEATON: *"Sex without love is an empty experience."*

WOODY ALLEN: *"Yes, but as empty experiences go, it's one of the best."*

I HAVE ARGUED that, among humans, there are species-typical sex differences in sexual desires and dispositions and that these differences tend to be masked by the compromises heterosexual relations entail (as well as by moral injunctions). Two independent kinds of evidence constitute test cases for this claim: (1) In mammals, species-typical sex differences result from the action of hormones (Caspari 1972), hence women who have been exposed to abnormally high levels of androgens (male sex hormones) should tend to exhibit a "masculinized" sexuality. (2) Sexual relations among homosexuals are not constrained by the necessity to compromise male and female desires and dispositions, hence the sexual relations of lesbians should differ profoundly from the sexual relations of homosexual men.

Hormones

A normal, genetically male mammal develops male reproductive anatomy because the fetal testes secrete high levels of the androgen testosterone which masculinzes specific target tissues during morphogenesis. (In the absence of high levels of testosterone a mammalian fetus, whether genetically female [XX] or genetically male [XY], develops female reproductive anatomy.) The masculinizing effects of testosterone apparently are not confined to reproductive anatomy, but include certain brain structures as well.

While many sex differences are not manifested until they are needed, at reproductive maturity, natural selection acts at all stages of the life cycle to promote reproductive success, and in many species there are sex differences in behavior among immature animals that presage adult sex differences. Among rhesus monkeys, for example, immature males exhibit much higher frequencies of aggressive play (playfighting and playchasing), play initiation, mounting, and threatening than immature females do, and, when raised without mothers in groups of peers, males outrank females in the dominance hierarchy. In terms of ultimate causation, these sex differences (with the exception of mounting) almost certainly result from the far greater importance of aggressive skills to male than to female reproductive success: aggressive play appears to function primarily as practice or training for adult aggression (see Symons 1978a). In terms of proximate causation, these sex differences appear to originate in the prenatal masculinization of the male brain by testosterone.

When pregnant rhesus females are injected with the androgen testosterone propionate during the middle trimester of gestation, their genetically male offspring are normal, since males are normally exposed to high levels of androgen *in utero*, but their genetically female offspring are genitally masculinized "pseudohermaphrodites." These pseudohermaphrodite females exhibit frequencies of aggressive play, play initiation, mounting, and threatening intermediate between those of normal males and normal females (Goy 1968, Goy and Resko 1972, Phoenix 1974) and, as adults, exhibit higher levels of aggression than normal adult females do (Eaton et al. 1973). The behavior of immature pseudohermaphrodite females is not masculinized completely either because testosterone propionate is not injected throughout the gestation period (Goy and Resko 1972), or because of the high levels of progesterone (which antagonizes androgen activity) secreted by the placenta containing a female (Resko 1974), or for both reasons.

Several lines of evidence indicate that the masculine behaviors of normal immature rhesus males (and pseudohermaphrodite females) result from prenatal modification of the brain by testosterone, not from postnatal hormonal action. Soon after birth male plasma testosterone falls to nondetectable amounts, remaining low until puberty (Resko 1970), and males castrated at birth exhibit typical male behaviors as infants and juveniles (Goy 1968). Postnatal testosterone injections do not increase the frequency of aggressive play (Goy and Resko 1972), although females thus injected do become more aggressive and replace males in the top positions in the dominance hierarchy (Joslyn 1973). The anatomical research of Goldman et al. (1974) confirms the existence of a sex difference in rhesus cortical development. These data do not prove that postnatal experience is unimportant in the development of rhesus sex-typical behavior (Goy 1968); on the contrary, experience is crucial to the development of normal behavior in both sexes. But the evidence does suggest that experience acts on a brain already biased in a male or a female direction.

As with rhesus monkeys, immature human males typically are more aggressive and engage in more frequent and intense "rough-and-tumble" play than immature females do (Freedman 1972, Hutt 1972a, 1972b, Brindley et al. 1973, Maccoby and Jacklin 1974, Aldis 1975). While the nature and extent of sex differences among immature humans varies substantially in cross-cultural perspective, sex differences in play and aggression appear to be universal (see Whiting, ed. 1963, Whiting and Pope 1973, Blurton-Jones and Konner 1973, Maccoby and Jacklin 1974). In a detailed comparison of London and Bushman children, for example, many sex differences commonly reported in British and North American studies were not found among the Bushmen; yet in both the London and the Bushman samples, boys were more aggressive than girls and exhibited a higher frequency of rough-and-tumble play (Blurton-Jones and Konner 1973). Also, North American boys notice and retain more details of modeled aggression and have more aggressive fantasies than girls do. The greater aggressiveness of North American boys apparently is not the result of more frequent rewards for aggression; on the contrary, boys are more frequently and severely punished for aggression (Maccoby and Jacklin 1974).

The exposure of human female fetuses to excess androgen—the human counterpart of the experiments on rhesus monkeys cited above—has occurred in two ways: (1) in the adrenogenital syndrome (AGS), the genetically defective adrenal cortex of the fetus does not synthesize cortisol but instead releases too much androgen; (2) before the masculinizing side effects were discovered, synthetic progestins—androgen-like hormones—were given as a miscarriage preventative to some pregnant women with histories of spontaneous abortion. As with rhesus monkeys, prenatal exposure to excess androgen results in the genital masculinization (clitoral enlargement and some labial fusion) of ge-

CityCollege HANDSWORTH

Learning Resource Service

From September 2000 a fines system will be introduced for items returned after their due date as follows:

3 week loan	**5p per day**
1 week loan	**15p per day**
Overnight loan	**50p per day**
Term loan	**5p per day**
Maximum fine	**£5.00**

PLEASE NOTE THE FINES SYSTEM APPLIES TO BOTH STAFF AND STUDENTS

Thank you for your co-operation

netic female offspring. Such girls are normally, but not invariably, surgically feminized at birth. Their internal reproductive anatomy is normal, and, at puberty, their ovaries produce female hormones which induce menstruation and feminize the body, although AGS girls require permanent cortisone therapy for normal feminization.

Girls exposed to excess prenatal androgen have been found to differ from matched controls in several ways (Money and Ehrhardt 1972, Ehrhardt and Baker 1974, Reinisch 1974). Compared to controls, such girls exhibit higher levels of physical energy in rough outdoor play; are less interested in dolls and other typically female toys, and consistently prefer boys' toys; are more often self-identified and identified by others as tomboys; prefer boys to girls as playmates; prefer utilitarian boys' clothes to chic or fashionable girls' clothes, and have little interest in hairdo or jewelry; are relatively indifferent to infants; and are more concerned with a future career than with plans for being a wife and mother. This "tomboyism" is not considered abnormally masculine by the girls or by their parents and does not interfere with the development of a female gender identity, nor do the girls give evidence of homosexuality.

Since the girls' parents were aware that their daughters were born with masculinized genitals, it is possible that tomboyism resulted from parental expectations rather than from masculinization of the fetal brain (Quadagno, Briscoe, and Quadagno 1977). Yet this hypothesis has not been compelling to the investigators who actually conducted the interviews with the girls and their parents. Money and Ehrhardt (1972:103) conclude: "The most likely hypothesis to explain the various features of tomboyism in fetally masculinized genetic females is that their tomboyism is a sequel to a masculinizing effect on the fetal brain." In accounting for the unproblematical nature of tomboyism, Money and Ehrhardt note that "so much gender-identity differentiation remains to take place postnatally, that prenatally determined traits or dispositions can be incorporated into the postnatally differentiated schema, whether it be masculine or feminine" (p. 103). Furthermore, the similarity of the human and the monkey findings, and the universality of human male-female differences in play, provide additional support for the brain masculinization hypothesis.

These data do not, of course, indicate that human males are inevitably violent, but they do suggest that the universal differences between men and women in fighting are presaged by corresponding differences between boys and girls, and that it may be easier for boys than for girls to learn fighting skills. Although the proximate causes of human and rhesus monkey violence are so different that they virtually defy comparison (Symons 1978a), the ultimate causes of sex differences in violence probably are similar in these species: in natural habitats human males and rhesus males fight far more frequently and intensely than females do because fighting typically has been far more important to male than to female reproductive success. And in both species there are corresponding sex differences in juvenile play and aggression because males and females are training for different kinds of adult activities.

The behaviors discussed so far are not specifically sexual, and, indeed, there is no obvious a priori reason to expect natural selection to have produced differences between boys and girls in sexuality, since children's sexual activities are nonreproductive. But there is evidence that certain aspects of adult male sexuality result from the effects of prenatal and postpubertal androgens: before the discovery of cortisone therapy, women with the adrenogenital syndrome were exposed to abnormally high levels of androgen throughout their lives, and clinical data on late-treated AGS women indicate clear-cut tendencies toward a male pattern of sexuality.

Pubertal boys' wet dreams, accompanied by strong visual imagery, have no counterpart among pubertal girls; when women do have strongly erotic dreams with orgasm, such dreams tend to occur later in life (Money and Ehrhardt 1972) and presumably require prior sexual experience. But late-treated AGS women tended to have histories of dream eroticism paralleling those of normal males, although the dream imagery was not homosexual but appropriate for heterosexual females (Money and Ehrhardt 1972, Lev-Ran 1974). In some cases, cortisone therapy markedly reduced the frequency of such dreams (Lev-Ran 1974). In addition, late-treated AGS women reported visual and narrative stimuli to be erotically arousing as often as touching and caressing; such arousal was specifically genital and, in the absence of a partner, frequently led to masturbation (Ehrhardt, Evers, and Money 1968, Money 1973). These women tended to exhibit clitoral hypersensitivity and an autonomous, initiatory, appetitive sexuality which investigators have characterized as evidencing a high sex drive or libido (Money 1961, 1965, Ehrhardt, Evers, and Money 1968, Lev-Ran 1974). In some cases, cortisone therapy reduced clitoral hypersensitivity and spontaneous sex drive without reducing sexual responsiveness:

It is noteworthy that none reported a post-treatment cessation of erotic sensitivity in the clitoral zone—only of erectile autonomy and hypersensitivity of the clitoris, or of its amputated stump. What they lost, therefore, was that autonomous initiatory eroticism of the phallus which seems to be so basic in the eroticism of men. The women were all unequivocally pleased to be relieved of clitoral hypersensitivity; it was the pleasure of being able to feel like a normal woman, several of them explained (Money 1961:1392).

These data underline the necessity of distinguishing between sexual responsiveness (or consummatory behavior) and autonomous libido (or appetitive behavior); for example, among peoples such as the Mangaians and Trobrianders, women may typically have stronger sexual responses than men but weaker sexual drives.

Money (1965) sums up the evidence on eroticism among AGS women as follows:

Some of these patients, in adulthood, have reported experiences more typically reported by normal males than by females, namely, erotic arousal with a strong genitopelvic component from the stimulation of visual and narrative perceptual material. Such arousal is more than the ordinary woman's arousal of romantic feeling and desire to be with her husband or boy friend, with the ensuing possibility of tactile and kinesthetic arousal. Rather, it is arousal that is likely to be accompanied by erection of the clitoris, hypertrophied in this syndrome, and masturbation or the willingness for sexual intercourse even with a transitory partner. The imagery of the erotic thoughts and desires is all suitably feminine in keeping with the sex of rearing and the psychosexual identity. The unfeminine aspect of the experience applies only to the threshold and the frequency of arousal, and to the amount of sexual initiative that it might engender. The reaction has occurred in the treated as well as the untreated state of the syndrome, but is attenuated by treatment which consists of feminizing clitoral surgery and hormonal correction with cortisone. There is a possibility, therefore, of a residual androgenic effect, even after the high fetal and childhood levels are regulated to normal. The informative cases will be those of infants whose excessive adrenal androgens were cortisone-controlled from birth onward, but these patients are still too young to be valid informants (pp. 69-70).

Women who were masculinized *in utero* by progestins will also be of interest, since they too will not have been exposed to excess androgens postnatally.

Data on late-treated AGS women suggest that some aspects of human sexuality, such as object choice, result largely from postnatal experiences; but these data also suggest that the male's tendencies to be sexually aroused by visual stimuli, the specifically genital focus of male sexual arousal and relief, and the autonomous, fantasizing, initiatory, appetitive, driving aspects of male sexuality result largely from interactions of the effects of prenatal androgens on the developing brain; the activating effects of postpubertal androgens on a brain already biased in a male direction; and peripheral stimulation from the genitals. These aspects of male sexuality develop in a relatively "innate" fashion because the tendencies to be sexually aroused by the sight of females,[1] to seek out opportunities to experience visual arousal, and to desire sexual intercourse with arousing objects were generally adaptive for males in ancestral populations. The function of these male characteristics is to generate reproductive opportunities in a milieu in which such opportunities almost always were competitive. Nothing in male sexuality—insofar as it contrasts with female sexuality—cries out for a more intricate functional interpretation or hints of an adaptation to monogamy.

Homosexuals

There is no reason to suppose that homosexuals differ systematically from heterosexuals in any way other than sexual object choice; as Tripp (1975:119) points out, "homosexual" is "a behavioral category of individuals who are about as diffusely allied with each other as the world's smokers or coffee drinkers, and who are defined more by social opinion than by any fundamental consistency among themselves." I have argued that male sexuality and female sexuality are fundamentally different, and that sexual relationships between men and women compromise these differences; if so, the sex lives of homosexual men and women—who need not compromise sexually with members of the opposite sex—should provide dramatic insight into male sexuality and female sexuality in their undiluted states. Homosexuals are the acid test for hypotheses about sex differences in sexuality.

Evidence on sexual arousal by visual stimuli reveals striking male-female differences: a substantial industry produces pornographic books, magazines, and motion pictures for a male homosexual audience; but no pornography is produced for a lesbian audience. Moreover, while

---

[1] I assume that in natural habitats human males are no more likely than other male mammals to develop exclusive erotic preferences for objects other than conspecific females.

there is reason to believe that homosexual men comprise much of the audience for the photographs of nude men in *Playgirl* magazine, there is no reason to believe that lesbians exhibit a corresponding interest in magazines such as *Playboy;* on the contrary,

> Most homosexual women laugh at or respond negatively to erotic pictures of women. "The sexuality is so exaggerated," they say. They assume that the pictures are published for men and think it "hysterically funny that men can be turned on by this." By way of "proof," they point out that these photos are published in men's magazines, not in magazines for women. You can be certain that if there were even a hint of a potential market, some enterprising businessman would supply the product—but the market simply doesn't exist (Nicholson 1972:16).

Heterosexual men are, of course, aware that the female sexuality portrayed in men's magazines reflects male fantasy more than female reality, just as heterosexual women are aware that the happy endings of stories in romance magazines exist largely in the realm of fantasy. It is precisely the fantasy that is appealing. But male homosexual pornography probably does reflect much of the reality of male sexuality, and it would be interesting to know whether the photographs of women in women's magazines appeal erotically to lesbians.

Fundamental male-female differences also are apparent in variety-seeking. The search for new sexual partners is a striking feature of the male homosexual world: the most frequent form of sexual activity is the one-night stand in which sex occurs, without obligation or commitment, between strangers (Hooker 1967, Leznoff and Westley 1967, West 1967, Hoffman 1968, 1977, Sonenschein 1968, Saghir and Robins 1973). In one-night stands and in longer liaisons the basis of the male homosexual relationship usually is sexual activity and orgasm (Hooker 1967, Sonenschein 1968, Saghir and Robins 1973) and the focus is on the genitals (Kinsey *et al.* 1953, Hoffman 1977). Sexual partners are found by "cruising" bars, street corners, hotel lobbies, parks, and public restrooms (Leznoff and Westley 1967, Hoffman 1968, 1977, Saghir and Robins 1973, Weinberg and Williams 1974); conversation and preliminaries are at a minimum, and sex occurs almost immediately (Hoffman 1968, 1977, Weinberg and Williams 1974). While more enduring relationships may develop from such encounters, relationships nonetheless begin with sex.

The male gay (homosexual) bar in American cities is a sexual marketplace where men go primarily to seek a sex partner for the night (Hooker 1967, Leznoff and Westley 1967, Hoffman 1968, 1977, Saghir and Robins 1973). Hooker (1967:174) writes that in the gay bar "one may observe one of the most standardized and characteristic patterns of social interaction in the 'gay' world: the meeting of strangers for the essential purpose of making an agreement to engage in sexual activity known as the 'one night stand.'" Such liaisons often do not last a night; in a few minutes or hours the individuals may be back in the bars again, cruising (Hooker 1967). Many American cities have steam baths that cater exclusively to homosexual men. A bath consists of individual rooms for private sexual activity and a large chamber for group sex; in either place, there is little socializing and a great deal of anonymous sex (Hoffman 1968, 1977, Saghir and Robins 1973). Fast, impersonal, anonymous sex between men in public restrooms is described by Hooker (1967), Leznoff and Westley (1967), Hoffman (1968), Humphreys (1970, 1971, 1972), and Saghir and Robins (1973). Contact also can be made in this way between a man and a male prostitute: "The entrepreneur and his customer in fact can meet with little more than an exchange of non-verbal gestures, transact their business with a minimum of verbal communication and part without a knowledge of one another's identity" (Reiss 1967:209).

Male homosexuals are often said to be "promiscuous." If nondiscrimination is the essence of promiscuity, some homosexual men are, indeed, sometimes promiscuous; for example, the man who reported being sodomized by forty-eight men in one evening in a gay bath (Hoffman 1968) presumably was fairly indiscriminate. Moreover, among homosexual men, as among heterosexual men, lust and ejaculation apparently can profoundly affect the perception of a sexual partner's attractiveness. A striking example is provided by the English novelist and playwright J. R. Ackerley (1968), who describes in his autobiography a period of his life during which he suffered from ejaculatory incontinence. Ackerley writes that ejaculation "put an end to my own pleasure before it had begun and, with the expiry of my desire, which was never soon renewed, my interest in the situation, even in the person, causing me to behave inconsiderately to him; I have not been above putting an abrupt end to affairs with new and not highly attractive boys in whose first close embrace, and before taking off our clothes, I had already had my own complete, undisclosed satisfaction" (pp. 210-11).

But for a number of reasons, it is misleading to characterize homosexual men as generally promiscuous. For one thing, as discussed in connection with the Coolidge Effect, the seeking of sexual variety is itself based on extraordinarily well-developed powers of discrimination. Hoffman (1968) notes that while most homosexual men are very interested in sexual activity, they do not necessarily engage in a great deal of it owing to the constant search for new partners. And novelty is by no means the only criterion of sexual desirability. Homosexual men often are extremely choosy, and impersonal sex "frequently entails a remarkable amount of discrimination. Even a person who never wants a second contact with any of his partners may spend much time carefully selecting each from dozens or even hundreds of possibilities. In fact, some of the most promiscuous individuals sustain considerable frustration not from any lack of opportunity but from being exceedingly selective" (Tripp 1975:142).

Physical attractiveness is the most important determinant of sexual desirability (Tripp 1975, Hoffman 1977), hence the emphasis on physical condition, dress, and grooming among homosexual men; and a major determinant of physical attractiveness is youth. Ackerley (1968: 115) writes: "Instinctively evading older men who seemed to desire me, I could not approach the younger ones whom I desired." As John Rechy has remarked, "Age is the monster figure of the gay world." Social class and status, on the other hand, appear to be relatively unimportant determinants of sexual desirability (Ackerley 1968, Tripp 1975). Finally, Tripp (1975) notes that a brief sexual encounter can be affectionate and romantic, a kind of telescoped love affair: "Each contact may proceed so rapidly from meeting to parting as to look to the casual observer like a leaf in the wind. But to the participants, each experience may be intensely romantic" (p. 148). In fact, Tripp (1975) and Hoffman (1977) point out that for many men one of the primary attractions of impersonal sex is that it allows each participant to imagine he is having sex with the ideal partner, a fantasy which may be vulnerable even to a small amount of preliminary conversation. The human male's ability to fall rapidly in love with an idealized fantasy— created solely from the data of physical appearance—is not unknown to heterosexual women, who may capitalize on it or fear and mistrust it. The difference between men and women in this respect perhaps has never been more incisively drawn than it is in Renée Néré's musings on her admirer in Colette's novel *The Vagabond:*

> How is it that he, who is in love with me, is not in the least disturbed
> that he knows me so little? He clearly never gives that a thought, and
> his one idea is first to reassure me and afterwards to conquer me. For if
> he has very quickly learnt . . . to hide his desire and subdue his look

and his voice when he speaks to me, if he pretends, cunning as an animal, to have forgotten that he wants to possess me, neither does he show any eagerness to find out what I am like, to question me or read my character, and I notice that he pays more attention to the play of light on my hair than to what I am saying.[2]

Among male homosexuals, friends are not usually sexual partners; sex rarely occurs within the social group (Leznoff and Westley 1967, Hoffman 1968, Sonenschein 1968, Weinberg and Williams 1974), and a common, but not universal, goal is to find a permanent partner (Hooker 1965, 1967, Hoffman 1968, Sonenschein 1968, Saghir and Robins 1973). In describing his (unsuccessful) lifelong search for the "ideal friend," Ackerley (1968:124-25) remarks: "Though two or three hundred young men were to pass through my hands in the course of years, I did not consider myself promiscuous but monogamous, it was all a run of bad luck. . . ." In an eight-year study of 30 homosexual men who were not seeking psychological help, showed no signs of psychological disturbances, and were gainfully employed, Hooker (1965) found that 27 out of 30 sought stable, dyadic relationships that would include sex, intimacy, love, and affection, but only 4 had sustained an exclusive sexual relationship for as long as two years. Weinberg and Williams (1974) report that 37 percent of their sample of 1057 American homosexual men have had a relationship in which sex was primarily (but not necessarily exclusively) restricted to one person for more than one year. Sonenschein (1968) found that the desire for a permanent sexual partner was more common among homosexual men over thirty; younger informants said they preferred extended encounters to a permanent relationship. Older homosexual men are much less successful in finding sex partners (Hoffman 1968, 1977, Weinberg and Williams 1974), and this may be partly responsible for their interest in developing a permanent relationship (Sonenschein 1968).

A few homosexual men are able to maintain long-term monogamous relationships (Hooker 1967, Hoffman 1968, Tripp 1975), and such relationships may have been underestimated in the literature (Tripp 1975); but clearly the majority revert to having sex with strangers as sexual interest in their partner wanes, while maintaining the original

[2] Translated by Enid McLeod. Copyright © 1955 by Farrar, Straus and Young. Reprinted by permission of Farrar, Straus & Giroux, Inc., and Martin Secker and Warburg Ltd.

living arrangements (Hooker 1967, West 1967, Hoffman 1968, Saghir and Robins 1973). And eventually, most seek all sexual activity outside of the relationship with their partner (Hooker 1967, Hoffman 1968, Saghir and Robins 1973). The instability of sexual relationships among male homosexuals has been frequently remarked (Kinsey *et al.* 1948, Hooker 1967, West 1967, Hoffman 1968, 1977, Sonenschein 1968, Saghir and Robins 1973, Weinberg and Williams 1974). Although homosexual men, like most people, usually want to have intimate relationships, such relationships are difficult to maintain, largely owing to the male desire for sexual variety; the unprecedented opportunity to satisfy this desire in a world of men; and the male tendency toward sexual jealousy (Hoffman 1968, Weinberg and Williams 1974).

Tripp (1975) suggests that long-term male homosexual couples owe the stability of their relationship to their understanding that sexual intensity with a single partner wanes, and that an appetite for new partners is inevitable. In the following passage Tripp implies that sexual jealousy can sometimes be overcome because of each partner's intuitive insight into the peculiarities of male sexuality:

> The sophisticated [male] homosexual couple (usually having gained that sophistication through previous relationships) tends to anticipate the problem and build a bulwark against it before their initial fascination with each other begins to subside. They may carefully avoid setting up a "fidelity contract" with each other and gear their expectations to include sexual contacts on the side, contacts in which an emotional investment in any new partner is deliberately avoided. Often more inventive arrangements are made. These may include threesomes in which one or both partners bring home a person who is shared in bed but who is not permitted to intrude on the basic relationship. There may be foursomes, or orgy dates, or conservative variations on the common heterosexual solutions such as the spoken or unspoken arrangement that any side-contact is to go unmentioned—or that almost any side-contact is all right if it is *always* mentioned. Not infrequently, partners who have been together for some time and who are secure in their affection go considerably further. Each may bring home partners who are not to be shared. Sometimes one or even both partners have hot, short-range romances which are discussed at home, often with amusement and a certain seasoned benevolence. While the possible arrangements vary considerably, most have several features in common. There tends to be an aboveboard recognition by both partners of the value of what is fleeting as well as of what is enduring, along with a realization that these appetites are far safer if not placed in competition (pp. 154-55).

Like homosexual men, lesbians tend to place a great deal of importance on sex and sex-related activities (Hoffman 1968, Hedblom 1973) although, unlike men, their sexual activities are not focused on the genitals (Kinsey *et al.* 1953, Tripp 1975). In his six-year study of lesbians in Philadelphia, Hedblom (1973) asked 65 informants about orgasm; of the 62 women who answered the question, all reported that they had been orgasmic in homosexual relations. Hedblom also reports a greater average frequency of sexual activity among lesbians than has been reported for heterosexual women. Indeed, the sexual activities of homosexuals of both sexes appear to be especially intense, varied, and satisfying. Tripp (1975) writes that "when two men are excited and unrestrained in their sexual interaction, the fire that is fed from both sides often does whip up levels of eroticism that are rarely reached elsewhere" (p. 117); and "among lesbians, sex is geared toward a diversified emphasis on what nearly all women consider most important: a build-up starting with peripheral stimulation that eventually concentrates on genital actions last, if at all" (p. 100).

But lesbians form lasting, intimate, paired relationships far more frequently and easily than male homosexuals do; stable relationships are overwhelmingly preferred to any other, and monogamy is the ideal (Stearn 1964, West 1967, Bass-Hass 1968, Hoffman 1968, Riess 1969, Hedblom 1972, 1973, Saghir and Robins 1973). In Hedblom's (1972) study, 64 of 65 informants said that they preferred a stable relationship and 71 percent had had a homosexual marriage. Kinsey *et al.* (1953) report that of males who had had any homosexual experience, 16 percent had 21 or more male partners, while no females had more than 20 female partners, and only 3 percent had 11 to 20 partners. Saghir and Robins report that only 15 percent of the lesbians but 94 percent of the male homosexuals in their sample had more than 15 sex partners. Although Saghir and Robins (1973) report that the 57 lesbians in their sample were more likely than unmarried heterosexual controls to have had short-term sexual relationships, the lesbians also were more likely to have had long-term relationships. Riess (1969) compared 226 lesbian women with 233 heterosexual women matched for age, place of birth and adolescence, education, education of parent, and socioeconomic level, and found that the average duration of sexual partnerships was about the same for both groups. Despite the value that lesbians place on sexuality, there is evidently little tendency to seek constant variation in sex partners; heterosexuals may, in fact, become sexually involved more rapidly than lesbians owing to male sexual initiative. Gagnon and Simon (1973:185) write that "given the absence of a male who conventionally begins or initiates physical expression in the course of interaction there . . . is a greater delay in the beginning of physical sexual involvement for the lesbian than for the heterosexual female."

Among lesbians sex is generally associated with enduring emotion and a loving partner (Gagnon and Simon 1973, Hedblom 1972, 1973, Saghir and Robins 1973). As among heterosexuals, lesbian dating and courting may lead to sexual relations; that is, a social relationship is the basis for a sexual relationship, whereas the opposite is true among male homosexuals. Hedblom (1972, 1973) reports that only 20 percent of lesbian dates resulted in a sexual liaison. Lesbian bars are far fewer in number than male gay bars, and—unlike male gay bars or even heterosexual singles' bars—they are not sexual marketplaces; the primary activity in lesbian bars is socializing with friends. Lesbians rarely pick up partners for one-night stands, do not cruise, do not have anonymous sex in public places, and there are no lesbian baths (Hoffman 1968, 1977, Saghir and Robins 1973). Ward and Kassebaum (1970) report that when women prisoners were asked what aspect of imprisonment was hardest to bear, only 5 of 293 cited lack of sexual contact with men, while 120 cited absence of home and family. Although homosexual contacts are more frequent among female than among male prisoners, not a single woman prisoner thought that "sex hunger" was the primary motive for her own affairs or for those of any woman she knew; homosexual activities tended to occur most frequently at the beginning of a sentence, when a woman's need for comfort, support, and reassurance was greatest (Ward and Kassebaum 1970).

The similarity of heterosexual and lesbian relationships and their fundamental difference from the relations of male homosexuals (Stearn 1964, Hooker 1967, Riess 1969, Gagnon and Simon 1973, Hedblom 1972, 1973) imply that the sexual proclivities of heterosexual males are very rarely manifested in behavior. Saghir and Robins (1973) report that less than 1 percent of their sample of 89 male homosexuals, but 72 percent of the unmarried heterosexual male controls, had fewer than 8 sex partners, while over 75 percent of the homosexual men, but no heterosexual man, had more than 30 partners. Hoffman's (1968) informant who was sodomized by 48 men in a gay bath had more partners in a single evening than most lesbians and heterosexual men have in a lifetime. The editor-publisher of *Playboy* magazine is alleged to have copulated with over 2000 young, attractive women during a twenty-year period (Nobile 1974); while this possibly represents an idiosyncrasy, or indicates that success in publishing such magazines selects for un-usual dispositions, this man probably differs from most men primarily in opportunity. I am suggesting that heterosexual men would be as likely as homosexual men to have sex most often with strangers, to par-ticipate in anonymous orgies in public baths, and to stop off in public restrooms for five minutes of fellatio on the way home from work if women were interested in these activities. But women are not inter-ested. Furthermore, even those homosexual men who do not engage in such activities do not necessarily refrain for the same reasons women do. A man may shun impersonal sex and the search for sexual variety for many reasons other than lack of interest: moral repugnance; fear of disease; fear of public disclosure or legal repercussions; fear of jeop-ardizing an important relationship; inability to obtain desired partners owing to age or physical unattractiveness; a preference to channel his time and energy in nonsexual directions. Thus there may be major sex differences in the psychological mechanisms by which long-term mo-nogamous relationships are maintained, whether these relationships are male homosexual, lesbian, or heterosexual.

Kinsey *et al.* (1948:633) write: "Long-time relationships between two males are notably few. Long-time relationships in the heterosexual would probably be less frequent than they are, if there were no social custom or legal restraints to enforce continued relationships in mar-riage." Since adult men wield the lion's share of political power every-where, one might suspect that the customs and laws which regulate marital and nonmarital sexual activities are in large part accumulated compromises made in the course of competition for nubile females, compromises which are manifested in male-male alliances, public rec-ognition and acknowledgment of sexual rights, moral injunctions against "promiscuity," and so forth. Following this line of reasoning, one could plausibly argue that long-term heterosexual relationships are the results of male dominance and male coalitions; however, there is enormous cross-cultural variation in sexual customs and laws and in the extent of male control, yet nowhere in the world do heterosexual rela-tions begin to approximate those typical of homosexual men. Even where women are relatively free of male constraints and children not at issue, as among lesbians, women very rarely behave sexually as men do. This suggests that, in addition to custom and law, heterosexual relations are structured to a substantial degree by the nature and inter-ests of the human female.

In conclusion, available data on the sex lives of contemporary homosexuals may have far-reaching implications for understanding human sexuality. These data imply that male sexuality and female sexuality differ much more profoundly than might be inferred from observing only the heterosexual world. That there is a substantial male homosexual market for pornography and no lesbian market whatsoever suggests that the tendency to be sexually aroused by "objectified" visual stimuli is simply a male tendency, not, as is often claimed, an expression of contempt for women. Similarly, the tremendous importance of physical attractiveness and youth in determining sexual desirability among homosexual men implies that these are relatively "innate" male criteria: heterosexual men tend to see women as sex objects and to desire young, beautiful women; homosexual men tend to see men as sex objects and to desire young, handsome men; but women, whether heterosexual or homosexual, are much less likely to be sexually aroused by objectified visual stimuli or to experience sexual arousal primarily on the basis of cosmetic qualities. Knowledge of a potential partner's character—even via brief conversation—can sometimes diminish a male's sexual interest by interfering with his fantasy; but a female's sexual interest not only is not diminished by, but usually requires, both some knowledge of the partner's character and some prior emotional involvement. Among men, sex sometimes results in intimacy; among women, intimacy sometimes results in sex. The tendencies to experience profound changes in perception following orgasm, to focus on the genitals in sexual activity, and to desire and enjoy sexual variety also appear to be male proclivities, manifested by homosexual men to unprecedented degree only because their behavior is not constrained by the necessity to compromise with women.

In previous chapters I argued that the ultimate causation of these male-female differences is relatively simple and straightforward if one assumes that sexual impulses and desires were designed by selection primarily to take advantage of rare opportunities and to motivate the effort required to compete for scarce resources. Ultimate causation has been obscured by the assumptions that sexual impulses and desires were designed to promote human happiness or to grease the wheels of marriage or society. "Innate" sex differences in sexuality are extreme because, however similar their typical parental investments may be, males and females differ enormously in their minimum investments and thus encounter completely different reproductive opportunities and constraints.

To call certain male-female differences in sexuality "relatively innate" does not contribute much toward their proximate explication. But it does suggest that inquiry into the effects of prenatal and post-pubertal testosterone on the male's brain are likely to be profitable lines of research and, furthermore, that some current discussions of sex differences are perhaps worth reexamining. Male-female differences in sexuality often are said to result from: (1) the differential access of men and women to economic resources and political power; (2) different norms of sexual behavior for men and women; or (3) minor "innate" sex differences that are greatly magnified by social experience. In each case, the data on contemporary homosexuals casts some doubt on these hypotheses.

(1) The data on lesbian sexuality do not support the hypothesis that heterosexual women have "innate" malelike sexual urges which they repress in order to trade sex for security or power. Lesbians—among whom economic trade-offs and pregnancy are not at issue—seem rather less malelike sexually than heterosexual women; perhaps when heterosexual women, consciously or unconsciously, exchange sexual access for money, security, or power their sexuality actually is compromised in a male direction. Prostitution represents the extreme case: the female prostitute may boldly initiate brief, genitally focused sexual encounters with strangers. These encounters resemble male homosexual encounters more closely than do almost any other sexual activities in the heterosexual world; but unlike the homosexual man, the prostitute almost always is feigning sexual interest and pleasure and is simulating a male fantasy of female sexuality.

(2) The striking differences between male homosexual and lesbian sexual behavior are usually attributed to different ideals of male and female sexuality in Western societies (for example, Gagnon and Simon 1973). It is said, for example, that boys are taught that it is "manly" to have intercourse with many partners, while girls are taught to desire a home and family and to be content with a single partner. Such explanations tend to ignore the fact that the messages each individual is exposed to, about how the world is and should be, are frequently in conflict; furthermore, by treating society as an entity from which beliefs and norms emanate, such explanations cannot locate the actual sources of beliefs and norms or discover why they persist or change. As an illustration of this point, consider that most individuals in the United States are exposed, during their formative years, to messages which either state or imply that: (1) most people have a sweet tooth; and (2) people ought to avoid refined sugar because it is un-

healthful. The first message is descriptive, the second prescriptive. Few of us, I assume, would wish to argue that the human sweet tooth exists because people believe it does. Now consider another pair of messages: (1) men tend to desire a variety of sexual partners; and (2) mature, sexually secure, "manly" men (mensch) tend to prefer a wife and family and to channel most of their time and energy into socially responsible, nonsexual pursuits. Once again, the first message is descriptive and the second largely prescriptive, although it is thinly disguised as description. It is true that men are commonly believed to desire sexual variety, but it is also true that the great majority of prescriptive messages concerning this desire are intended to suppress it, not to foster it.

To interpret male homosexual variety-seeking and impersonal sex as the acting out of prescriptively based norms strikes me as tenuous at best. The primary emotional problem in the male homosexual world is the difficulty of maintaining intimate, long-term relationships (Hoffman 1977), a problem that homosexual men are well aware results largely from the desire for variety. And whatever condemnation there may be in Western societies of intimacy between two men, which may mitigate against long-term relationships (Hoffman 1977), surely it is nothing compared with the condemnation of sex in public restrooms: no one asserts that such sex represents desirable, manly behavior, and even its participants may find it repugnant as well as pleasurable (Humphreys 1970).

If homosexual men were acting out social norms or expectations of desirable male behavior they would be cultural heroes (although perhaps condemned for their partner choice), but they are not. In fact, extremes of malelike sexual behavior are not considered manly and almost inevitably are played down by homosexual spokesmen who are attempting to sway public opinion toward acceptance of homosexuality. It is precisely these aspects of male homosexual behavior that some segments of the public find most threatening; many homosexual men achieve in reality the kind of sexual contacts that most heterosexual men can only fantasize about. Most prescriptive messages about male sexuality are not attempts to glorify these male fantasies but to suppress them. Lesbian sexual behavior does not similarly challenge social norms, which probably is one reason that females are never prosecuted for homosexual behavior. In the following passage Tripp (1975) argues that public hostility toward homosexual men results from the psychic threat they constitute:

Even in the most conventional heterosexual settings, one violates basic codes by pursuing sex for fun, for variety, for conquest, and for still other "purely" erotic and personal desires. To do so is to hear charges of shallowness and adulteration—if not the adulteration of one's marriage then of love itself, frequently with lectures on what constitutes "mature" relationships. In short, the philosophic basis of our heterosexuality is still essentially ascetic, with the curse fully lifted off of sex when, and only when, it is transcended by affection and social commitments.

Very many people retain these attitudes and this whole way of viewing sex. If they have held to rigid sex codes, the loss of interest they have sustained in the bedroom has usually been made more tolerable by being rationalized—often with the idea that sex is not all that important anyway, and that through their privations they have earned moral credits and met family obligations. From this point of comparison, homosexuality not only seems personally unappealing (as "opposite" choices always are) but thoroughly contemptible, especially when pictured as lasciviously free (p. 227).

(3) Weitz (1977) grants that small "innate" sex differences probably exist in the tendencies to be sexually aroused by visual stimuli, but goes on to argue that these initial differences are greatly magnified in Western societies by the widespread use of pictures of women in advertising, men's magazines, etc. Weitz's hypothesis is attractive because it seems to represent a balanced and sensible integration of "biological" and "social" factors; however, there is no guarantee that truth lies between extremes. I propose an alternative hypothesis: pictures of attractive women are used to sell products because these pictures appeal to men (and perhaps to women as well), not the other way around. There may be no positive feedback at all; on the contrary, constant exposure to pictures of nude and nearly nude female bodies may to some extent habituate men to these stimuli and thus make men and women *more*, rather than less, alike. That homosexual men are at least as likely as heterosexual men to be interested in pornography, cosmetic qualities, and youth seems to me to imply that these interests are no more the result of advertising than adultery and alcohol consumption are the result of country and western music.

The existence of large numbers of exclusive homosexuals in contemporary Western societies attests to the importance of social experience in determining the objects that humans sexually desire; but the fact that homosexual men behave in many ways like heterosexual men, only more so, and lesbians behave like heterosexual women, only more so, indicates that some other aspects of human sexuality are not so plastic. And even when men and women appear to be similar in behavior, as in forming long-term sexual partnerships, the behavioral similarities are not necessarily brought about or maintained by the same psychological mechanisms.

TEN

Conclusions

Polygamy may well be held in dread,
 Not only as a sin, but as a bore:
Most wise men with one moderate woman wed,
 Will scarcely find philosophy for more . . .

* * *

. . . how the devil is it that fresh features
Have such a charm for us poor human creatures?
 LORD BYRON, *Don Juan*

ACCORDING TO RASMUSSEN (1931), Eskimo men will "have intercourse with any woman whenever there is an opportunity" (p. 195); but neither Eskimo women nor women of other human communities will have intercourse at every opportunity. The ultimate causes of such sex differences are the differing reproductive opportunities and constraints males and females typically encountered during the course of evolutionary history. Shaw makes John Tanner say, "if women could do without our work, and we ate their children's bread instead of making it, they would kill us as the spider kills her mate or as the bees kill the drone." But although evolutionary theory provides unparalleled ultimate explanations of many data on human sexuality, theory is in no sense more "real" than data. I argued, for example, that men tend to be sexually jealous of their wives because in ancestral populations the emotion of jealousy (in concert with other emotions) increased the probability that men would sire their wives' offspring; that is, I attempted to explain why this emotion typically exists. But the evidence for its widespread existence comes from ethnography, not evolutionary biology, and it would be inaccurate to infer that a furious, cuckolded husband only imagines himself to be angry at his wife's sexual pecca-dilloes when, in some more profound sense, what he is "really" doing is promoting the survival of his genes. In fact, the opposite would be more accurate: sexual jealousy is real; this jealousy may or may not affect reproductive success; and how selection operated in times past is still more conjectural. Furthermore, an evolutionary explanation of why males tend to be sexually jealous has no implications for the question of how "free" they are to act or not to act jealously.

Throughout the Pleistocene boys and girls must have been reared differently, but it is most unlikely that these different rearing condi-tions were the sole developmental mechanism responsible for sex dif-ferences in sexuality. The data presented in previous chapters, and summarized in the last chapter, suggest some developmental fixity in sexuality (there are no myths of sleeping males who require a princess' kiss to awaken them: if males are still dozing at puberty they are awakened by nature). Very likely, many of these sex differences would prove to be innate—without apologetic quotation marks—if the envi-ronment were held constant. That is, males and females exposed to identical environmental conditions during ontogeny would develop different sexual behaviors, attitudes, and feelings. This does not neces-sarily mean that it would be impossible to rear boys and girls so that they developed identical sexualities, but simply that identical sexualities would not result from identical rearing conditions.

Because human sexual behavior is determined less by genes and gonadal hormones and more by learning than is the sexual behavior of any other animal species, human sexuality is often said to be released or emancipated from genes and hormones—culture and society, the great emancipators, having marched through the evolving cerebral cortex to sexual freedom. But culture and society are not entities: they are the cumulative material and symbolic products of individual hu-man beings, no two of whom had identical reproductive "interests." Plasticity is a double-edged sword: the more flexible an organism is the greater the variety of maladaptive, as well as adaptive, behaviors it can develop; the more teachable it is the more fully it can profit from the experiences of its ancestors and associates and the more it risks being exploited by its ancestors and associates; the greater its capacity for learning morality the more worthless superstitions, as well as tradi-tions of social wisdom, it can acquire; the more cooperatively inter-dependent the members of a group become the greater is their collec-tive power and the more fulsome are the opportunities for individuals to manipulate one another; the more sophisticated language becomes the more subtle are the lies, as well as the truths, that can be told. Hence I argued that the evolutionary elaboration of the cerebral cortical superstructure that makes human plasticity possible entailed a concomitant elaboration of a nonplastic motivational substructure. If selection has always been potent at the level of the individual, individuals must have "innate" mechanisms, probably best conceived as emotional/motivational mechanisms, to recognize and look after their own reproductive "interests." Thus humans cannot be merely passive vehicles by which society and culture perpetuate themselves, whether society and culture are understood as systems, as they often are, or as collections of discrete components, as Dawkins (1976) understands them. Dawkins argues that bits of culture are, like viruses, self-replicating parasites on human beings, but his analogy shows precisely why this view must be incomplete: in environments containing pathogenic viruses, selection favors the most resistant individuals.

Unlike most other mammals, humans mate year round. Unlike all other mammals, human females conceal, rather than advertise, ovulation. Unlike all other mammals, human reproductive competition occurred in social milieus of enormous complexity. It was, I believe, the complexity of sexual opportunity and constraint in natural human environments that made adaptive a human psyche uniquely informed by sexuality. That individual reproductive "interests" must in some degree conflict with one another may account for the intensity of human sexual emotions, the pervasive interest in other people's sex lives, the frequency with which sex is a subject of gossip, the universal seeking of privacy for sexual intercourse, the secrecy and deception that surround sexual activities and make the scientific study of sex so difficult, the universal existence of sexual laws or rules, and the fact that in our own society "morals" has come to refer almost exclusively to sexual matters. Neither adaptation to monogamous pair-bonds nor a history of noncompetitive promiscuity can easily account for the above facts about human sexuality, and these facts also constitute a challenge to group selection theories and to theories in which society is the source of human emotion.

The relations of society and culture to organic evolution are likely to be debated in the biological and social sciences for many years to come. Even at present, however, views of society that ignore organic evolution entirely can be seen to be inadequate, at least with respect to sexuality. It is generally believed, for example, that young women tend to be more sexually attractive than older women. But what is the source of this belief, and why is it maintained? Does a powerful, secret cabal of twenty-year-old women control propaganda? Do men promulgate this belief in order to reduce the competition for middle-aged women, whom they lust after in their hearts? In actuality, if one considers such concepts as the dirty old man, statutory rape, and psychosexual immaturity, it seems fairly clear that young women are perceived as attractive in spite of, not because of, normative and prescriptive rhetoric.

As discussed in Chapter Two, many social scientists, and probably most economists and psychologists, view society and culture as the cumulative products of individuals pursuing their own interests. But it has proved difficult to define "self-interest" in a way that is neither circular nor dependent on intuition and to specify the mechanisms by which individuals initiate, perpetuate, and change social forms. Although Bloch (1977) and Brown (n.d.) argue that inaccurate notions of time, society, and history are tools for perpetuating inequalities, these writers are appropriately vague about the actual mechanisms involved. Bloch writes that the perpetuation of institutionalized hierarchy is what the cognitive system that he calls social structure "is about." And Brown calls attention to the correlation between quality of historiography and openness of social stratification, but he does not argue that powerful individuals in hereditarily stratified societies necessarily either consciously perceive that accurate history would endanger their positions or make conscious efforts to suppress accurate history (though they may).

One reason the concept of self-interest is so difficult may be that, for the most part, self-interest is perceived and pursued unconsciously, making conspiracies without conspirators possible. Alexander (1974, 1975) has even argued that selection favored individuals who were ignorant of the "selfish" effects of their own behavior, since the sincere belief in one's own "altruism" makes one's deceptive performances more believable. Obviously selection could not have opposed awareness of abstract scientific notions like inclusive fitness any more than it could have opposed awareness of the atomic structure of matter, but even if "selfish" and "altruistic" are understood in their ordinary senses, Alexander's argument is not compelling. Our typically keen insight into other people's motives implies intense selection for social perceptiveness in times past (among preliterate peoples, reproductively successful headmen seem to be uncommonly politically astute and socially perceptive). But our failure to note that social perceptiveness is grounded in projection does not necessarily imply that selection actually disfavored self-insight. Karl Lashley pointed out that we are conscious primarily of the results, not the processes, of thought. Our ability to make almost any kind of judgment or calculation far exceeds our ability to understand how we make them. To know others is an adaptive necessity; to know thyself is an acquired taste.

The sex differences in human sexuality discussed in this book originated in the greater variability of male than of female reproductive success during the course of evolutionary history. One might, therefore, expect male sexuality to be more plastic and variable than female sexuality; for example, high- and low-ranking males might be expected to pursue different reproductive "strategies." Indeed, Crook (1971, 1972) suggests that among nonhuman primates high-ranking males freely use scarce resources, such as estrous females, while low-ranking males adopt "behavioral subterfuges" to gain access to these resources. Kaufmann (1965) characterizes some low-ranking male rhesus monkeys as "opportunistic" because they mate furtively and in concealment, and he notes that a low-ranking male may copulate when a female's regular partner is temporarily out of sight (also see Symons 1978a). Trivers (1972:146) writes: "If males within a relatively monogamous species are, in fact, adapted to pursue a mixed strategy, the optimal is likely to differ for different males. . . . psychology might well benefit from attempting to view human sexual plasticity as an adaptation to permit the individual to choose the mixed strategy best suited to local conditions and his own attributes." And I suggested that the human male's desire for sexual variety might vary to some extent with opportunities to satisfy this desire (Chapter Seven). Nevertheless, contrary to expectation, the data on human sexuality indicate "that the range of variation in the female far exceeds the range of variation in the male" (Kinsey et al. 1953:537-38).

Some women in Kinsey's sample had never been aroused erotically, while others were aroused almost daily; of those who had been aroused, some responded only mildly to tactile or psychologic stimulation (visual and narrative stimuli and fantasy), while others responded instantaneously and intensely, and reached orgasm quickly; some who had been aroused by tactile stimuli had never been aroused by psychologic stimuli, while others could reach orgasm from psychologic stimuli alone. "There were females in the sample who had been more responsive to psychologic stimulation than any male we have known"

(p. 540). Although the women in Kinsey's sample very rarely were interested in sexual variety *per se*, a few were as interested as any man. And, in cross-cultural perspective, among some peoples there is no concept of female orgasm, while among others all women are said to experience multiple orgasms.

Female sexuality seems to be generally less rigidly channeled than male sexuality. At swingers' parties in the United States, for example, over 90 percent of the (presumably heterosexual) women find that they enjoy sex with other women, while male swingers almost never have sex with other men (Bartell 1971). Recall, too, that AGS women were unequivocally happy about the changes cortisone therapy induced in their sexuality. They said that they liked being able to feel like normal women, but perhaps they also enjoyed the increased freedom from reflexlike responses to external stimuli and from internal sexual pressures. Neither their clitoral sensitivity nor, presumably, their capacity for sexual pleasure were impaired by cortisone: in essence, they lost sexual compulsion without losing sexual possibility.

Because the sexual variability of the human female far exceeds that of the male it is harder for women than for men to understand intuitively the sexual experiences and feelings of some members of their own sex:

> Because there is such wide variation in the sexual responsiveness and frequencies of overt activity among females, many females are incapable of understanding other females. There are fewer males who are incapable of understanding other males. Even the sexually least responsive of the males can comprehend something of the meaning of the frequent and continuous arousal which some other males experience. But the female who goes through life or for any long period of years with little or no experience in orgasm, finds it very difficult to comprehend the female who is capable of several orgasms every time she has sexual contact, and who may, on occasion, have a score or more orgasms in an hour. To the third or more of the females who have rarely been aroused by psychologic stimuli, it may seem fantastic to believe that there are females who come to orgasm as the result of sexual fantasy, without any physical stimulation of their genitalia or of any other part of their body (Kinsey *et al.* 1953:538-39).

Perhaps female sexual variability accounts for the fact that one woman psychiatrist can argue, on the basis of the female's capacity for multiple orgasms, that human females are sexually insatiable (Sherfey 1972), while a second woman psychiatrist can question the very existence of multiple orgasms (Shainess 1976).

Some of the sexual variability of the human female probably represents adaptation. For example, although men and women are equally
capable of experiencing intense sexual jealousy of a spouse, learning
may play a greater role in determining the circumstances in which
females experience jealousy; that is, sexual jealousy may be a facultative adaptation in the human female and an obligate adaptation in the
human male (Chapter Seven). The probable ultimate explanation for
this sex difference is that it has always been adaptive for men to be
sexually jealous of their wives, while in some polygynous marriages it
has not been adaptive for women to be sexually jealous of their husbands; furthermore, husbands' extramarital adventures have not *necessarily* constituted threats to their wives' reproductive success, hence
females are adapted to learn to discriminate threatening from nonthreatening adultery. Similarly, criteria for evaluating sexual attractiveness probably develop in a more "innate" fashion in the human
male than in the human female. For example, certain physical characteristics (especially skin quality) universally correlate with female age,
and males very likely have "innate" psychological mechanisms for
detecting and responding to these characteristics, whereas the evaluation of male status and prowess presumably depends more on learning.

But facultative adaptations cannot, in my opinion, begin to account
for the sexual variability of the human female. The fact of female
sexual plasticity, which makes variability possible, is not in itself evidence for adaptation to exhibit variable sexual behavior (see Chapter
Two); the enormous range of sexual variation observed among females
may be primarily an artifact of artificial, postagricultural habitats. If
one adopts Williams's dictum, "adaptation is a special and onerous
concept that should be used only where it is really necessary," available
evidence does not justify the conclusion that the female orgasm is an
adaptation (Chapter Three). Parsimoniously interpreted, the data
suggest that with sufficient clitoral stimulation any female mammal can
experience orgasm, but that sufficient stimulation rarely or never occurs
in a state of nature. With respect to humans, what happened in a state
of nature is obviously conjectural, but since among most peoples sexual
intercourse is completed primarily in terms of the man's passions and
pleasures (Davenport 1977), it is a reasonable hypothesis that the human female's capacity for orgasm is no more an adaptation than is the
ability to learn to read. If, throughout most of human evolutionary
history, the potentials of females sexuality were very rarely realized,
these potentials would have been largely "invisible" to natural selec-

tion, and this may account for the astonishing sexual plasticity of the human female.

There are, I believe, several general implications in the line of reasoning pursued here. First, data, not theory and not analogies with nonhuman animals, reveal what human beings are like. Second, evolutionary analyses must consider the question of the environments for which organisms have been designed, however speculative such consideration may be. Structures, behaviors, and psyches that develop in unnatural environments may not have ultimate causes at all. Third, the tendencies to equate "natural" and "good" and to find dignity in biological adaptation can only impede understanding of ultimate causation and distort perceptions of nonhuman animals, preliterate peoples, and history. Finally, the *potentials* of a biological mechanism are not necessarily constrained by, and cannot necessarily be predicted from, the *purposes* for which the mechanism was designed by natural selection. Perhaps it is not excessively naïve to hope that a creature capable of perceiving the plowshare in the sword is also capable of freeing itself from the nightmare of the past.

References

ABELE, L. G., and S. GILCHRIST
  1977 Homosexual rape and sexual selection in acanthocephalan worms. *Science* 197:81-83.
ACKERLEY, J. R.
  1968 *My Father and Myself.* New York: Coward-McCann.
AGAR, E., and G. MITCHELL
  1975 Behavior of free-ranging adult rhesus macaques: a review. Pp. 323-42 in G. H. Bourne, ed., *The Rhesus Monkey*, vol. 1. New York: Academic Press.
ALCOCK, J.
  1975 *Animal Behavior: An Evolutionary Approach.* Sunderland, Massachusetts: Sinauer Associates.
ALDIS, O.
  1975 *Play Fighting.* New York: Academic Press.
ALEXANDER, R. D.
  1971 The search for an evolutionary philosophy of man. *Proceedings of the Royal Society of Victoria* 84:99-120.
  1974 The evolution of social behavior. *Annual Review of Ecology and Systematics* 5:325-83.
  1975 The search for a general theory of behavior. *Behavioral Science* 20:77-100.
ALLEN, E. *et al.*
  1975 Against sociobiology. *New York Review of Books*, November 13.
AMIS, K.
  1958 *Lucky Jim.* New York: The Viking Press.
ANONYMOUS ("Walter")
  1966 *My Secret Life.* New York: Grove Press.
BALIKCI, A.
  1970 *The Netsilik Eskimo.* Garden City, New York: The Natural History Press.
BARASH, D. P.
  1977a *Sociobiology and Behavior.* New York: Elsevier North-Holland, Inc.
  1977b Sociobiology and rape in mallards (*Anas platyrhynchos*): responses of the mated male. *Science* 197:788-89.
BARRETT, P. H.
  1974 Darwin's early and unpublished notebooks. Pp. 259-474 in H. E.

Gruber, ed., *Darwin on Man: A Psychological Study of Scientific Creativity*. New York: E. P. Dutton & Co.

BARTELL, G. D.

1971 *Group Sex: A Scientist's Eyewitness Report on the American Way of Swinging*. New York: Peter H. Wyden.

BASS-HASS, R.

1968 The lesbian dyad. *The Journal of Sex Research* 4:108-26.

BAUM, M. J.; B. J. EVERITT; J. HERBERT; and E. B. KEVERNE

1977 Hormonal basis of proceptivity and receptivity in female primates. *Archives of Sexual Behavior* 6:173-92.

BEACH, F. A.

1965 Retrospect and prospect. Pp. 535-69 in F. A. Beach, ed., *Sex and Behavior*. New York: John Wiley and Sons.

1974 Human sexuality and evolution. Pp. 333-65 in W. Montagna and W. A. Sadler, eds., *Reproductive Behavior*. New York: Plenum.

1976a Cross-species comparisons and the human heritage. *Archives of Sexual Behavior* 5:469-85.

1976b Sexual attractivity, proceptivity, and receptivity in female mammals. *Hormones and Behavior* 7:105-38.

BEAMER, W.; G. BERMANT; and M. T. CLEGG

1969 Copulatory behaviour of the ram, *Ovis aries* II: factors affecting copulatory satiation. *Animal Behavior* 17:706-11.

BELL, R. R.

1974 Female sexual satisfaction as related to levels of education. Pp. 3-11 in L. Gross, ed., *Sexual Behavior—Current Issues: An Interdisciplinary Perspective*. Flushing, New York: Spectrum.

BELL, R. R., and D. PELTZ

1974 Extramarital sex among women. *Medical Aspects of Human Sexuality* 8:10-39.

BELL, R. R., S. TURNER, and L. ROSEN

1975 A multivariate analysis of female extramarital coitus. *Journal of Marriage and the Family* 37:375-84.

BELLOW, S.

1973 *Humboldt's Gift*. New York: The Viking Press.

BENGIS, I.

1973 *Combat in the Erogenous Zone*. New York: Bantam.

BERMANT, G.

1976 Sexual behavior: hard times with the Coolidge Effect. Pp. 76-103 in M. H. Siegel and H. P. Zeigler, eds., *Psychological Research: The Inside Story*. New York: Harper & Row.

BERMANT, G.; M. T. CLEGG; and W. BEAMER

1969 Copulatory behaviour of the ram, *Ovis aires* I: a normative study. *Animal Behaviour* 17:700-705.

BERNARD, J.

1945 Observation and generalization in cultural anthropology. *The American Journal of Sociology* 50:284-91.

1968 *The Sex Game*. Englewood Cliffs, New Jersey: Prentice-Hall.

1972   *The Future of Marriage.* New York: World.

BERNDT, R. M.

1962   *Excess and Restraint.* Chicago: University of Chicago Press.

BERNDT, R. M., and C. H. BERNDT

1951   *Sexual Behavior in Western Arnhem Land.* New York: Viking Fund.

BERSCHEID, E., and E. WALSTER

1974   Physical attractiveness. Pp. 157-215 in L. Berkowitz, ed., *Advances in Experimental Social Psychology,* vol. 7. New York: Academic Press.

BIGELOW, R.

1973   The evolution of cooperation, aggression, and self-control. Pp. 1-57 in J. K. Cole and D. D. Jensen, eds., *Nebraska Symposium on Motivation 1972.* Lincoln, Nebraska: University of Nebraska Press.

BLAU, P. M.

1964   *Exchange and Power in Social Life.* New York: John Wiley and Sons.

BLOCH, M.

1977   The past and the present in the present. *Man* (N.S.) 12: 278-92.

BLURTON-JONES, N. G., and M. J. KONNER

1973   Sex differences in behaviour of London and Bushman children. Pp. 689-750 in R. P. Michael and J. H. Crook, eds., *Comparative Ecology and Behaviour of Primates.* New York: Academic Press.

BOLTON, R.

1973   Tawanku: intercouple bonds in a Qolla village (Peru). *Anthropos* 68: 145-55.

BRADY, J. V.

1975   Toward a behavioral biology of emotion. Pp. 17-45 in L. Levi, ed., *Emotions—Their Parameters and Measurement.* New York: Raven Press.

BRINDLEY, C.; P. CLARKE; C. HUTT; I. ROBINSON; and E. WETHLI

1973   Sex differences in the activities and social interactions of nursery school children. Pp. 799-828 in R. P. Michael and J. H. Crook, eds., *Comparative Ecology and Behaviour of Primates.* New York: Academic Press.

BROCKELMAN, W. Y.; B. A. ROSS; and S. PANTUWATANA

1973   Social correlates of reproductive success in the gibbon colony on Ko Klet Kaeo, Thailand. *American Journal of Physical Anthropology* 38:637-40.

1974   Social interactions of adult gibbons (*Hylobates lar*) in an experimental colony. *Gibbon and Siamang* 3:137-56.

BROWN, D. E.

n.d.   Social stratification and historiography.

BROWNMILLER, S.

1975   *Against Our Will: Men, Women and Rape.* New York: Simon and Schuster.

BRYANT, C. D., and C. E. PALMER

 1975 Massage parlors and "hand whores": some sociological observations. *Journal of Sex Research* 11:227-41.

BURGESS, E. W., and P. WALLIN

 1953 *Engagement and Marriage.* Chicago: J. B. Lippincott.

BURTON, F. D.

 1971 Sexual climax in female *Macaca mulatta. Proceedings of the Third International Congress of Primatology,* Zurich 1970, 3: 180-91. Basel: Karger.

BUTLER, H.

 1974 Evolutionary trends in primate sex cycles. *Contributions to Primatology* 3:2-35.

BUTLER, R. A.

 1954 Incentive conditions which influence visual exploration. *Journal of Experimental Psychology* 48:19-23.

BYGOTT, J. D.

 in press Agonistic behaviour, dominance, and social structure in wild chimpanzees of the Gombe National Park. In B. Hamburg and E. McCown, eds., *The Great Apes.* Menlo Park, California: Benjamin/Cummings.

CAMPBELL, B.

 1971 *Human Evolution: An Introduction to Man's Adaptations.* Chicago: Aldine.

 1974 *Human Evolution: An Introduction to Man's Adaptations* (2nd ed.). Chicago: Aldine.

CAMPBELL, D. T.

 1975 On the conflicts between biological and social evolution and between psychology and moral tradition. *American Psychologist* 30:1103-26.

CARNEIRO, R.

 1958 Extra-marital sex freedom among the Kuikuru Indians of Mato Grosso. *Revista do Museu Paulista, São Paulo* 10:135-42.

CARPENTER, C. R.

 1940 A field study in Siam of the behaviour and social relations of the gibbon (*Hylobates lar*). *Comparative Psychology Monographs* 16:1-212.

 1942 Sexual behavior of free-ranging rhesus monkeys. *Journal of Comparative Psychology* 33:113-62.

CASPARI, E.

 1972 Sexual selection in human evolution. Pp. 332-56 in B. Campbell, ed., *Sexual Selection and the Descent of Man 1871-1971.* Chicago: Aldine.

CHAGNON, N. A.

 1968a *Yanomamö: The Fierce People.* New York: Holt, Rinehart and Winston.

 1968b Yanomamö social organization and warfare. Pp. 109-59 in M. Fried, M. Harris, and R. Murphy, eds., *War: The Anthropology of Armed Conflict and Aggression.* Garden City, New York: The Natural History Press.

in press Is reproductive success "equal" in egalitarian societies? In N. A. Chagnon and W. Irons, eds., *Evolutionary Biology and Human Social Behavior: An Anthropological Perspective.* North Scituate, Massachusetts: Duxbury Press.

CHANCE, M. R. A., and A. P. MEAD

1953 Social behaviour and primate evolution. Society for Experimental Biology, *Symposia* no. 7:395-439.

CHAPPELL, D.; R. GEIS; and G. GEIS, eds.

1977 *Forcible Rape: The Crime, the Victim, and the Offender.* New York: Columbia University Press.

CHESSER, E.

1956 *The Sexual, Marital and Family Relationships of the English Woman.* Great Britain: Hutchinson's Medical Publications.

CHEVALIER-SKOLNIKOFF, S.

1974 Male-female, female-female, and male-male sexual behavior in the stumptail monkey, with special attention to the female orgasm. *Archives of Sexual Behavior* 3:95-116.

CHRISTENSEN, H. T.

1960 Cultural relativism and premarital sex norms. *American Sociological Review* 25:31-39.

CLARK, J. D.

1976 The African origins of man the toolmaker. Pp. 1-53 in G. Ll. Isaac and E. R. McCown, eds., *Human Origins: Louis Leakey and the East African Evidence.* Menlo Park, California: W. A. Benjamin.

CLASTRES, P.

1972 *Chronique Des Indiens Guayaki: Ce Que Savent Les Aché, Chasseurs Nomades Du Paraguay.* Paris: Librairie Plon.

CLUTTON-BROCK, T. H., and P. H. HARVEY

1976 Evolutionary rules and primate societies. Pp. 195-237 in P. P. G. Bateson and R. A. Hinde, eds., *Growing Points in Ethology.* Cambridge: Cambridge University Press.

COHEN, M. L.; R. GAROFALO; R. B. BOUCHER; and T. SEGHORN

1977 [1971] The psychology of rapists. Pp. 291-314 in D. Chappell, R. Geis, and G. Geis, eds., *Forcible Rape: The Crime, the Victim, and the Offender.* New York: Columbia University Press.

COLETTE

1955 *The Vagabond.* Translated by E. McLeod. New York: Farrar, Straus & Giroux.

1958 The Kepi. In *The Tender Shoot and Other Stories by Colette.* Translated by A. White. New York: Farrar, Straus & Giroux.

COLSON, E.

1974 *Tradition and Contract: The Problem of Order.* Chicago: Aldine.

Cox, C. R., and B. J. Le Boeuf

1977 Female incitation of male competition: a mechanism in sexual selection. *The American Naturalist* 111:317-35.

Crook, J. H.

1971 Sources of cooperation in animals and man. Pp. 237-60 in J. F. Eisenberg and W. S. Dillon, eds., *Man and Beast: Comparative Social Behavior.* Washington: Smithsonian Institution Press.

1972 Sexual selection, dimorphism, and social organization in the primates. Pp. 231-81 in B. Campbell, ed., *Sexual Selection and the Descent of Man 1871-1971.* Chicago: Aldine.

Cuber, J. F.

1969 Adultery: reality versus stereotype. Pp. 190-96 in G. Neubeck, ed., *Extramarital Relations.* Englewood Cliffs, New Jersey: Prentice-Hall.

1975 The natural history of sex in marriage. *Medical Aspects of Human Sexuality* 9:51-73.

Cuber, J. F., and P. B. Harroff

1965 *Sex and the Significant Americans: A Study of Sexual Behavior among the Affluent.* New York: Penguin Books.

D'Andrade, R. G.

1966 Sex differences and cultural institutions. Pp. 174-204 in E. E. Maccoby, ed., *The Development of Sex Differences.* Stanford: Stanford University Press.

Darwin, C.

1859 *On the Origin of Species by Means of Natural Selection, or the Preservation of Favoured Races in the Struggle for Life.* London: Watts & Co.

1871 *The Descent of Man and Selection in Relation to Sex.* London: John Murray.

Davenport, W. H.

1965 Sexual patterns and their regulation in a society of the southwest Pacific. Pp. 161-203 in F. A. Beach, ed., *Sex and Behavior.* New York: John Wiley and Sons.

1977 Sex in cross-cultural perspective. Pp. 115-63 in F. A. Beach, ed., *Human Sexuality in Four Perspectives.* Baltimore: The Johns Hopkins University Press.

Dawkins, R.

1976 *The Selfish Gene.* Oxford: Oxford University Press.

Degler, C. N.

1974 What ought to be and what was: women's sexuality in the nineteenth century. *American Historical Review* 79:1467-90.

DeVore, I.

1977 The new science of genetic self-interest. *Psychology Today,* February: 42.

De Vries, P.

1958 *The Mackerel Plaza.* Boston: Little, Brown and Company.

1978   *The Tunnel of Love.* New York: Popular Library.

DIAKOW, C.

1974   Male-female interactions and the organization of mammalian mating patterns. *Advances in the Study of Behavior* 5:227-68.

DURHAM, W. H.

1976   Resource competition and human aggression, part I: a review of primitive war. *Quarterly Review of Biology* 51:385-415.

DYSON-HUDSON, R., and E. A. SMITH

1978   Human territoriality: an ecological reassessment. *American Anthropologist* 80:21-41.

EATON, G. G.

1973   Social and endocrine determinants of sexual behavior in simian and prosimian females. Pp. 20-35 in C. H. Phoenix, ed., *Fourth International Congress of Primatology,* vol. 2. Basel: S. Karger.

EATON, G. G.; R. W. GOY; and C. H. PHOENIX

1973   Effects of testosterone treatment in adulthood on sexual behaviour of female pseudohermaphrodite rhesus monkeys. *Nature New Biology* 242:119-20.

EDWARDS, J. N.

1973   Extramarital involvement: fact and theory. *Journal of Sex Research* 9:210-24.

EDWARDS, J. N., and A. BOOTH

1976   Sexual behavior in and out of marriage: an assessment of correlates. *Journal of Marriage and the Family* 38:73-81.

EDWARDS, L.

1976   *Lover: The Confessions of a One-Night Stand.* New York: Farrar, Straus & Giroux.

EHRHARDT, A. A., and S. W. BAKER

1974   Fetal androgens, human central nervous system differentiation, and behavior sex differences. Pp. 33-51 in R. C. Friedman, R. M. Richart, and R. L. Vande Wiele, eds., *Sex Differences in Behavior.* New York: John Wiley and Sons.

EHRHARDT, A.; K. EVERS; and J. MONEY

1968   Influence of androgen and some aspects of sexually dimorphic behavior in women with the late-treated adrenogenital syndrome. *Johns Hopkins Medical Journal* 123:115-22.

EHRMANN, W.

1963   Social determinants of human sexual behavior. Pp. 142-63 in G. Winokur, ed., *Determinants of Human Sexual Behavior.* Springfield, Illinois: Charles C. Thomas.

EIBL-EIBESFELDT, I.

1974   The myth of the aggression-free hunter and gatherer society. Pp. 435-57 in R. L. Holloway, ed., *Primate Aggression, Territoriality, and Xenophobia.* New York: Academic Press.

1975   *Ethology: The Biology of Behavior.* New York: Holt, Rinehart and Winston.

EISENBERG, J. F.
  1966 The social organizations of mammals. *Handbuch der Zoologie*
        10:1-92.
ELLEFSON, J. O.
  1968 Territorial behavior in the common white-handed gibbon *Hylo-
        bates lar Linn.* Pp. 180-99 in P. C. Jay, ed., *Primates: Studies in
        Adaptation and Variability.* New York: Holt, Rinehart and
        Winston.
ELWIN, V.
  1968 *The Kingdom of the Young.* London: Oxford University Press.
EMLEN, S. T.
  1976 An alternative case for sociobiology. *Science* 192:736-38.
EMLEN, S. T., and L. W. ORING
  1977 Ecology, sexual selection, and the evolution of mating systems.
        Science 197:215-23.
ERASMUS, C. J.
  1977 *In Search of the Common Good: Utopian Experiments Past and
        Future.* New York: The Free Press.
EVANS-PRITCHARD, E. E.
  1965 The position of women in primitive societies and in our own. Pp.
        37-58 in E. E. Evans-Pritchard, *The Position of Women in Prim-
        itive Societies and Other Essays in Social Anthropology.* New
        York: The Free Press.
FAIRBANKS, L. A.
  1977 Animal and human behavior: guidelines for generalization across
        species. Pp. 87-110 in M. T. McGuire and L. A. Fairbanks, eds.,
        *Ethological Psychiatry: Psychopathology in the Context of Evo-
        lution Biology.* New York: Grune & Stratton.
FEE, E.
  1976 Science and the woman problem: historical perspectives. Pp.
        175-223 in M. S. Teitelbaum, ed., *Sex Differences: Social and
        Biological Perspectives.* Garden City, New York: Anchor Press/
        Doubleday.
FIRESTONE, S.
  1970 *The Dialectic of Sex: The Case for Feminist Revolution.* New
        York: William Morrow and Company.
FISHER, S.
  1973 *The Female Orgasm: Psychology, Physiology, Fantasy.* New
        York: Basic Books.
FLAUBERT, G.
  1950 *Madame Bovary.* Translated by A. Russell. New York: Penguin
        Books.
FLEW, A.
  1967 *Evolutionary Ethics.* New York: St. Martin's Press.
FORD, C. S.
  1945 *A Comparative Study of Human Reproduction.* New Haven:
        Yale University Press.

FORD, C. S., and F. A. BEACH
  1951   *Patterns of Sexual Behavior.* New York: Harper & Row.
FOX, C. A., and B. FOX
  1971   A comparative study of coital physiology, with special reference to the sexual climax. *Journal of Reproduction and Fertility* 24: 319-36.
FOX, R.
  1967   In the beginning: aspects of hominid behavioural evolution. *Man* 2:415-33.
FREEDMAN, D. G.
  1972   Genetic variations on the hominid theme: individual, sex and ethnic differences. Pp. 121-41 in F. J. Mönks, W. W. Hartup, and J. deWit, eds., *Determinants of Behavioral Development.* New York: Academic Press.
FREEDMAN, M. B.
  1970   The sexual behavior of American college women: an empirical study and an historical survey. Pp. 135-50 in A. Shiloh, ed., *Studies in Human Sexual Behavior: The American Scene.* Springfield, Illinois: Charles C. Thomas.
FREMONT, J.
  1975   Rapists speak for themselves. Pp. 241-56 in D. E. H. Russell, *The Politics of Rape: The Victim's Perspective.* New York: Stein and Day.
FREUD, S.
  1961   *Civilization and Its Discontents.* Translated by J. Strachey (The Standard Edition of the Complete Psychological Works, vol. 21). London: The Hogarth Press.
GAGNON, J. H.
  1973   Scripts and the coordination of sexual conduct. Pp. 27-59 in J. K. Cole and R. Dienstbier, eds., *Nebraska Symposium on Motivation 1973.* Lincoln: University of Nebraska Press.
  1977   *Human Sexualities.* Glenview, Illinois: Scott, Foresman and Company.
GAGNON, J. H., and W. SIMON
  1973   *Sexual Conduct.* Chicago: Aldine.
GALDIKAS, B. M. F.
  1978   Orangutan Adaptation at Tanjung Puting Reserve, Central Borneo. Ph.D. thesis, University of California, Los Angeles.
  in press   Orangutan adaptation at Tanjung Puting Reserve: mating and ecology. In B. Hamburg and E. McCown, eds., *The Great Apes.* Menlo Park, California: Benjamin/Cummings.
GALTON, F.
  1883   *Inquiries into Human Faculty and Its Development.* London: Macmillan.
GAZZANIGA, M. S.
  1970   *The Bisected Brain.* New York: Appleton-Century-Crofts.

GEBHARD, P. H.

1965   Situational factors affecting human sexual behavior. Pp. 483-95 in F. A. Beach, ed., *Sex and Behavior*. New York: John Wiley and Sons.

1971a   Foreword. Pp. xi-xiv in D. S. Marshall and R. C. Suggs, eds., *Human Sexual Behavior*. New York: Basic Books.

1971b   The anthropological study of sexual behavior. Pp. 250-60 in D. S. Marshall and R. C. Suggs, eds., *Human Sexual Behavior*. New York: Basic Books.

GEERTZ, C.

1965   The impact of the concept of culture on the concept of man. Pp. 93-118 in J. R. Platt, ed., *New Views of the Nature of Man*. Chicago: University of Chicago Press.

GEIS, G.

1977   Forcible rape: an introduction. Pp. 1-44 in D. Chappell, R. Geis, and G. Geis, eds., *Forcible Rape: The Crime, the Victim, and the Offender*. New York: Columbia University Press.

GENG, V.

1976   Requiem for the women's movement. *Harpers* 253:49-68.

GHISELIN, M. T.

1973   Darwin and evolutionary psychology. *Science* 179:964-68.

1974   *The Economy of Nature and the Evolution of Sex*. Berkeley: University of California Press.

GLACKEN, C. J.

1967   *Traces on the Rhodian Shore*. Berkeley: University of California Press.

GLADWIN, T., and S. B. SARASON

1953   *Truk: Man in Paradise*. New York: The Viking Fund.

GOFFMAN, E.

1969   *Strategic Interaction*. Philadelphia: University of Pennsylvania Press.

GOLDMAN, P. S.; H. T. CRAWFORD; L. P. STOKES; T. W. GALKIN; and H. E. ROSVOLD

1974   Sex-dependent behavioral effects of cerebral cortical lesions in the developing rhesus monkey. *Science* 186:540-42.

GOODALE, J. C.

1971   *Tiwi Wives: A Study of the Women of Melville Island, North Australia*. Seattle: University of Washington Press.

GOODALL, J.

1965   Chimpanzees of the Gombe Stream Reserve. Pp. 425-73 in I. De-Vore, ed., *Primate Behavior: Field Studies of Monkeys and Apes*. New York: Holt, Rinehart and Winston.

1976   Continuities between chimpanzee and human behavior. Pp. 81-95 in G. Ll. Isaac and E. R. McCown, eds., *Human Origins: Louis Leakey and the East African Evidence*. Menlo Park, California: W. A. Benjamin.

GOODALL, J.; A. BANDORA; E. BERGMANN; C. BUSSE; H. MATAMA; E. MPONGO; A. PIERCE; and D. RISS

in press Inter-community interactions in the chimpanzee population of the Gombe National Park. In B. Hamburg and E. McCown, eds., *The Great Apes*. Menlo Park, California; Benjamin/ Cummings.

GOODENOUGH, W. H.

1949 Premarital freedom on Truk: theory and practice. *American Anthropologist* 51:615-19.

GOUGH, K.

1971 The origin of the family. *Journal of Marriage and the Family* 33:760-71.

GOY, R. W.

1968 Organizing effects of androgen on the behaviour of rhesus monkeys. Pp. 12-31 in R. P. Michael, ed., *Endocrinology & Human Behaviour*. London: Oxford University Press.

GOY, R. W., and J. A. RESKO

1972 Gonadal hormones and behavior of normal and pseudohermaphroditic nonhuman female primates. *Recent Progress in Hormone Research* 28:707-33. New York: Academic Press.

GRABURN, N.

1968 Inuriat: the killings. Paper presented to the Symposium on Primitive Law at the Annual Meetings of the American Anthropological Association, Seattle, Washington, 1968.

GREER, G.

1971 *The Female Eunuch*. New York: McGraw-Hill.

GREGOR, T.

1973 Privacy and extra-marital affairs in a tropical forest community. Pp. 242-60 in D. R. Gross, ed., *Peoples and Cultures of Native South America*. Garden City, New York: The Natural History Press.

GROAT, H. T.

1976 Community and conflict in mass society. Pp. 49-77 in A. G. Neal, ed., *Violence in Animal and Human Societies*. Chicago: Nelson Hall.

GROSS, D. R.

1975 Protein capture and cultural development in the Amazon Basin. *American Anthropologist* 77:526-49.

GURIN, J.

1976 Is society hereditary? *Harvard Magazine* 79:21-25.

HALPERIN, S. D.

in press Temporary association patterns in free ranging chimpanzees: an assessment of individual grouping preferences. In B. Hamburg and E. McCown, eds., *The Great Apes*. Menlo Park, California: Benjamin/Cummings.

HAMBURG, B. A.

1978 The biosocial basis of sex differences. Pp. 155-213 in S. L. Washburn and E. R. McCown, eds., *Human Evolution: Biosocial Perspectives*. Menlo Park, California: Benjamin/Cummings.

HAMBURG, D. A.

1971   Aggressive behavior of chimpanzees and baboons in natural habitats. *Journal of Psychiatric Research* 8:385-90.

1973   An evolutionary and developmental approach to human aggressiveness. *The Psychoanalytic Quarterly* 42:185-96.

1974   Ethological perspectives on human aggressive behaviour. Pp. 209-19 in N. F. White, ed., *Ethology and Psychiatry*. Toronto: University of Toronto Press.

HAMES, R.

n.d.   A comparison of the efficiencies of the shotgun and bow in neotropical forest hunting.

HAMILTON, W. D.

1964   The genetical evolution of social behavior. *Journal of Theoretical Biology* 7:1-52.

1975   Innate social aptitudes of man: an approach from evolutionary genetics. Pp. 133-55 in R. Fox, ed., *Biosocial Anthropology*. New York: John Wiley and Sons.

1977   The play by nature. *Science* 196:757-59.

HANBY, J.

1976   Sociosexual development in primates. Pp. 1-67 in P. P. G. Bateson and P. H. Klopfer, eds., *Perspectives in Ethology*. New York: Plenum.

HARPER, R. A.

1961   Extramarital sex relations. Pp. 384-91 in A. Ellis and A. Abarbanel, eds., *The Encyclopedia of Sexual Behavior*. New York: Hawthorn Books.

HART, C. W. M., and A. R. PILLING

1960   *The Tiwi of North Australia*. New York: Holt, Rinehart and Winston.

HATCH, E.

1973   *Theories of Man and Culture*. New York: Columbia University Press.

HEDBLOM, J. H.

1972   The female homosexual: social and attitudinal dimensions. Pp. 31-64 in J. A. McCaffrey, ed., *The Homosexual Dialect*. Englewood Cliffs, New Jersey: Prentice-Hall.

1973   Dimensions of lesbian sexual experience. *Archives of Sexual Behavior* 2:329-41.

HEIDER, K. G.

1976   Dani sexuality: a low energy system. *Man* (N.S.) 2:188-201.

HEIMAN, J. R.

1975   The physiology of erotica: women's sexual arousal. *Psychology Today* 8:90-94.

HELLER, J.

1955   *Catch-22*. New York: Simon and Schuster.

HINDE, R. A.

1975 The concept of function. Pp. 3-15 in G. Bearends, C. Beer, and A. Manning, eds., *Function and Evolution in Behaviour.* Oxford: Clarendon Press.

HINDELANG, M. J., and B. J. DAVIS

1977 Forcible rape in the United States: a statistical profile. Pp. 87-114 in D. Chappell, R. Geis, and G. Geis, eds., *Forcible Rape: The Crime, the Victim, and the Offender.* New York: Columbia University Press.

HITE, S.

1974 *Sexual Honesty: By Women for Women.* New York: Warner Paperback Library.

1976 *The Hite Report.* New York: Macmillan Publishing Co.

HODGEN, G. D.; A. L. GOODMAN; A. O'CONNOR; and D. K. JOHNSON

1977 Menopause in rhesus monkeys: model for study of disorders in the human climacteric. *American Journal of Obstetrics and Gynecology* 127:581-84.

HOFFMAN, M.

1968 *The Gay World.* New York: Basic Books.

1977 Homosexuality. Pp. 164-89 in F. A. Beach, ed., *Human Sexuality in Four Perspectives.* Baltimore: The Johns Hopkins University Press.

HOLMBERG, A. R.

1950 *Nomads of the Long Bow: The Siriono of Eastern Bolivia.* Washington, D.C.: United States Government Printing Office.

HOOKER, E.

1965 An empirical study of some relations between sexual patterns and gender identity in male homosexuals. Pp. 24-52 in J. Money, ed., *Sex Research: New Developments.* New York: Holt, Rinehart and Winston.

1967 The homosexual community. Pp. 167-84 in J. H. Gagnon and W. Simon, eds., *Sexual Deviance.* New York: Harper & Row.

HRDY, S. B.

1974 Male-male competition and infanticide among the langurs (*Presbytis entellus*) of Abu, Rajasthan. *Folia Primatologica* 22:19-58.

HUBER, J. T.

1969 Discussion. Pp. 234-41 in G. D. Goldman and D. S. Milman, eds., *Modern Woman: Her Psychology and Sexuality.* Springfield, Illinois: Charles C. Thomas.

HUMPHREYS, L.

1970 *Tearoom Trade: Impersonal Sex in Public Places.* Chicago: Aldine.

1971 Impersonal sex and perceived satisfaction. Pp. 351-74 in J. M. Henslin, ed., *Studies in the Sociology of Sex.* New York: Appleton-Century-Crofts.

1972 New styles in homosexual manliness. Pp. 65-83 in J. A. McCaffrey, ed., *The Homosexual Dialect*. Englewood Cliffs, New Jersey: Prentice-Hall.

HUNT, M.
1974 *Sexual Behavior in the 1970's*. Chicago: Playboy Press.

HUTT, C.
1972a Sex differences in human development. *Human Development* 15:153-70.
1972b Sexual dimorphism: its significance in human development. Pp. 169-96 in F. J. Mönks, W. W. Hartup, and J. deWit, eds., *Determinants of Behavioral Development*. New York: Academic Press.

HUXLEY, T. H.
1897 *Evolution and Ethics and Other Essays*. New York: D. Appleton.

HYNES, S.
1968 *The Edwardian Turn of Mind*. Princeton: Princeton University Press.

JAMES, A., and R. PIKE
1967 Sexual behavior of couples receiving marriage counseling at a family agency. *The Journal of Sex Research* 3:232-38.

JARVIE, I. C.
1964 *The Revolution in Anthropology*. New York: The Humanities Press.

JENNI, D. A.
1974 Evolution of polyandry in birds. *American Zoologist* 14:129-44.

JOHNSON, R. E.
1970 Some correlates of extramarital coitus. *Journal of Marriage and the Family* 32:449-56.

JONES, F. C.
1975 The post-reproductive phase in mammals. Pp. 1-19 in P. A. van Keep and C. Lauritzen, eds., *Estrogens in the Post-Menopause: Frontiers of Hormone Research*, vol. 3. Basel: S. Karger.

JONG, E.
1973 *Fear of Flying*. New York: Holt, Rinehart and Winston.

JOSLYN, W. D.
1973 Androgen-induced social dominance in infant female rhesus monkeys. *Journal of Child Psychiatry* 14:137-45.

JUNOD, H. A.
1962 *The Life of a South African Tribe*. New Hyde Park: University Books.

KANIN, E. J.; K. R. DAVIDSON; and S. R. SCHECK
1970 A research note on male-female differentials in the experience of heterosexual love. *Journal of Sex Research* 6:64-72.

KAUFMANN, J. H.
1965 A three-year study of mating behavior in a free-ranging band of rhesus monkeys. *Ecology* 46:500-512.

KIM, Y. H.
1969 The Kinsey findings. Pp. 65-73 in G. Neubeck, ed., *Extramarital Relations*. Englewood Cliffs, New Jersey: Prentice-Hall.

KING, M. C., and A. C. WILSON
  1975 Evolution at two levels in humans and chimpanzees. *Science* 188: 107-16.
KINSEY, A. C.; W. B. POMEROY; and C. E. MARTIN
  1948 *Sexual Behavior in the Human Male.* Philadelphia: W. B. Saunders.
KINSEY, A. C.; W. B. POMEROY; C. E. MARTIN; and P. H. GEBHARD
  1953 *Sexual Behavior in the Human Female.* Philadelphia: W. B. Saunders.
KIRKENDALL, L. A.
  1961 *Premarital Intercourse and Interpersonal Relationships.* New York: The Julian Press.
Kleiman, D. G.
  1977 Monogamy in mammals. *Quarterly Review of Biology* 52:39-69.
LACK, D.
  1969 Of birds and men. *New Scientist,* January 16:121-22.
LANCASTER, J. B.
  in press Sex and gender in evolutionary perspective. Pp. 51-80 in H. A. Katchadourian, ed., *Human Sexuality: A Comparative and Developmental Perspective.* Berkeley: University of California Press.
LANCASTER, J. B., and R. B. LEE
  1965 The annual reproductive cycle in monkeys and apes. Pp. 486-513 in I. DeVore, ed., *Primate Behavior: Field Studies of Monkeys and Apes.* New York: Holt, Rinehart and Winston.
LAUGHLIN, W. S.
  1968 Hunting: an integrating biobehavior system and its evolutionary importance. Pp. 304-20 in R. B. Lee and I. DeVore, eds., *Man the Hunter.* Chicago: Aldine.
LAWICK-GOODALL, J. VAN
  1968 *The Behavior of Free-Living Chimpanzees in the Gombe Stream Reserve. Animal Behaviour Monographs* 1(3).
  1971 *In the Shadow of Man.* Boston: Houghton Mifflin.
  1973 Cultural elements of a chimpanzee community. Pp. 144-84 in E. W. Menzel, Jr., ed., *Precultural Primate Behavior.* New York: S. Karger.
  1975 Behaviour of the chimpanzee. Pp. 74-136 in Kurth and I. Eibl-Eibesfeldt, eds., *Hominisation und Verhalten.* Stuttgart: Fischer.
LEACH, E.
  1966 Virgin birth. *Proceedings of the Royal Anthropological Institute of Great Britain and Ireland for 1966*:39-49.
LE BOEUF, B. J.
  1974 Male-male competition and reproductive success in elephant seals. *American Zoologist* 14:163-76.
LEE, R. B.
  1968 What hunters do for a living or, how to make out on scarce resources. Pp. 30-48 in R. B. Lee and I. DeVore, eds., *Man the Hunter.* Chicago: Aldine.

1969 !Kung Bushman violence. Paper presented at the meeting of the American Anthropological Association, November 1969.

LeGrand, C. E.
1977 [1973] Rape and rape laws: sexism in society and law. Pp. 65-86 in D. Chappell, R. Geis, and G. Geis, eds., *Forcible Rape: The Crime, the Victim, and the Offender.* New York: Columbia University Press.

Lehrman, D. S.
1970 Semantic and conceptual issues in the nature-nurture problem. Pp. 17-52 in L. R. Aronson and E. Tobach, eds., *Development and Evolution of Behavior.* New York: W. H. Freeman & Company.

LeVine, R. A.
1977 [1959] Gusii sex offenses: a study in social control. Pp. 189-226 in D. Chappell, R. Geis, and G. Geis, eds., *Forcible Rape: The Crime, the Victim, and the Offender.* New York: Columbia University Press.

Lévi-Strauss, C.
1944 The social and psychological aspects of chieftainship in a primitive tribe: the Nambikuara of northwestern Mato Grosso. *Transactions of the New York Academy of Sciences* 7:16-32.
1969 *The Elementary Structures of Kinship.* Boston: Beacon Press.

Lev-Ran, A.
1974 Sexuality and educational levels of women with the late-treated adrenogenital syndrome. *Archives of Sexual Behavior* 3:27-32.

Leznoff, M., and W. A. Westley
1967 The homosexual community. Pp. 184-96 in J. H. Gagnon and W. Simon, eds., *Sexual Deviance.* New York: Harper & Row.

Lindburg, D. G.
1971 The rhesus monkey in north India: an ecological and behavioral study. Pp. 2-106 in L. A. Rosenblum, ed., *Primate Behavior 2.* New York: Academic Press.

Livingstone, F. B.
1967 The effects of warfare on the biology of the human species. Pp. 3-15 in M. Fried, M. Harris, and R. Murphy, eds., *War: The Anthropology of Armed Conflict and Aggression.* Garden City, New York: The Natural History Press.

Loy, J.
1971 Estrous behavior of free-ranging rhesus monkeys. *Primates* 12:1-31.

Lumholtz, C.
1889 *Among Cannibals.* New York: Scribner's.

Maccoby, E. E., and C. N. Jacklin
1974 *The Psychology of Sex Differences.* Stanford: Stanford University Press.

MacKinnon, J.
in press Reproductive behaviour in wild orang-utan populations. In

B. Hamburg and E. McCown, eds., *The Great Apes*. Menlo Park, California: Benjamin/Cummings.

MacLean, P. D.

1970 The triune brain, emotion, and scientific bias. Pp. 336-49 in F. O. Schmitt, ed., *The Neurosciences Second Study Program*. New York: Rockefeller University Press.

Magar, M. E.

1972 *Adultery and Its Compatibility with Marriage*. Monona, Wisconsin: Nefertiti.

Malinowski, B.

1927 *Sex and Repression in Savage Society*. London: Routledge & Kegan Paul.

1929 *The Sexual Life of Savages in North-Western Melanesia*. New York: Halcyon House.

1962 *Sex, Culture, and Myth*. New York: Harcourt, Brace & World.

Marcus, S.

1966 *The Other Victorians: A Study of Sexuality and Pornography in Mid-Nineteenth-Century England*. New York: Basic Books.

Marks, S. A.

1977 Hunting behavior and strategies of the Valley Bisa in Zambia. *Human Ecology* 5:1-36.

Mark Twain

1938 *Letters from the Earth*. Edited by B. DeVoto. New York: Harper & Row.

Marler, P.

1976 On animal aggression. *American Psychologist* 31:239-46.

Marler, P., and W. J. Hamilton

1966 *Mechanisms of Animal Behavior*. New York: John Wiley and Sons.

Marshall, D. S.

1971 Sexual behavior on Mangaia. Pp. 103-62 in D. S. Marshall and R. C. Suggs, eds., *Human Sexual Behavior*. New York: Basic Books.

Marshall, D. S., and R. C. Suggs, eds.

1971 *Human Sexual Behavior*. New York: Basic Books.

Martin, M. K., and B. Voorhies

1975 *Female of the Species*. New York: Columbia University Press.

Martindale, D.

1965 Limits of and alternatives to functionalism in sociology. Pp. 144-62 in D. Martindale, ed., *Functionalism in the Social Sciences: The Strength and Limits of Functionalism in Anthropology, Economics, Political Science, and Sociology*. Philadelphia: The American Academy of Political and Social Science.

Masters, W. H., and V. E. Johnson

1966 *Human Sexual Response*. Boston: Little, Brown and Company.

1970 *Human Sexual Inadequacy*. Boston: Little, Brown and Company.

MATHEWS, A. M.; J. H. J. BANCROFT; and P. SLATER
    1972   The principal components of sexual preference. *British Journal of Social and Clinical Psychology* 11:35-43.

MAYBURY-LEWIS, D.
    1967   *Akwe-Shavante Society*. Oxford: Clarendon Press.

MAYNARD SMITH, J.
    1958   *The Theory of Evolution*. Baltimore: Penguin Books.
    1972   Game theory and the evolution of fighting. Pp. 8-28 in J. Maynard Smith, *On Evolution*. Edinburgh: Edinburgh University Press.
    1976   Evolution and the theory of games. *American Scientist* 64:41-45.

MAYNARD SMITH, J., and G. R. PRICE
    1973   The logic of animal conflict. *Nature* 246:15-18.

MAYR, E.
    1961   Cause and effect in biology. *Science* 134:1501-6.
    1972   Sexual selection and natural selection. Pp. 87-104 in B. Campbell, ed., *Sexual Selection and the Descent of Man 1871-1971*. Chicago: Aldine.

McGINNIS, P. R.
    in press   Sexual behavior in free-living chimpanzees: consort relationships. In B. Hamburg and E. McCown, eds., *The Great Apes*. Menlo Park, California: Benjamin/Cummings.

McGREW, W. C.
    in press   Evolutionary implications of sex differences in chimpanzee predation and tool use. In B. Hamburg and E. McCown, eds., *The Great Apes*. Menlo Park, California: Banjamin/Cummings.

McKENZIE, R. B., and G. TULLOCK
    1975   *The New World of Economics: Explorations into the Human Experience*. Homewod, Illinois: Richard D. Irwin.

MEAD, M.
    1935   *Sex and Temperament in Three Primitive Societies*. New York: William Morrow and Company.
    1961   Cultural determinants of sexual behavior. Pp. 1433-79 in W. C. Young, ed., *Sex and Internal Secretions* (3rd ed.). Baltimore: Williams and Wilkins.
    1967   *Male and Female: A Study of the Sexes in a Changing World*. New York: William Morrow and Company.

MEGGITT, M.
    1977   *Blood Is Their Argument: Warfare among the Mae Enga Tribesmen of the New Guinea Highlands*. Palo Alto, California: Mayfield.

MELGES, F. T., and D. A. HAMBURG
    1977   Psychological effects of hormonal changes in women. Pp. 269-95 in F. A. Beach, ed., *Human Sexuality in Four Perspectives*. Baltimore: The Johns Hopkins University Press.

MENZEL, E. W., JR.; R. K. DAVENPORT; and C. M. ROGERS
1972 Protocultural aspects of chimpanzees' responsiveness to novel objects. *Folia Primatologica* 17:161-70.

MESSENGER, J. C.
1971 Sex and repression in an Irish folk community. Pp. 3-37 in D. S. Marshall and R. C. Suggs, eds., *Human Sexual Behavior*. New York: Basic Books.

MICHAEL, R. P.
1971 Neuroendocrine factors regulating primate behaviour. Pp. 359-98 in L. Martini and W. F. Ganong, eds., *Frontiers in Neuroendocrinology*. New York: Oxford University Press.

MICHAEL, R. P., and R. W. BONSALL
1977 Chemical signals and primate behavior. Pp. 251-71 in D. Müller-Schwarze and M. M. Mozell, eds., *Chemical Signals in Vertebrates*. New York: Plenum.

MICHAEL, R. P.; R. W. BONSALL; and P. WARNER
1974 Human vaginal secretions: volatile fatty acid content. *Science* 186:1217-19.

MILLER, H.
1959 *The World of Sex*. New York: Grove Press.

MILNER, C., and R. MILNER
1973 *Black Players: The Secret World of Black Pimps*. New York: Bantam Books.

MONEY, J.
1961 Sex hormones and other variables in human eroticism. Pp. 1383-1400 in W. C. Young and G. W. Corner, eds., *Sex and Internal Secretions*, vol. II. Baltimore: Williams and Wilkins.

1965 Influence of hormones on sexual behavior. *Annual Review of Medicine* 16:67-82.

1973 Prenatal hormones and postnatal socialization in gender identity differentiation. Pp. 221-95 in J. K. Cole and R. Dienstbier, eds., *Nebraska Symposium on Motivation*. Lincoln, Nebraska: University of Nebraska Press.

MONEY, J., and A. A. EHRHARDT
1972 *Man & Woman Boy & Girl*. Baltimore: The Johns Hopkins University Press.

MONTAGU, A.
1957 *The Reproductive Development of the Female, with Special Reference to the Period of Adolescent Sterility: A Study in the Comparative Physiology of Infecundity of the Adolescent Organism*. New York: Julian Press.

MONTAIGNE
1958 *The Complete Essays of Montaigne*. Translated by D. M. Frame. Stanford: Stanford University Press.

MORRIS, D.
1967 *The Naked Ape*. New York: Dell Publishing Co.

MURDOCK, G. P.
  1972 Anthropology's mythology. *Proceedings of the Royal Anthropological Institute of Great Britain and Ireland for 1971*:17-24.

MURSTEIN, B. I.
  1972 Physical attractiveness and marital choice. *Journal of Personality and Social Psychology* 22:8-12.

NEEL, J. V.
  1970 Lessons from a "primitive" people. *Science* 170:815-22.

NEEL, J. V.; F. M. SALZANO; P. C. JUNQUEIRA; F. KEITER; and D. MAYBURY-LEWIS
  1964 Studies on the Xavante Indians of the Brazilian Mato Grosso. *Human Genetics* 16:52-140.

NEUBECK, G.
  1969 Other societies: an anthropological review of extramarital relations. Pp. 108-26 in G. Neubeck, ed., *Extramarital Relations*. Englewood Cliffs, New Jersey: Prentice-Hall.

NEWTON, N.
  1973 Interrelationships between sexual responsiveness, birth, and breast feeding. Pp. 77-98 in J. Zubin and J. Money, eds., *Contemporary Sexual Behavior: Critical Issues in the 1970s*. Baltimore: The Johns Hopkins University Press.

NICHOLSON, J.
  1972 Foreword. In M. Gabor, *The Pin-Up: A Modest History*. New York: Bell Publishing Co.

NISHIDA, T.
  1968 The social group of wild chimpanzees in the Mahali Mountains. *Primates* 9:167-219.
  in press The social structure of chimpanzees of the Mahali Mountains. In B. Hamburg and E. McCown, eds., *The Great Apes*. Menlo Park, California: Benjamin/Cummings.

NOBILE, P.
  1974 Review of *Hefner*. *New York Times Book Review*, December 15:4-5.

ORIANS, G. H.
  1969 On the evolution of mating systems in birds and mammals. *The American Naturalist* 103:589-603.

ORWELL, G.
  1961 *Down and Out in Paris and London*. New York: Harcourt, Brace & World.
  1968 Looking Back on the Spanish War. Pp. 249-67 in S. Orwell and I. Angus, eds., *The Collected Essays, Journalism and Letters of George Orwell, II: My Country Right or Left 1940-1943*. New York: Harcourt, Brace & World.

PARKER, G. A.
  1974 Assessment strategy and the evolution of fighting behaviour. *Journal of Theoretical Biology* 47:223-43.

PERETTI, P. O.

1969 Premarital sexual behavior between females and males of two middle-sized midwestern cities. *The Journal of Sex Research* 5: 218-25.

PETER, PRINCE OF GREECE AND DENMARK, H.R.H.

1963 *A Study of Polyandry.* The Hague: Mouton.

PHOENIX, C. H.

1974 Prenatal testosterone in the nonhuman primate and its consequences for behavior. Pp. 19-32 in R. C. Friedman, R. M. Richart, and R. L. Vande Wiele, eds., *Sex Differences in Behavior.* New York: John Wiley and Sons.

PIETROPINTO, A., and J. SIMENAUER

1977 *Beyond the Male Myth.* New York: Times Books.

POPP, J. L., and I. DeVORE

in press Aggressive competition and social dominance theory. In B. Hamburg and E. McCown, eds., *The Great Apes.* Menlo Park, California: Benjamin/Cummings.

POPPER, K. R., and J. C. ECCLES

1977 *The Self and Its Brain: An Argument for Interactionism.* New York: Springer International.

PROUST, M.

1934 *Remembrance of Things Past.* Translated by C. K. S. Moncrieff. New York: Random House.

PUSEY, A.

in press Intercommunity transfer of chimpanzees in Gombe National Park. In B. Hamburg and E. McCown, eds., *The Great Apes.* Menlo Park, California: Benjamin/Cummings.

QUADAGNO, D. M.; R. BRISCOE; and J. S. QUADAGNO

1977 Effect of perinatal gonadal hormones on selected nonsexual behavior patterns: a critical assessment of the nonhuman and human literature. *Psychological Bulletin* 84:62-80.

RADCLIFFE-BROWN, A. R.

1935 On the concept of function in social science. *American Anthropologist* 37:394-402.

RALLS, K.

1976 Mammals in which females are larger than males. *The Quarterly Review of Biology* 51:245-76.

1977 Sexual dimorphism in mammals: avian models and unanswered questions. *The American Naturalist* 111:917-38.

RASMUSSEN, K.

1931 *The Netsilik Eskimos: Social Life and Spiritual Culture.* Copenhagen: Gyldendalske Boghandel, Nordisk Forlag.

READ, K. E.

1955 Morality and concept of the person among the Gahuku-Gama. *Oceania* 25:233-82.

REINISCH, J. M.

1974 Fetal hormones, the brain, and human sex differences: a heuristic, integrative review of the recent literature. *Archives of Sexual Behavior* 3:51-90.

REISS, A. J., JR.

1967   The social integration of queers and peers. Pp. 197-228 in J. H. Gagnon and W. Simon, eds., *Sexual Deviance*. New York: Harper & Row.

RESKO, J. A.

1970   Androgen secretion by the fetal and neonatal rhesus monkey. *Endocrinology* 87:680-87.

1974   The relationship between fetal hormones and the differentiation of the central nervous system in primates. Pp. 211-22 in W. Montagna and W. A. Sadler, eds., *Reproductive Behavior*. New York: Plenum.

RICHERSON, P. J., and R. BOYD

1978   A dual inheritance model of the human evolutionary process I: basic postulates and a simple model. *Journal of Social and Biological Structures* 1:127-54.

RIESS, B. F.

1969   Discussion. Pp. 268-71 in G. D. Goldman and D. S. Milman, eds., *Modern Woman: Her Psychology and Sexuality*. Springfield, Illinois: Charles C. Thomas.

RINGER, R.

1976   *Winning Through Intimidation*. New York: Fawcett World Library.

RISS, D., and J. GOODALL

1977   The recent rise to the alpha-rank in a population of free-living chimpanzees. *Folia Primatologica* 27:134-51.

Robinson, J. H.

1921   *The Mind in the Making: The Relation of Intelligence to Social Reform*. New York: Harper & Brothers.

ROBINSON, P. A.

1969   *The Freudian Left: Wilhelm Reich, Geza Roheim, Herbert Marcuse*. New York: Harper & Row.

1976   *The Modernization of Sex*. New York: Harper & Row.

ROGERS, C. M.

1973   Implications of a primate early rearing experiment for the concept of culture. Pp. 185-91 in E. W. Menzel, Jr., ed., *Precultural Primate Behavior*. New York: S. Karger.

ROSE, F. G. G.

1968   Australian marriage, land-owning groups, and initiations. Pp. 200-208 in R. B. Lee and I. DeVore, eds., *Man the Hunter*. Chicago: Aldine.

ROSENBLATT, P. C.

1974   Cross-cultural perspective on attraction. Pp. 79-95 in T. L. Huston, ed., *Foundations of Interpersonal Attraction*. New York: Academic Press.

ROSSI, A. S.

1973   Maternalism, sexuality, and the new feminism. Pp. 145-73 in J.

Zubin and J. Money, eds., *Contemporary Sexual Behavior: Critical Issues in the 1970s.* Baltimore: The Johns Hopkins University Press.

ROTH, P.
1969 *Portnoy's Complaint.* New York: Random House.

ROWELL, T. E.
1972a Female reproduction cycles and social behavior in primates. Pp. 69-105 in D. S. Lehrman, ed., *Advances in the Study of Behavior,* vol. 4. New York: Academic Press.
1972b *The Social Behaviour of Monkeys.* Baltimore: Penguin Books.

RUSSELL, D. E. H.
1975 *The Politics of Rape: The Victim's Perspective.* New York: Stein and Day.

SAAYMAN, G. S.
1970 The menstrual cycle and sexual behaviour in a troop of free ranging Chacma baboons (*Papio ursinus*). *Folia Primatologica* 12:81-110.
1975 The influence of hormonal and ecological factors upon sexual behavior and social organization in Old World primates. Pp. 181-204 in R. H. Tuttle, ed., *Socioecology and Psychology of Primates.* The Hague: Mouton.

SAFILIOS-ROTHSCHILD, C.
1969 Attitudes of Greek spouses toward marital infidelity. Pp. 77-93 in G. Neubeck, ed., *Extramarital Relations.* Englewood Cliffs, New Jersey: Prentice-Hall.

SAGARIN, E.
1971 Sex research and sociology: retrospective and prospective. Pp. 337-408 in J. M. Henslin, ed., *Studies in the Sociology of Sex.* New York: Appleton-Century-Crofts.

SAGHIR, M. T., and E. ROBINS
1973 *Male and Female Homosexuality.* Baltimore: Williams and Wilkins.

SAHLINS, M.
1976 *The Use and Abuse of Biology: An Anthropological Critique of Sociobiology.* Ann Arbor, Michigan: University of Michigan Press.

SCHALLER, G. B., and G. R. LOWTHER
1969 The relevance of carnivore behavior to the study of early hominids. *Southwestern Journal of Anthropology* 25:307-41.

SCHAPERA, I.
1940 *Married Life in an African Tribe.* London: Faber and Faber.

SCHEIN, M. W., and E. B. HALE
1965 Stimuli eliciting sexual behavior. Pp. 440-82 in F. Beach, ed., *Sex and Behavior.* New York: John Wiley and Sons.

SCHLEGEL, A.
1972 *Male Dominance and Female Autonomy: Domestic Authority in Matrilineal Societies.* HRAF Press.

SCHMIDT, G., and V. SIGUSCH
   1970   Sex differences in responses to psychosexual stimulation by films
          and slides. *The Journal of Sex Research* 6:268-83.
   1973   Woman's sexual arousal. Pp. 117-43 in J. Zubin and J. Money,
          eds., *Contemporary Sexual Behavior: Critical Issues in the 1970s.*
          Baltimore: The Johns Hopkins University Press.
SCHNEIDER, H. K.
   1971   Romantic love among the Turu. Pp. 59-70 in D. S. Marshall and
          R. C. Suggs, eds., *Human Sexual Behavior.* New York: Basic
          Books.
SCHOFIELD, M.
   1965   *The Sexual Behaviour of Young People.* Boston: Little, Brown
          and Company.
SCHULTZ, A. H.
   1969   *The Life of Primates.* London: Weidenfeld and Nicolson.
SEILER, M.
   1976   Monogamy is "unnatural," man with 9 wives says. *Los Angeles
          Times,* part II, February 9:1.
SELANDER, R. K.
   1972   Sexual selection and dimorphism in birds. Pp. 180-230 in B. Camp-
          bell, ed., *Sexual Selection and the Descent of Man 1871-1971.*
          Chicago: Aldine.
SERR, D. M.; A. PORATH-FUREDI; E. RABAU; H. ZAKUT; and S. M. MANNOR
   1968   Recording of electrical activity from the human cervix. *Journal
          of Obstetrics and Gynaecology of the British Commonwealth* 75:
          360-63.
SERVICE, E. R.
   1967   War and our contemporary ancestors. Pp. 160-67 in M. Fried,
          M. Harris, and R. Murphy, eds., *War: The Anthropology of
          Armed Conflict and Aggression.* Garden City, New York: The
          Natural History Press.
   1975   *Origins of the State and Civilization: The Process of Cultural
          Evolution.* New York: W. W. Norton.
SHAINESS, N.
   1976   How "sex experts" debase sex. Pp. 122-25 in *Focus: Human Sex-
          uality.* Guilford, Connecticut: The Dushkin Publishing Group.
SHAND, A. F.
   1914   *The Foundations of Character: Being a Study of the Tendencies
          of the Emotions and Sentiments.* London: Macmillan.
SHERFEY, M. J.
   1972   *The Nature and Evolution of Female Sexuality.* New York:
          Random House.
SHILOH, A., ed.
   1970   *Studies in Human Sexual Behavior: The American Scene.* Spring-
          field, Illinois: Charles C. Thomas.
SIGUSCH, V., and G. SCHMIDT
   1971   Lower-class sexuality: some emotional and social aspects in West

German males and females. *Archives of Sexual Behavior* 1:29-44.

SIGUSCH, V.; G. SCHMIDT; A. REINFELD; and I. WIEDEMANN-SUTOR

1970 Psychosexual stimulation: sex differences. *The Journal of Sex Research* 6:10-14.

SIMON, W.

1973 The social, the erotic, and the sensual: the complexities of sexual scripts. Pp: 61-82 in J. K. Cole and R. Dienstbier, eds., *Nebraska Symposium on Motivation 1973.* Lincoln: University of Nebraska Press.

SISKIND, J.

1973a *To Hunt in the Morning.* New York: Oxford University Press.

1973b Tropical forest hunters and the economy of sex. Pp. 226-40 in D. R. Gross, ed., *Peoples and Cultures of Native South America.* Garden City, New York: The Natural History Press.

SMITH, D. D.

1976 The social content of pornography. *Journal of Communication* 26:16-24.

SONENSCHEIN, D.

1968 The ethnography of male homosexual relationships. *The Journal of Sex Research* 4:69-83.

SPENCER, R. F.

1968 Spouse-exchange among the North Alaskan Eskimo. Pp. 130-44 in P. Bohannan and J. Middleton, eds., *Marriage, Family and Residence.* Garden City, New York: The Natural History Press.

SPERRY, R. W.

1969 A modified concept of consciousness. *Psychological Review* 76: 532-36.

1977 Bridging science and human values. *American Psychologist* 32: 237-45.

SPIRO, M. E.

1968 Virgin birth, parthenogenesis and physiological paternity: an essay in cultural interpretation. *Man* 3:242-61.

STAUFFER, J., and R. FROST

1976 Male and female interest in sexually-oriented magazines. *Journal of Communication* 26:25-30.

STEADMAN, L. B.

1971 Neighbours and Killers: Residence and Dominance among the Hewa of New Guinea. Ph.D. thesis, Australian National University.

n.d. The killing of witches.

STEARN, J.

1964 *The Grapevine.* New York: Doubleday.

STEBBING, L. S.

1937 *Philosophy and the Physicists.* London: Methuen & Co.

STEELE, D. G., and C. E. WALKER

1974 Male and female differences in reaction to erotic stimuli as related to sexual adjustment. *Archives of Sexual Behavior* 3:459-70.

STEPHENS, W. N.
    1963   *The Family in Cross-cultural Perspective.* New York: Holt, Rinehart and Winston.
STEVENSON, H. W.
    1972   *Children's Learning.* New York: Appleton-Century-Crofts.
STYRON, W.
    1977   *Esquire* 82:81.
SUGGS, R. C.
    1966   *Marquesan Sexual Behavior.* New York: Harcourt, Brace & World.
    1971a Sex and personality in the Marquesas: a discussion of the Linton-Kardiner report. Pp. 163-86 in D. S. Marshall and R. C. Suggs, eds., *Human Sexual Behavior.* New York: Basic Books.
    1971b A critique of some anthropological methods and theory. Pp. 272-94 in D. S. Marshall and R. C. Suggs, eds., *Human Sexual Behavior.* New York: Basic Books.
SUGGS, R. C., and D. S. MARSHALL
    1971   Anthropological perspectives on human sexual behavior. Pp. 218-43 in D. S. Marshall and R. C. Suggs, eds., *Human Sexual Behavior.* New York: Basic Books.
SUGIYAMA, Y.
    1969   Social behavior of chimpanzees in the Budongo Forest, Uganda. *Primates* 10:197-225.
SYMONS, D.
    1978a *Play and Aggression: A Study of Rhesus Monkeys.* New York: Columbia University Press.
    1978b The question of function: dominance and play. Pp. 193-230 in E. O. Smith, ed., *Social Play in Primates.* New York: Academic Press.
TAVRIS, C., and S. SADD
    1977   *The Redbook Report on Female Sexuality.* New York: Delacorte Press.
TELEKI, G.
    1973   *The Predatory Behavior of Wild Chimpanzees.* Lewisburg, Pennsylvania: Bucknell University Press.
    1974   Chimpanzee subsistence technology: materials and skills. *Journal of Human Evolution* 3:575-94.
TENAZA, R. R.
    1975   Territory and monogamy among Kloss gibbons in Siberut Island, Indonesia. *Folia Primatologica* 24:60-80.
TERMAN, L. M.
    1938   *Psychological Factors in Marital Happiness.* New York: Mc-Graw-Hill.
THURNWALD, R. C.
    1936   Review of *Sex and Temperament in Three Primitive Societies.* *American Anthropologist* 38:663-67.
TIGER, L.
    1969   *Men in Groups.* New York: Random House.

1975 Somatic factors and social behaviour. Pp. 115-32 in R. Fox, ed., *Biosocial Anthropology*. New York: John Wiley and Sons.

TOBIAS, P. V.

1964 Bushman hunter-gatherers: a study in human ecology. In D. H. S. Davis, ed., *Ecological Studies in Southern Africa*. The Hague: W. Junk.

TOLSTOY, L.

1960 *Anna Karenina*. Translated by J. Carmichael. New York: Bantam Books.

TRIPP, C. A.

1975 *The Homosexual Matrix*. New York: Signet.

TRIVERS, R. L.

1971 The evolution of reciprocal altruism. *Quarterly Review of Biology* 46:35-57.

1972 Parental investment and sexual selection. Pp. 136-79 in B. Campbell, ed., *Sexual Selection and the Descent of Man 1871-1971*. Chicago: Aldine.

1974 Parent-offspring conflict. *American Zoologist* 14:249-64.

TUTIN, C. E. G.

1975 Exceptions to promiscuity in a feral chimpanzee community. Pp. 445-49 in S. Kondo, M. Kawai, and A. Ehara, eds., *Contemporary Primatology: Fifth International Congress of Primatology, Nagoya*. Basel: Karger.

UDRY, J. R.; K. E. BAUMAN; and N. M. MORRIS

1975 Changes in premarital coital experience of recent decade-of-birth cohorts of urban American women. *Journal of Marriage and the Family* 37:783-87.

UDRY, J. R., and N. M. MORRIS

1968 Distribution of coitus in the menstrual cycle. *Nature* 220:593-96.

U.S. COMMISSION ON OBSCENITY AND PORNOGRAPHY

1970 *The Report of the U.S. Commission on Obscenity and Pornography*. New York: Random House.

VALLOIS, H. V.

1961 The social life of early man: the evidence of skeletons. Pp. 214-35 in S. L. Washburn, ed., *Social Life of Early Man*. Chicago: Aldine.

VAN DEN BERGHE, P. L., and D. P. BARASH

1977 Inclusive fitness and human family structure. *American Anthropologist* 79:809-23.

VENABLE, V.

1966 *Human Nature: The Marxian View*. Cleveland: The World Publishing Company.

VENER, A. M., and C. S. STEWART

1974 Adolescent sexual behavior in middle America revisited: 1970-1973. *Journal of Marriage and the Family* 36:728-35.

VICKERS, W. T.

1975 Meat is meat: the Siona-Secoya and the hunting prowess-sexual reward hypothesis. *Latinamericanist* 11 (1).

WADDINGTON, C. H.
  1960   *The Ethical Animal.* Chicago: University of Chicago Press.
  1976   Review of E. O. Wilson's *Sociobiology. New York Review of Books,* August 7.
WADE, N.
  1976   Sociobiology: troubled birth for a new discipline. *Science* 191: 1151-55.
WALLACE, B. J.
  1969   Pagan Gaddang spouse exchange. *Ethnology* 8:183-88.
WARD, D. A., and G. G. KASSEBAUM
  1970   Lesbian liaisons. Pp. 125-36 in J. H. Gagnon and W. Simon, eds., *The Sexual Scene.* Chicago: Aldine.
WASHBURN, S. L.
  1970   Comment on: "A possible evolutionary basis for aesthetic appreciation in men and apes." *Evolution* 24:824-25.
  1973   Human evolution: science or game? *Yearbook of Physical Anthropology* 17:67-70.
WASHBURN, S. L.; P. C. JAY; and J. B. LANCASTER
  1965   Field studies of Old World monkeys and apes. *Science* 150: 1541-47.
WASHBURN, S. L., and C. S. LANCASTER
  1968   The evolution of hunting. Pp. 293-303 in R. B. Lee and I. De-Vore, eds., *Man the Hunter.* Chicago: Aldine.
WASHBURN, S. L., and S. C. STRUM
  1972   Concluding comments. Pp. 469-91 in S. L. Washburn and P. Dolhinow, eds., *Perspectives on Human Evolution 2.* New York: Holt, Rinehart and Winston.
WEINBERG, M. S., and C. J. WILLIAMS
  1974   *Male Homosexuals: Their Problems and Adaptations.* New York: Oxford University Press.
WEINRICH, J. D.
  1977   Human sociobiology: pair-bonding and resource predictability (effects of social class and race). *Behavioral Ecology and Sociobiology* 2:91-118.
WEITZ, S.
  1977   *Sex Roles: Biological, Psychological, and Social Foundations.* New York: Oxford University Press.
WEST, D. J.
  1967   *Homosexuality.* Chicago: Aldine.
WHITING, B. B., ed.
  1963   *Six Cultures: Studies of Child Rearing.* New York: John Wiley and Sons.
WHITING, B. B., and C. P. EDWARDS
  1973   A cross-cultural analysis of sex-differences in the behavior of children aged three through 11. *The Journal of Social Psychology* 91:171-88.
WILLIAMS, G. C.
  1966   *Adaptation and Natural Selection: A Critique of Some Current*

Evolutionary Thought. Princeton, New Jersey: Princeton University Press.

1975   *Sex and Evolution*. Princeton, New Jersey: Princeton University Press.

WILSON, E. O.

1975   *Sociobiology: The New Synthesis*. Cambridge, Massachusetts: The Belknap Press of Harvard University Press.

WILSON, J. R.; R. E. KUEHN; and F. R. BEACH

1963   Modification in the sexual behavior of male rats produced by changing the stimulus female. *Journal of Comparative and Physiological Psychology* 56:636-44.

WOLFE, L.

1975a   *Playing Around: Women and Extramarital Sex*. New York: William Morrow and Company.

1975b   The consequences of playing around. *New York Magazine*, June 2:49-55.

WOODBURN, J.

1968   An introduction to Hadza ecology. Pp. 49-55 in R. B. Lee and I. DeVore, eds., *Man the Hunter*. Chicago: Aldine.

WRANGHAM, R. W.

in press   Sex differences in chimpanzee dispersion. In B. Hamburg and E. McCown, eds., *The Great Apes*. Menlo Park, California: Benjamin/Cummings.

ZUCKERMAN, S.

1932   *The Social Life of Monkeys and Apes*. London: Butler & Tanner Ltd.

ZUMPE, D., and R. P. MICHAEL

1968   The clutching reaction and orgasm in the female rhesus monkey (*Macaca mulatta*). *Journal of Endocrinology* 40:117-23.

1977   Effects of ejaculations by males on the sexual invitations of female rhesus monkeys (*Macaca mulatta*). *Behaviour* 60:260-77.

Index